Urusei Yatsura

1

Story & Art by
RUMIKO TAKAHASHI

Urusei Yatsura

Part 1

Part 1 Contents

CHAPTER 1: YOUNG LOVE ON THE RUN

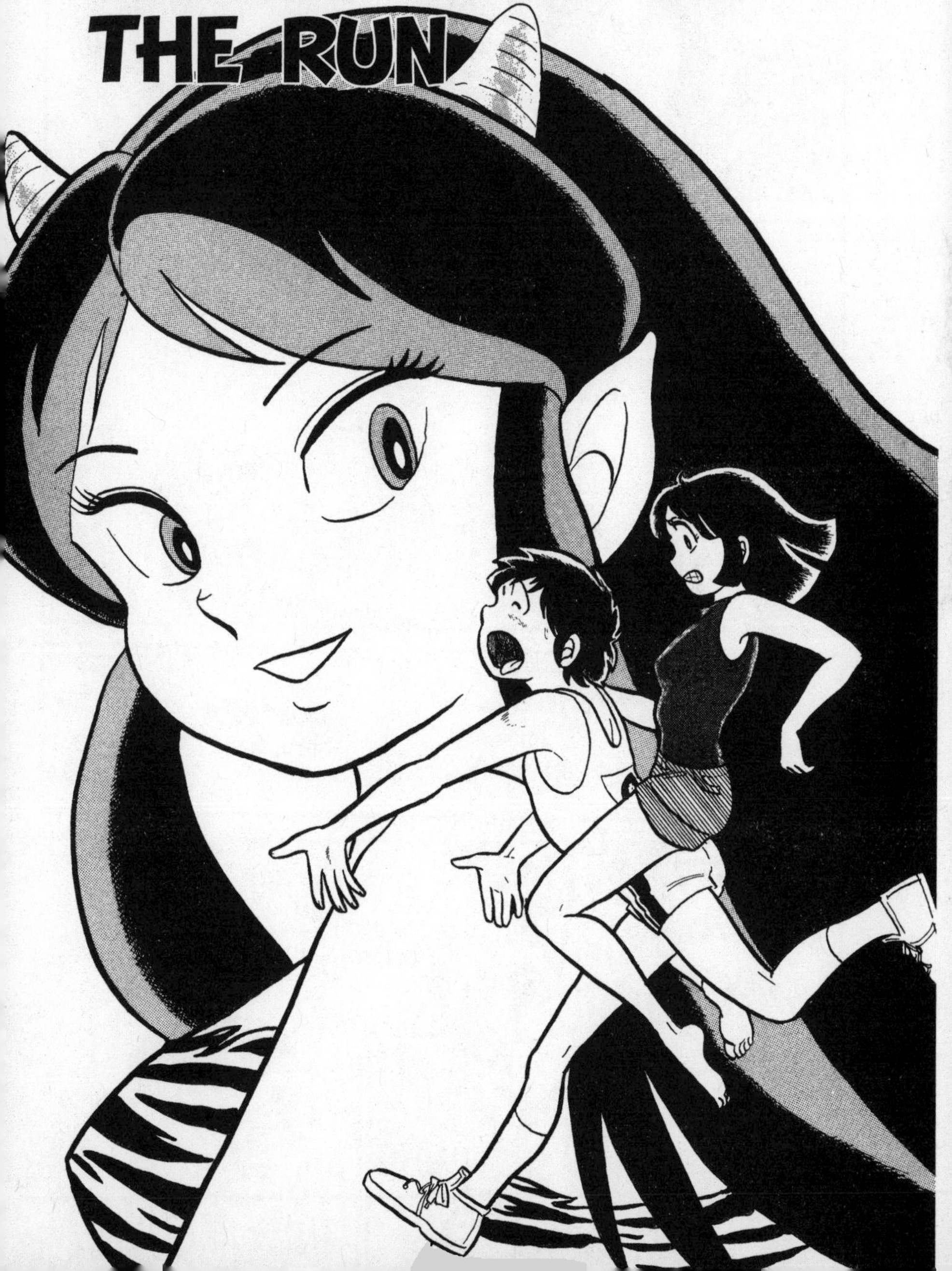

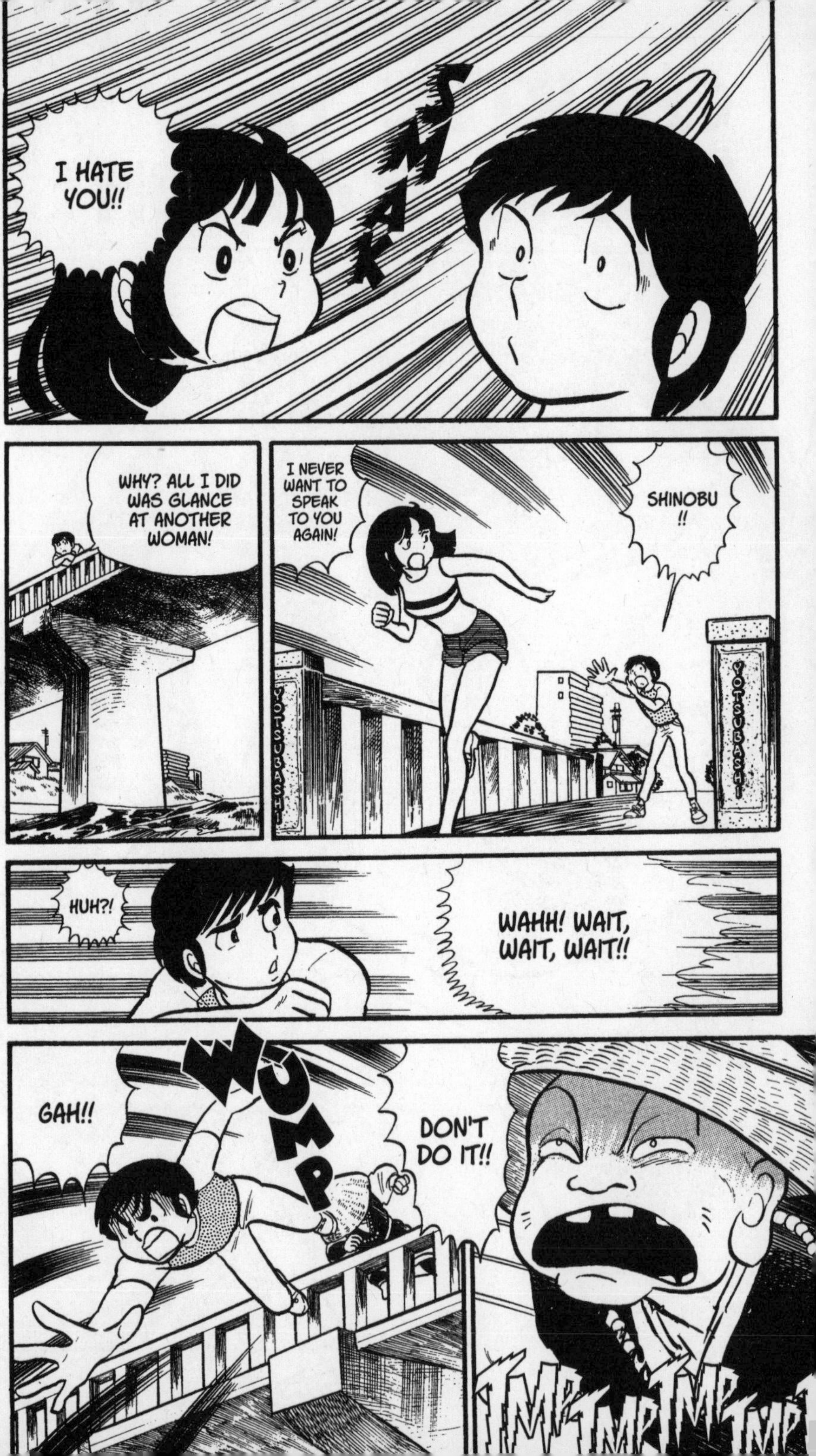
SMAK
I HATE YOU!!
SHINOBU !!
YOTSUBASHI
I NEVER WANT TO SPEAK TO YOU AGAIN!
YOTSUBASHI
WHY? ALL I DID WAS GLANCE AT ANOTHER WOMAN!
WAHH! WAIT, WAIT, WAIT!!
HUH?!
DON'T DO IT!!
TMP TMP TMP TMP
WUMP
GAH!!

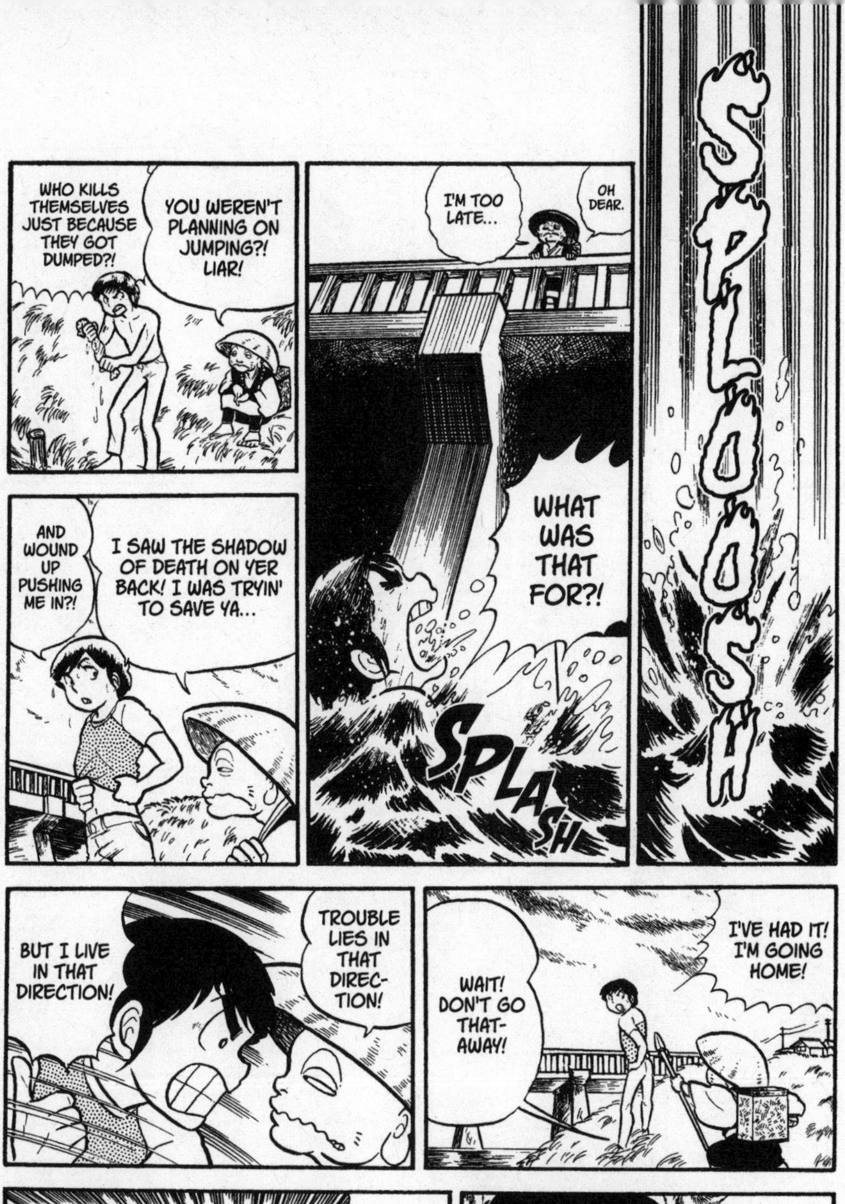
SPLOOSH
OH DEAR.
I'M TOO LATE...
WHAT WAS THAT FOR?!
SPLASH
YOU WEREN'T PLANNING ON JUMPING?! LIAR!
WHO KILLS THEMSELVES JUST BECAUSE THEY GOT DUMPED?!
I SAW THE SHADOW OF DEATH ON YER BACK! I WAS TRYIN' TO SAVE YA...
AND WOUND UP PUSHING ME IN?!
I'VE HAD IT! I'M GOING HOME!
WAIT! DON'T GO THAT-AWAY!
TROUBLE LIES IN THAT DIREC-TION!
BUT I LIVE IN THAT DIRECTION!
YER...YER FACE...
...IS HORRIBLE!

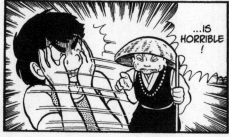

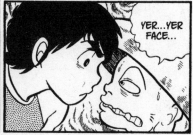

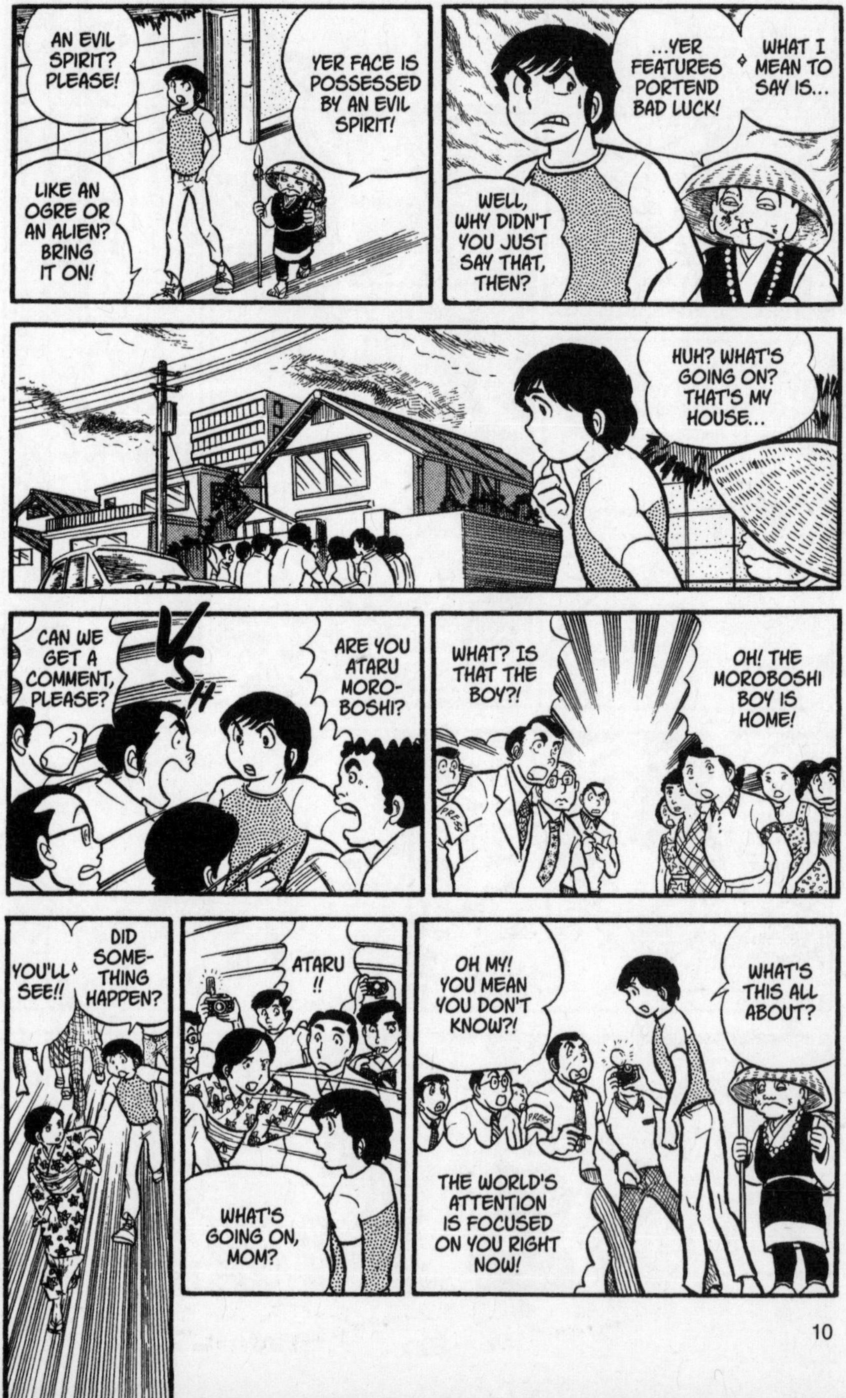
WHAT I MEAN TO SAY IS...
...YER FEATURES PORTEND BAD LUCK!
WELL, WHY DIDN'T YOU JUST SAY THAT, THEN?
YER FACE IS POSSESSED BY AN EVIL SPIRIT!
AN EVIL SPIRIT? PLEASE!
LIKE AN OGRE OR AN ALIEN? BRING IT ON!
HUH? WHAT'S GOING ON? THAT'S MY HOUSE...
OH! THE MOROBOSHI BOY IS HOME!
WHAT? IS THAT THE BOY?!
ARE YOU ATARU MORO-BOSHI?
VSH
CAN WE GET A COMMENT, PLEASE?
WHAT'S THIS ALL ABOUT?
OH MY! YOU MEAN YOU DON'T KNOW?!
THE WORLD'S ATTENTION IS FOCUSED ON YOU RIGHT NOW!
ATARU!!
WHAT'S GOING ON, MOM?
DID SOME-THING HAPPEN?
YOU'LL SEE!!

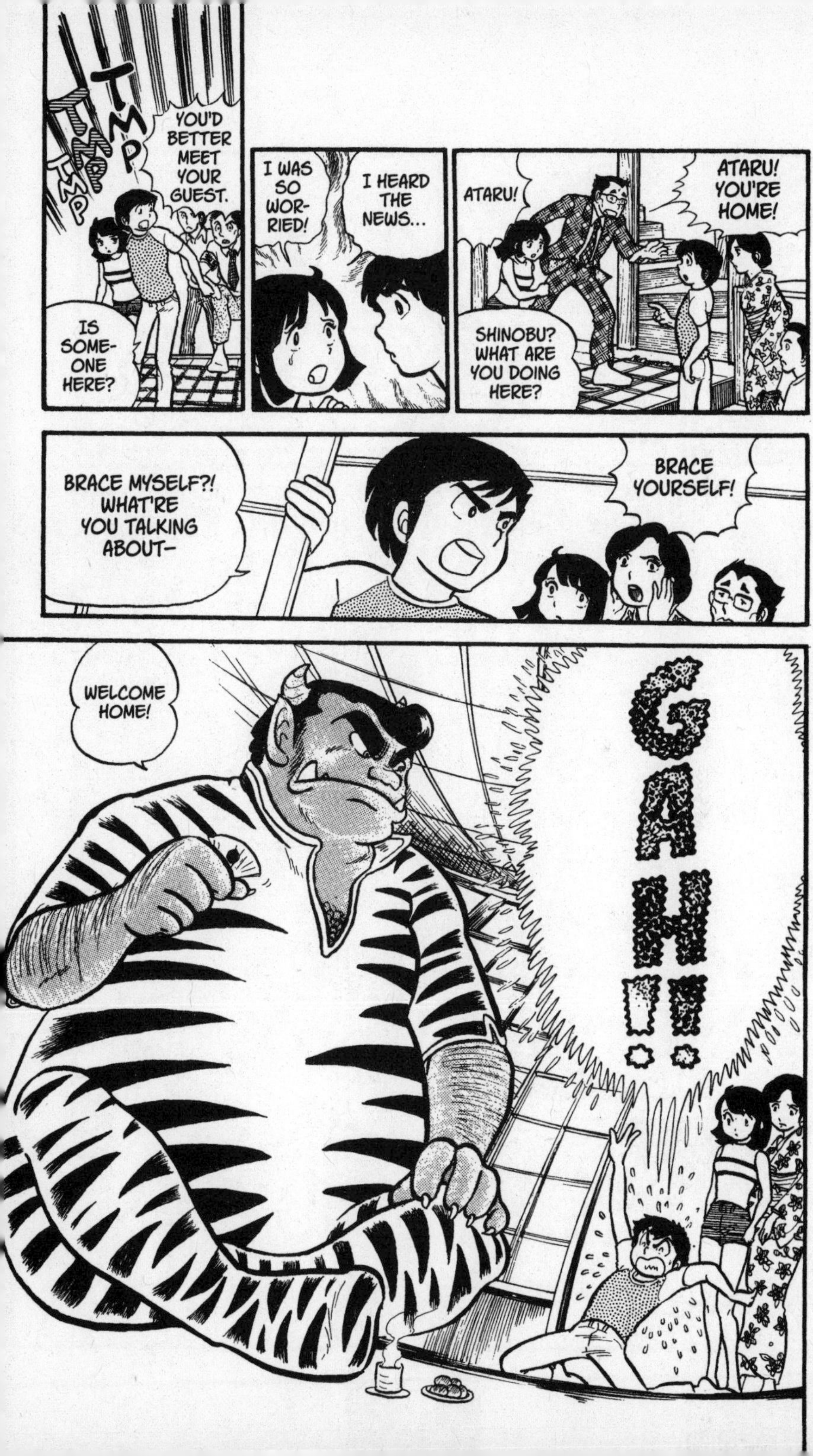
ATARU! YOU'RE HOME!
ATARU!
SHINOBU? WHAT ARE YOU DOING HERE?
I HEARD THE NEWS...
I WAS SO WOR-RIED!
TMP TMP TMP
YOU'D BETTER MEET YOUR GUEST.
IS SOME-ONE HERE?
BRACE YOURSELF!
BRACE MYSELF?! WHAT'RE YOU TALKING ABOUT-
GAH!!
WELCOME HOME!

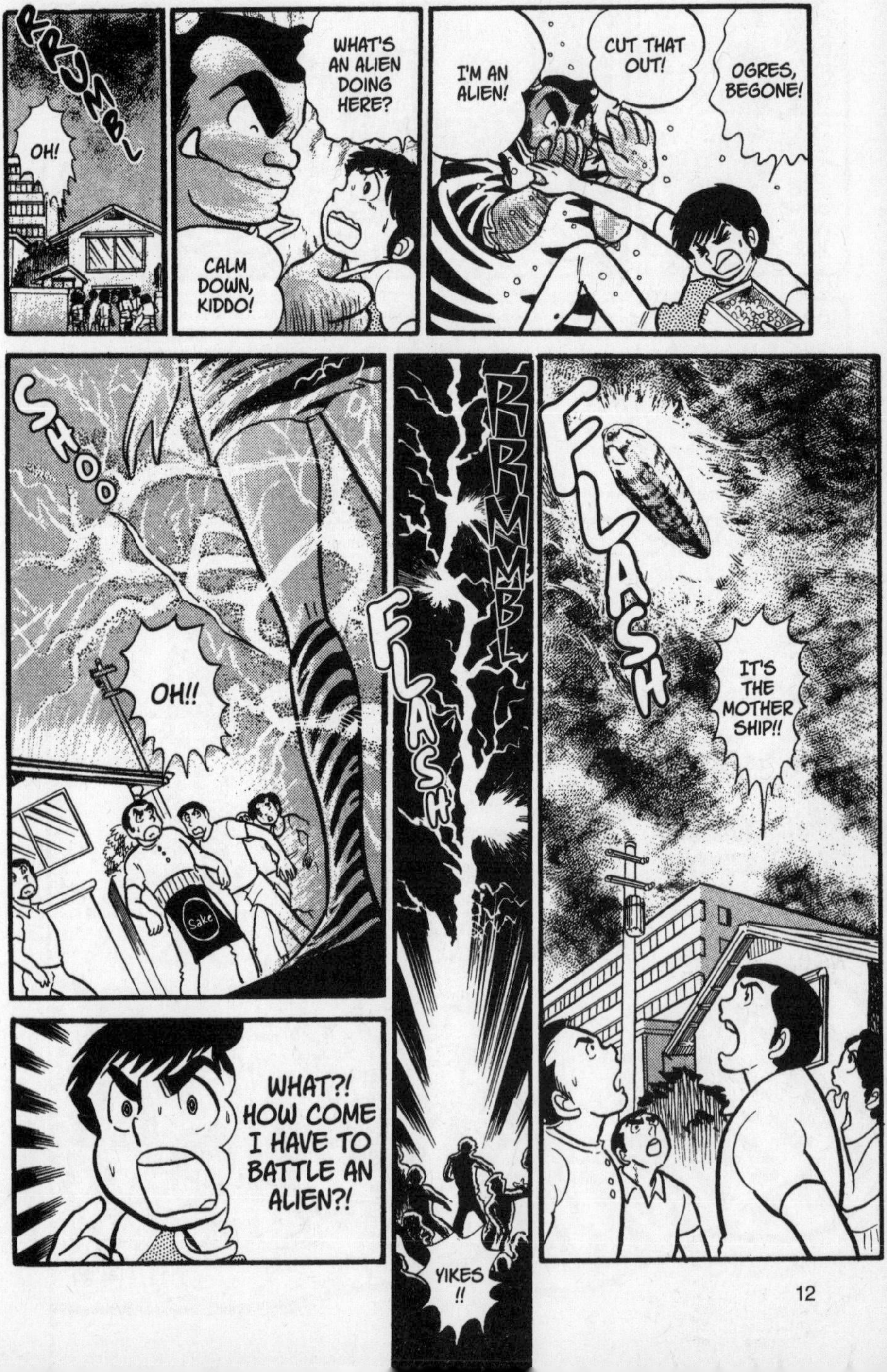
OGRES, BEGONE!
CUT THAT OUT!
I'M AN ALIEN!
WHAT'S AN ALIEN DOING HERE?
CALM DOWN, KIDDO!
RRUMBL
OH!
FLASH
IT'S THE MOTHER SHIP!!
RRRMMBL
FLASH
YIKES!!
SHOOO
OH!!
Sake
WHAT?! HOW COME I HAVE TO BATTLE AN ALIEN?!

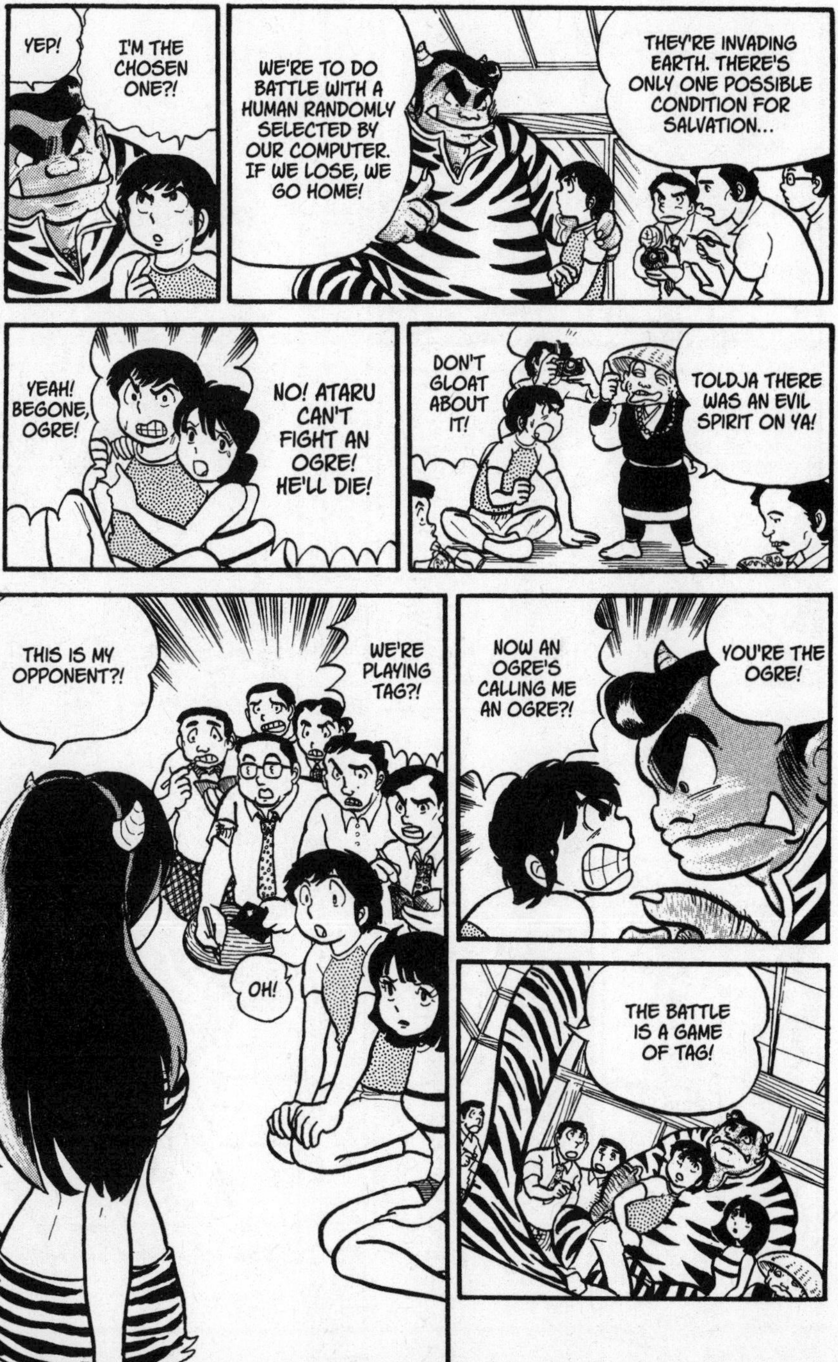
THEY'RE INVADING EARTH. THERE'S ONLY ONE POSSIBLE CONDITION FOR SALVATION...
WE'RE TO DO BATTLE WITH A HUMAN RANDOMLY SELECTED BY OUR COMPUTER. IF WE LOSE, WE GO HOME!
I'M THE CHOSEN ONE?!
YEP!
TOLDJA THERE WAS AN EVIL SPIRIT ON YA!
DON'T GLOAT ABOUT IT!
NO! ATARU CAN'T FIGHT AN OGRE! HE'LL DIE!
YEAH! BEGONE, OGRE!
YOU'RE THE OGRE!
NOW AN OGRE'S CALLING ME AN OGRE?!
THE BATTLE IS A GAME OF TAG!
WE'RE PLAYING TAG?!
THIS IS MY OPPONENT?!
OH!

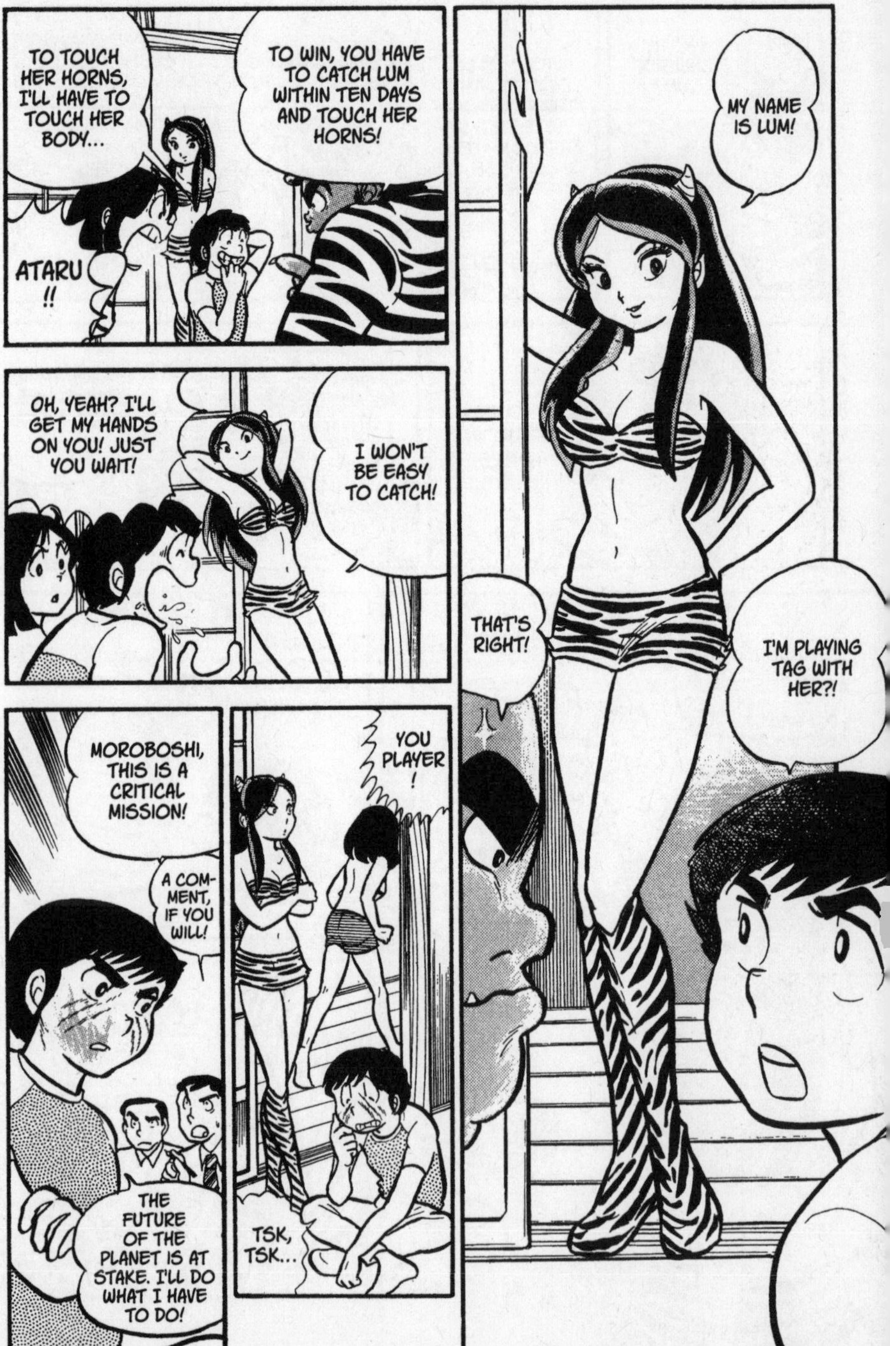
MY NAME IS LUM!
I'M PLAYING TAG WITH HER?!
THAT'S RIGHT!
TO WIN, YOU HAVE TO CATCH LUM WITHIN TEN DAYS AND TOUCH HER HORNS!
TO TOUCH HER HORNS, I'LL HAVE TO TOUCH HER BODY...
ATARU !!
I WON'T BE EASY TO CATCH!
OH, YEAH? I'LL GET MY HANDS ON YOU! JUST YOU WAIT!
YOU PLAYER !
TSK, TSK...
MOROBOSHI, THIS IS A CRITICAL MISSION!
A COMMENT, IF YOU WILL!
THE FUTURE OF THE PLANET IS AT STAKE. I'LL DO WHAT I HAVE TO DO!

SAKURANBO MEANS CHERRY IN JAPANESE.

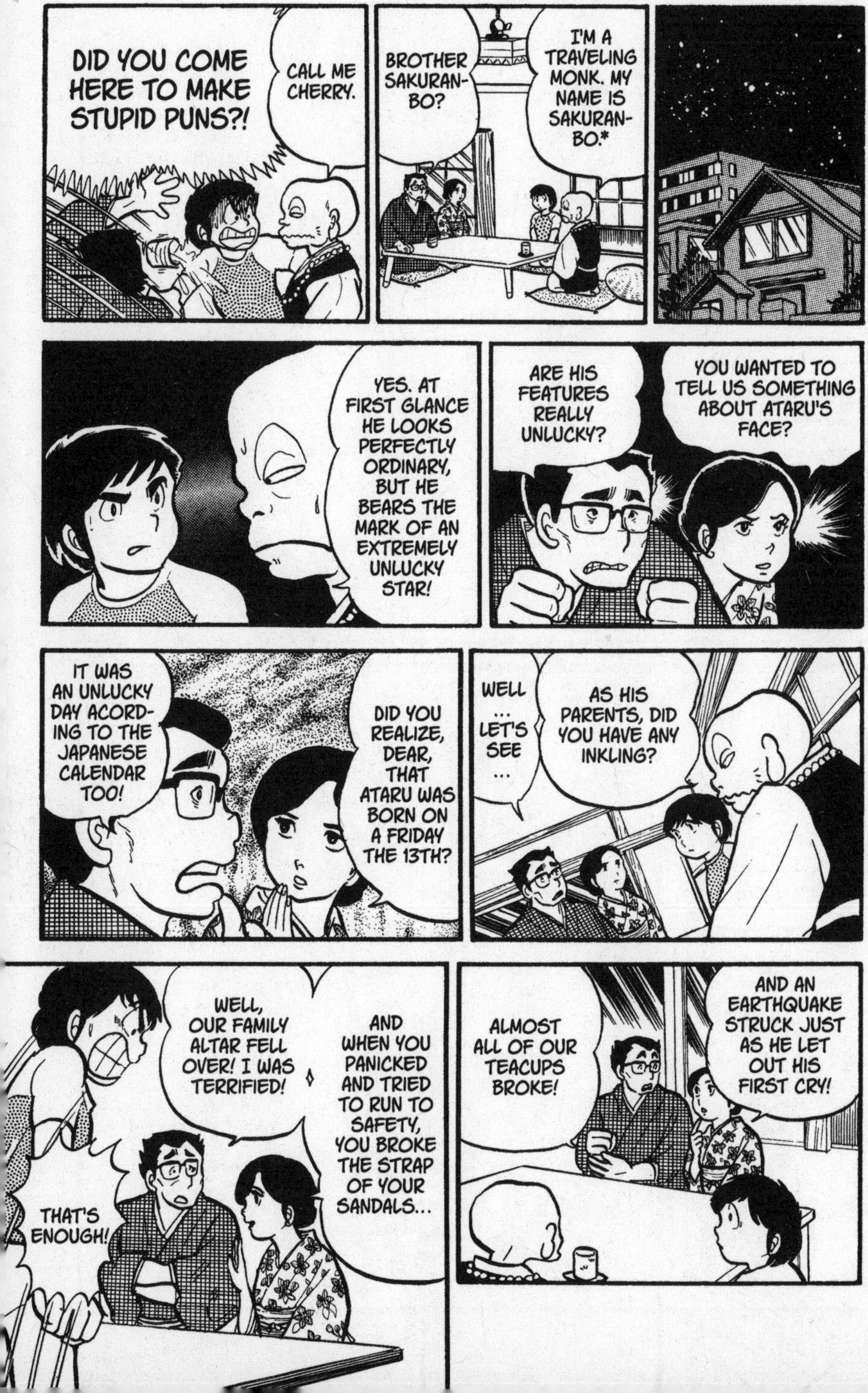
I'M A TRAVELING MONK. MY NAME IS SAKURANBO.*
BROTHER SAKURANBO?
CALL ME CHERRY.
DID YOU COME HERE TO MAKE STUPID PUNS?!
YOU WANTED TO TELL US SOMETHING ABOUT ATARU'S FACE?
ARE HIS FEATURES REALLY UNLUCKY?
YES. AT FIRST GLANCE HE LOOKS PERFECTLY ORDINARY, BUT HE BEARS THE MARK OF AN EXTREMELY UNLUCKY STAR!
AS HIS PARENTS, DID YOU HAVE ANY INKLING?
WELL ... LET'S SEE ...
DID YOU REALIZE, DEAR, THAT ATARU WAS BORN ON A FRIDAY THE 13TH?
IT WAS AN UNLUCKY DAY ACORDING TO THE JAPANESE CALENDAR TOO!
AND AN EARTHQUAKE STRUCK JUST AS HE LET OUT HIS FIRST CRY!
ALMOST ALL OF OUR TEACUPS BROKE!
WELL, OUR FAMILY ALTAR FELL OVER! I WAS TERRIFIED!
AND WHEN YOU PANICKED AND TRIED TO RUN TO SAFETY, YOU BROKE THE STRAP OF YOUR SANDALS...
THAT'S ENOUGH!

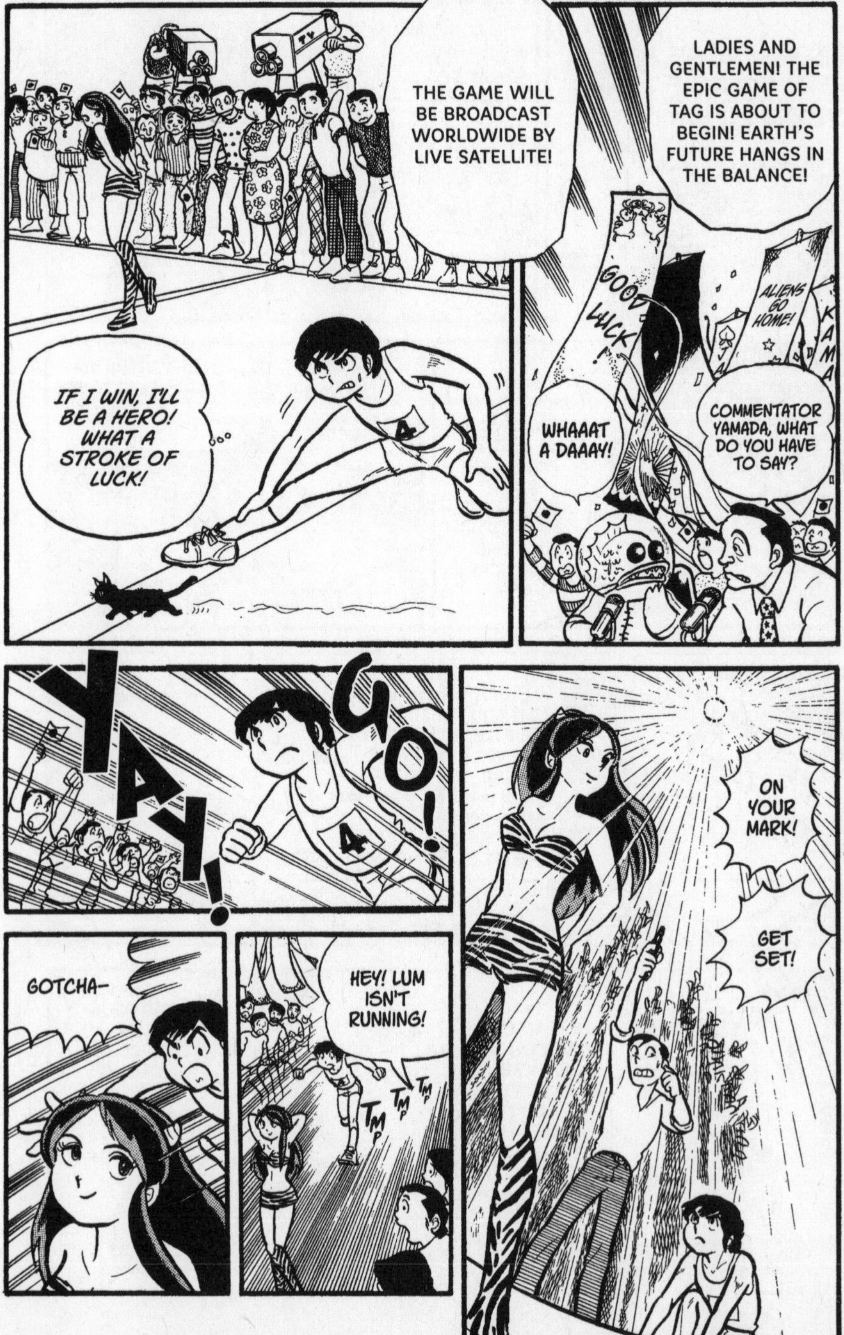
LADIES AND GENTLEMEN! THE EPIC GAME OF TAG IS ABOUT TO BEGIN! EARTH'S FUTURE HANGS IN THE BALANCE!
ALIENS GO HOME!
GOOD LUCK!
COMMENTATOR YAMADA, WHAT DO YOU HAVE TO SAY?
WHAAAT A DAAAY!
THE GAME WILL BE BROADCAST WORLDWIDE BY LIVE SATELLITE!
IF I WIN, I'LL BE A HERO! WHAT A STROKE OF LUCK!
ON YOUR MARK!
GET SET!
GO!
YAY!
HEY! LUM ISN'T RUNNING!
TMP TMP TMP
GOTCHA-

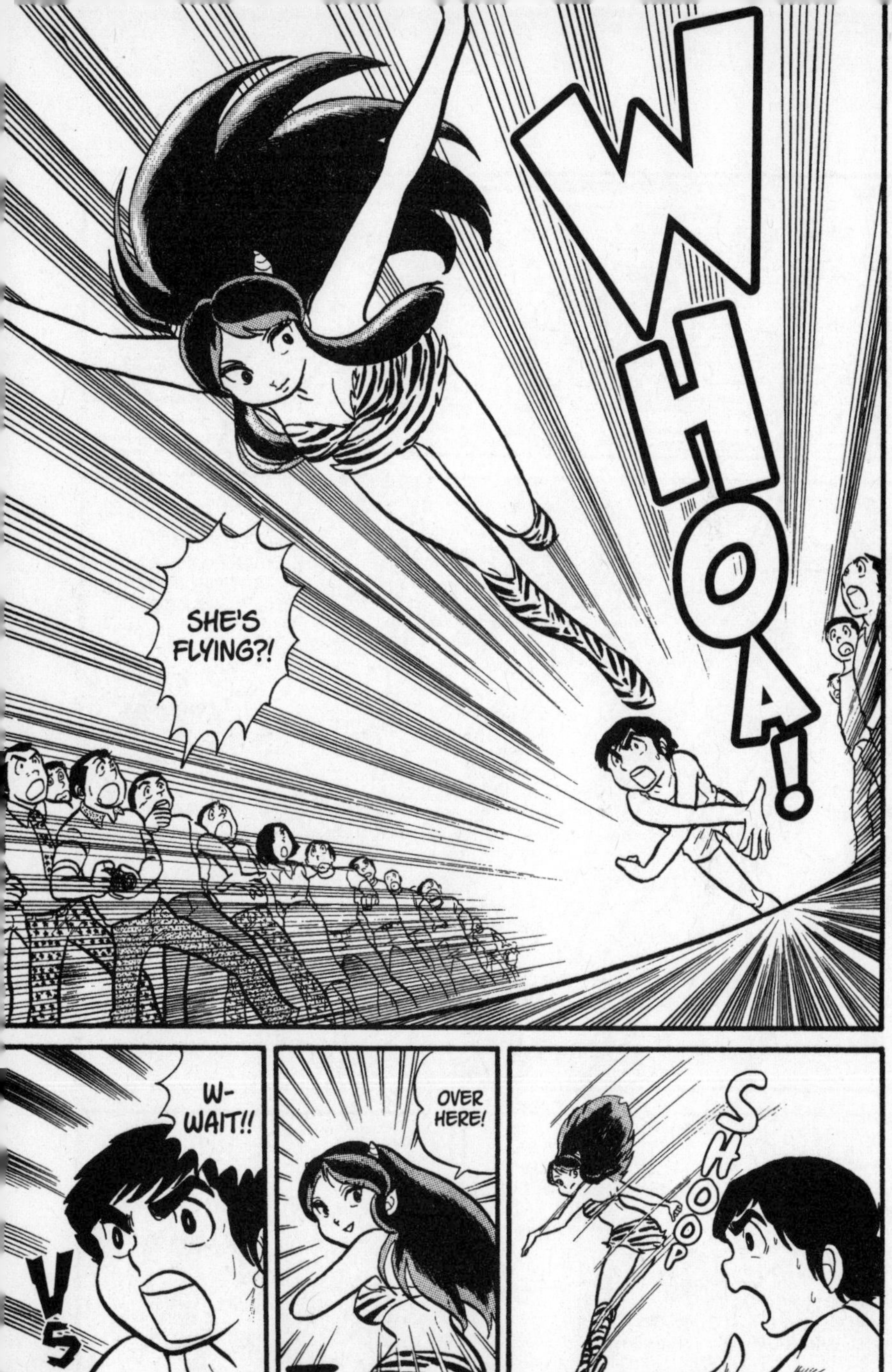
WHOA!
SHE'S FLYING?!
SHOOP
OVER HERE!
TMP
W-WAIT!!
VSH

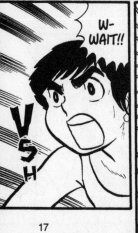

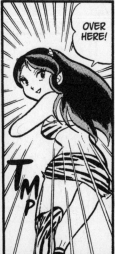

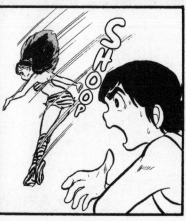

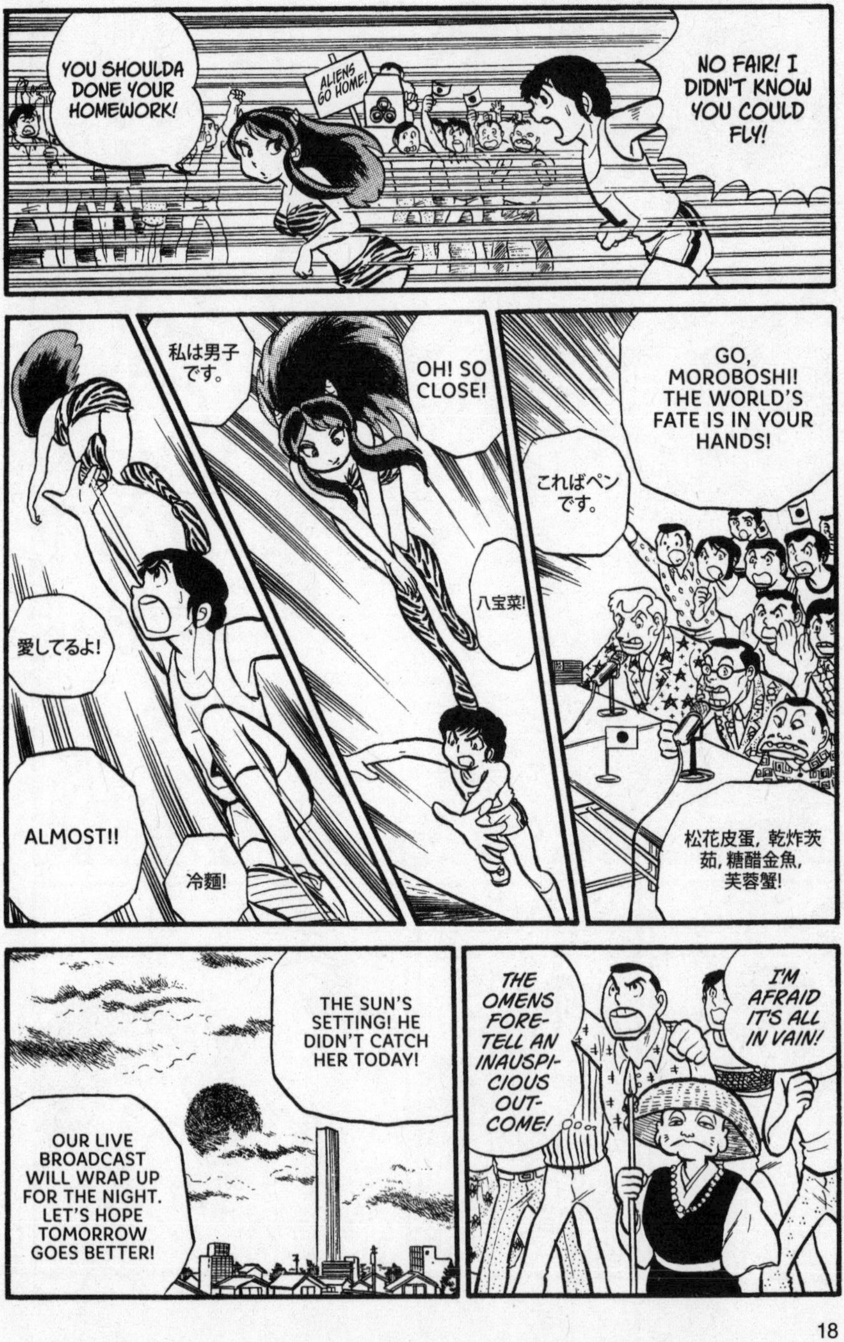
NO FAIR! I DIDN'T KNOW YOU COULD FLY!
ALIENS GO HOME!
YOU SHOULDA DONE YOUR HOMEWORK!
GO, MOROBOSHI!! THE WORLD'S FATE IS IN YOUR HANDS!
こればペンです。
松花皮蛋, 乾炸茨茹, 糖醋金魚, 芙蓉蟹!
OH! SO CLOSE!
私は男子です。
八宝菜!
愛してるよ!
ALMOST!!
冷麵!
I'M AFRAID IT'S ALL IN VAIN!
THE OMENS FORETELL AN INAUSPICIOUS OUTCOME!
THE SUN'S SETTING! HE DIDN'T CATCH HER TODAY!
OUR LIVE BROADCAST WILL WRAP UP FOR THE NIGHT. LET'S HOPE TOMORROW GOES BETTER!

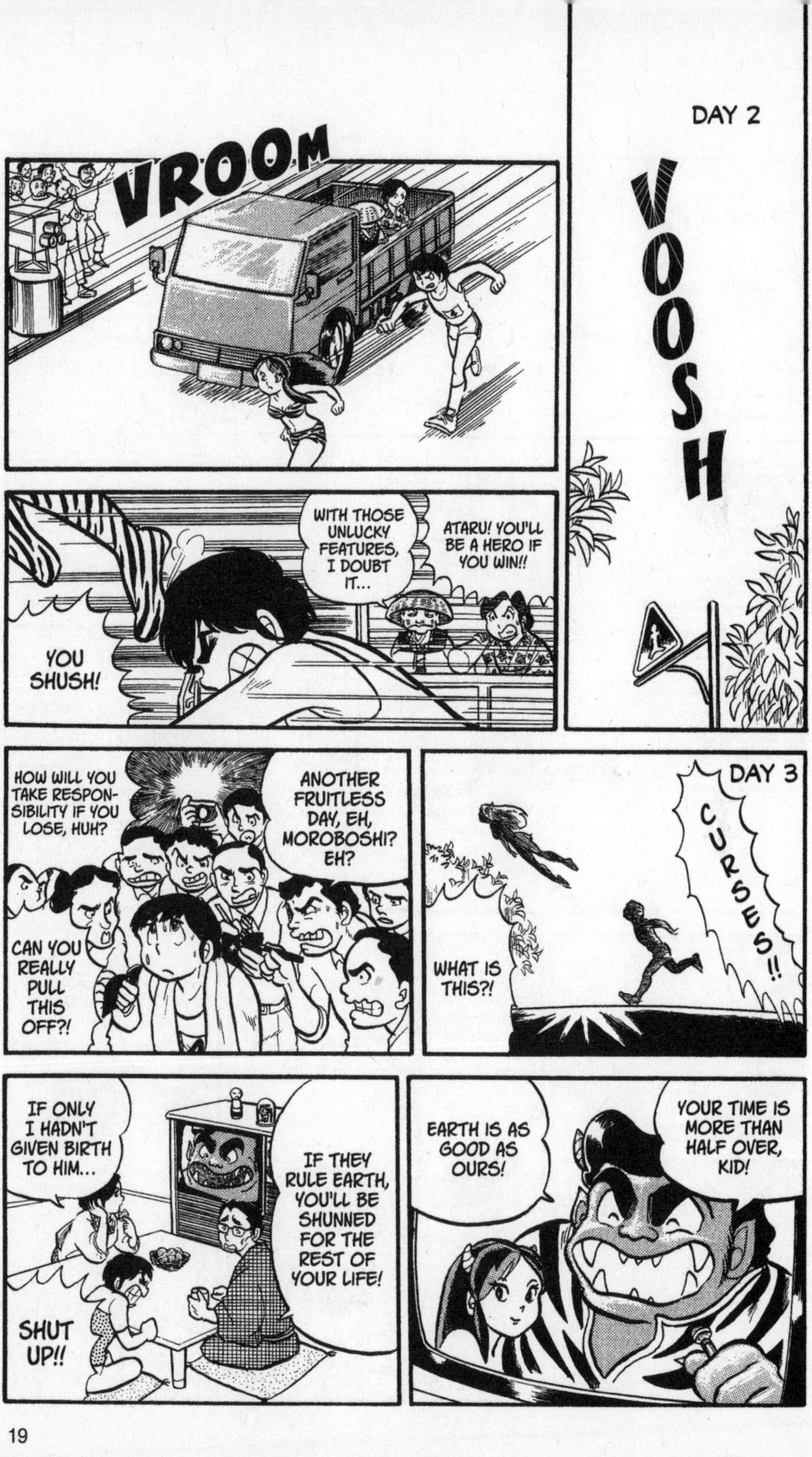
DAY 2
VOOSH
VROOM
ATARU! YOU'LL BE A HERO IF YOU WIN!!
WITH THOSE UNLUCKY FEATURES, I DOUBT IT...
YOU SHUSH!
DAY 3
CURSES!!
WHAT IS THIS?!
ANOTHER FRUITLESS DAY, EH, MOROBOSHI? EH?
HOW WILL YOU TAKE RESPONSIBILITY IF YOU LOSE, HUH?
CAN YOU REALLY PULL THIS OFF?!
YOUR TIME IS MORE THAN HALF OVER, KID!
EARTH IS AS GOOD AS OURS!
IF THEY RULE EARTH, YOU'LL BE SHUNNED FOR THE REST OF YOUR LIFE!
IF ONLY I HADN'T GIVEN BIRTH TO HIM...
SHUT UP!!

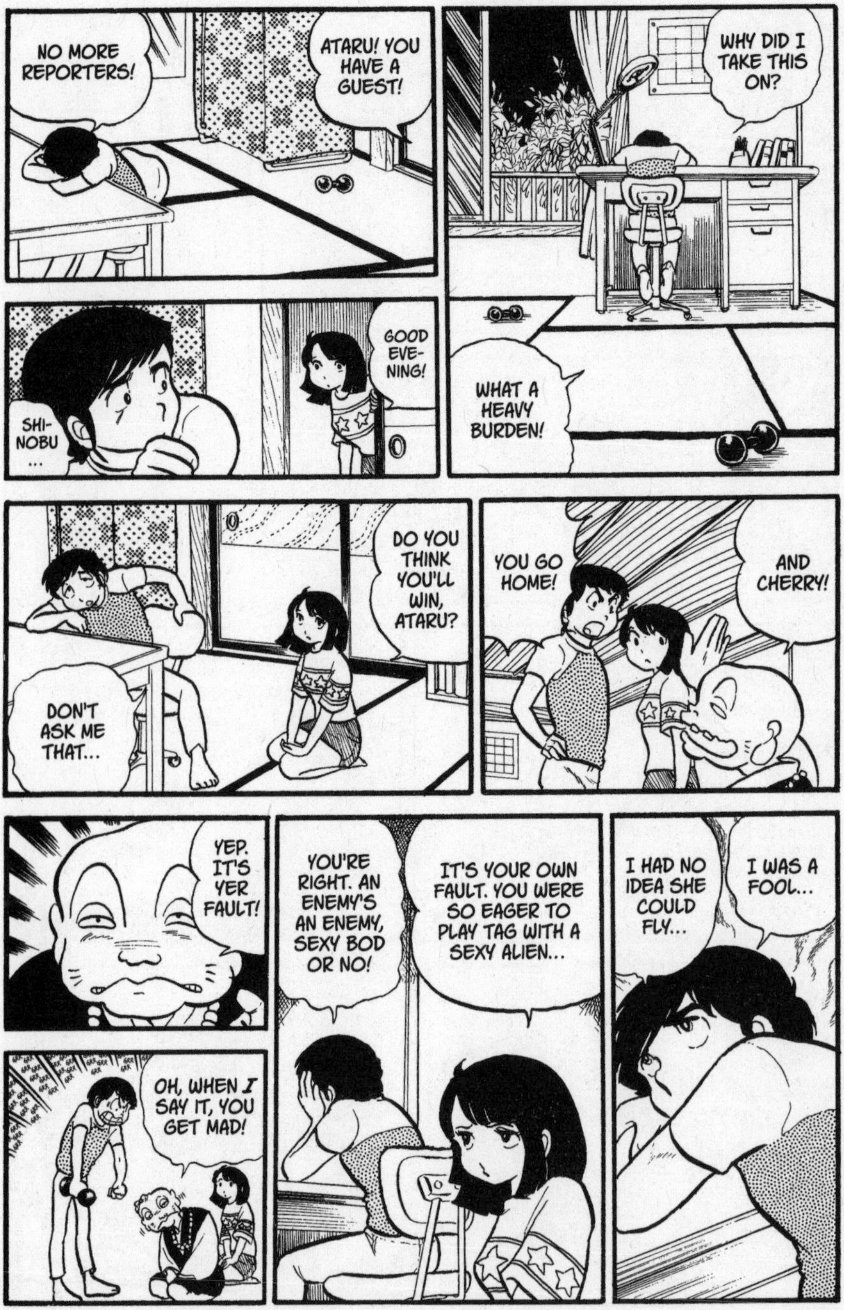

WHY DID I TAKE THIS ON?
WHAT A HEAVY BURDEN!
ATARU! YOU HAVE A GUEST!
NO MORE REPORTERS!
GOOD EVE-NING!
SHI-NOBU...
AND CHERRY!
YOU GO HOME!
DO YOU THINK YOU'LL WIN, ATARU?
DON'T ASK ME THAT...
I WAS A FOOL...
I HAD NO IDEA SHE COULD FLY...
IT'S YOUR OWN FAULT. YOU WERE SO EAGER TO PLAY TAG WITH A SEXY ALIEN...
YOU'RE RIGHT. AN ENEMY'S AN ENEMY, SEXY BOD OR NO!
YEP. IT'S YER FAULT!
OH, WHEN I SAY IT, YOU GET MAD!

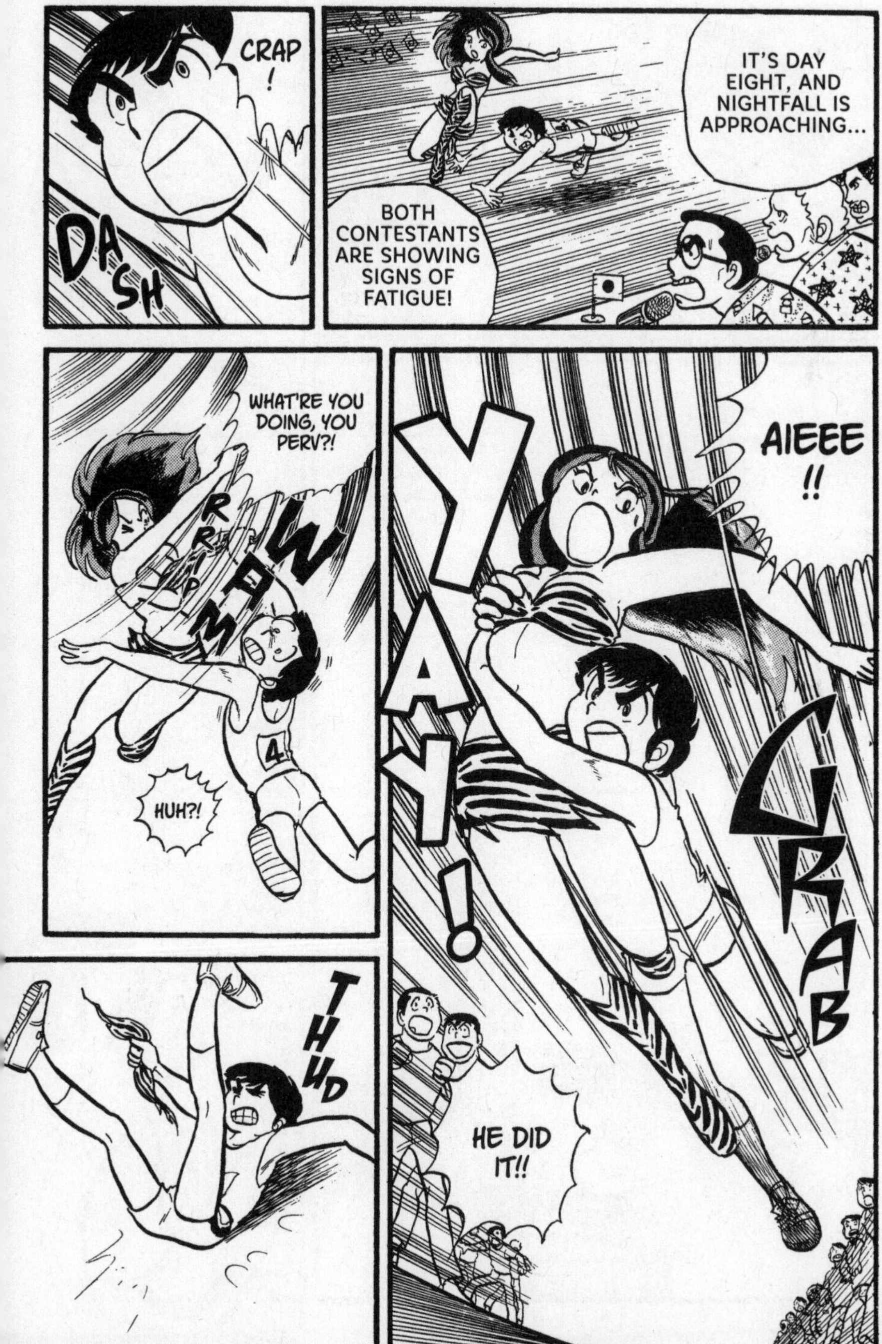
IT'S DAY EIGHT, AND NIGHTFALL IS APPROACHING...
BOTH CONTESTANTS ARE SHOWING SIGNS OF FATIGUE!
CRAP!
DASH
YAY!
AIEEE!!
GRAB
HE DID IT!!
WHAT'RE YOU DOING, YOU PERV?!
RRRIP
WAM
HUH?!
THUD

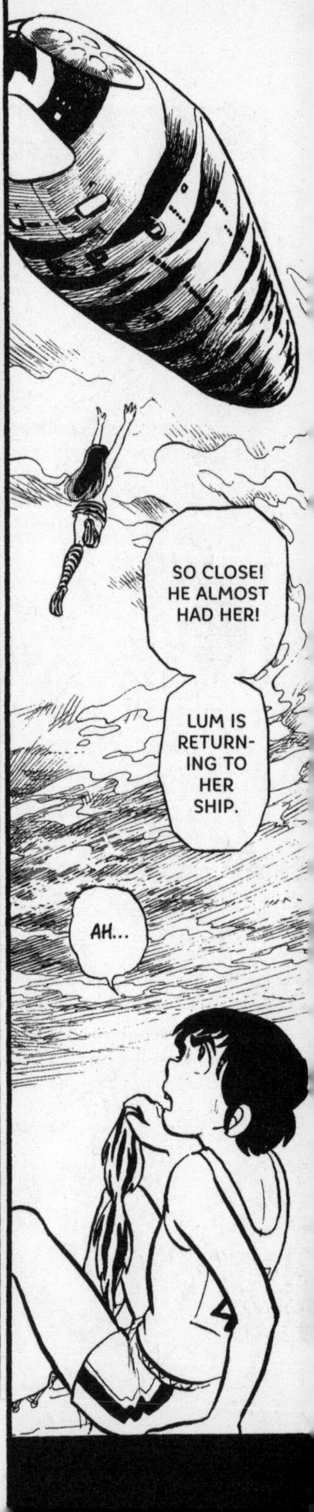
SO CLOSE! HE ALMOST HAD HER!
LUM IS RETURNING TO HER SHIP.
AH...

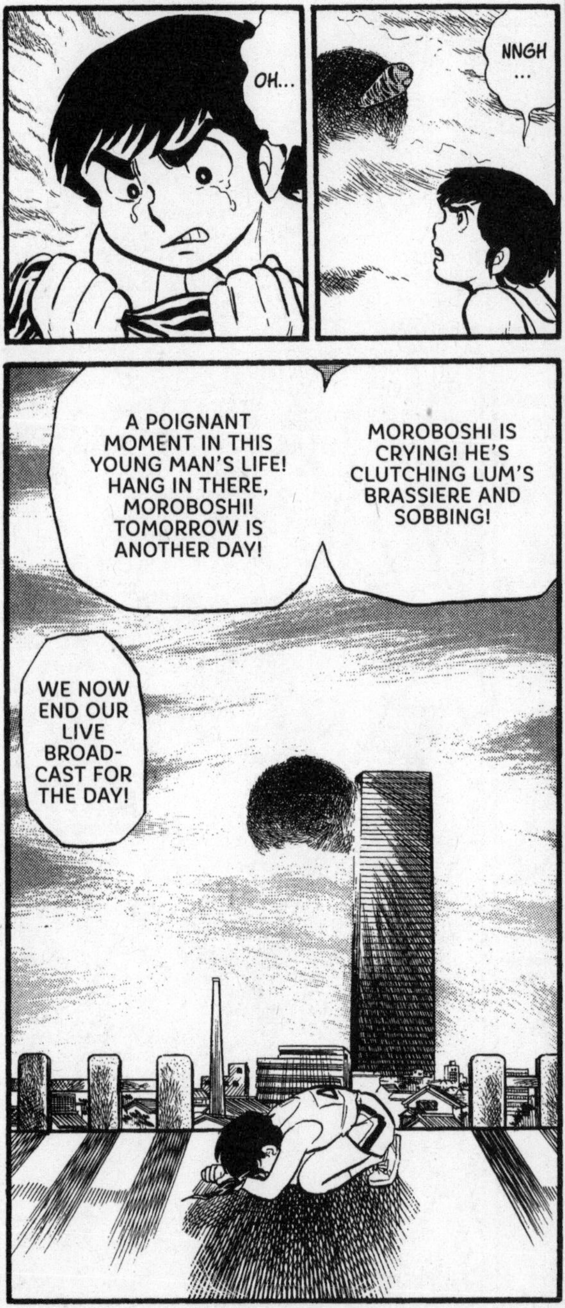
NNGH ...
OH...
MOROBOSHI IS CRYING! HE'S CLUTCHING LUM'S BRASSIERE AND SOBBING!
A POIGNANT MOMENT IN THIS YOUNG MAN'S LIFE! HANG IN THERE, MOROBOSHI! TOMORROW IS ANOTHER DAY!
WE NOW END OUR LIVE BROADCAST FOR THE DAY!

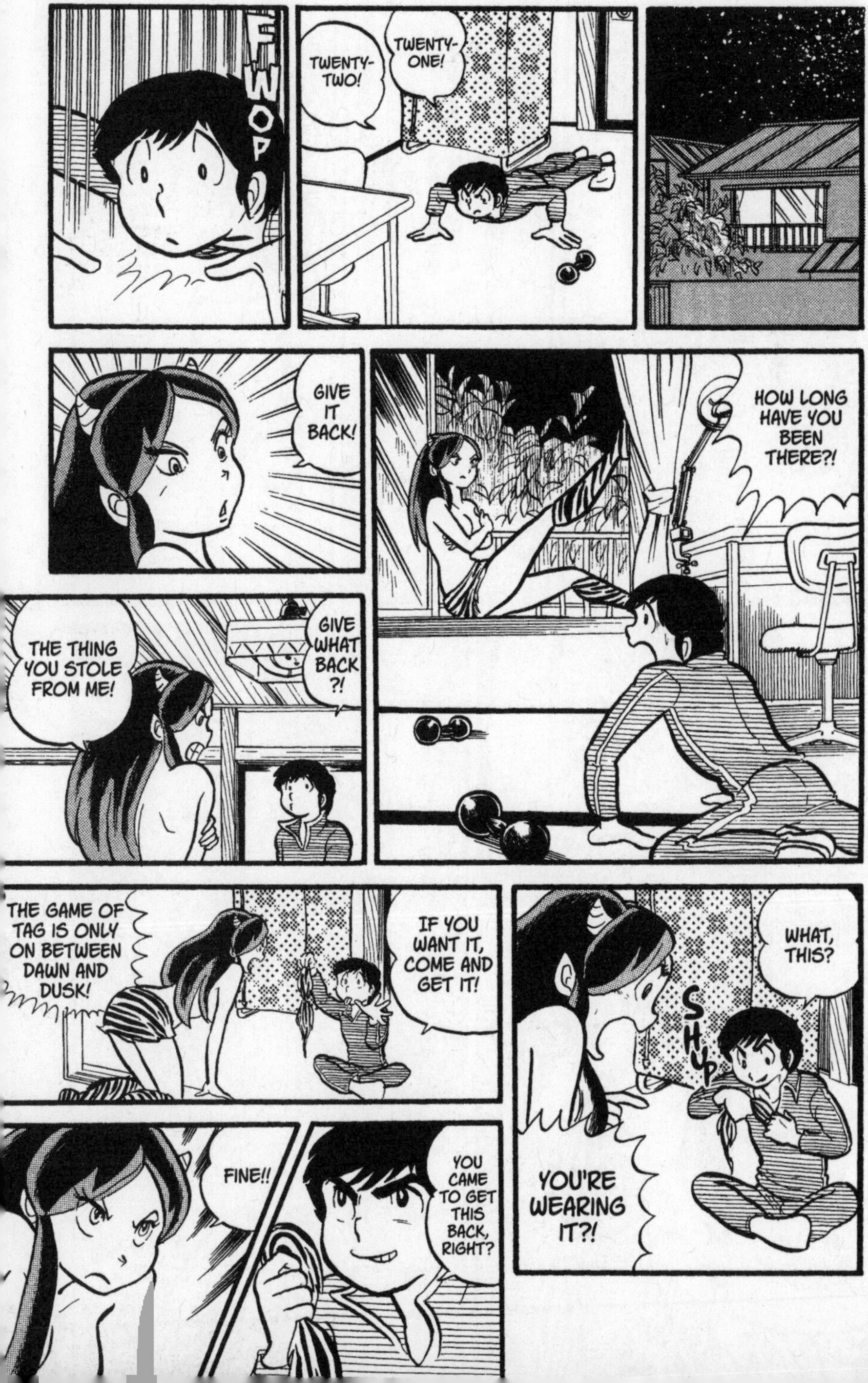
TWENTY-ONE!
TWENTY-TWO!
FWOP
HOW LONG HAVE YOU BEEN THERE?!
GIVE IT BACK!
GIVE WHAT BACK?!
THE THING YOU STOLE FROM ME!
WHAT, THIS?
SHUP
YOU'RE WEARING IT?!
IF YOU WANT IT, COME AND GET IT!
THE GAME OF TAG IS ONLY ON BETWEEN DAWN AND DUSK!
YOU CAME TO GET THIS BACK, RIGHT?
FINE!!

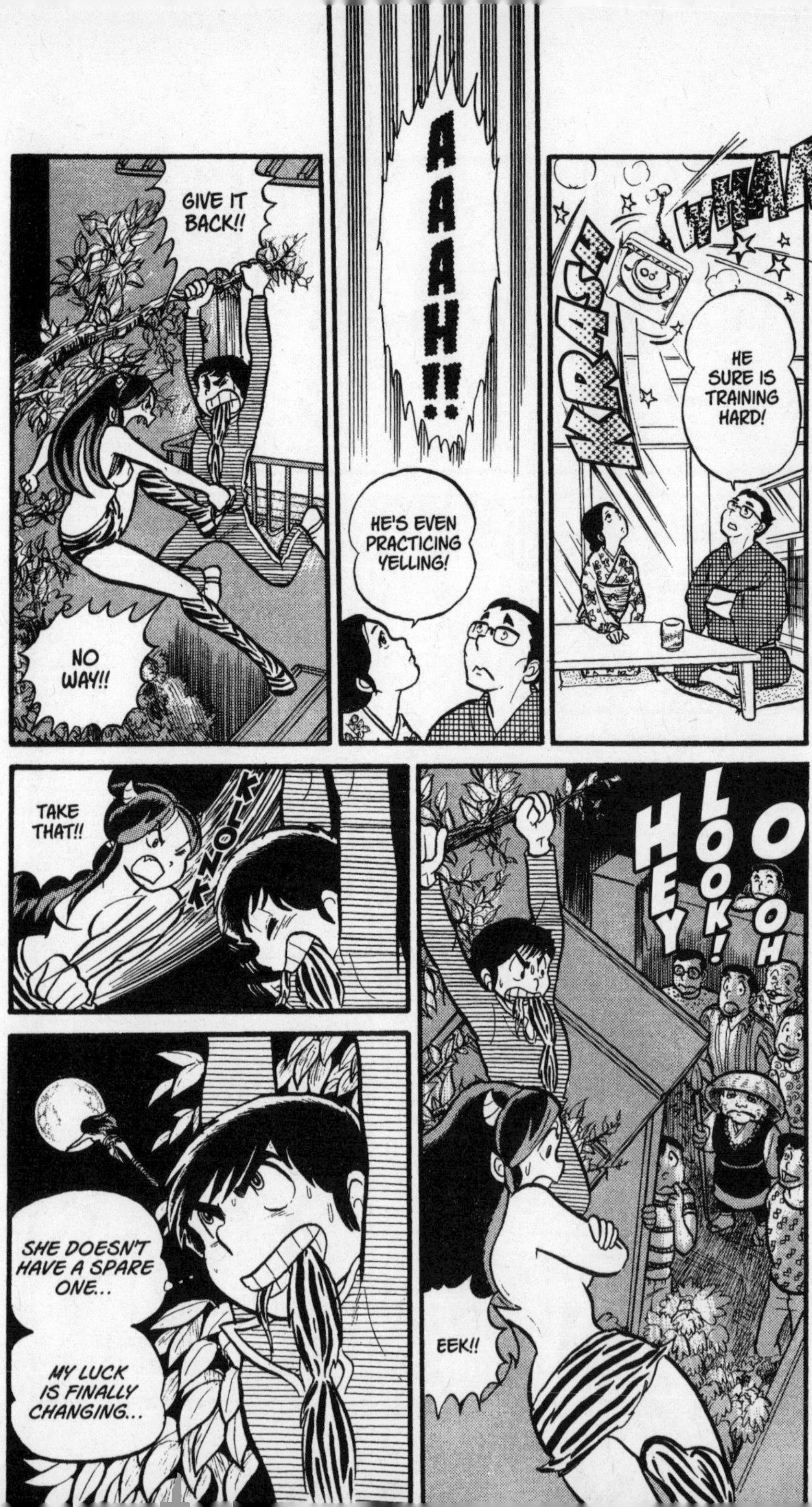
WHAM
KRASH
HE SURE IS TRAINING HARD!
AAAAH!!
HE'S EVEN PRACTICING YELLING!
GIVE IT BACK!!
NO WAY!!
OOH
LOOK!
HEY
EEK!!
TAKE THAT!!
KLONK
SHE DOESN'T HAVE A SPARE ONE...
MY LUCK IS FINALLY CHANGING...

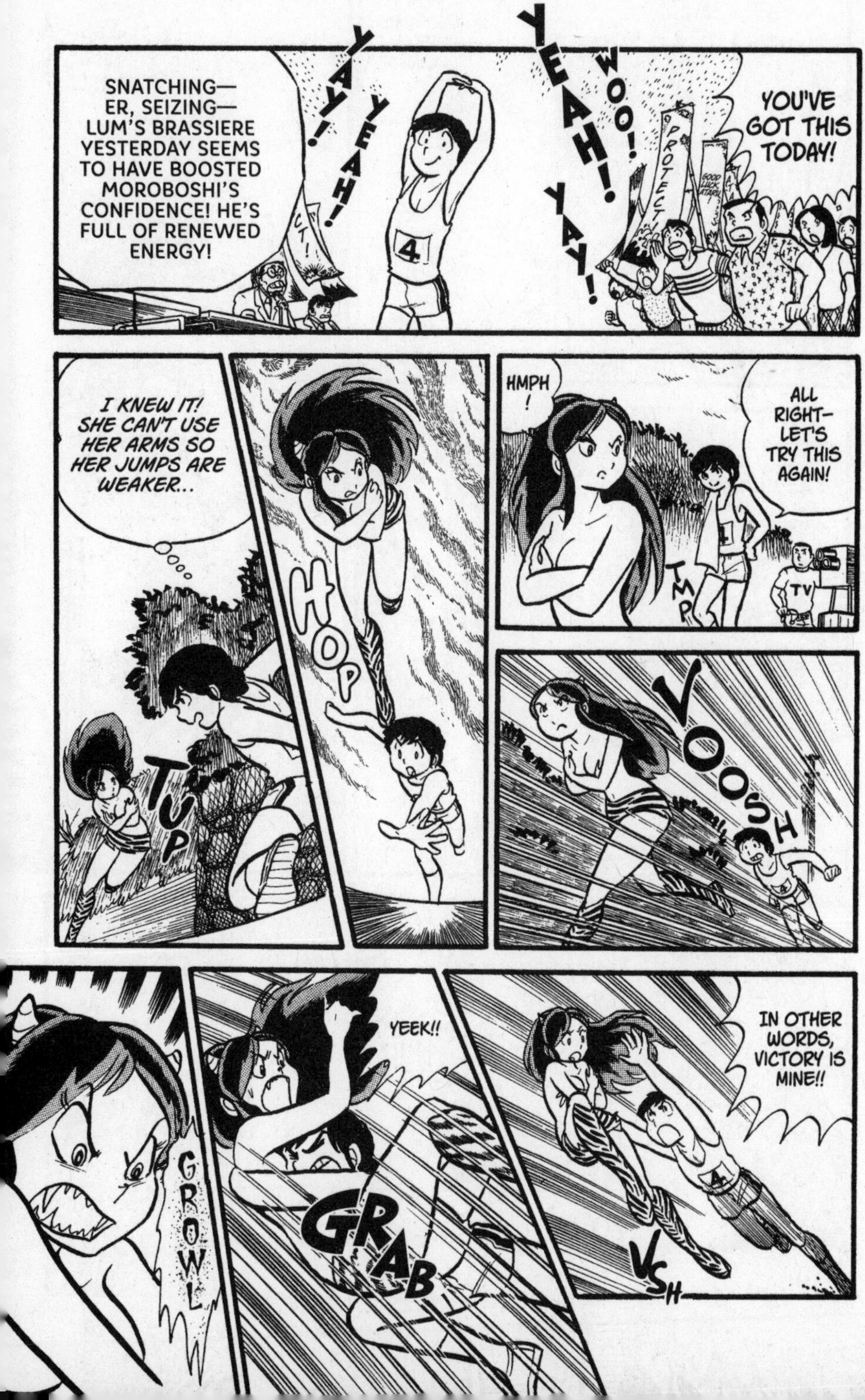
YOU'VE GOT THIS TODAY!
PROTECT
GOOD LUCK ATARU!
WOO!
YEAH!
YAY!
YEAH!
YAY!
SNATCHING— ER, SEIZING— LUM'S BRASSIERE YESTERDAY SEEMS TO HAVE BOOSTED MOROBOSHI'S CONFIDENCE! HE'S FULL OF RENEWED ENERGY!
ALL RIGHT— LET'S TRY THIS AGAIN!
HMPH!
TMP
TV
VOOSH
HOP
I KNEW IT! SHE CAN'T USE HER ARMS SO HER JUMPS ARE WEAKER...
TUP
IN OTHER WORDS, VICTORY IS MINE!!
VSH
YEEK!!
GRAB
GROWL

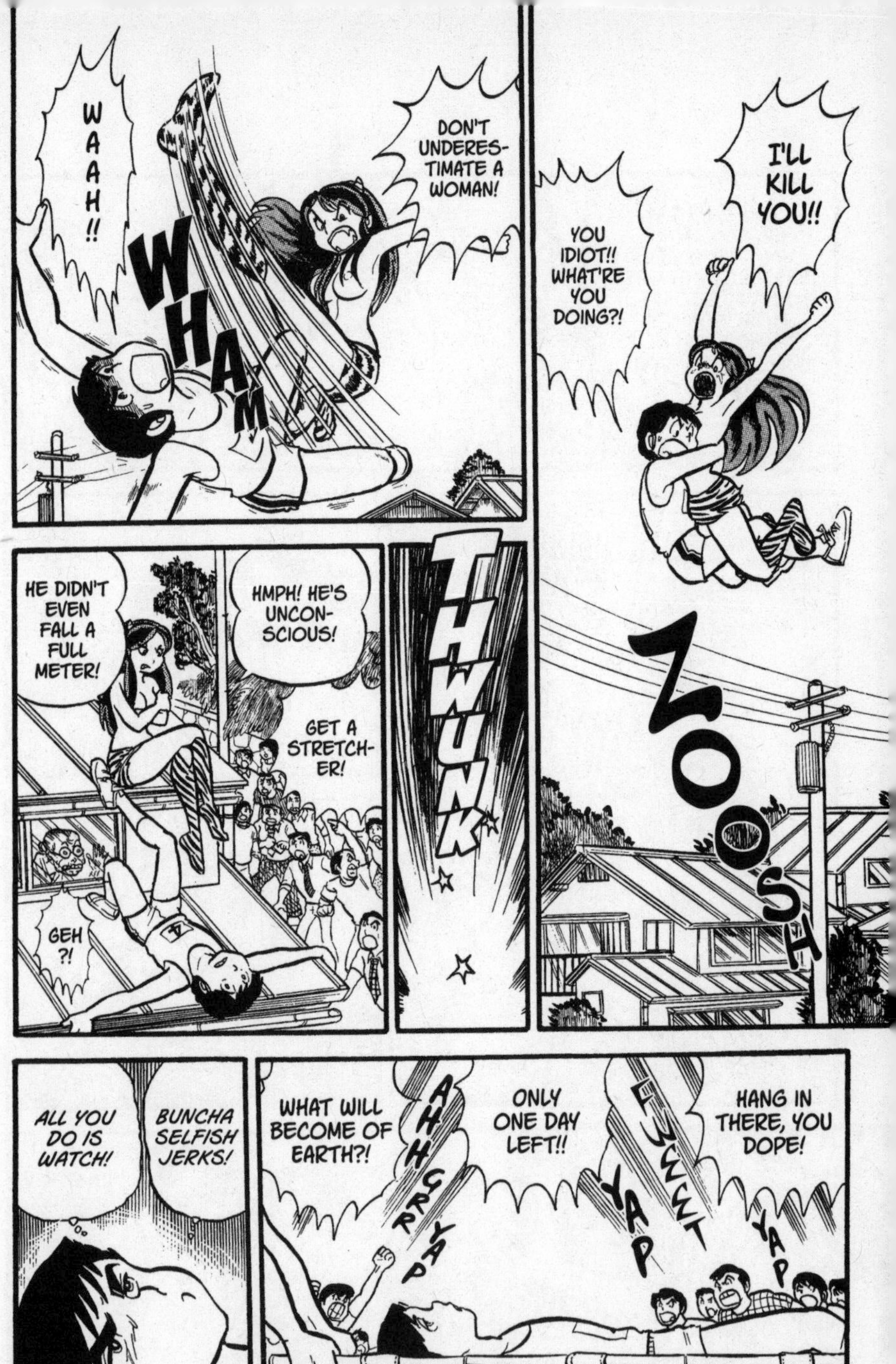
I'LL KILL YOU!!
YOU IDIOT!! WHAT'RE YOU DOING?!
ZOOSH
DON'T UNDERES-TIMATE A WOMAN!
WHAM
WAAAH!!
THWUNK
HMPH! HE'S UNCON-SCIOUS!
HE DIDN'T EVEN FALL A FULL METER!
GET A STRETCH-ER!
GEH ?!
HANG IN THERE, YOU DOPE!
YAP
FWEET
YAP
ONLY ONE DAY LEFT!!
AHHH
GRRR
YAP
WHAT WILL BECOME OF EARTH?!
BUNCHA SELFISH JERKS!
ALL YOU DO IS WATCH!

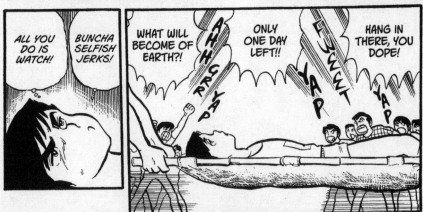

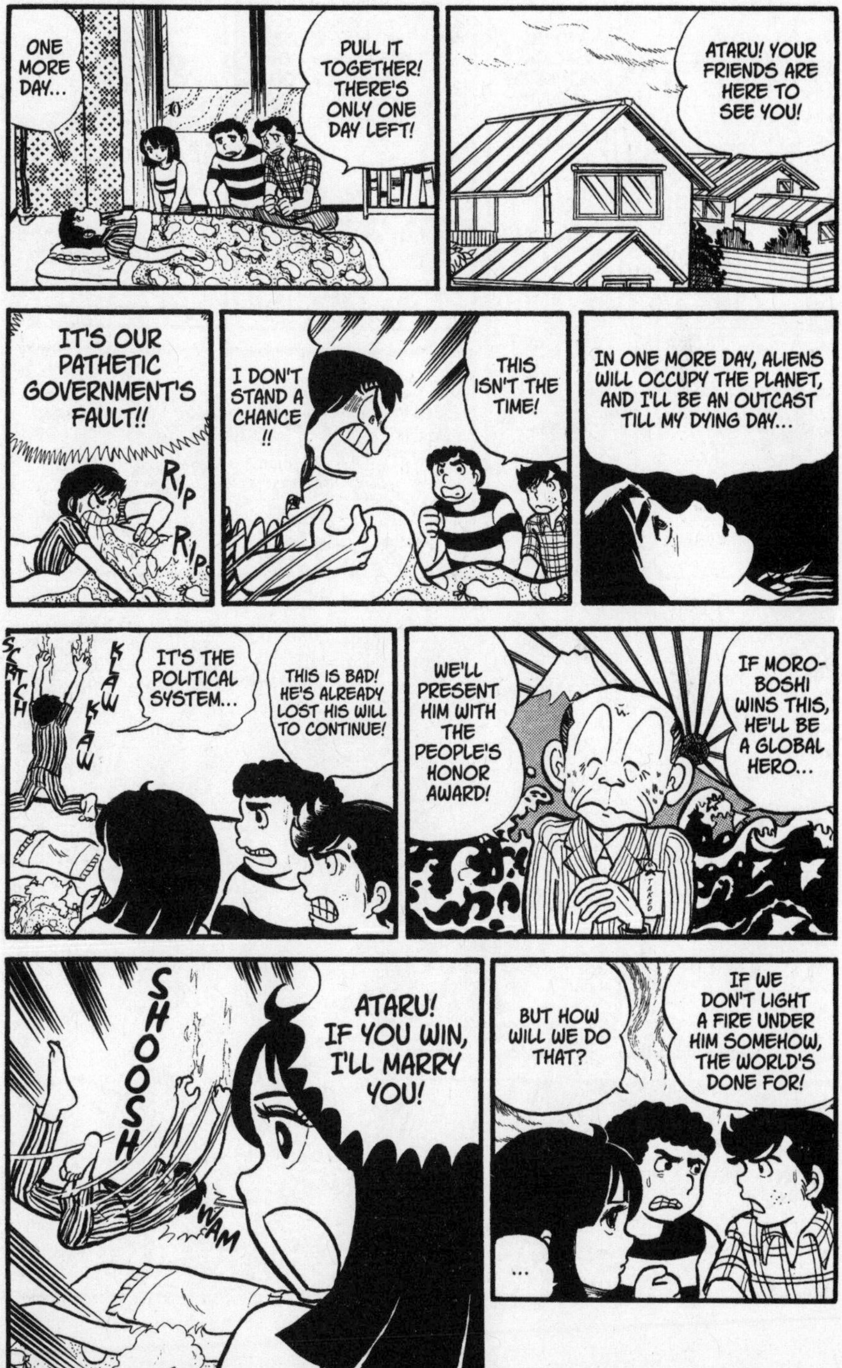
ATARU! YOUR FRIENDS ARE HERE TO SEE YOU!
PULL IT TOGETHER! THERE'S ONLY ONE DAY LEFT!
ONE MORE DAY...
IN ONE MORE DAY, ALIENS WILL OCCUPY THE PLANET, AND I'LL BE AN OUTCAST TILL MY DYING DAY...
THIS ISN'T THE TIME!
I DON'T STAND A CHANCE !!
IT'S OUR PATHETIC GOVERNMENT'S FAULT!!
RIP
RIP
IF MORO-BOSHI WINS THIS, HE'LL BE A GLOBAL HERO...
WE'LL PRESENT HIM WITH THE PEOPLE'S HONOR AWARD!
THIS IS BAD! HE'S ALREADY LOST HIS WILL TO CONTINUE!
IT'S THE POLITICAL SYSTEM...
KLAW
KLAW
SCRTCH
IF WE DON'T LIGHT A FIRE UNDER HIM SOMEHOW, THE WORLD'S DONE FOR!
BUT HOW WILL WE DO THAT?
...
ATARU! IF YOU WIN, I'LL MARRY YOU!
SHOOOSH
WAM

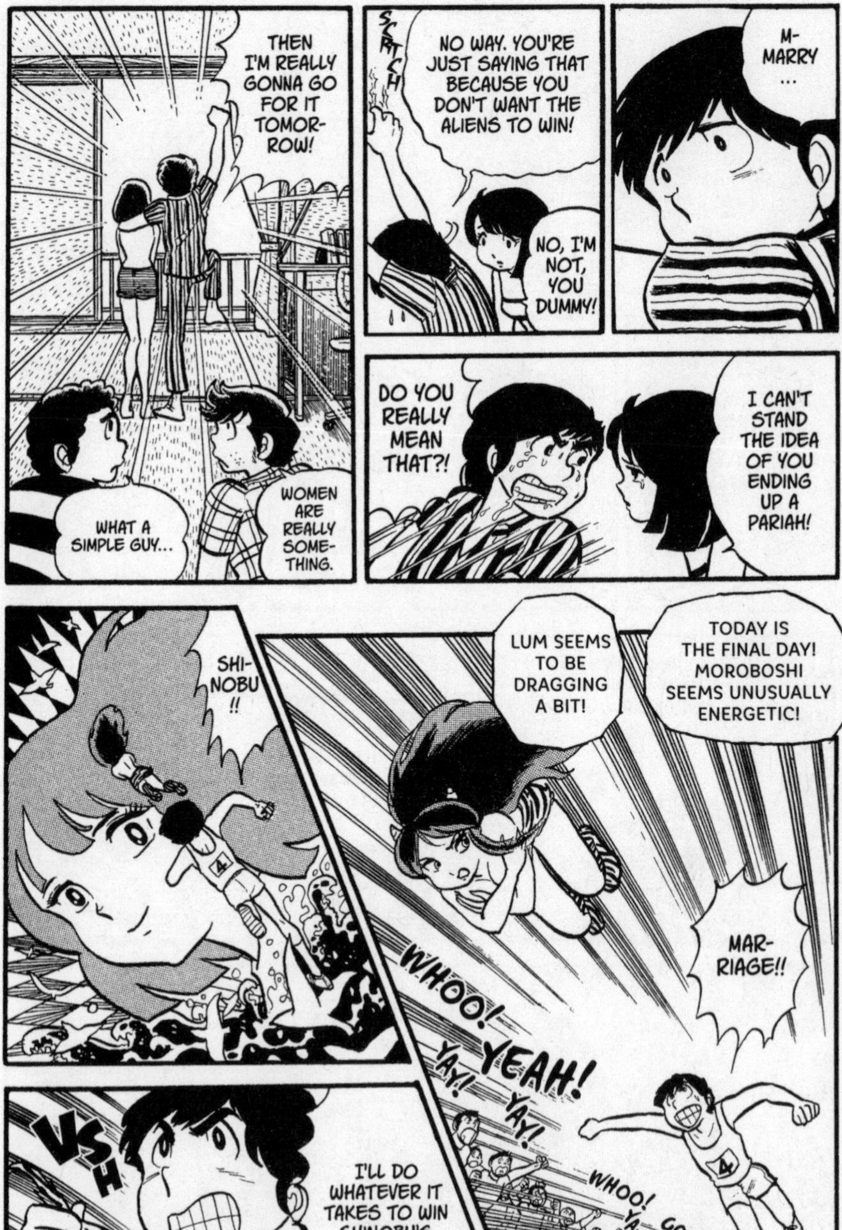
M-MARRY ...
SCRTCH
NO WAY. YOU'RE JUST SAYING THAT BECAUSE YOU DON'T WANT THE ALIENS TO WIN!
NO, I'M NOT, YOU DUMMY!
I CAN'T STAND THE IDEA OF YOU ENDING UP A PARIAH!
DO YOU REALLY MEAN THAT?!
THEN I'M REALLY GONNA GO FOR IT TOMORROW!
WOMEN ARE REALLY SOMETHING.
WHAT A SIMPLE GUY...
TODAY IS THE FINAL DAY! MOROBOSHI SEEMS UNUSUALLY ENERGETIC!
LUM SEEMS TO BE DRAGGING A BIT!
MARRIAGE!!
WHOO!
YEAH!
YAY!
YAY!
WHOO! YAY!!
GOOO! YAY!!
SHINOBU!!
VSH
I'LL DO WHATEVER IT TAKES TO WIN SHINOBU'S HAND!

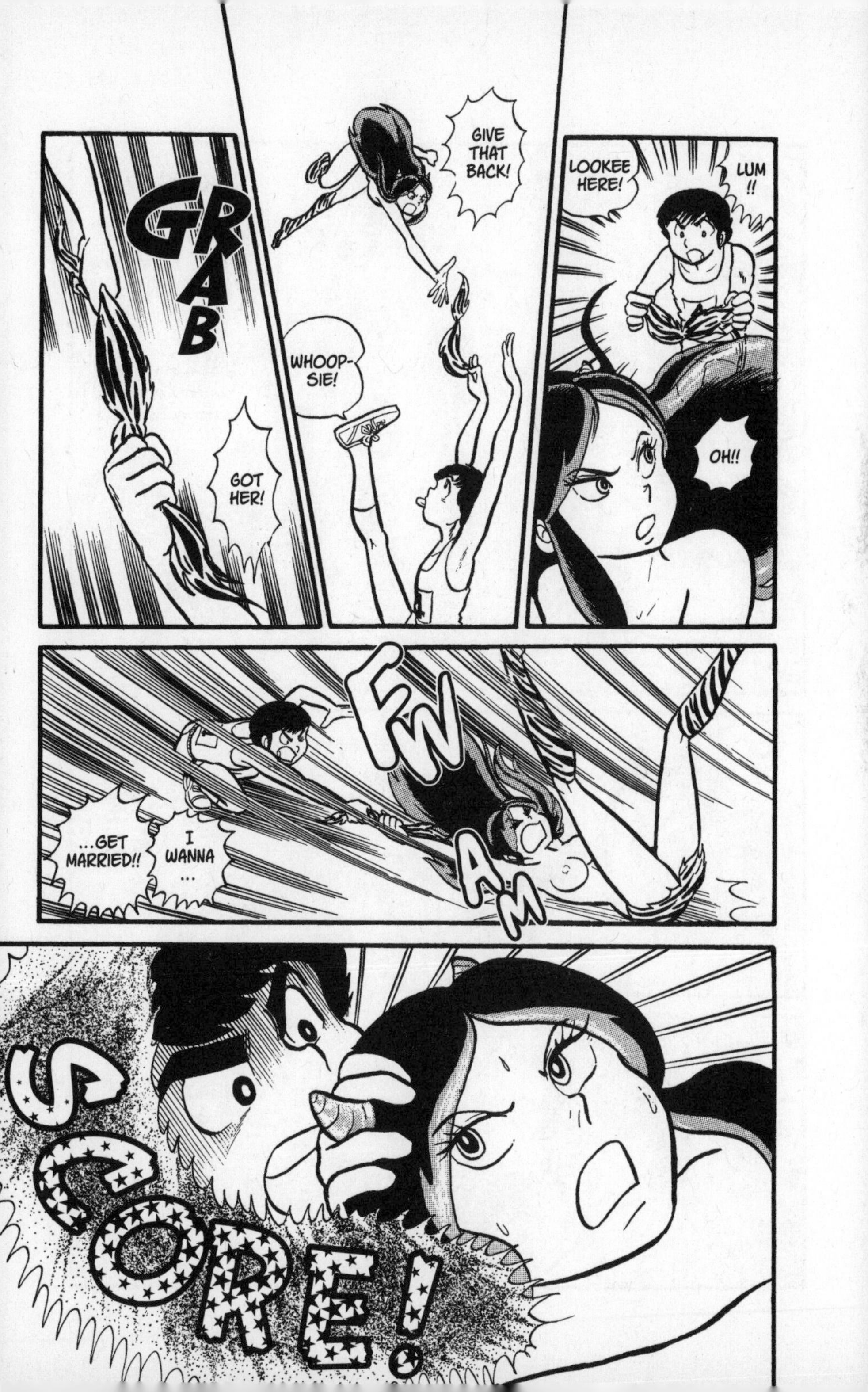
LUM !!
LOOKEE HERE!
OH!!
GIVE THAT BACK!
WHOOP-SIE!
GRAB
GOT HER!
FWAM
I WANNA ...
...GET MARRIED!!
SCORE!

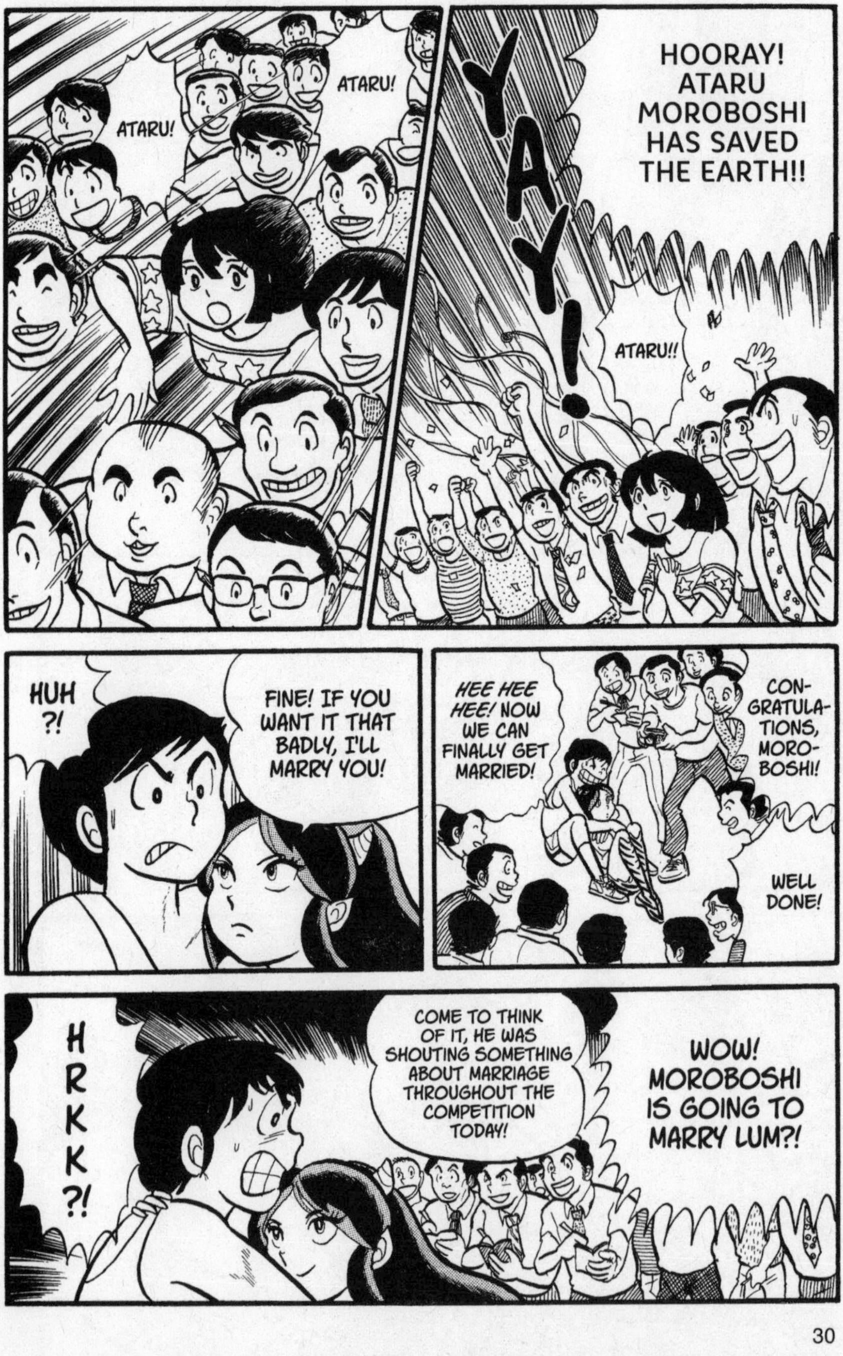
HOORAY! ATARU MOROBOSHI HAS SAVED THE EARTH!!
YAY!
ATARU!!
ATARU!
ATARU!
CON-GRATULA-TIONS, MORO-BOSHI!
HEE HEE HEE! NOW WE CAN FINALLY GET MARRIED!
WELL DONE!
FINE! IF YOU WANT IT THAT BADLY, I'LL MARRY YOU!
HUH ?!
WOW! MOROBOSHI IS GOING TO MARRY LUM?!
COME TO THINK OF IT, HE WAS SHOUTING SOMETHING ABOUT MARRIAGE THROUGHOUT THE COMPETITION TODAY!
HRKK ?!

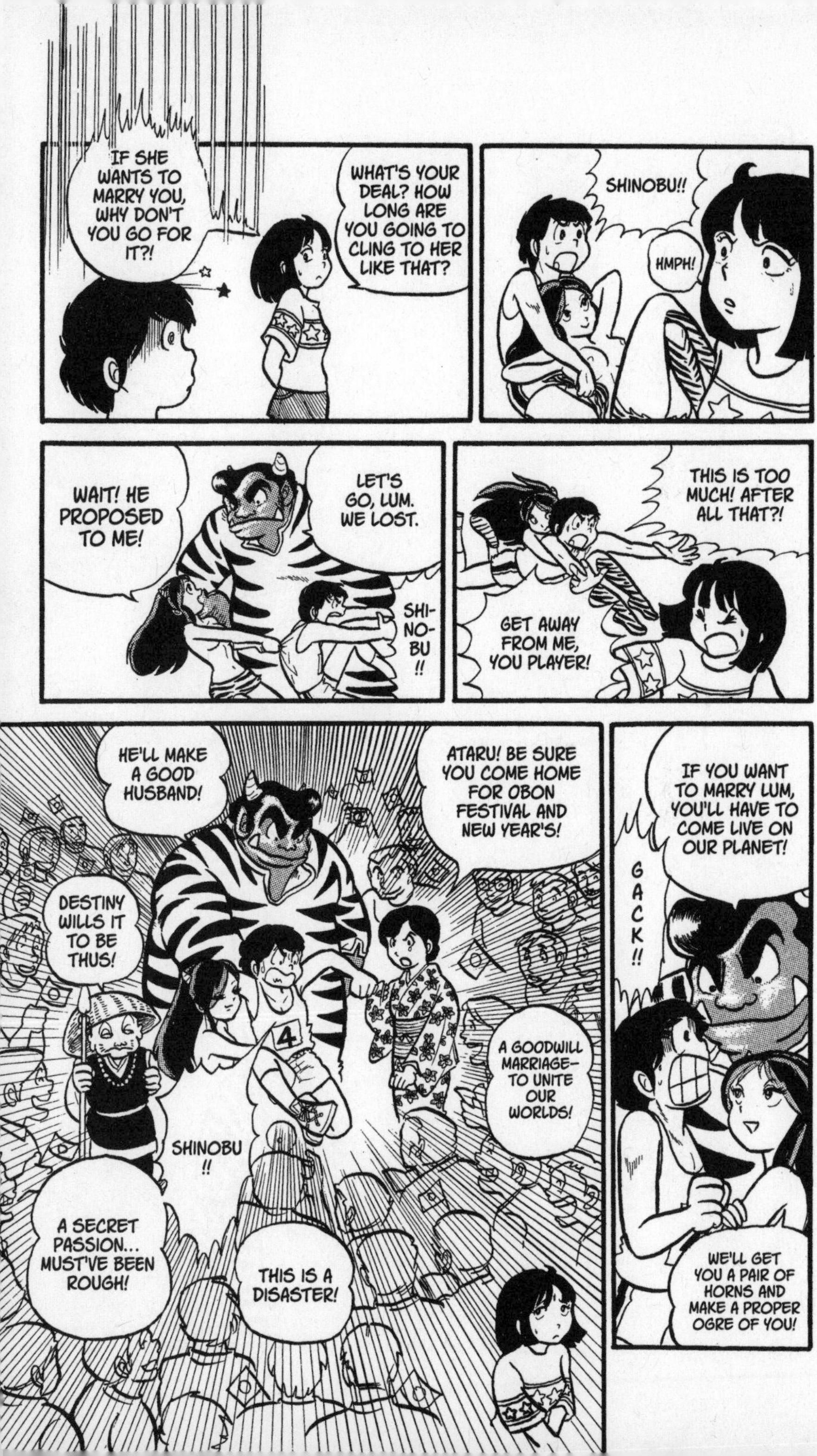
SHINOBU!!
HMPH!
WHAT'S YOUR DEAL? HOW LONG ARE YOU GOING TO CLING TO HER LIKE THAT?
IF SHE WANTS TO MARRY YOU, WHY DON'T YOU GO FOR IT?!
THIS IS TOO MUCH! AFTER ALL THAT?!
GET AWAY FROM ME, YOU PLAYER!
LET'S GO, LUM. WE LOST.
WAIT! HE PROPOSED TO ME!
SHI-NO-BU!!
IF YOU WANT TO MARRY LUM, YOU'LL HAVE TO COME LIVE ON OUR PLANET!
GACK!!
WE'LL GET YOU A PAIR OF HORNS AND MAKE A PROPER OGRE OF YOU!
ATARU! BE SURE YOU COME HOME FOR OBON FESTIVAL AND NEW YEAR'S!
HE'LL MAKE A GOOD HUSBAND!
DESTINY WILLS IT TO BE THUS!
A GOODWILL MARRIAGE-TO UNITE OUR WORLDS!
SHINOBU!!
THIS IS A DISASTER!
A SECRET PASSION... MUST'VE BEEN ROUGH!

CHAPTER 2: GENTLE IMP

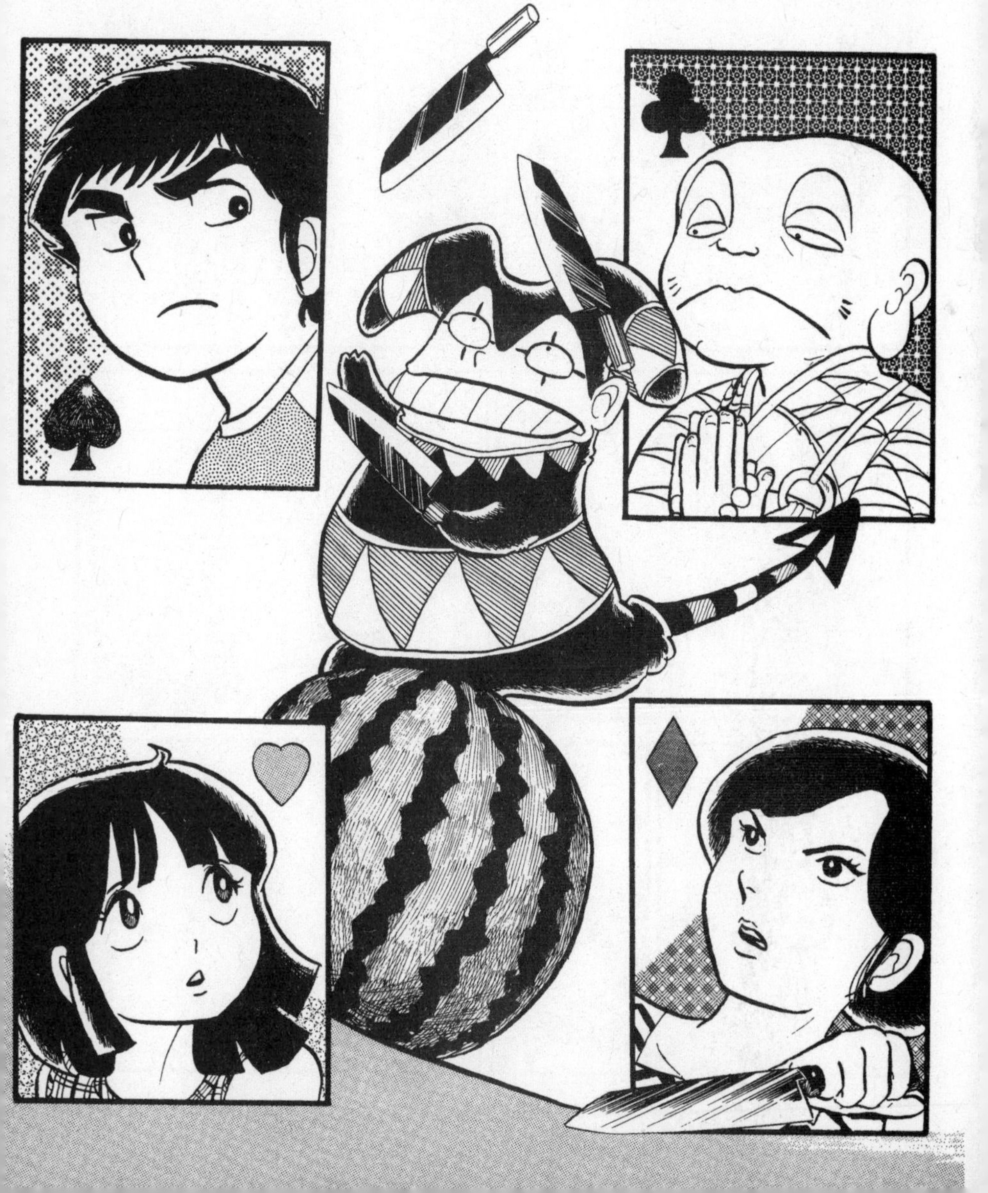

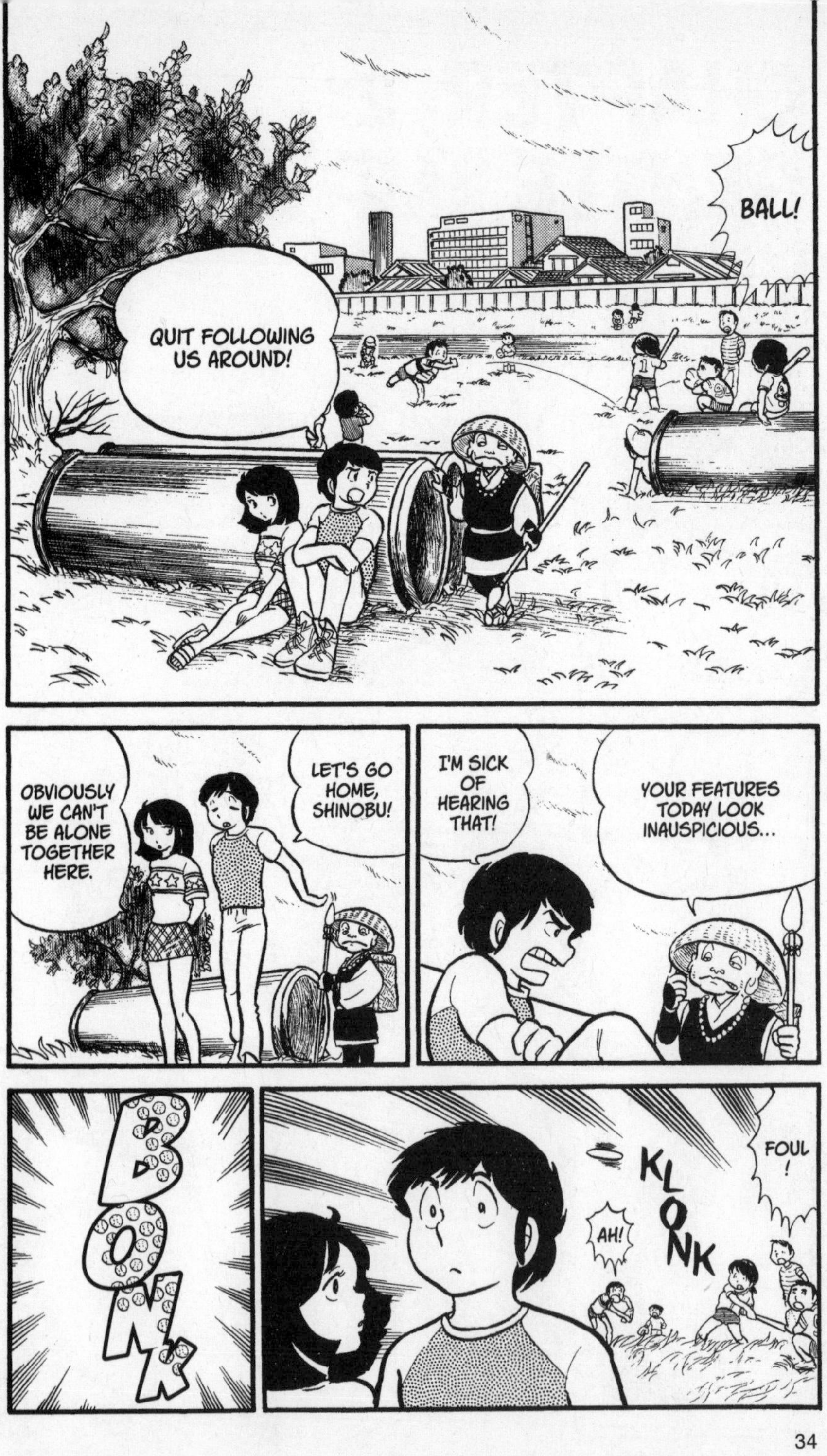
BALL!
QUIT FOLLOWING US AROUND!
YOUR FEATURES TODAY LOOK INAUSPICIOUS...
I'M SICK OF HEARING THAT!
LET'S GO HOME, SHINOBU!
OBVIOUSLY WE CAN'T BE ALONE TOGETHER HERE.
FOUL!
KLONK
AH!
BONK

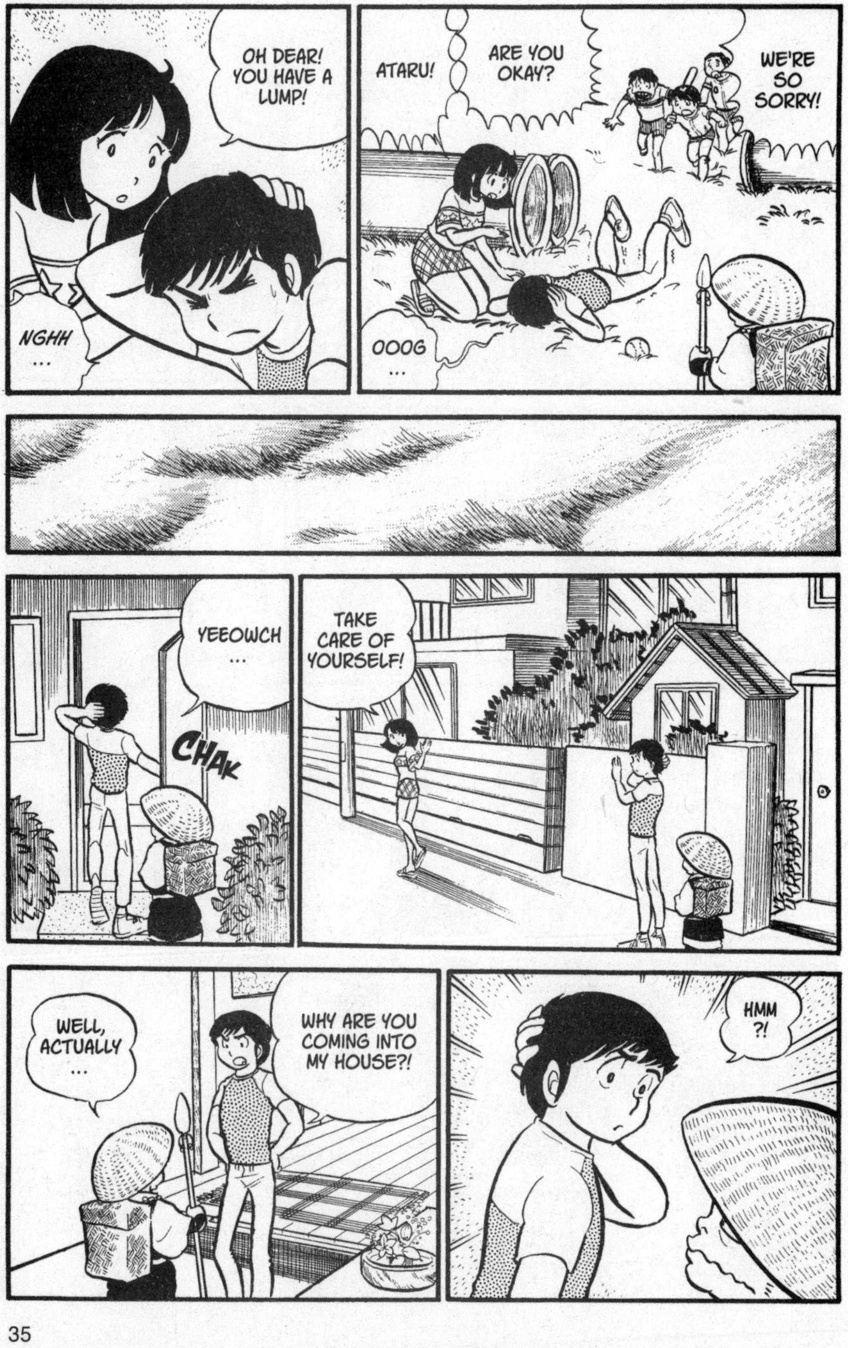
WE'RE SO SORRY!
ARE YOU OKAY?
ATARU!
OOOG ...
OH DEAR! YOU HAVE A LUMP!
NGHH ...
TAKE CARE OF YOURSELF!
YEEOWCH ...
CHAK
HMM ?!
WHY ARE YOU COMING INTO MY HOUSE?!
WELL, ACTUALLY ...

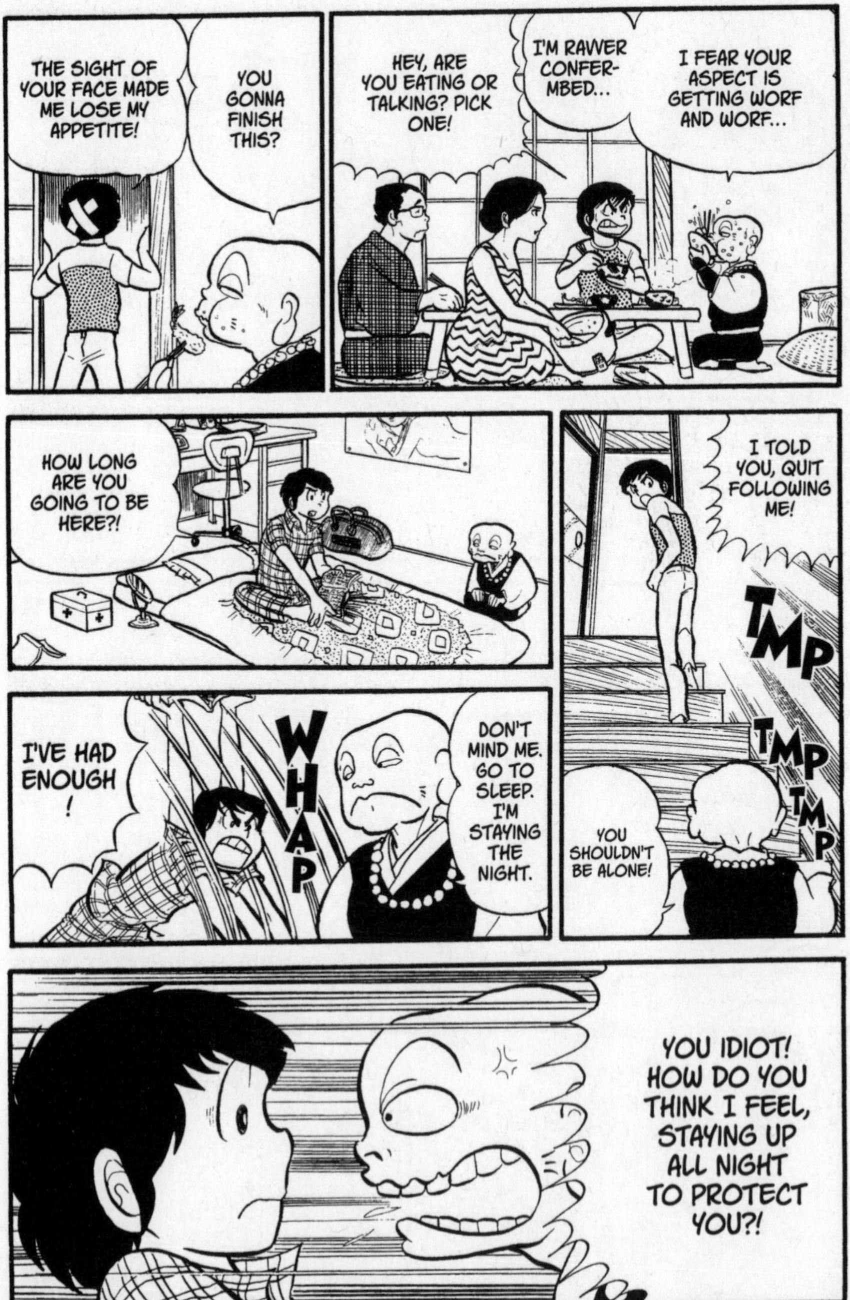
I FEAR YOUR ASPECT IS GETTING WORF AND WORF...
I'M RAWVER CONFERMBED...
HEY, ARE YOU EATING OR TALKING? PICK ONE!
YOU GONNA FINISH THIS?
THE SIGHT OF YOUR FACE MADE ME LOSE MY APPETITE!
I TOLD YOU, QUIT FOLLOWING ME!
TMP
TMP
TMP
TMP
YOU SHOULDN'T BE ALONE!
HOW LONG ARE YOU GOING TO BE HERE?!
DON'T MIND ME. GO TO SLEEP. I'M STAYING THE NIGHT.
WHAP
I'VE HAD ENOUGH!
YOU IDIOT! HOW DO YOU THINK I FEEL, STAYING UP ALL NIGHT TO PROTECT YOU?!

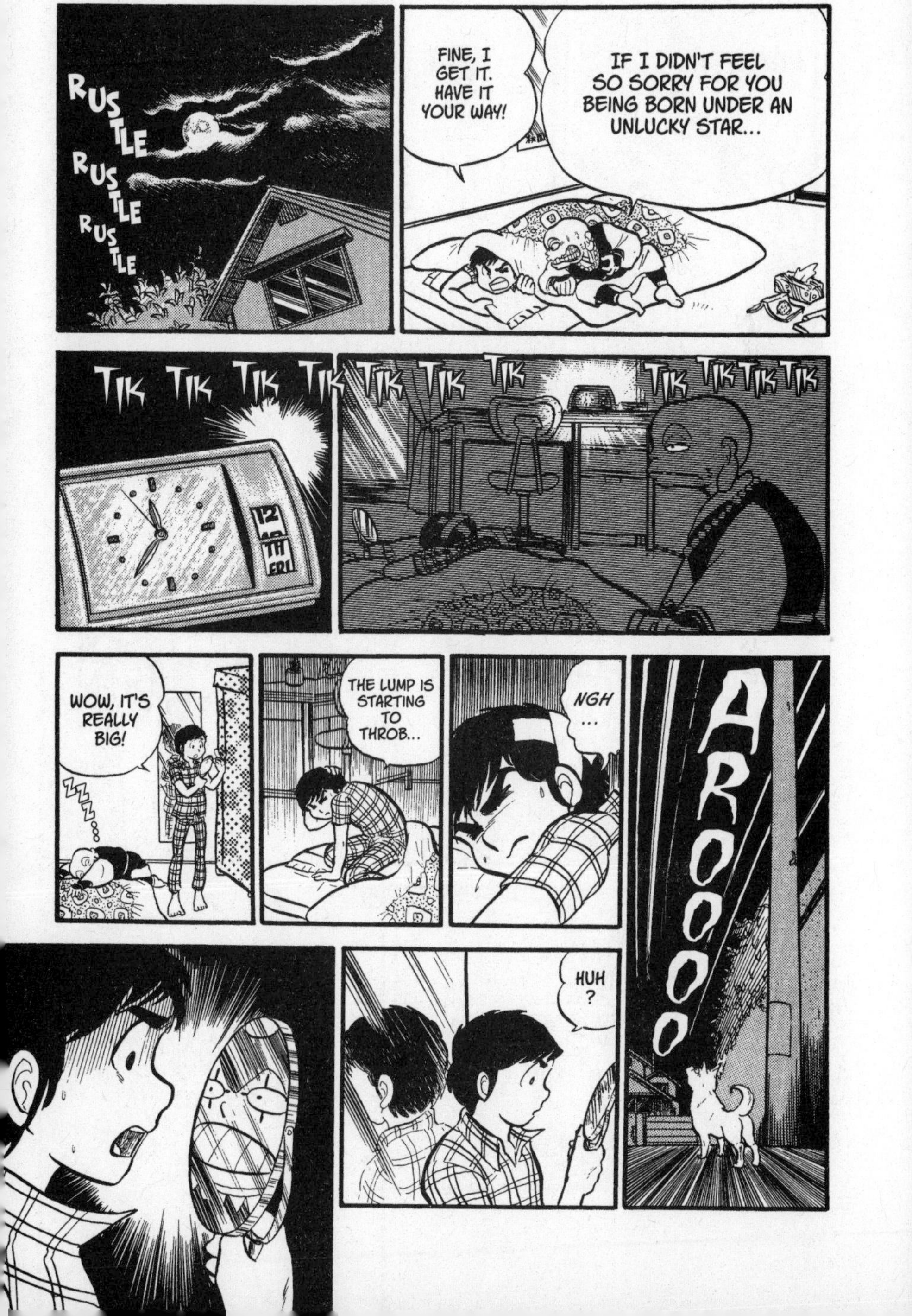
IF I DIDN'T FEEL SO SORRY FOR YOU BEING BORN UNDER AN UNLUCKY STAR...
FINE, I GET IT. HAVE IT YOUR WAY!
RUSTLE RUSTLE RUSTLE
TIK TIK TIK TIK TIK
TIK TIK TIK TIK TIK TIK TIK
AROOOOO
NGH...
THE LUMP IS STARTING TO THROB...
WOW, IT'S REALLY BIG!
ZZZ...
HUH?

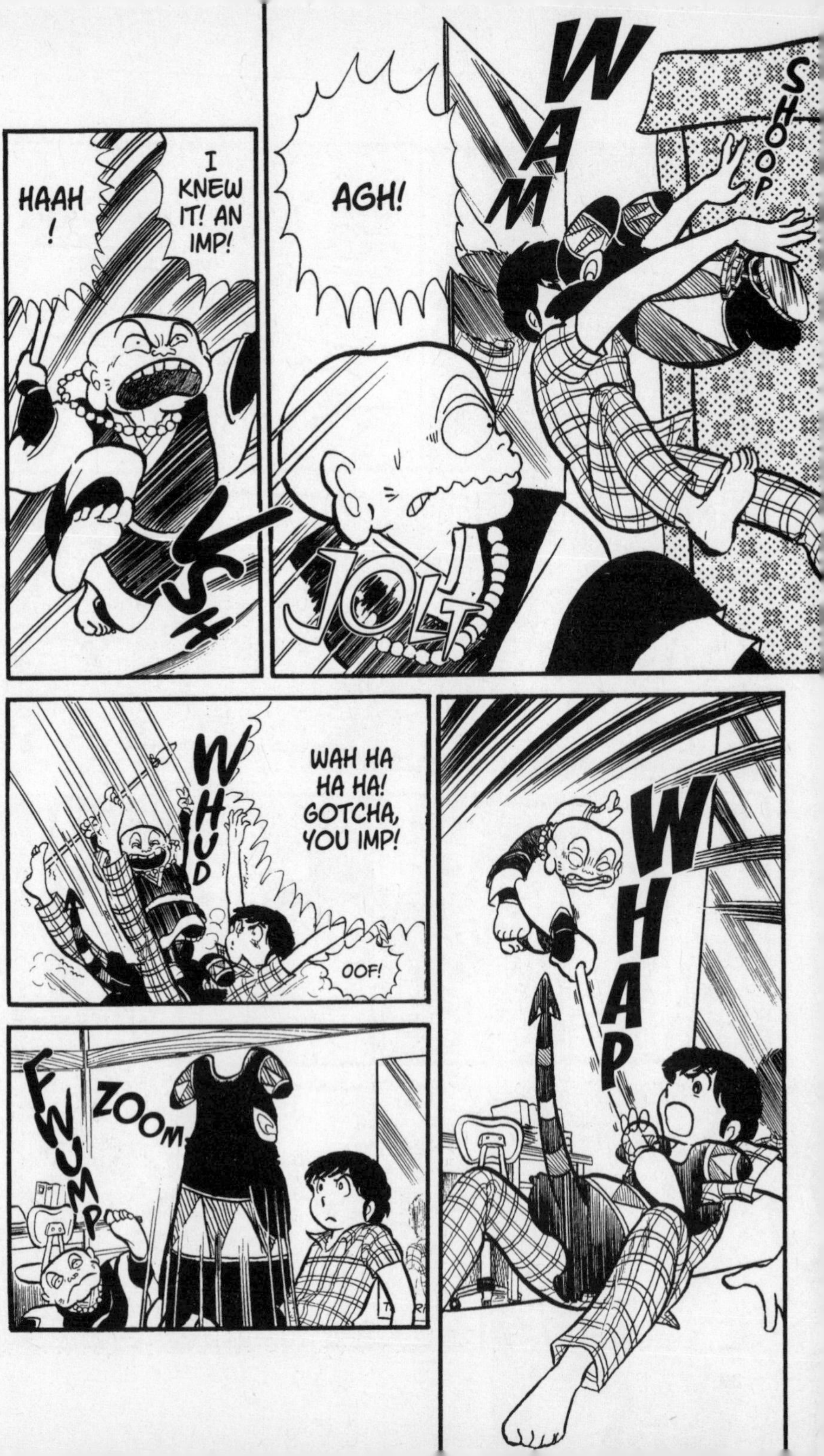
SHOOP
WAM
AGH!
JOLT
I KNEW IT! AN IMP!
HAAH!
KSH
WHAP
WAH HA HA HA! GOTCHA, YOU IMP!
WHUD
OOF!
ZOOM
FWUMP

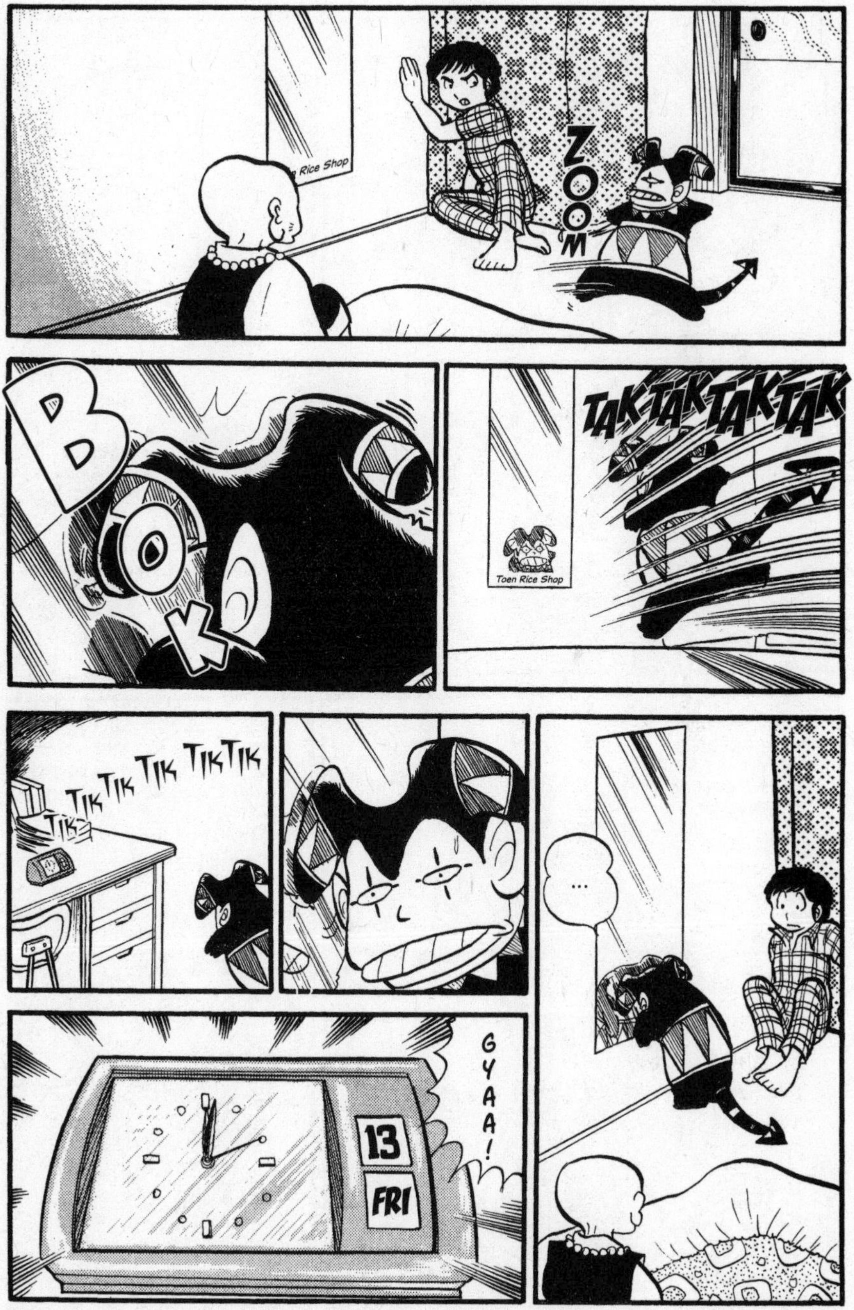
Rice Shop
ZOOM
TAKTAKTAKTAK
Toen Rice Shop
BOK
...
TIK TIK TIK TIK TIKTIK
13
FRI
GYAAA!

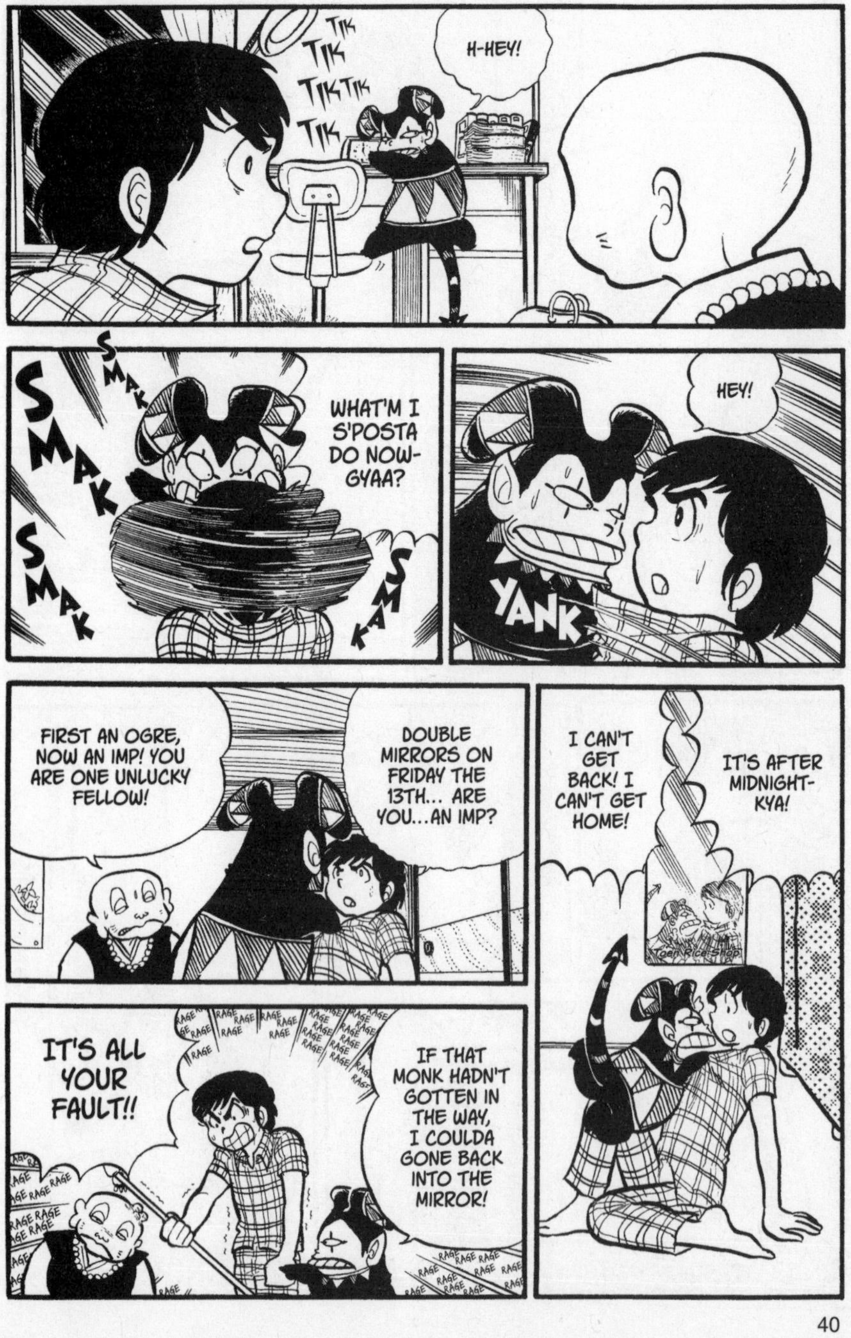
H-HEY!
TIK TIK TIKTIK TIK
HEY!
YANK
WHAT'M I S'POSTA DO NOW-GYAA?
SMAK SMAK SMAK SMAK SMAK
IT'S AFTER MIDNIGHT-KYA!
I CAN'T GET BACK! I CAN'T GET HOME!
Toen Rice Shop
DOUBLE MIRRORS ON FRIDAY THE 13TH... ARE YOU...AN IMP?
FIRST AN OGRE, NOW AN IMP! YOU ARE ONE UNLUCKY FELLOW!
IF THAT MONK HADN'T GOTTEN IN THE WAY, I COULDA GONE BACK INTO THE MIRROR!
IT'S ALL YOUR FAULT!!
RAGE RAGE RAGE RAGE

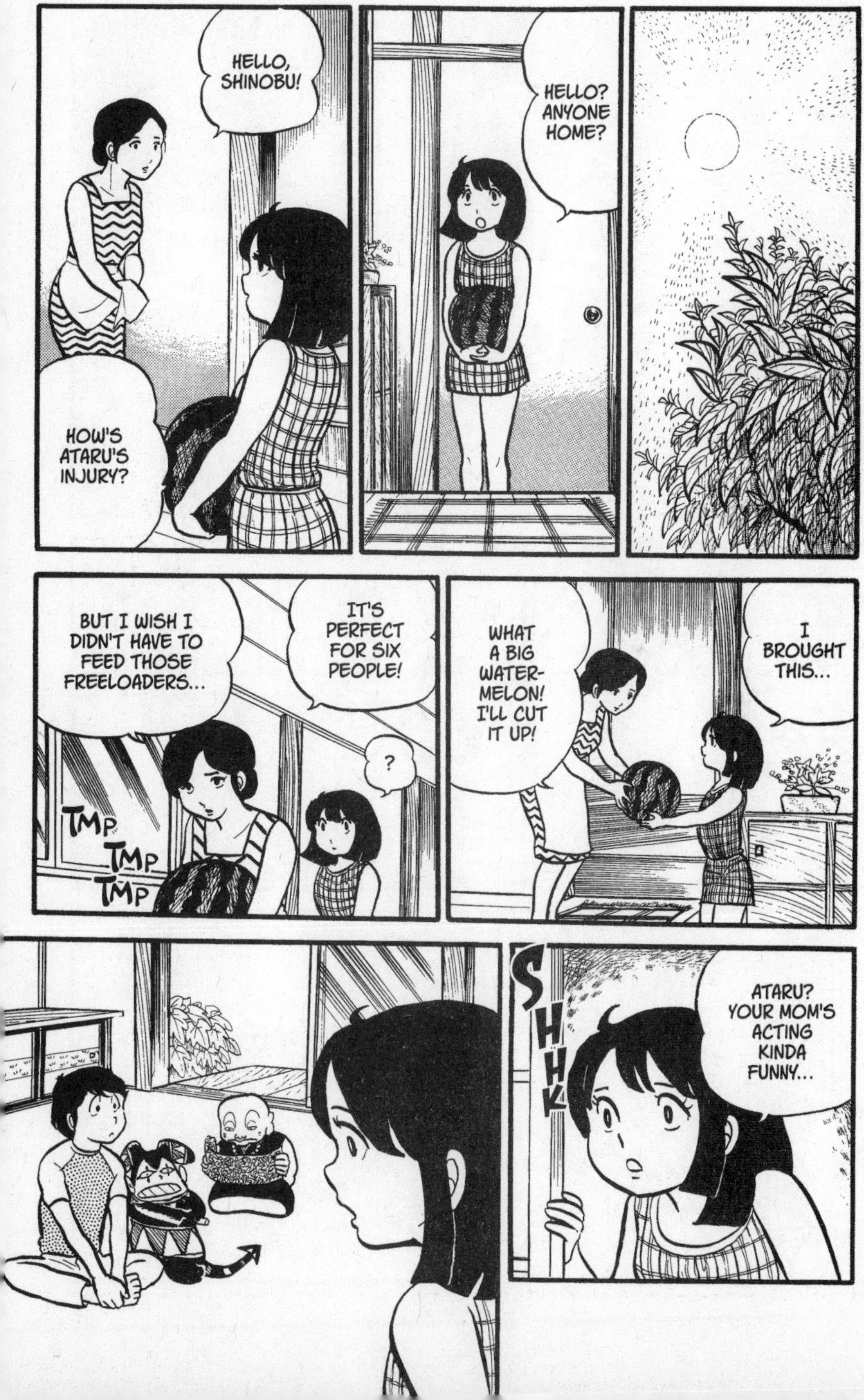
HELLO? ANYONE HOME?
HELLO, SHINOBU!
HOW'S ATARU'S INJURY?
I BROUGHT THIS...
WHAT A BIG WATER-MELON! I'LL CUT IT UP!
IT'S PERFECT FOR SIX PEOPLE!
BUT I WISH I DIDN'T HAVE TO FEED THOSE FREELOADERS...
?
TMP TMP TMP
SHHK
ATARU? YOUR MOM'S ACTING KINDA FUNNY...

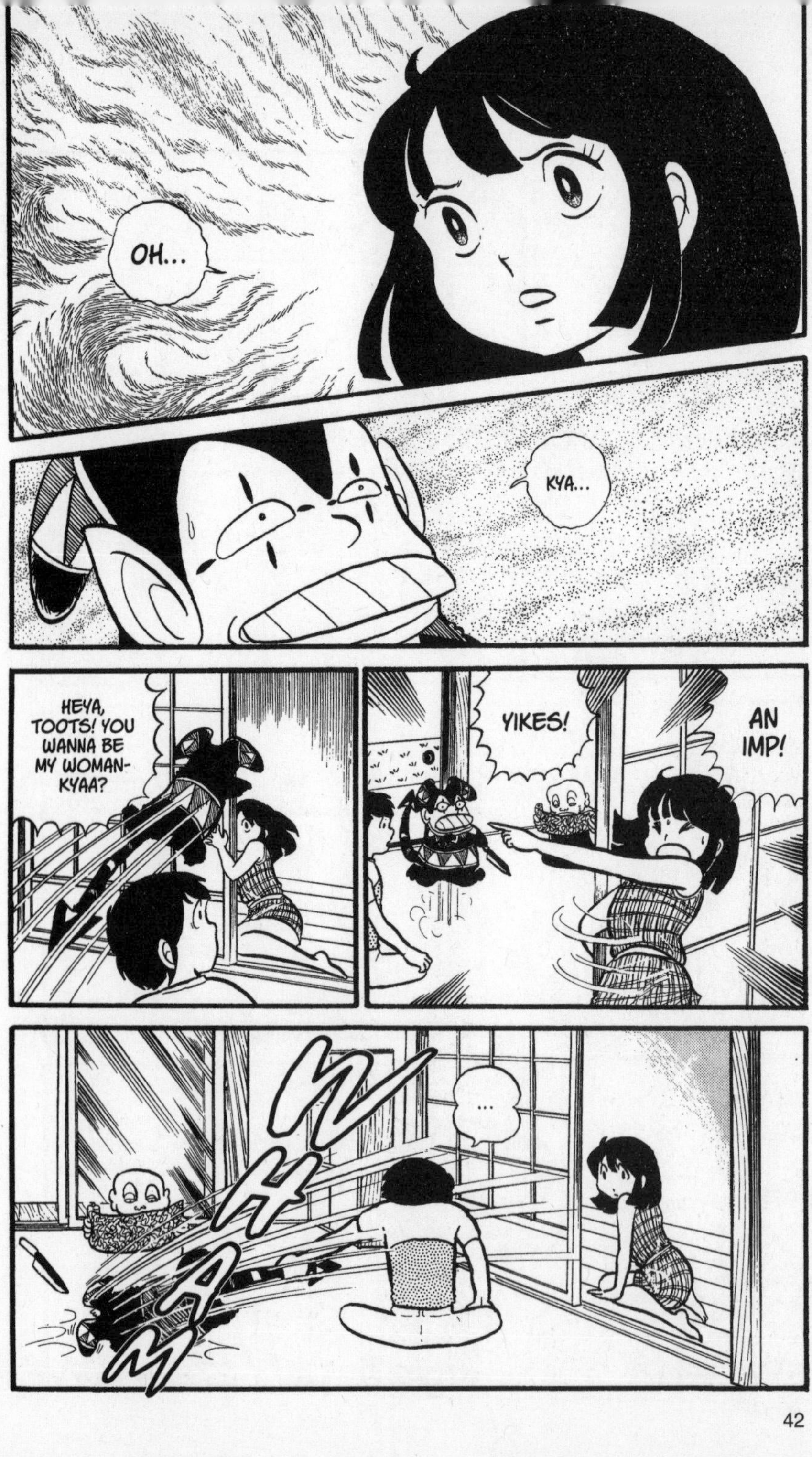
OH...
KYA...
AN IMP!
YIKES!
HEYA, TOOTS! YOU WANNA BE MY WOMAN-KYAA?
...
WHAM

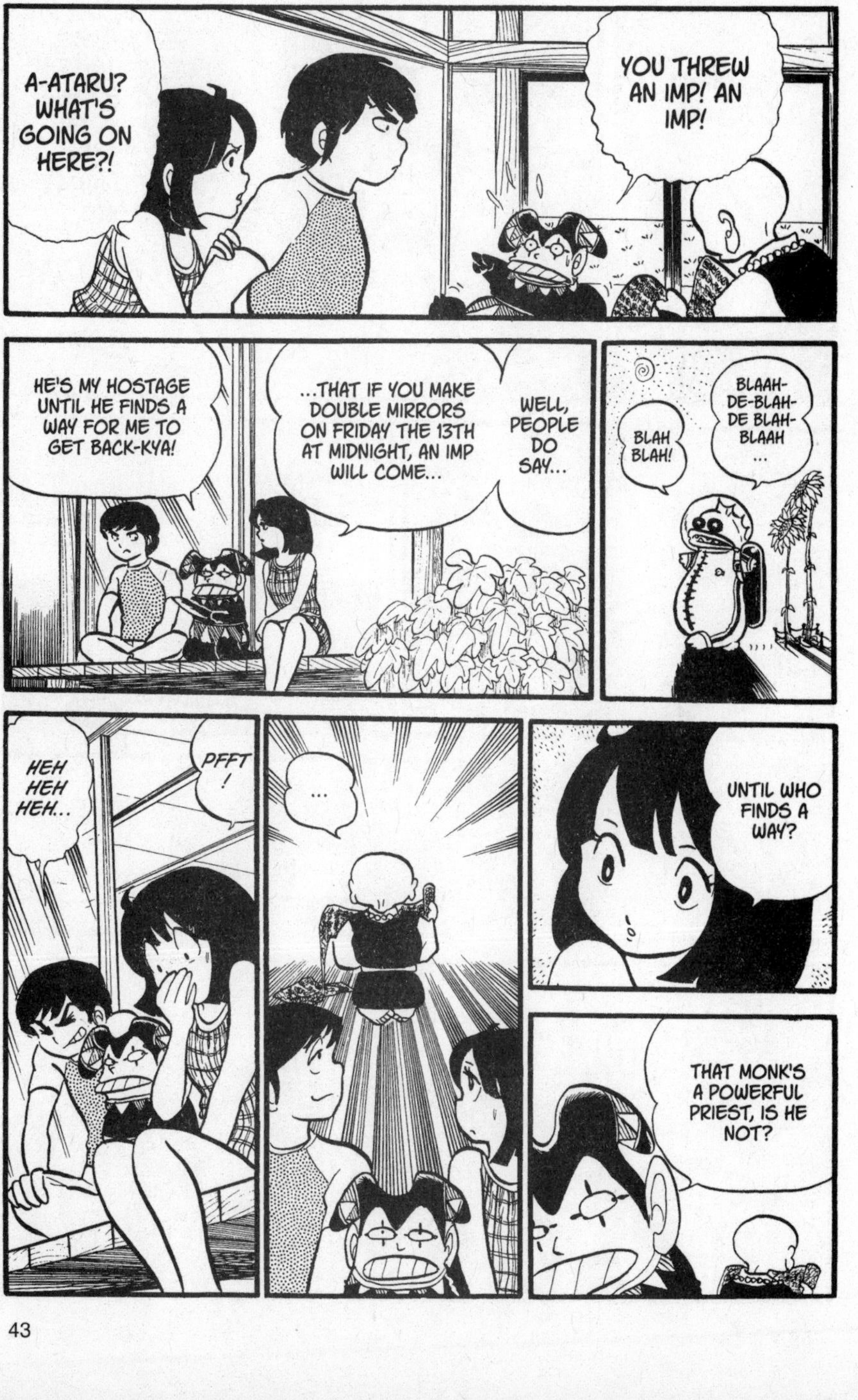
YOU THREW AN IMP! AN IMP!
A-ATARU? WHAT'S GOING ON HERE?!
BLAAH-DE-BLAH-DE BLAH-BLAAH ...
BLAH BLAH!
WELL, PEOPLE DO SAY...
...THAT IF YOU MAKE DOUBLE MIRRORS ON FRIDAY THE 13TH AT MIDNIGHT, AN IMP WILL COME...
HE'S MY HOSTAGE UNTIL HE FINDS A WAY FOR ME TO GET BACK-KYA!
UNTIL WHO FINDS A WAY?
THAT MONK'S A POWERFUL PRIEST, IS HE NOT?
...
PFFT!
HEH HEH HEH...

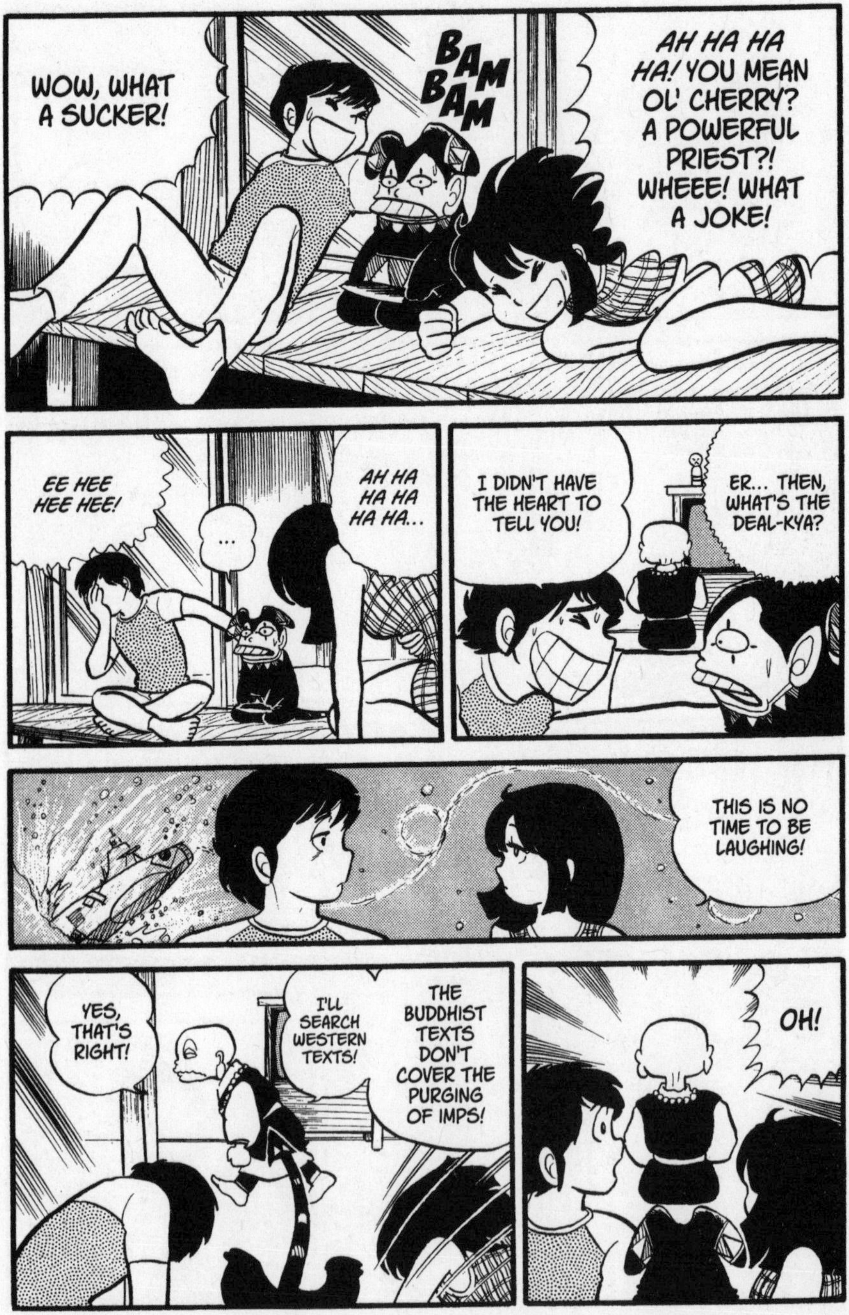
AH HA HA HA! YOU MEAN OL' CHERRY? A POWERFUL PRIEST?! WHEEE! WHAT A JOKE!
BAM BAM
WOW, WHAT A SUCKER!
ER... THEN, WHAT'S THE DEAL-KYA?
I DIDN'T HAVE THE HEART TO TELL YOU!
AH HA HA HA HA HA...
...
EE HEE HEE HEE!
THIS IS NO TIME TO BE LAUGHING!
OH!
THE BUDDHIST TEXTS DON'T COVER THE PURGING OF IMPS!
I'LL SEARCH WESTERN TEXTS!
YES, THAT'S RIGHT!

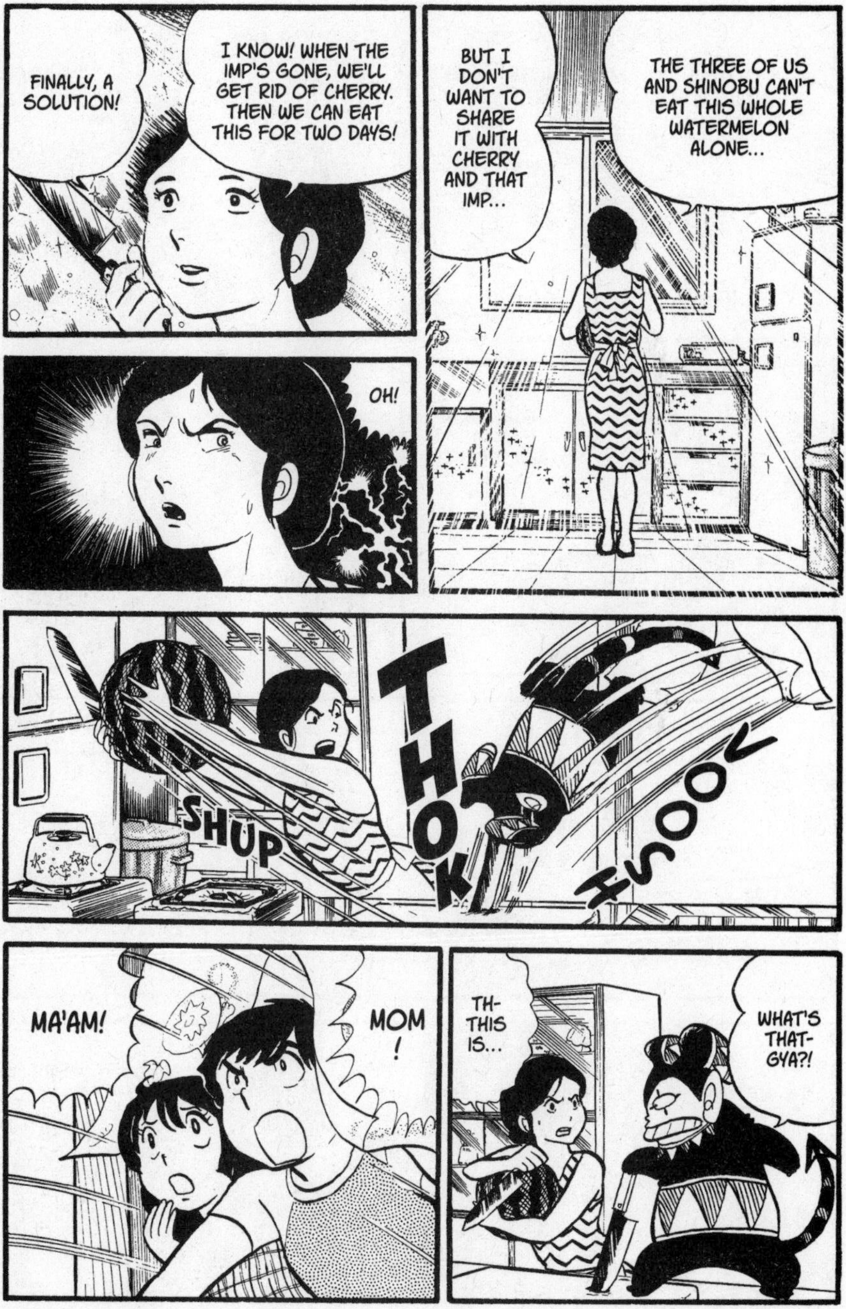
THE THREE OF US AND SHINOBU CAN'T EAT THIS WHOLE WATERMELON ALONE...
BUT I DON'T WANT TO SHARE IT WITH CHERRY AND THAT IMP...
I KNOW! WHEN THE IMP'S GONE, WE'LL GET RID OF CHERRY. THEN WE CAN EAT THIS FOR TWO DAYS!
FINALLY, A SOLUTION!
OH!
WHOOSH
THOK
SHUP
WHAT'S THAT-GYA?!
TH-THIS IS...
MOM!
MA'AM!

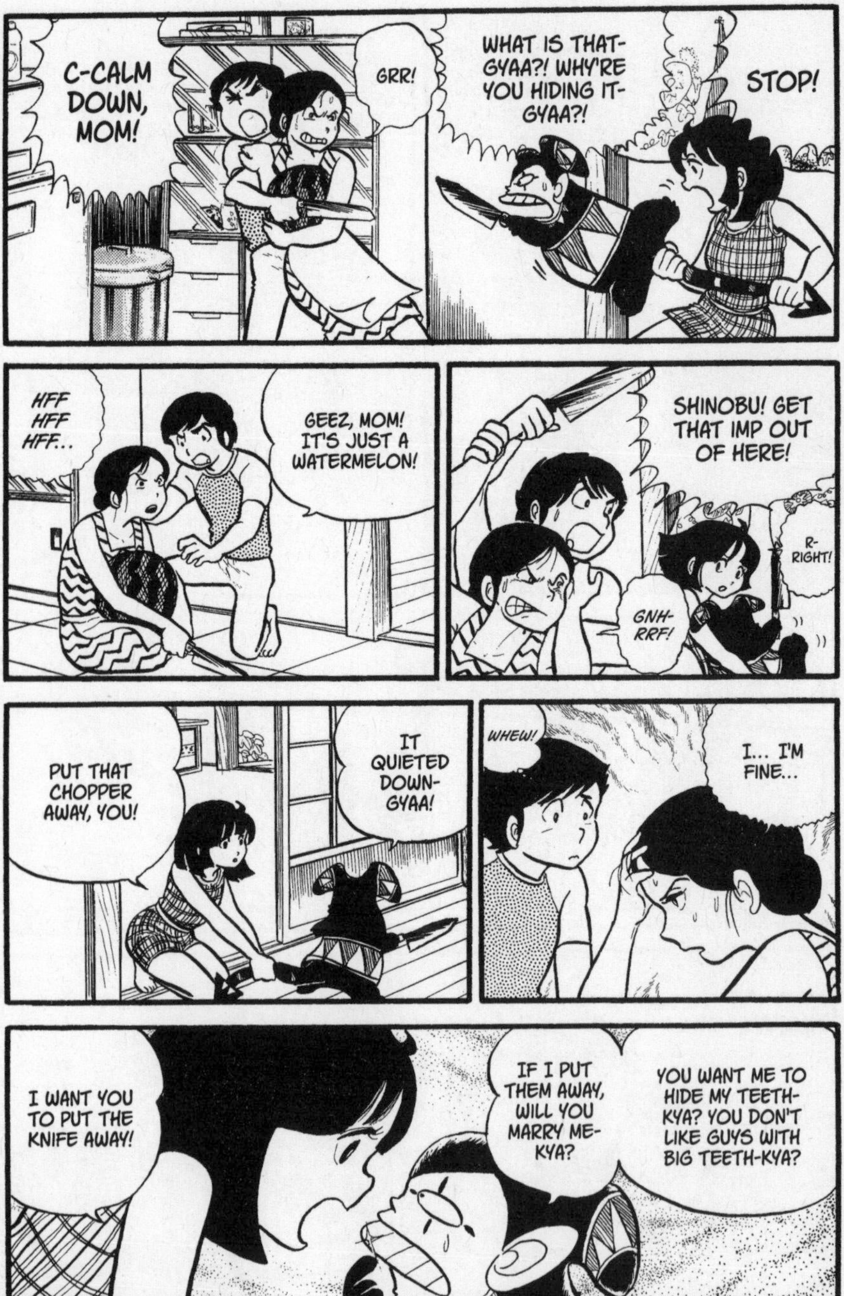
WHAT IS THAT-GYAA?! WHY'RE YOU HIDING IT-GYAA?!
STOP!
GRR!
C-CALM DOWN, MOM!
SHINOBU! GET THAT IMP OUT OF HERE!
R-RIGHT!
GNH-RRF!
GEEZ, MOM! IT'S JUST A WATERMELON!
HFF HFF HFF...
I... I'M FINE...
WHEW!
IT QUIETED DOWN-GYAA!
PUT THAT CHOPPER AWAY, YOU!
YOU WANT ME TO HIDE MY TEETH-KYA? YOU DON'T LIKE GUYS WITH BIG TEETH-KYA?
IF I PUT THEM AWAY, WILL YOU MARRY ME-KYA?
I WANT YOU TO PUT THE KNIFE AWAY!

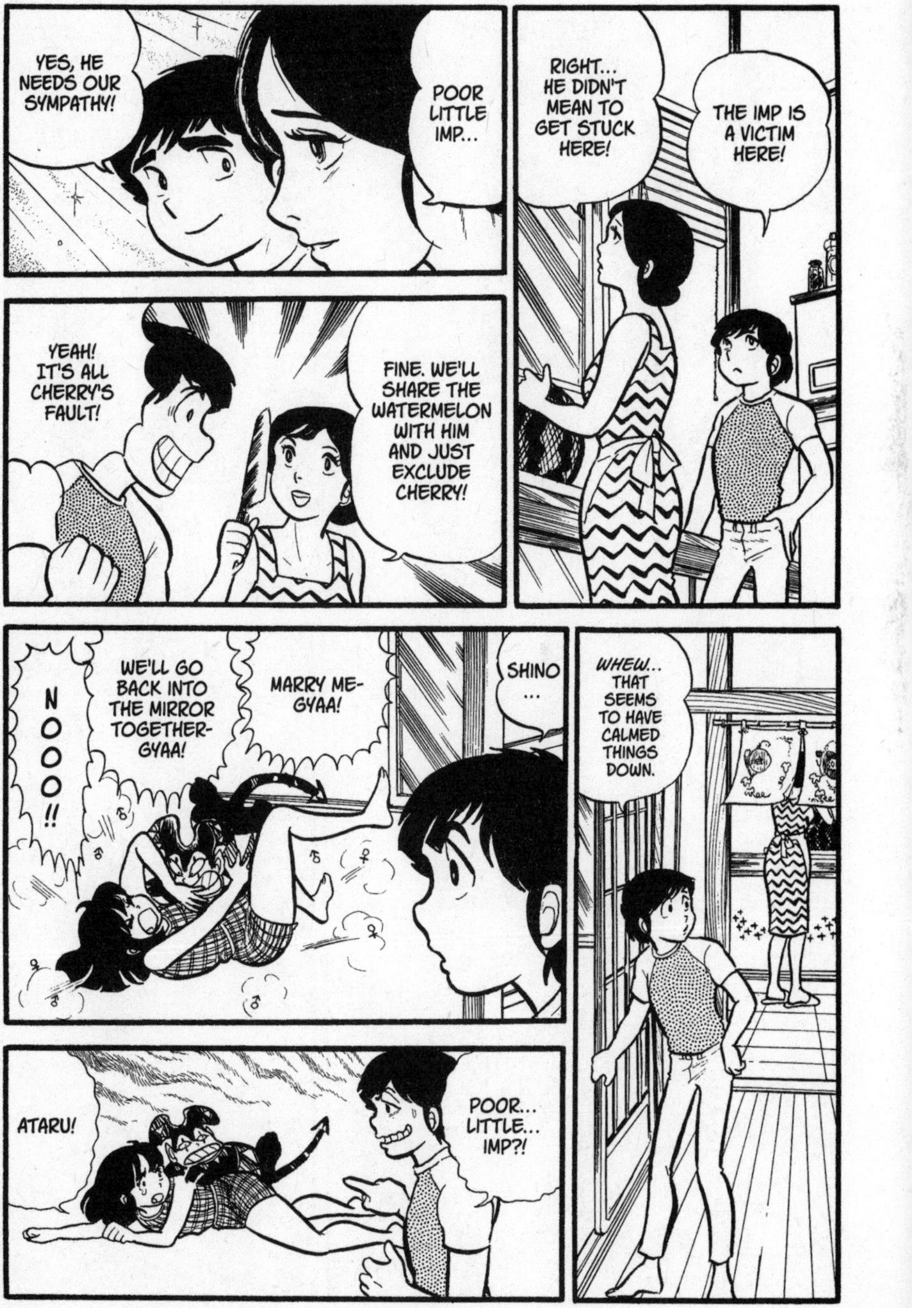
THE IMP IS A VICTIM HERE!
RIGHT... HE DIDN'T MEAN TO GET STUCK HERE!
POOR LITTLE IMP...
YES, HE NEEDS OUR SYMPATHY!
FINE. WE'LL SHARE THE WATERMELON WITH HIM AND JUST EXCLUDE CHERRY!
YEAH! IT'S ALL CHERRY'S FAULT!
WHEW... THAT SEEMS TO HAVE CALMED THINGS DOWN.
SHINO ...
MARRY ME-GYAA!
WE'LL GO BACK INTO THE MIRROR TOGETHER-GYAA!
NOOOO!!
POOR... LITTLE... IMP?!
ATARU!

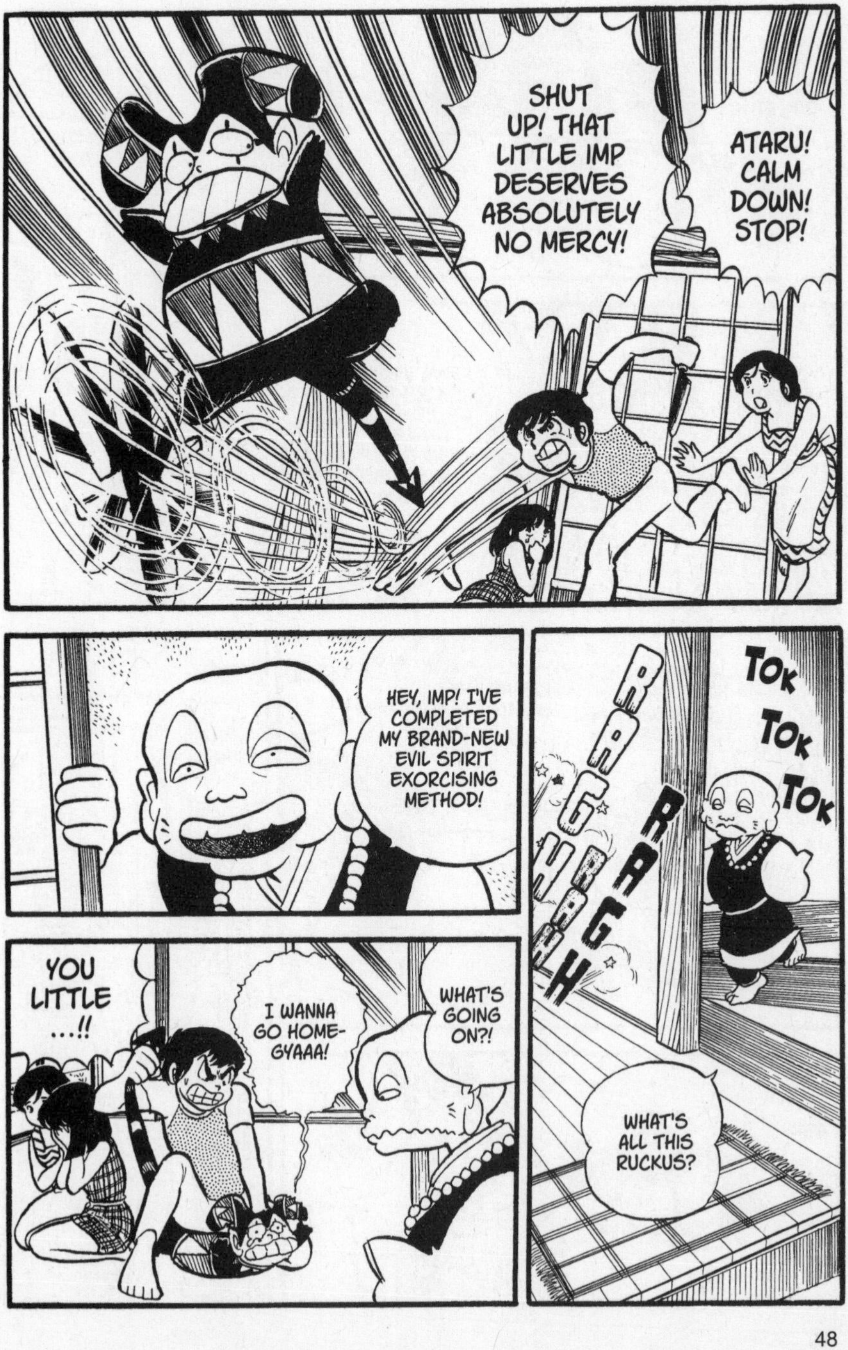
ATARU! CALM DOWN! STOP!
SHUT UP! THAT LITTLE IMP DESERVES ABSOLUTELY NO MERCY!
TOK TOK TOK
RAGH
RAGH
WHAT'S ALL THIS RUCKUS?
HEY, IMP! I'VE COMPLETED MY BRAND-NEW EVIL SPIRIT EXORCISING METHOD!
WHAT'S GOING ON?!
I WANNA GO HOME-GYAAA!
YOU LITTLE ...!!

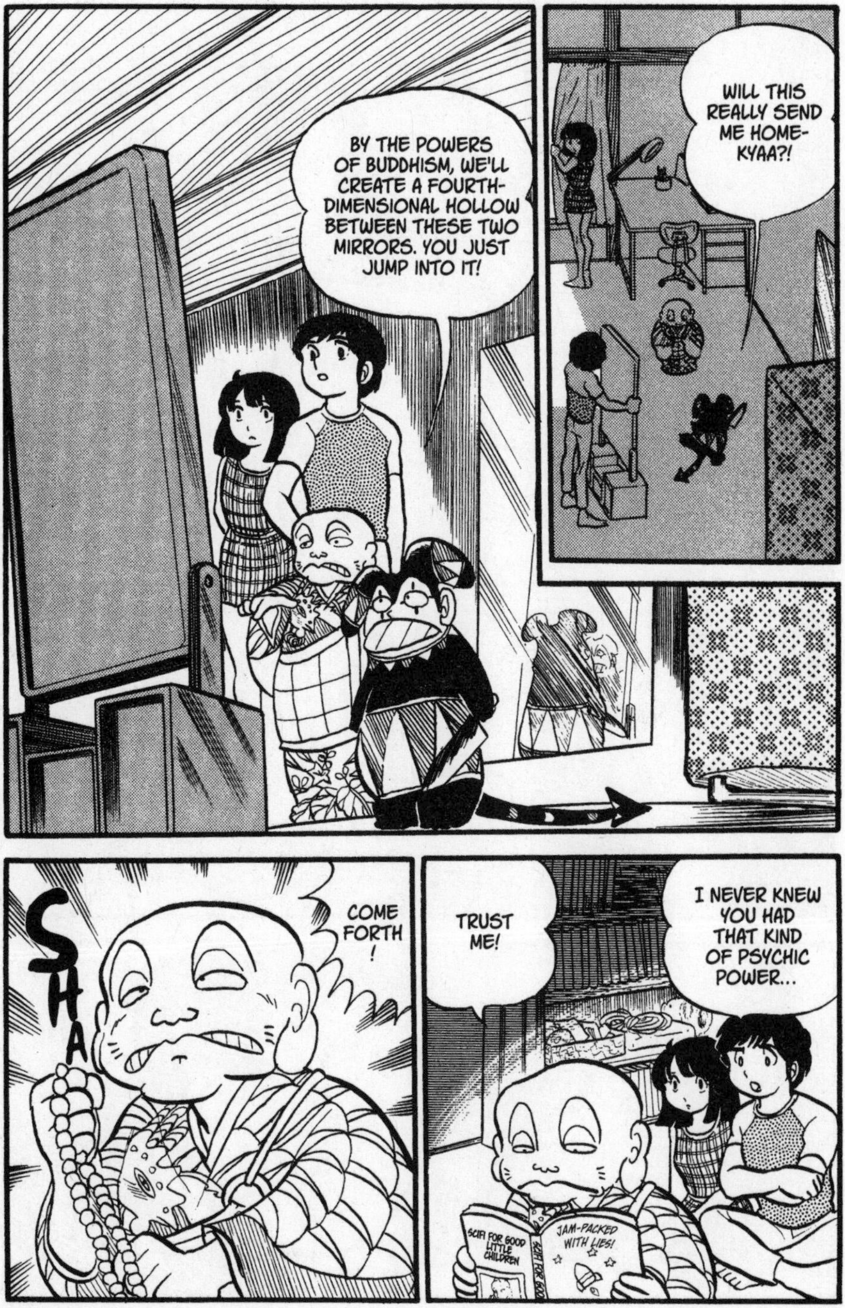
WILL THIS REALLY SEND ME HOME-KYAA?!
BY THE POWERS OF BUDDHISM, WE'LL CREATE A FOURTH-DIMENSIONAL HOLLOW BETWEEN THESE TWO MIRRORS. YOU JUST JUMP INTO IT!
I NEVER KNEW YOU HAD THAT KIND OF PSYCHIC POWER...
TRUST ME!
JAM-PACKED WITH LIES!
SCIFI FOR GOOD LITTLE CHILDREN
COME FORTH!
SHA

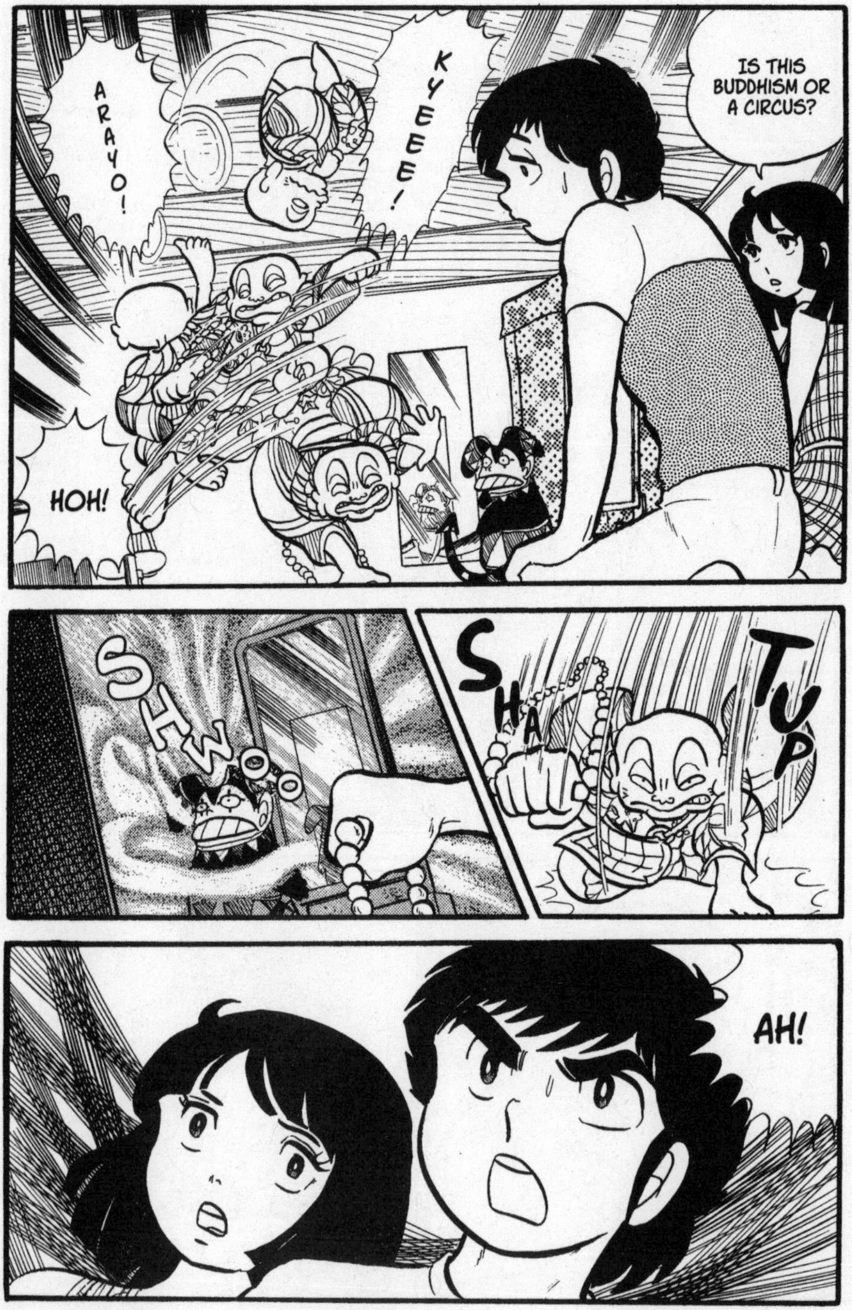
IS THIS BUDDHISM OR A CIRCUS?
KYEEEE!
ARAYO!
HOH!
TUP
SHA
SHWOOO
AH!

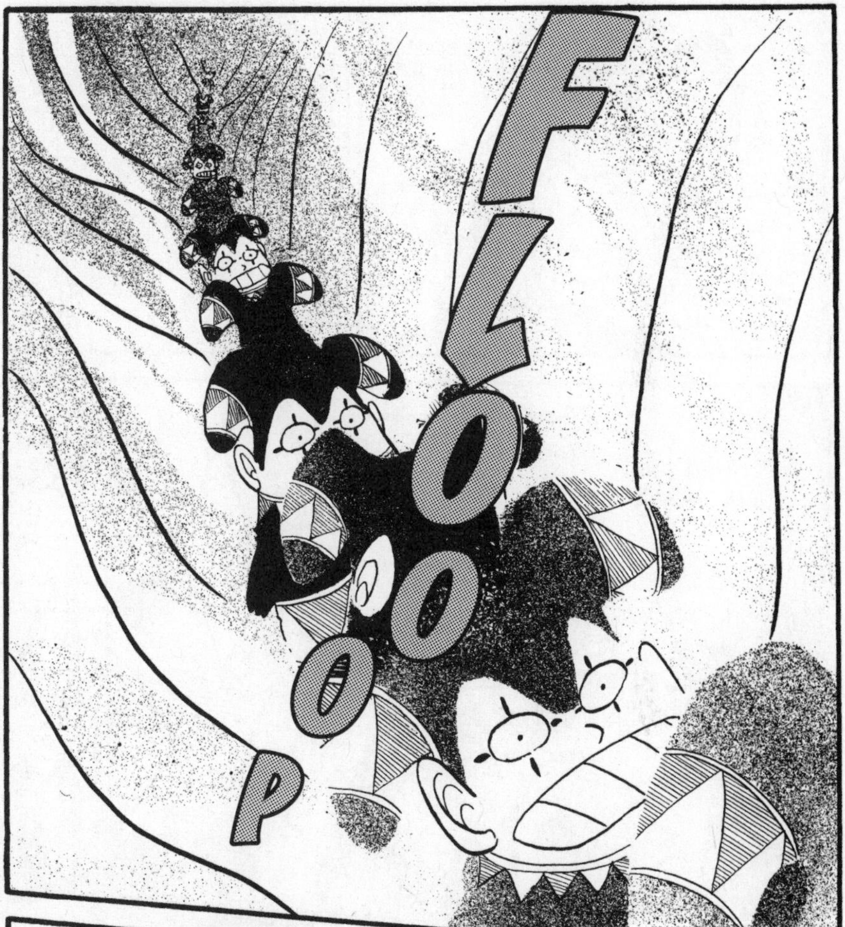
FLOOOOP
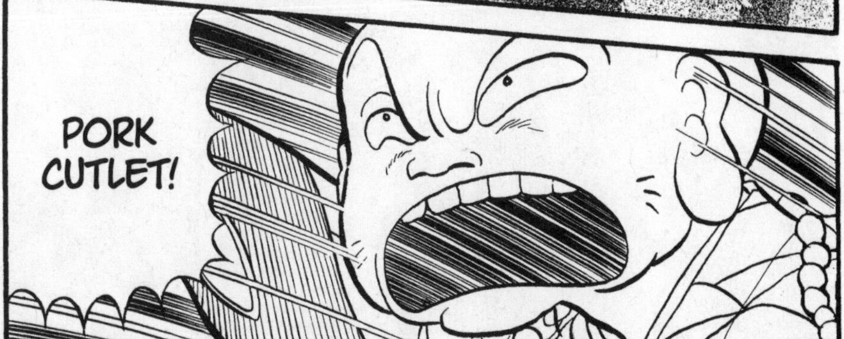
PORK CUTLET!

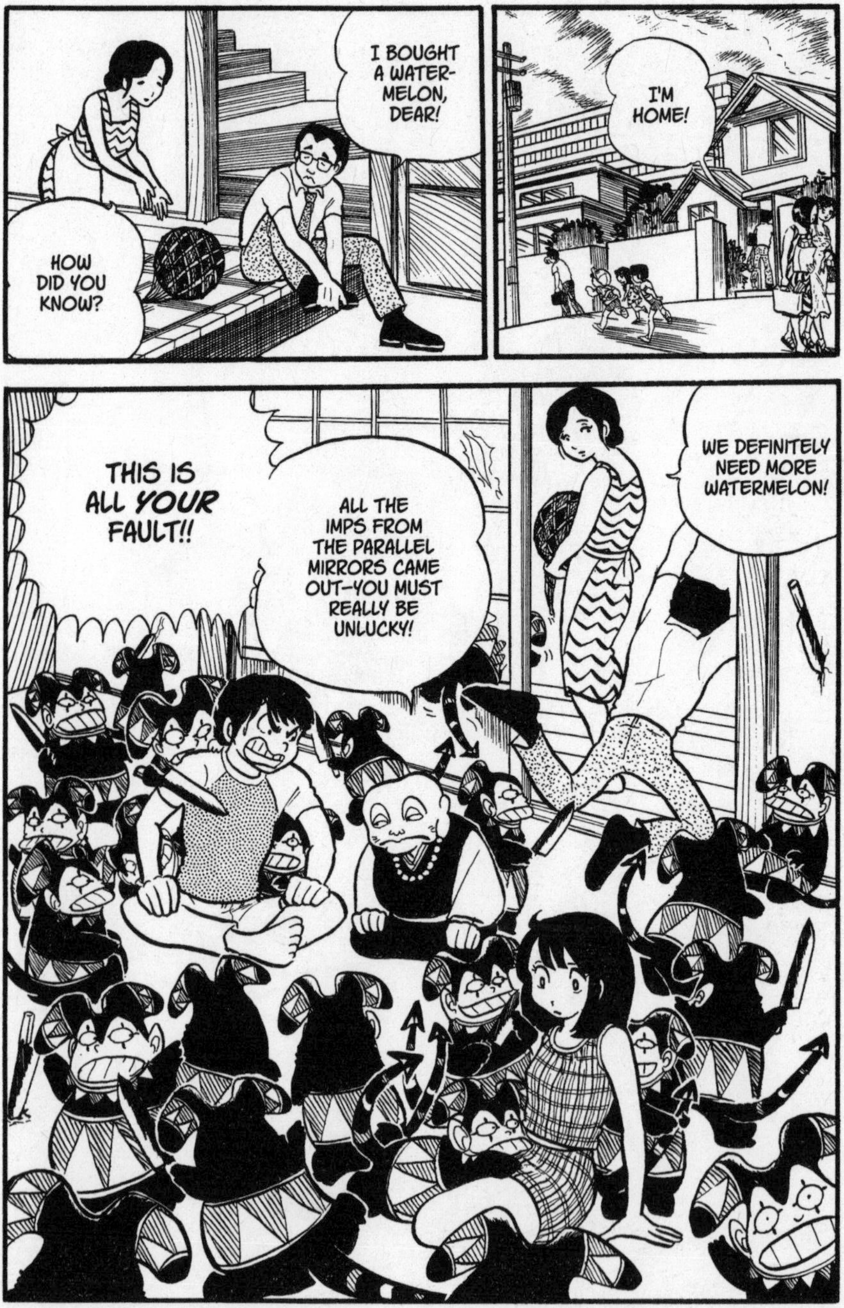

I'M HOME!
I BOUGHT A WATER-MELON, DEAR!
HOW DID YOU KNOW?
WE DEFINITELY NEED MORE WATERMELON!
ALL THE IMPS FROM THE PARALLEL MIRRORS CAME OUT—YOU MUST REALLY BE UNLUCKY!
THIS IS ALL *YOUR* FAULT!!

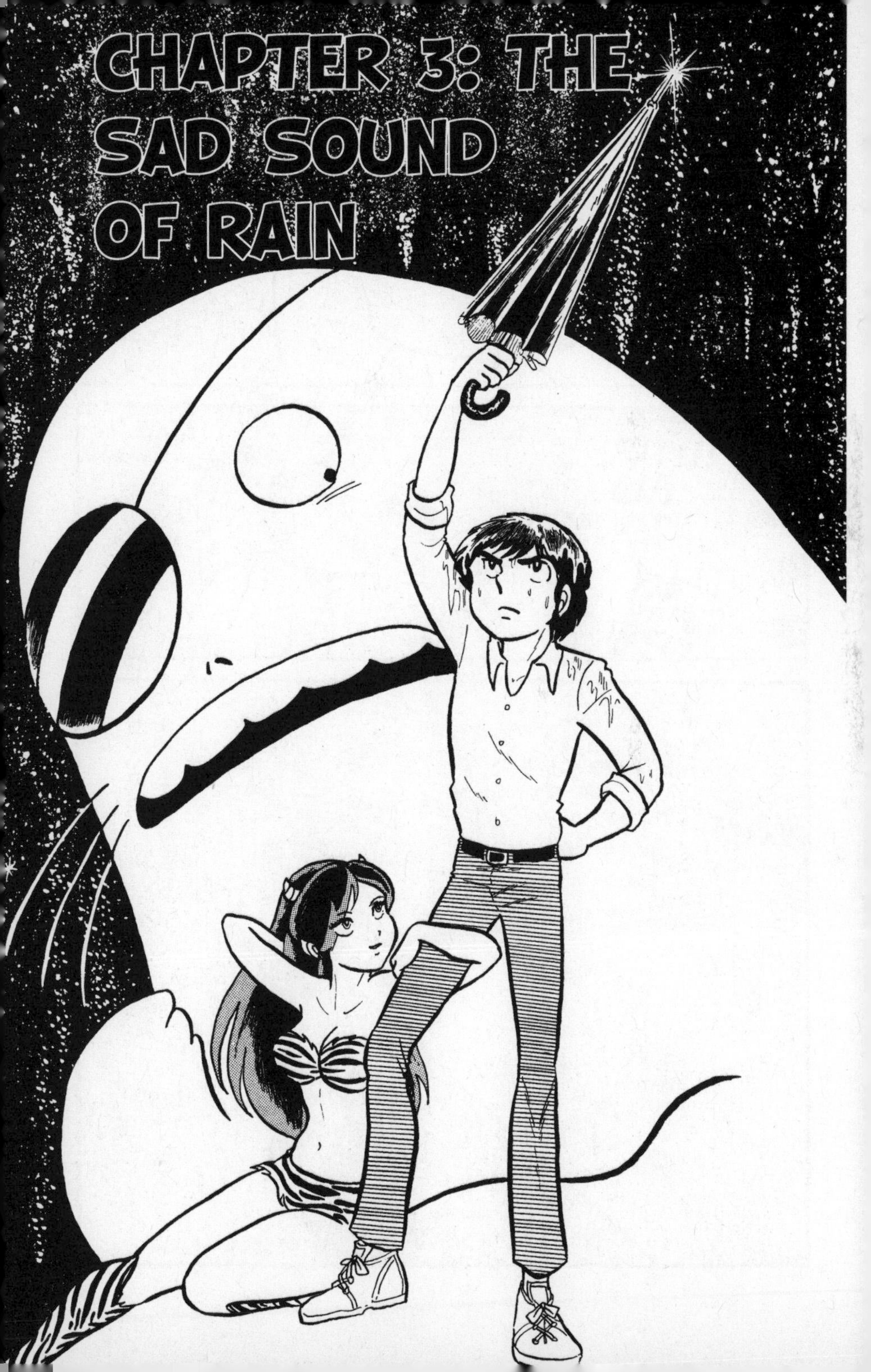
CHAPTER 3: THE SAD SOUND OF RAIN

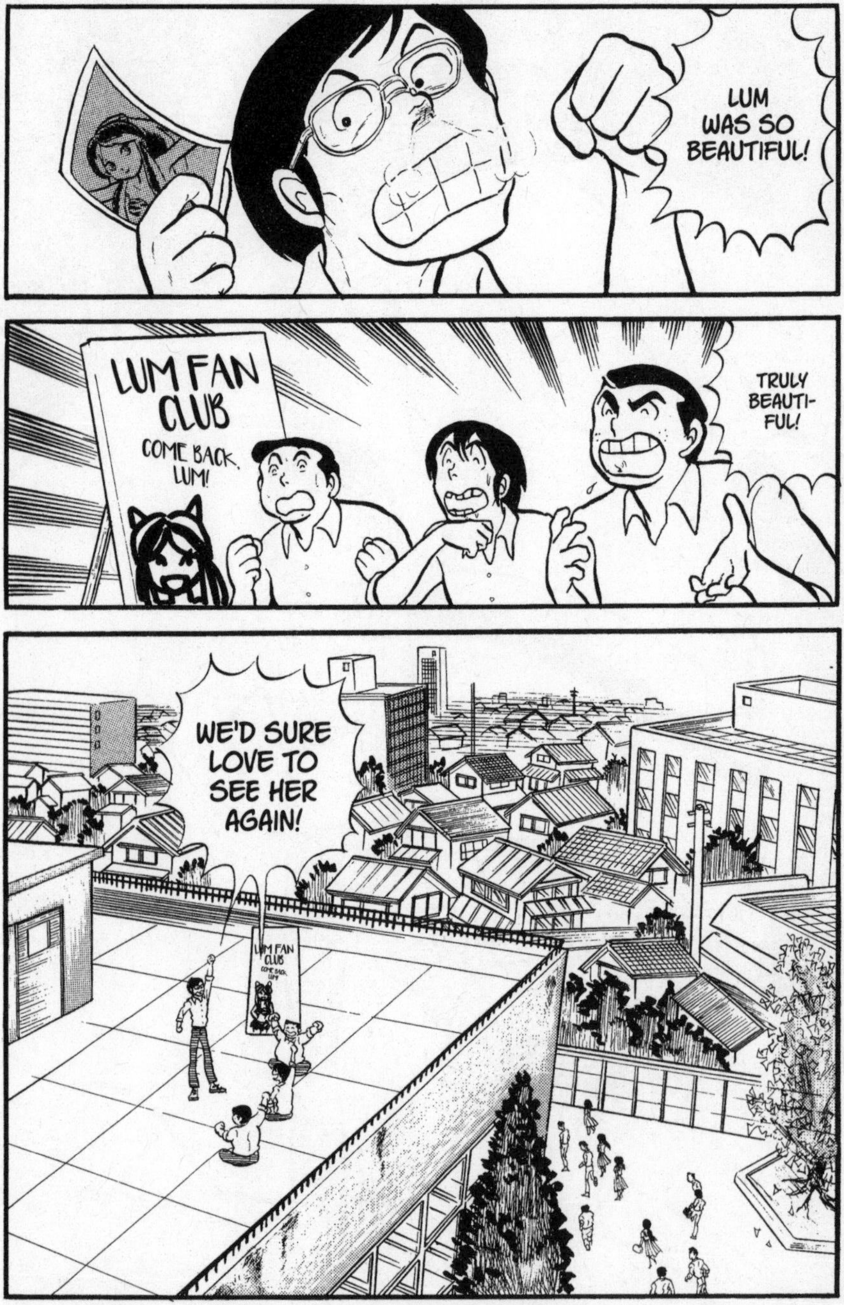
LUM WAS SO BEAUTIFUL!
TRULY BEAUTI-FUL!
LUM FAN CLUB
COME BACK, LUM!
WE'D SURE LOVE TO SEE HER AGAIN!

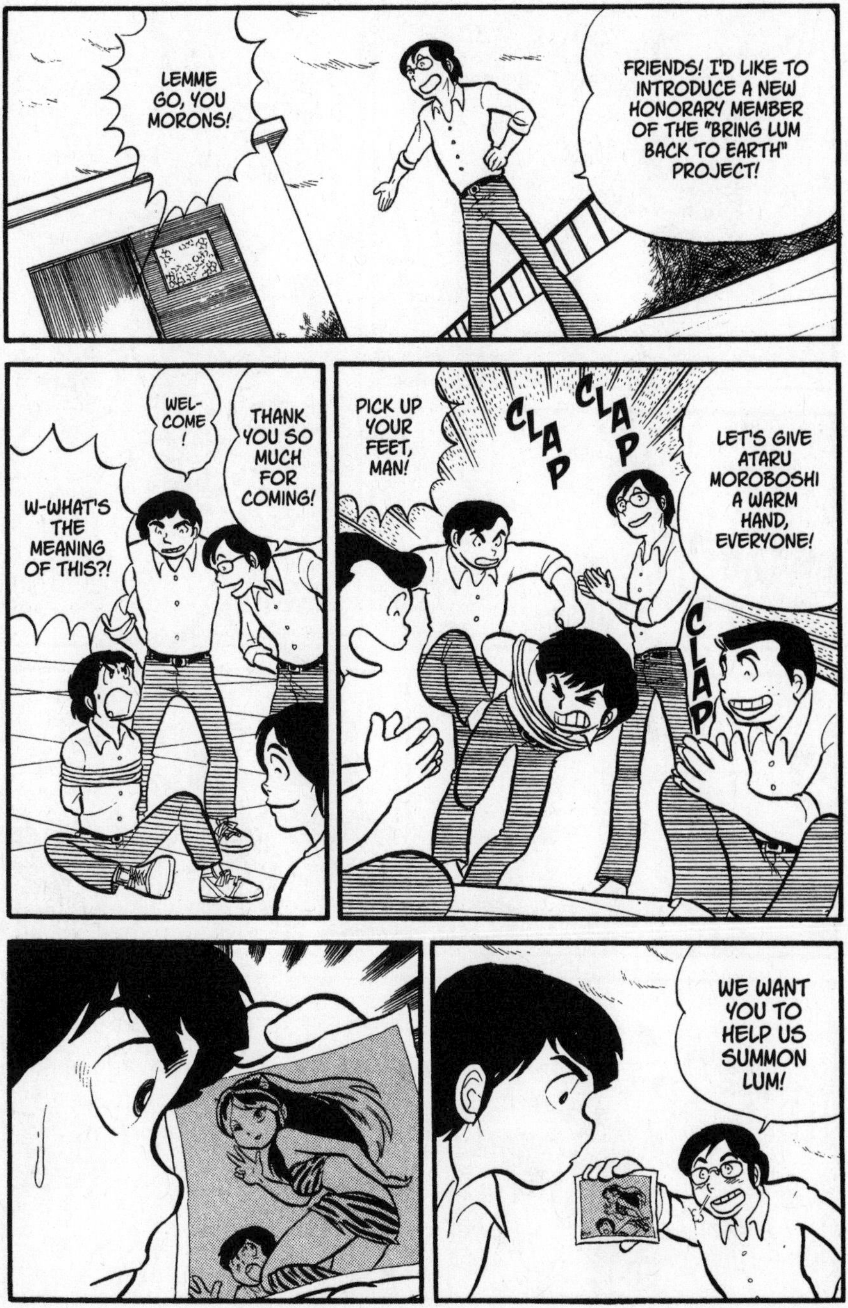

FRIENDS! I'D LIKE TO INTRODUCE A NEW HONORARY MEMBER OF THE "BRING LUM BACK TO EARTH" PROJECT!
LEMME GO, YOU MORONS!
LET'S GIVE ATARU MOROBOSHI A WARM HAND, EVERYONE!
CLAP
CLAP
PICK UP YOUR FEET, MAN!
CLAP
THANK YOU SO MUCH FOR COMING!
WEL-COME!
W-WHAT'S THE MEANING OF THIS?!
WE WANT YOU TO HELP US SUMMON LUM!

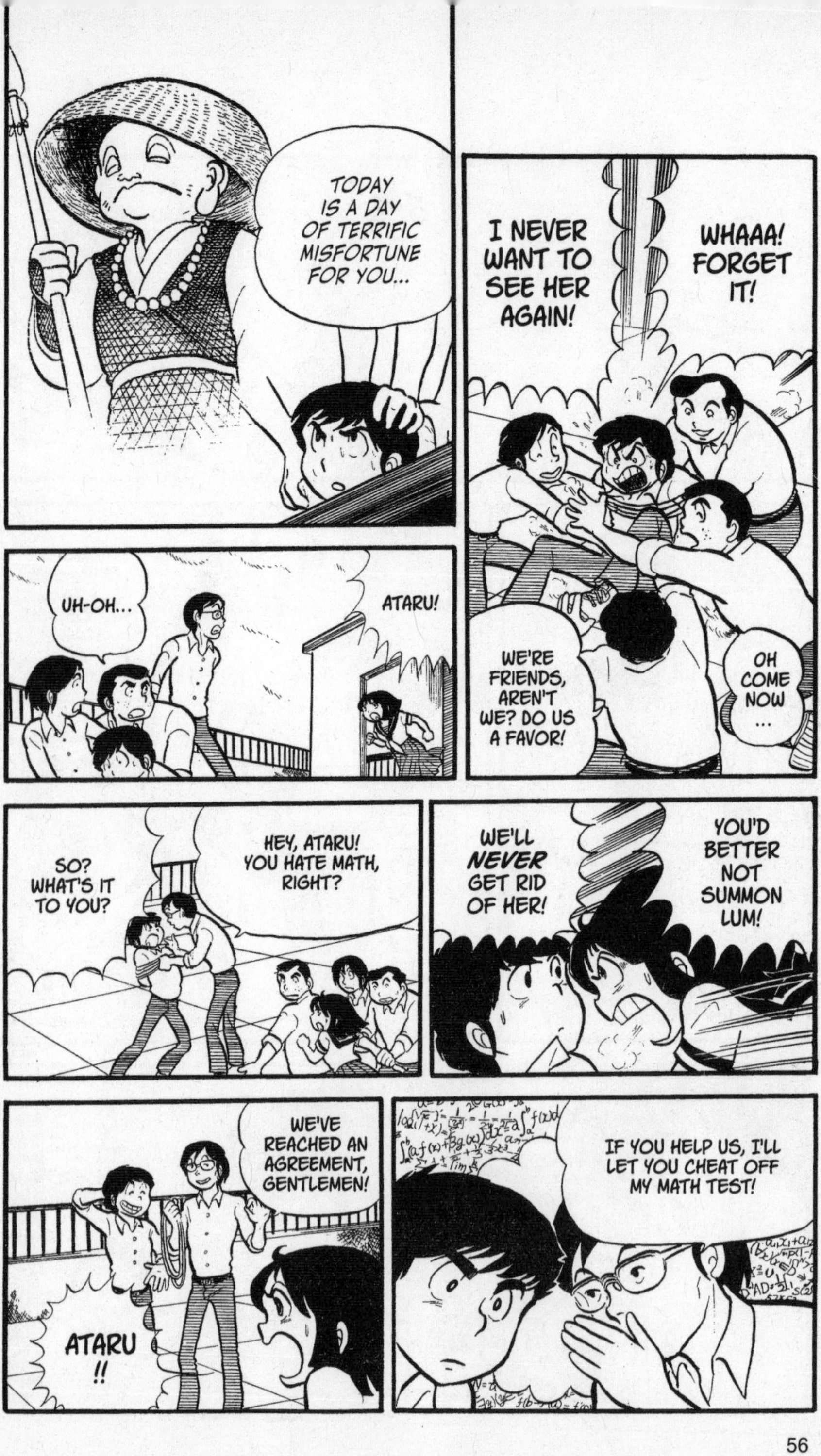
WHAAA! FORGET IT!
I NEVER WANT TO SEE HER AGAIN!
OH COME NOW ...
WE'RE FRIENDS, AREN'T WE? DO US A FAVOR!
TODAY IS A DAY OF TERRIFIC MISFORTUNE FOR YOU...
ATARU!
UH-OH...
YOU'D BETTER NOT SUMMON LUM!
WE'LL NEVER GET RID OF HER!
HEY, ATARU! YOU HATE MATH, RIGHT?
SO? WHAT'S IT TO YOU?
IF YOU HELP US, I'LL LET YOU CHEAT OFF MY MATH TEST!
WE'VE REACHED AN AGREEMENT, GENTLEMEN!
ATARU !!

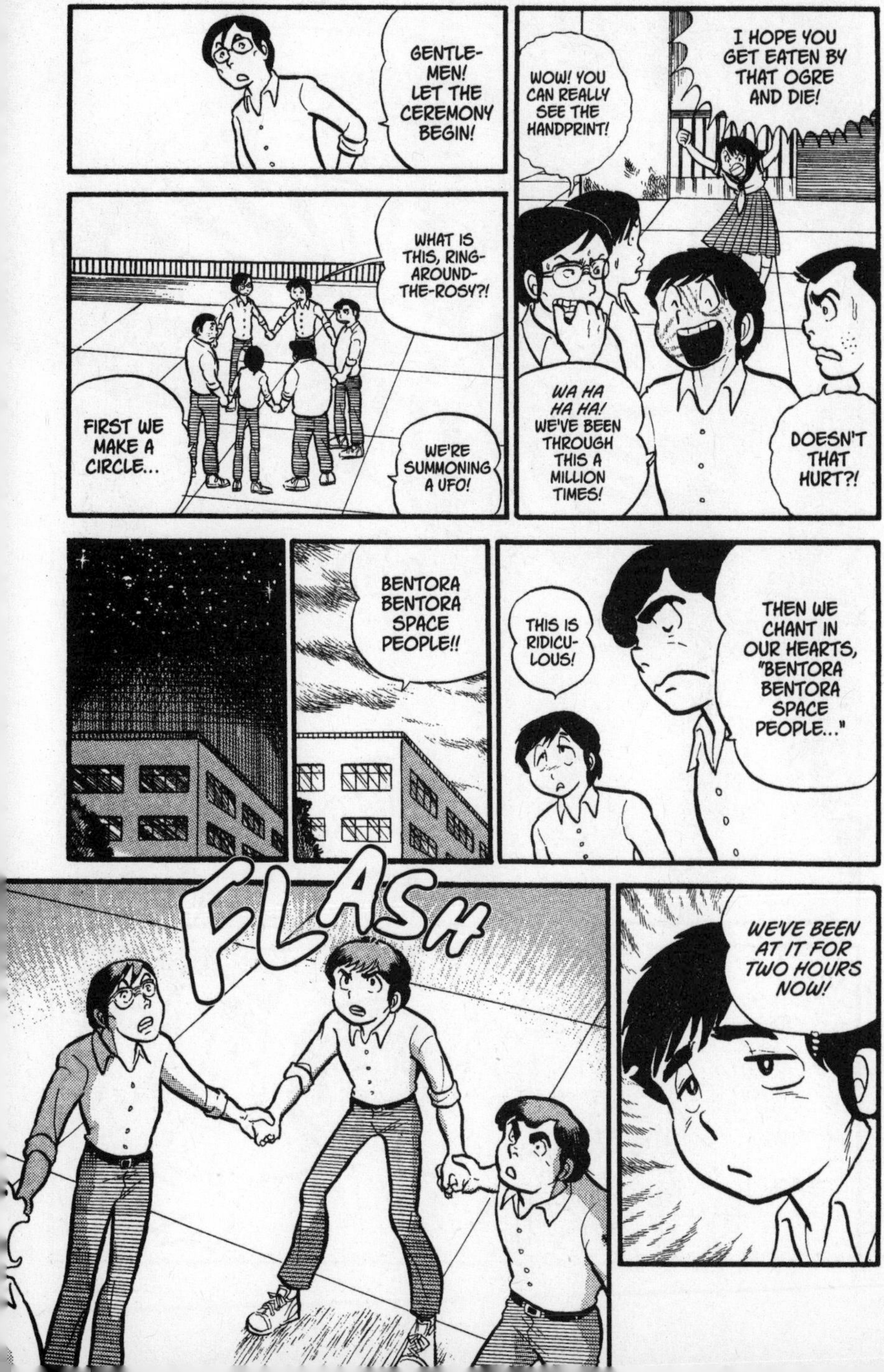
I HOPE YOU GET EATEN BY THAT OGRE AND DIE!
WOW! YOU CAN REALLY SEE THE HANDPRINT!
DOESN'T THAT HURT?!
WA HA HA HA! WE'VE BEEN THROUGH THIS A MILLION TIMES!
GENTLE-MEN! LET THE CEREMONY BEGIN!
WHAT IS THIS, RING-AROUND-THE-ROSY?!
WE'RE SUMMONING A UFO!
FIRST WE MAKE A CIRCLE...
THEN WE CHANT IN OUR HEARTS, "BENTORA BENTORA SPACE PEOPLE..."
THIS IS RIDICU-LOUS!
BENTORA BENTORA SPACE PEOPLE!!
WE'VE BEEN AT IT FOR TWO HOURS NOW!
FLASH

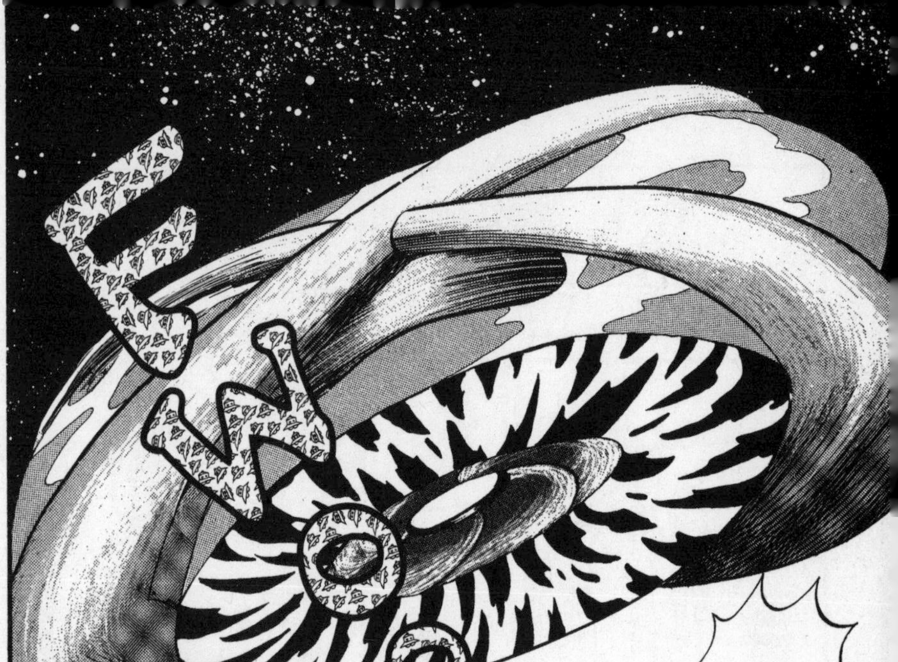
FWOOM
WAH! IT'S HERE!!
THAT'S NOT LUM'S UFO!!
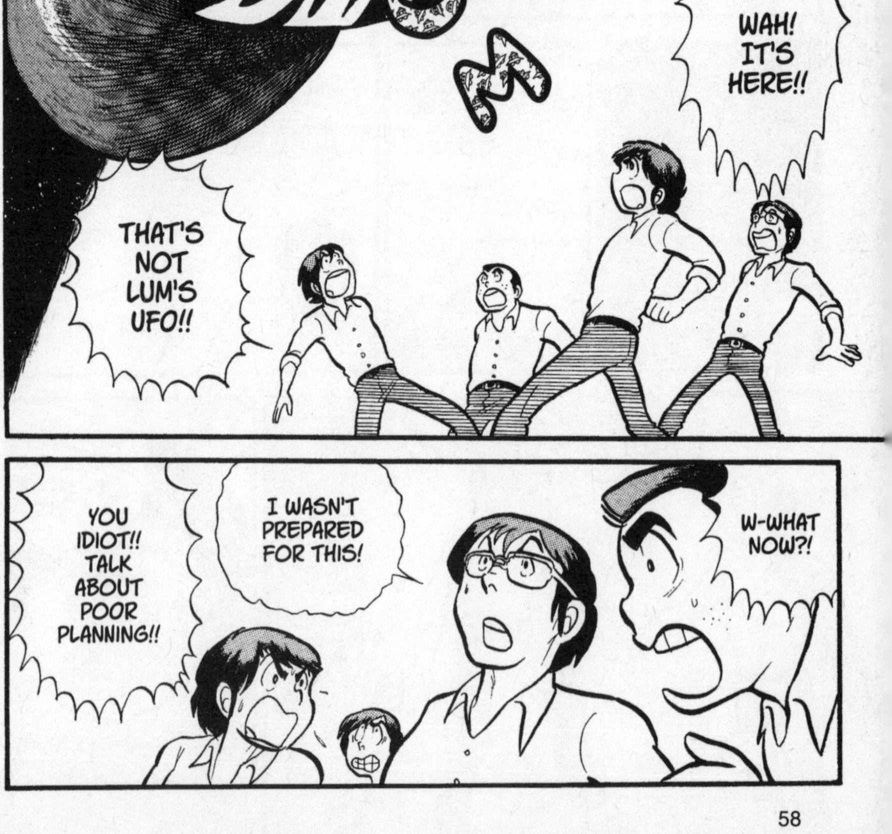
W-WHAT NOW?!
I WASN'T PREPARED FOR THIS!
YOU IDIOT!! TALK ABOUT POOR PLANNING!!

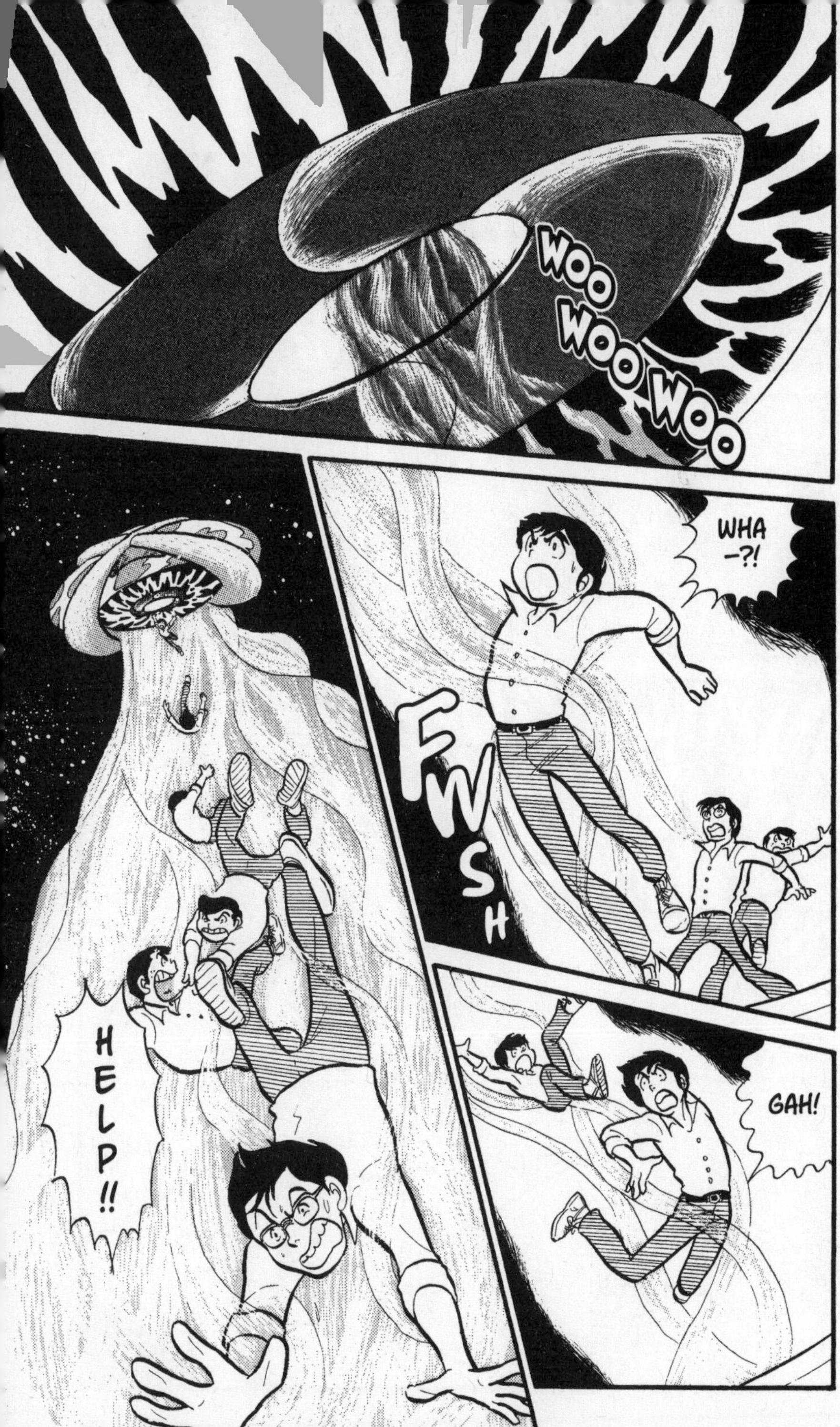
WOO WOO WOO
WHA
-?!
FWSH
GAH!
HELP!!

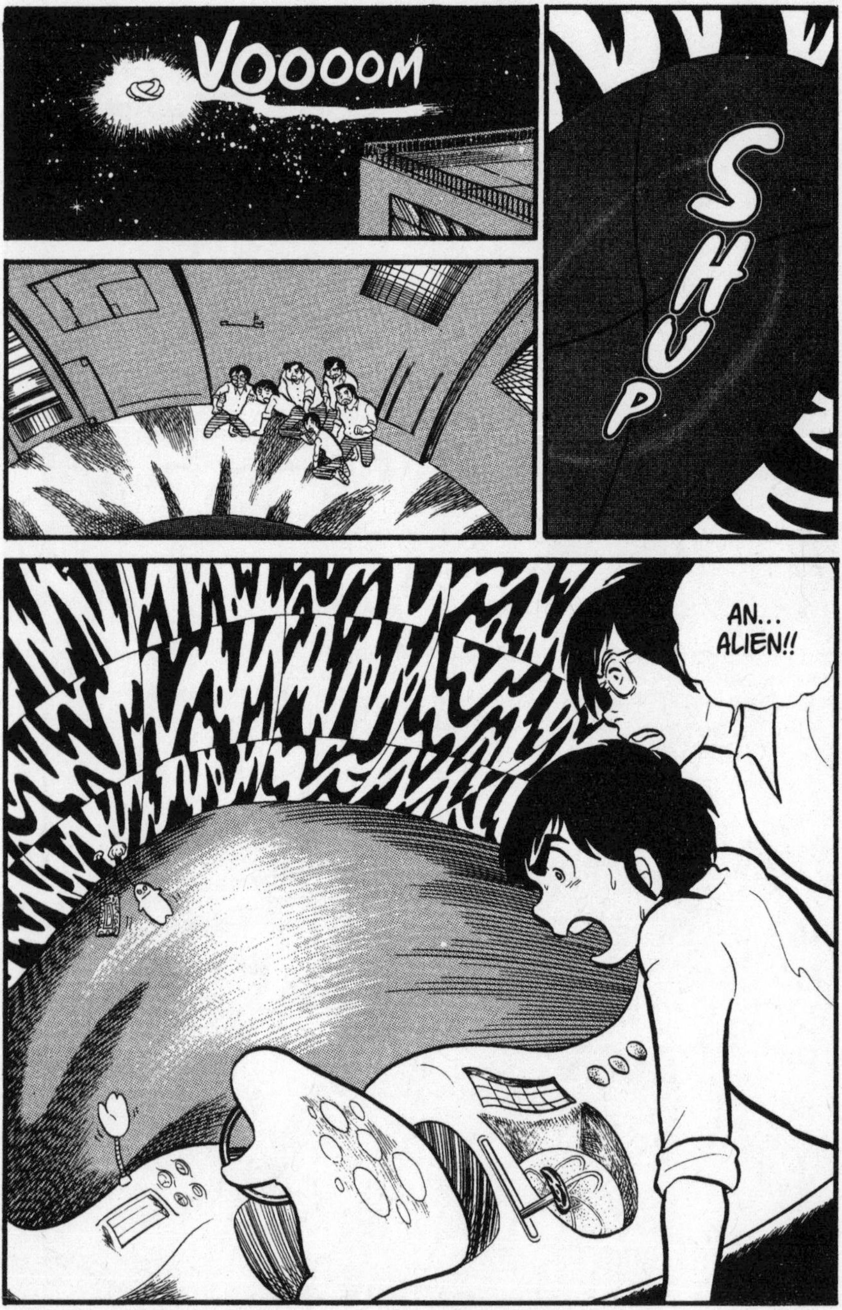
SHUP
VOOOOM
AN... ALIEN!!

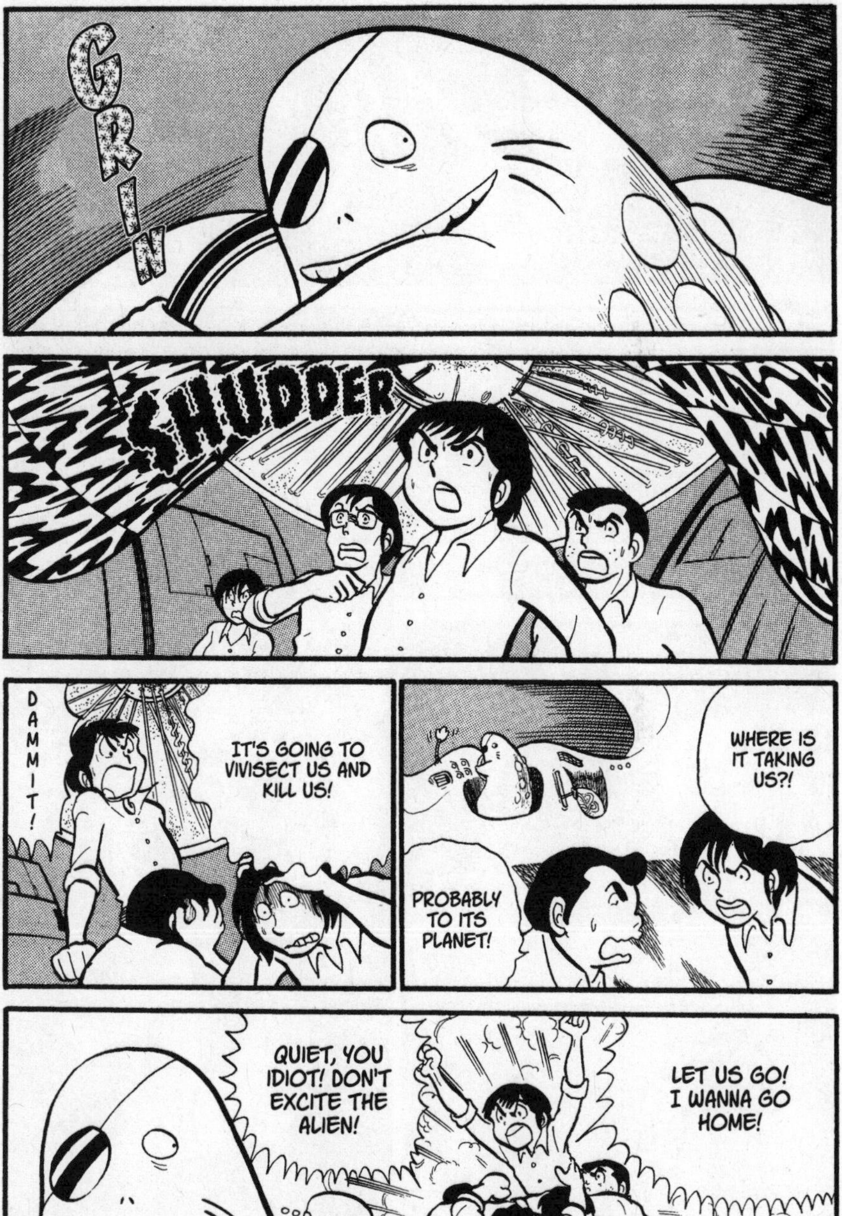
GRIN
SHUDDER
WHERE IS IT TAKING US?!
PROBABLY TO ITS PLANET!
IT'S GOING TO VIVISECT US AND KILL US!
DAMMIT!
LET US GO! I WANNA GO HOME!
QUIET, YOU IDIOT! DON'T EXCITE THE ALIEN!
HOME, HUH?

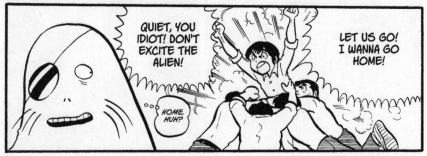

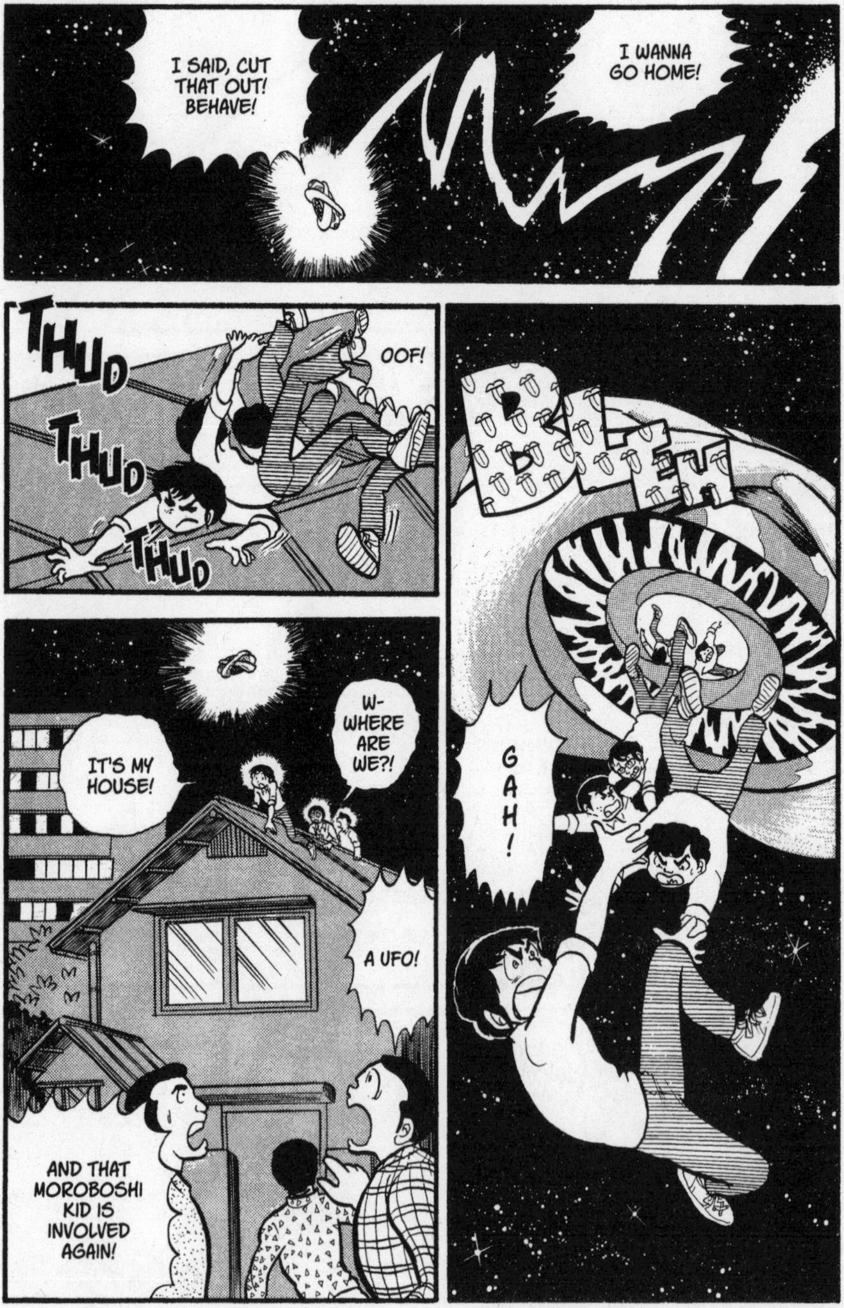
I WANNA GO HOME!
I SAID, CUT THAT OUT! BEHAVE!
BLEH
GAH!
THUD
OOF!
THUD
THUD
W-WHERE ARE WE?!
IT'S MY HOUSE!
A UFO!
AND THAT MOROBOSHI KID IS INVOLVED AGAIN!

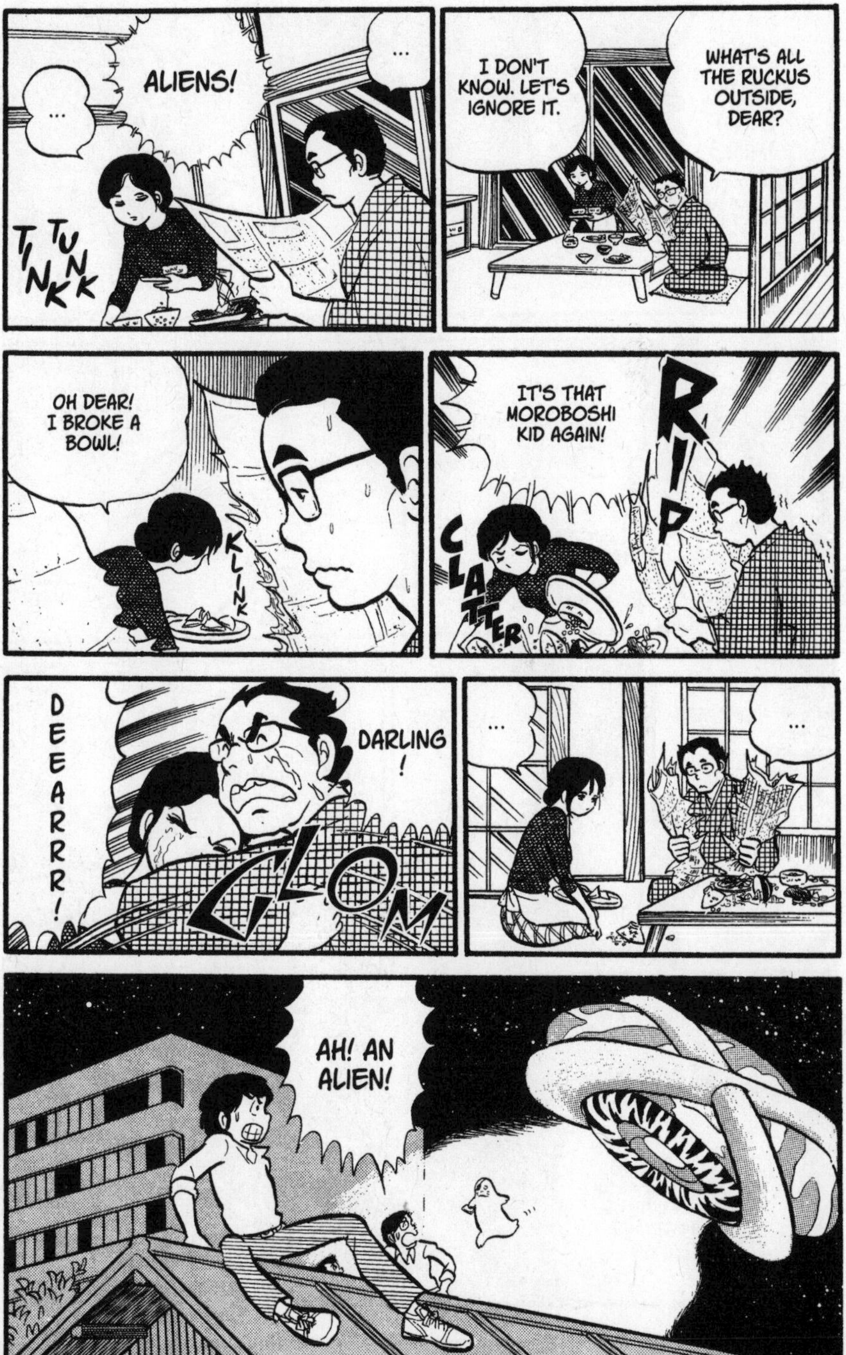
WHAT'S ALL THE RUCKUS OUTSIDE, DEAR?
I DON'T KNOW. LET'S IGNORE IT.
...
ALIENS!
...
TUNK
TINK
RIP
IT'S THAT MOROBOSHI KID AGAIN!
CLATTER
OH DEAR! I BROKE A BOWL!
KLINK
...
...
DARLING!
DEEEARRRR!
CLOM
AH! AN ALIEN!

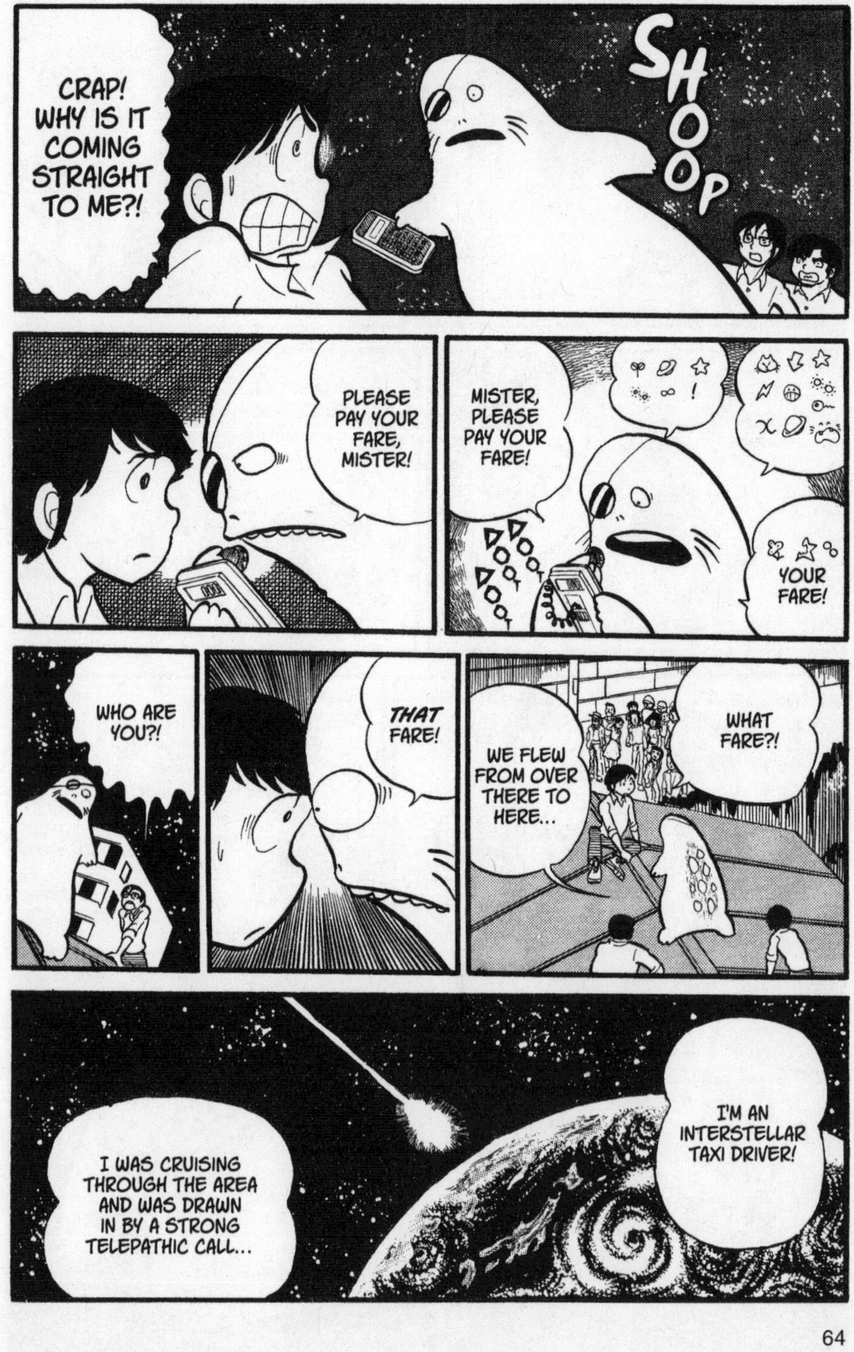
SHOOP
CRAP! WHY IS IT COMING STRAIGHT TO ME?!
MISTER, PLEASE PAY YOUR FARE!
YOUR FARE!
PLEASE PAY YOUR FARE, MISTER!
WHAT FARE?!
WE FLEW FROM OVER THERE TO HERE...
THAT FARE!
WHO ARE YOU?!
I'M AN INTERSTELLAR TAXI DRIVER!
I WAS CRUISING THROUGH THE AREA AND WAS DRAWN IN BY A STRONG TELEPATHIC CALL...

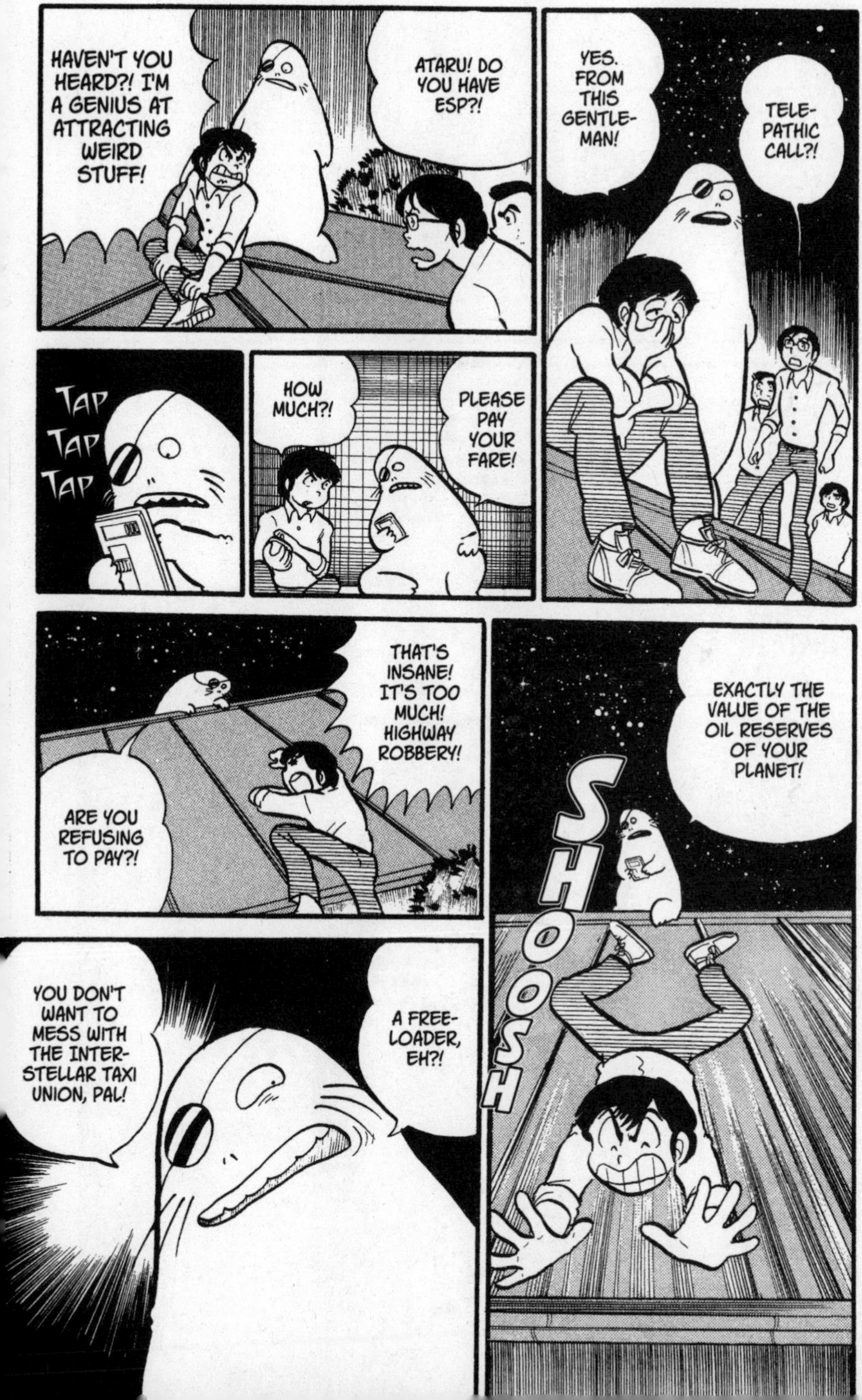
TELE-PATHIC CALL?!
YES. FROM THIS GENTLE-MAN!
ATARU! DO YOU HAVE ESP?!
HAVEN'T YOU HEARD?! I'M A GENIUS AT ATTRACTING WEIRD STUFF!
PLEASE PAY YOUR FARE!
HOW MUCH?!
TAP TAP TAP
EXACTLY THE VALUE OF THE OIL RESERVES OF YOUR PLANET!
SHOOOSH
THAT'S INSANE! IT'S TOO MUCH! HIGHWAY ROBBERY!
ARE YOU REFUSING TO PAY?!
A FREE-LOADER, EH?!
YOU DON'T WANT TO MESS WITH THE INTER-STELLAR TAXI UNION, PAL!

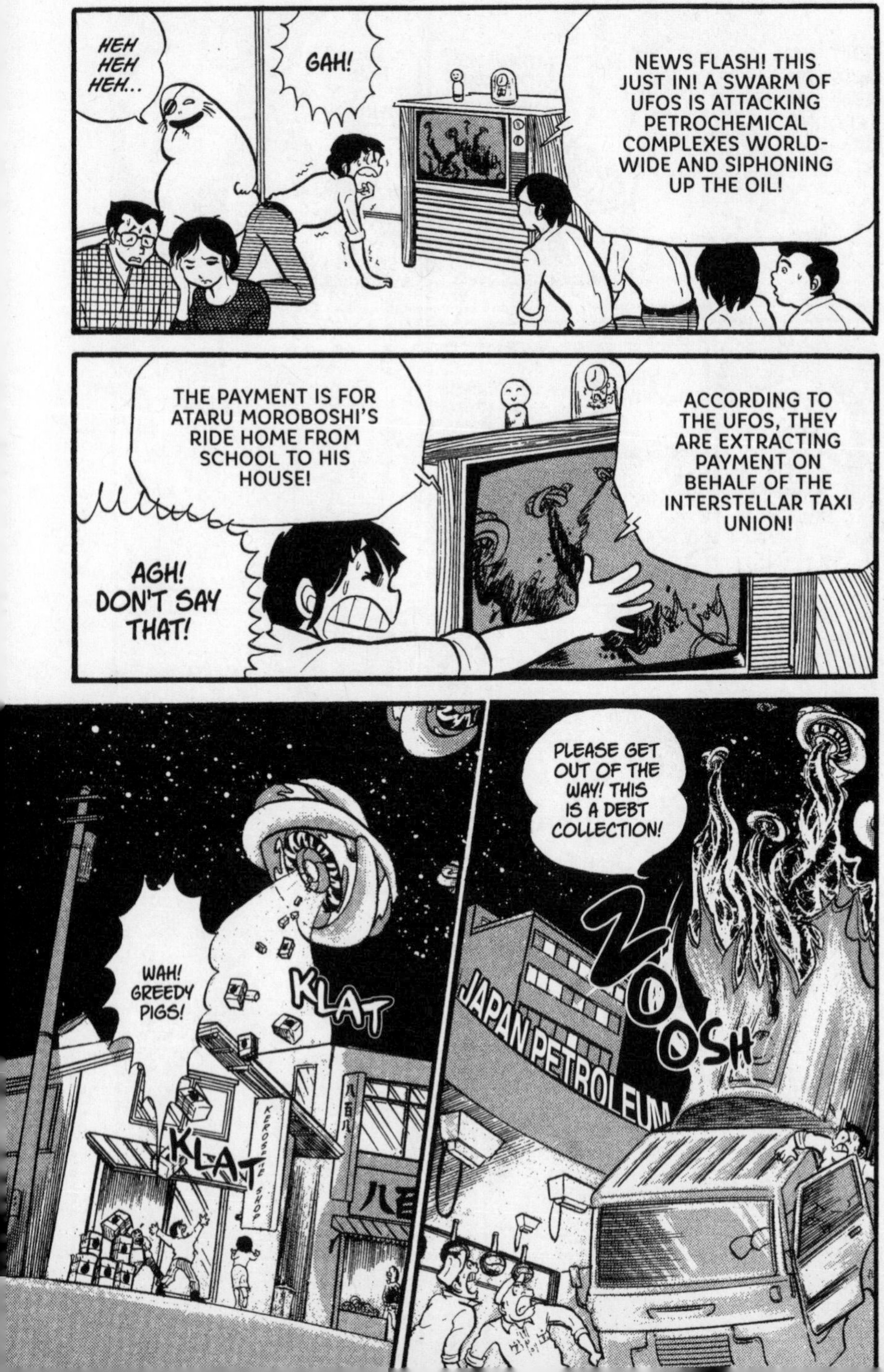
NEWS FLASH! THIS JUST IN! A SWARM OF UFOS IS ATTACKING PETROCHEMICAL COMPLEXES WORLD-WIDE AND SIPHONING UP THE OIL!
GAH!
HEH HEH HEH...
ACCORDING TO THE UFOS, THEY ARE EXTRACTING PAYMENT ON BEHALF OF THE INTERSTELLAR TAXI UNION!
THE PAYMENT IS FOR ATARU MOROBOSHI'S RIDE HOME FROM SCHOOL TO HIS HOUSE!
AGH! DON'T SAY THAT!
PLEASE GET OUT OF THE WAY! THIS IS A DEBT COLLECTION!
ZOOOSH
JAPAN PETROLEUM
KLAT
WAH! GREEDY PIGS!
KLAT

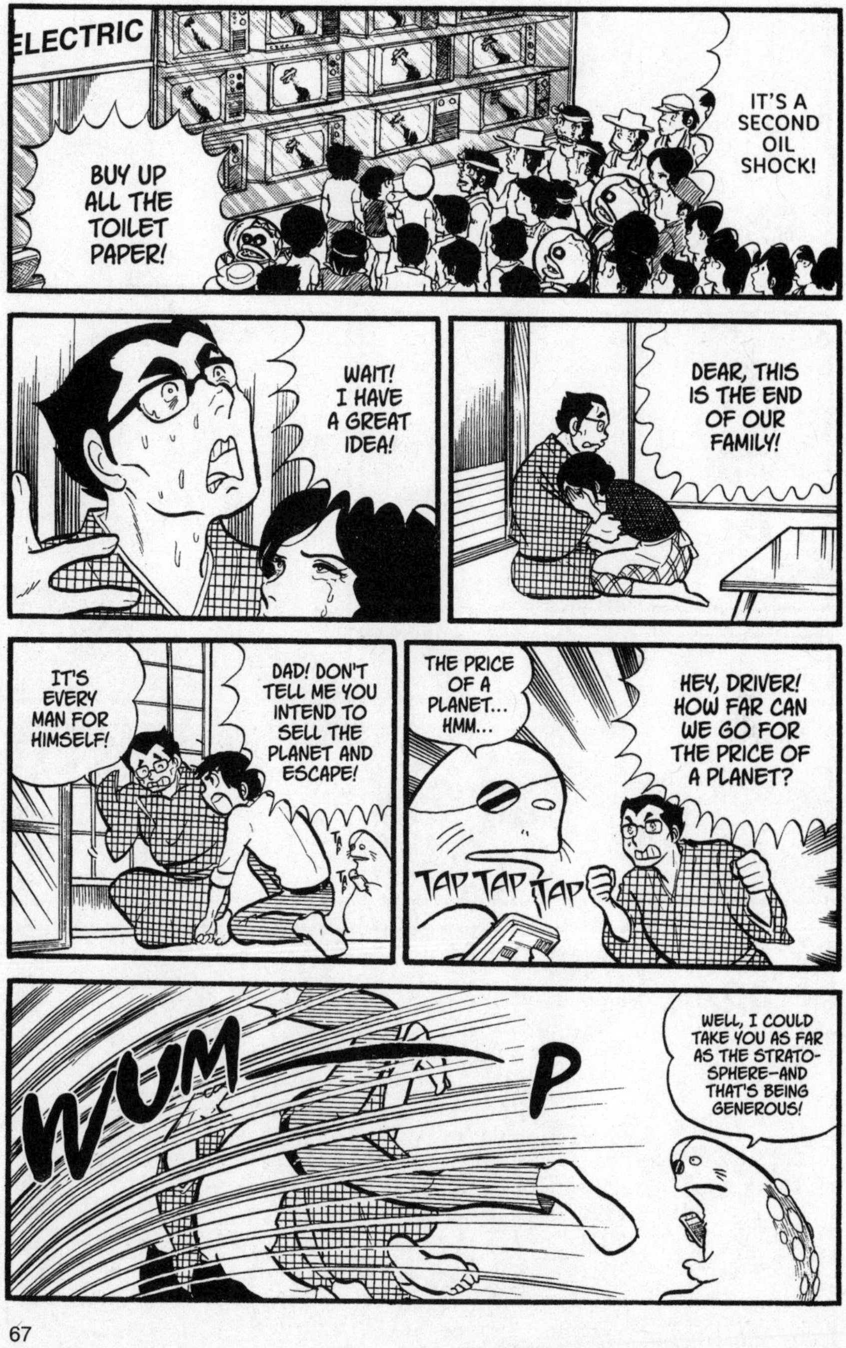
IT'S A SECOND OIL SHOCK!
BUY UP ALL THE TOILET PAPER!
ELECTRIC
DEAR, THIS IS THE END OF OUR FAMILY!
WAIT! I HAVE A GREAT IDEA!
HEY, DRIVER! HOW FAR CAN WE GO FOR THE PRICE OF A PLANET?
THE PRICE OF A PLANET... HMM...
TAP TAP TAP
DAD! DON'T TELL ME YOU INTEND TO SELL THE PLANET AND ESCAPE!
IT'S EVERY MAN FOR HIMSELF!
TAP TAP
WELL, I COULD TAKE YOU AS FAR AS THE STRATO-SPHERE—AND THAT'S BEING GENEROUS!
WUMP

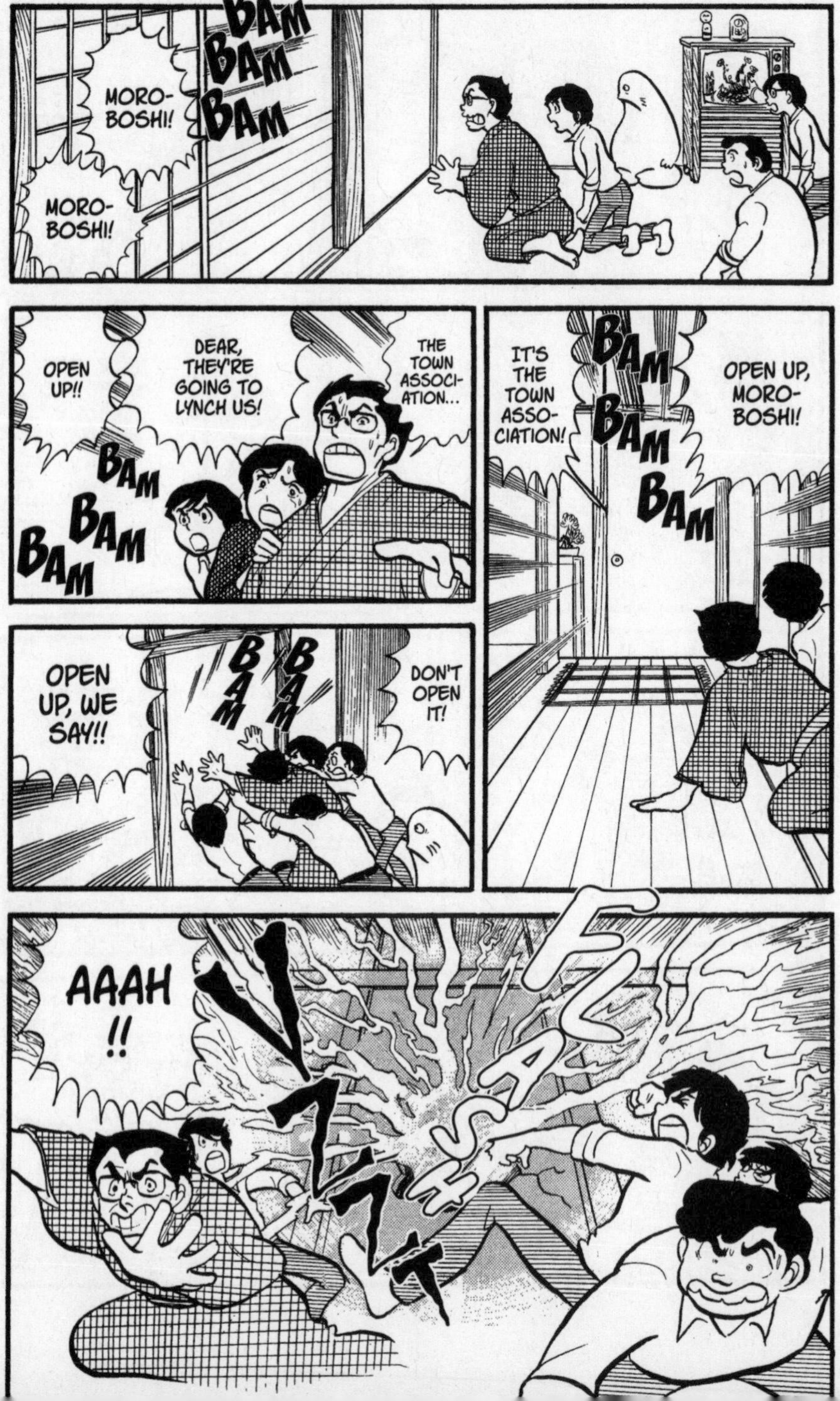
BAM BAM BAM
MORO-BOSHI!
MORO-BOSHI!
OPEN UP, MORO-BOSHI!
BAM BAM BAM
IT'S THE TOWN ASSOCIATION!
THE TOWN ASSOCIATION...
DEAR, THEY'RE GOING TO LYNCH US!
OPEN UP!!
BAM BAM BAM
DON'T OPEN IT!
BAM BAM
OPEN UP, WE SAY!!
FLASH
VZZZT
AAAH !!

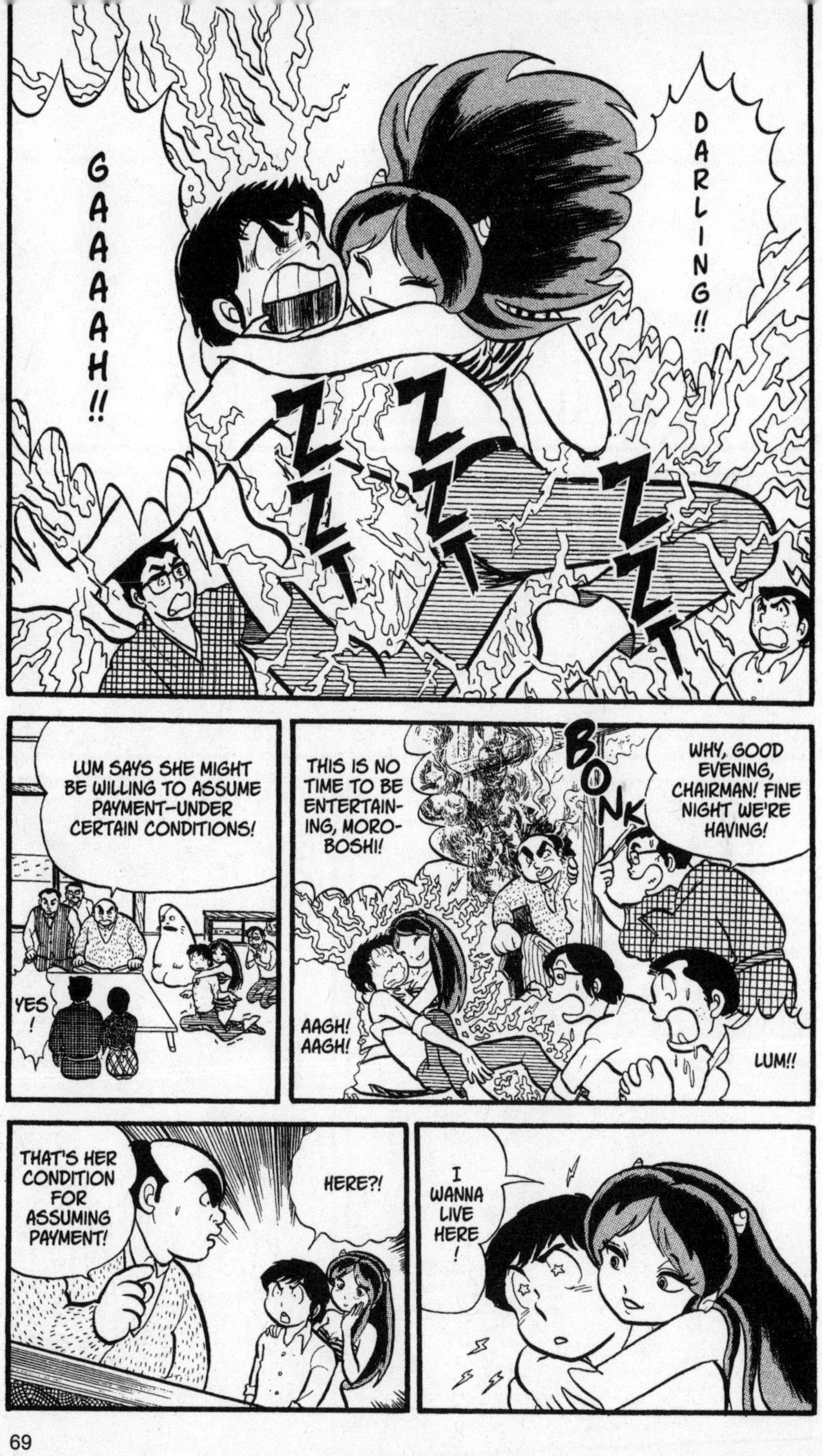
DARLING!!
GAAAAAH!!
ZZZT
ZZZT
ZZZT
WHY, GOOD EVENING, CHAIRMAN! FINE NIGHT WE'RE HAVING!
BONK
THIS IS NO TIME TO BE ENTERTAIN-ING, MORO-BOSHI!
LUM!!
AAGH! AAGH!
LUM SAYS SHE MIGHT BE WILLING TO ASSUME PAYMENT—UNDER CERTAIN CONDITIONS!
YES!
I WANNA LIVE HERE!
HERE?!
THAT'S HER CONDITION FOR ASSUMING PAYMENT!

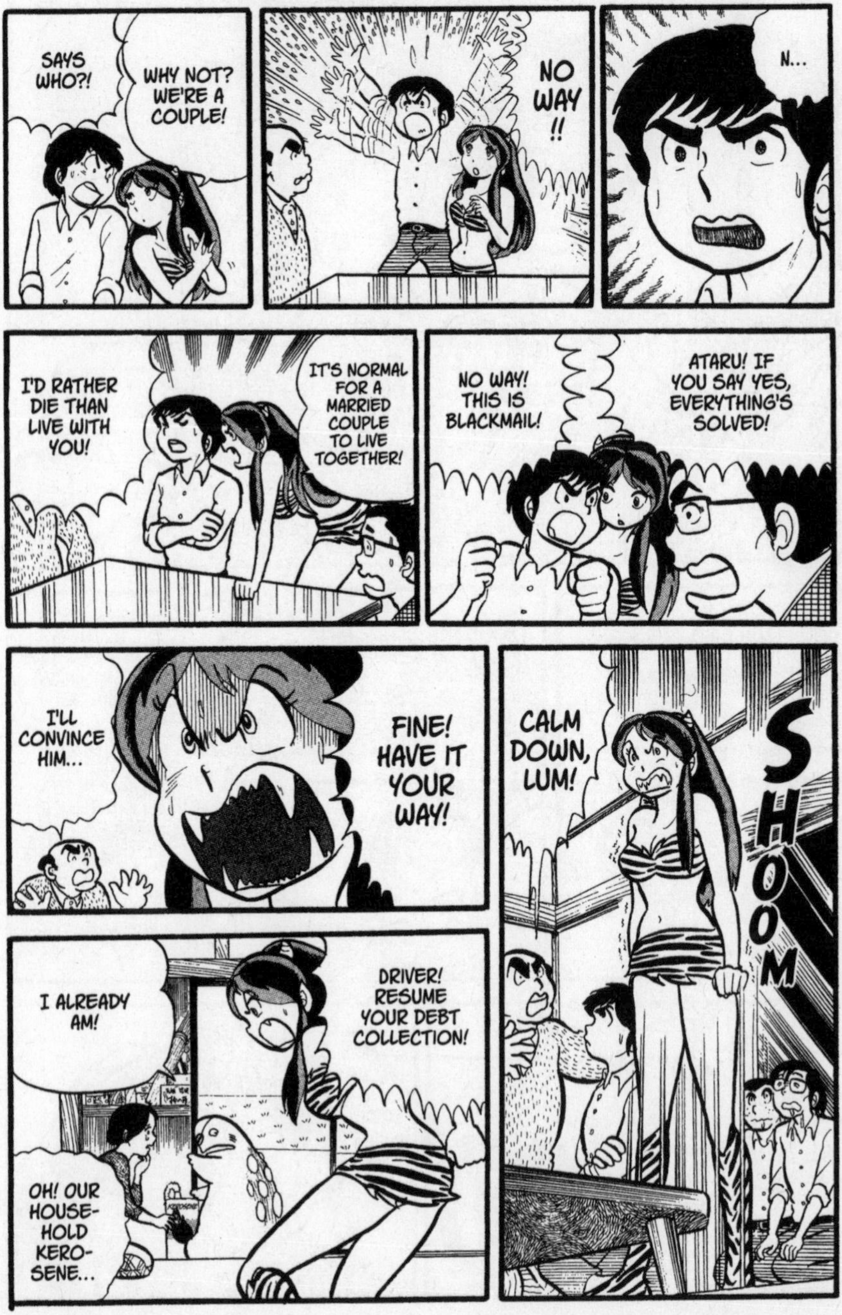
N...
NO WAY !!
WHY NOT? WE'RE A COUPLE!
SAYS WHO?!
ATARU! IF YOU SAY YES, EVERYTHING'S SOLVED!
NO WAY! THIS IS BLACKMAIL!
IT'S NORMAL FOR A MARRIED COUPLE TO LIVE TOGETHER!
I'D RATHER DIE THAN LIVE WITH YOU!
SHOOM
CALM DOWN, LUM!
FINE! HAVE IT YOUR WAY!
I'LL CONVINCE HIM...
DRIVER! RESUME YOUR DEBT COLLECTION!
I ALREADY AM!
OH! OUR HOUSE-HOLD KERO-SENE...

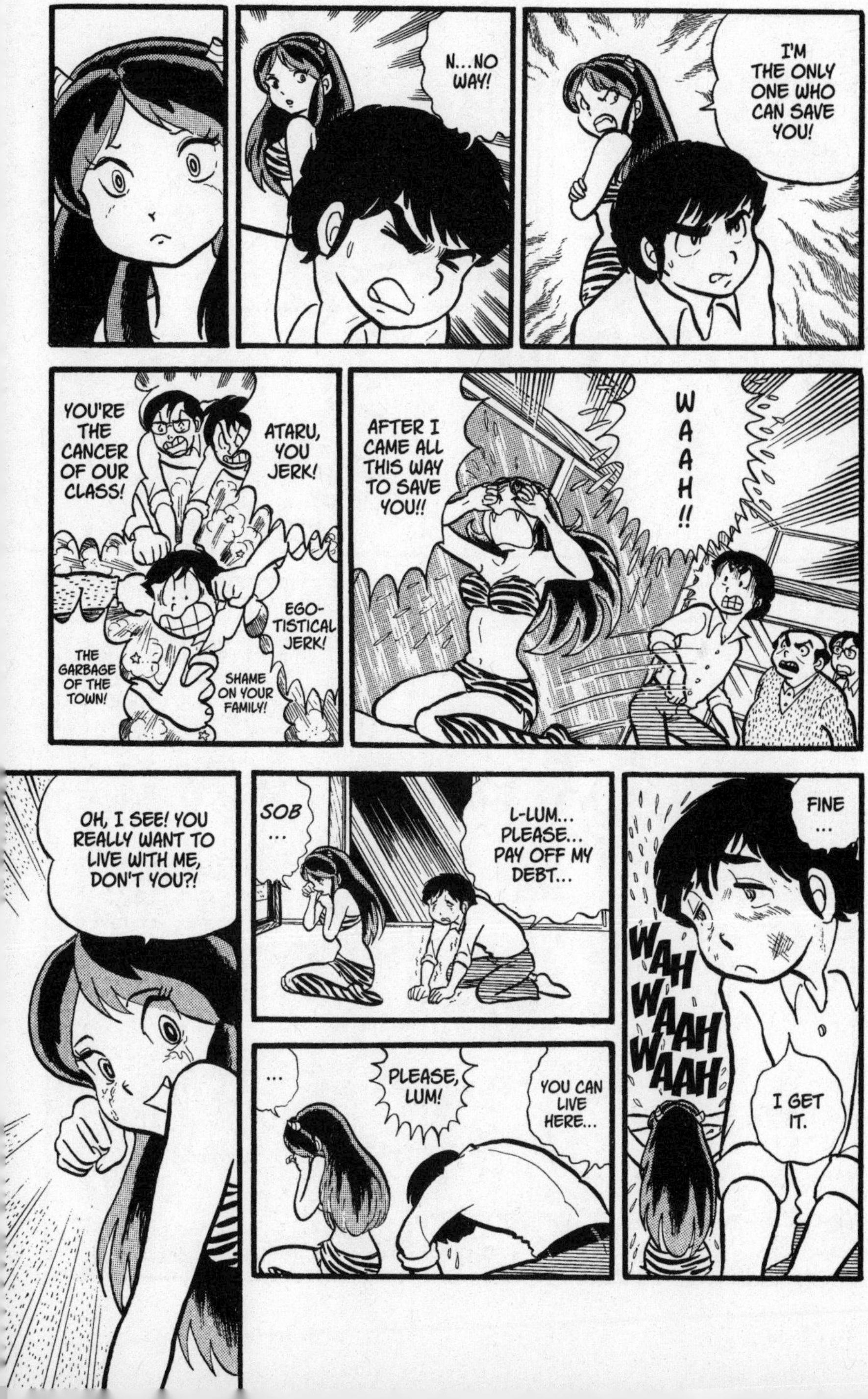
I'M THE ONLY ONE WHO CAN SAVE YOU!
N...NO WAY!
WAAH!!
AFTER I CAME ALL THIS WAY TO SAVE YOU!!
ATARU, YOU JERK!
YOU'RE THE CANCER OF OUR CLASS!
EGO-TISTICAL JERK!
SHAME ON YOUR FAMILY!
THE GARBAGE OF THE TOWN!
FINE ...
WAH WAAH WAAH
I GET IT.
L-LUM... PLEASE... PAY OFF MY DEBT...
SOB ...
YOU CAN LIVE HERE...
PLEASE, LUM!
...
OH, I SEE! YOU REALLY WANT TO LIVE WITH ME, DON'T YOU?!

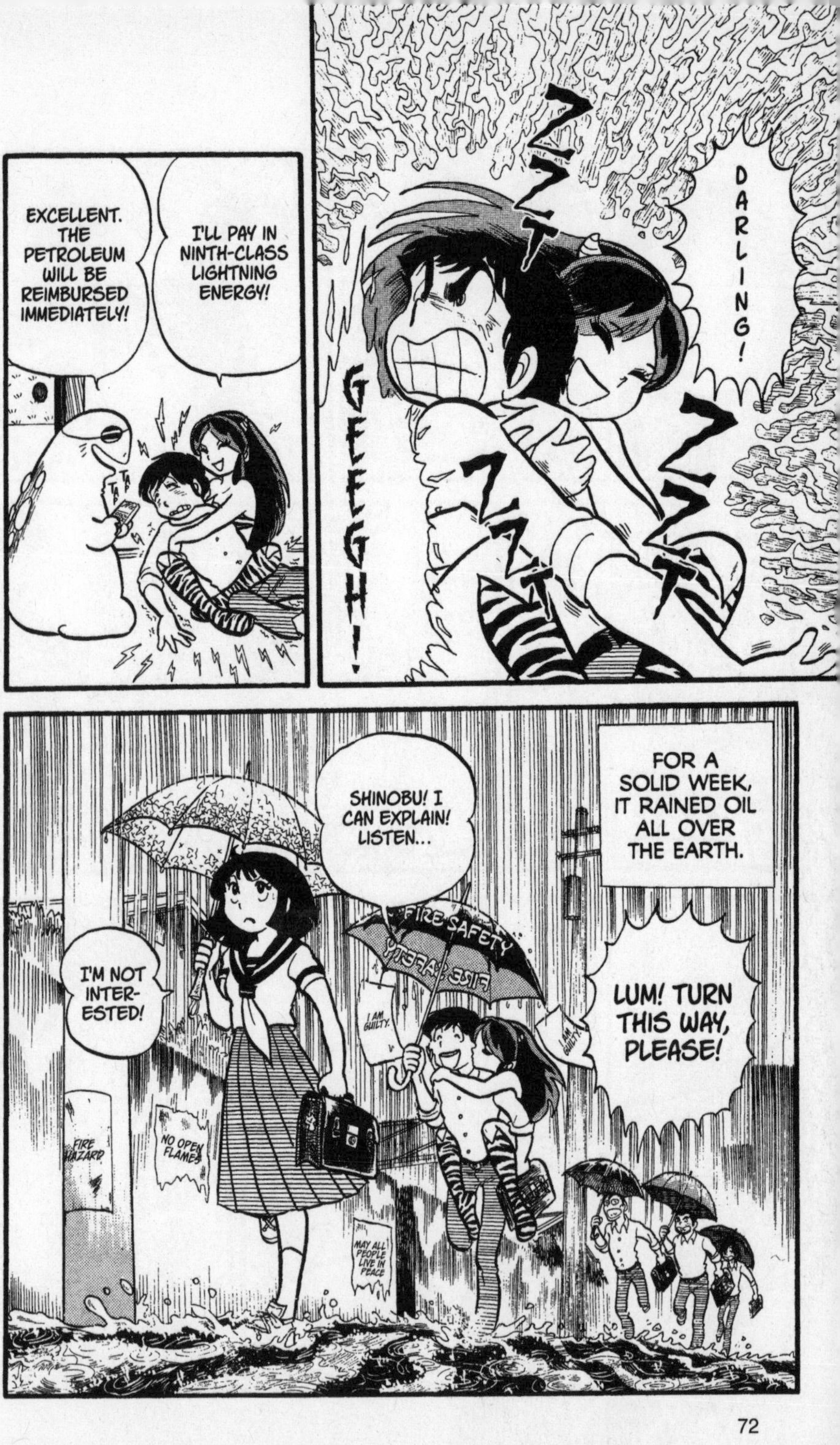
ZZZT
DARLING!
ZZZT
ZZZT
GFEEGH!
I'LL PAY IN NINTH-CLASS LIGHTNING ENERGY!
EXCELLENT. THE PETROLEUM WILL BE REIMBURSED IMMEDIATELY!
FOR A SOLID WEEK, IT RAINED OIL ALL OVER THE EARTH.
LUM! TURN THIS WAY, PLEASE!
SHINOBU! I CAN EXPLAIN! LISTEN...
FIRE SAFETY
I AM GUILTY.
I AM GUILTY.
I'M NOT INTER-ESTED!
NO OPEN FLAMES
FIRE HAZARD
MAY ALL PEOPLE LIVE IN PEACE

CHAPTER 4: PRESENT FOR YOU

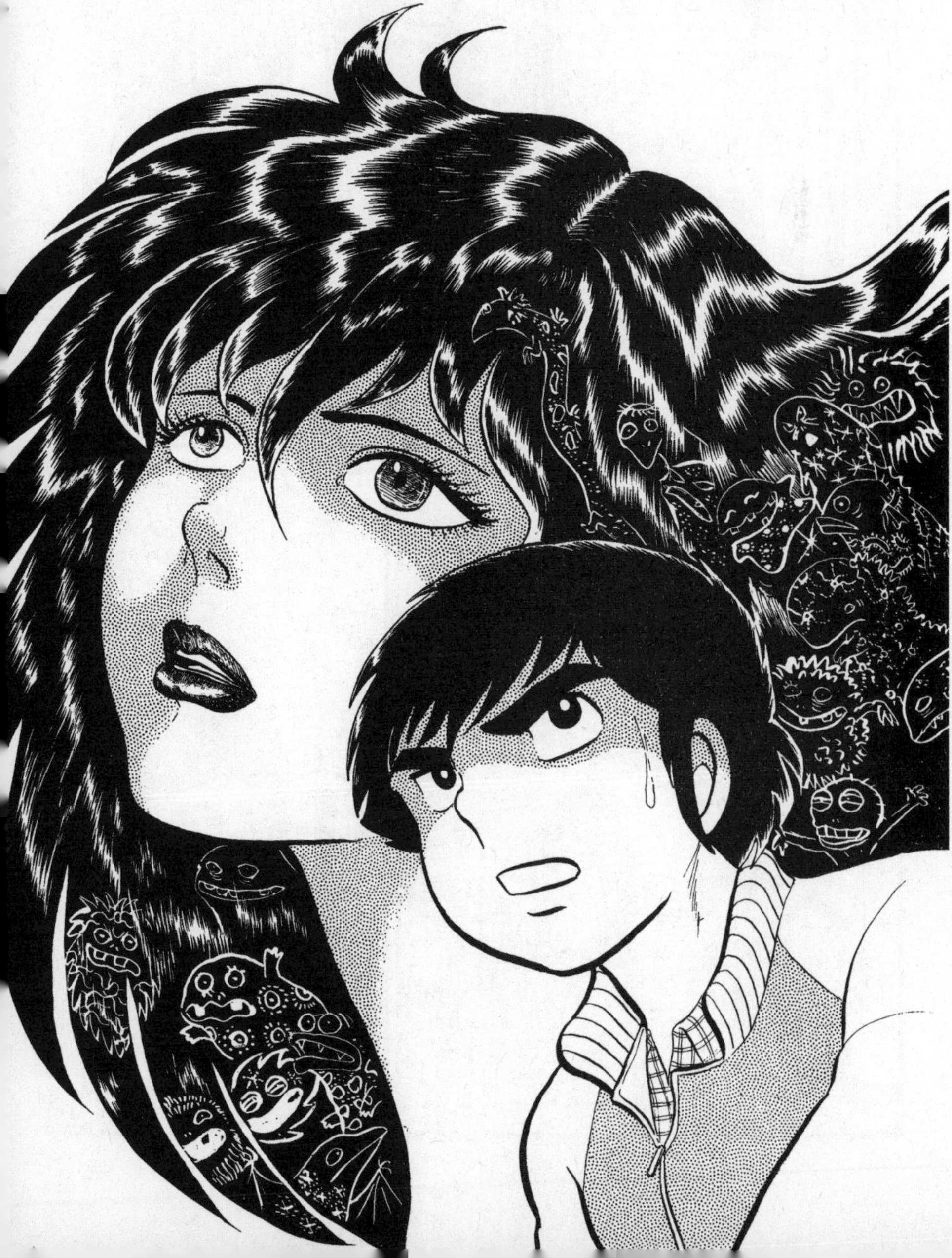

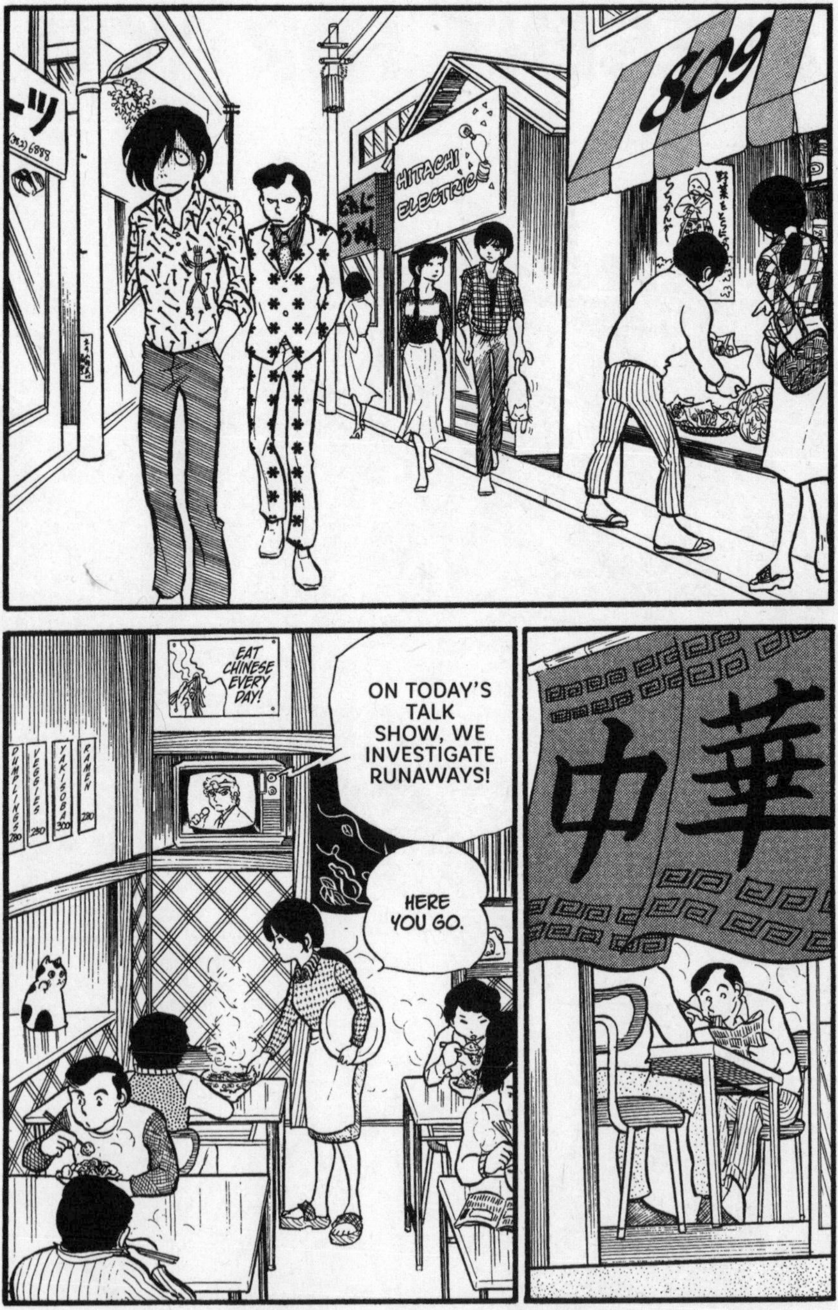
809
HITACHI ELECTRIC
中華
EAT CHINESE EVERY DAY!
RAMEN 280
YAKISOBA 300
VEGGIES 280
DUMPLINGS 280
ON TODAY'S TALK SHOW, WE INVESTIGATE RUNAWAYS!
HERE YOU GO.

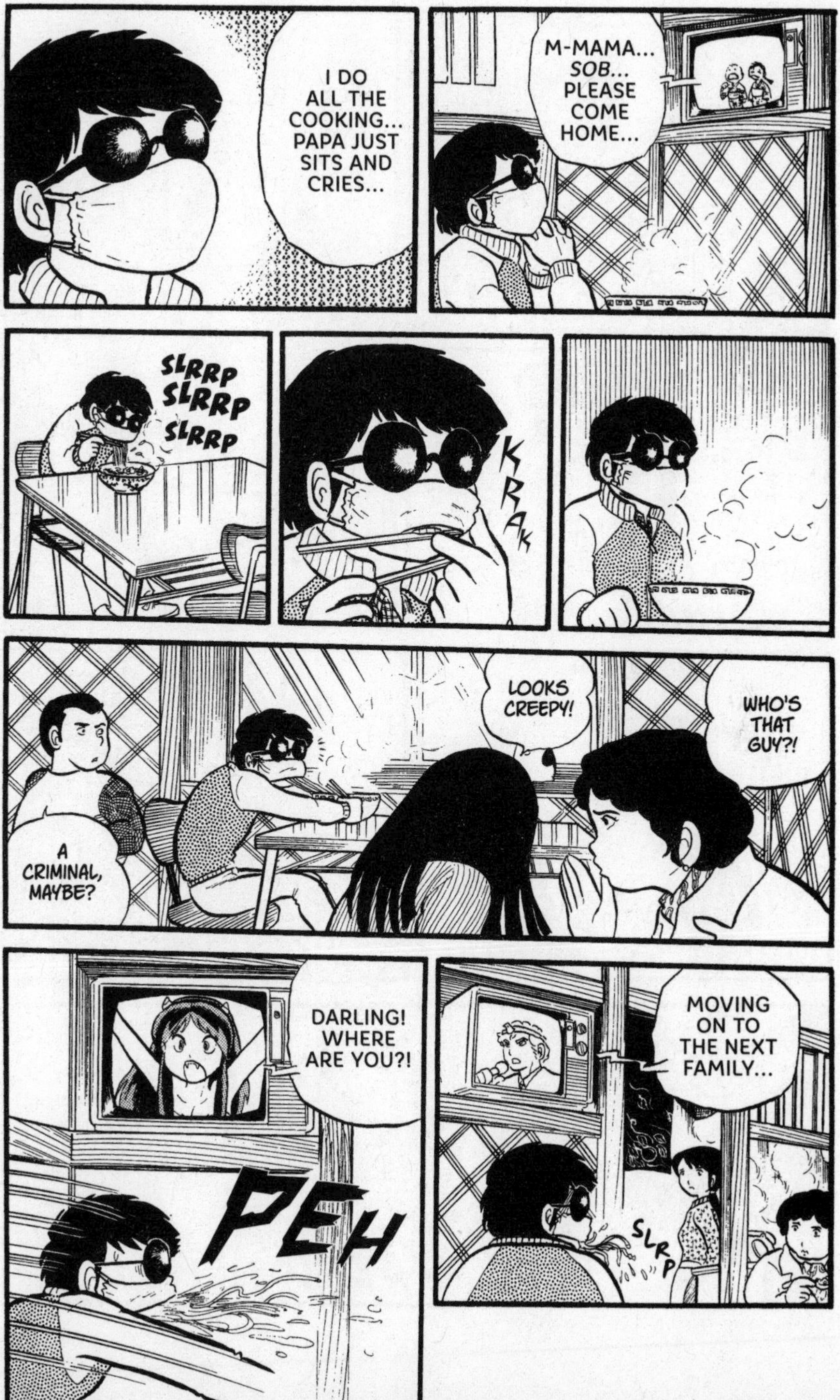
M-MAMA... *SOB*... PLEASE COME HOME...
I DO ALL THE COOKING... PAPA JUST SITS AND CRIES...
KRAK
SLRRP SLRRP SLRRP
WHO'S THAT GUY?!
LOOKS CREEPY!
A CRIMINAL, MAYBE?
MOVING ON TO THE NEXT FAMILY...
SLRP
DARLING! WHERE ARE YOU?!
PEH

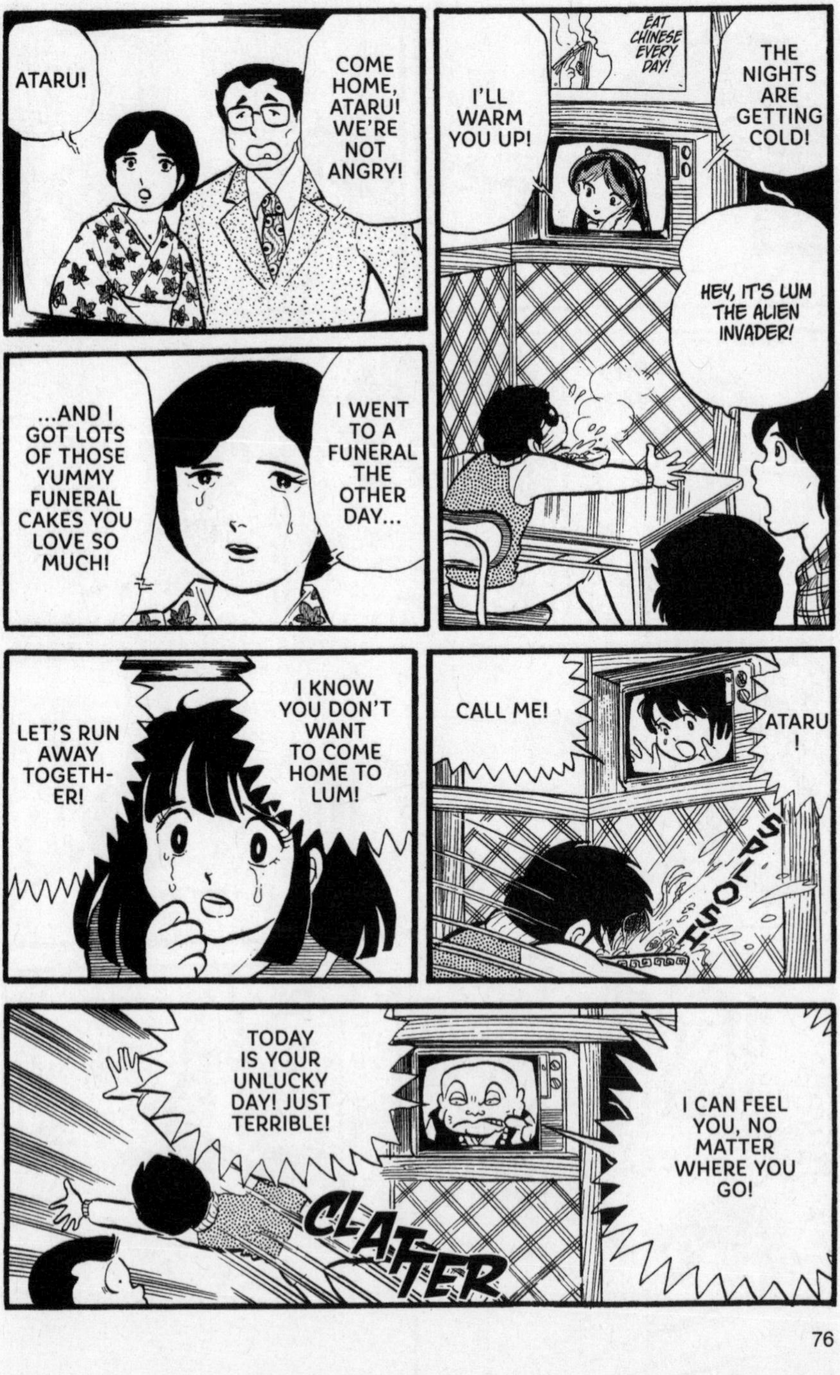
THE NIGHTS ARE GETTING COLD!
EAT CHINESE EVERY DAY!
I'LL WARM YOU UP!
HEY, IT'S LUM THE ALIEN INVADER!
COME HOME, ATARU! WE'RE NOT ANGRY!
ATARU!
I WENT TO A FUNERAL THE OTHER DAY...
...AND I GOT LOTS OF THOSE YUMMY FUNERAL CAKES YOU LOVE SO MUCH!
ATARU!
CALL ME!
SPLOOSH
I KNOW YOU DON'T WANT TO COME HOME TO LUM!
LET'S RUN AWAY TOGETHER!
I CAN FEEL YOU, NO MATTER WHERE YOU GO!
TODAY IS YOUR UNLUCKY DAY! JUST TERRIBLE!
CLATTER

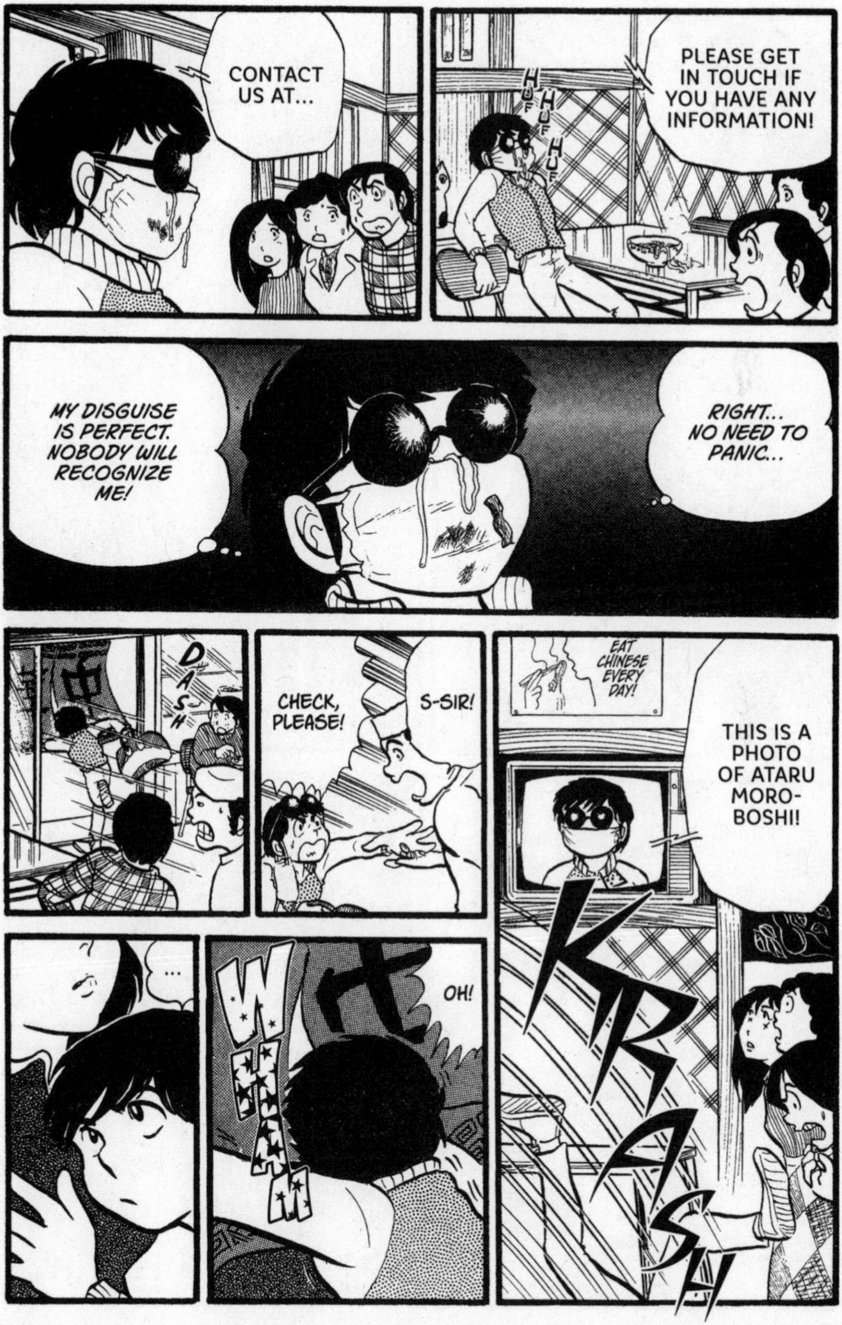
PLEASE GET IN TOUCH IF YOU HAVE ANY INFORMATION!
HUF HUF HUF
CONTACT US AT...
RIGHT... NO NEED TO PANIC...
MY DISGUISE IS PERFECT. NOBODY WILL RECOGNIZE ME!
EAT CHINESE EVERY DAY!
THIS IS A PHOTO OF ATARU MORO-BOSHI!
KRASH
S-SIR!
CHECK, PLEASE!
DASH
OH!
WHAM
...

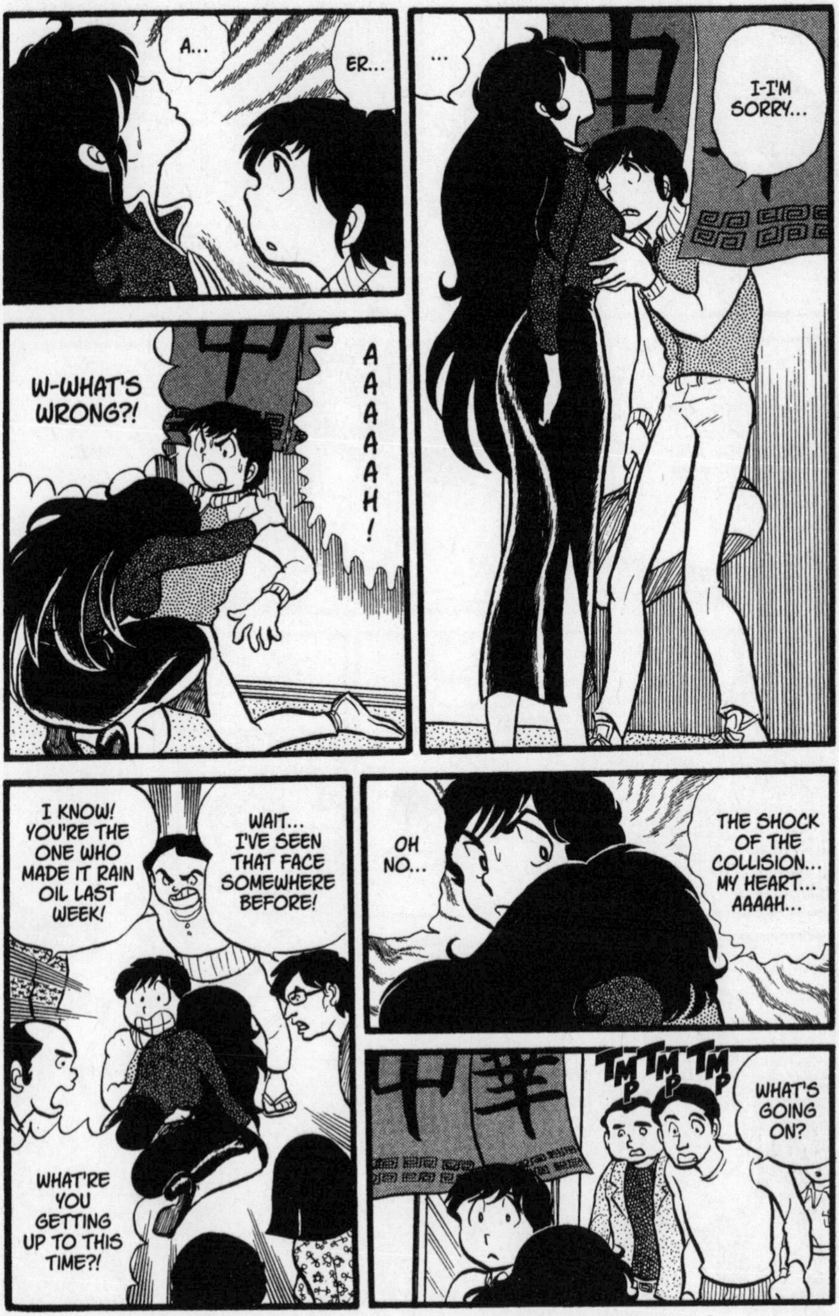

I-I'M SORRY...
...
ER...
A...
AAAAAAH!
W-WHAT'S WRONG?!
THE SHOCK OF THE COLLISION... MY HEART... AAAAH...
OH NO...
WHAT'S GOING ON?
TMP TMP TMP TMP
WAIT... I'VE SEEN THAT FACE SOMEWHERE BEFORE!
I KNOW! YOU'RE THE ONE WHO MADE IT RAIN OIL LAST WEEK!
WHAT'RE YOU GETTING UP TO THIS TIME?!

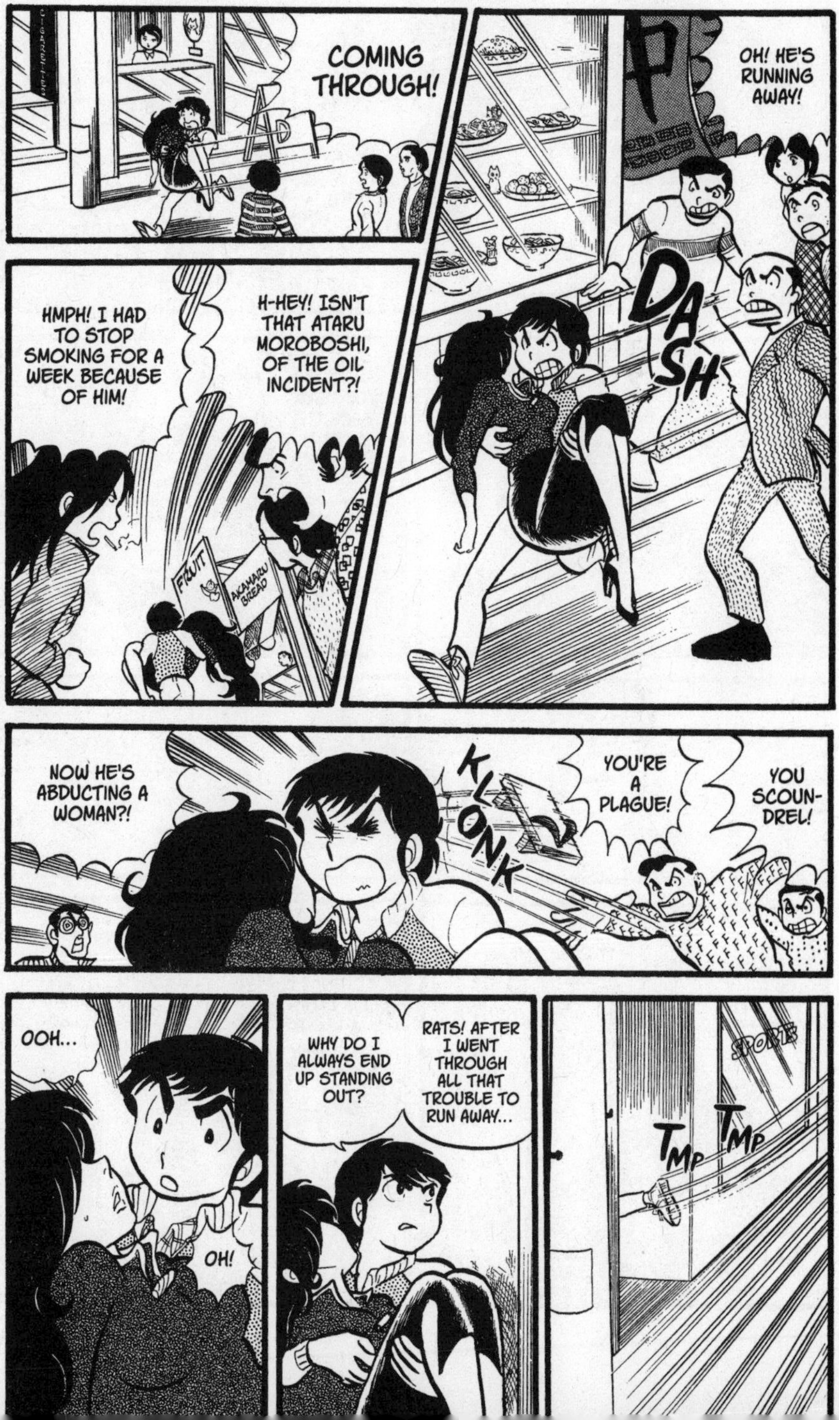
OH! HE'S RUNNING AWAY!
DASH
COMING THROUGH!
H-HEY! ISN'T THAT ATARU MOROBOSHI, OF THE OIL INCIDENT?!
HMPH! I HAD TO STOP SMOKING FOR A WEEK BECAUSE OF HIM!
FRUIT
AKAMARU BREAD
YOU SCOUN-DREL!
YOU'RE A PLAGUE!
KLONK
NOW HE'S ABDUCTING A WOMAN?!
SPORTS
TMP TMP
RATS! AFTER I WENT THROUGH ALL THAT TROUBLE TO RUN AWAY...
WHY DO I ALWAYS END UP STANDING OUT?
OOH...
OH!

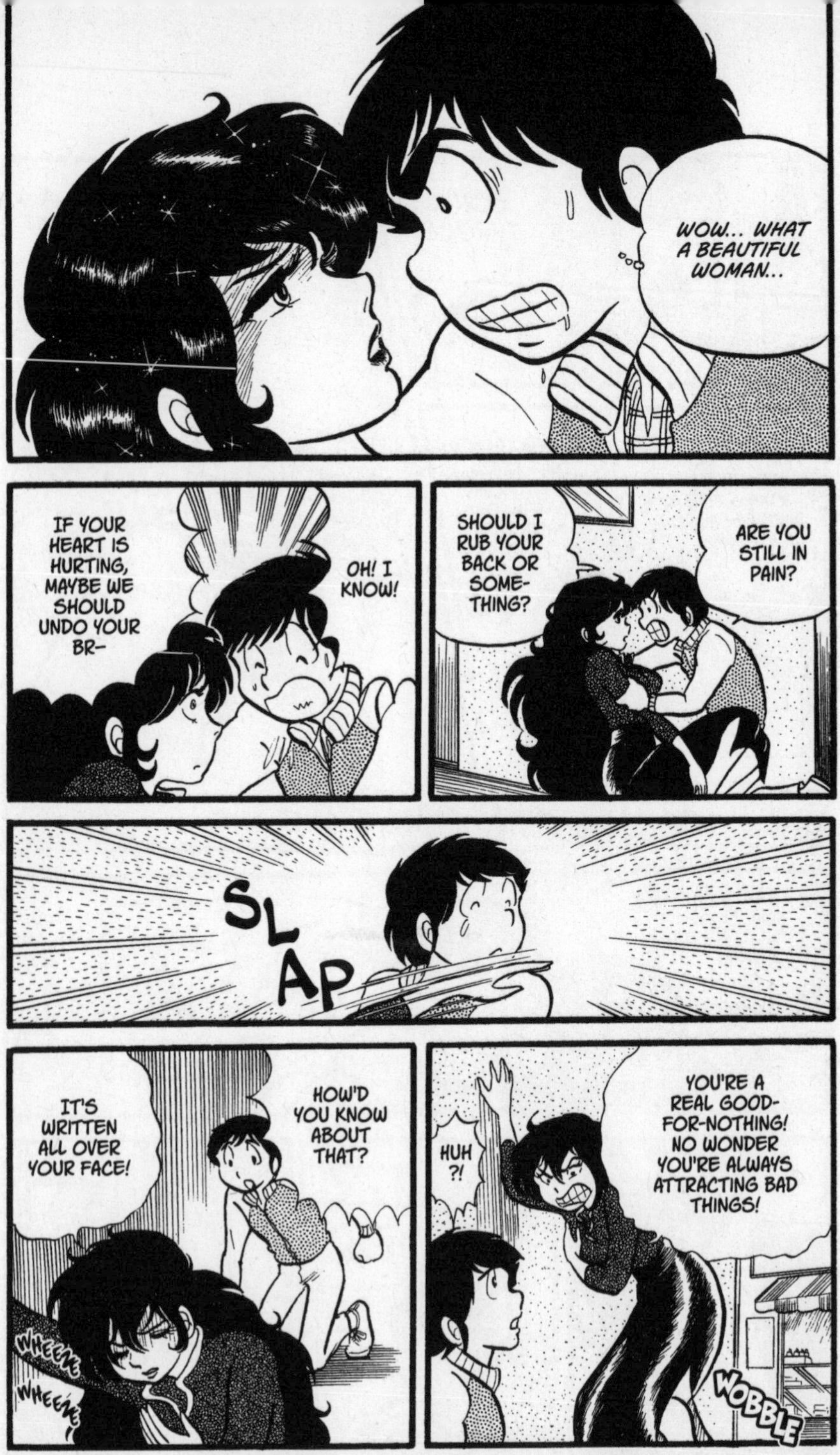
WOW... WHAT A BEAUTIFUL WOMAN...
ARE YOU STILL IN PAIN?
SHOULD I RUB YOUR BACK OR SOME-THING?
OH! I KNOW!
IF YOUR HEART IS HURTING, MAYBE WE SHOULD UNDO YOUR BR-
SLAP
YOU'RE A REAL GOOD-FOR-NOTHING! NO WONDER YOU'RE ALWAYS ATTRACTING BAD THINGS!
HUH ?!
WOBBLE
HOW'D YOU KNOW ABOUT THAT?
IT'S WRITTEN ALL OVER YOUR FACE!
WHEENE
WHEENE

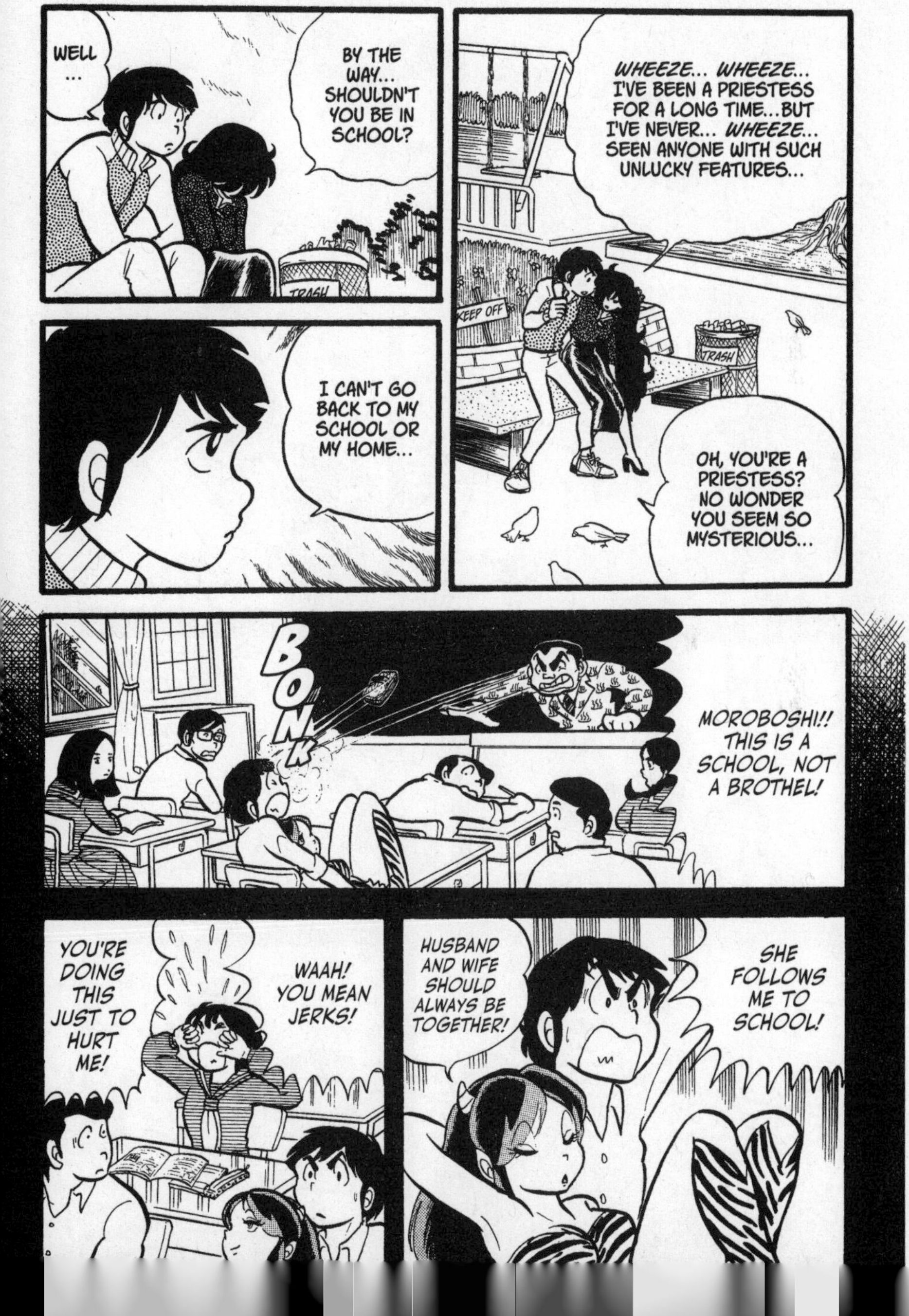
WHEEZE... WHEEZE... I'VE BEEN A PRIESTESS FOR A LONG TIME...BUT I'VE NEVER... WHEEZE... SEEN ANYONE WITH SUCH UNLUCKY FEATURES...
OH, YOU'RE A PRIESTESS? NO WONDER YOU SEEM SO MYSTERIOUS...
KEEP OFF
TRASH
BY THE WAY... SHOULDN'T YOU BE IN SCHOOL?
WELL ...
TRASH
I CAN'T GO BACK TO MY SCHOOL OR MY HOME...
MOROBOSHI!! THIS IS A SCHOOL, NOT A BROTHEL!
BONK
SHE FOLLOWS ME TO SCHOOL!
HUSBAND AND WIFE SHOULD ALWAYS BE TOGETHER!
WAAH! YOU MEAN JERKS!
YOU'RE DOING THIS JUST TO HURT ME!

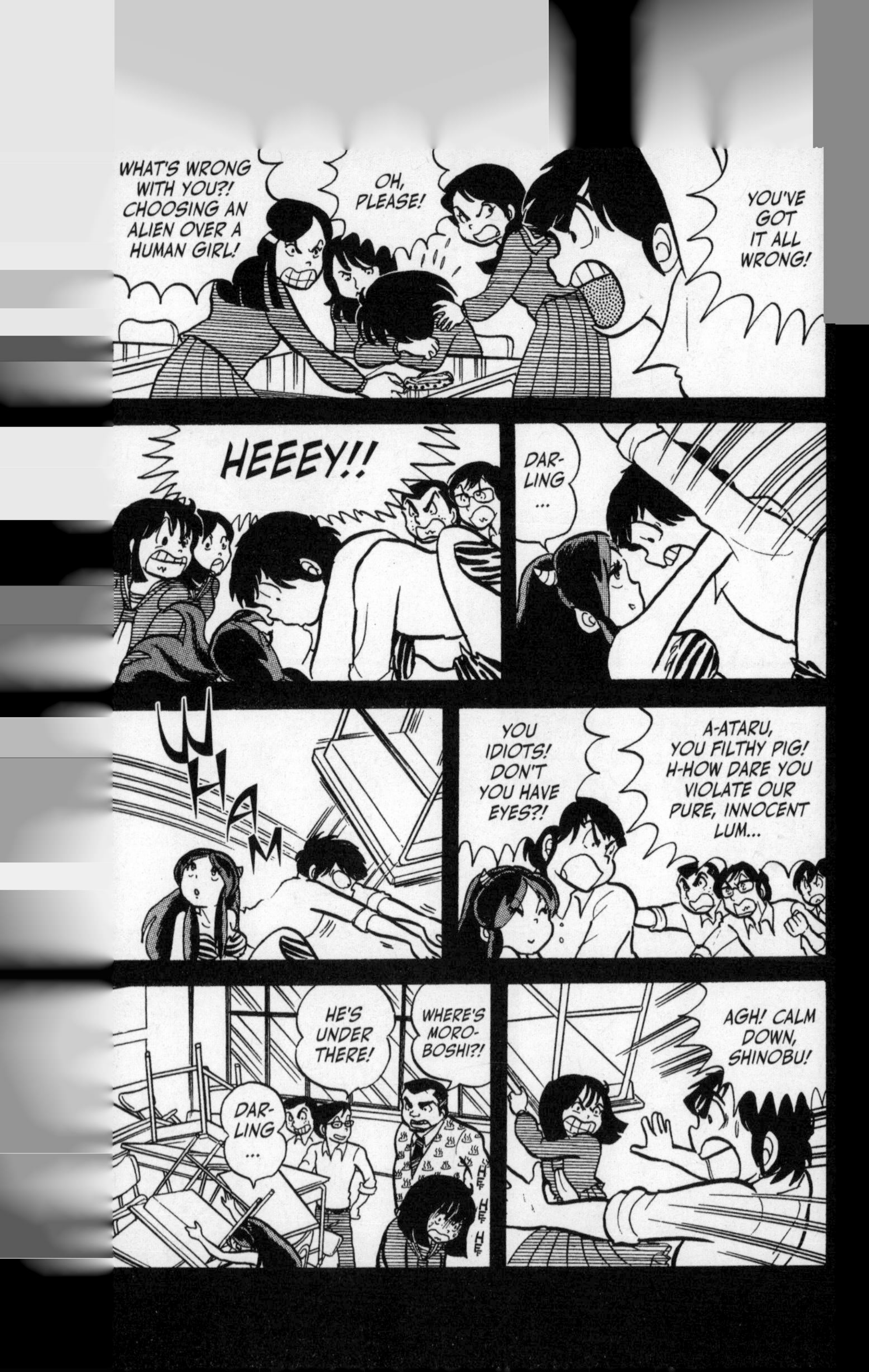
YOU'VE GOT IT ALL WRONG!
OH, PLEASE!
WHAT'S WRONG WITH YOU?! CHOOSING AN ALIEN OVER A HUMAN GIRL!
DAR-LING ...
HEEEY!!
A-ATARU, YOU FILTHY PIG! H-HOW DARE YOU VIOLATE OUR PURE, INNOCENT LUM...
YOU IDIOTS! DON'T YOU HAVE EYES?!
WHAM
AGH! CALM DOWN, SHINOBU!
WHERE'S MORO-BOSHI?!
HE'S UNDER THERE!
DAR-LING ...

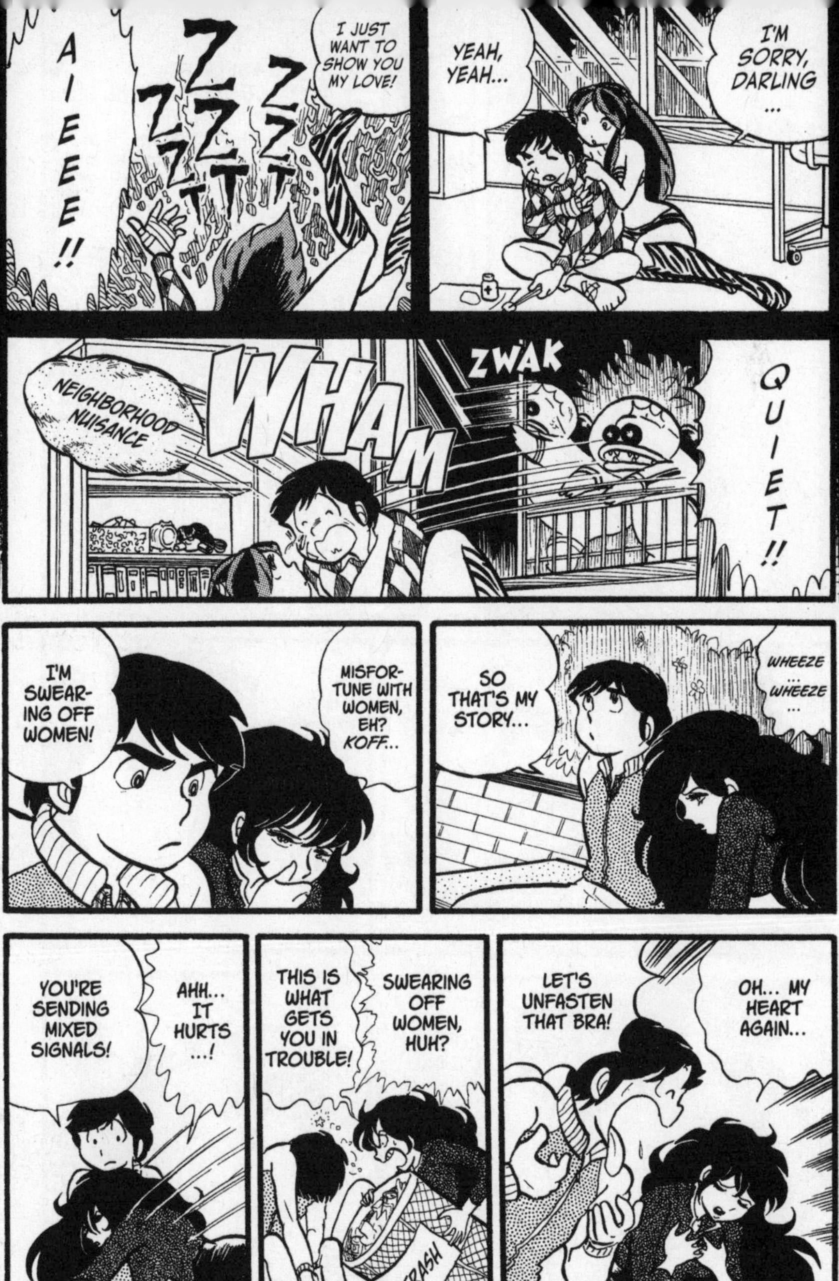
I'M SORRY, DARLING ...
YEAH, YEAH...
I JUST WANT TO SHOW YOU MY LOVE!
ZZZZT ZZT
AIEEEE!!
QUIET!!
ZWAK
WHAM
NEIGHBORHOOD NUISANCE
WHEEZE ... WHEEZE ...
SO THAT'S MY STORY...
MISFORTUNE WITH WOMEN, EH? KOFF...
I'M SWEARING OFF WOMEN!
OH... MY HEART AGAIN...
LET'S UNFASTEN THAT BRA!
SWEARING OFF WOMEN, HUH?
THIS IS WHAT GETS YOU IN TROUBLE!
TRASH
AHH... IT HURTS ...!
YOU'RE SENDING MIXED SIGNALS!

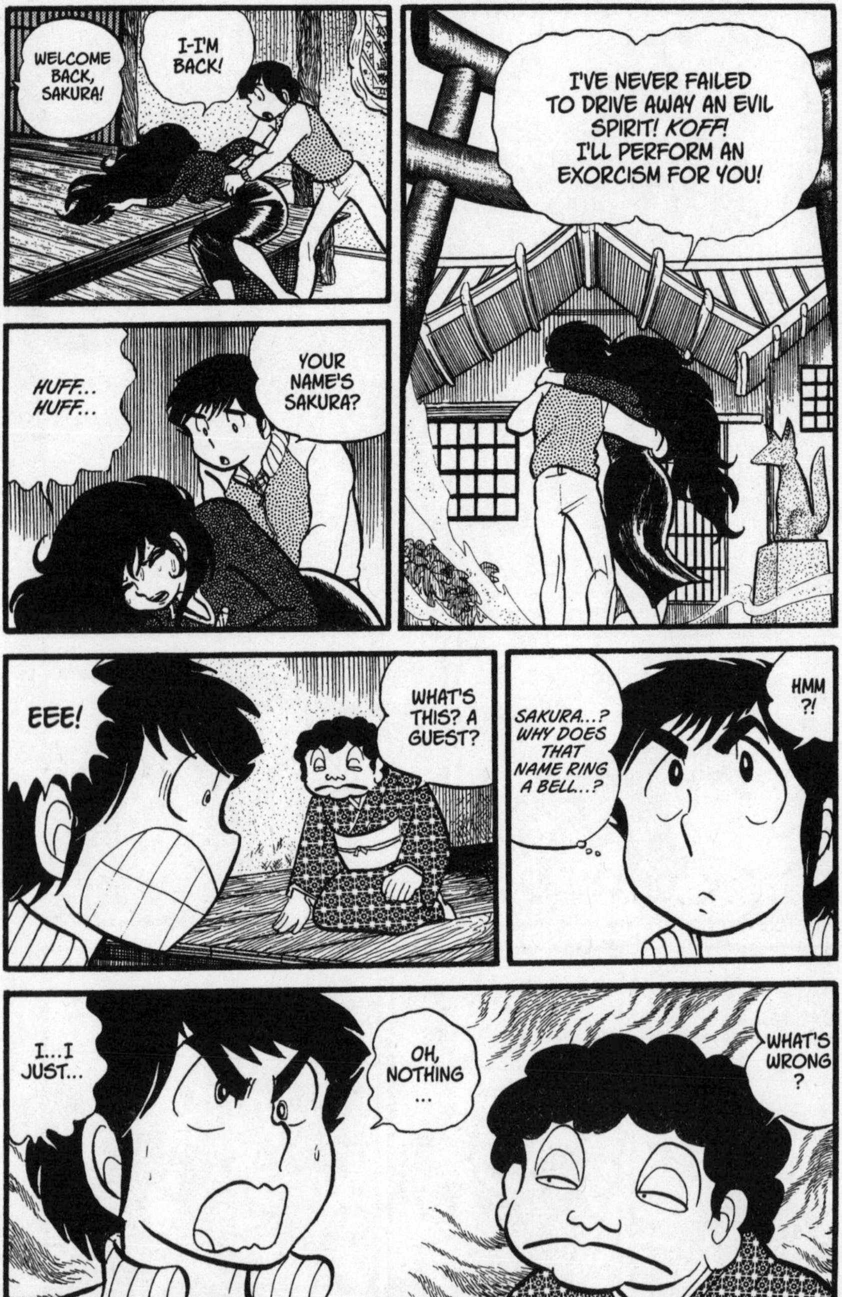
I'VE NEVER FAILED TO DRIVE AWAY AN EVIL SPIRIT! *KOFF!* I'LL PERFORM AN EXORCISM FOR YOU!
I-I'M BACK!
WELCOME BACK, SAKURA!
YOUR NAME'S SAKURA?
HUFF... HUFF...
HMM ?!
SAKURA...? WHY DOES THAT NAME RING A BELL...?
WHAT'S THIS? A GUEST?
EEE!
WHAT'S WRONG ?
OH, NOTHING ...
I...I JUST...

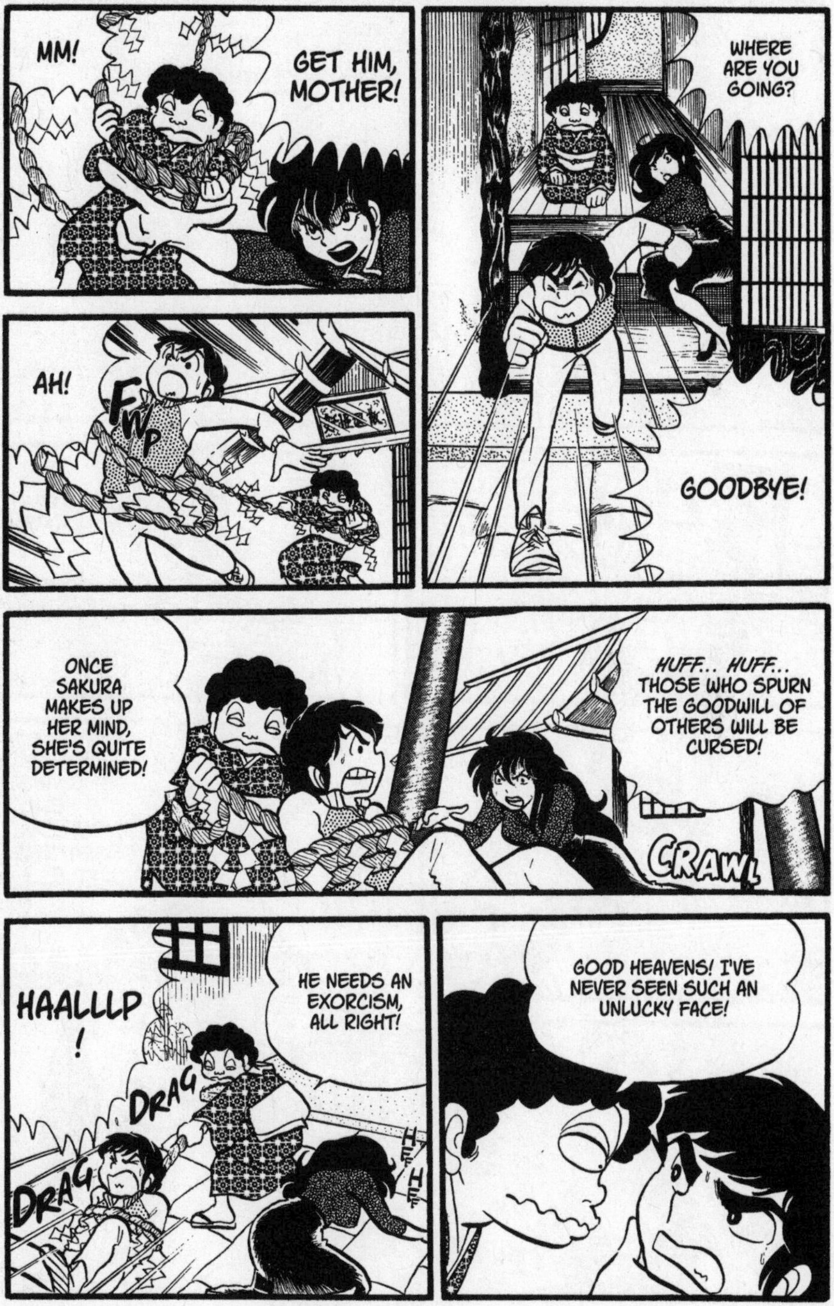

WHERE ARE YOU GOING?
GOODBYE!
GET HIM, MOTHER!
MM!
AH!
FWP
HUFF... HUFF... THOSE WHO SPURN THE GOODWILL OF OTHERS WILL BE CURSED!
CRAWL
ONCE SAKURA MAKES UP HER MIND, SHE'S QUITE DETERMINED!
GOOD HEAVENS! I'VE NEVER SEEN SUCH AN UNLUCKY FACE!
HE NEEDS AN EXORCISM, ALL RIGHT!
HAALLLP!
DRAG
HFF HFF
DRAG

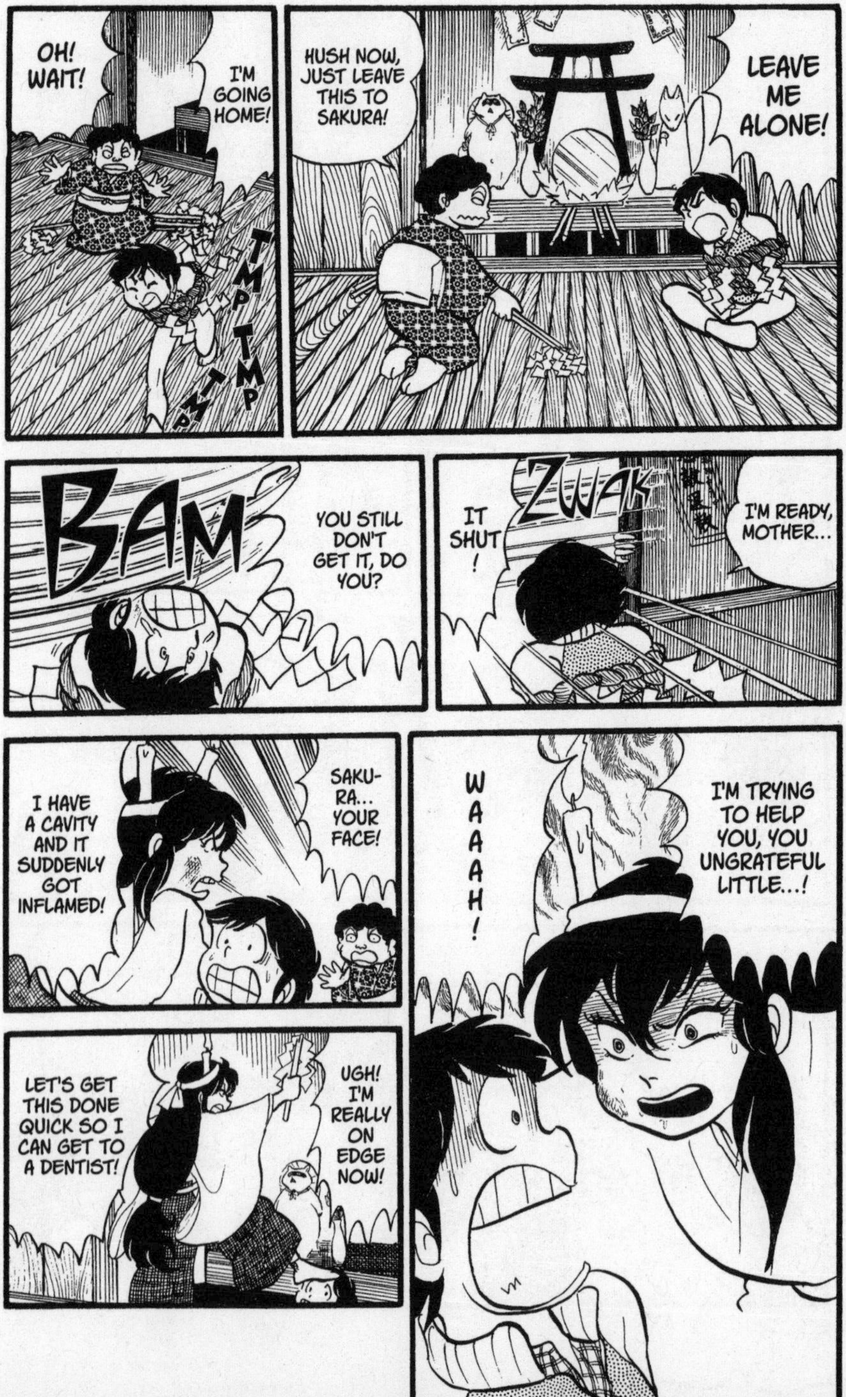
LEAVE ME ALONE!
HUSH NOW, JUST LEAVE THIS TO SAKURA!
I'M GOING HOME!
OH! WAIT!
TMP TMP TMP
I'M READY, MOTHER...
ZWAK
IT SHUT!
YOU STILL DON'T GET IT, DO YOU?
BAM
I'M TRYING TO HELP YOU, YOU UNGRATEFUL LITTLE...!
WAAAAH!
SAKU-RA... YOUR FACE!
I HAVE A CAVITY AND IT SUDDENLY GOT INFLAMED!
UGH! I'M REALLY ON EDGE NOW!
LET'S GET THIS DONE QUICK SO I CAN GET TO A DENTIST!

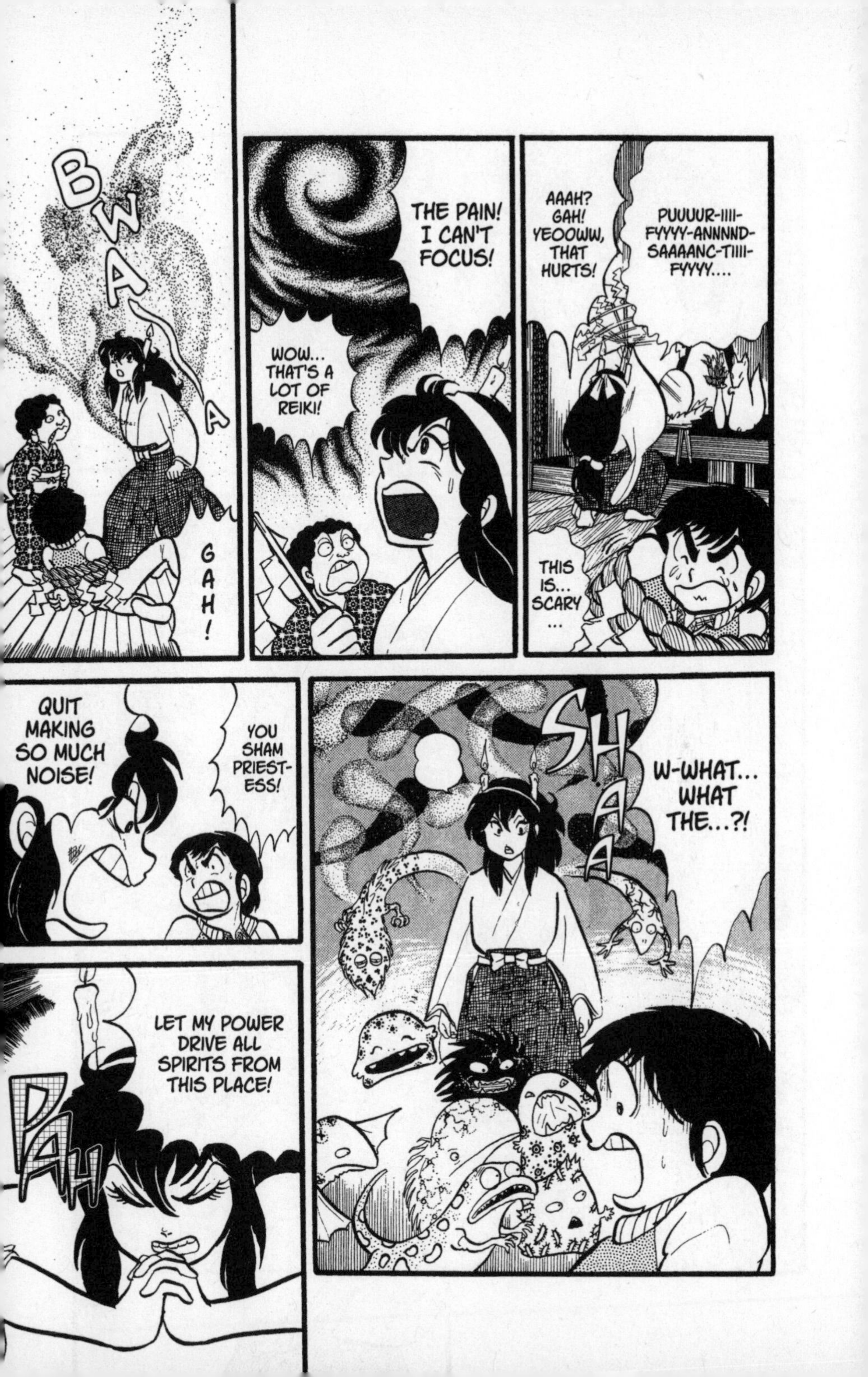
PUUUUR-IIII-FYYYY-ANNNND-SAAAANC-TIIII-FYYYY....
AAAH? GAH! YEOOWW, THAT HURTS!
THIS IS... SCARY ...
THE PAIN! I CAN'T FOCUS!
WOW... THAT'S A LOT OF REIKI!
BWAA
GAH!
SHAA
W-WHAT... WHAT THE...?!
YOU SHAM PRIEST-ESS!
QUIT MAKING SO MUCH NOISE!
LET MY POWER DRIVE ALL SPIRITS FROM THIS PLACE!
DAH

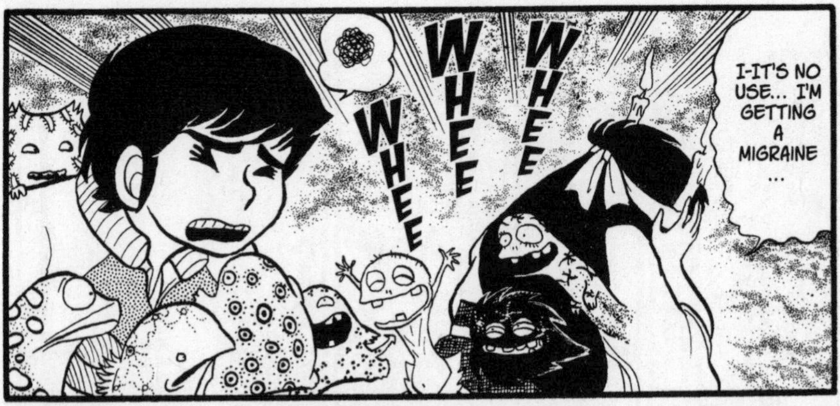
I-IT'S NO USE... I'M GETTING A MIGRAINE ...
WHEE
WHEE
WHEE
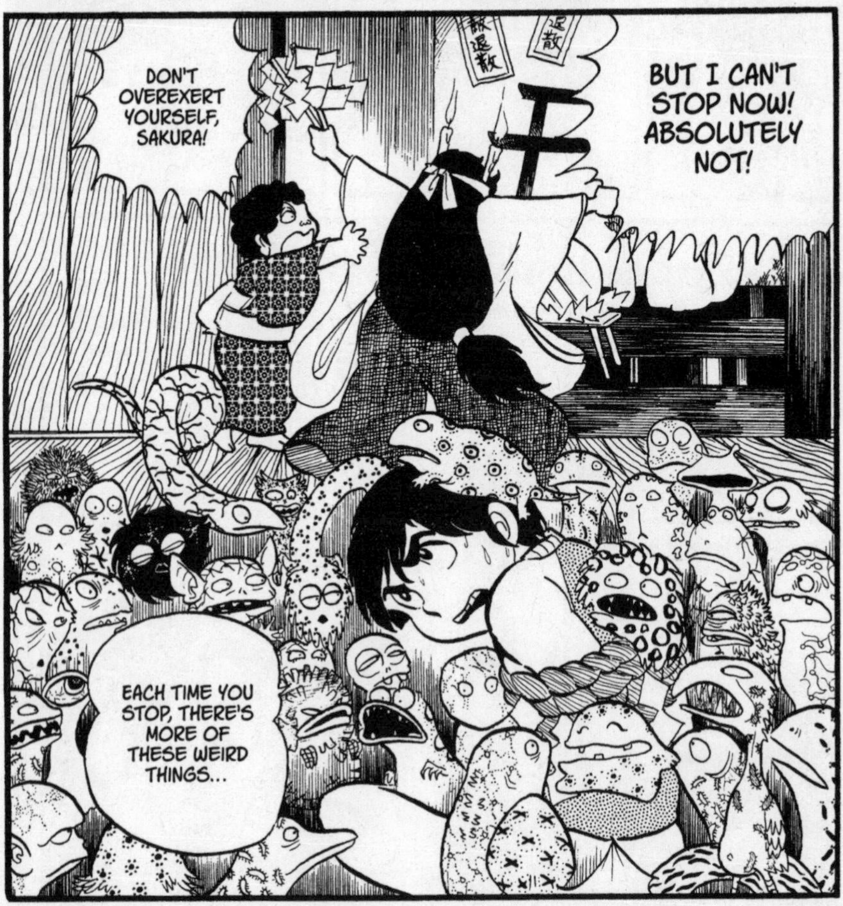
BUT I CAN'T STOP NOW! ABSOLUTELY NOT!
DON'T OVEREXERT YOURSELF, SAKURA!
EACH TIME YOU STOP, THERE'S MORE OF THESE WEIRD THINGS...

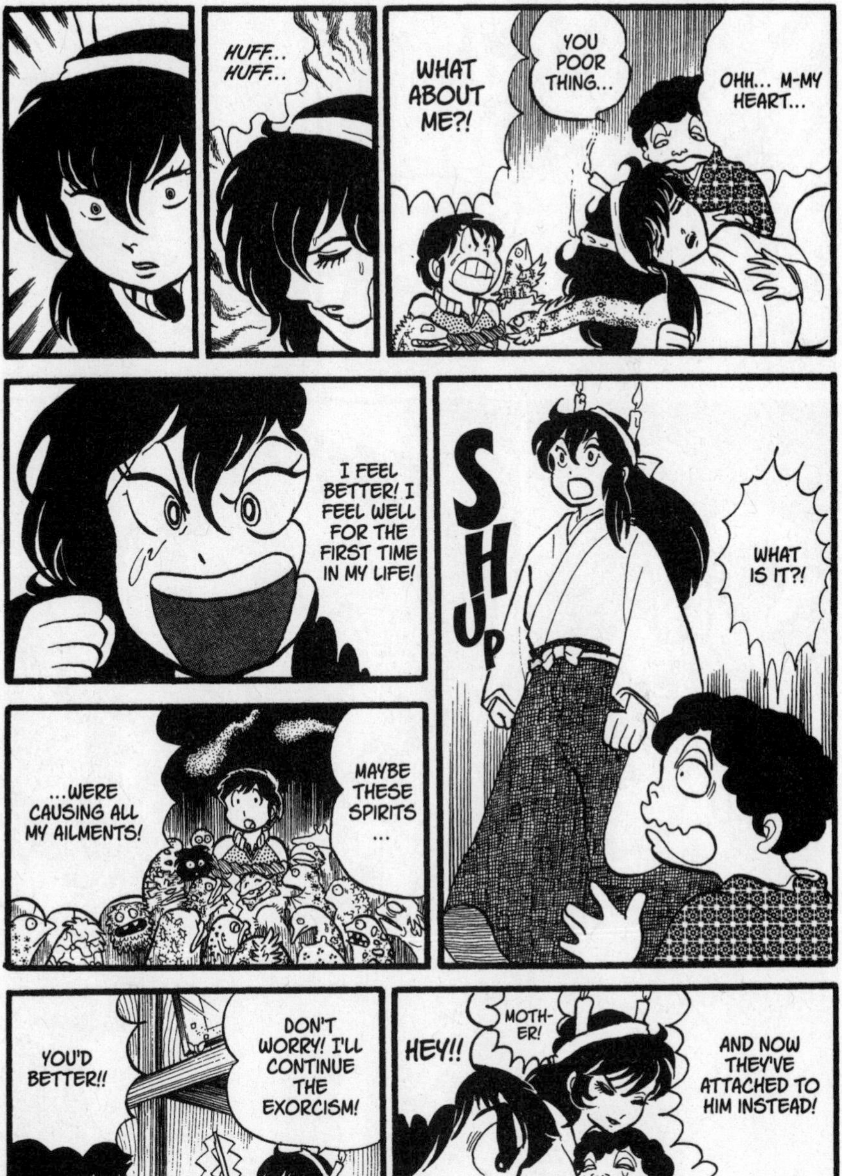
OHH... M-MY HEART...
YOU POOR THING...
WHAT ABOUT ME?!
HUFF... HUFF...
WHAT IS IT?!
SHUP
I FEEL BETTER! I FEEL WELL FOR THE FIRST TIME IN MY LIFE!
MAYBE THESE SPIRITS ...
...WERE CAUSING ALL MY AILMENTS!
AND NOW THEY'VE ATTACHED TO HIM INSTEAD!
MOTH-ER!
HEY!!
I'M SO HAPPY FOR YOU, SAKURA!
DON'T WORRY! I'LL CONTINUE THE EXORCISM!
YOU'D BETTER!!

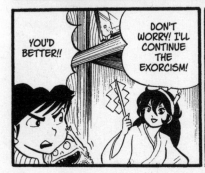

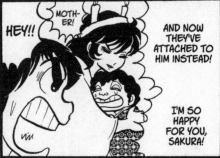

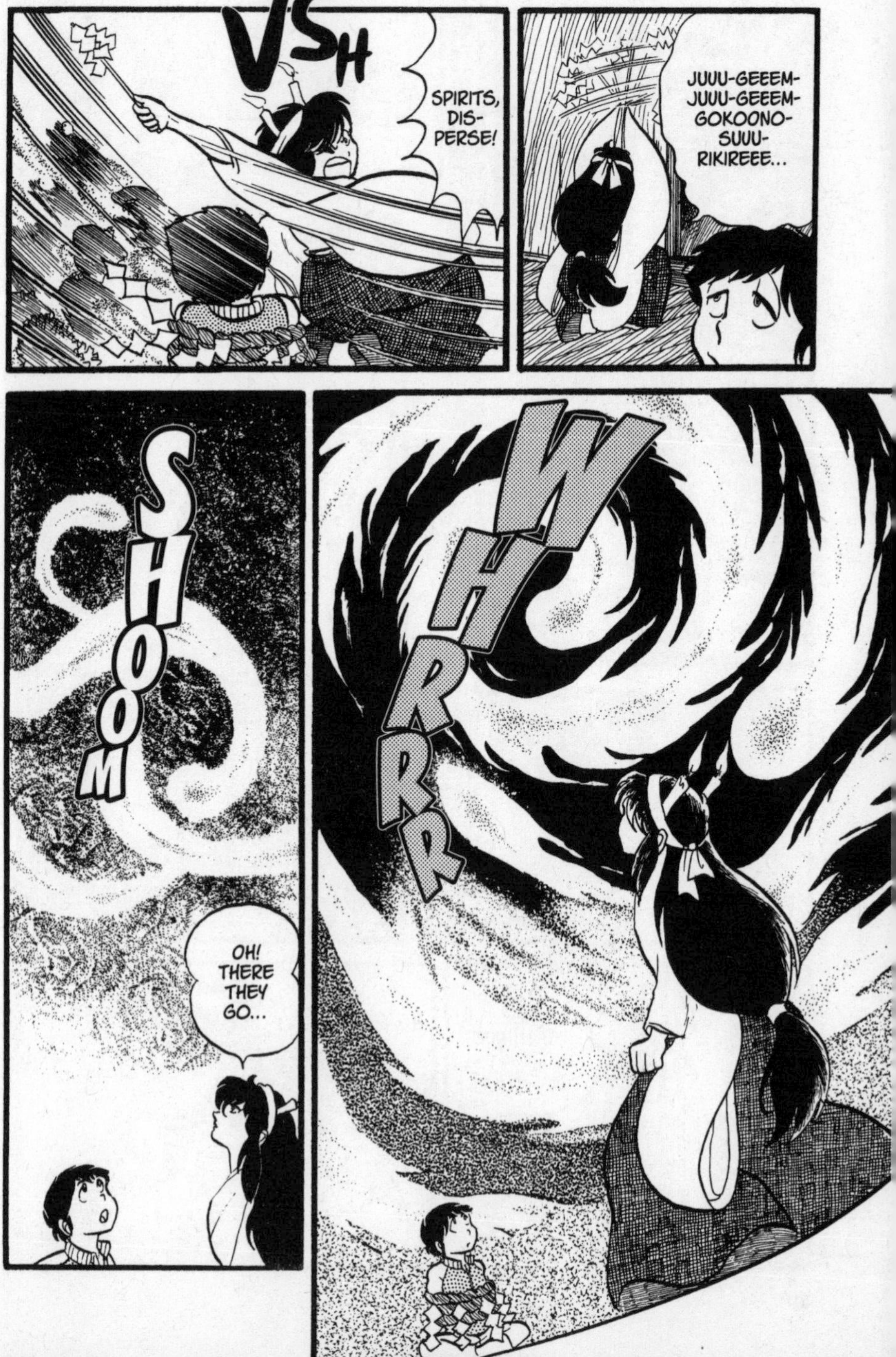
JUUU-GEEEM-JUUU-GEEEM-GOKOONO-SUUU-RIKIREEE...
VSH
SPIRITS, DIS-PERSE!
WHRRRR
SHOOM
OH! THERE THEY GO...

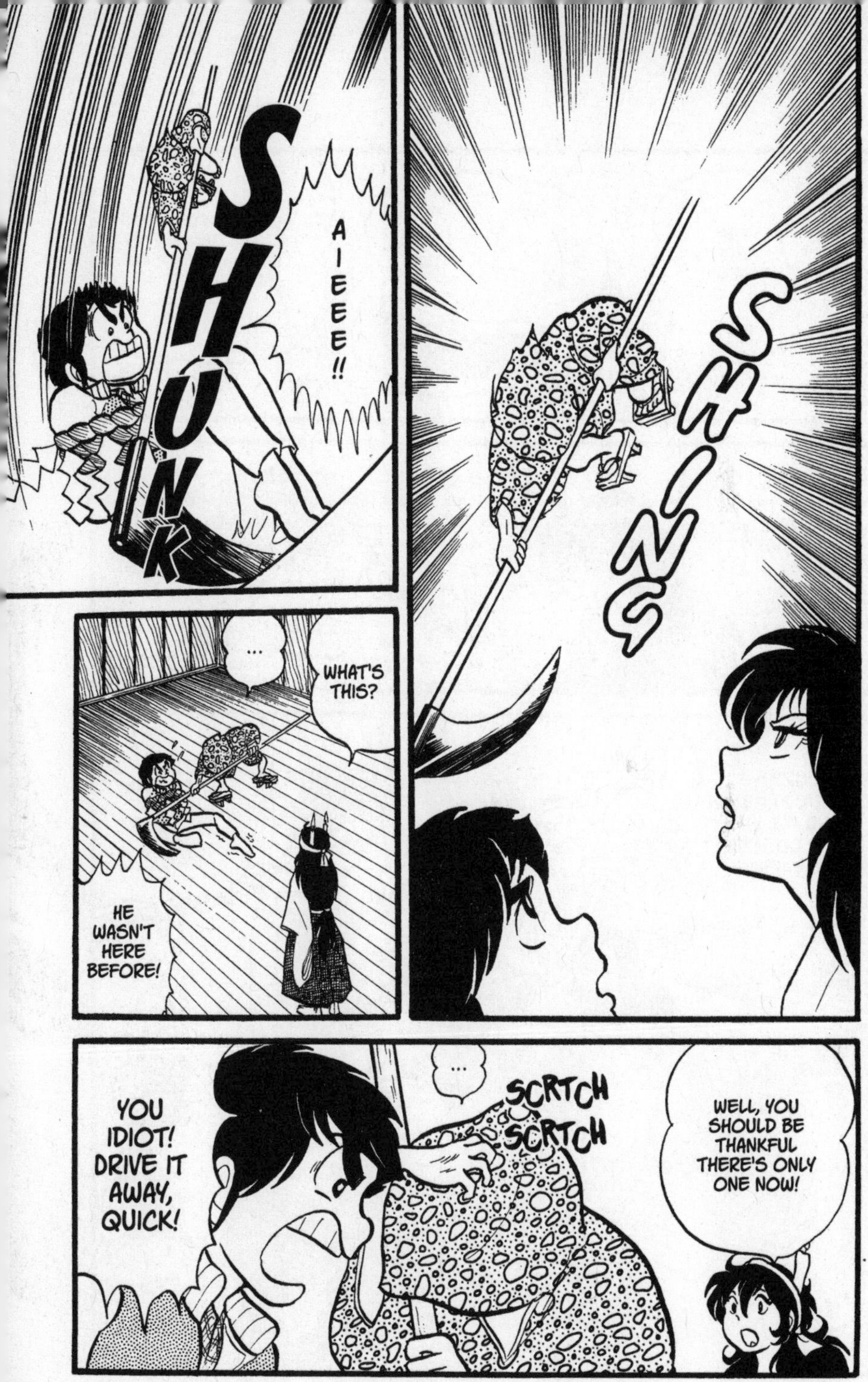
SHING
AIEEE!!
SHUNK
WHAT'S THIS?
...
HE WASN'T HERE BEFORE!
WELL, YOU SHOULD BE THANKFUL THERE'S ONLY ONE NOW!
...
SCRTCH SCRTCH
YOU IDIOT! DRIVE IT AWAY, QUICK!

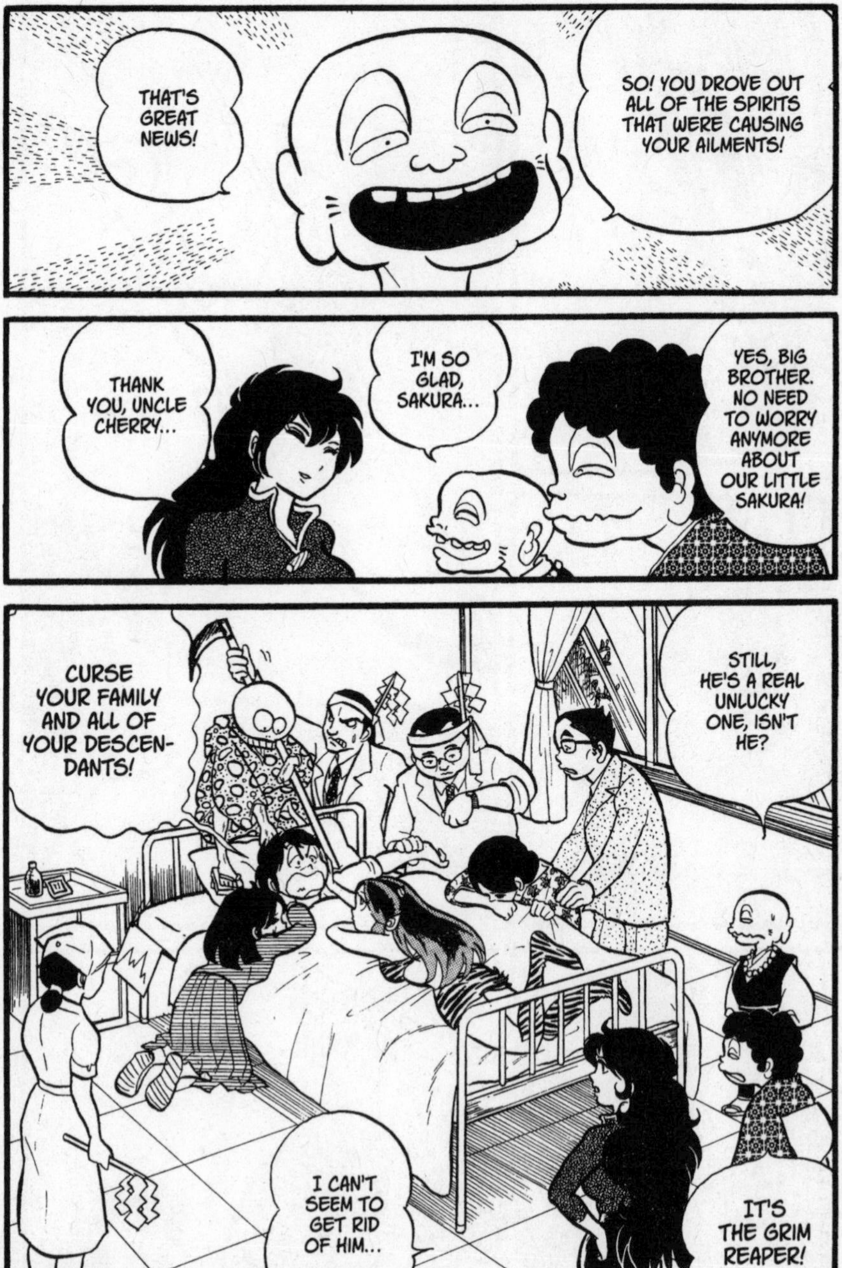
SO! YOU DROVE OUT ALL OF THE SPIRITS THAT WERE CAUSING YOUR AILMENTS!
THAT'S GREAT NEWS!
YES, BIG BROTHER. NO NEED TO WORRY ANYMORE ABOUT OUR LITTLE SAKURA!
I'M SO GLAD, SAKURA...
THANK YOU, UNCLE CHERRY...
STILL, HE'S A REAL UNLUCKY ONE, ISN'T HE?
CURSE YOUR FAMILY AND ALL OF YOUR DESCEN-DANTS!
IT'S THE GRIM REAPER!
I CAN'T SEEM TO GET RID OF HIM...

CHAPTER 5: BETWEEN A ROCK AND A HARD PLACE

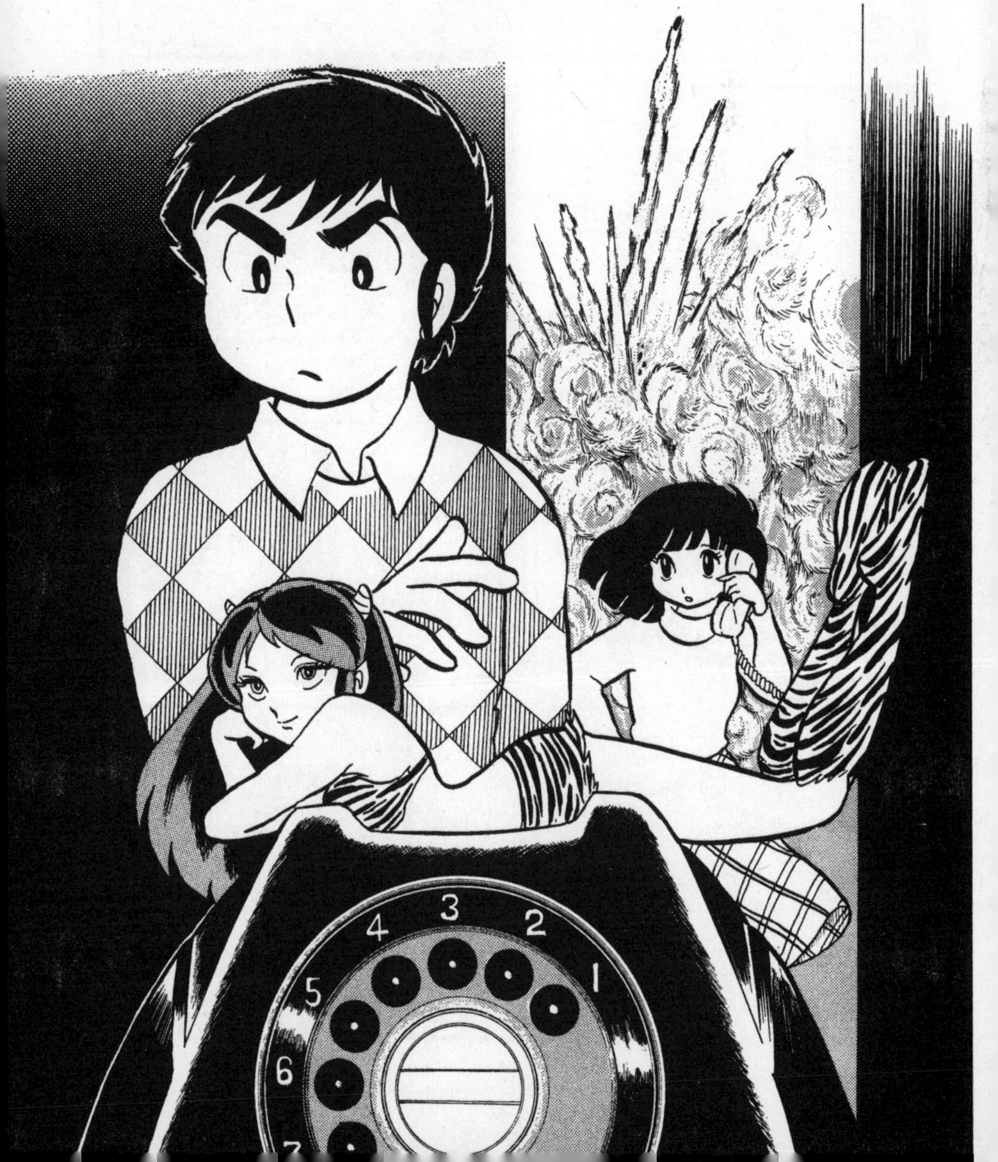

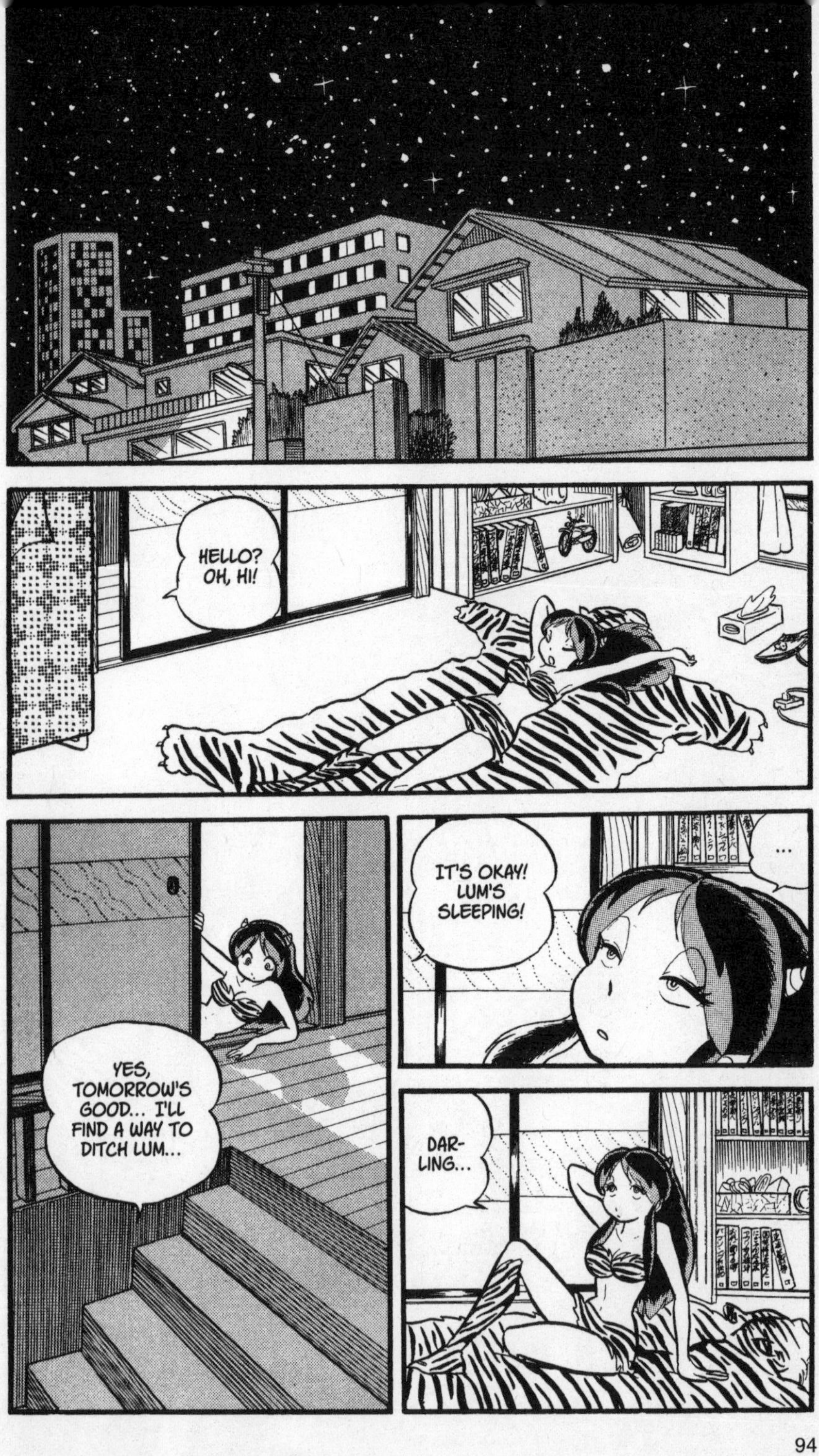
HELLO? OH, HI!
...
IT'S OKAY! LUM'S SLEEPING!
DAR-LING...
YES, TOMORROW'S GOOD... I'LL FIND A WAY TO DITCH LUM...

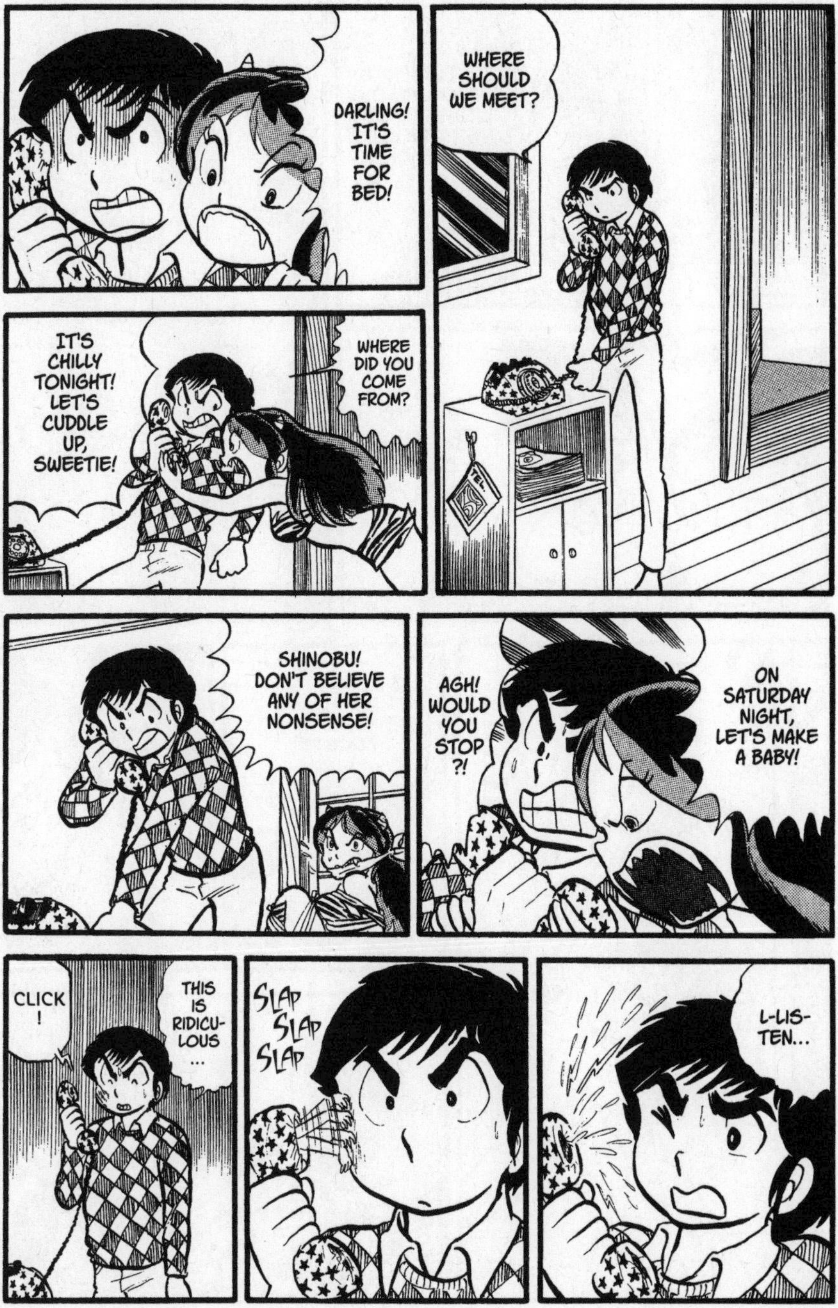
WHERE SHOULD WE MEET?
DARLING! IT'S TIME FOR BED!
WHERE DID YOU COME FROM?
IT'S CHILLY TONIGHT! LET'S CUDDLE UP, SWEETIE!
ON SATURDAY NIGHT, LET'S MAKE A BABY!
AGH! WOULD YOU STOP ?!
SHINOBU! DON'T BELIEVE ANY OF HER NONSENSE!
L-LIS-TEN...
SLAP SLAP SLAP
THIS IS RIDICU-LOUS ...
CLICK !

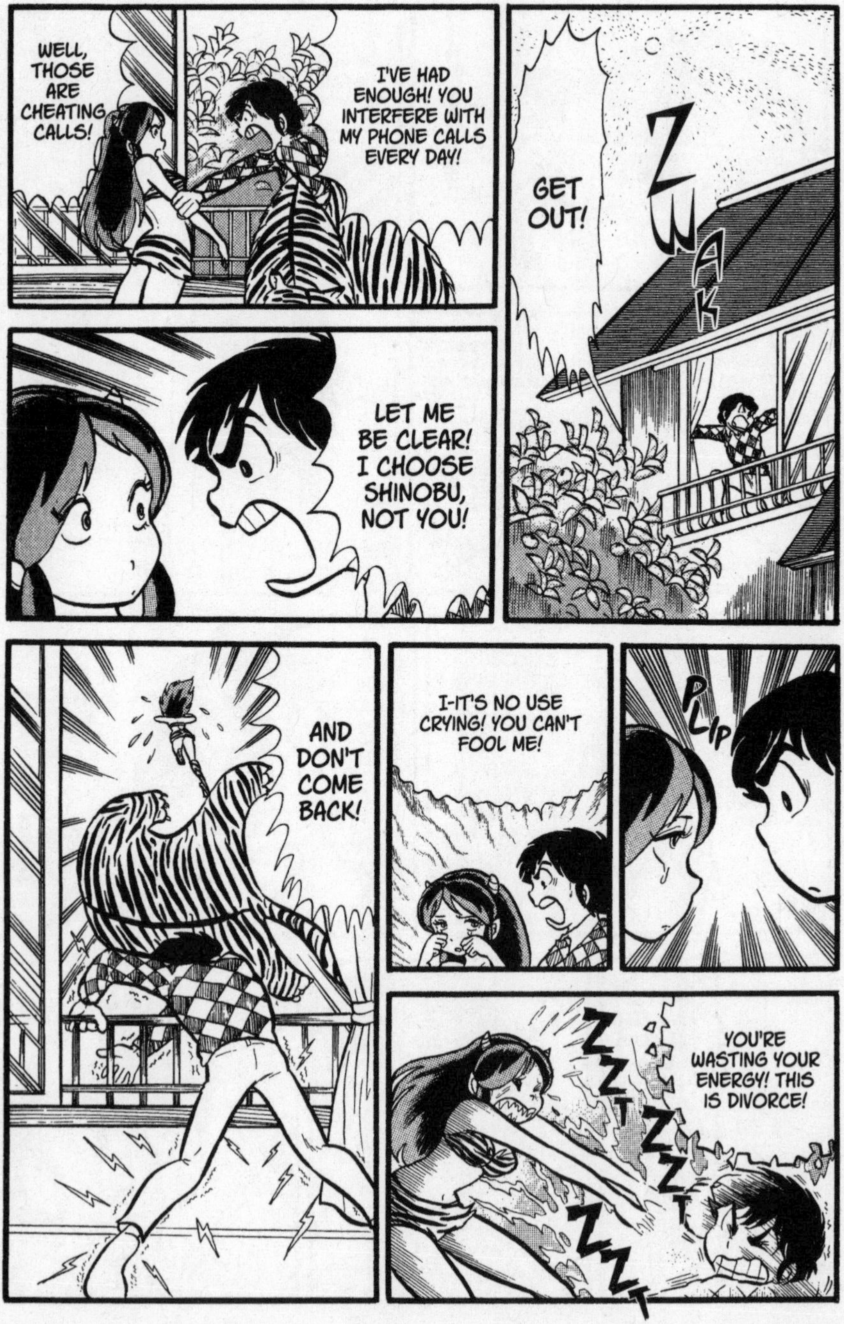
ZWAK
GET OUT!
I'VE HAD ENOUGH! YOU INTERFERE WITH MY PHONE CALLS EVERY DAY!
WELL, THOSE ARE CHEATING CALLS!
LET ME BE CLEAR! I CHOOSE SHINOBU, NOT YOU!
PLIP
I-IT'S NO USE CRYING! YOU CAN'T FOOL ME!
YOU'RE WASTING YOUR ENERGY! THIS IS DIVORCE!
ZZZT ZZZT ZZZT ZZZT
AND DON'T COME BACK!

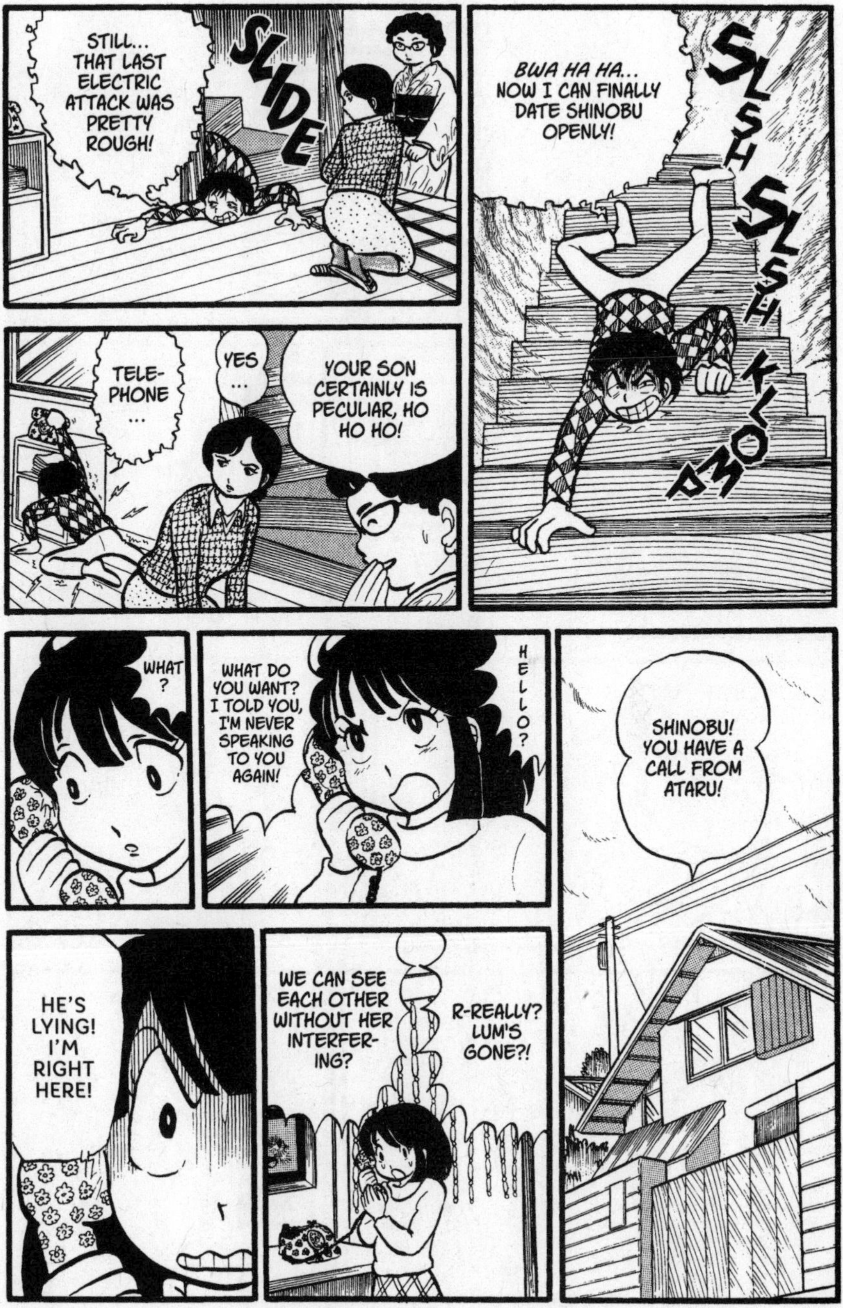
BWA HA HA... NOW I CAN FINALLY DATE SHINOBU OPENLY!
SLSH
SLSH
KLOMP
SLIDE
STILL... THAT LAST ELECTRIC ATTACK WAS PRETTY ROUGH!
YOUR SON CERTAINLY IS PECULIAR, HO HO HO!
YES ...
TELE-PHONE ...
SHINOBU! YOU HAVE A CALL FROM ATARU!
HELLO?
WHAT DO YOU WANT? I TOLD YOU, I'M NEVER SPEAKING TO YOU AGAIN!
WHAT ?
R-REALLY? LUM'S GONE?!
WE CAN SEE EACH OTHER WITHOUT HER INTERFER-ING?
HE'S LYING! I'M RIGHT HERE!

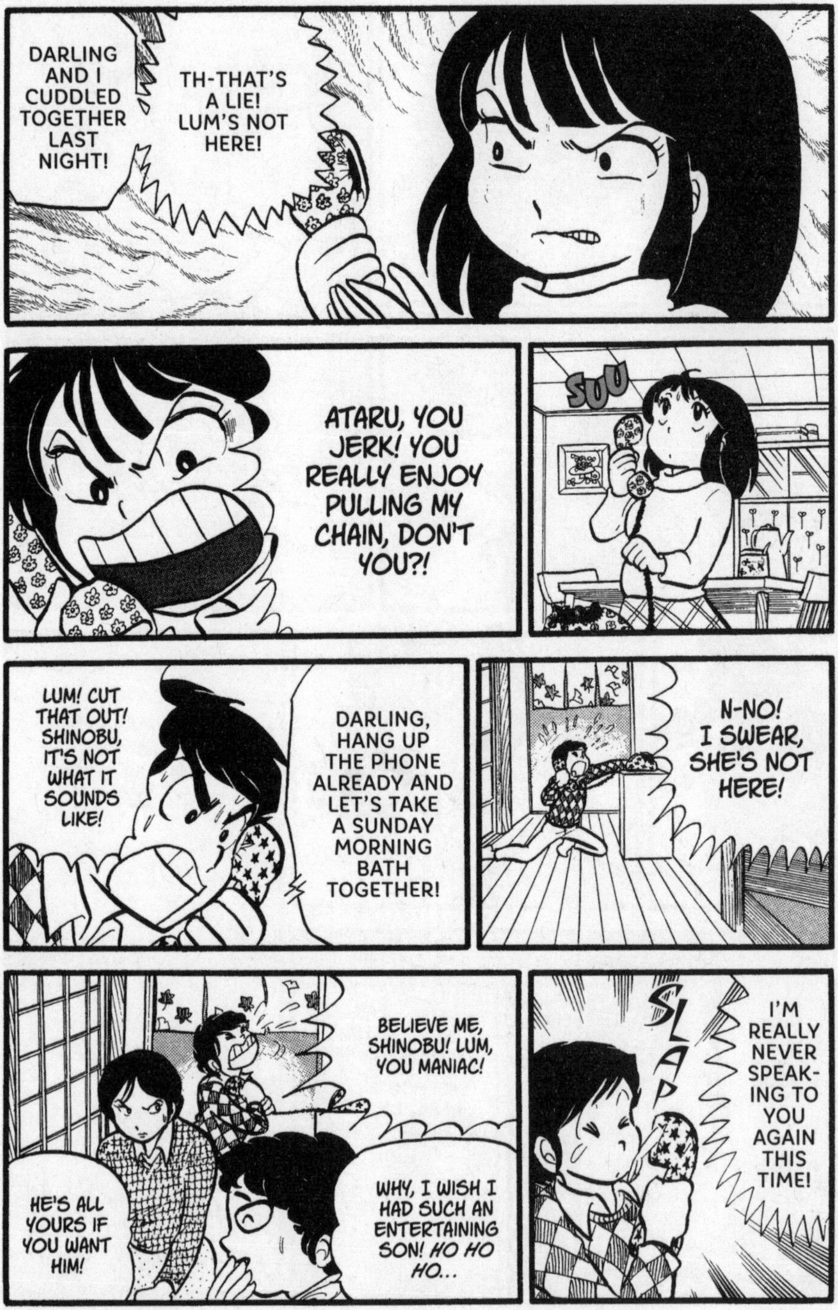
TH-THAT'S A LIE! LUM'S NOT HERE!
DARLING AND I CUDDLED TOGETHER LAST NIGHT!
SUU
ATARU, YOU JERK! YOU REALLY ENJOY PULLING MY CHAIN, DON'T YOU?!
N-NO! I SWEAR, SHE'S NOT HERE!
DARLING, HANG UP THE PHONE ALREADY AND LET'S TAKE A SUNDAY MORNING BATH TOGETHER!
LUM! CUT THAT OUT! SHINOBU, IT'S NOT WHAT IT SOUNDS LIKE!
SLAP
I'M REALLY NEVER SPEAK-ING TO YOU AGAIN THIS TIME!
BELIEVE ME, SHINOBU! LUM, YOU MANIAC!
WHY, I WISH I HAD SUCH AN ENTERTAINING SON! *HO HO HO...*
HE'S ALL YOURS IF YOU WANT HIM!

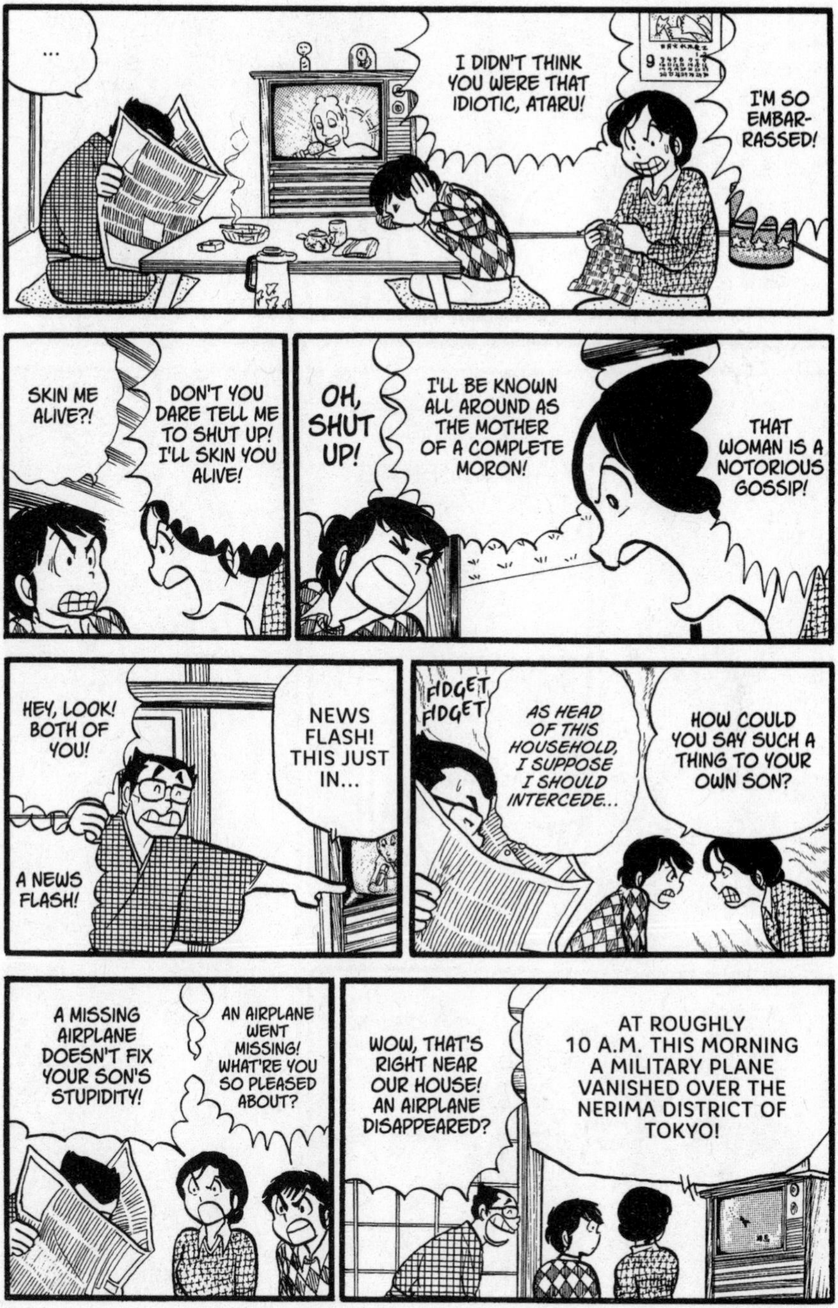
I'M SO EMBARRASSED!
I DIDN'T THINK YOU WERE THAT IDIOTIC, ATARU!
...
THAT WOMAN IS A NOTORIOUS GOSSIP!
I'LL BE KNOWN ALL AROUND AS THE MOTHER OF A COMPLETE MORON!
OH, SHUT UP!
DON'T YOU DARE TELL ME TO SHUT UP! I'LL SKIN YOU ALIVE!
SKIN ME ALIVE?!
HOW COULD YOU SAY SUCH A THING TO YOUR OWN SON?
AS HEAD OF THIS HOUSEHOLD, I SUPPOSE I SHOULD INTERCEDE...
FIDGET FIDGET
NEWS FLASH! THIS JUST IN...
HEY, LOOK! BOTH OF YOU!
A NEWS FLASH!
AT ROUGHLY 10 A.M. THIS MORNING A MILITARY PLANE VANISHED OVER THE NERIMA DISTRICT OF TOKYO!
WOW, THAT'S RIGHT NEAR OUR HOUSE! AN AIRPLANE DISAPPEARED?
AN AIRPLANE WENT MISSING! WHAT'RE YOU SO PLEASED ABOUT?
A MISSING AIRPLANE DOESN'T FIX YOUR SON'S STUPIDITY!

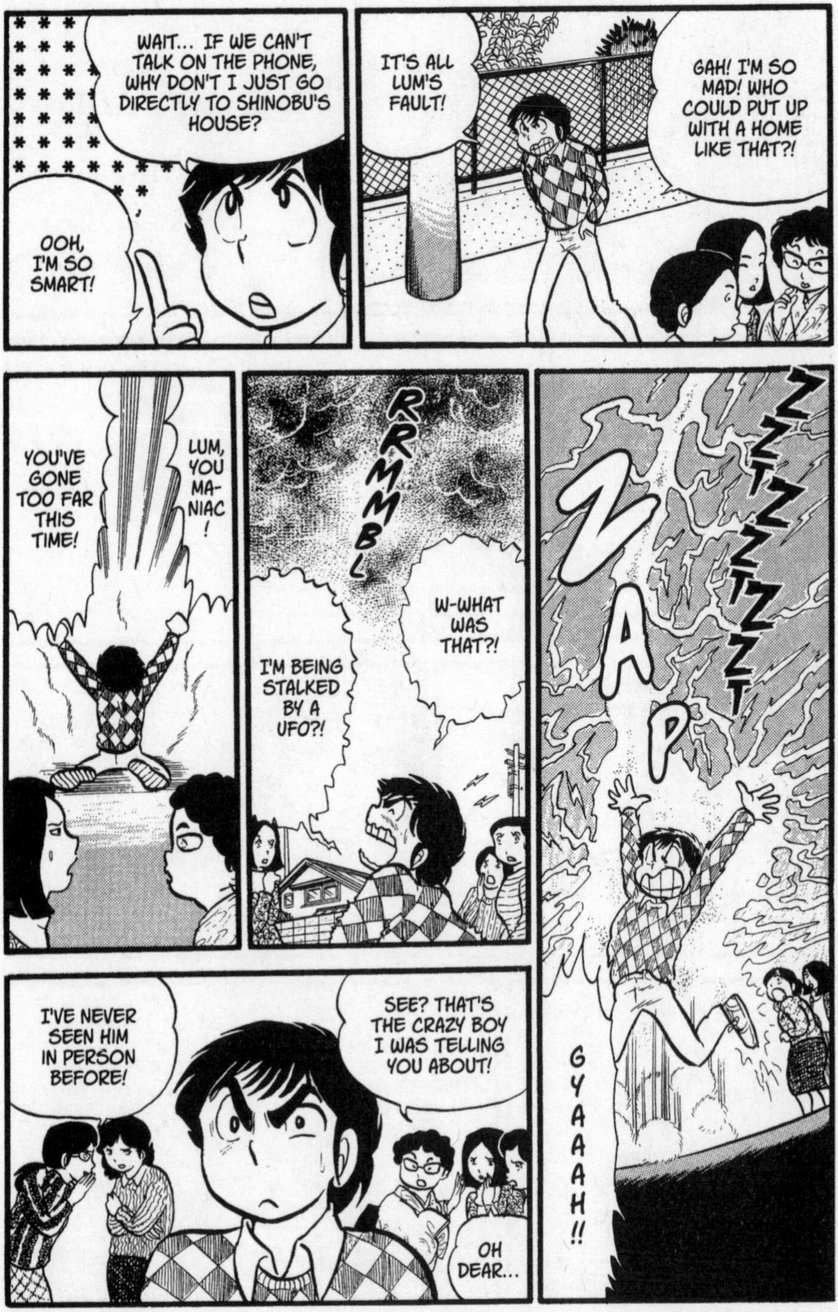
GAH! I'M SO MAD! WHO COULD PUT UP WITH A HOME LIKE THAT?!
IT'S ALL LUM'S FAULT!
WAIT... IF WE CAN'T TALK ON THE PHONE, WHY DON'T I JUST GO DIRECTLY TO SHINOBU'S HOUSE?
OOH, I'M SO SMART!
ZZZTZZZTZZZT
ZAP
GYAAAAH!!
RRMMBL
W-WHAT WAS THAT?!
I'M BEING STALKED BY A UFO?!
LUM, YOU MA-NIAC!
YOU'VE GONE TOO FAR THIS TIME!
SEE? THAT'S THE CRAZY BOY I WAS TELLING YOU ABOUT!
I'VE NEVER SEEN HIM IN PERSON BEFORE!
OH DEAR...

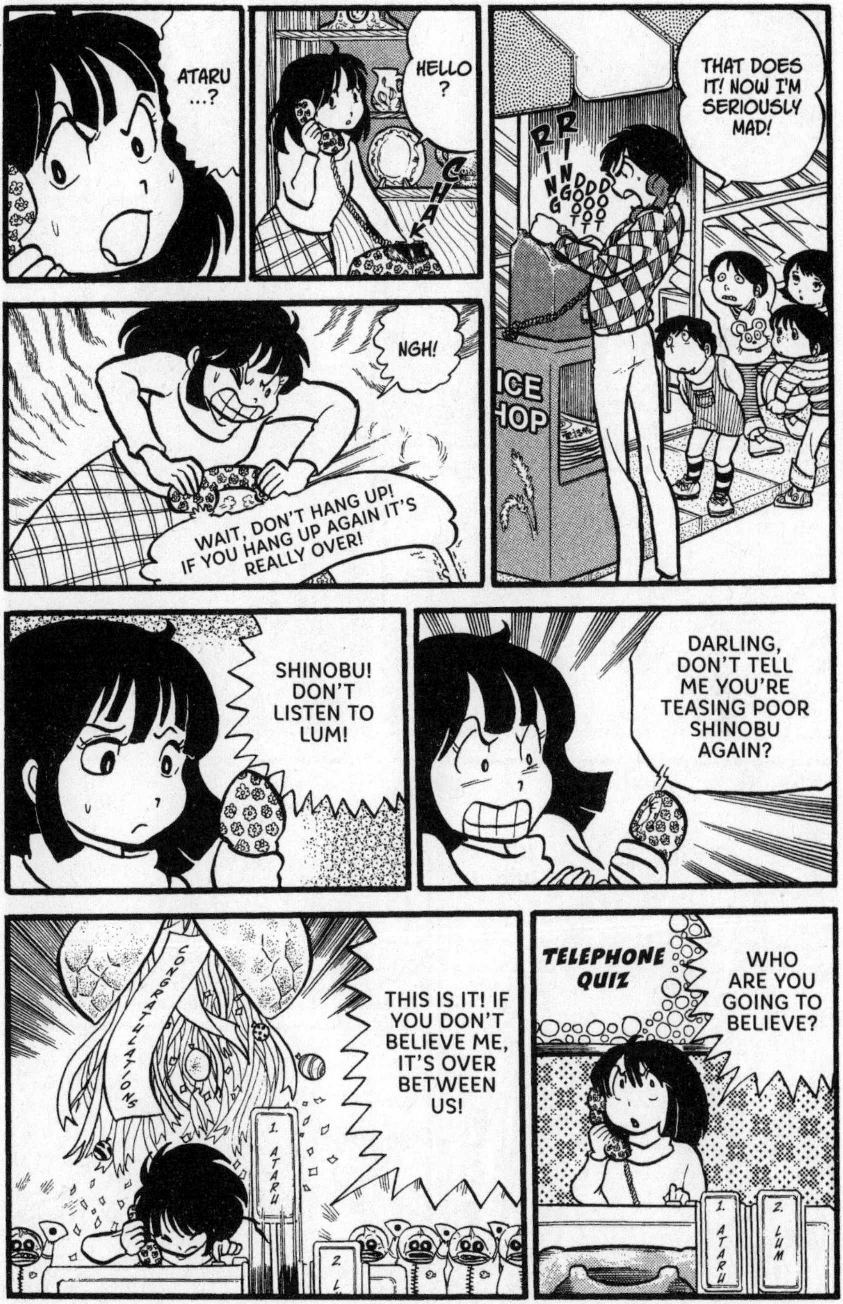
THAT DOES IT! NOW I'M SERIOUSLY MAD!
RRING
RING
DOOOT
DOOOT
ICE
HOP
HELLO?
CHAK
ATARU...?
NGH!
WAIT, DON'T HANG UP! IF YOU HANG UP AGAIN IT'S REALLY OVER!
DARLING, DON'T TELL ME YOU'RE TEASING POOR SHINOBU AGAIN?
SHINOBU! DON'T LISTEN TO LUM!
TELEPHONE QUIZ
WHO ARE YOU GOING TO BELIEVE?
1. ATARU
2. LUM
THIS IS IT! IF YOU DON'T BELIEVE ME, IT'S OVER BETWEEN US!
CONGRATULATIONS
1. ATARU

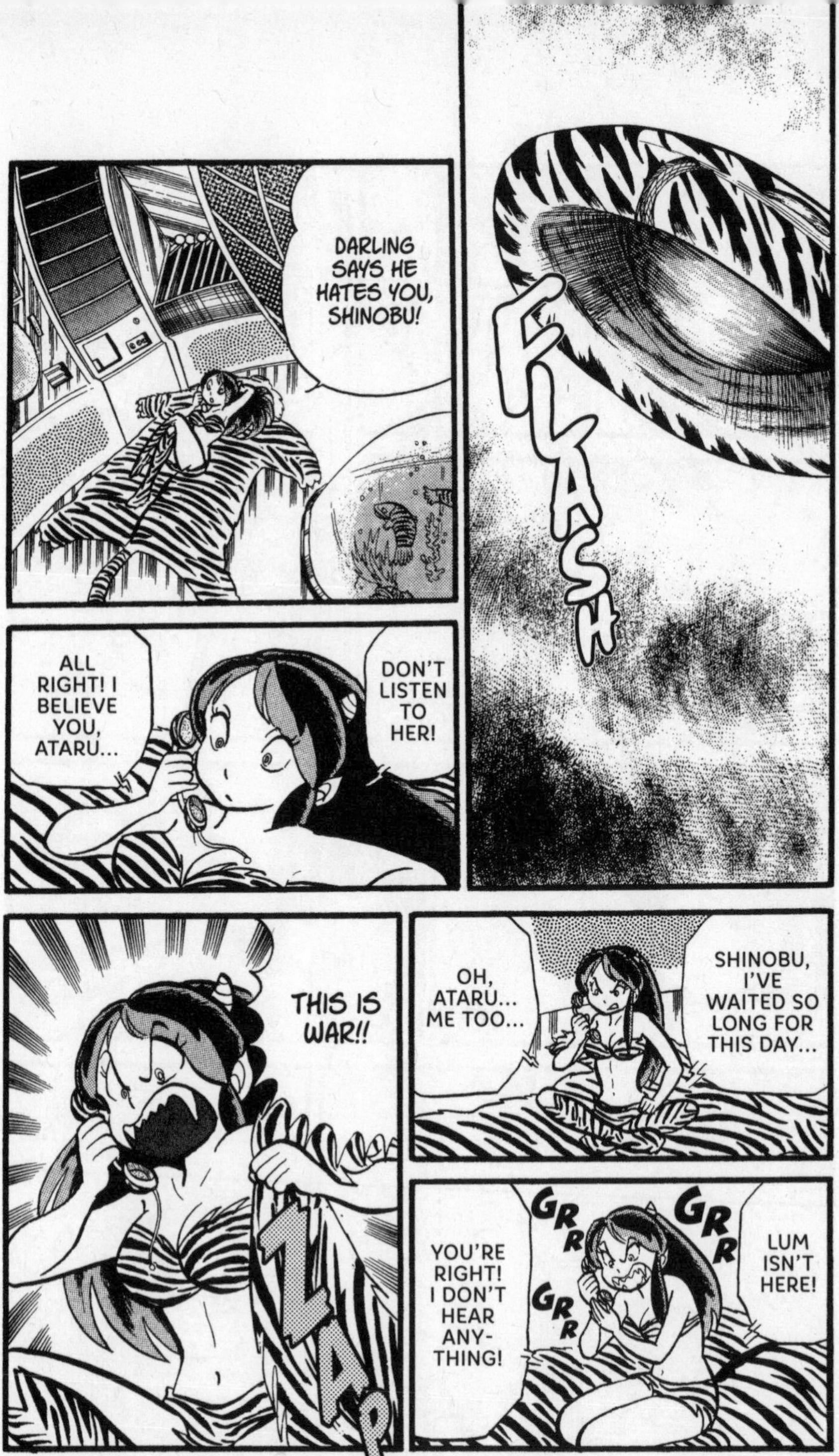
FLASH
DARLING SAYS HE HATES YOU, SHINOBU!
DON'T LISTEN TO HER!
ALL RIGHT! I BELIEVE YOU, ATARU...
SHINOBU, I'VE WAITED SO LONG FOR THIS DAY...
OH, ATARU... ME TOO...
LUM ISN'T HERE!
GRR
GRR
GRR
YOU'RE RIGHT! I DON'T HEAR ANY-THING!
THIS IS WAR!!
ZAP

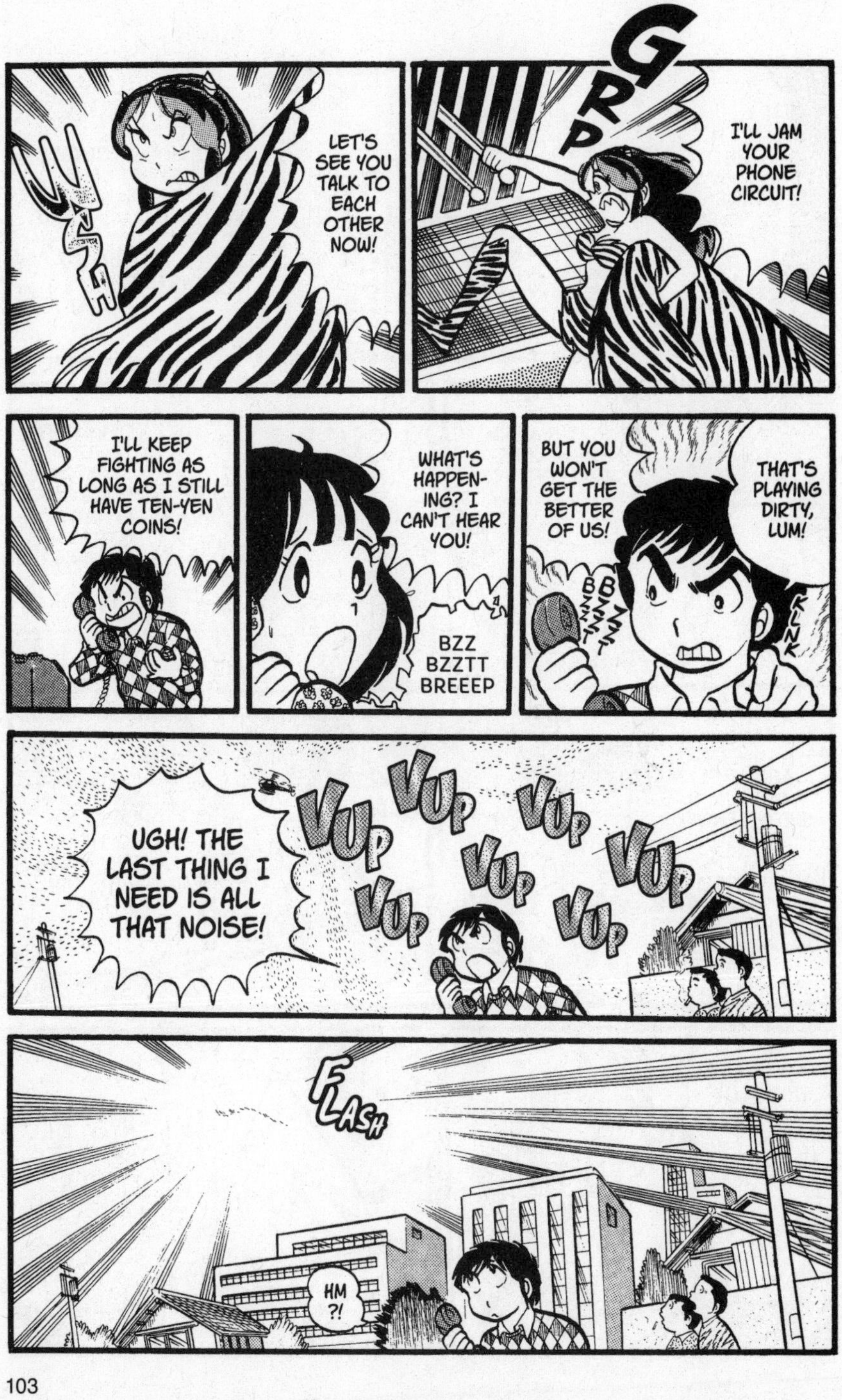
GRP
I'LL JAM YOUR PHONE CIRCUIT!
LET'S SEE YOU TALK TO EACH OTHER NOW!
THAT'S PLAYING DIRTY, LUM!
BUT YOU WON'T GET THE BETTER OF US!
WHAT'S HAPPEN-ING? I CAN'T HEAR YOU!
BZZ BZZTT BREEEP
I'LL KEEP FIGHTING AS LONG AS I STILL HAVE TEN-YEN COINS!
VUP VUP VUP VUP VUP VUP VUP VUP
UGH! THE LAST THING I NEED IS ALL THAT NOISE!
FLASH
HM ?!

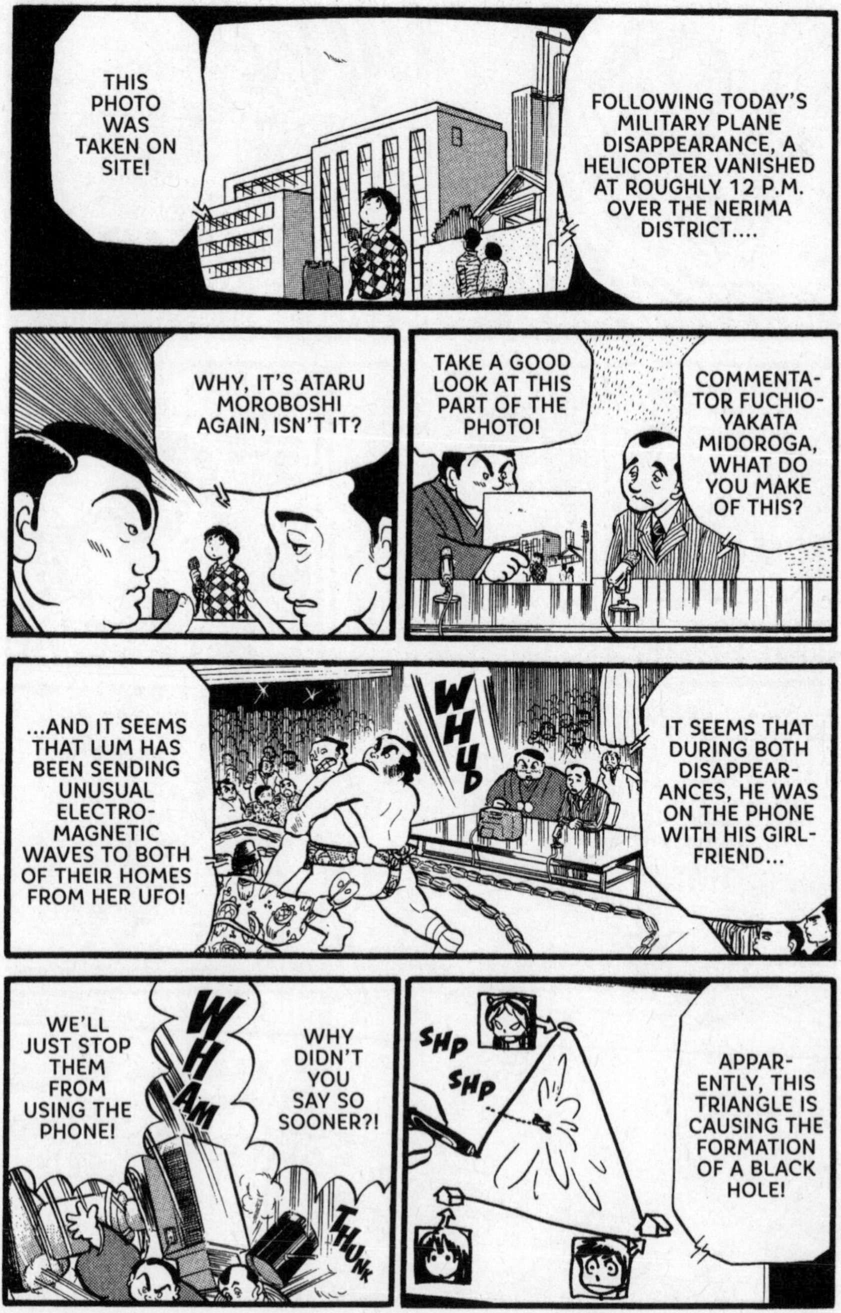
FOLLOWING TODAY'S MILITARY PLANE DISAPPEARANCE, A HELICOPTER VANISHED AT ROUGHLY 12 P.M. OVER THE NERIMA DISTRICT....
THIS PHOTO WAS TAKEN ON SITE!
COMMENTATOR FUCHIO-YAKATA MIDOROGA, WHAT DO YOU MAKE OF THIS?
TAKE A GOOD LOOK AT THIS PART OF THE PHOTO!
WHY, IT'S ATARU MOROBOSHI AGAIN, ISN'T IT?
IT SEEMS THAT DURING BOTH DISAPPEARANCES, HE WAS ON THE PHONE WITH HIS GIRLFRIEND...
WHUD
...AND IT SEEMS THAT LUM HAS BEEN SENDING UNUSUAL ELECTROMAGNETIC WAVES TO BOTH OF THEIR HOMES FROM HER UFO!
APPARENTLY, THIS TRIANGLE IS CAUSING THE FORMATION OF A BLACK HOLE!
SHP
SHP
WHY DIDN'T YOU SAY SO SOONER?!
WHAM
WE'LL JUST STOP THEM FROM USING THE PHONE!
THUNK

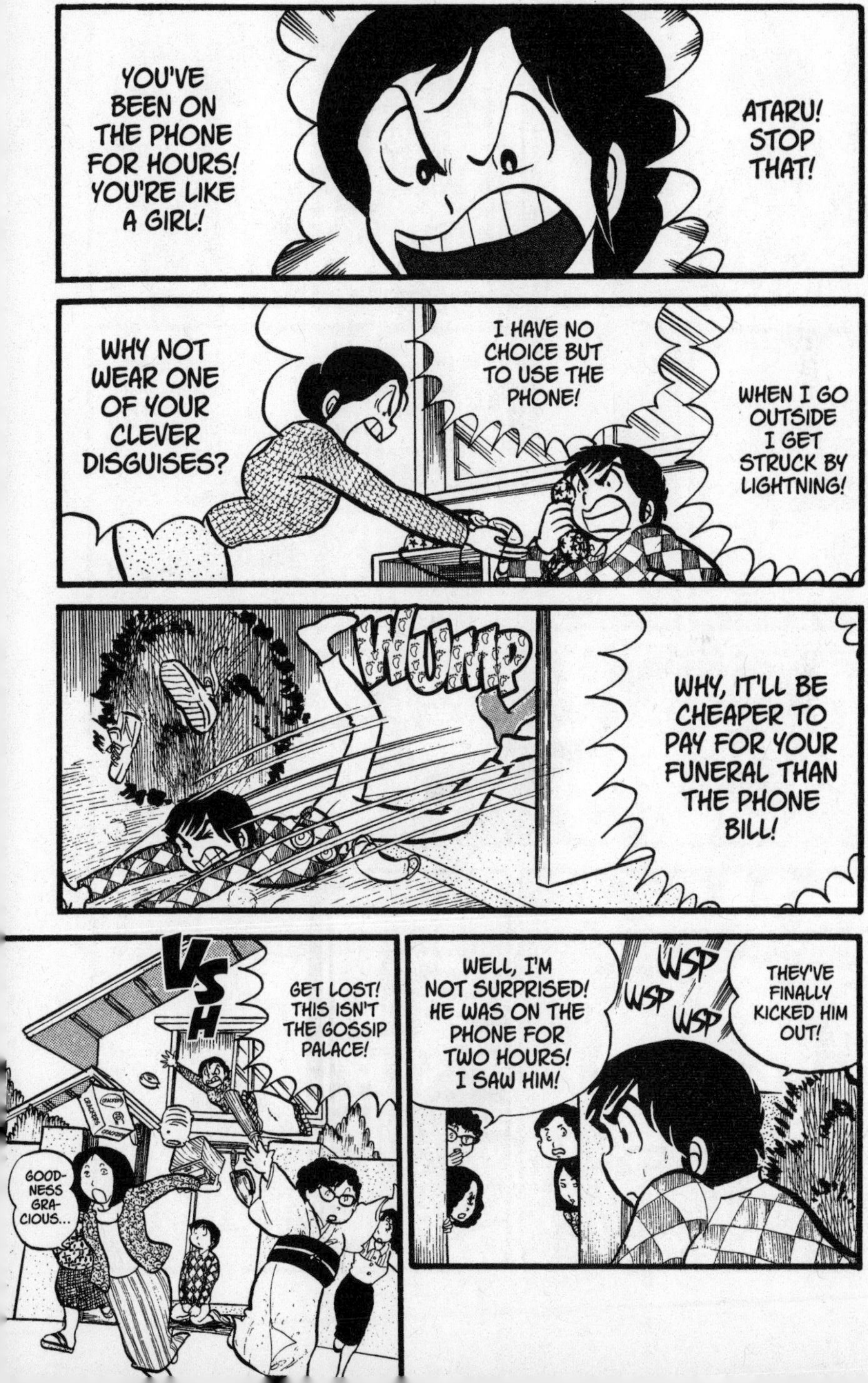
ATARU! STOP THAT!
YOU'VE BEEN ON THE PHONE FOR HOURS! YOU'RE LIKE A GIRL!
WHEN I GO OUTSIDE I GET STRUCK BY LIGHTNING!
I HAVE NO CHOICE BUT TO USE THE PHONE!
WHY NOT WEAR ONE OF YOUR CLEVER DISGUISES?
WHY, IT'LL BE CHEAPER TO PAY FOR YOUR FUNERAL THAN THE PHONE BILL!
WUMP
THEY'VE FINALLY KICKED HIM OUT!
WSP
WSP
WSP
WELL, I'M NOT SURPRISED! HE WAS ON THE PHONE FOR TWO HOURS! I SAW HIM!
GET LOST! THIS ISN'T THE GOSSIP PALACE!
VSH
GOOD-NESS GRA-CIOUS...

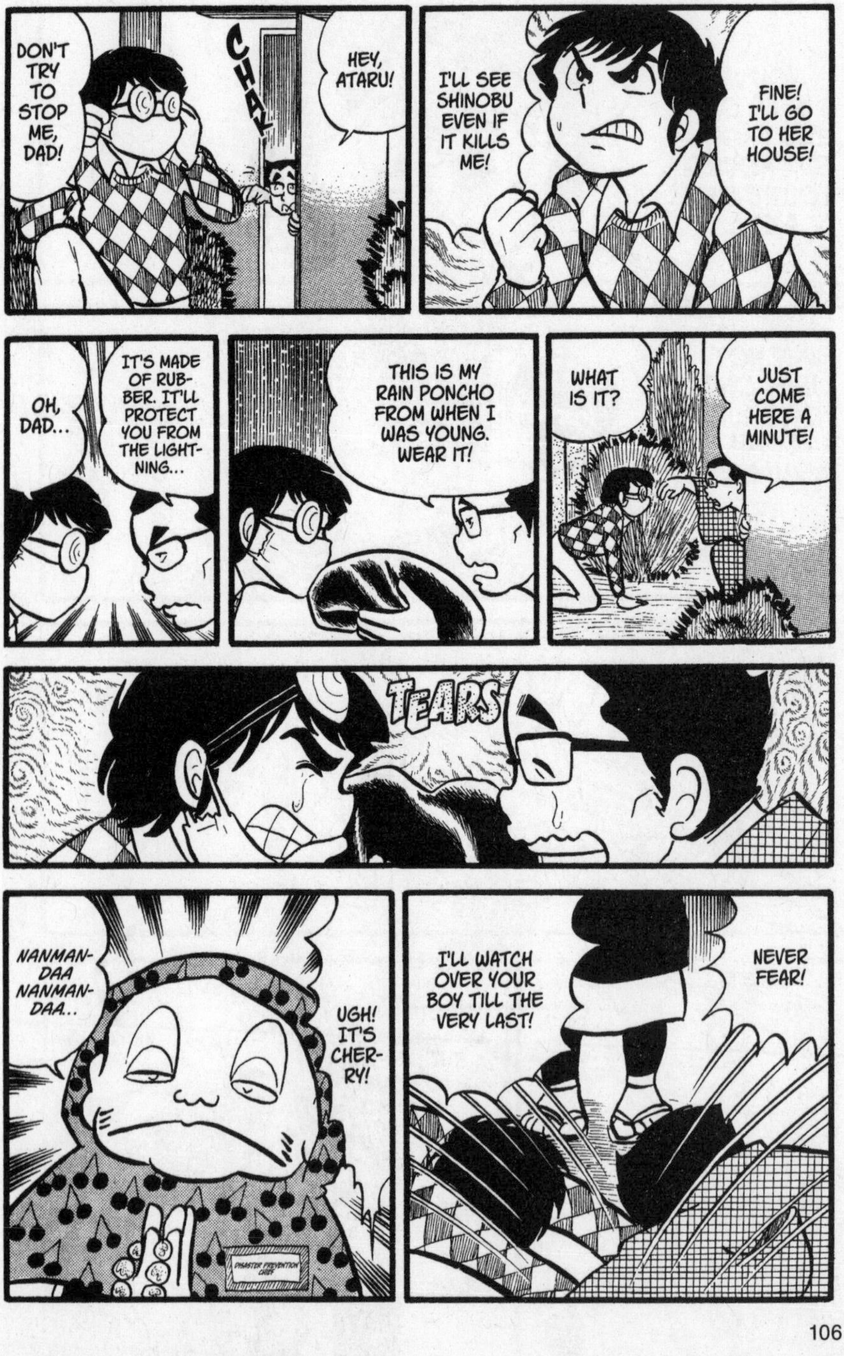
FINE! I'LL GO TO HER HOUSE!
I'LL SEE SHINOBU EVEN IF IT KILLS ME!
HEY, ATARU!
CHA
DON'T TRY TO STOP ME, DAD!
JUST COME HERE A MINUTE!
WHAT IS IT?
THIS IS MY RAIN PONCHO FROM WHEN I WAS YOUNG. WEAR IT!
IT'S MADE OF RUB-BER. IT'LL PROTECT YOU FROM THE LIGHT-NING...
OH, DAD...
TEARS
NEVER FEAR!
I'LL WATCH OVER YOUR BOY TILL THE VERY LAST!
UGH! IT'S CHER-RY!
NANMAN-DAA NANMAN-DAA...
DISASTER PREVENTION CHIEF

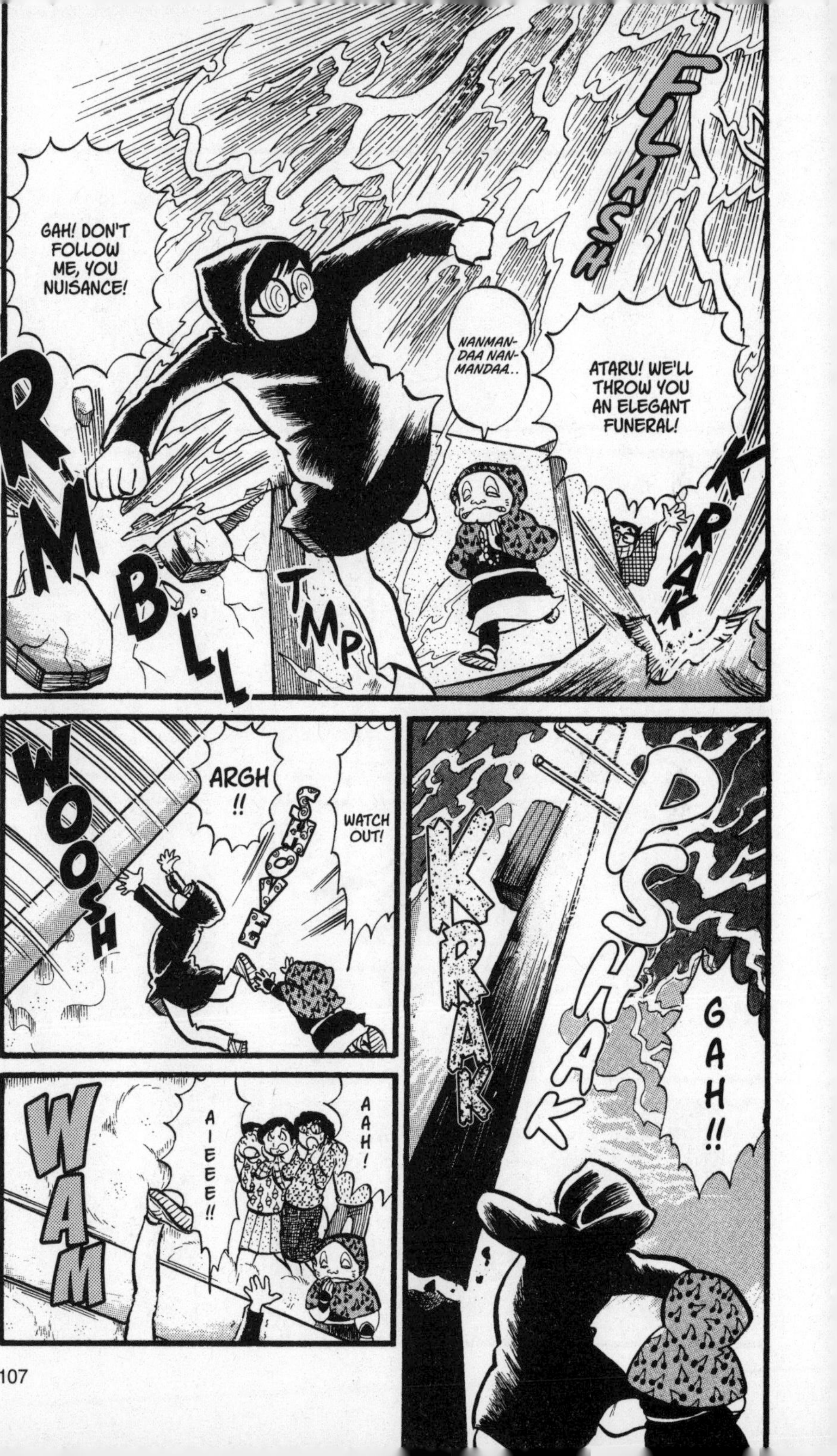
FLASH
KRAK
ATARU! WE'LL THROW YOU AN ELEGANT FUNERAL!
NANMANDAA NANMANDAA...
TMP
GAH! DON'T FOLLOW ME, YOU NUISANCE!
RMBLL
PSHAAK
KRAK
GAH!!
WATCH OUT!
SHOVE
ARGH!!
WOOSH
AAH!
AIEEE!!
WAM

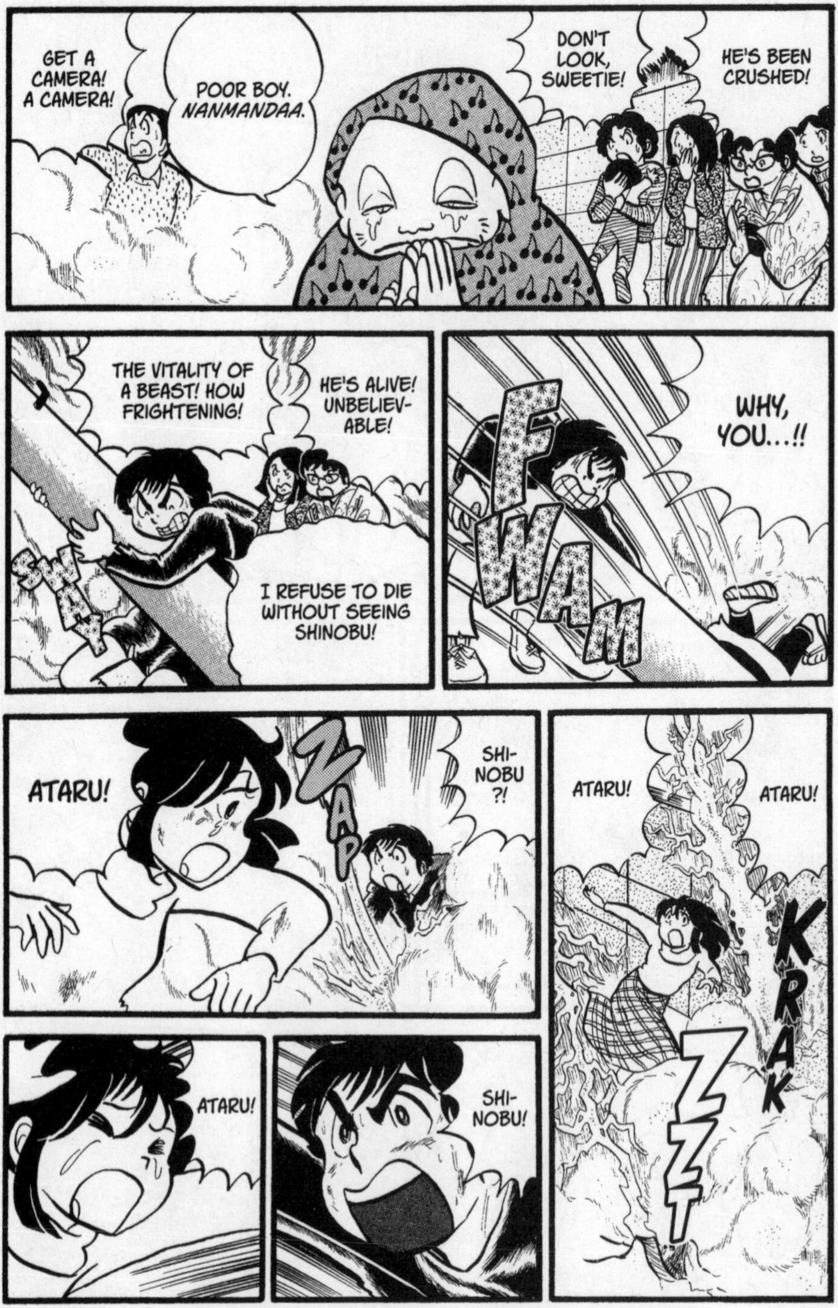
HE'S BEEN CRUSHED!
DON'T LOOK, SWEETIE!
POOR BOY. *NANMANDAA.*
GET A CAMERA! A CAMERA!
WHY, YOU...!!
FWAM
HE'S ALIVE! UNBELIEV-ABLE!
THE VITALITY OF A BEAST! HOW FRIGHTENING!
I REFUSE TO DIE WITHOUT SEEING SHINOBU!
SWAY
ATARU!
ATARU!
KRAK
ZZZT
SHI-NOBU ?!
ZAP
ATARU!
SHI-NOBU!
ATARU!

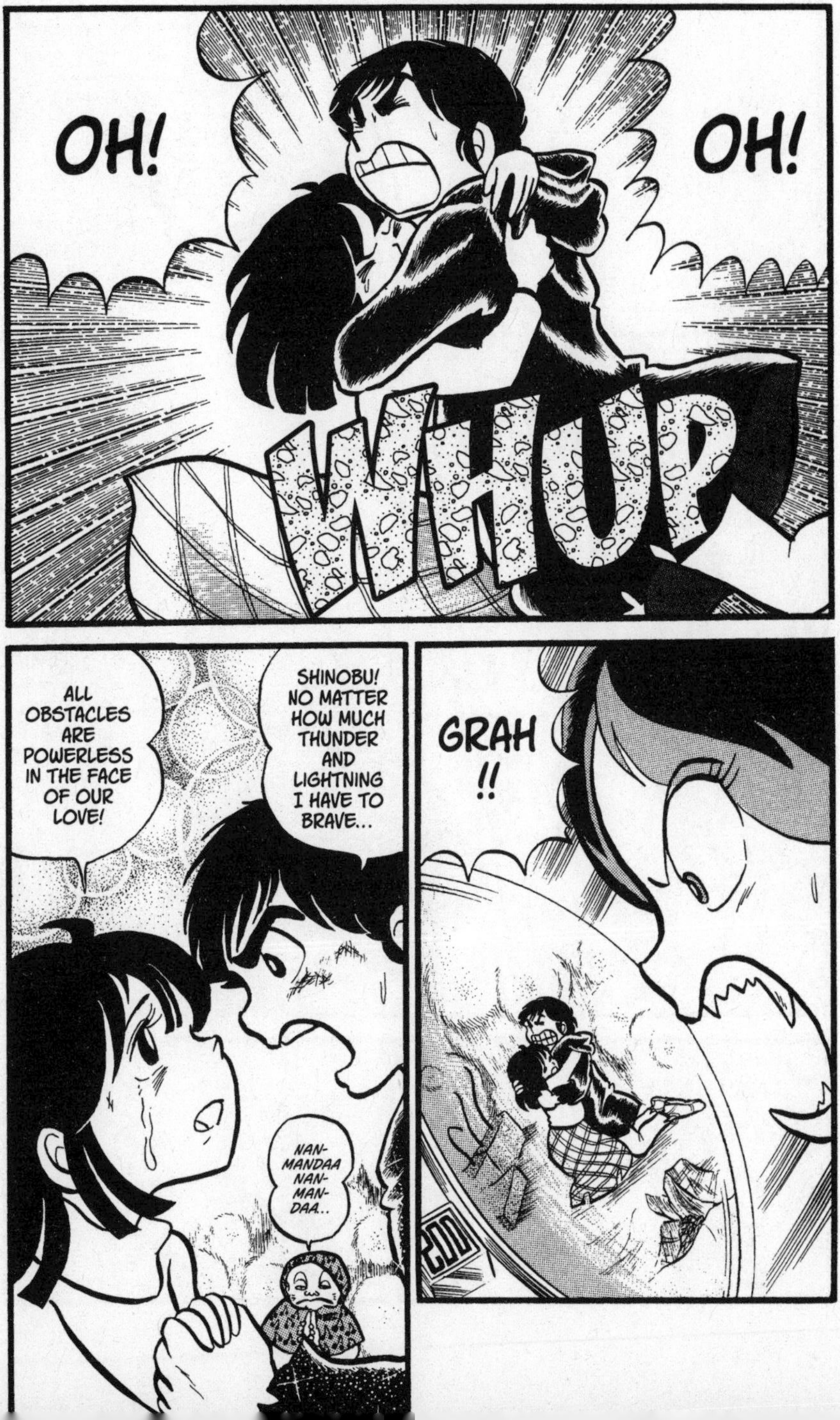
OH!
OH!
WHUP
GRAH !!
SHINOBU! NO MATTER HOW MUCH THUNDER AND LIGHTNING I HAVE TO BRAVE...
ALL OBSTACLES ARE POWERLESS IN THE FACE OF OUR LOVE!
NAN-MANDAA NAN-MAN-DAA...

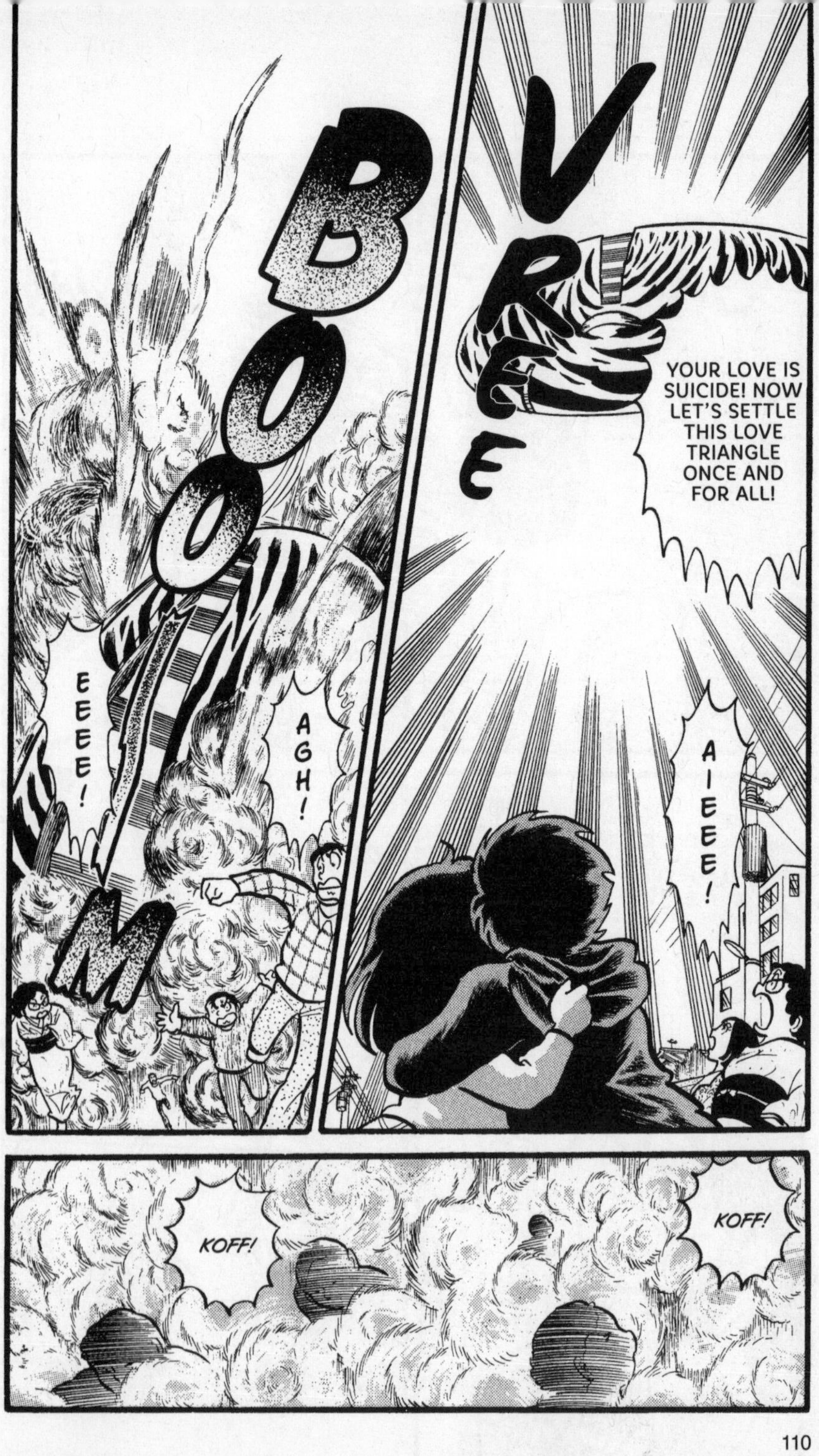
VREE
YOUR LOVE IS SUICIDE! NOW LET'S SETTLE THIS LOVE TRIANGLE ONCE AND FOR ALL!
AIEEEE!
BOOOM
AGH!
EEEE!
KOFF!
KOFF!

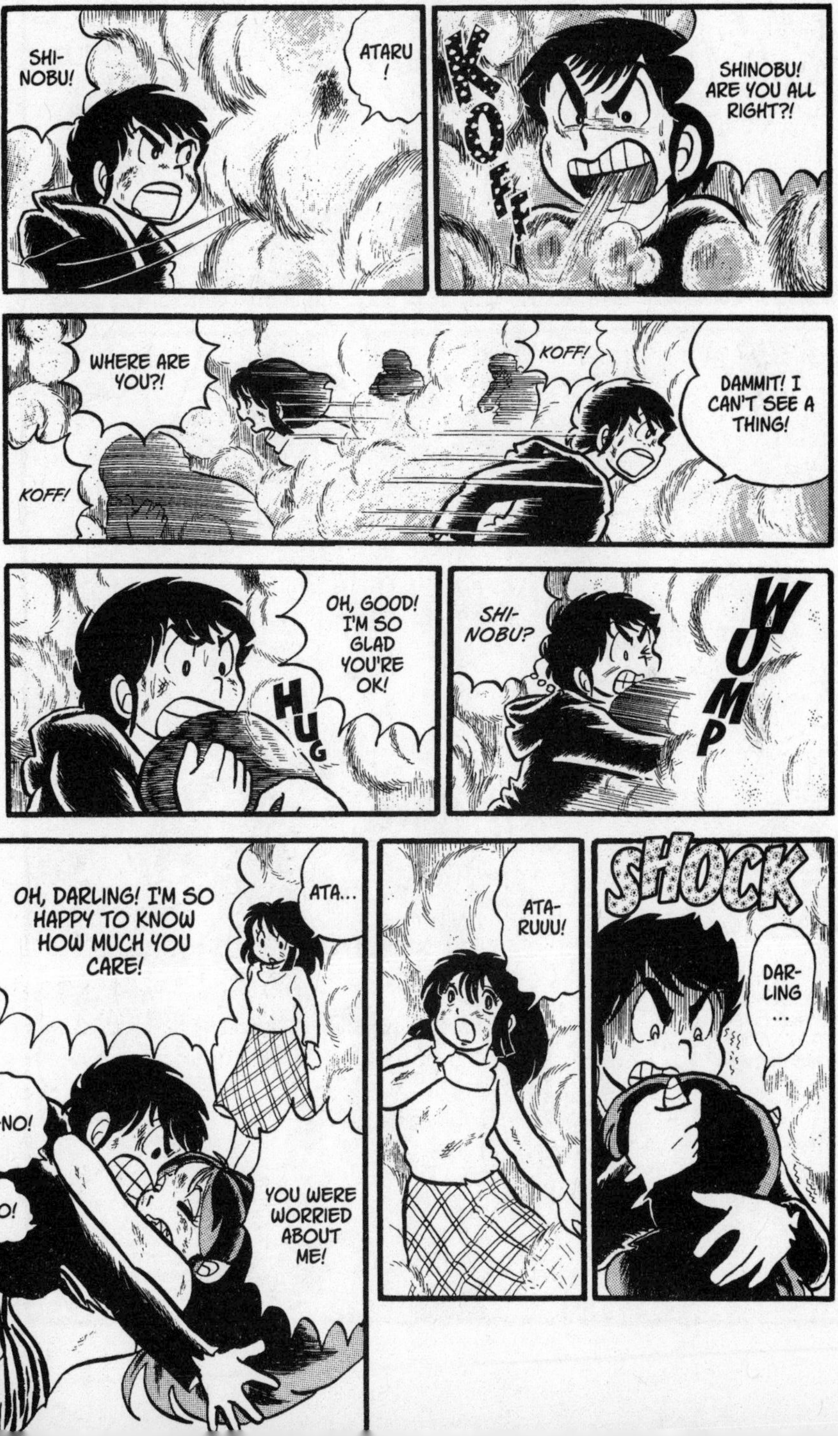

KOFF
SHINOBU! ARE YOU ALL RIGHT?!
ATARU!
SHI-NOBU!
DAMMIT! I CAN'T SEE A THING!
KOFF!
WHERE ARE YOU?!
KOFF!
WUMP
SHI-NOBU?
OH, GOOD! I'M SO GLAD YOU'RE OK!
HUG
SHOCK
DAR-LING...
ATA-RUUU!
ATA...
OH, DARLING! I'M SO HAPPY TO KNOW HOW MUCH YOU CARE!
YOU WERE WORRIED ABOUT ME!
N-NO!
NO!

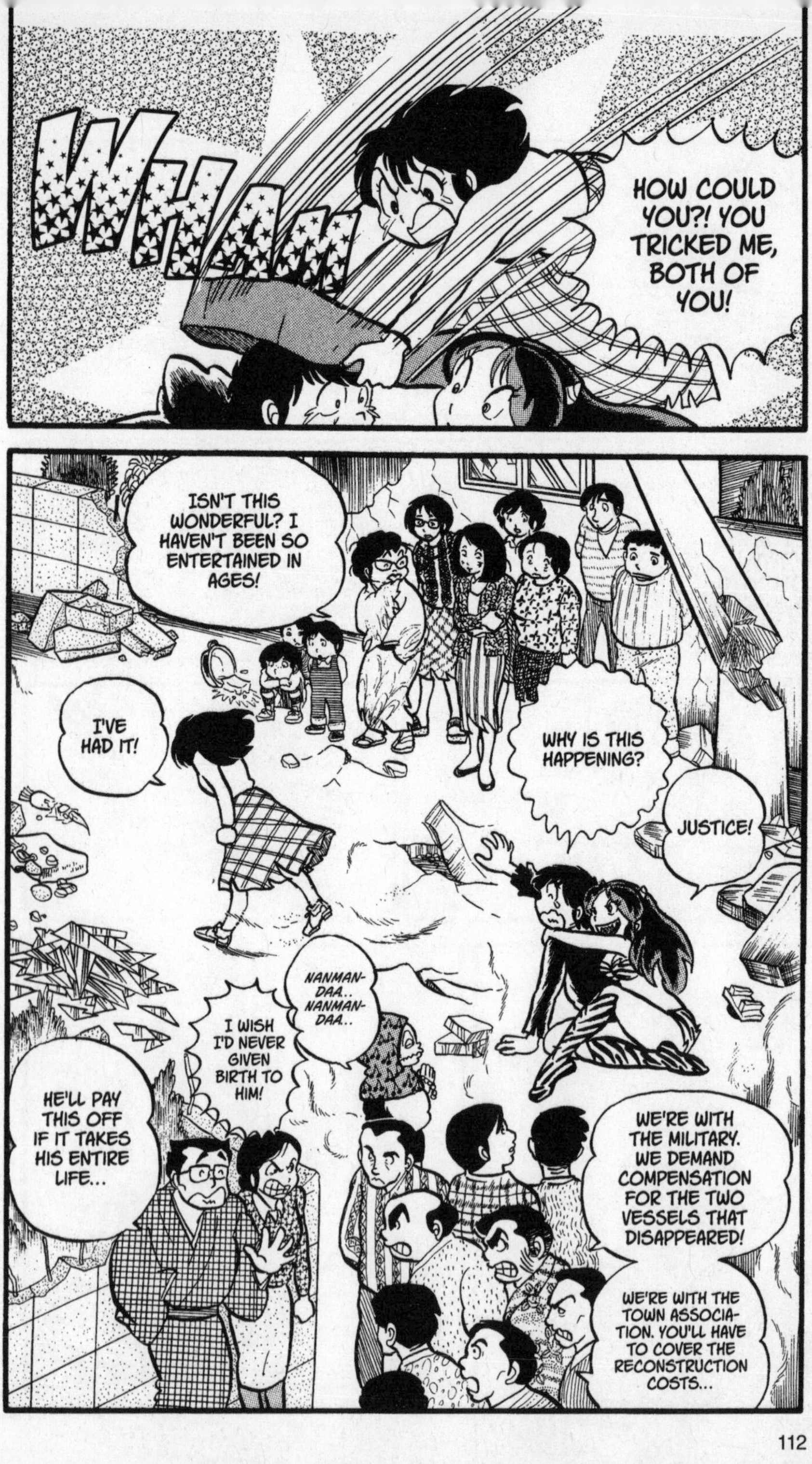
HOW COULD YOU?! YOU TRICKED ME, BOTH OF YOU!
WHAM
ISN'T THIS WONDERFUL? I HAVEN'T BEEN SO ENTERTAINED IN AGES!
WHY IS THIS HAPPENING?
I'VE HAD IT!
JUSTICE!
NANMAN-DAA... NANMAN-DAA...
I WISH I'D NEVER GIVEN BIRTH TO HIM!
WE'RE WITH THE MILITARY. WE DEMAND COMPENSATION FOR THE TWO VESSELS THAT DISAPPEARED!
HE'LL PAY THIS OFF IF IT TAKES HIS ENTIRE LIFE...
WE'RE WITH THE TOWN ASSOCIA-TION. YOU'LL HAVE TO COVER THE RECONSTRUCTION COSTS...

CHAPTER 6: TO KILL WITH LOVE

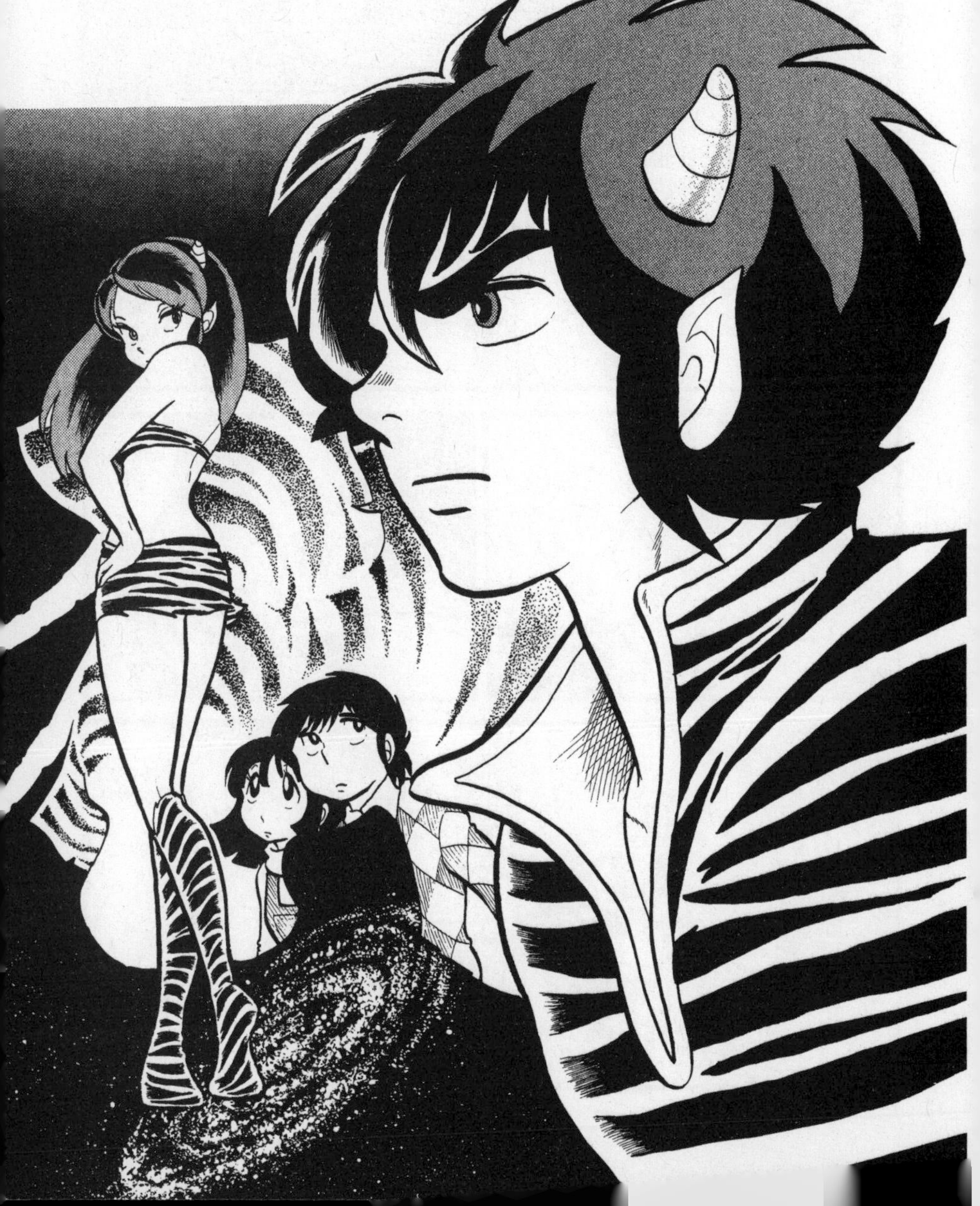

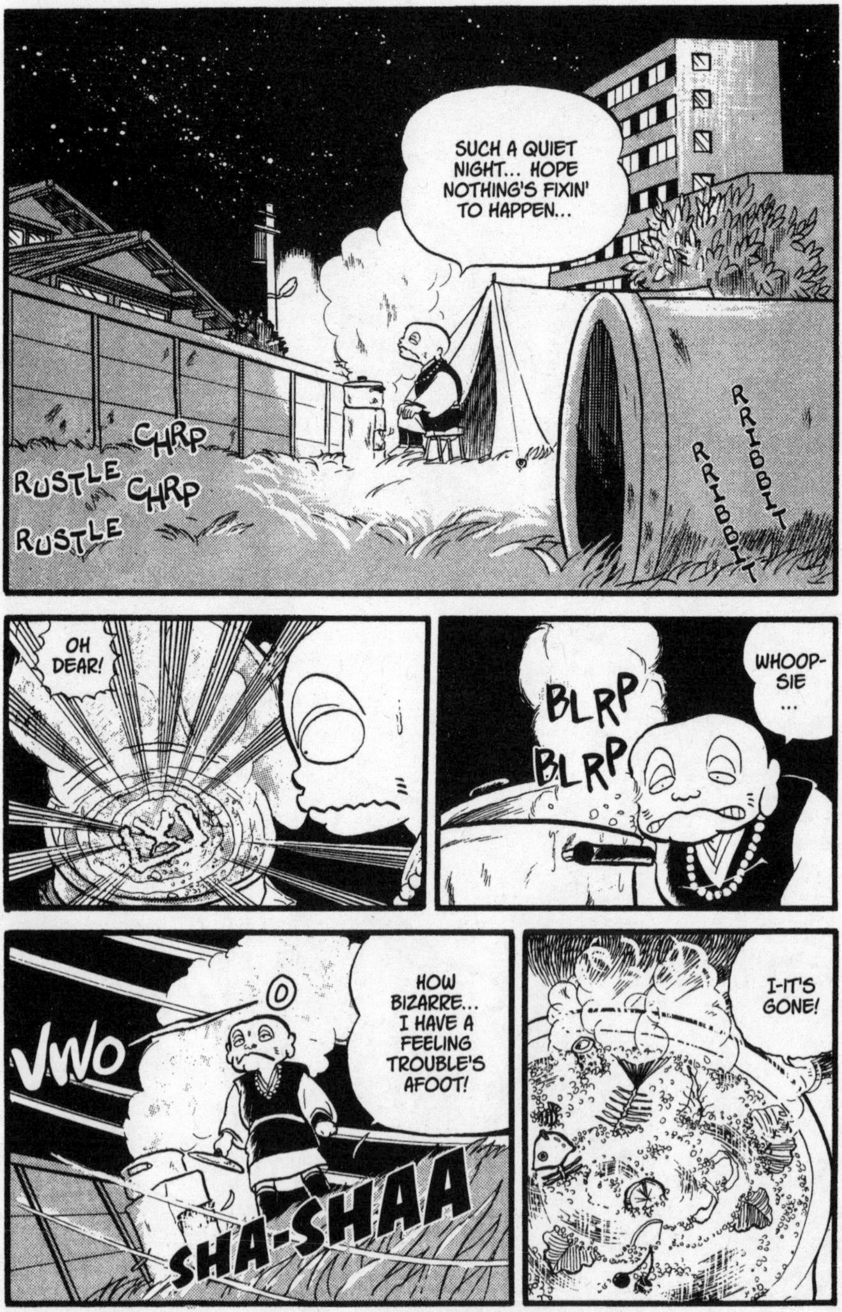
SUCH A QUIET NIGHT... HOPE NOTHING'S FIXIN' TO HAPPEN...
RRIBBIT
RRIBBIT
CHRP
RUSTLE
CHRP
RUSTLE
WHOOPSIE ...
BLRP
BLRP
OH DEAR!
I-IT'S GONE!
HOW BIZARRE... I HAVE A FEELING TROUBLE'S AFOOT!
VWO
SHA-SHAA

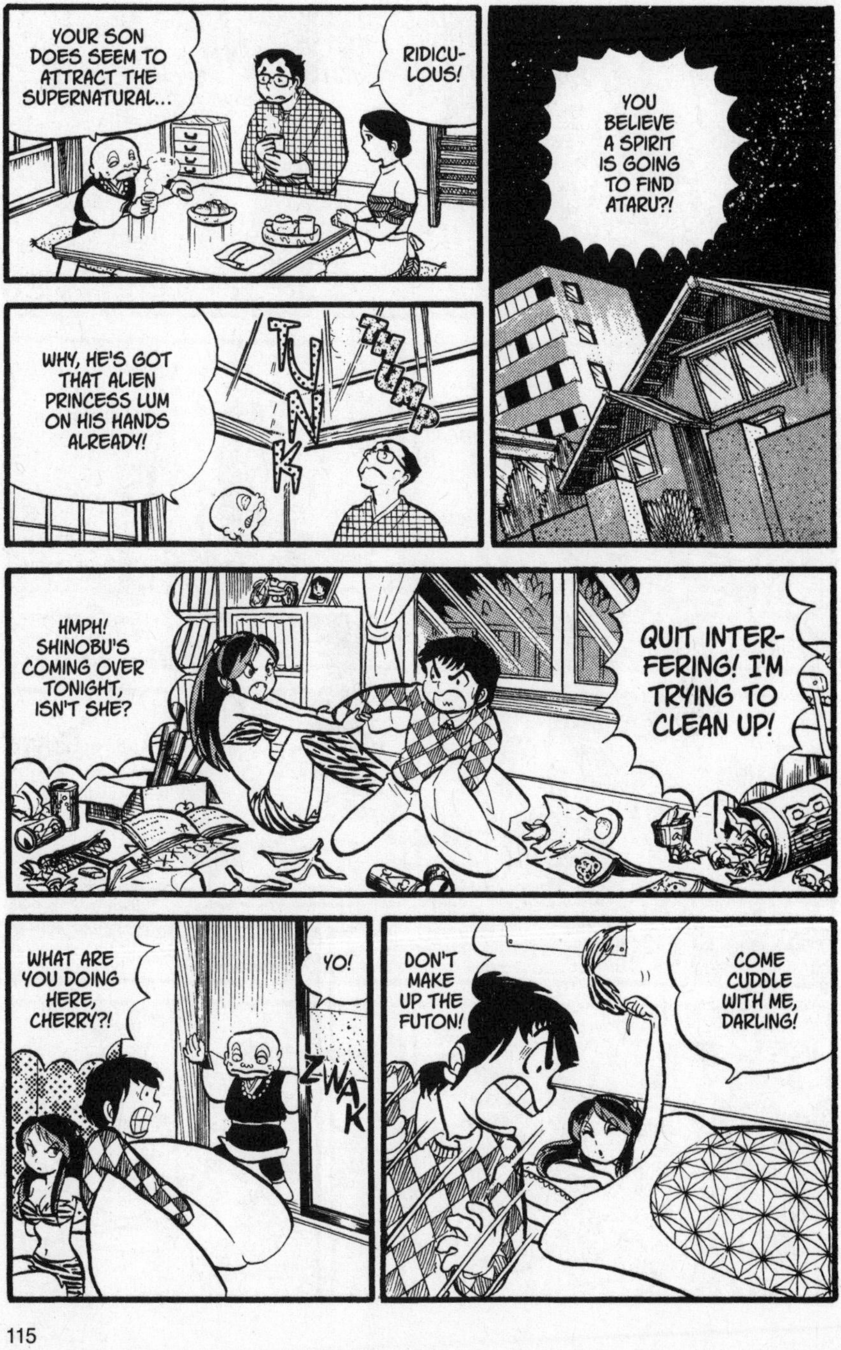
YOU BELIEVE A SPIRIT IS GOING TO FIND ATARU?!
RIDICU-LOUS!
YOUR SON DOES SEEM TO ATTRACT THE SUPERNATURAL...
THUMP
TUNK
WHY, HE'S GOT THAT ALIEN PRINCESS LUM ON HIS HANDS ALREADY!
QUIT INTER-FERING! I'M TRYING TO CLEAN UP!
HMPH! SHINOBU'S COMING OVER TONIGHT, ISN'T SHE?
COME CUDDLE WITH ME, DARLING!
DON'T MAKE UP THE FUTON!
YO!
ZWAK
WHAT ARE YOU DOING HERE, CHERRY?!

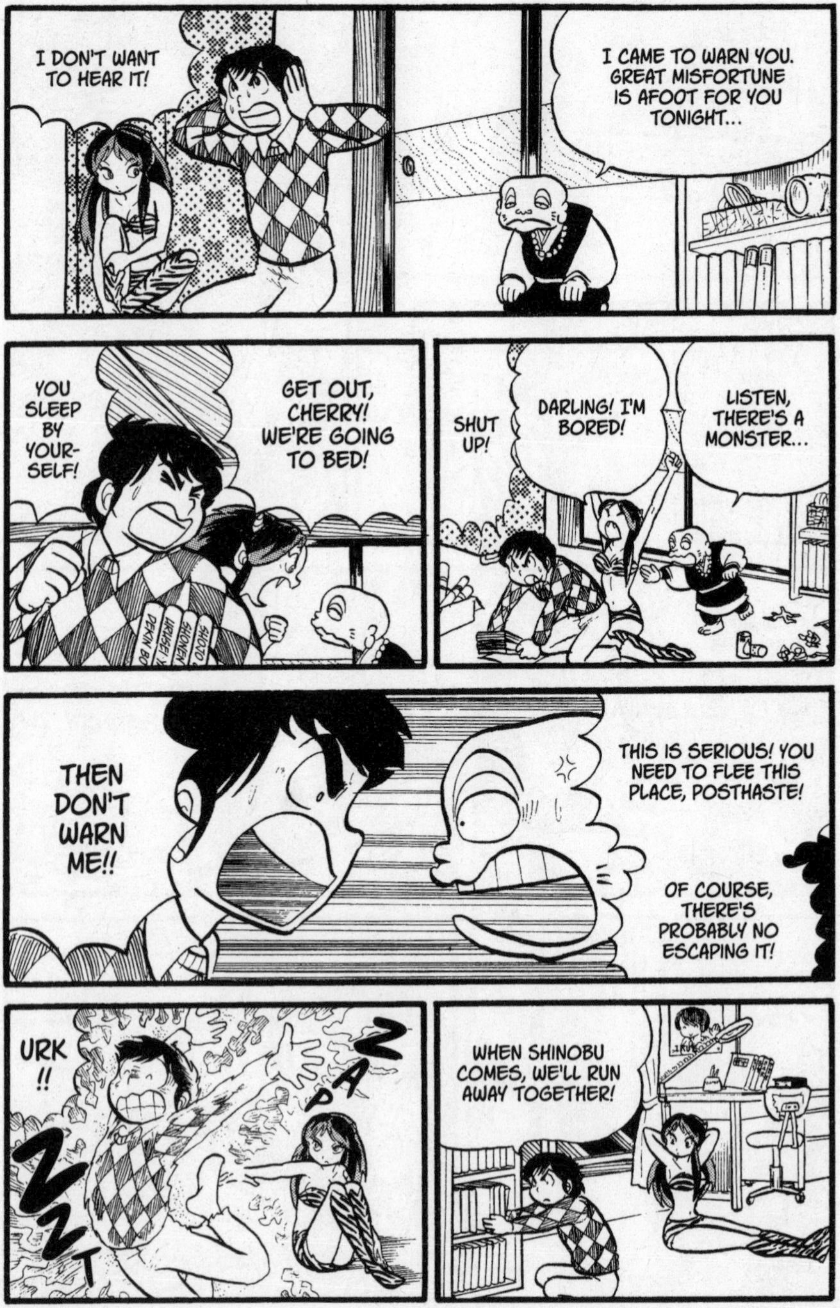
I CAME TO WARN YOU. GREAT MISFORTUNE IS AFOOT FOR YOU TONIGHT...
I DON'T WANT TO HEAR IT!
LISTEN, THERE'S A MONSTER...
DARLING! I'M BORED!
SHUT UP!
GET OUT, CHERRY! WE'RE GOING TO BED!
YOU SLEEP BY YOUR-SELF!
THIS IS SERIOUS! YOU NEED TO FLEE THIS PLACE, POSTHASTE!
OF COURSE, THERE'S PROBABLY NO ESCAPING IT!
THEN DON'T WARN ME!!
WHEN SHINOBU COMES, WE'LL RUN AWAY TOGETHER!
ZAP
URK !!
ZZZT

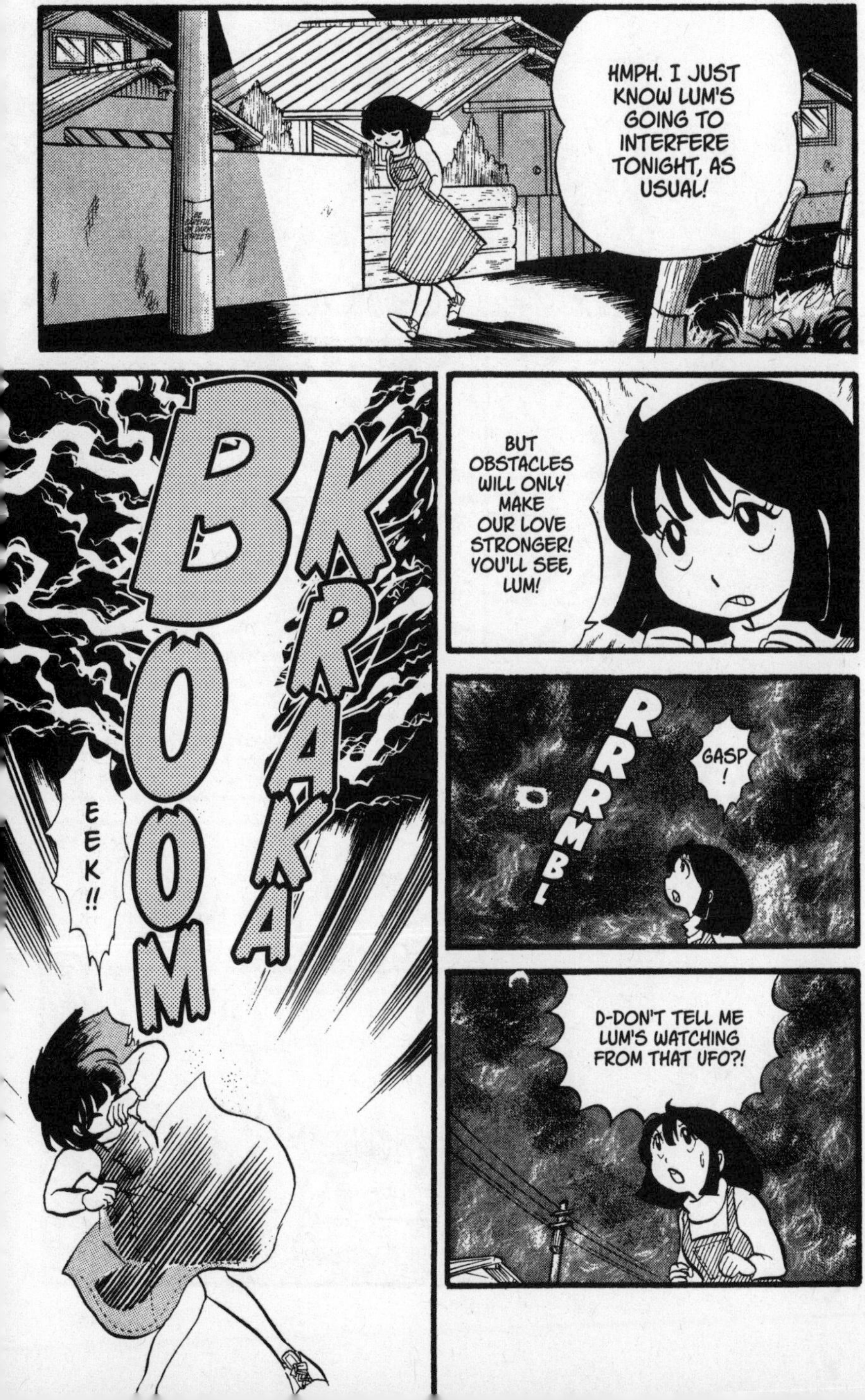
HMPH. I JUST KNOW LUM'S GOING TO INTERFERE TONIGHT, AS USUAL!
BUT OBSTACLES WILL ONLY MAKE OUR LOVE STRONGER! YOU'LL SEE, LUM!
RRRRMBL
GASP!
D-DON'T TELL ME LUM'S WATCHING FROM THAT UFO?!
BKRAKA
BOOM
EEK!!

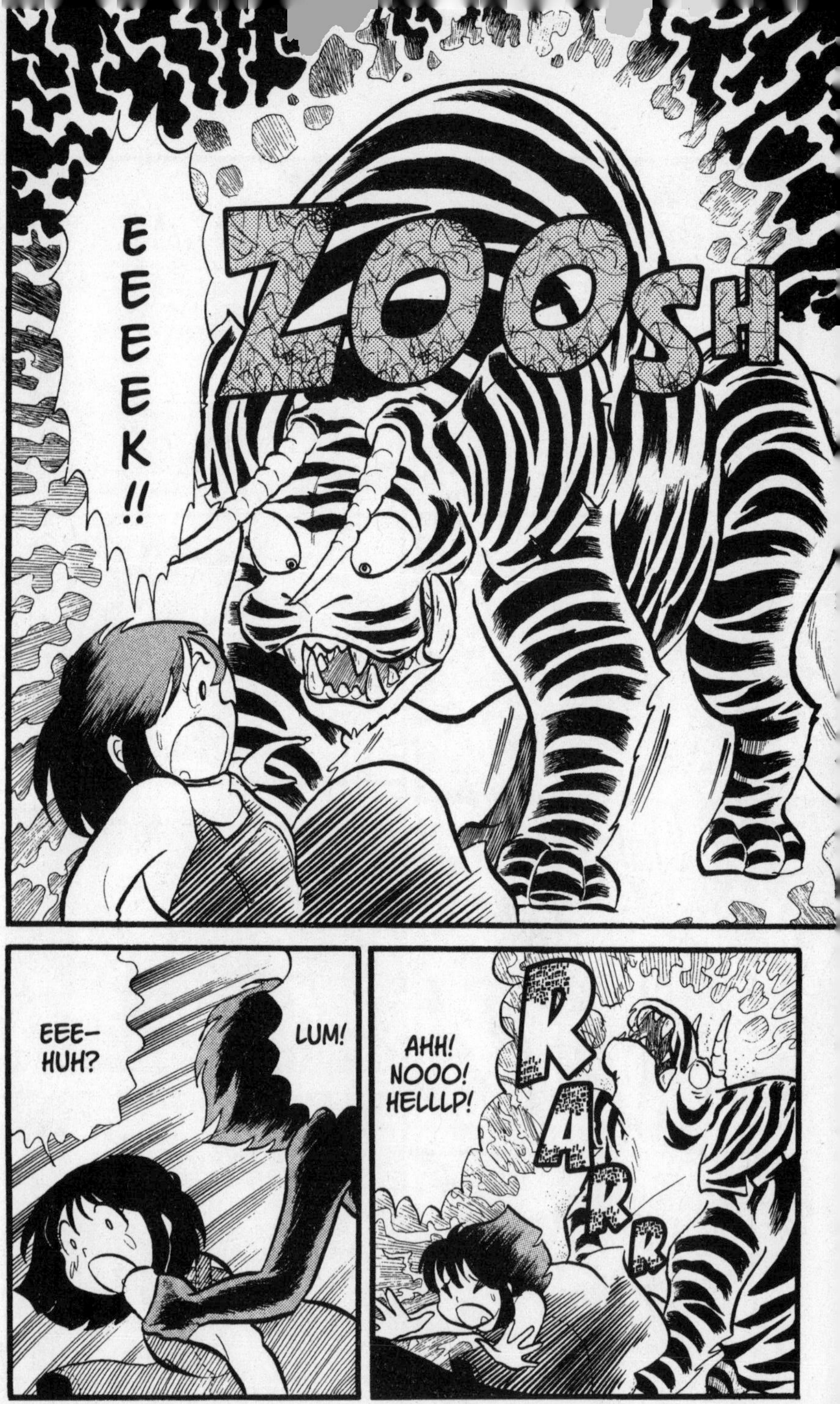
EEEEEK!!
ZOOSH
RARR
AHH! NOOO! HELLLP!
LUM!
EEE-HUH?

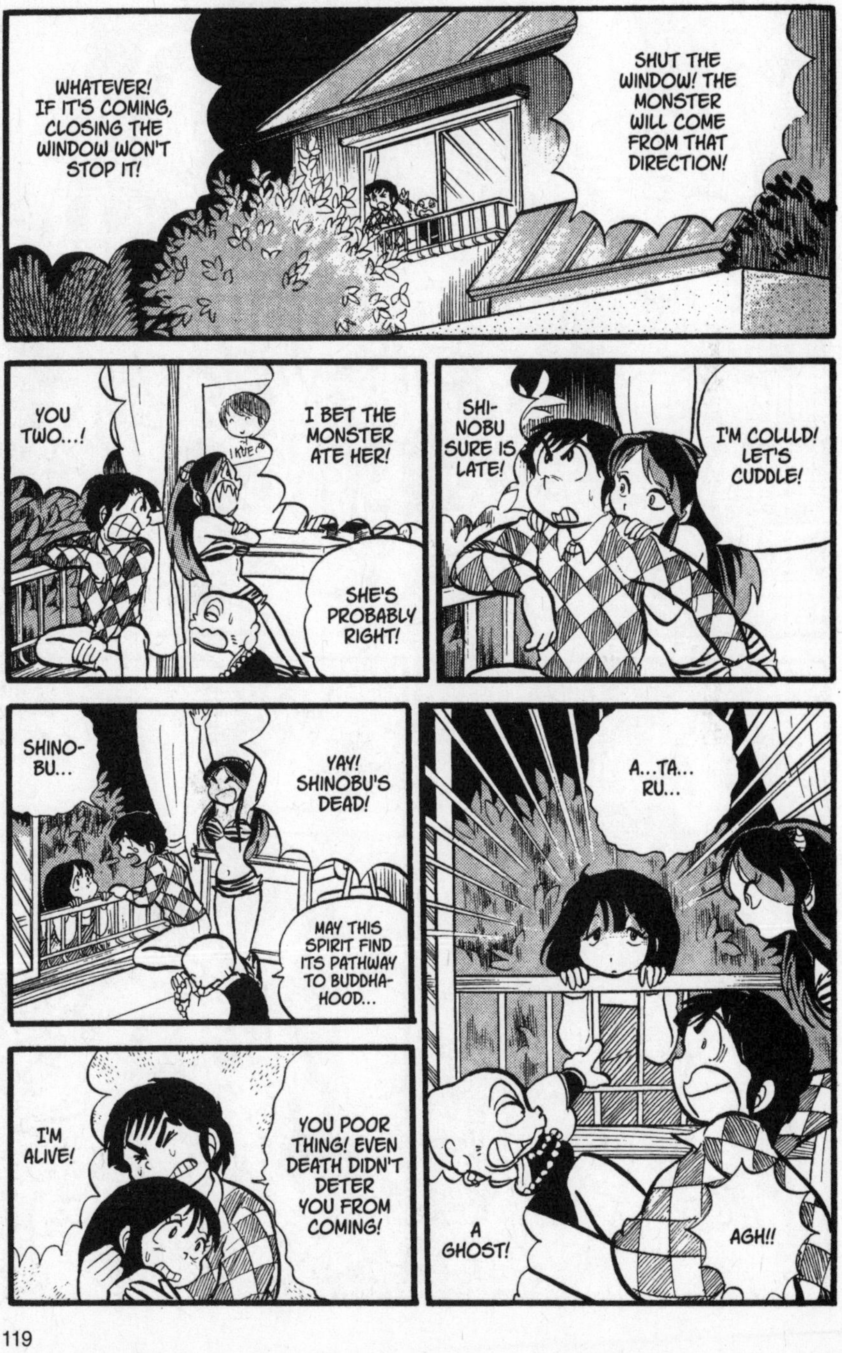
SHUT THE WINDOW! THE MONSTER WILL COME FROM THAT DIRECTION!
WHATEVER! IF IT'S COMING, CLOSING THE WINDOW WON'T STOP IT!
I'M COLLLD! LET'S CUDDLE!
SHI-NOBU SURE IS LATE!
I BET THE MONSTER ATE HER!
YOU TWO...!
SHE'S PROBABLY RIGHT!
A...TA... RU...
AGH!!
A GHOST!
YAY! SHINOBU'S DEAD!
SHINO-BU...
MAY THIS SPIRIT FIND ITS PATHWAY TO BUDDHA-HOOD...
YOU POOR THING! EVEN DEATH DIDN'T DETER YOU FROM COMING!
I'M ALIVE!

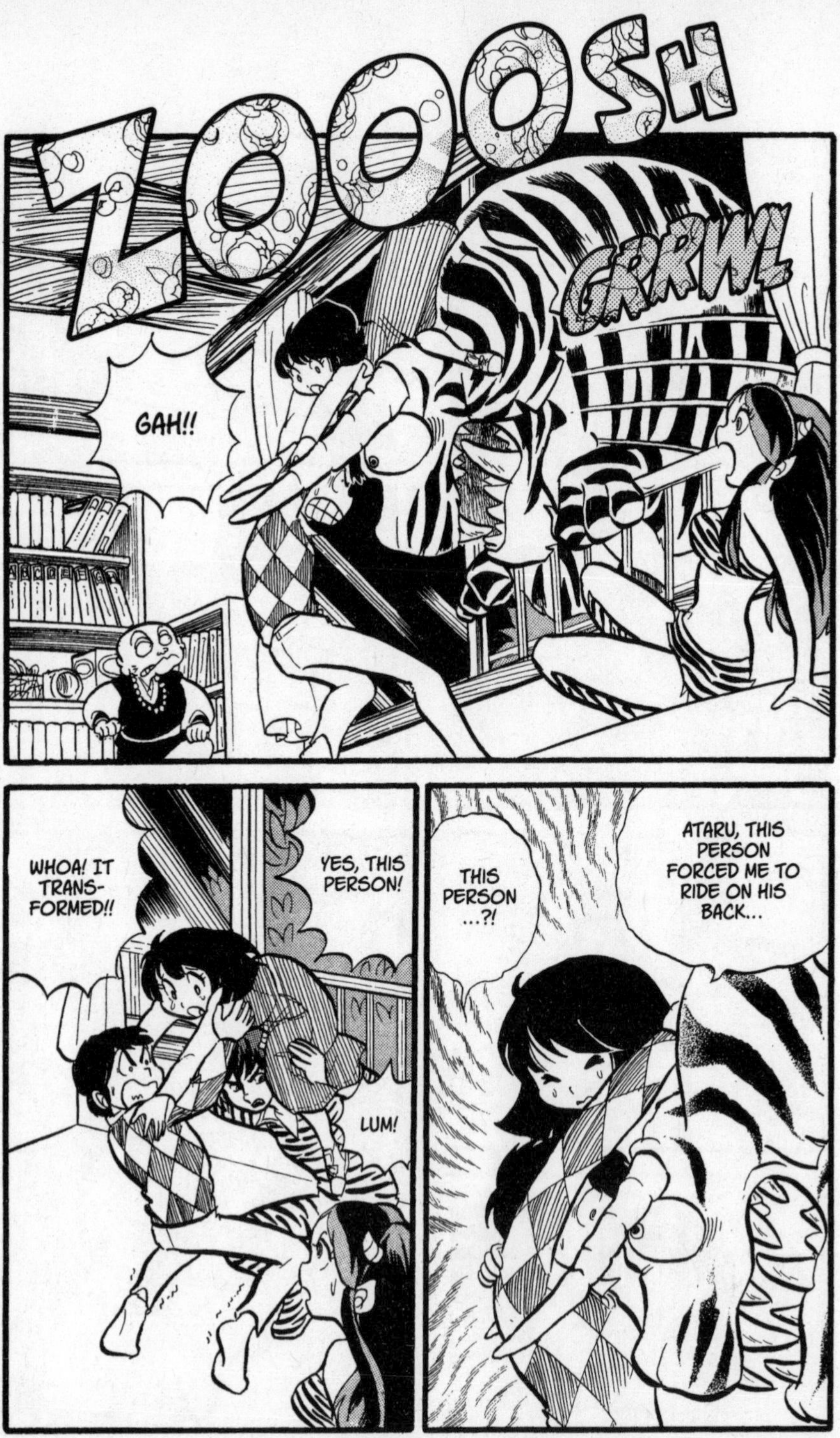
ZOOOSH
GRRWL
GAH!!
ATARU, THIS PERSON FORCED ME TO RIDE ON HIS BACK...
THIS PERSON ...?!
YES, THIS PERSON!
WHOA! IT TRANS-FORMED!!
LUM!

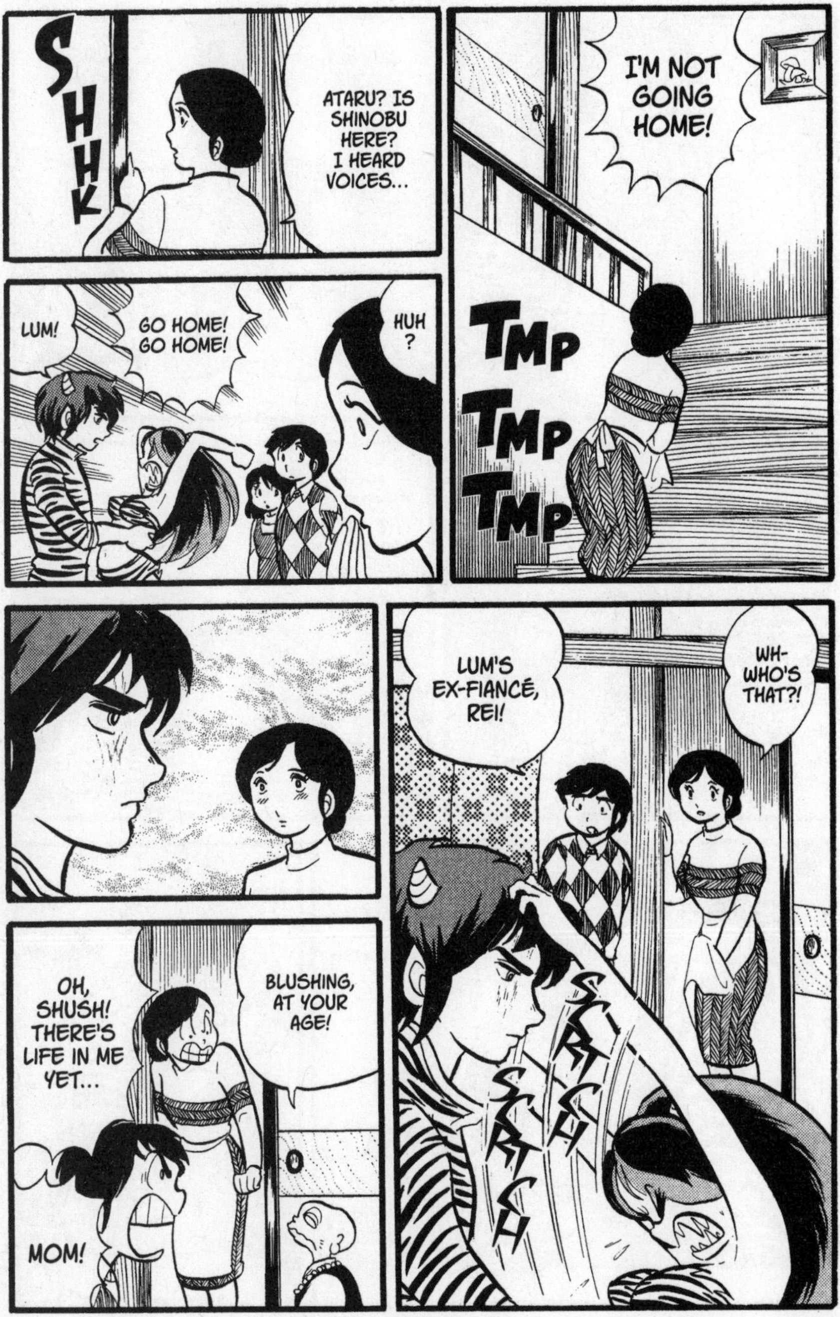
I'M NOT GOING HOME!
TMP TMP TMP
SHHK
ATARU? IS SHINOBU HERE? I HEARD VOICES...
HUH ?
GO HOME! GO HOME!
LUM!
WH- WHO'S THAT?!
LUM'S EX-FIANCÉ, REI!
SCRTCH SCRTCH
BLUSHING, AT YOUR AGE!
OH, SHUSH! THERE'S LIFE IN ME YET...
MOM!

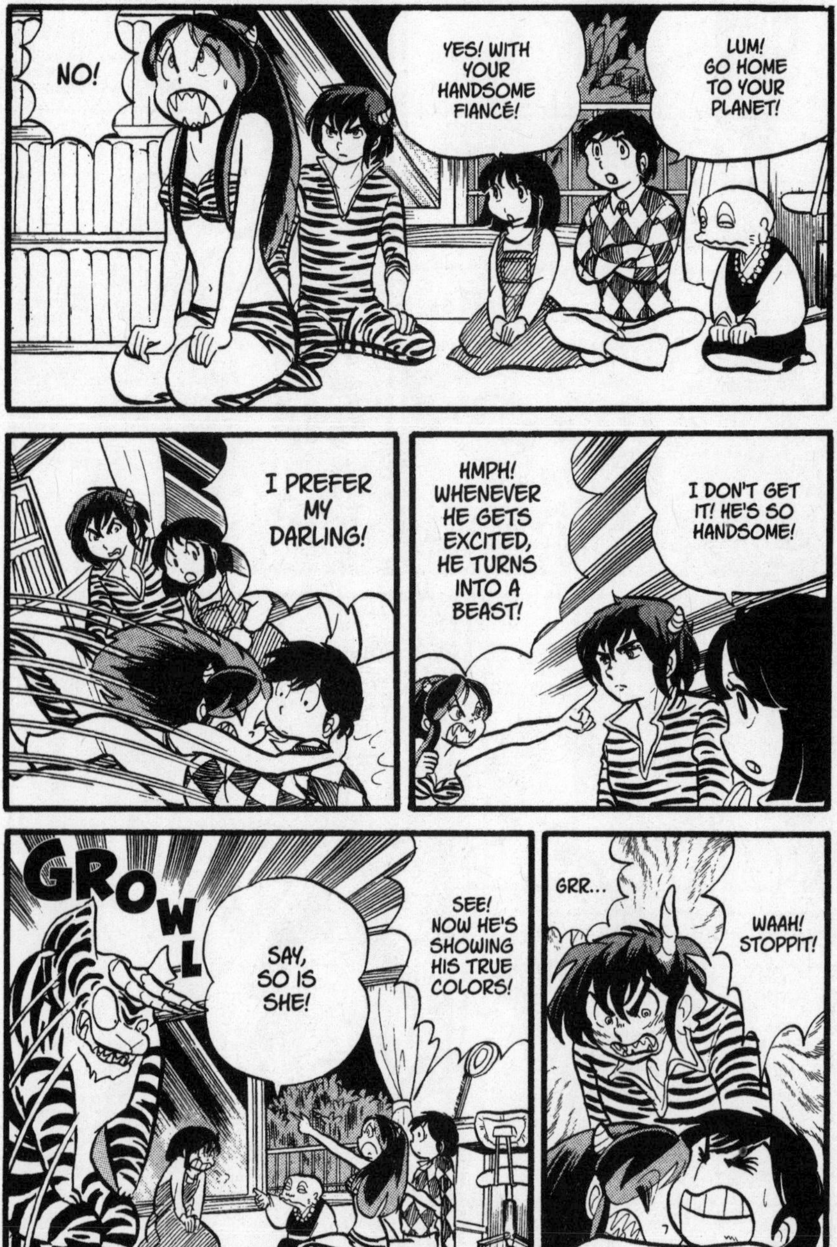
LUM! GO HOME TO YOUR PLANET!
YES! WITH YOUR HANDSOME FIANCÉ!
NO!
I DON'T GET IT! HE'S SO HANDSOME!
HMPH! WHENEVER HE GETS EXCITED, HE TURNS INTO A BEAST!
I PREFER MY DARLING!
WAAH! STOPPIT!
GRR...
SEE! NOW HE'S SHOWING HIS TRUE COLORS!
SAY, SO IS SHE!
GROWL

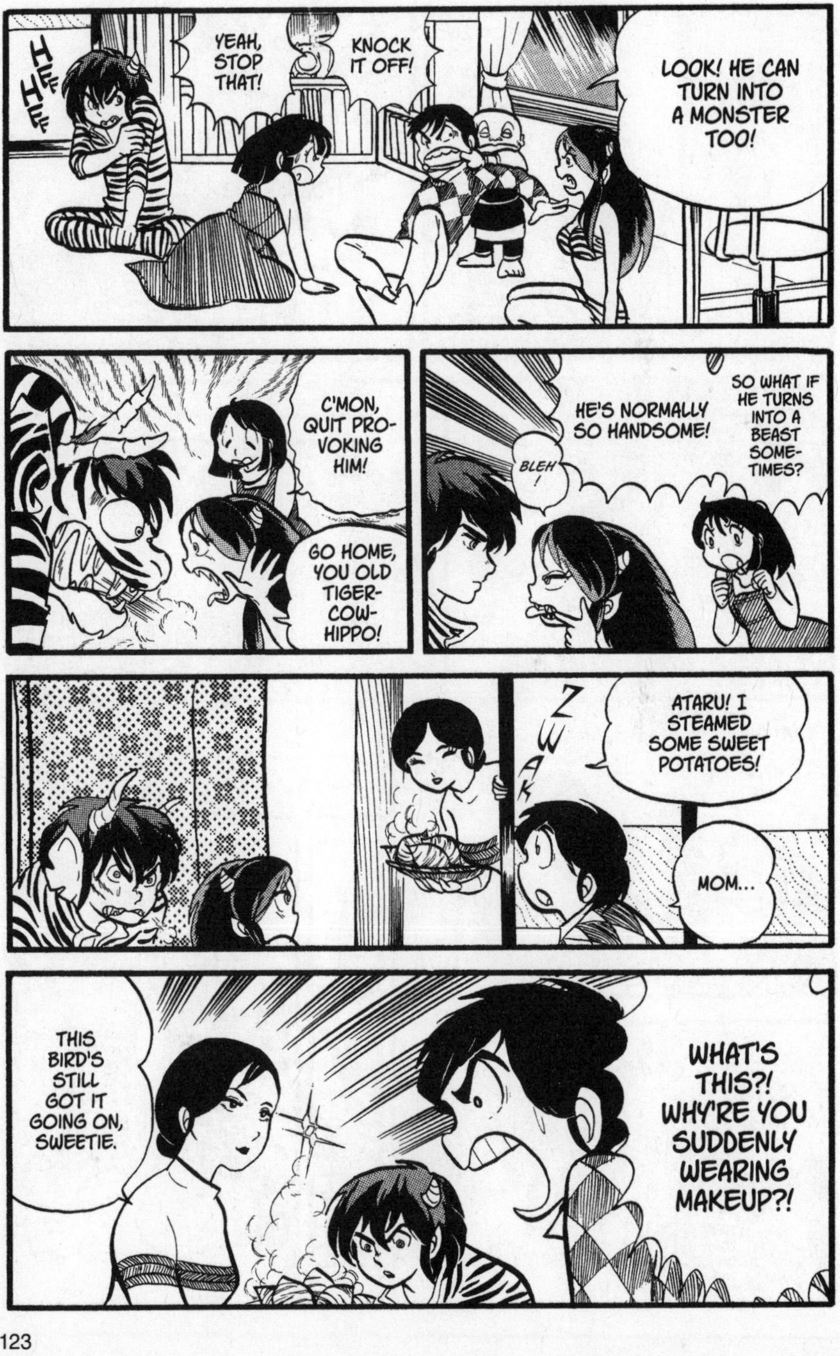
LOOK! HE CAN TURN INTO A MONSTER TOO!
KNOCK IT OFF!
YEAH, STOP THAT!
HEEE HEEE
SO WHAT IF HE TURNS INTO A BEAST SOMETIMES?
HE'S NORMALLY SO HANDSOME!
BLEH!
C'MON, QUIT PROVOKING HIM!
GO HOME, YOU OLD TIGER-COW-HIPPO!
ATARU! I STEAMED SOME SWEET POTATOES!
ZWAK
MOM...
WHAT'S THIS?! WHY'RE YOU SUDDENLY WEARING MAKEUP?!
THIS BIRD'S STILL GOT IT GOING ON, SWEETIE.

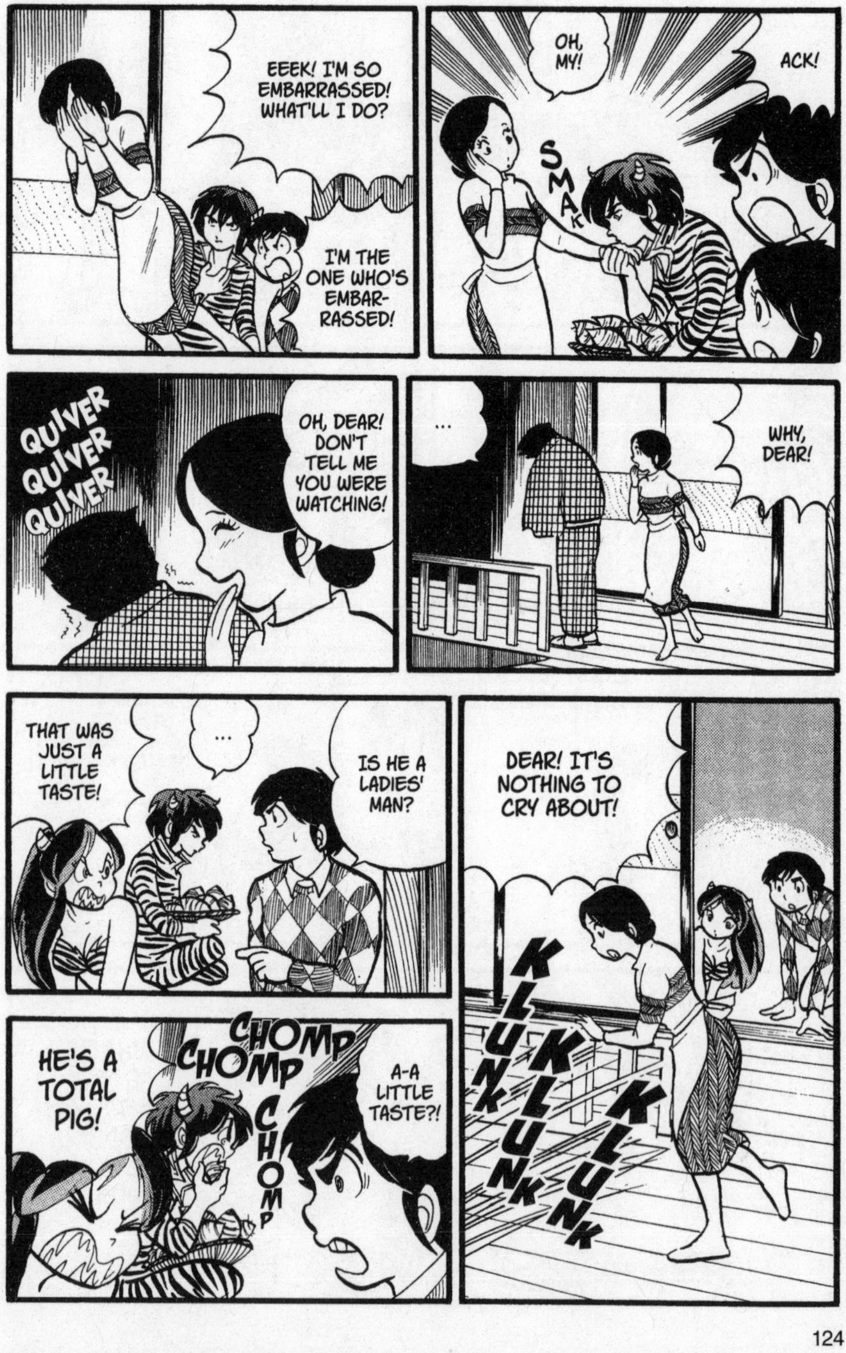
ACK!
OH, MY!
SMAK
EEEK! I'M SO EMBARRASSED! WHAT'LL I DO?
I'M THE ONE WHO'S EMBARRASSED!
WHY, DEAR!
...
OH, DEAR! DON'T TELL ME YOU WERE WATCHING!
QUIVER QUIVER QUIVER
DEAR! IT'S NOTHING TO CRY ABOUT!
KLUNK KLUNK KLUNK KLUNK
IS HE A LADIES' MAN?
...
THAT WAS JUST A LITTLE TASTE!
A-A LITTLE TASTE?!
CHOMP CHOMP CHOMP
HE'S A TOTAL PIG!

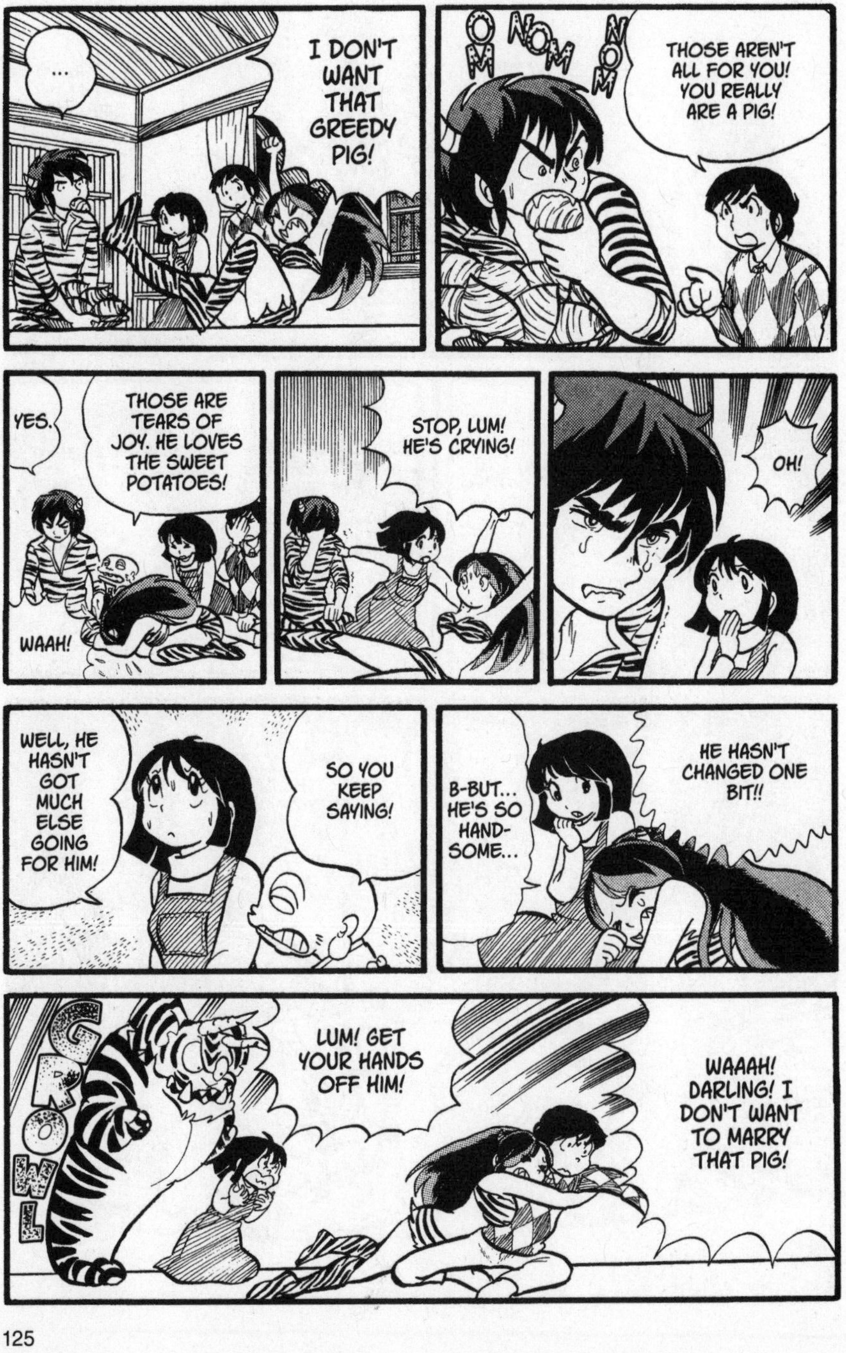
NOM NOM NOM
THOSE AREN'T ALL FOR YOU! YOU REALLY ARE A PIG!
I DON'T WANT THAT GREEDY PIG!
...
OH!
STOP, LUM! HE'S CRYING!
THOSE ARE TEARS OF JOY. HE LOVES THE SWEET POTATOES!
YES.
WAAH!
HE HASN'T CHANGED ONE BIT!!
B-BUT... HE'S SO HAND-SOME...
SO YOU KEEP SAYING!
WELL, HE HASN'T GOT MUCH ELSE GOING FOR HIM!
WAAAH! DARLING! I DON'T WANT TO MARRY THAT PIG!
LUM! GET YOUR HANDS OFF HIM!
GROWL

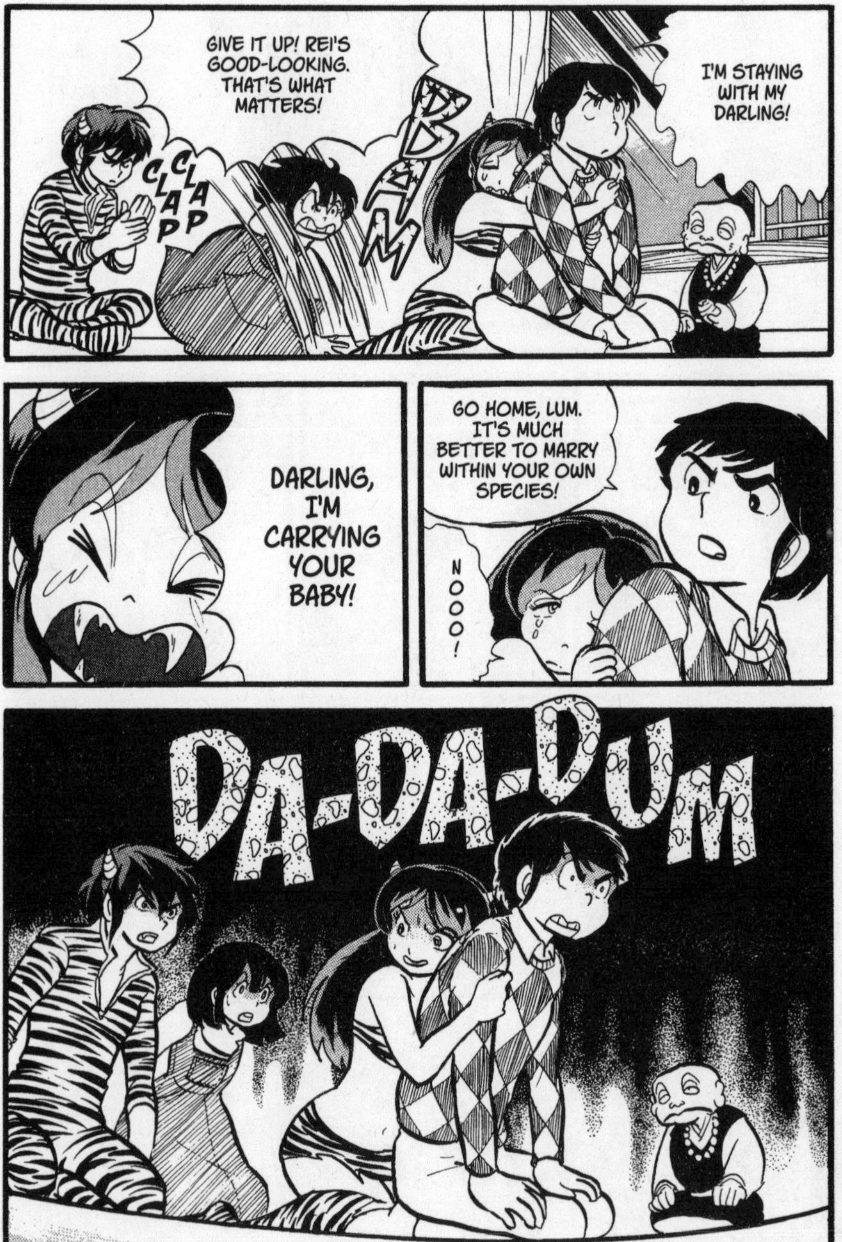
I'M STAYING WITH MY DARLING!
BDAM
GIVE IT UP! REI'S GOOD-LOOKING. THAT'S WHAT MATTERS!
CLAP CLAP
GO HOME, LUM. IT'S MUCH BETTER TO MARRY WITHIN YOUR OWN SPECIES!
NOOOO!
DARLING, I'M CARRYING YOUR BABY!
DA-DA-DUM

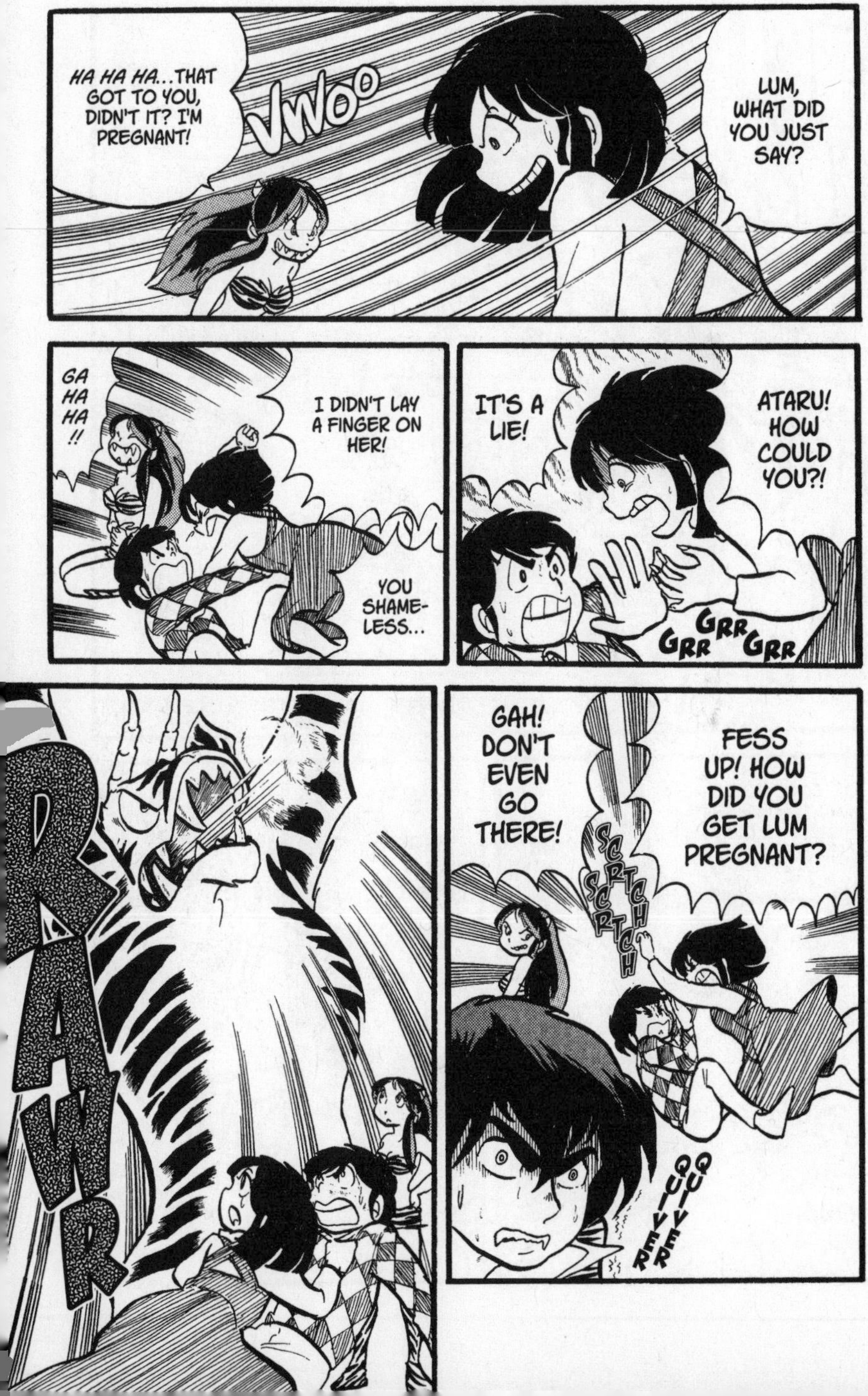
LUM, WHAT DID YOU JUST SAY?
VWOO
HA HA HA...THAT GOT TO YOU, DIDN'T IT? I'M PREGNANT!
ATARU! HOW COULD YOU?!
IT'S A LIE!
GRR GRR GRR GRR
I DIDN'T LAY A FINGER ON HER!
GA HA HA !!
YOU SHAMELESS...
FESS UP! HOW DID YOU GET LUM PREGNANT?
GAH! DON'T EVEN GO THERE!
SCRTCH SCRTCH
QUIVER QUIVER
RAWR

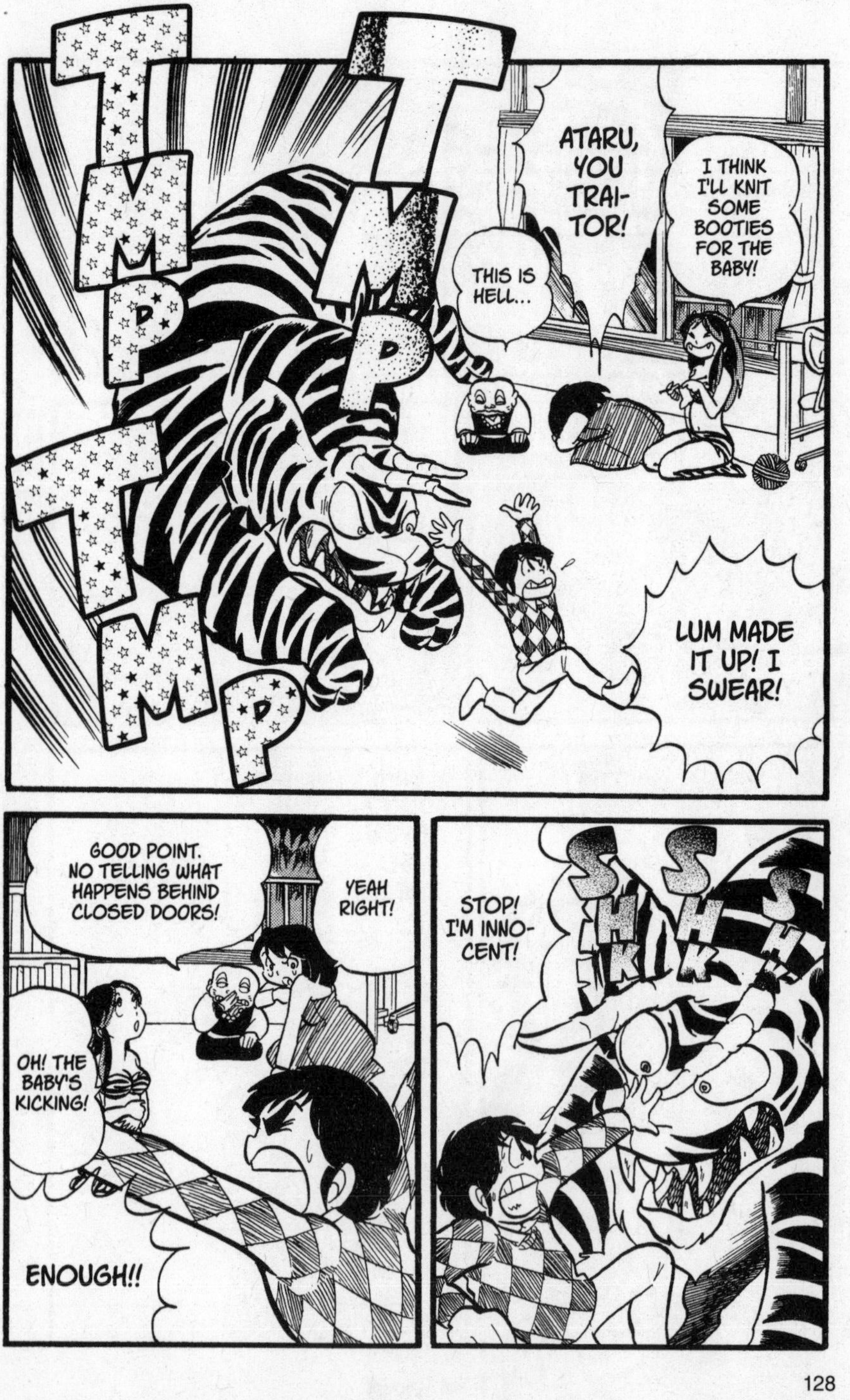

I THINK I'LL KNIT SOME BOOTIES FOR THE BABY!
ATARU, YOU TRAITOR!
THIS IS HELL...
TMP
TMP
TMP
LUM MADE IT UP! I SWEAR!
SHK
SHK
SHK
STOP! I'M INNOCENT!
YEAH RIGHT!
GOOD POINT. NO TELLING WHAT HAPPENS BEHIND CLOSED DOORS!
OH! THE BABY'S KICKING!
ENOUGH!!

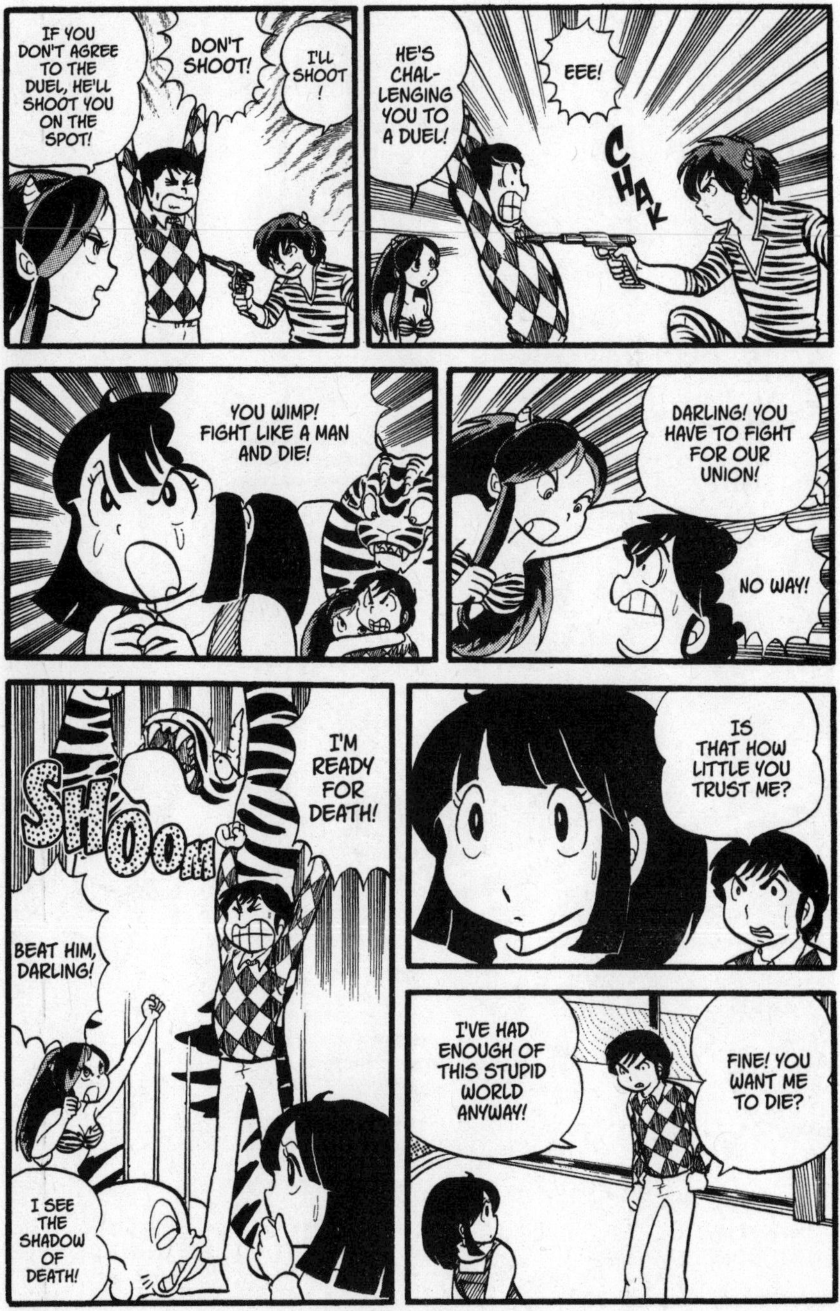
EEE!
CHAK
HE'S CHAL-LENGING YOU TO A DUEL!
I'LL SHOOT!
DON'T SHOOT!
IF YOU DON'T AGREE TO THE DUEL, HE'LL SHOOT YOU ON THE SPOT!
DARLING! YOU HAVE TO FIGHT FOR OUR UNION!
NO WAY!
YOU WIMP! FIGHT LIKE A MAN AND DIE!
IS THAT HOW LITTLE YOU TRUST ME?
FINE! YOU WANT ME TO DIE?
I'VE HAD ENOUGH OF THIS STUPID WORLD ANYWAY!
I'M READY FOR DEATH!
SHOOM
BEAT HIM, DARLING!
I SEE THE SHADOW OF DEATH!

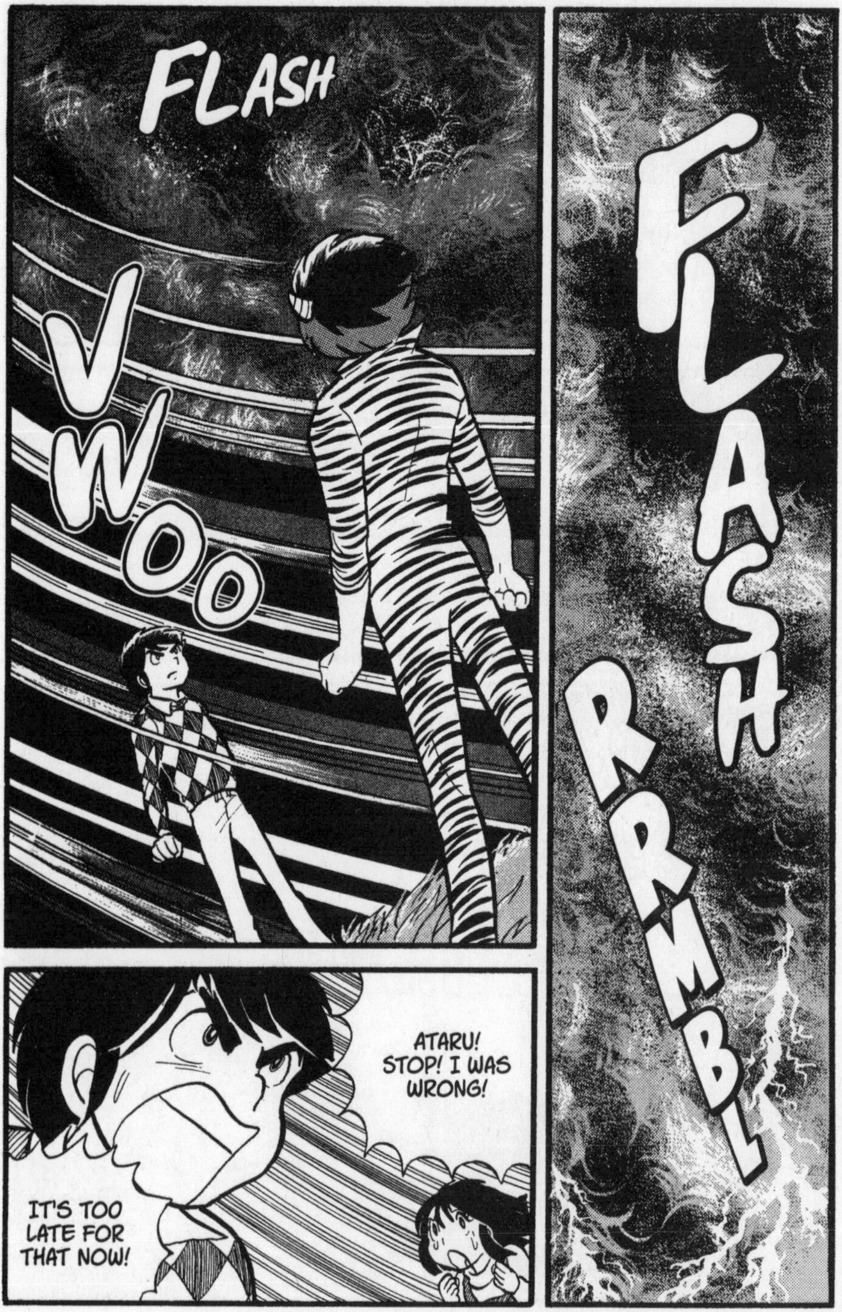
FLASH
RRMBL
FLASH
VWOOO
ATARU! STOP! I WAS WRONG!
IT'S TOO LATE FOR THAT NOW!

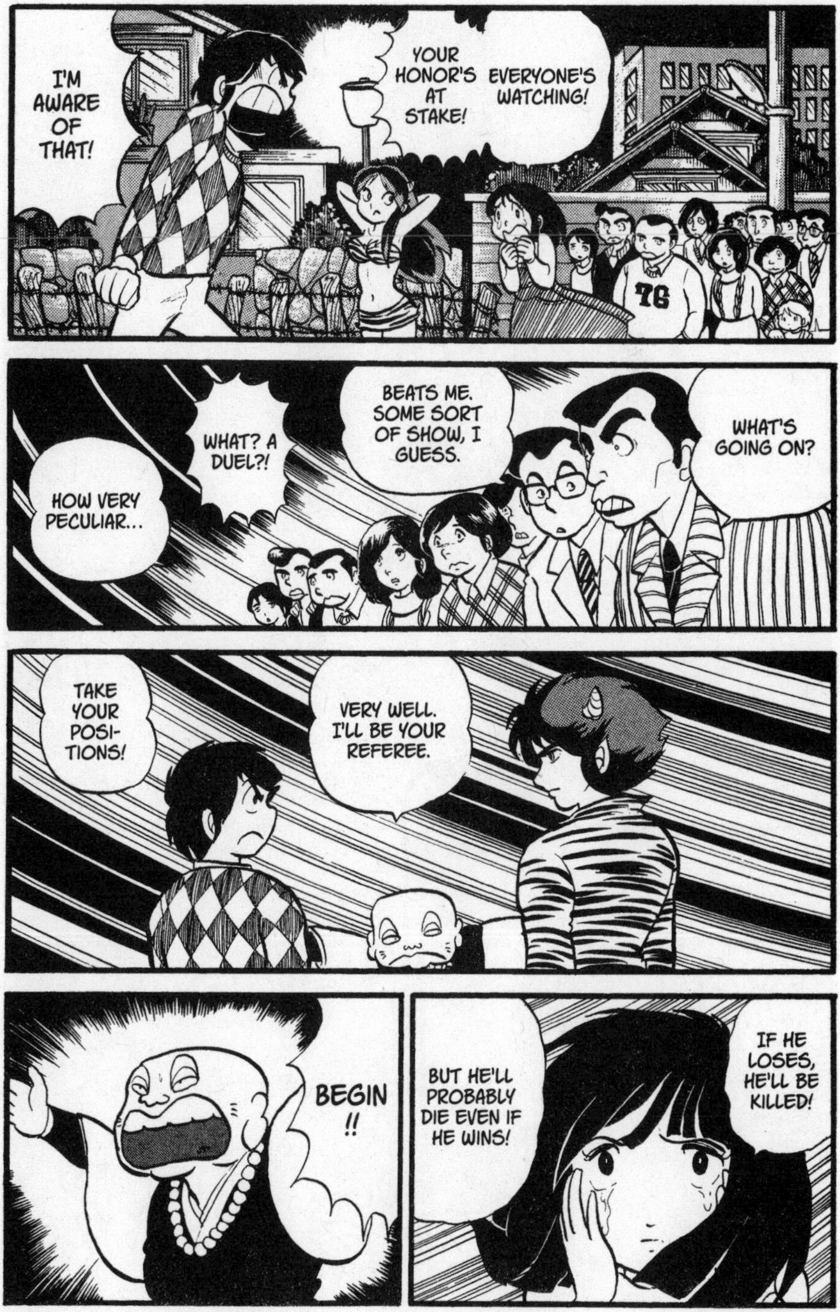
EVERYONE'S WATCHING!
YOUR HONOR'S AT STAKE!
I'M AWARE OF THAT!
76
WHAT'S GOING ON?
BEATS ME. SOME SORT OF SHOW, I GUESS.
WHAT? A DUEL?!
HOW VERY PECULIAR...
VERY WELL. I'LL BE YOUR REFEREE.
TAKE YOUR POSITIONS!
IF HE LOSES, HE'LL BE KILLED!
BUT HE'LL PROBABLY DIE EVEN IF HE WINS!
BEGIN !!

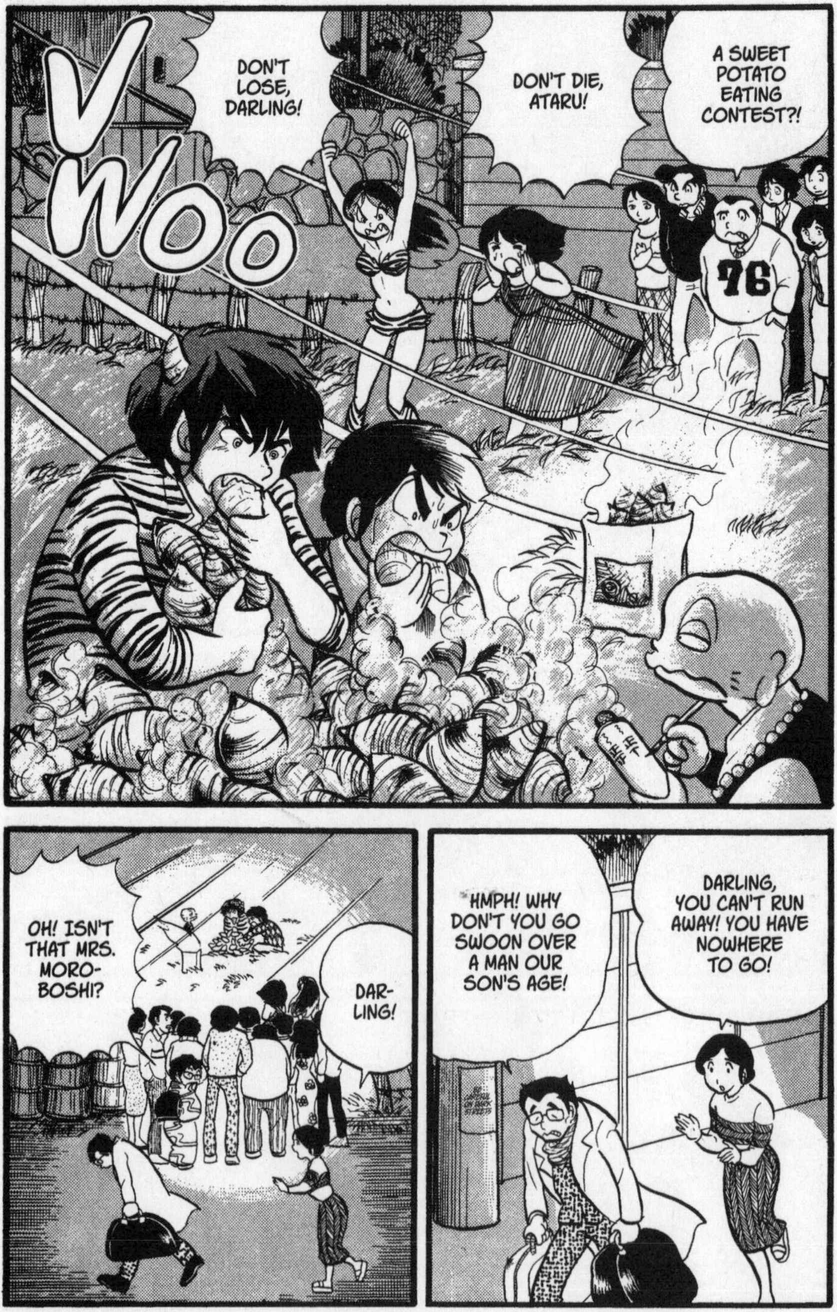
A SWEET POTATO EATING CONTEST?!
DON'T DIE, ATARU!
DON'T LOSE, DARLING!
VWOO
DARLING, YOU CAN'T RUN AWAY! YOU HAVE NOWHERE TO GO!
HMPH! WHY DON'T YOU GO SWOON OVER A MAN OUR SON'S AGE!
DAR-LING!
OH! ISN'T THAT MRS. MORO-BOSHI?

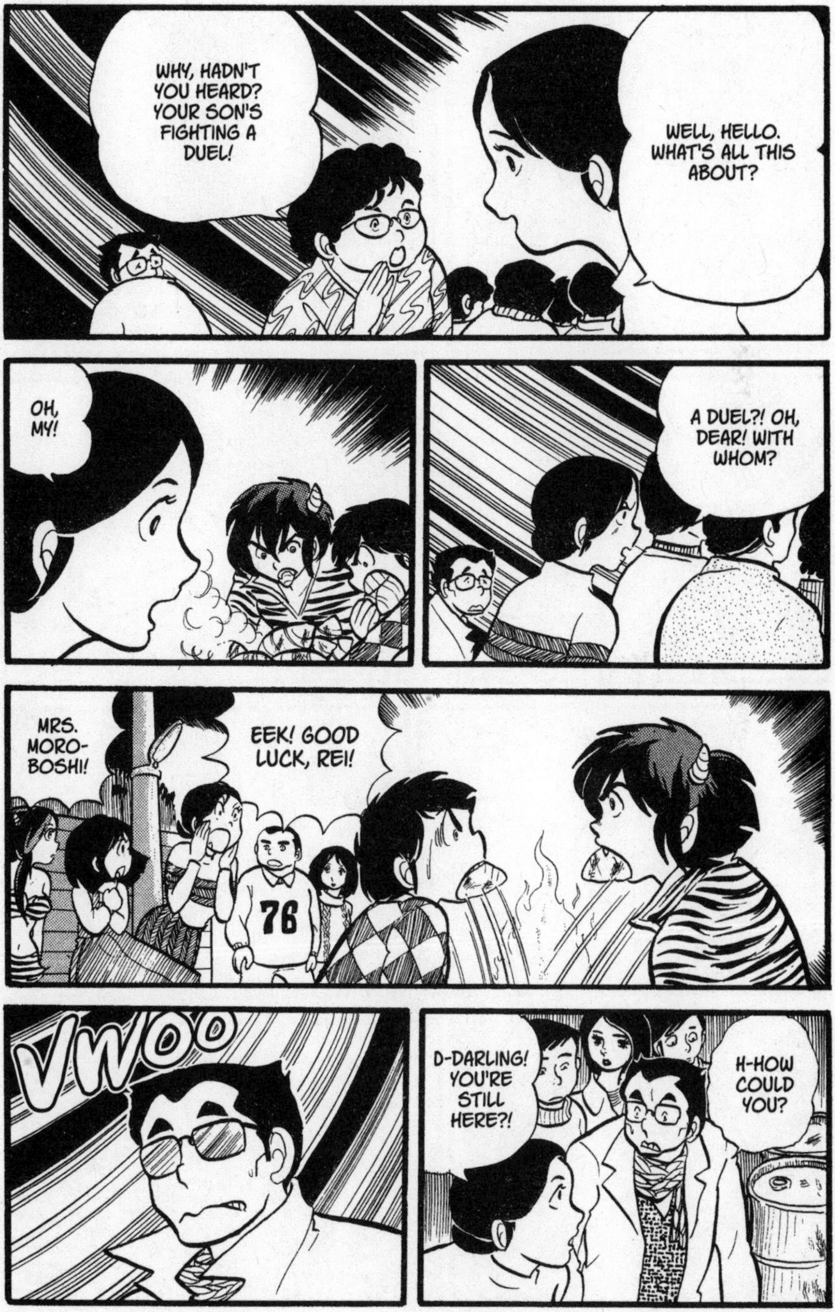
WELL, HELLO. WHAT'S ALL THIS ABOUT?
WHY, HADN'T YOU HEARD? YOUR SON'S FIGHTING A DUEL!
A DUEL?! OH, DEAR! WITH WHOM?
OH, MY!
EEK! GOOD LUCK, REI!
MRS. MORO-BOSHI!
H-HOW COULD YOU?
D-DARLING! YOU'RE STILL HERE?!
VWOO

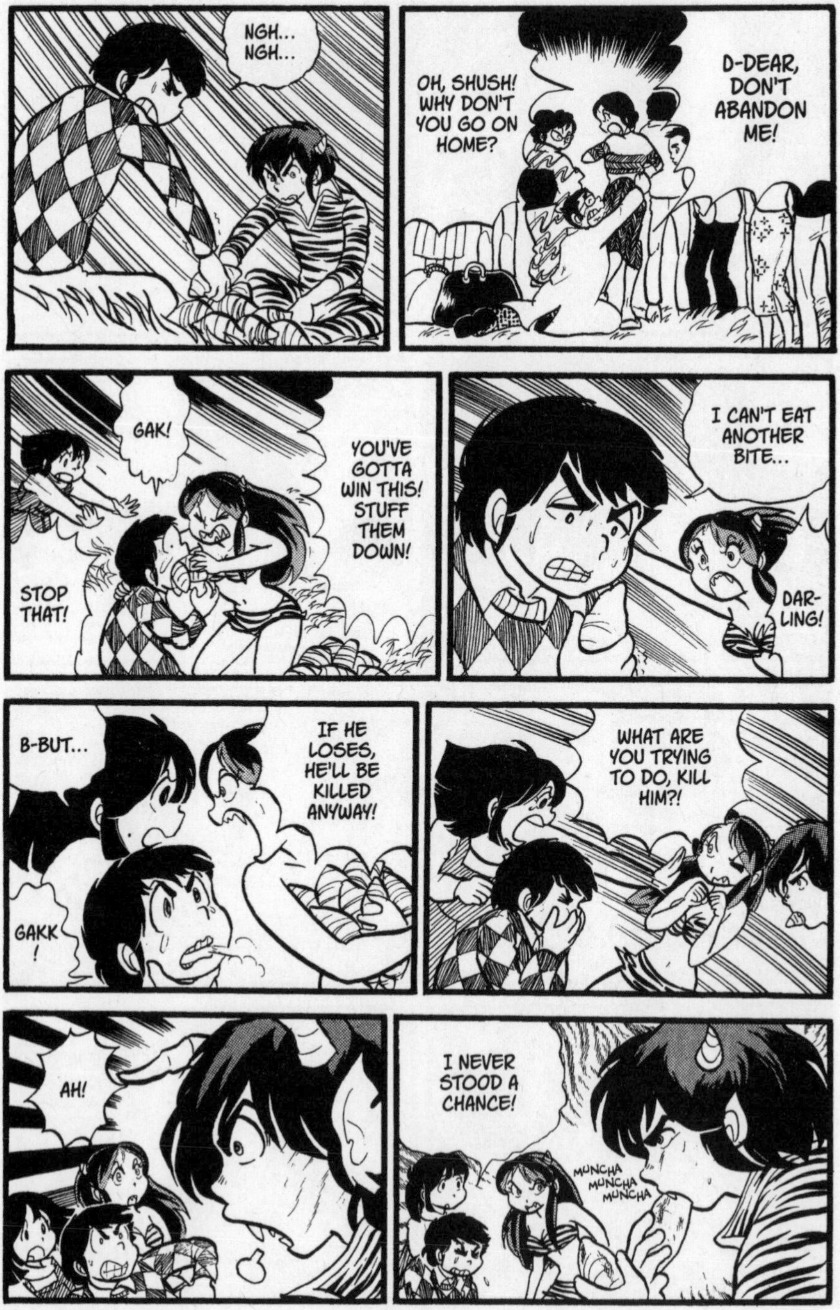
D-DEAR, DON'T ABANDON ME!
OH, SHUSH! WHY DON'T YOU GO ON HOME?
NGH... NGH...
I CAN'T EAT ANOTHER BITE...
DAR-LING!
YOU'VE GOTTA WIN THIS! STUFF THEM DOWN!
GAK!
STOP THAT!
WHAT ARE YOU TRYING TO DO, KILL HIM?!
IF HE LOSES, HE'LL BE KILLED ANYWAY!
B-BUT...
GAKK!
I NEVER STOOD A CHANCE!
MUNCHA MUNCHA MUNCHA
AH!

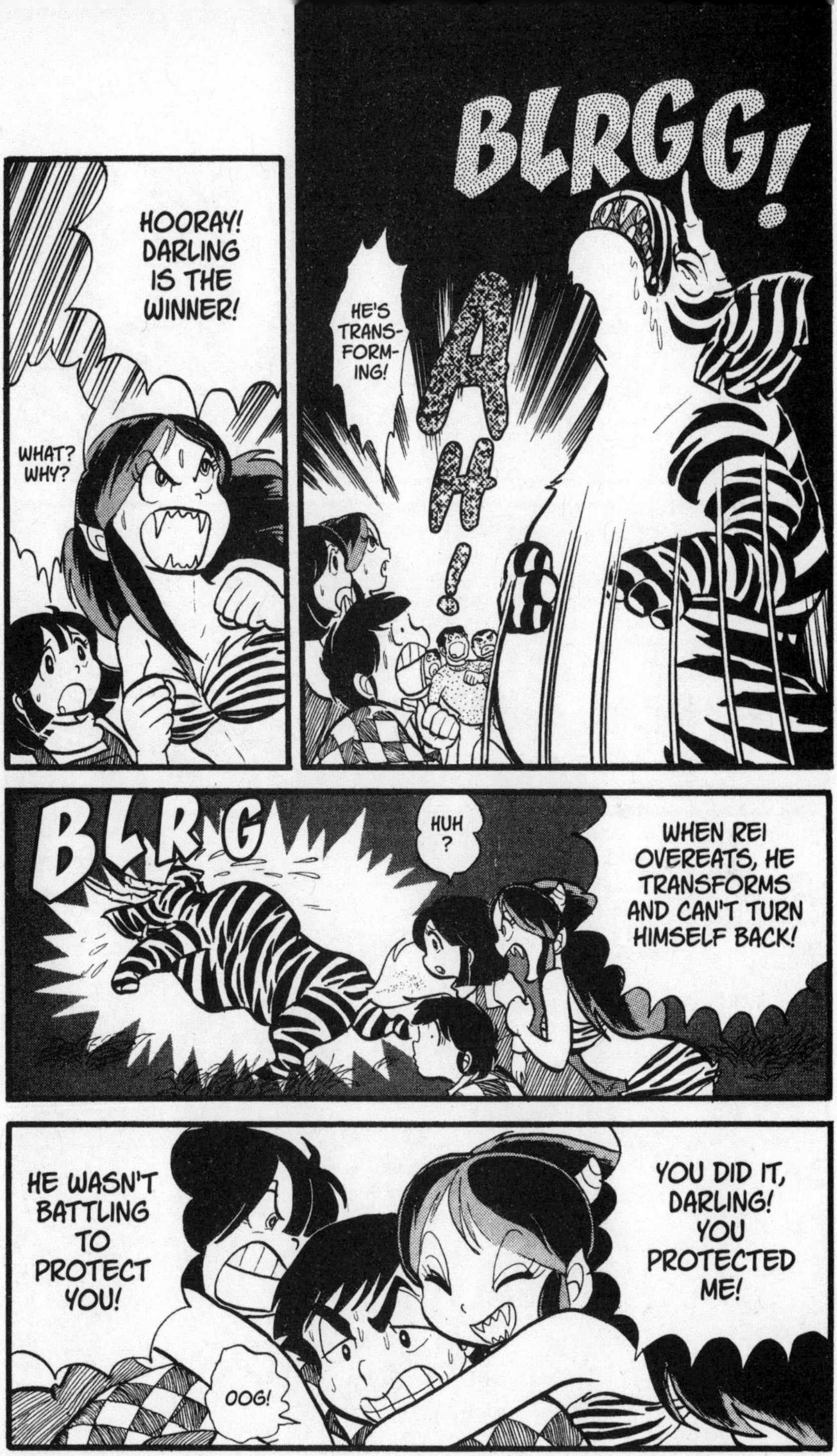
BLRGG!
HE'S TRANS-FORM-ING!
AH!
HOORAY! DARLING IS THE WINNER!
WHAT? WHY?
WHEN REI OVEREATS, HE TRANSFORMS AND CAN'T TURN HIMSELF BACK!
HUH?
BLRG
YOU DID IT, DARLING! YOU PROTECTED ME!
HE WASN'T BATTLING TO PROTECT YOU!
OOG!

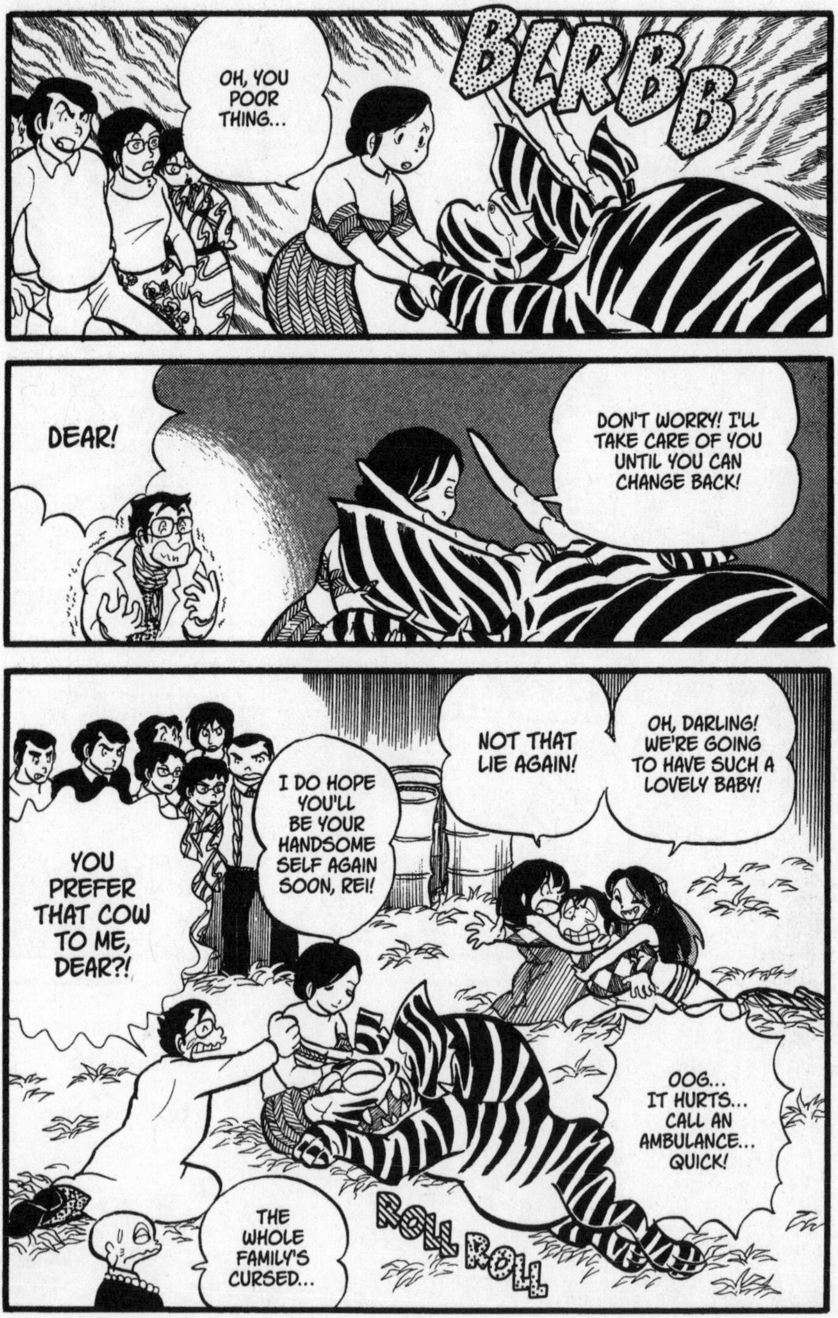
BLRBB
OH, YOU POOR THING...
DON'T WORRY! I'LL TAKE CARE OF YOU UNTIL YOU CAN CHANGE BACK!
DEAR!
OH, DARLING! WE'RE GOING TO HAVE SUCH A LOVELY BABY!
NOT THAT LIE AGAIN!
I DO HOPE YOU'LL BE YOUR HANDSOME SELF AGAIN SOON, REI!
YOU PREFER THAT COW TO ME, DEAR?!
OOG... IT HURTS... CALL AN AMBULANCE... QUICK!
ROLL ROLL
THE WHOLE FAMILY'S CURSED...

CHAPTER 7:
A CONTEMPTIBLE
GOOD-FOR-NOTHING

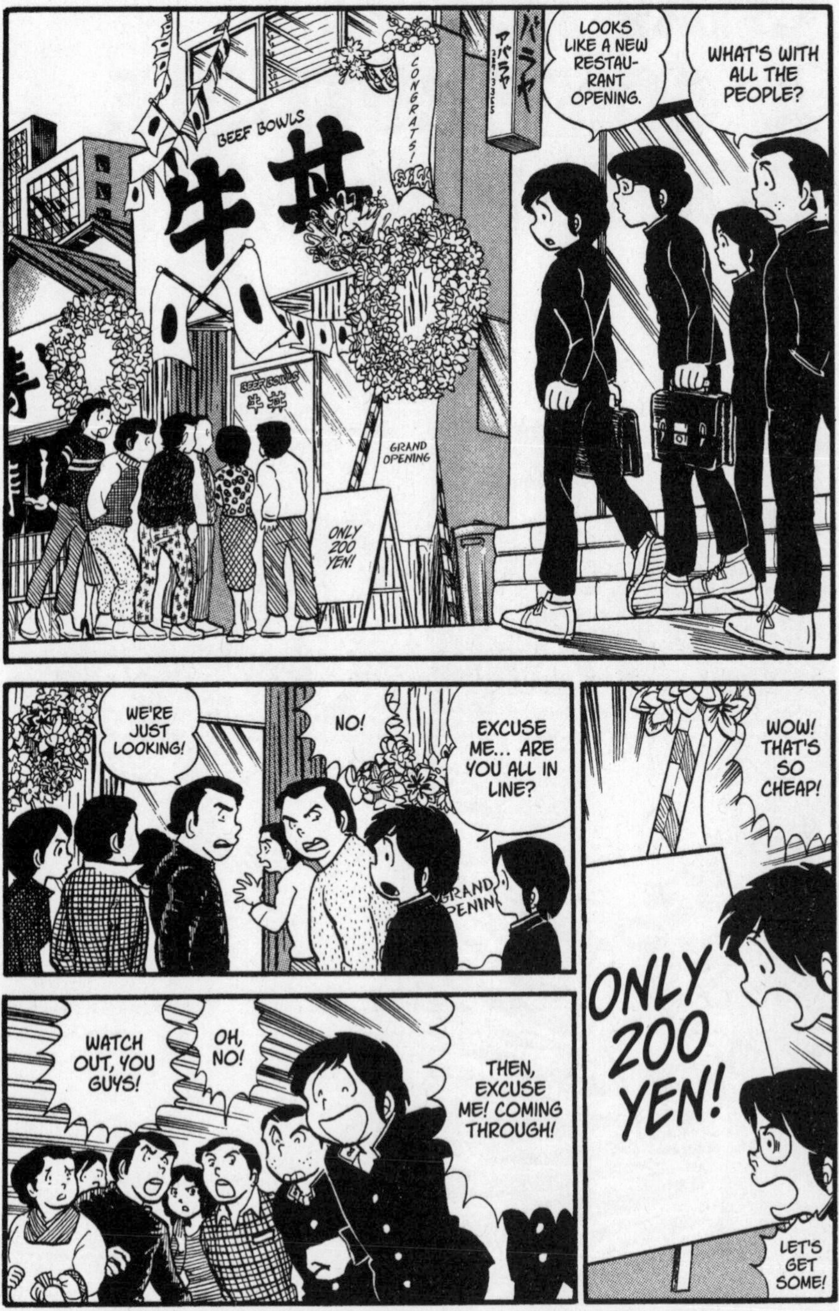
WHAT'S WITH ALL THE PEOPLE?
LOOKS LIKE A NEW RESTAU-RANT OPENING.
バラヤ
CONGRATS!
BEEF BOWLS
牛丼
BEEF BOWLS
牛丼
GRAND OPENING
ONLY 200 YEN!
WOW! THAT'S SO CHEAP!
ONLY 200 YEN!
LET'S GET SOME!
EXCUSE ME... ARE YOU ALL IN LINE?
NO!
WE'RE JUST LOOKING!
GRAND OPENIN
THEN, EXCUSE ME! COMING THROUGH!
OH, NO!
WATCH OUT, YOU GUYS!

*200 YEN = ABOUT $2

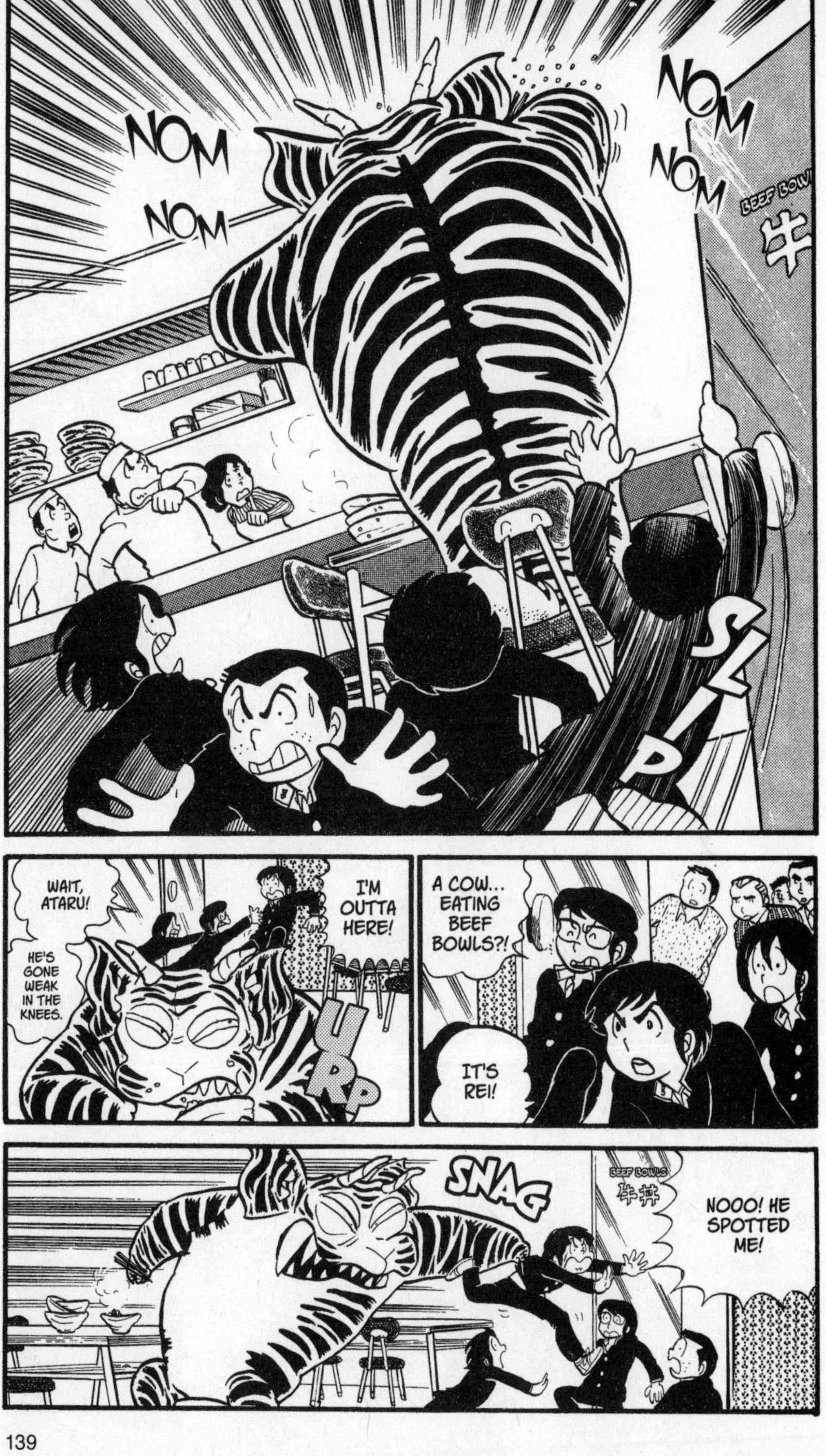
NOM
NOM
NOM
BEEF BOWL
牛
NOM
NOM
SLIP
A COW... EATING BEEF BOWLS?!
IT'S REI!
I'M OUTTA HERE!
WAIT, ATARU!
HE'S GONE WEAK IN THE KNEES.
URP
NOOO! HE SPOTTED ME!
BEEF BOWLS
牛丼
SNAG

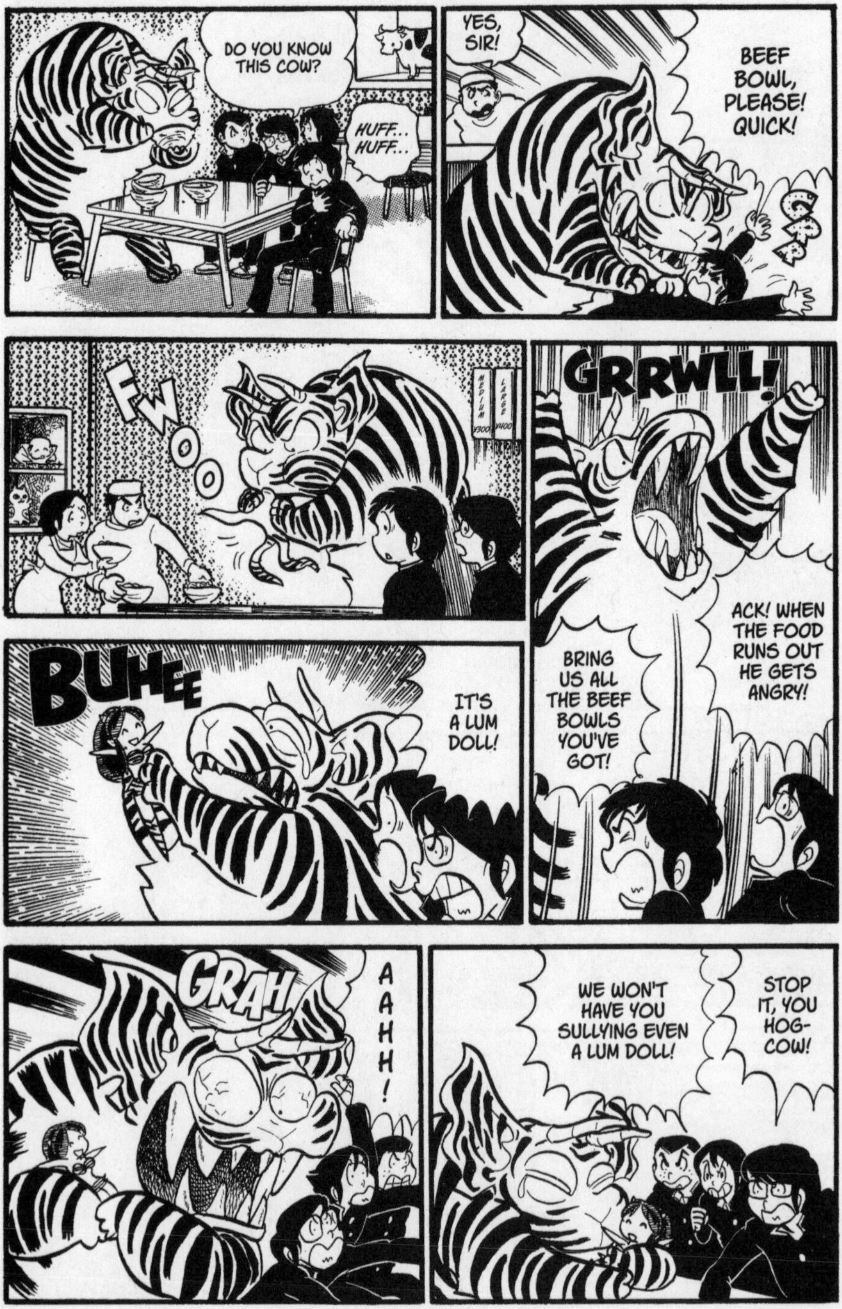
BEEF BOWL, PLEASE! QUICK!
YES, SIR!
GRRR
DO YOU KNOW THIS COW?
HUFF... HUFF...
GRRWLL!
ACK! WHEN THE FOOD RUNS OUT HE GETS ANGRY!
BRING US ALL THE BEEF BOWLS YOU'VE GOT!
MEDIUM ¥300
LARGE ¥400
FWOOO
IT'S A LUM DOLL!
BUHEE
STOP IT, YOU HOG-COW!
WE WON'T HAVE YOU SULLYING EVEN A LUM DOLL!
AAHH!
GRAH

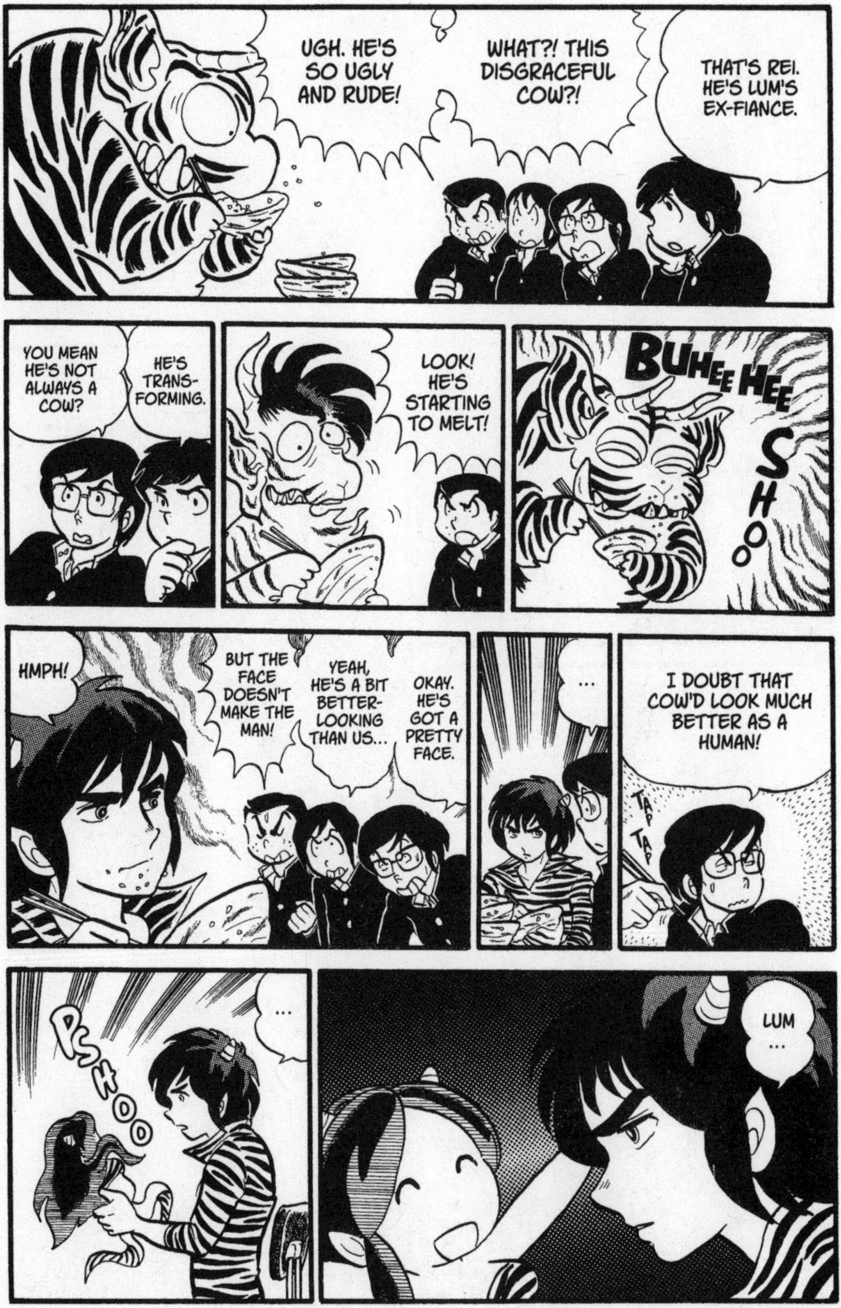

THAT'S REI. HE'S LUM'S EX-FIANCE.
WHAT?! THIS DISGRACEFUL COW?!
UGH. HE'S SO UGLY AND RUDE!
BUHEE HEE
SHOO
LOOK! HE'S STARTING TO MELT!
HE'S TRANS-FORMING.
YOU MEAN HE'S NOT ALWAYS A COW?
I DOUBT THAT COW'D LOOK MUCH BETTER AS A HUMAN!
TAP TAP
...
OKAY. HE'S GOT A PRETTY FACE.
YEAH, HE'S A BIT BETTER-LOOKING THAN US...
BUT THE FACE DOESN'T MAKE THE MAN!
HMPH!
LUM ...
...
PSHOO

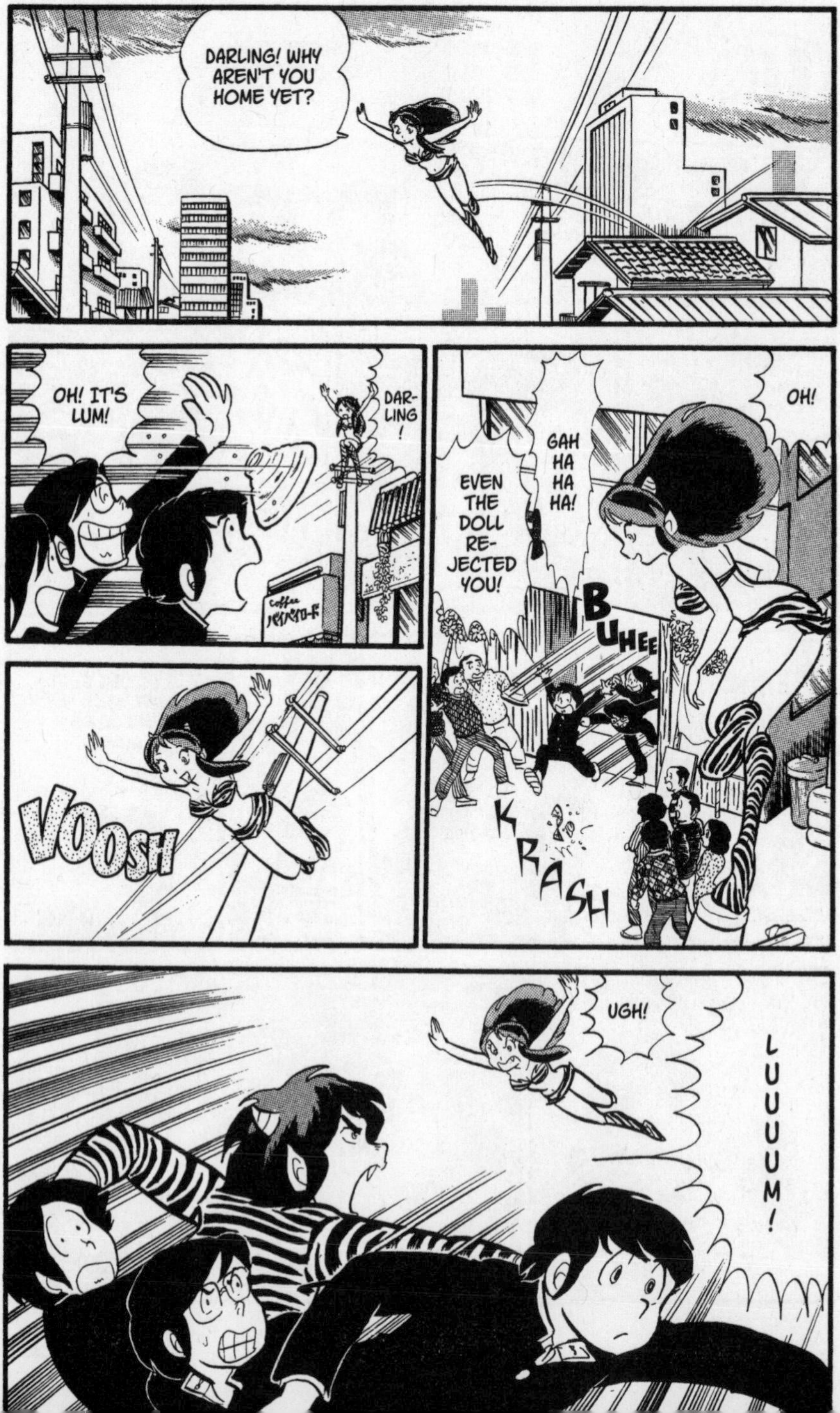
DARLING! WHY AREN'T YOU HOME YET?
OH!
GAH HA HA HA!
EVEN THE DOLL RE-JECTED YOU!
BUHEE
KRASH
DAR-LING!
OH! IT'S LUM!
VOOSH
LUUUUUM!
UGH!

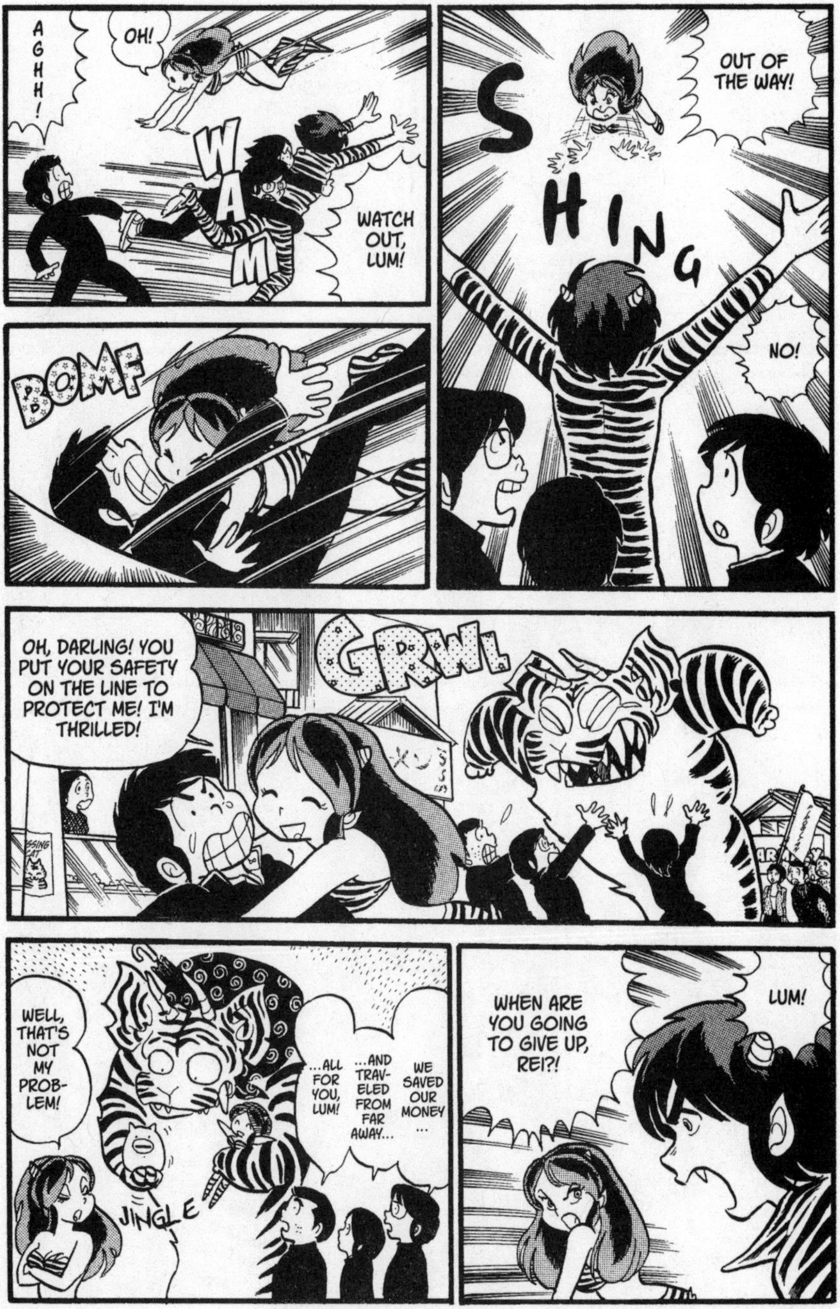
OUT OF THE WAY!
SHING
NO!
OH!
AGHH!
WAM
WATCH OUT, LUM!
DOMF
GRWL
OH, DARLING! YOU PUT YOUR SAFETY ON THE LINE TO PROTECT ME! I'M THRILLED!
LUM!
WHEN ARE YOU GOING TO GIVE UP, REI?!
WE SAVED OUR MONEY...
...AND TRAVELED FROM FAR AWAY...
...ALL FOR YOU, LUM!
WELL, THAT'S NOT MY PROBLEM!
JINGLE

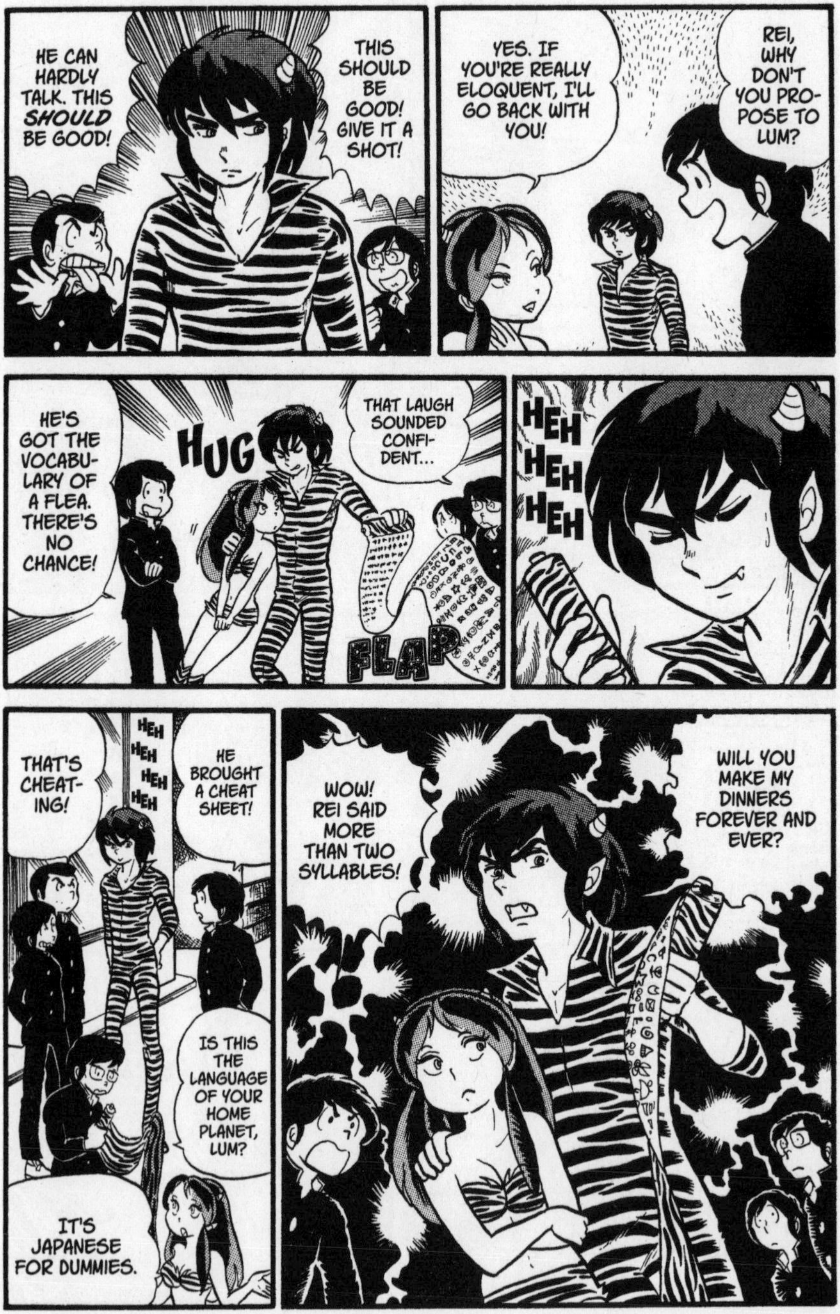
REI, WHY DON'T YOU PROPOSE TO LUM?
YES. IF YOU'RE REALLY ELOQUENT, I'LL GO BACK WITH YOU!
THIS SHOULD BE GOOD! GIVE IT A SHOT!
HE CAN HARDLY TALK. THIS *SHOULD* BE GOOD!
HEH HEH HEH
THAT LAUGH SOUNDED CONFIDENT...
HUG
FLAP
HE'S GOT THE VOCABULARY OF A FLEA. THERE'S NO CHANCE!
WILL YOU MAKE MY DINNERS FOREVER AND EVER?
WOW! REI SAID MORE THAN TWO SYLLABLES!
HE BROUGHT A CHEAT SHEET!
HEH HEH HEH HEH
THAT'S CHEATING!
IS THIS THE LANGUAGE OF YOUR HOME PLANET, LUM?
IT'S JAPANESE FOR DUMMIES.

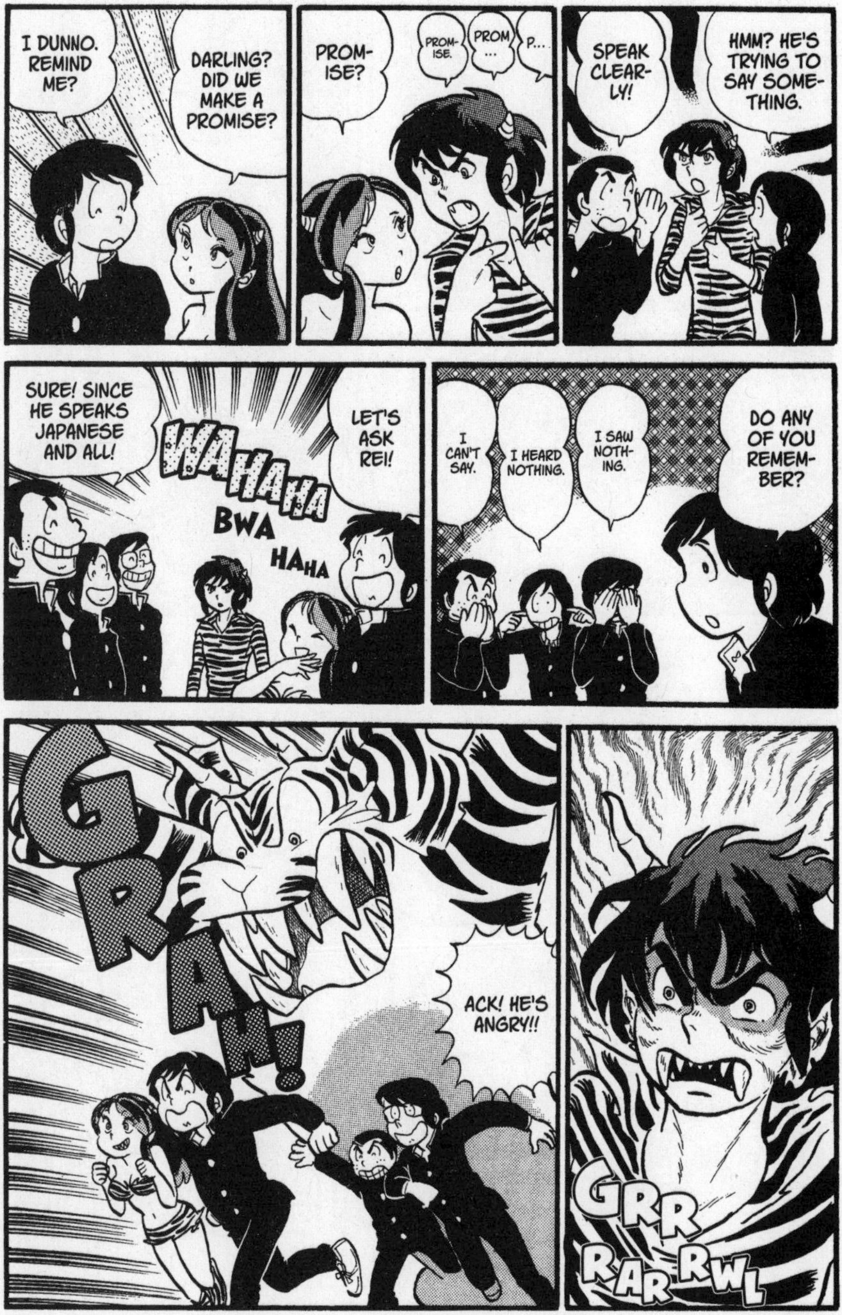
HMM? HE'S TRYING TO SAY SOMETHING.
SPEAK CLEARLY!
P...
PROM ...
PROMISE.
PROMISE?
DARLING? DID WE MAKE A PROMISE?
I DUNNO. REMIND ME?
DO ANY OF YOU REMEMBER?
I SAW NOTHING.
I HEARD NOTHING.
I CAN'T SAY.
LET'S ASK REI!
WAHAHA
BWA HAHA
SURE! SINCE HE SPEAKS JAPANESE AND ALL!
GRRRARRWL
GRAH!
ACK! HE'S ANGRY!!

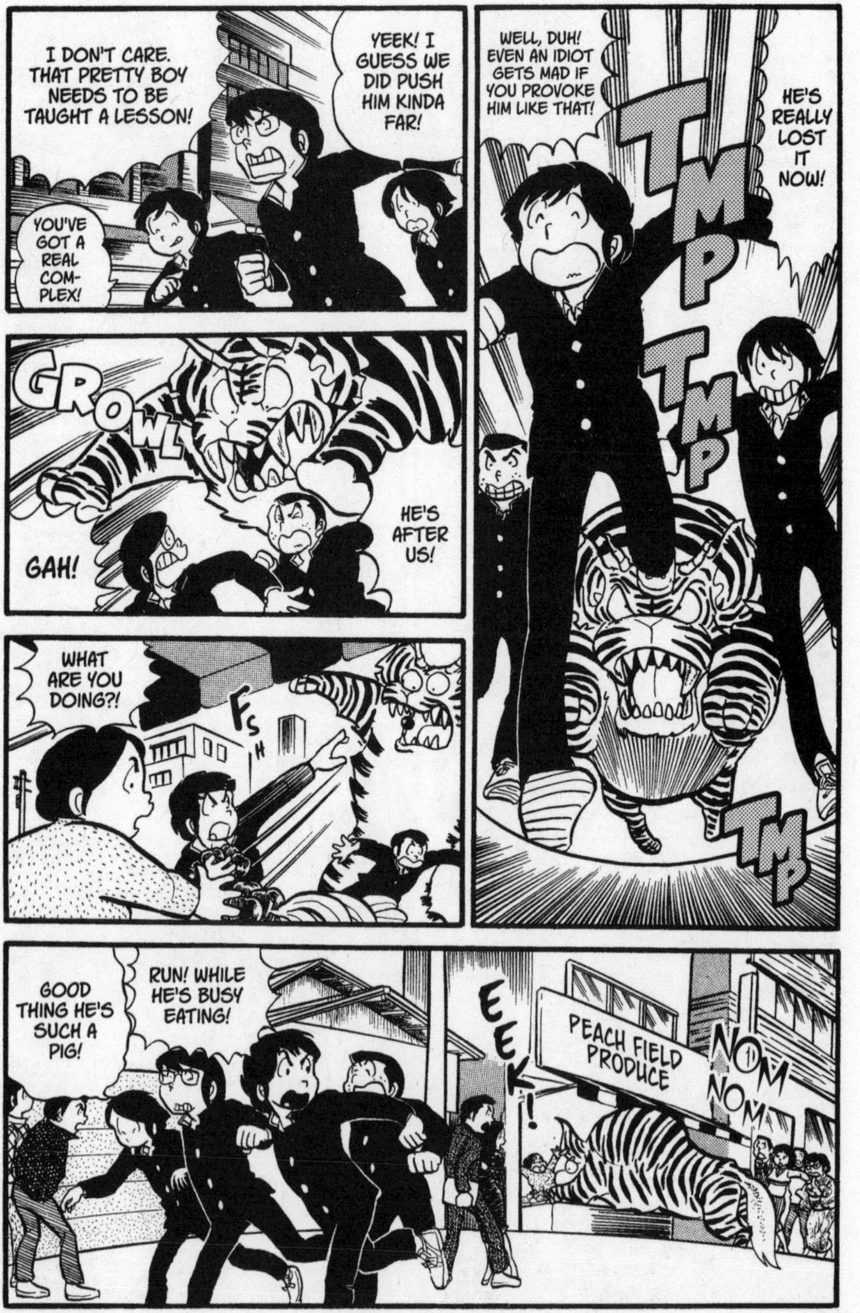
HE'S REALLY LOST IT NOW!
WELL, DUH! EVEN AN IDIOT GETS MAD IF YOU PROVOKE HIM LIKE THAT!
TMP TMP TMP TMP
YEEK! I GUESS WE DID PUSH HIM KINDA FAR!
I DON'T CARE. THAT PRETTY BOY NEEDS TO BE TAUGHT A LESSON!
YOU'VE GOT A REAL COM-PLEX!
GROWL
HE'S AFTER US!
GAH!
WHAT ARE YOU DOING?!
FSH
NOM NOM
PEACH FIELD PRODUCE
EEEK!
RUN! WHILE HE'S BUSY EATING!
GOOD THING HE'S SUCH A PIG!

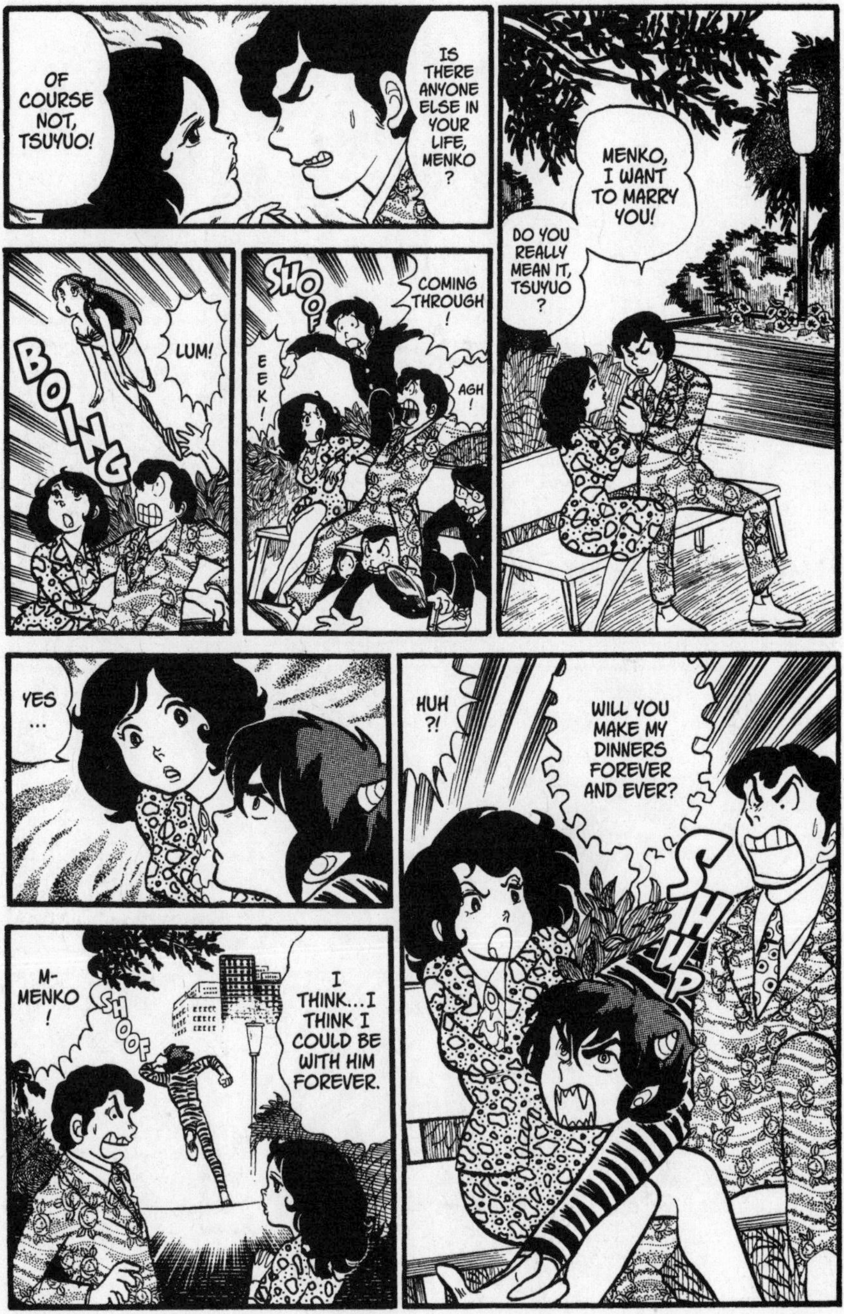
MENKO, I WANT TO MARRY YOU!
DO YOU REALLY MEAN IT, TSUYUO?
IS THERE ANYONE ELSE IN YOUR LIFE, MENKO?
OF COURSE NOT, TSUYUO!
COMING THROUGH!
SHOOF
AGH!
EEK!
LUM!
BOING
WILL YOU MAKE MY DINNERS FOREVER AND EVER?
HUH?!
SHUP
YES...
I THINK...I THINK I COULD BE WITH HIM FOREVER.
M-MENKO!
SHOOF

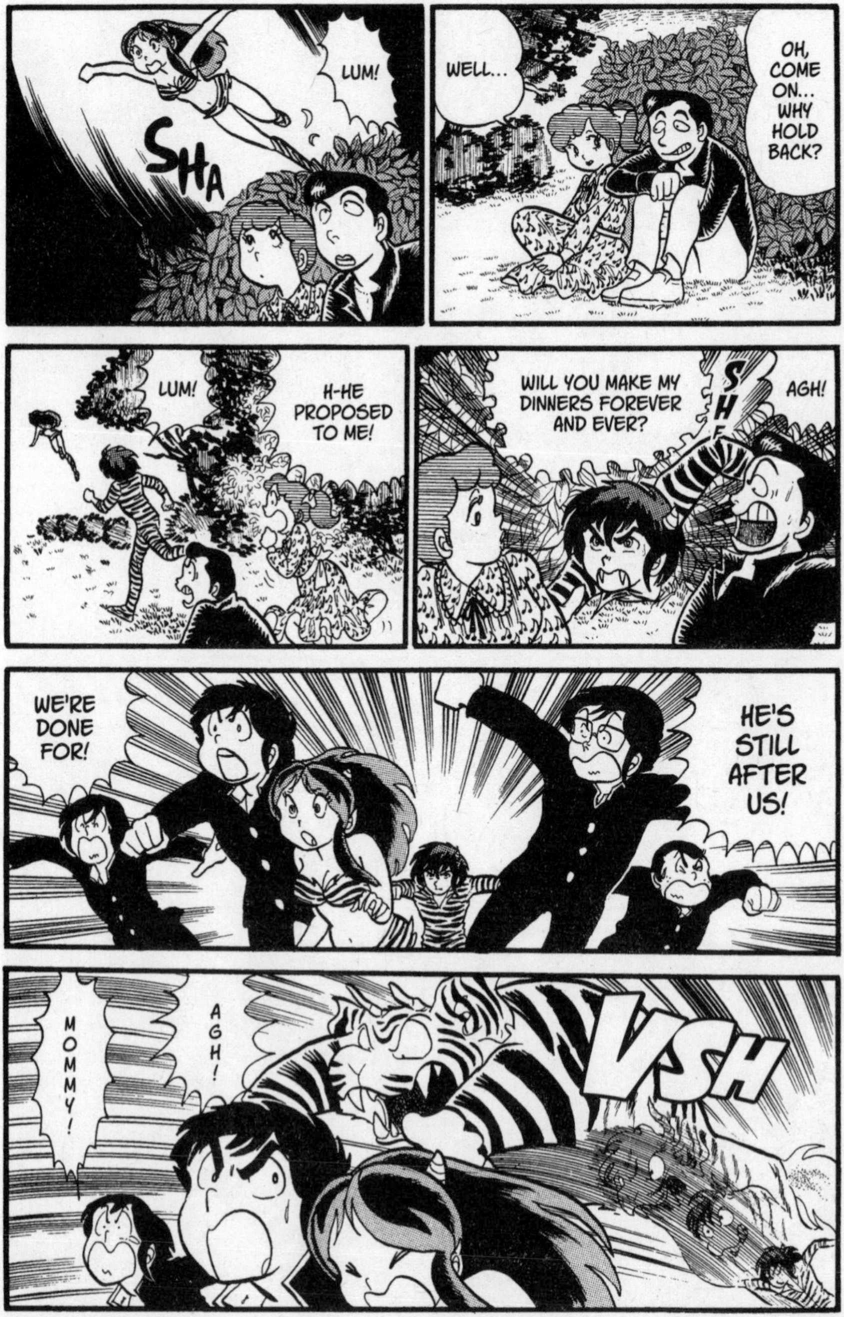
OH, COME ON... WHY HOLD BACK?
WELL...
LUM!
SHA
AGH!
SHF
WILL YOU MAKE MY DINNERS FOREVER AND EVER?
H-HE PROPOSED TO ME!
LUM!
HE'S STILL AFTER US!
WE'RE DONE FOR!
VSH
AGH!
MOMMY!

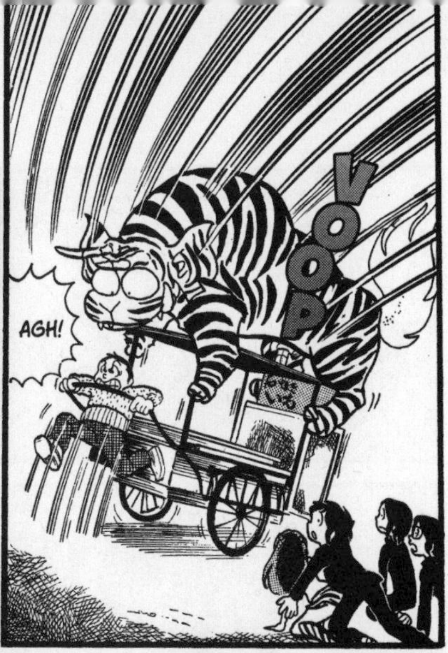
VOOP
AGH!

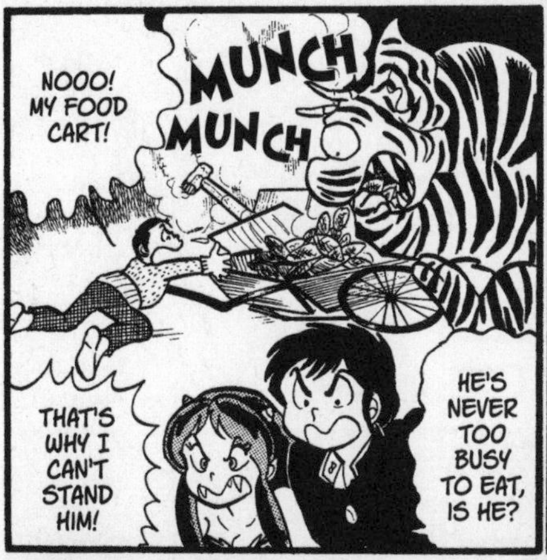
MUNCH
MUNCH
NOOO! MY FOOD CART!
HE'S NEVER TOO BUSY TO EAT, IS HE?
THAT'S WHY I CAN'T STAND HIM!

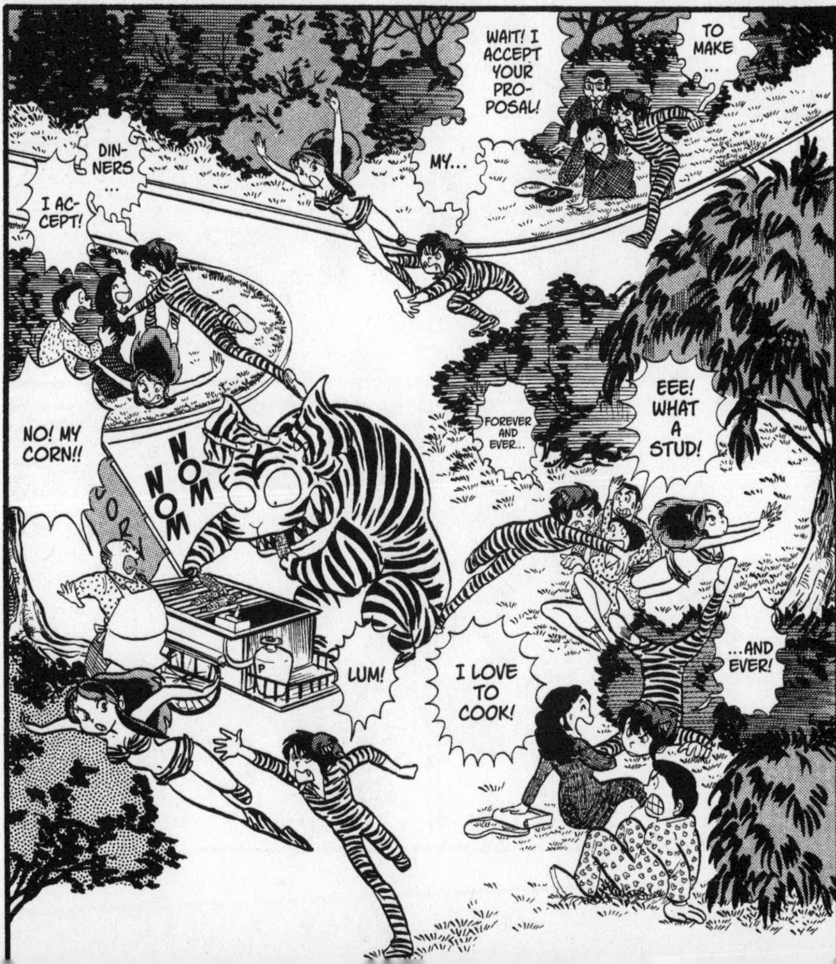
TO MAKE ...
WAIT! I ACCEPT YOUR PROPOSAL!
MY...
DINNERS ...
I ACCEPT!
EEE! WHAT A STUD!
FOREVER AND EVER...
NOM NOM NOM
NO! MY CORN!!
...AND EVER!
I LOVE TO COOK!
LUM!

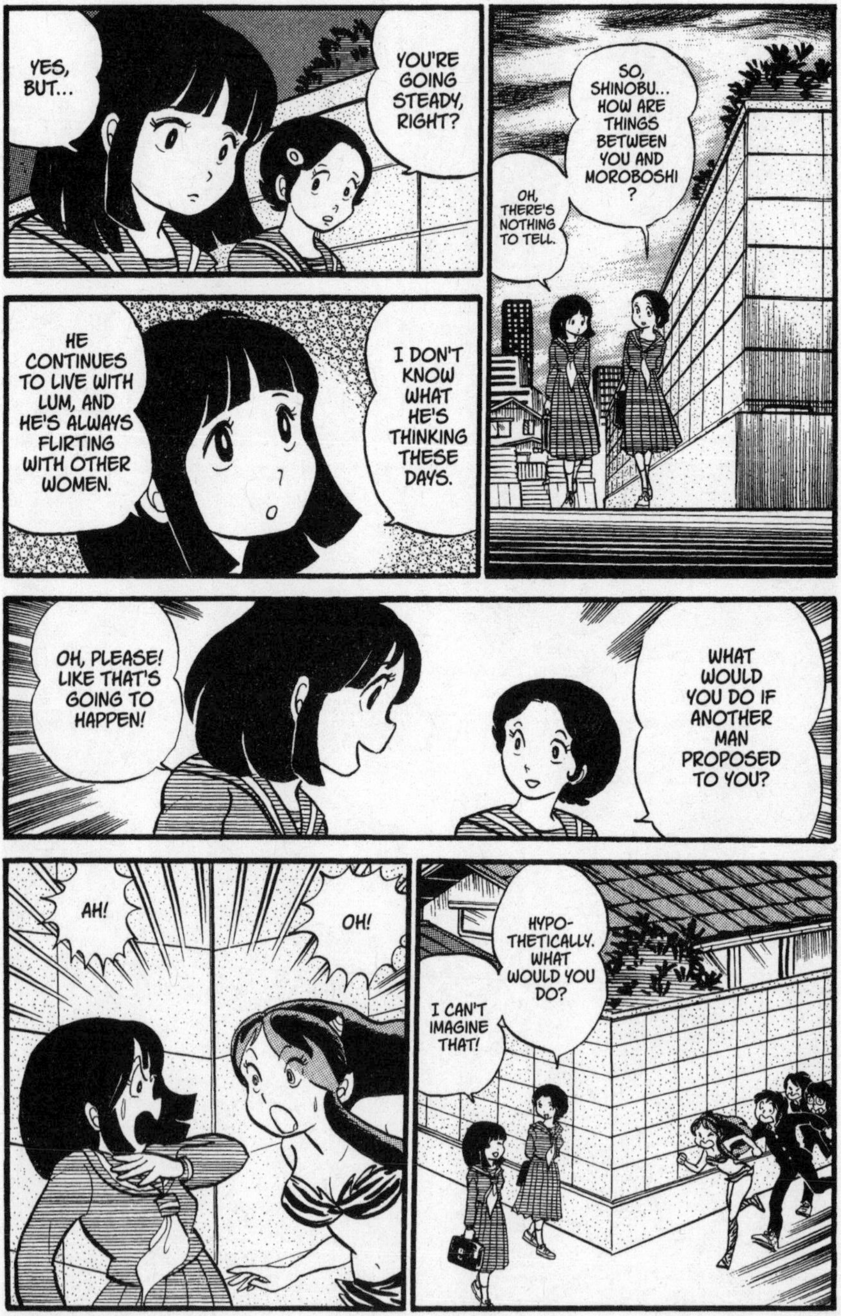
SO, SHINOBU... HOW ARE THINGS BETWEEN YOU AND MOROBOSHI?
OH, THERE'S NOTHING TO TELL.
YOU'RE GOING STEADY, RIGHT?
YES, BUT...
I DON'T KNOW WHAT HE'S THINKING THESE DAYS.
HE CONTINUES TO LIVE WITH LUM, AND HE'S ALWAYS FLIRTING WITH OTHER WOMEN.
WHAT WOULD YOU DO IF ANOTHER MAN PROPOSED TO YOU?
OH, PLEASE! LIKE THAT'S GOING TO HAPPEN!
HYPO-THETICALLY. WHAT WOULD YOU DO?
I CAN'T IMAGINE THAT!
OH!
AH!

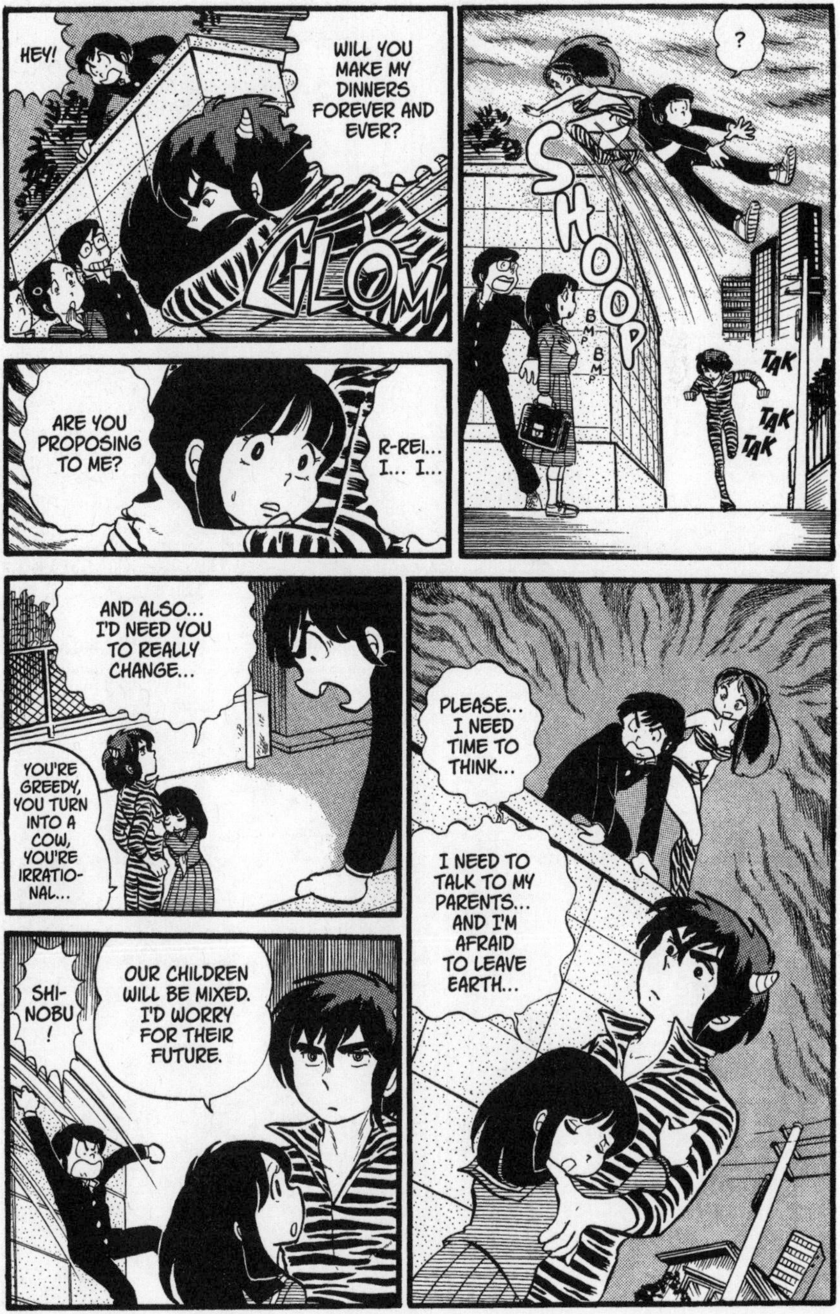
?
SHOOP
BMP BMP
TAK
TAK
TAK
WILL YOU MAKE MY DINNERS FOREVER AND EVER?
HEY!
GLOM
R-REI... I... I...
ARE YOU PROPOSING TO ME?
PLEASE... I NEED TIME TO THINK...
I NEED TO TALK TO MY PARENTS... AND I'M AFRAID TO LEAVE EARTH...
AND ALSO... I'D NEED YOU TO REALLY CHANGE...
YOU'RE GREEDY, YOU TURN INTO A COW, YOU'RE IRRATIO-NAL...
OUR CHILDREN WILL BE MIXED. I'D WORRY FOR THEIR FUTURE.
SHI-NOBU!

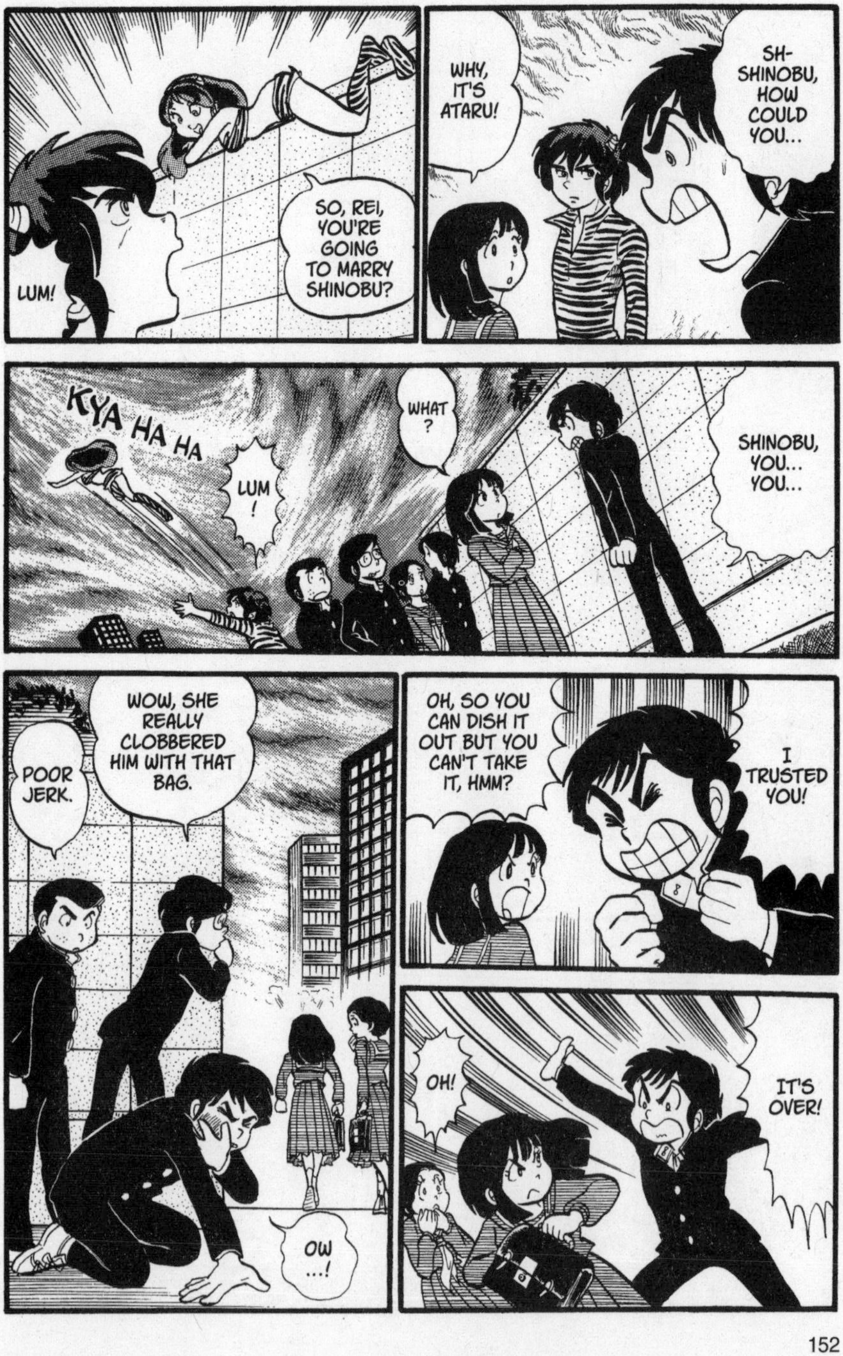
SH-SHINOBU, HOW COULD YOU...
WHY, IT'S ATARU!
SO, REI, YOU'RE GOING TO MARRY SHINOBU?
LUM!
SHINOBU, YOU... YOU...
WHAT?
LUM!
KYA HA HA
I TRUSTED YOU!
OH, SO YOU CAN DISH IT OUT BUT YOU CAN'T TAKE IT, HMM?
IT'S OVER!
OH!
WOW, SHE REALLY CLOBBERED HIM WITH THAT BAG.
POOR JERK.
OW...!

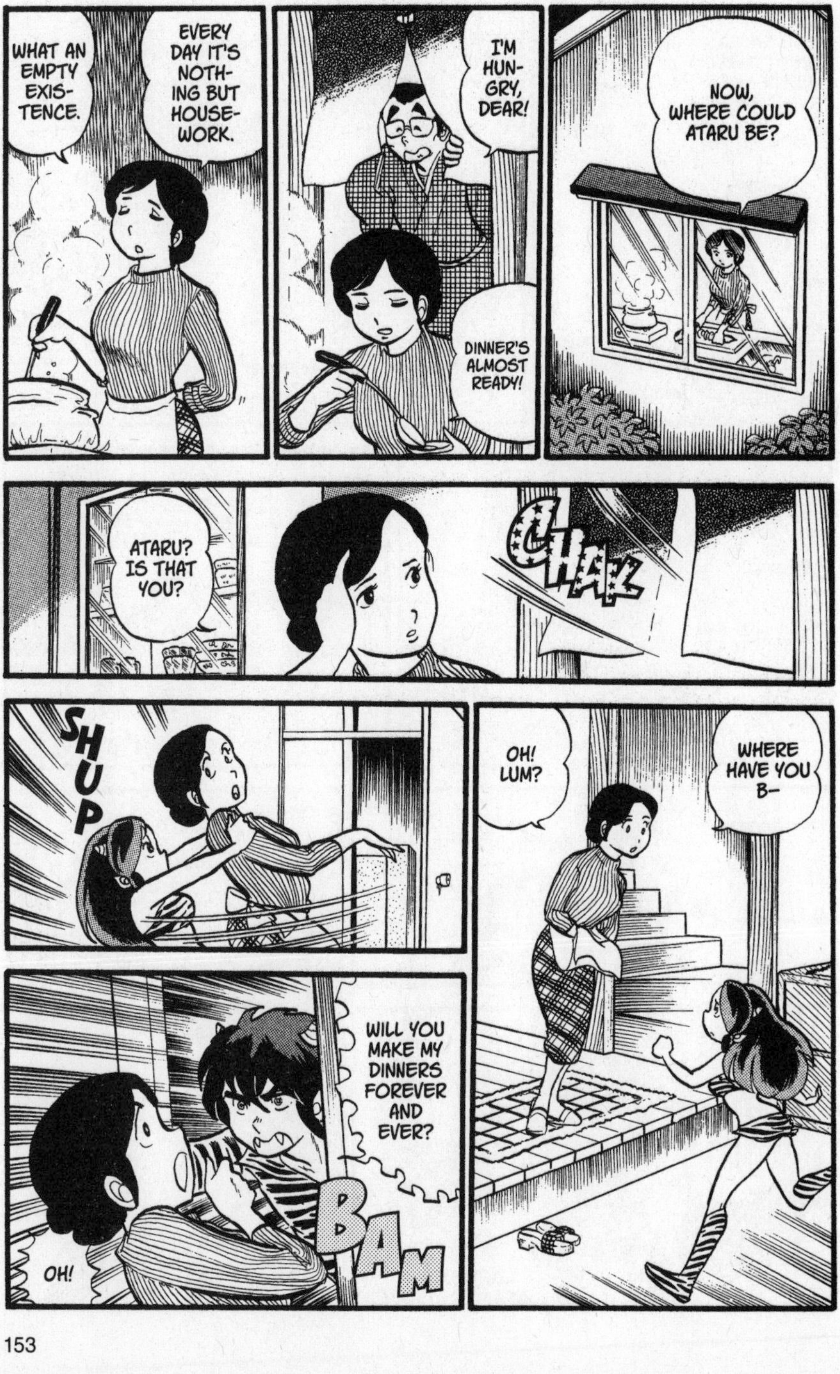
NOW, WHERE COULD ATARU BE?
I'M HUN-GRY, DEAR!
DINNER'S ALMOST READY!
EVERY DAY IT'S NOTH-ING BUT HOUSE-WORK.
WHAT AN EMPTY EXIS-TENCE.
CHAK
ATARU? IS THAT YOU?
WHERE HAVE YOU B—
OH! LUM?
SHUP
WILL YOU MAKE MY DINNERS FOREVER AND EVER?
BAM
OH!

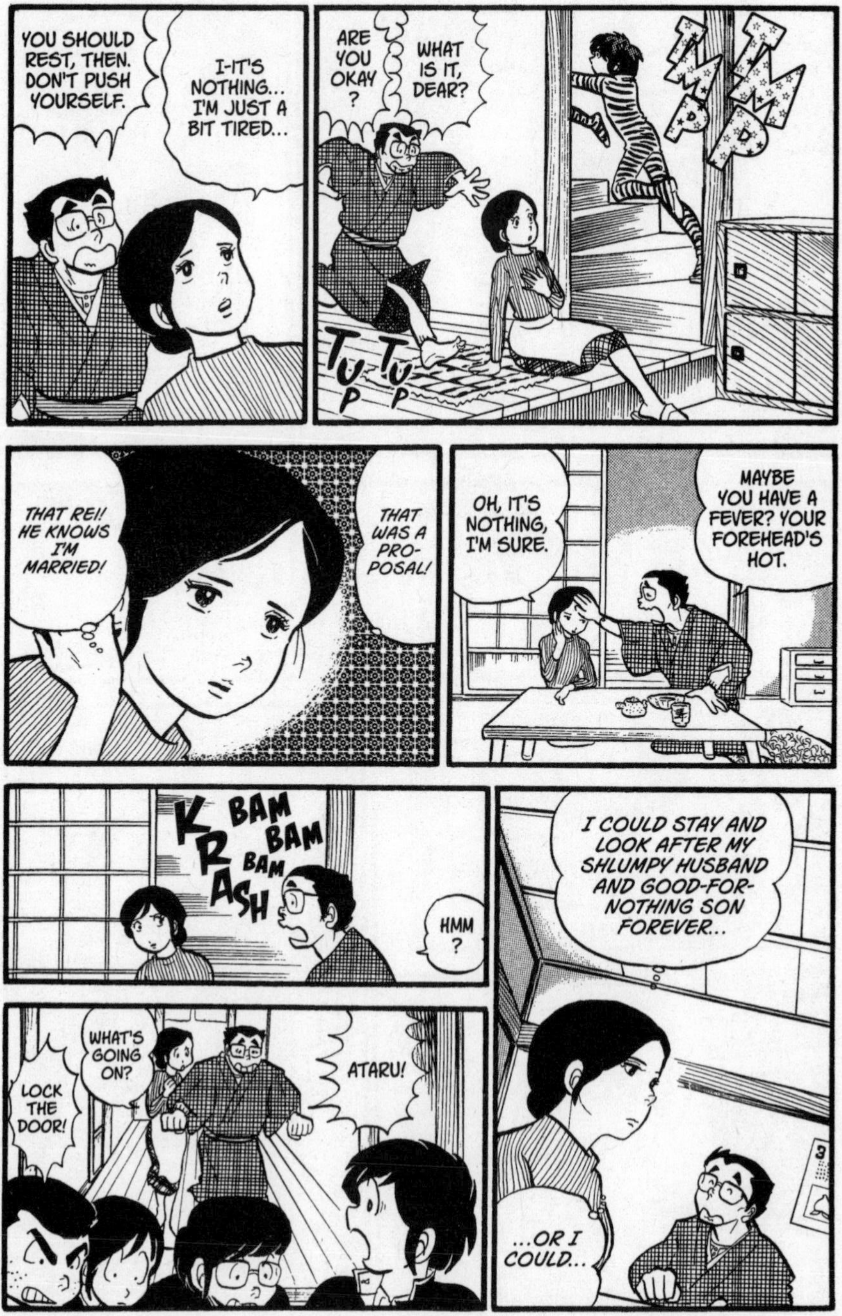
WHAT IS IT, DEAR?
ARE YOU OKAY?
TMP
TMP
TUP TUP
I-IT'S NOTHING... I'M JUST A BIT TIRED...
YOU SHOULD REST, THEN. DON'T PUSH YOURSELF.
MAYBE YOU HAVE A FEVER? YOUR FOREHEAD'S HOT.
OH, IT'S NOTHING, I'M SURE.
THAT WAS A PRO-POSAL!
THAT REI! HE KNOWS I'M MARRIED!
I COULD STAY AND LOOK AFTER MY SHLUMPY HUSBAND AND GOOD-FOR-NOTHING SON FOREVER...
...OR I COULD...
HMM ?
KRASH
BAM BAM BAM
ATARU!
WHAT'S GOING ON?
LOCK THE DOOR!

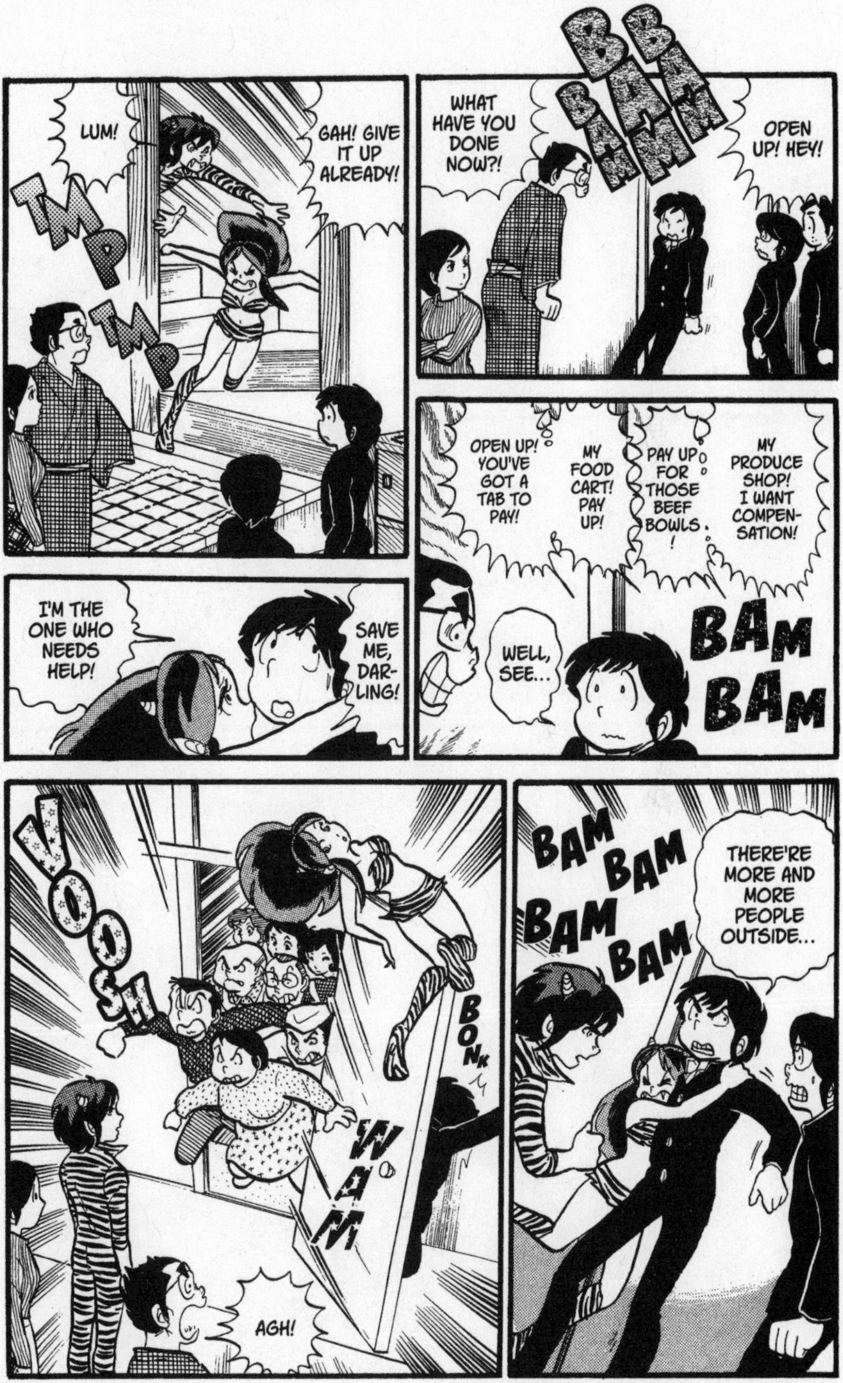
BBBAAAMMMM
OPEN UP! HEY!
WHAT HAVE YOU DONE NOW?!
GAH! GIVE IT UP ALREADY!
LUM!
TMP TMP
MY PRODUCE SHOP! I WANT COMPEN-SATION!
PAY UP FOR THOSE BEEF BOWLS!
MY FOOD CART! PAY UP!
OPEN UP! YOU'VE GOT A TAB TO PAY!
BAM BAM
WELL, SEE...
SAVE ME, DARLING!
I'M THE ONE WHO NEEDS HELP!
THERE'RE MORE AND MORE PEOPLE OUTSIDE...
BAM BAM BAM BAM
BONK
VOOSH
WAM
AGH!

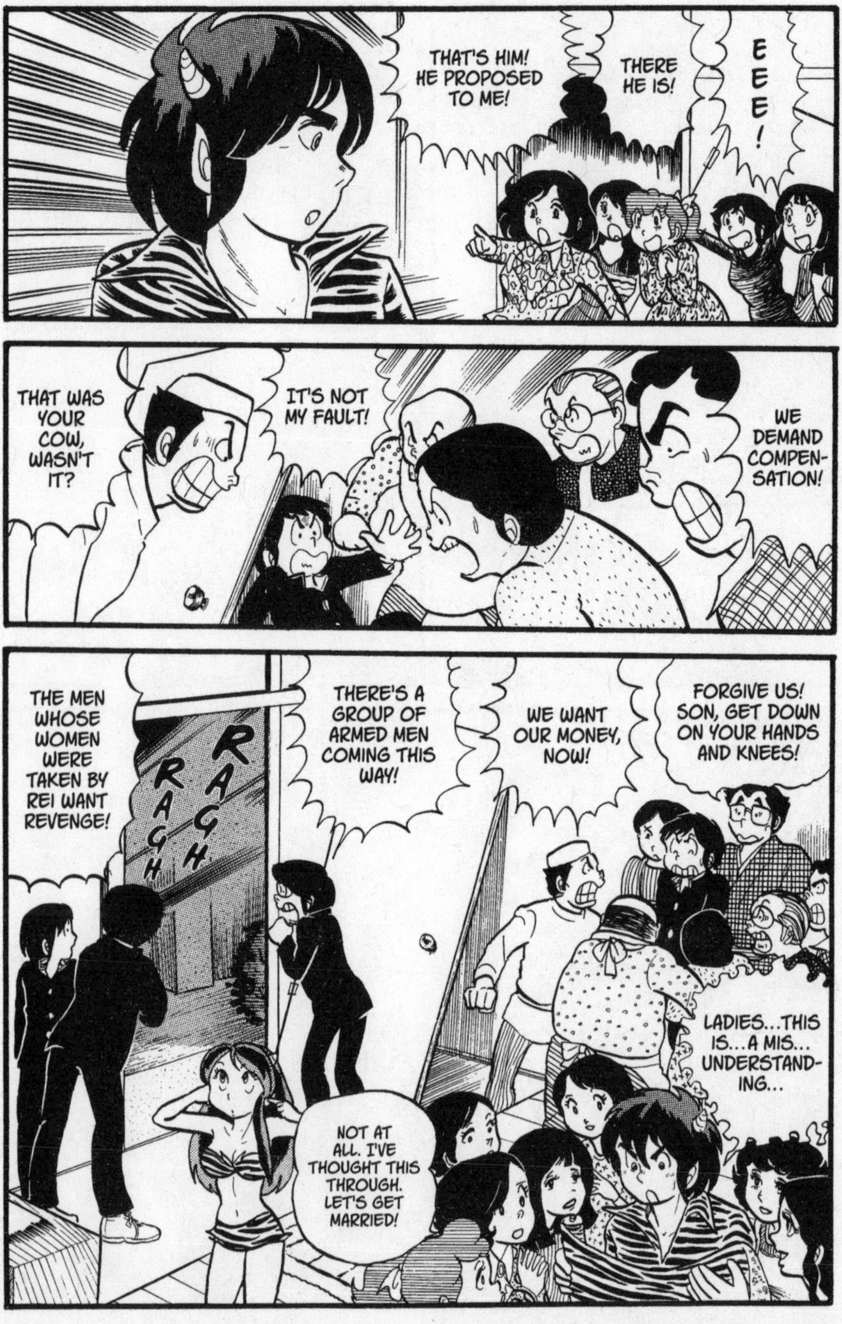
EEE!
THERE HE IS!
THAT'S HIM! HE PROPOSED TO ME!
WE DEMAND COMPENSATION!
IT'S NOT MY FAULT!
THAT WAS YOUR COW, WASN'T IT?
FORGIVE US! SON, GET DOWN ON YOUR HANDS AND KNEES!
WE WANT OUR MONEY, NOW!
THERE'S A GROUP OF ARMED MEN COMING THIS WAY!
THE MEN WHOSE WOMEN WERE TAKEN BY REI WANT REVENGE!
RAGH
RAGH
LADIES...THIS IS...A MIS...UNDERSTANDING...
NOT AT ALL. I'VE THOUGHT THIS THROUGH. LET'S GET MARRIED!

CHAPTER 8: GOOD DAY FOR A DEPARTURE

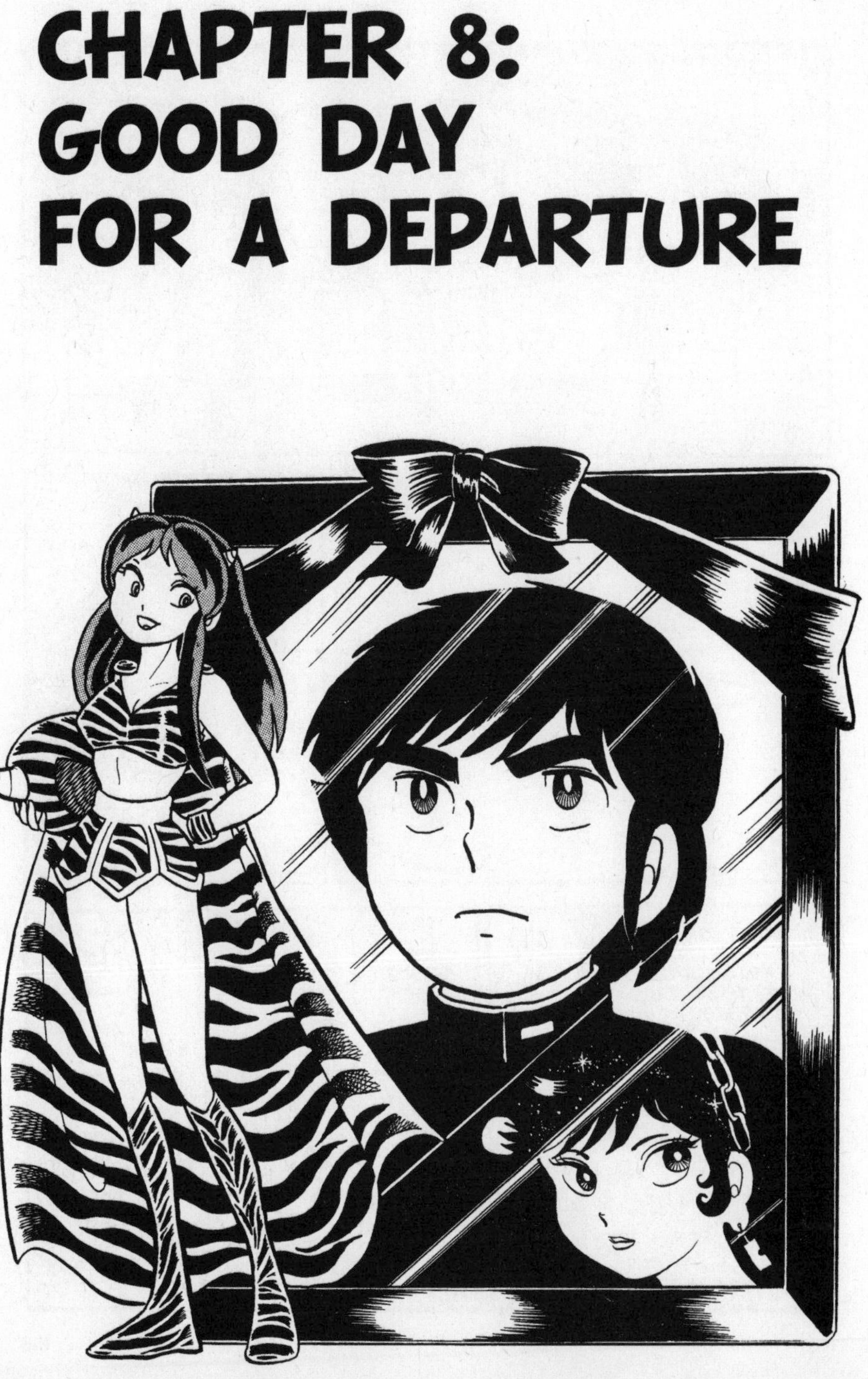

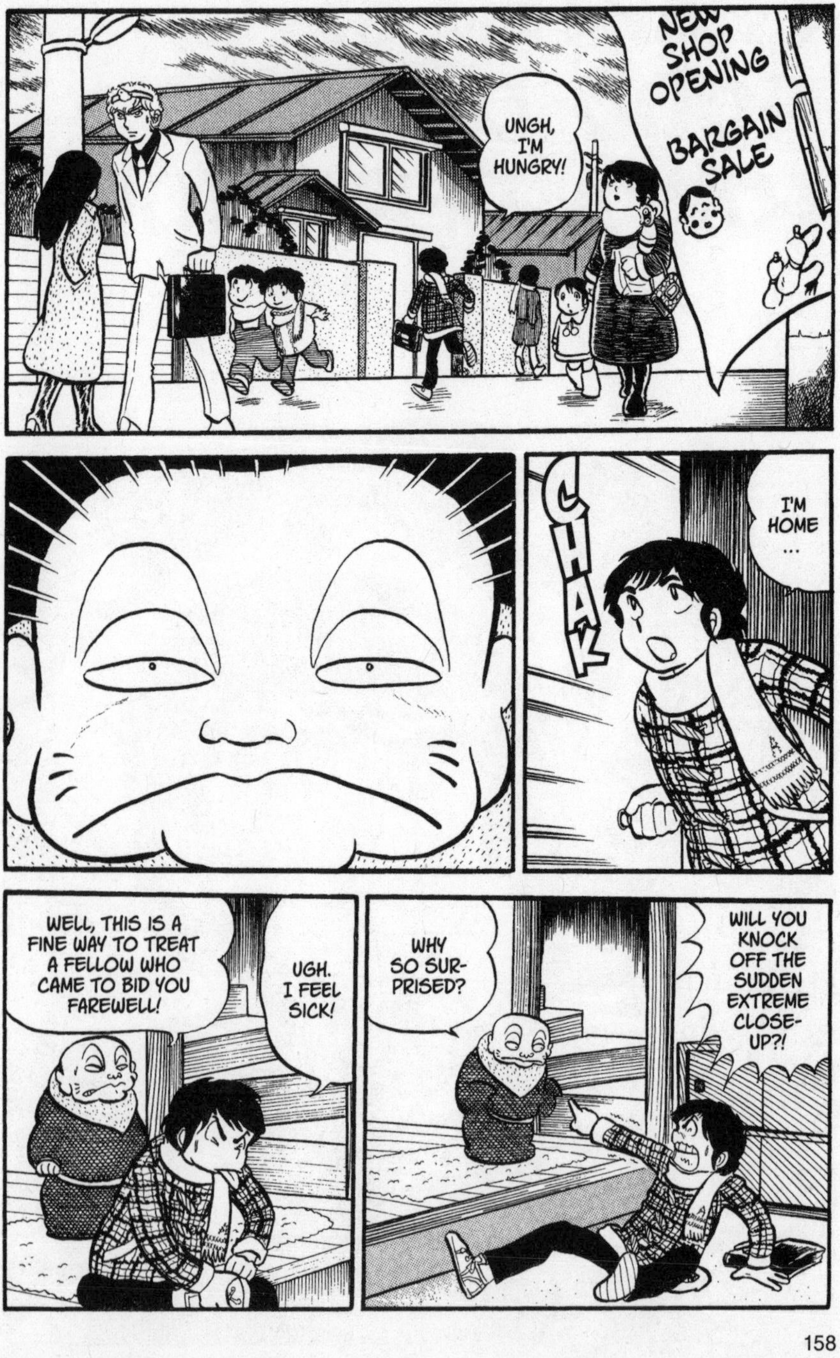
NEW SHOP OPENING
BARGAIN SALE
UNGH, I'M HUNGRY!
I'M HOME ...
CHAK
WILL YOU KNOCK OFF THE SUDDEN EXTREME CLOSE-UP?!
WHY SO SUR-PRISED?
UGH. I FEEL SICK!
WELL, THIS IS A FINE WAY TO TREAT A FELLOW WHO CAME TO BID YOU FAREWELL!

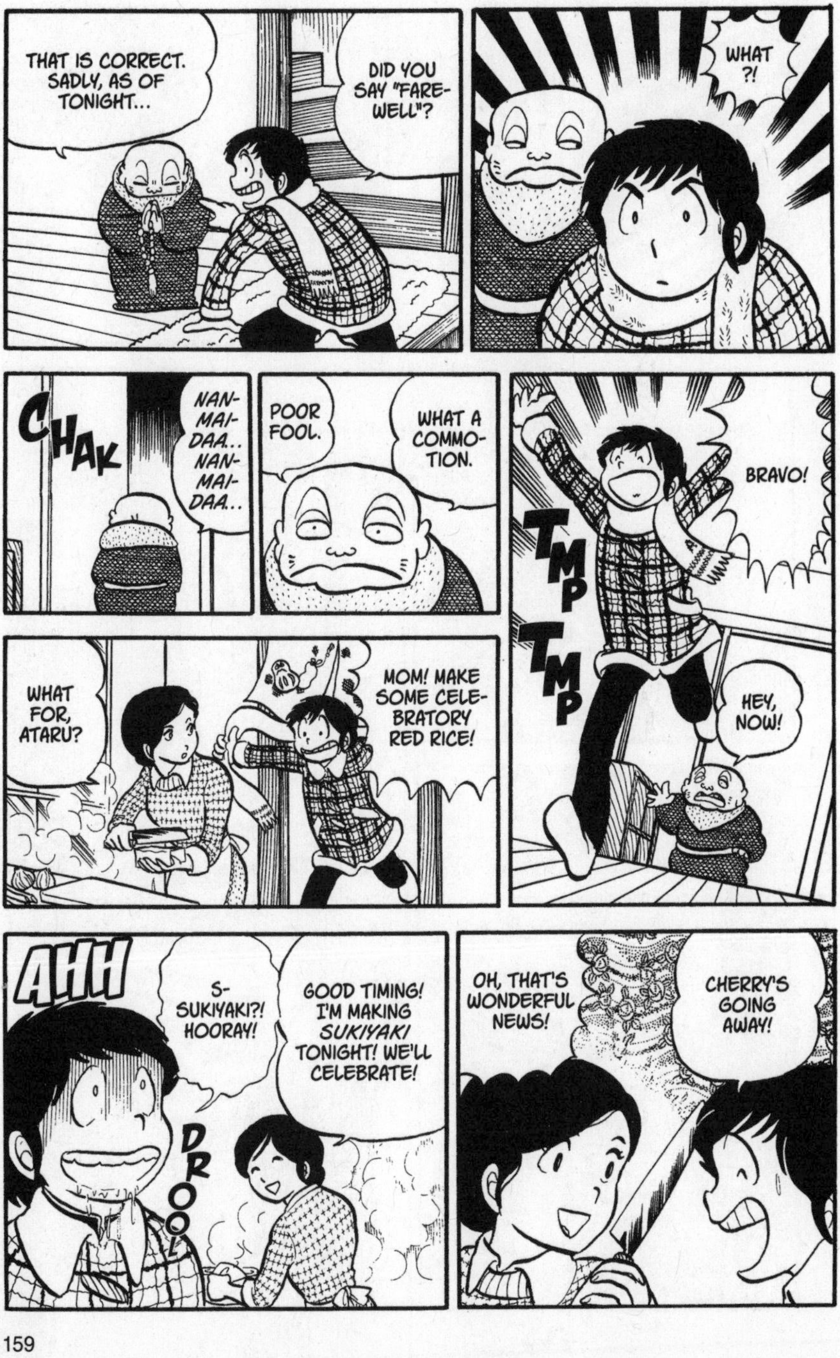
WHAT ?!
DID YOU SAY "FARE-WELL"?
THAT IS CORRECT. SADLY, AS OF TONIGHT...
BRAVO!
TMP TMP
HEY, NOW!
WHAT A COMMOTION.
POOR FOOL.
NAN-MAI-DAA... NAN-MAI-DAA...
CHAK
MOM! MAKE SOME CELEBRATORY RED RICE!
WHAT FOR, ATARU?
CHERRY'S GOING AWAY!
OH, THAT'S WONDERFUL NEWS!
GOOD TIMING! I'M MAKING *SUKIYAKI* TONIGHT! WE'LL CELEBRATE!
S-SUKIYAKI?! HOORAY!
AHH
DROOL

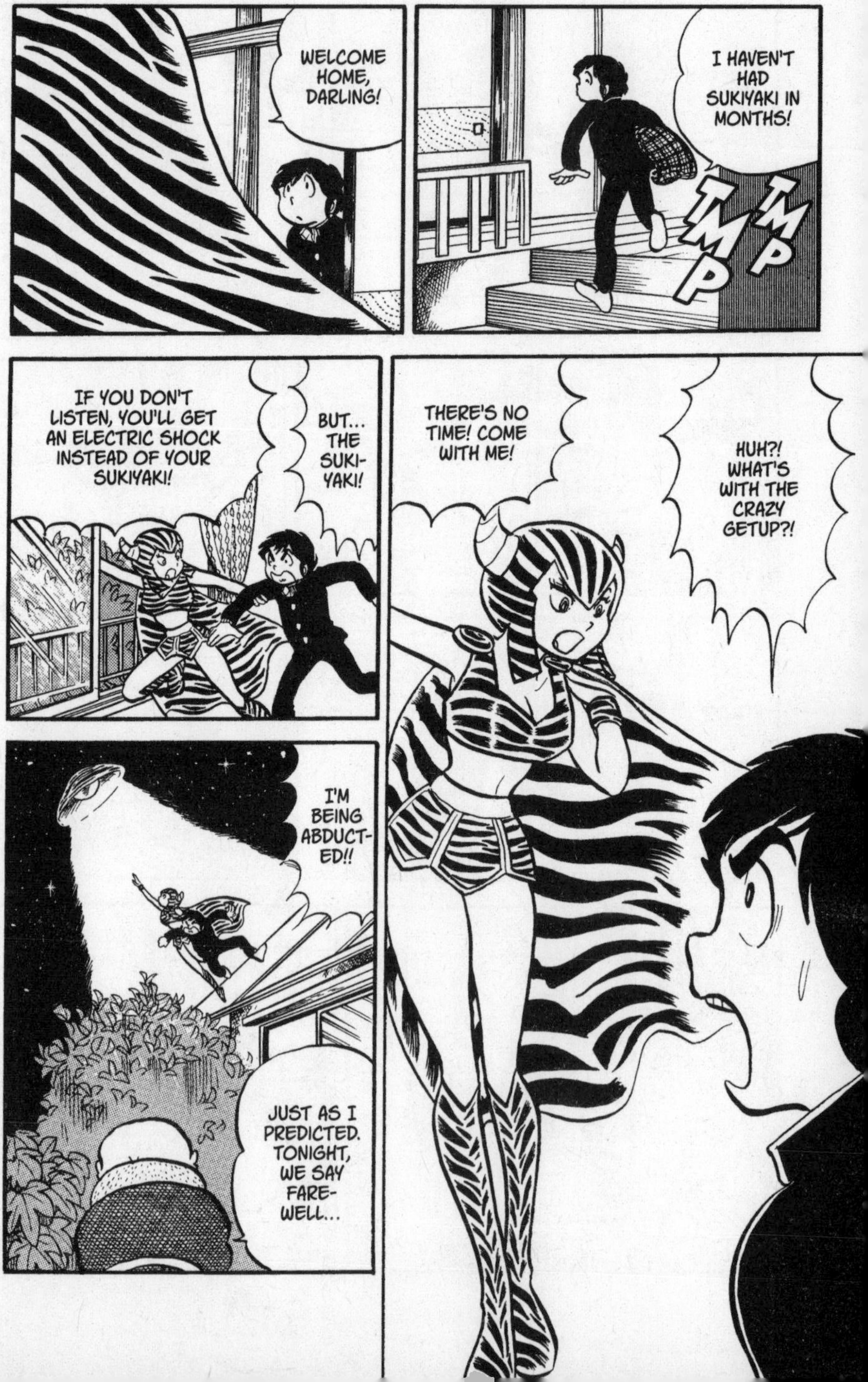
I HAVEN'T HAD SUKIYAKI IN MONTHS!
TMP
TMP
WELCOME HOME, DARLING!
HUH?! WHAT'S WITH THE CRAZY GETUP?!
THERE'S NO TIME! COME WITH ME!
BUT... THE SUKI-YAKI!
IF YOU DON'T LISTEN, YOU'LL GET AN ELECTRIC SHOCK INSTEAD OF YOUR SUKIYAKI!
I'M BEING ABDUCT-ED!!
JUST AS I PREDICTED. TONIGHT, WE SAY FARE-WELL...

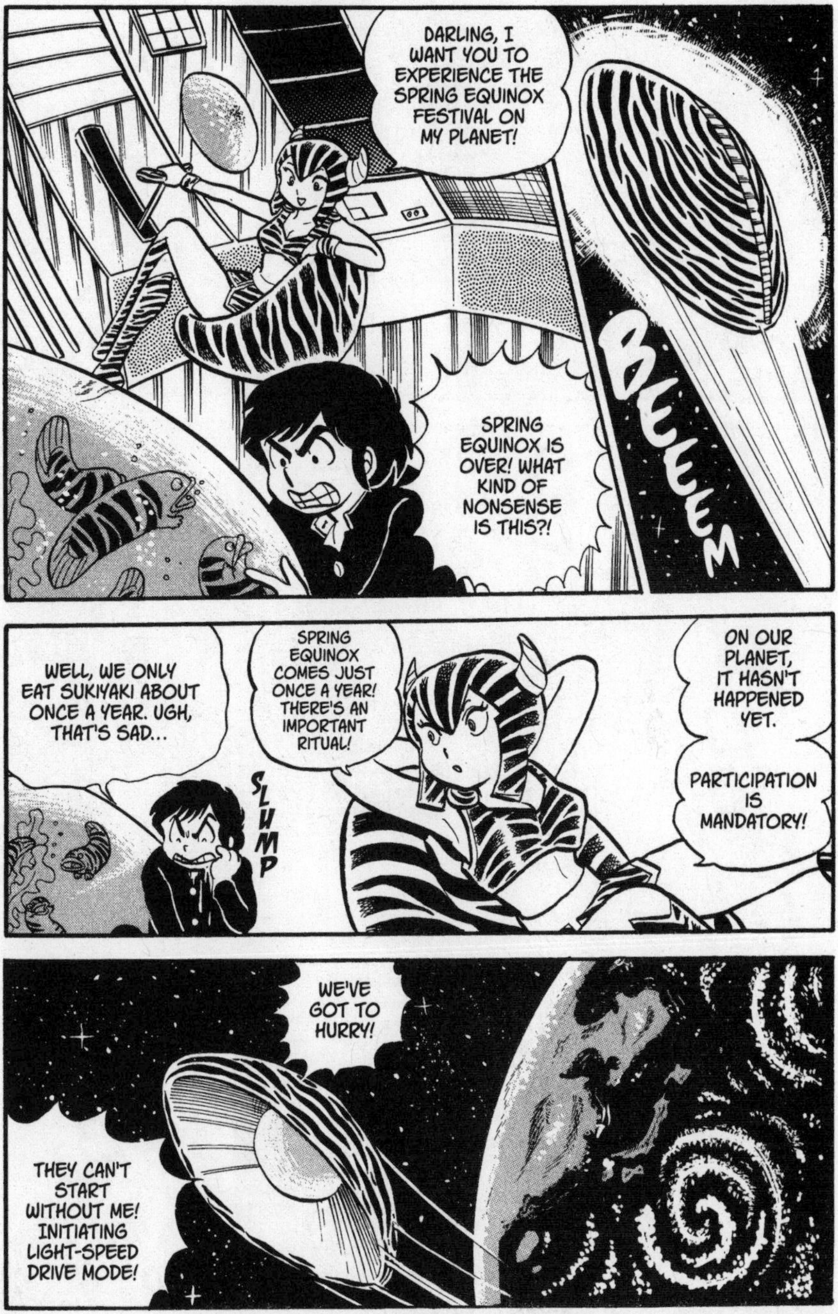

DARLING, I WANT YOU TO EXPERIENCE THE SPRING EQUINOX FESTIVAL ON MY PLANET!
BEEEM
SPRING EQUINOX IS OVER! WHAT KIND OF NONSENSE IS THIS?!
ON OUR PLANET, IT HASN'T HAPPENED YET.
PARTICIPATION IS MANDATORY!
SPRING EQUINOX COMES JUST ONCE A YEAR! THERE'S AN IMPORTANT RITUAL!
WELL, WE ONLY EAT SUKIYAKI ABOUT ONCE A YEAR. UGH, THAT'S SAD...
SLUMP
WE'VE GOT TO HURRY!
THEY CAN'T START WITHOUT ME! INITIATING LIGHT-SPEED DRIVE MODE!

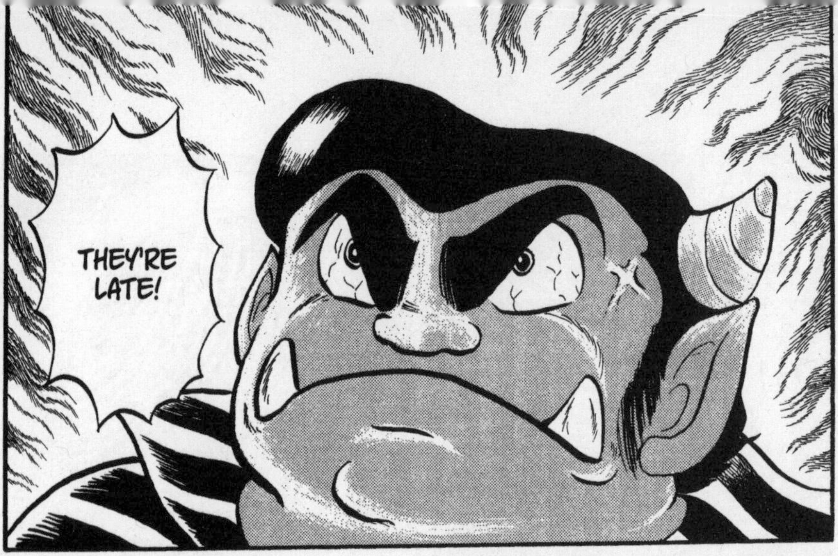
THEY'RE LATE!

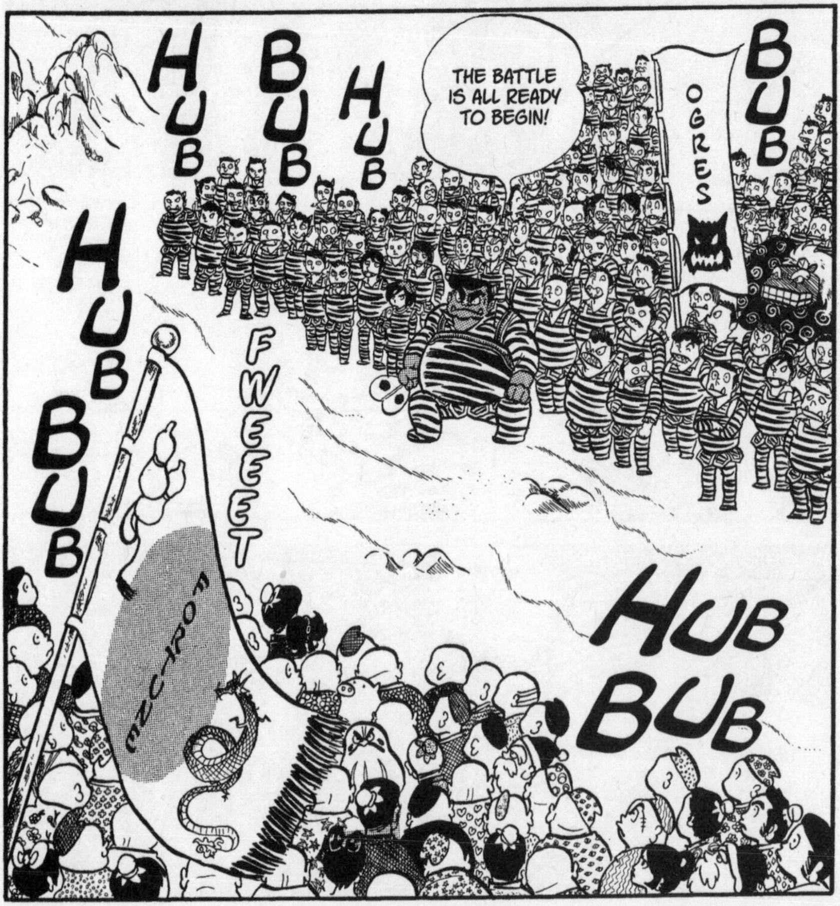
BUB BUB
OGRES
THE BATTLE IS ALL READY TO BEGIN!
HUB HUB
BUB BUB
HUB HUB
FWEEEET
HUB HUB BUB BUB
HUB BUB

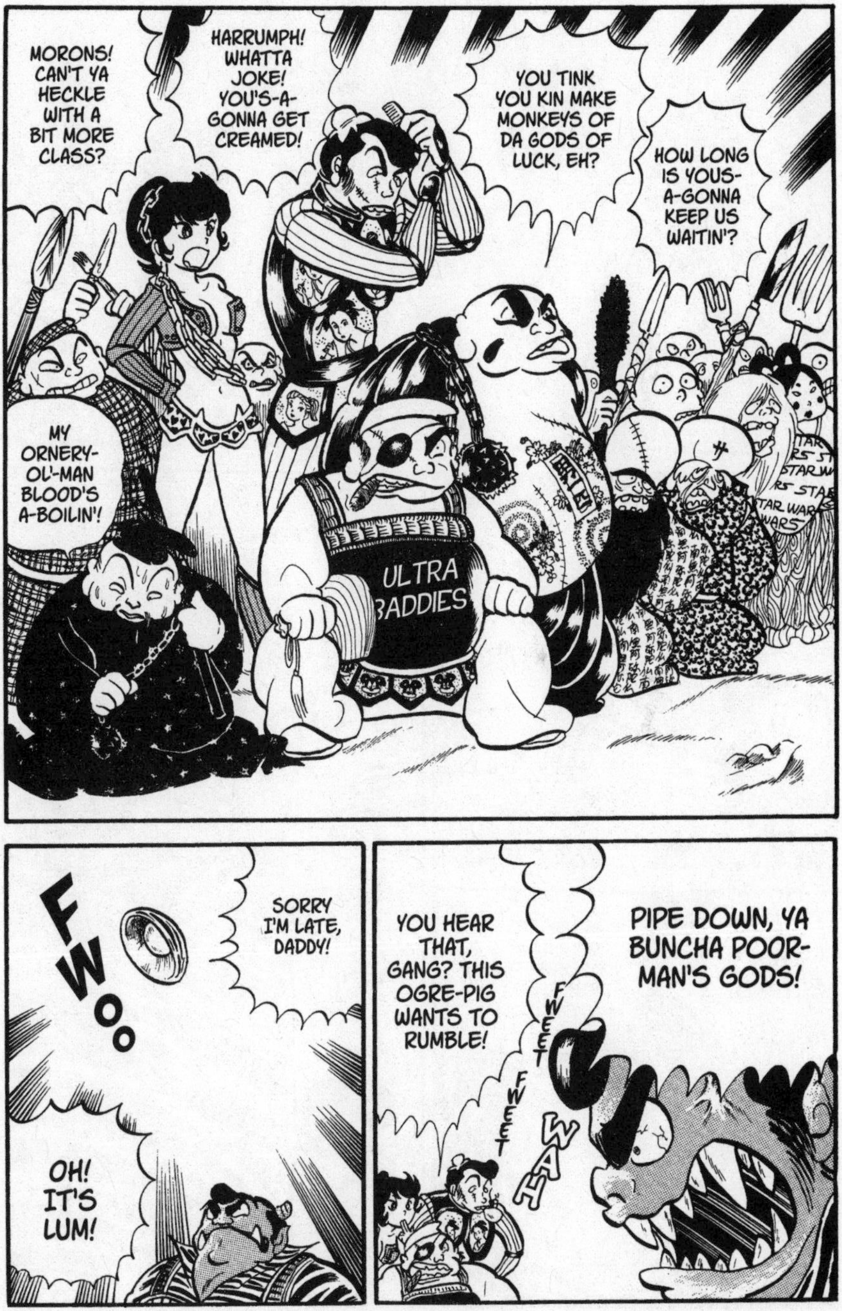
HOW LONG IS YOUS-A-GONNA KEEP US WAITIN'?
YOU TINK YOU KIN MAKE MONKEYS OF DA GODS OF LUCK, EH?
HARRUMPH! WHATTA JOKE! YOU'S-A-GONNA GET CREAMED!
MORONS! CAN'T YA HECKLE WITH A BIT MORE CLASS?
ULTRA BADDIES
MY ORNERY-OL'-MAN BLOOD'S A-BOILIN'!
PIPE DOWN, YA BUNCHA POOR-MAN'S GODS!
WAH
FWEET
FWEET
YOU HEAR THAT, GANG? THIS OGRE-PIG WANTS TO RUMBLE!
SORRY I'M LATE, DADDY!
FWOO
OH! IT'S LUM!

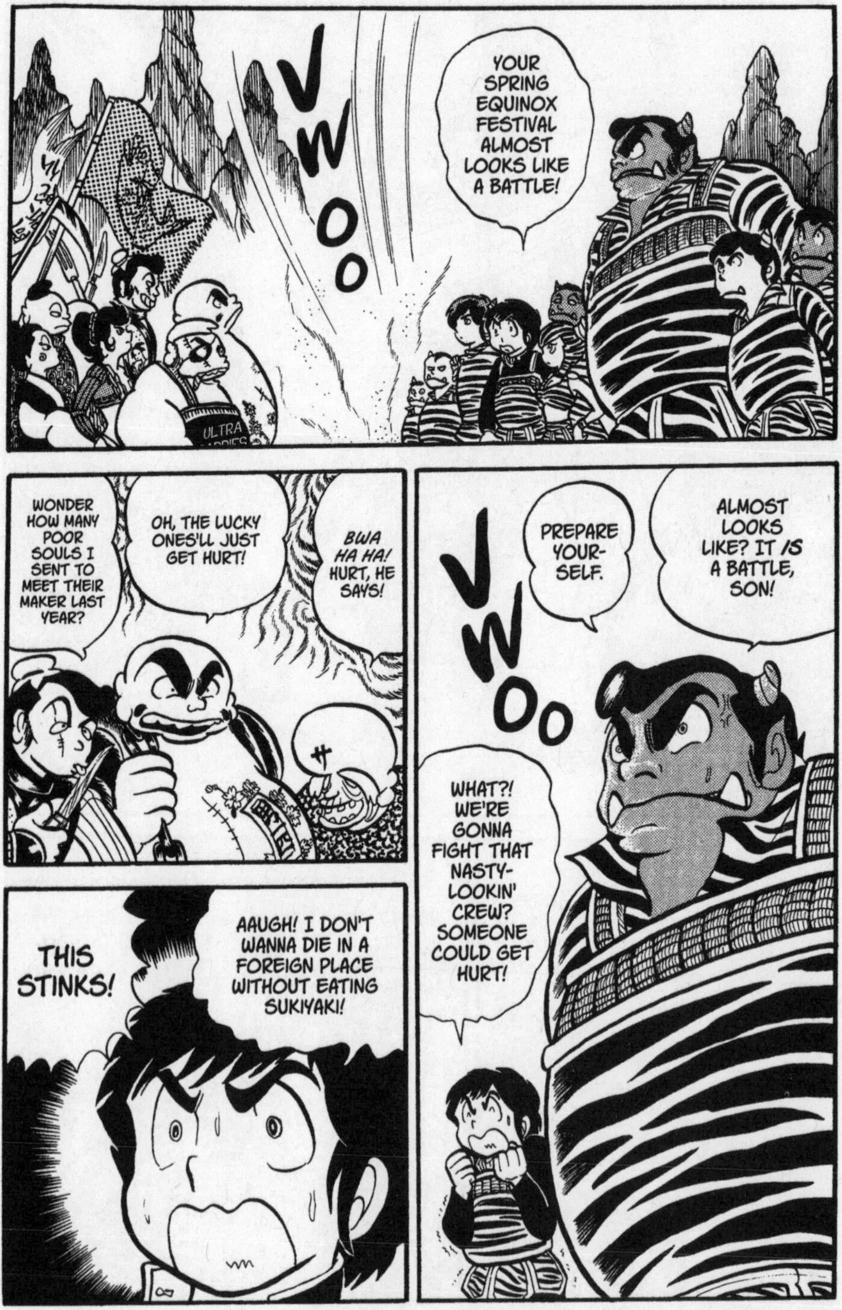
VWOOO
YOUR SPRING EQUINOX FESTIVAL ALMOST LOOKS LIKE A BATTLE!
ULTRA
ALMOST LOOKS LIKE? IT *IS* A BATTLE, SON!
PREPARE YOUR-SELF.
VWOOO
WHAT?! WE'RE GONNA FIGHT THAT NASTY-LOOKIN' CREW? SOMEONE COULD GET HURT!
BWA HA HA! HURT, HE SAYS!
OH, THE LUCKY ONES'LL JUST GET HURT!
WONDER HOW MANY POOR SOULS I SENT TO MEET THEIR MAKER LAST YEAR?
AAUGH! I DON'T WANNA DIE IN A FOREIGN PLACE WITHOUT EATING SUKIYAKI!
THIS STINKS!

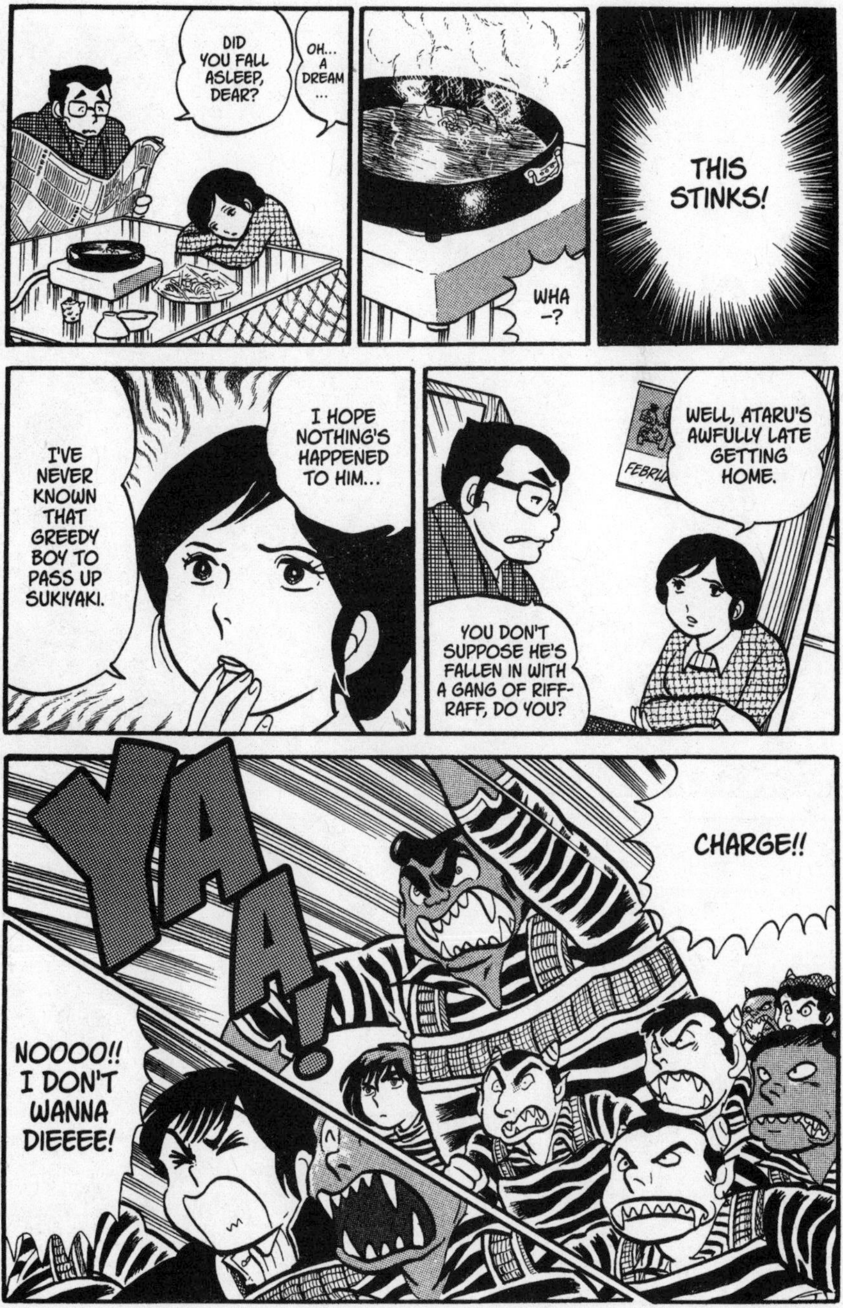
THIS STINKS!
WHA —?
OH... A DREAM ...
DID YOU FALL ASLEEP, DEAR?
WELL, ATARU'S AWFULLY LATE GETTING HOME.
YOU DON'T SUPPOSE HE'S FALLEN IN WITH A GANG OF RIFF-RAFF, DO YOU?
I HOPE NOTHING'S HAPPENED TO HIM...
I'VE NEVER KNOWN THAT GREEDY BOY TO PASS UP SUKIYAKI.
CHARGE!!
YAAA!
NOOOO!! I DON'T WANNA DIEEEE!

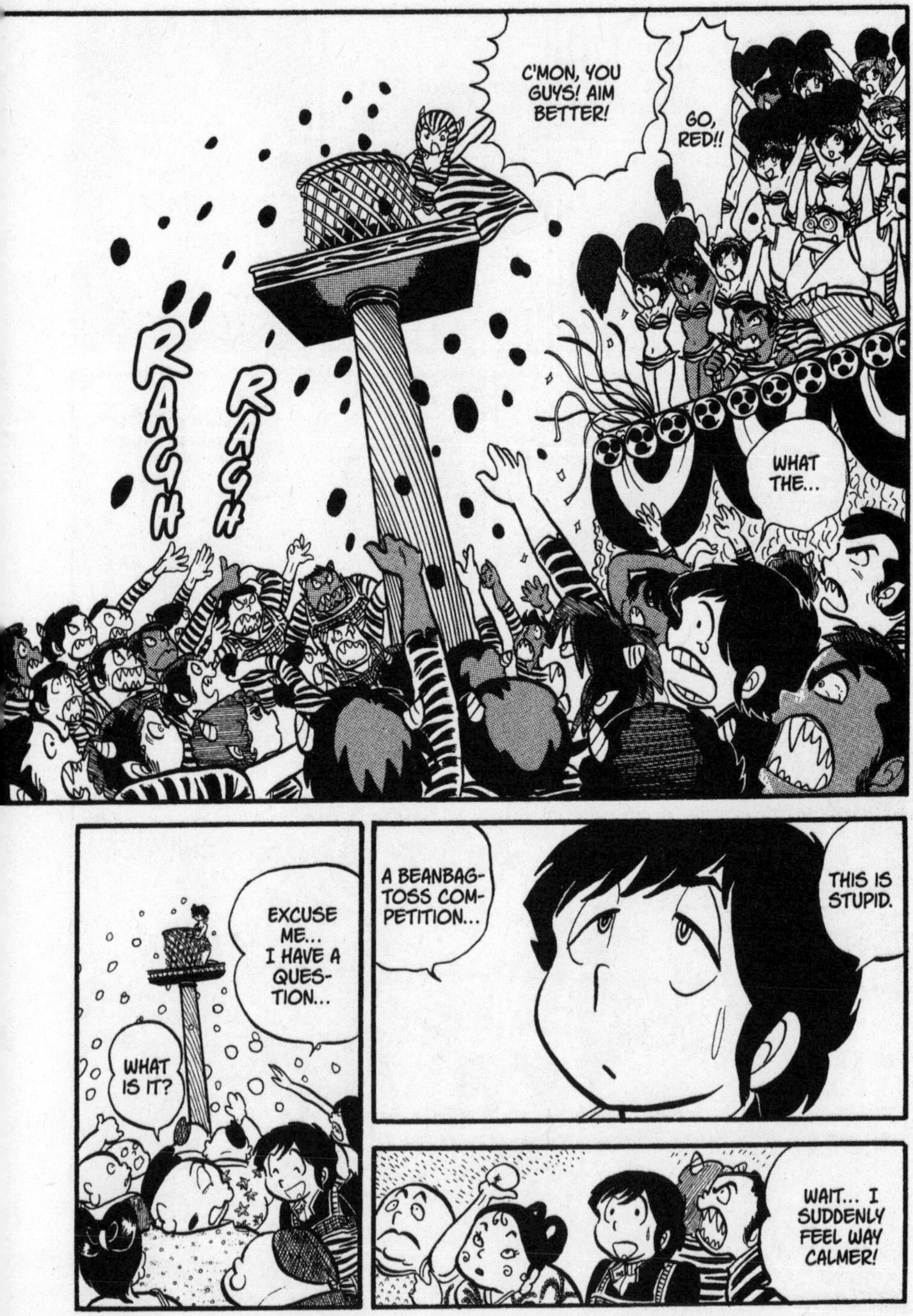
GO, RED!!
C'MON, YOU GUYS! AIM BETTER!
WHAT THE...
RAGH
RAGH
THIS IS STUPID.
A BEANBAG-TOSS COMPETITION...
WAIT... I SUDDENLY FEEL WAY CALMER!
EXCUSE ME... I HAVE A QUESTION...
WHAT IS IT?

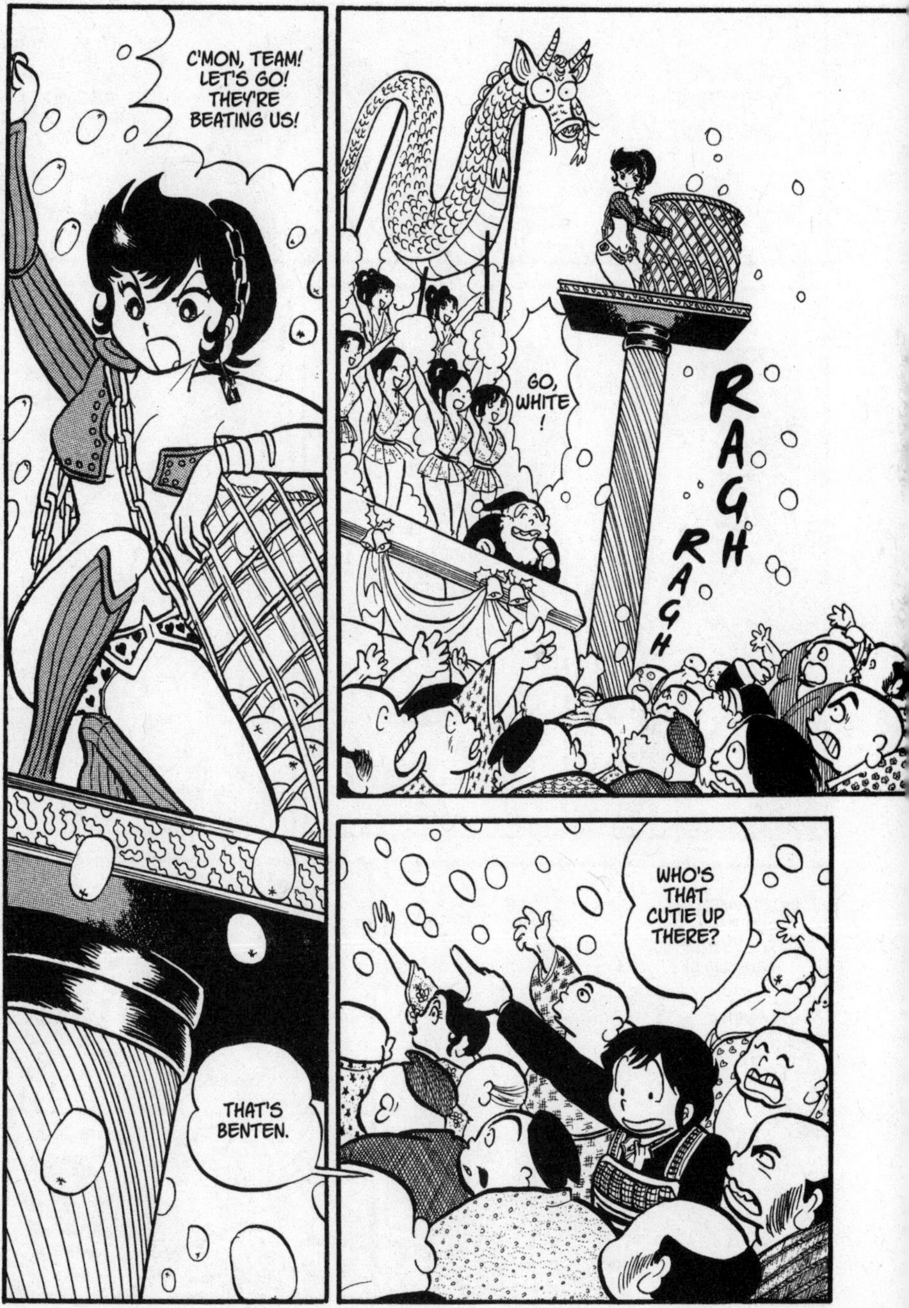
GO, WHITE!
RAGH
RAGH
WHO'S THAT CUTIE UP THERE?
C'MON, TEAM! LET'S GO! THEY'RE BEATING US!
THAT'S BENTEN.

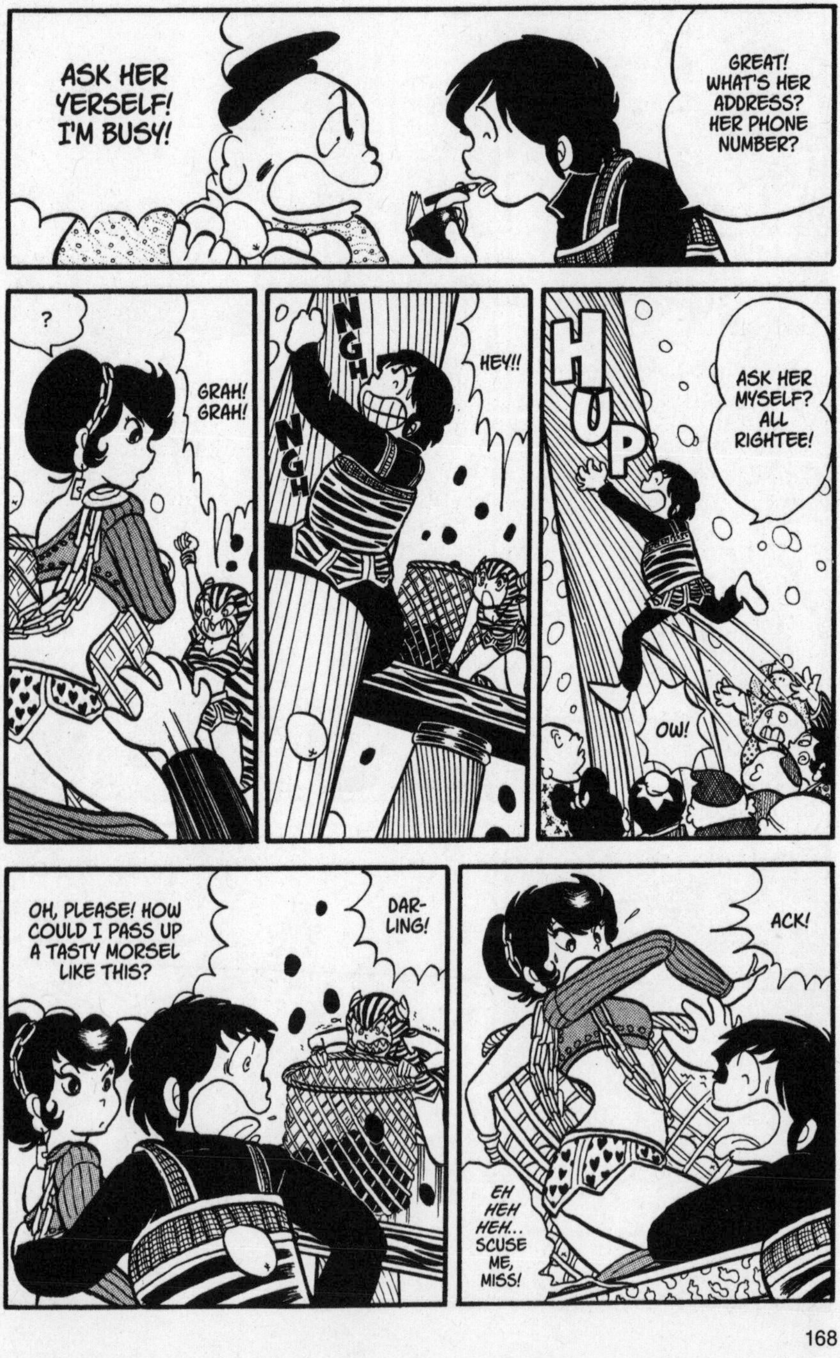
GREAT! WHAT'S HER ADDRESS? HER PHONE NUMBER?
ASK HER YERSELF! I'M BUSY!
ASK HER MYSELF? ALL RIGHTEE!
HUP
OW!
HEY!!
NGH
NGH
GRAH! GRAH!
?
ACK!
EH HEH HEH... SCUSE ME, MISS!
DAR-LING!
OH, PLEASE! HOW COULD I PASS UP A TASTY MORSEL LIKE THIS?

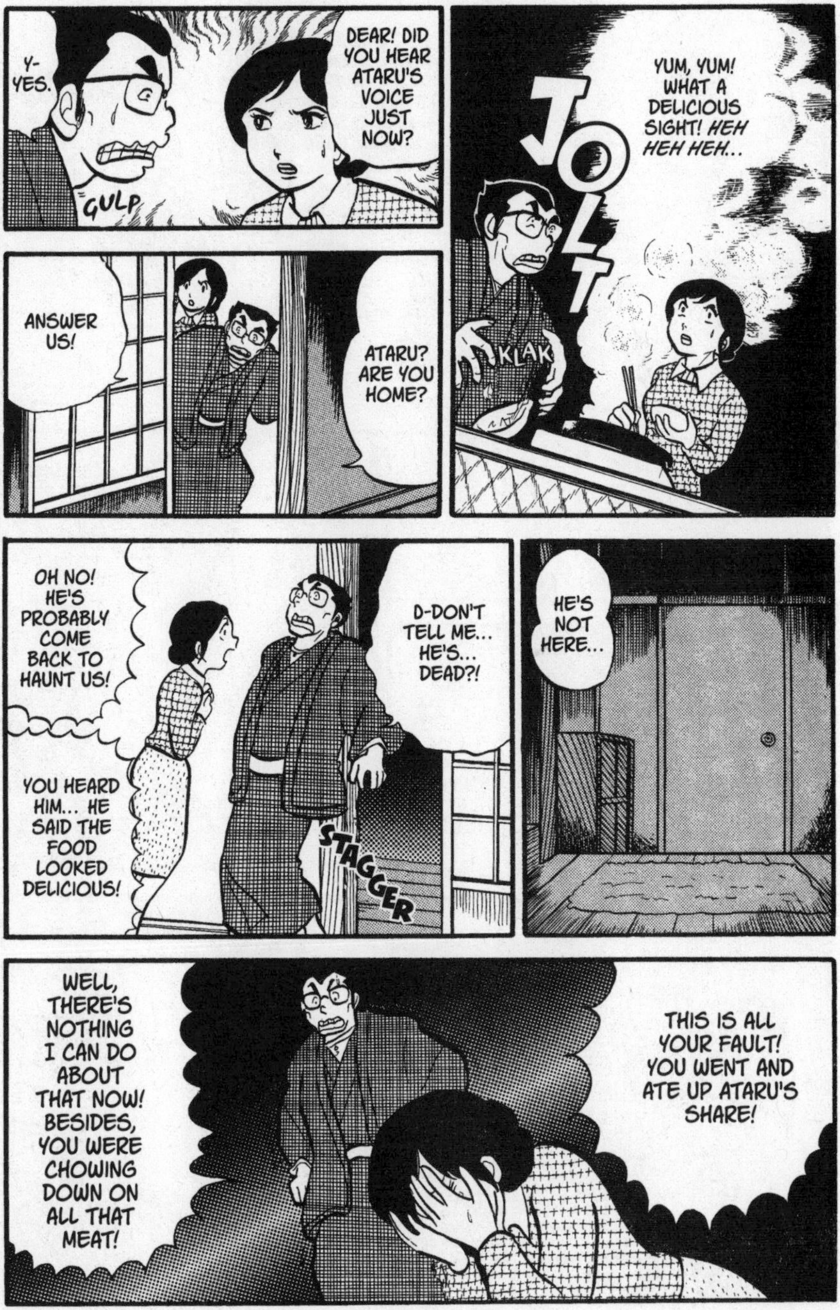
YUM, YUM! WHAT A DELICIOUS SIGHT! *HEH HEH HEH...*
JOLT
KLAK
DEAR! DID YOU HEAR ATARU'S VOICE JUST NOW?
Y- YES.
GULP
ATARU? ARE YOU HOME?
ANSWER US!
HE'S NOT HERE...
D-DON'T TELL ME... HE'S... DEAD?!
OH NO! HE'S PROBABLY COME BACK TO HAUNT US!
YOU HEARD HIM... HE SAID THE FOOD LOOKED DELICIOUS!
STAGGER
THIS IS ALL YOUR FAULT! YOU WENT AND ATE UP ATARU'S SHARE!
WELL, THERE'S NOTHING I CAN DO ABOUT THAT NOW! BESIDES, YOU WERE CHOWING DOWN ON ALL THAT MEAT!

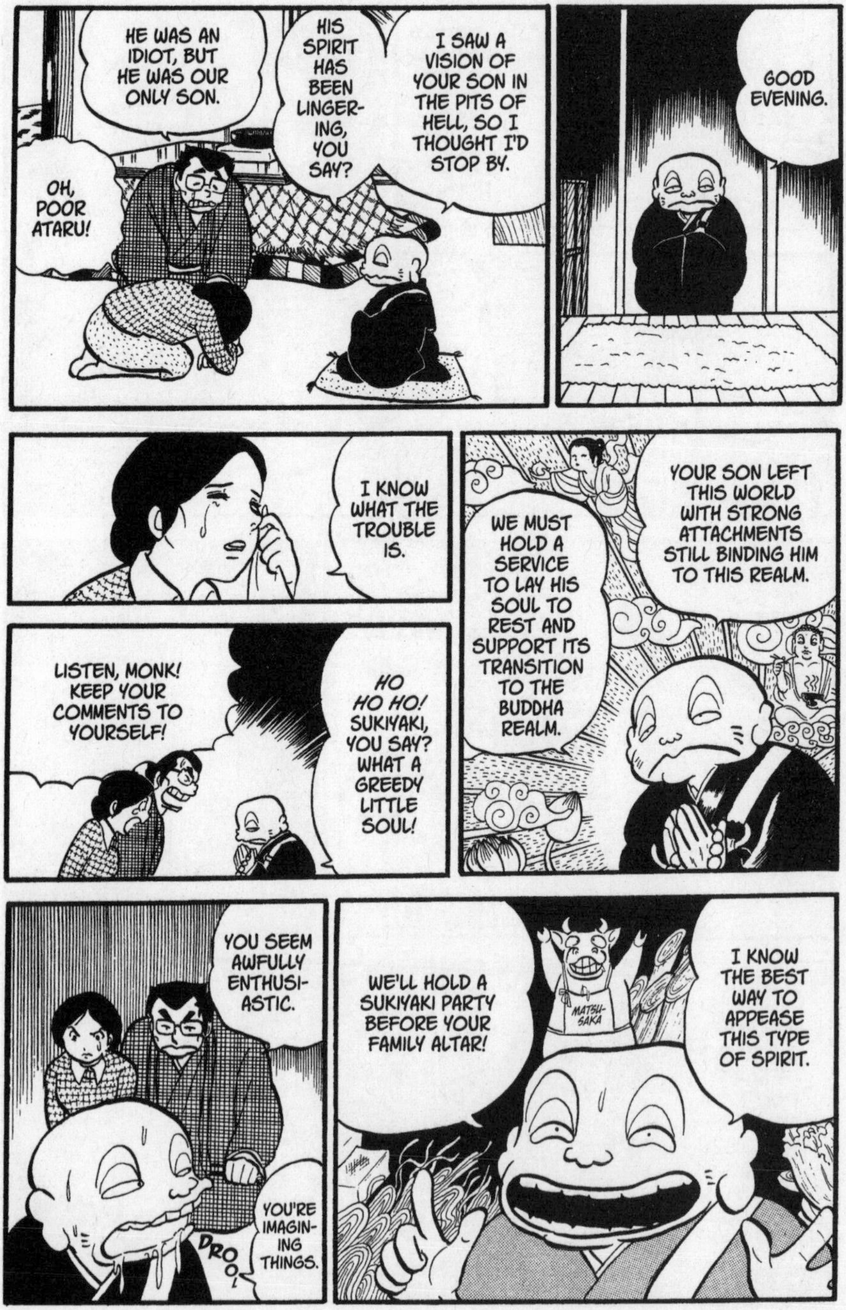
GOOD EVENING.
I SAW A VISION OF YOUR SON IN THE PITS OF HELL, SO I THOUGHT I'D STOP BY.
HIS SPIRIT HAS BEEN LINGERING, YOU SAY?
HE WAS AN IDIOT, BUT HE WAS OUR ONLY SON.
OH, POOR ATARU!
YOUR SON LEFT THIS WORLD WITH STRONG ATTACHMENTS STILL BINDING HIM TO THIS REALM.
WE MUST HOLD A SERVICE TO LAY HIS SOUL TO REST AND SUPPORT ITS TRANSITION TO THE BUDDHA REALM.
I KNOW WHAT THE TROUBLE IS.
HO HO HO! SUKIYAKI, YOU SAY? WHAT A GREEDY LITTLE SOUL!
LISTEN, MONK! KEEP YOUR COMMENTS TO YOURSELF!
I KNOW THE BEST WAY TO APPEASE THIS TYPE OF SPIRIT.
WE'LL HOLD A SUKIYAKI PARTY BEFORE YOUR FAMILY ALTAR!
MATSU-SAKA
YOU SEEM AWFULLY ENTHUSIASTIC.
YOU'RE IMAGINING THINGS.
DROOL

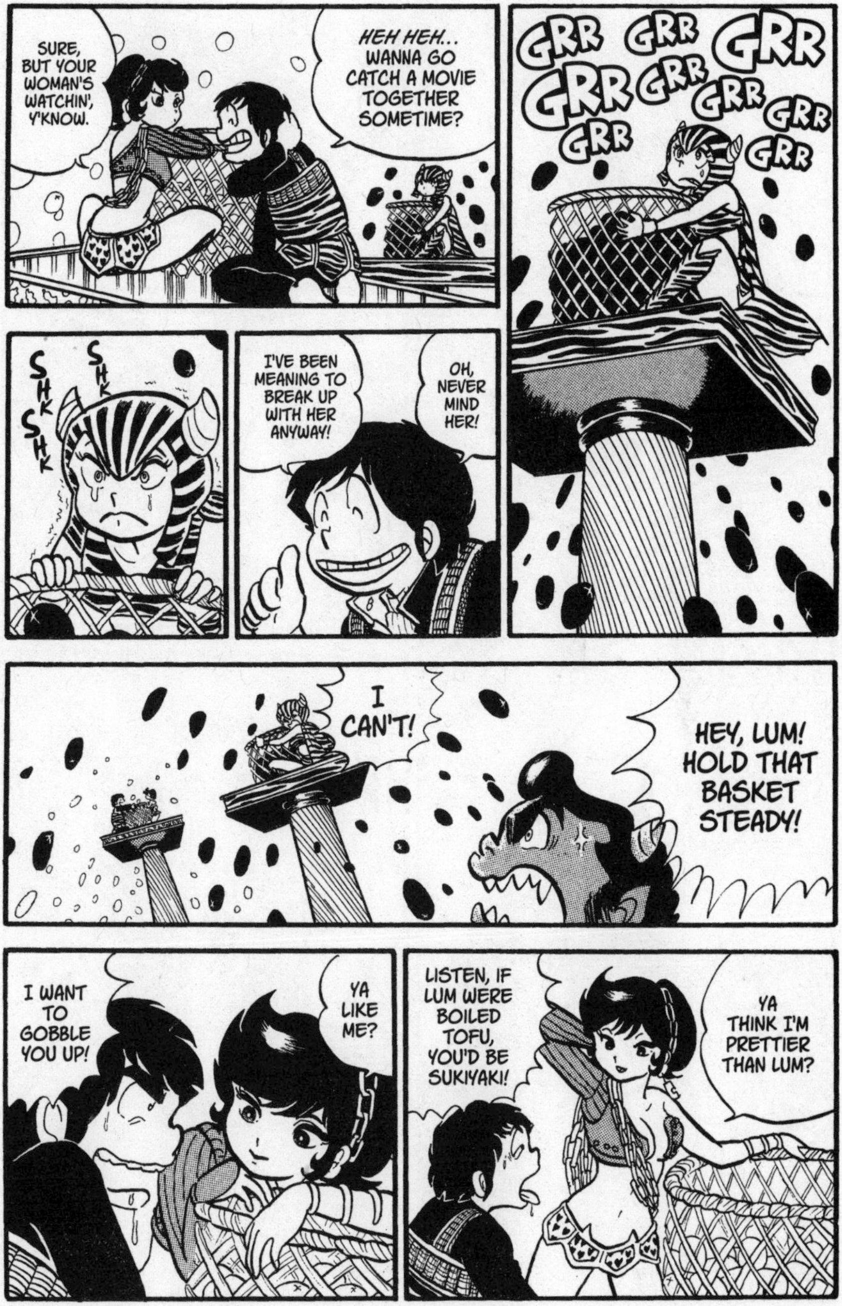
GRR GRR GRR GRR GRR GRR GRR GRR GRR GRR
HEH HEH... WANNA GO CATCH A MOVIE TOGETHER SOMETIME?
SURE, BUT YOUR WOMAN'S WATCHIN', Y'KNOW.
OH, NEVER MIND HER!
I'VE BEEN MEANING TO BREAK UP WITH HER ANYWAY!
SHK SHK SHK
HEY, LUM! HOLD THAT BASKET STEADY!
I CAN'T!
YA THINK I'M PRETTIER THAN LUM?
LISTEN, IF LUM WERE BOILED TOFU, YOU'D BE SUKIYAKI!
YA LIKE ME?
I WANT TO GOBBLE YOU UP!

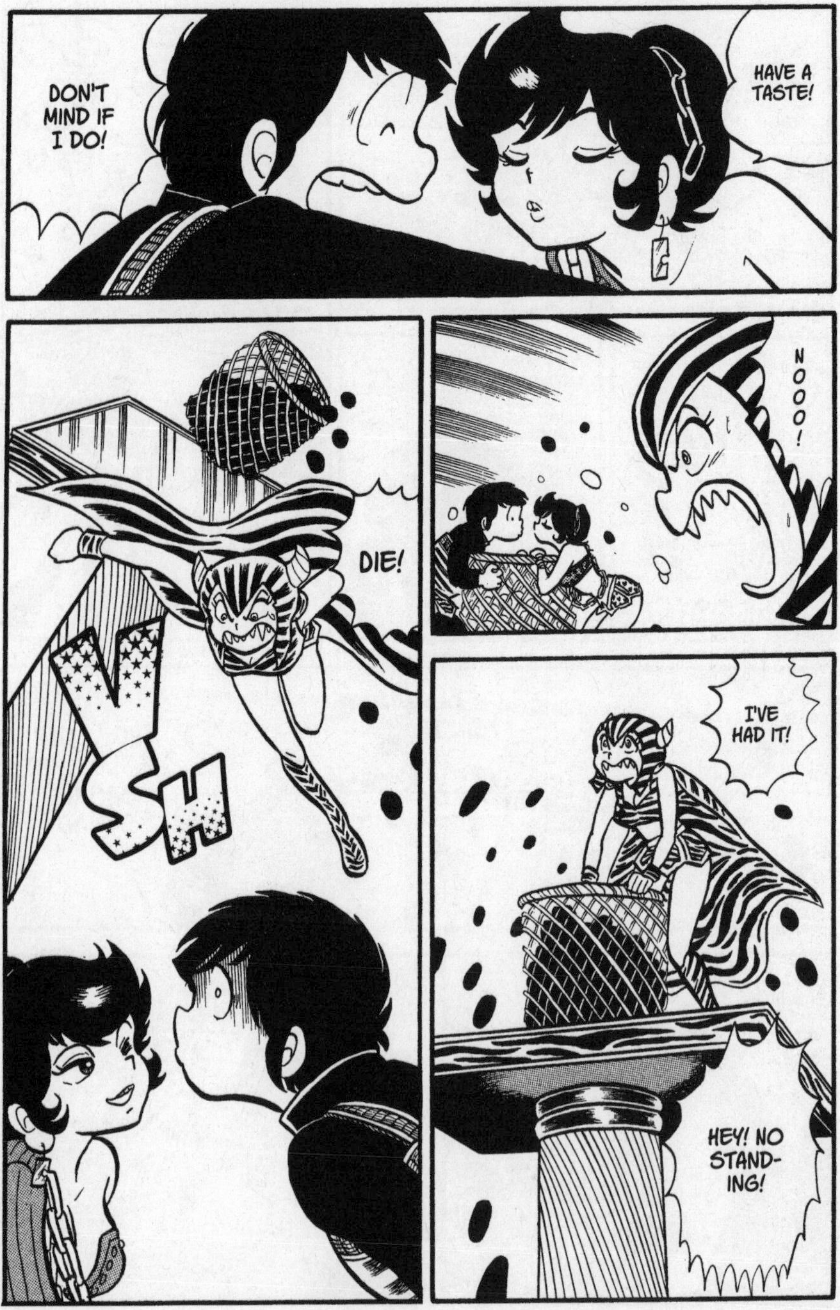
HAVE A TASTE!
DON'T MIND IF I DO!
NOOOO!
I'VE HAD IT!
HEY! NO STANDING!
DIE!
VSH

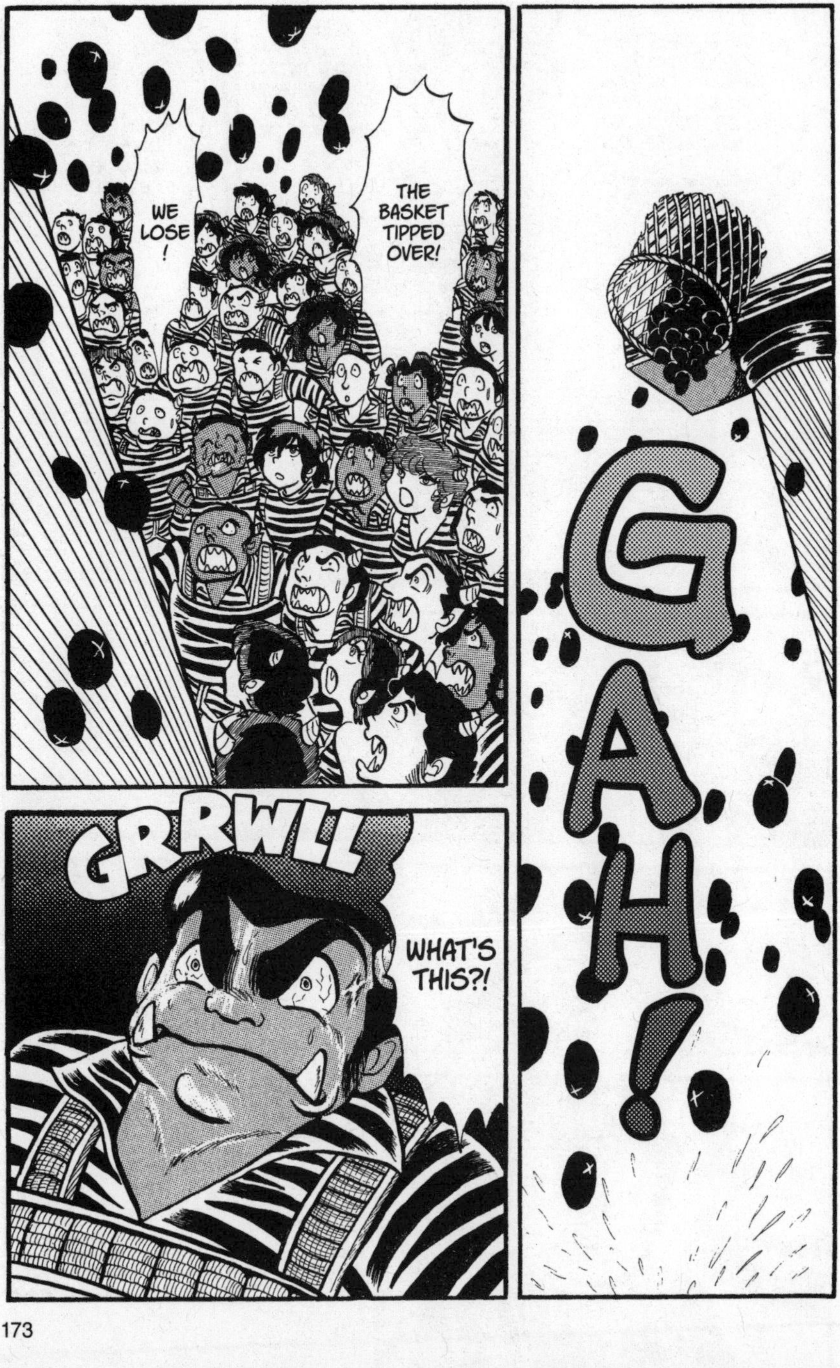
GAH!
THE BASKET TIPPED OVER!
WE LOSE!
GRRWLL
WHAT'S THIS?!

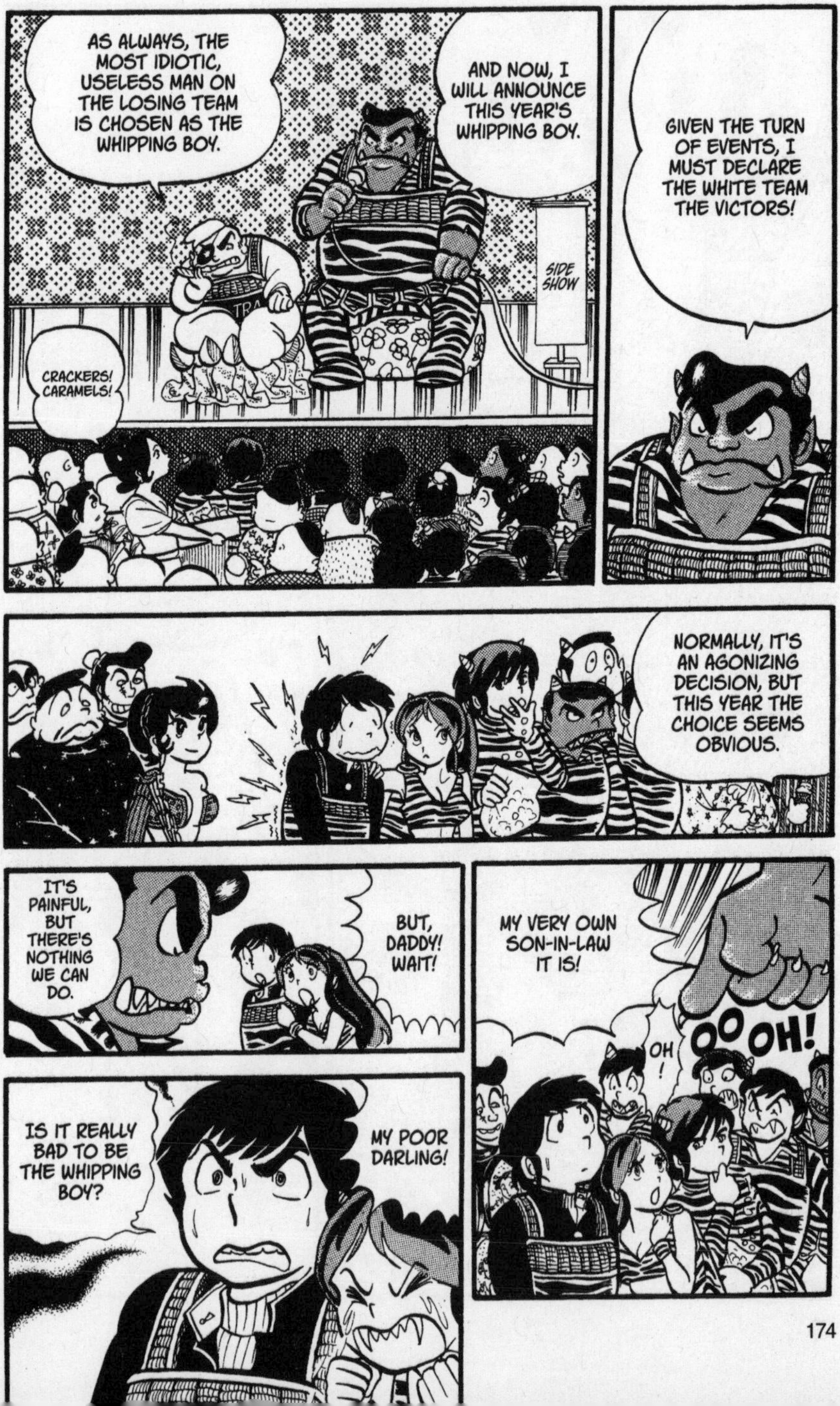
GIVEN THE TURN OF EVENTS, I MUST DECLARE THE WHITE TEAM THE VICTORS!
AND NOW, I WILL ANNOUNCE THIS YEAR'S WHIPPING BOY.
AS ALWAYS, THE MOST IDIOTIC, USELESS MAN ON THE LOSING TEAM IS CHOSEN AS THE WHIPPING BOY.
SIDE SHOW
CRACKERS! CARAMELS!
NORMALLY, IT'S AN AGONIZING DECISION, BUT THIS YEAR THE CHOICE SEEMS OBVIOUS.
MY VERY OWN SON-IN-LAW IT IS!
OOOH!
OH!
BUT, DADDY! WAIT!
IT'S PAINFUL, BUT THERE'S NOTHING WE CAN DO.
MY POOR DARLING!
IS IT REALLY BAD TO BE THE WHIPPING BOY?

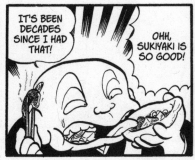

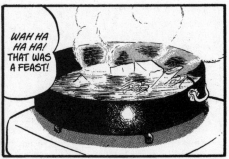

WAH HA HA HA! THAT WAS A FEAST!
OHH, SUKIYAKI IS SO GOOD!
IT'S BEEN DECADES SINCE I HAD THAT!
NOW THAT YOU'RE DONE EATING, IF WE COULD...
YES...
AH, YES, IT'S TIME...
I SHOULD BE GETTING HOME.
CHER-RY!!
KLONK
WHAT ABOUT ATARU'S SERVICE? YOU HAVEN'T LIT A SINGLE STICK OF INCENSE!
OH, YES! OF COURSE!
IT COMPLETELY SLIPPED MY MIND.
CALM DOWN, DEAR...
DAMNED HUNGRY MONK!
WE'LL USE THIS MANDALA TO GUIDE YOUR SON'S SPIRIT TOWARD SEPARATING FROM THIS REALM.

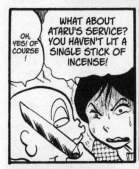

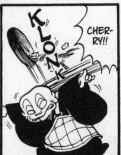

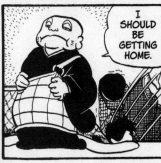

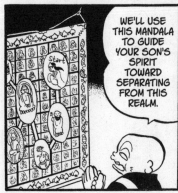

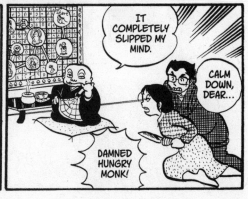

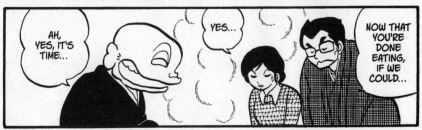

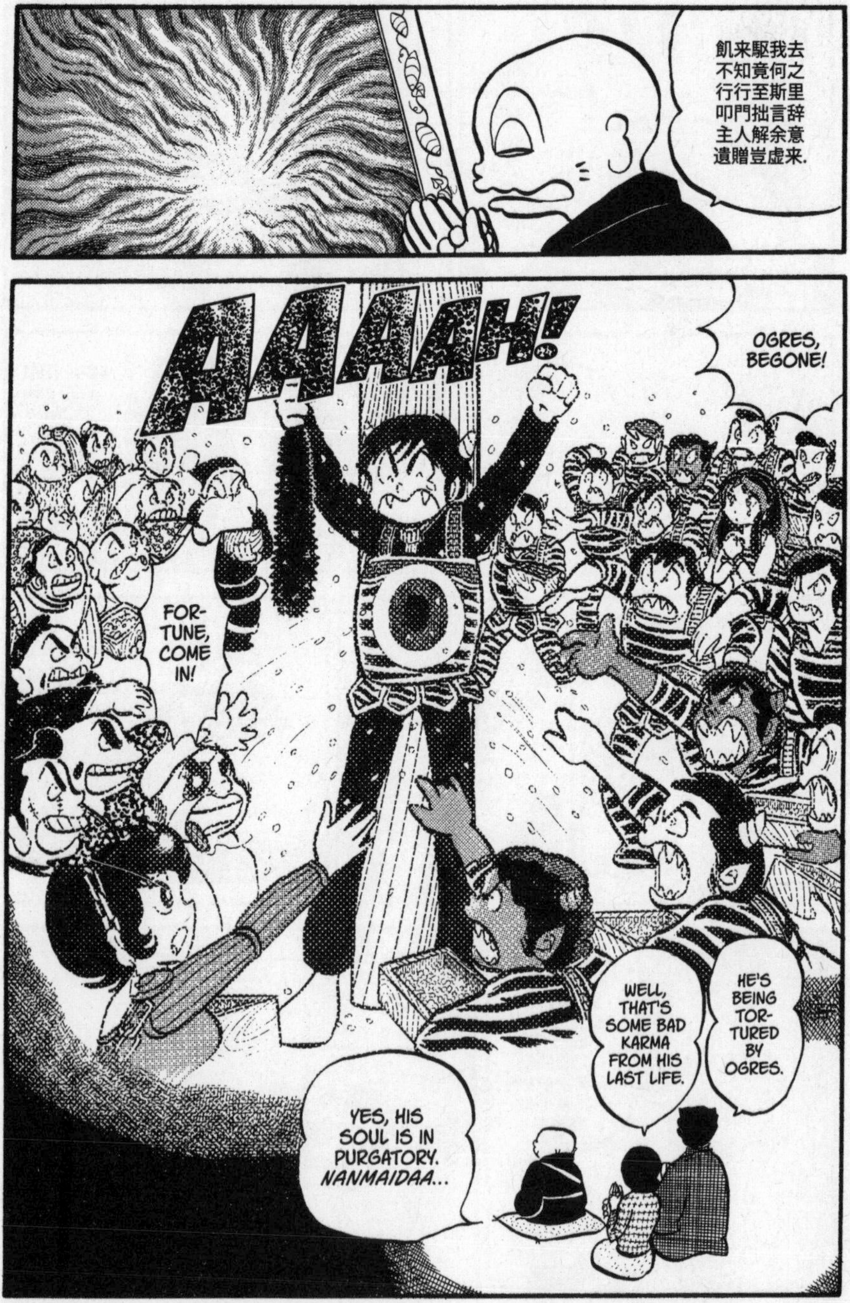
飢来駆我去
不知竟何之
行行至斯里
叩門拙言辞
主人解余意
遺贈豈虚来.
OGRES, BEGONE!
AAAAH!
FOR-TUNE, COME IN!
HE'S BEING TOR-TURED BY OGRES.
WELL, THAT'S SOME BAD KARMA FROM HIS LAST LIFE.
YES, HIS SOUL IS IN PURGATORY. *NANMAIDAA...*

CHAPTER 9: SHOWDOWN

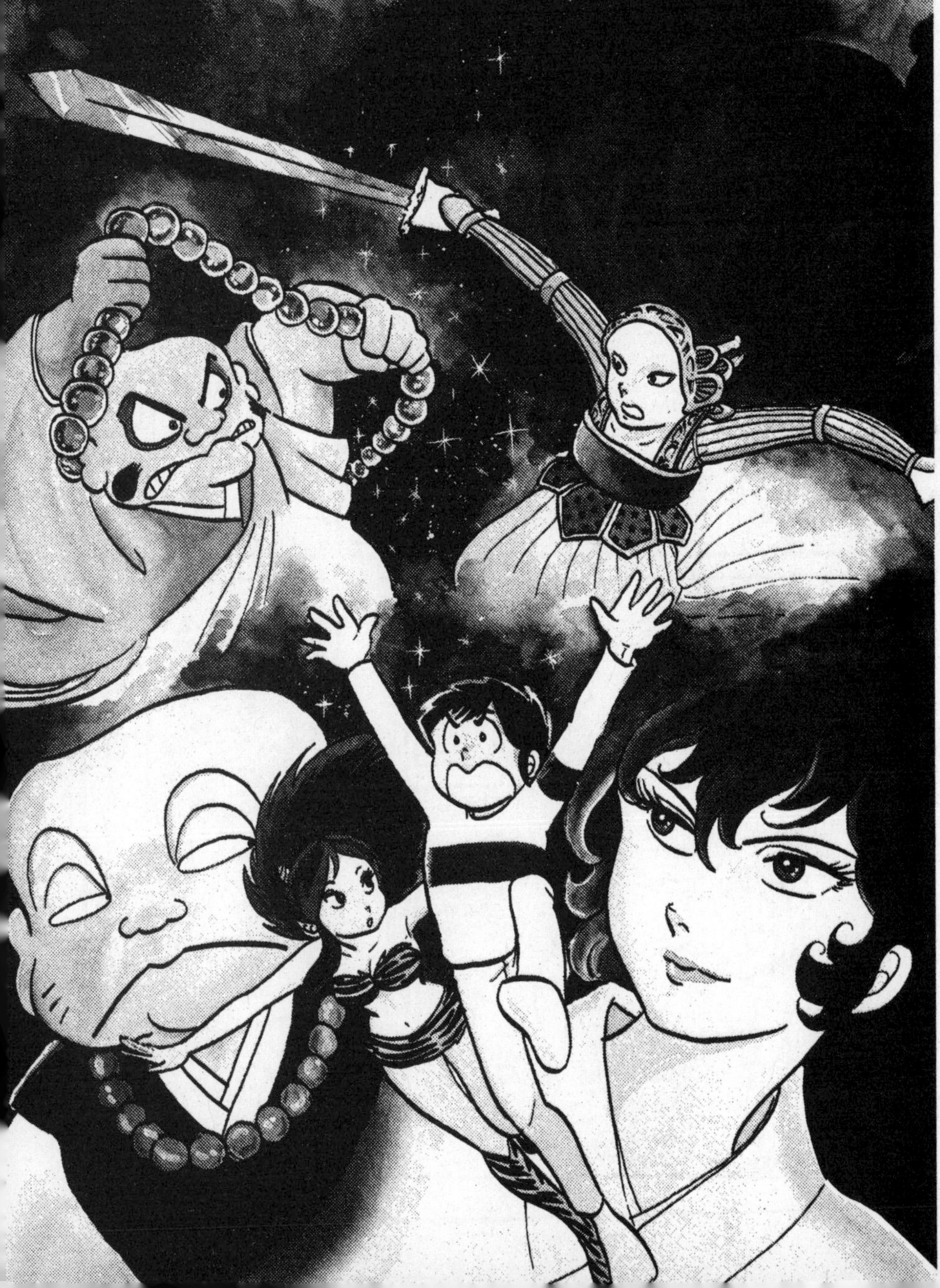

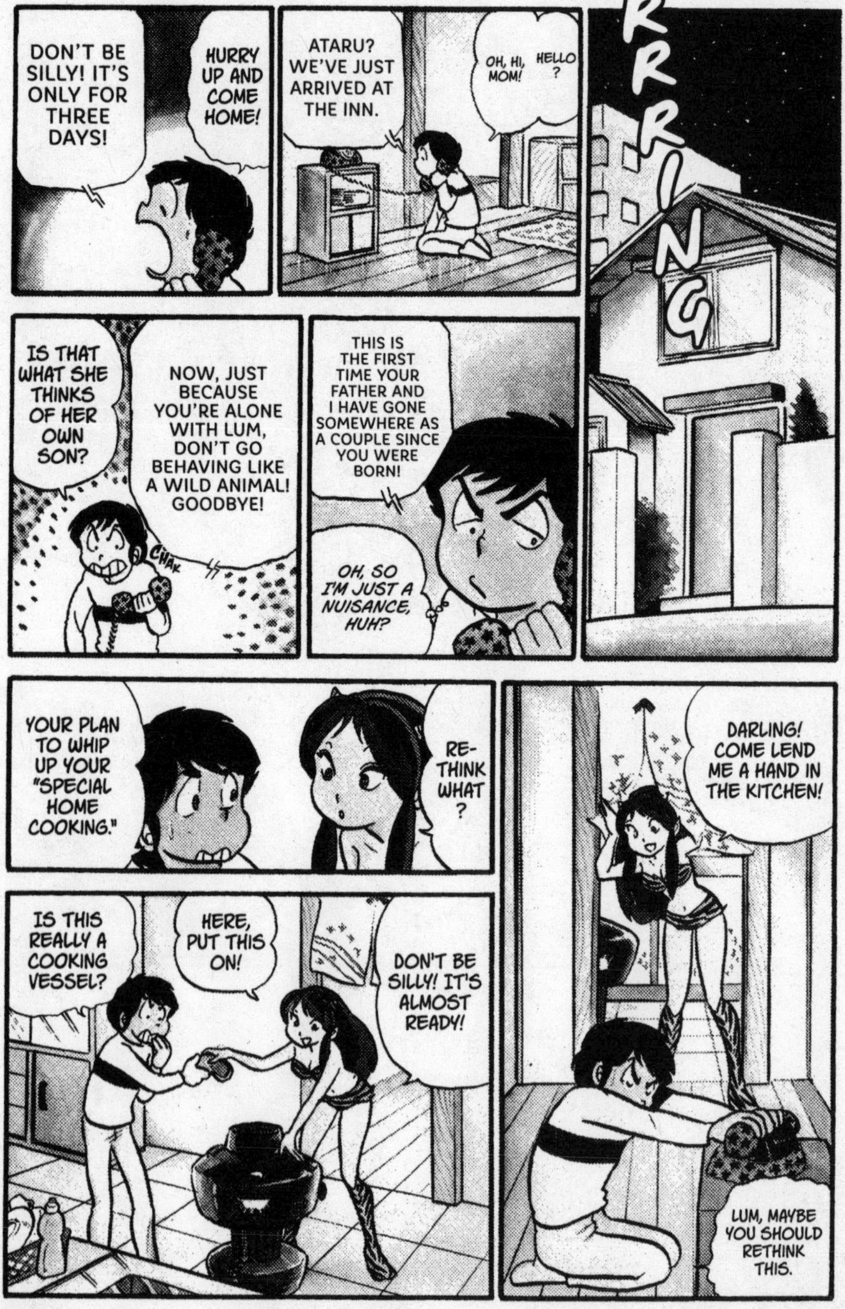
RRRING
HELLO?
OH, HI, MOM!
ATARU? WE'VE JUST ARRIVED AT THE INN.
HURRY UP AND COME HOME!
DON'T BE SILLY! IT'S ONLY FOR THREE DAYS!
THIS IS THE FIRST TIME YOUR FATHER AND I HAVE GONE SOMEWHERE AS A COUPLE SINCE YOU WERE BORN!
OH, SO I'M JUST A NUISANCE, HUH?
NOW, JUST BECAUSE YOU'RE ALONE WITH LUM, DON'T GO BEHAVING LIKE A WILD ANIMAL! GOODBYE!
CHAK
IS THAT WHAT SHE THINKS OF HER OWN SON?
DARLING! COME LEND ME A HAND IN THE KITCHEN!
LUM, MAYBE YOU SHOULD RETHINK THIS.
RE-THINK WHAT?
YOUR PLAN TO WHIP UP YOUR "SPECIAL HOME COOKING."
DON'T BE SILLY! IT'S ALMOST READY!
HERE, PUT THIS ON!
IS THIS REALLY A COOKING VESSEL?

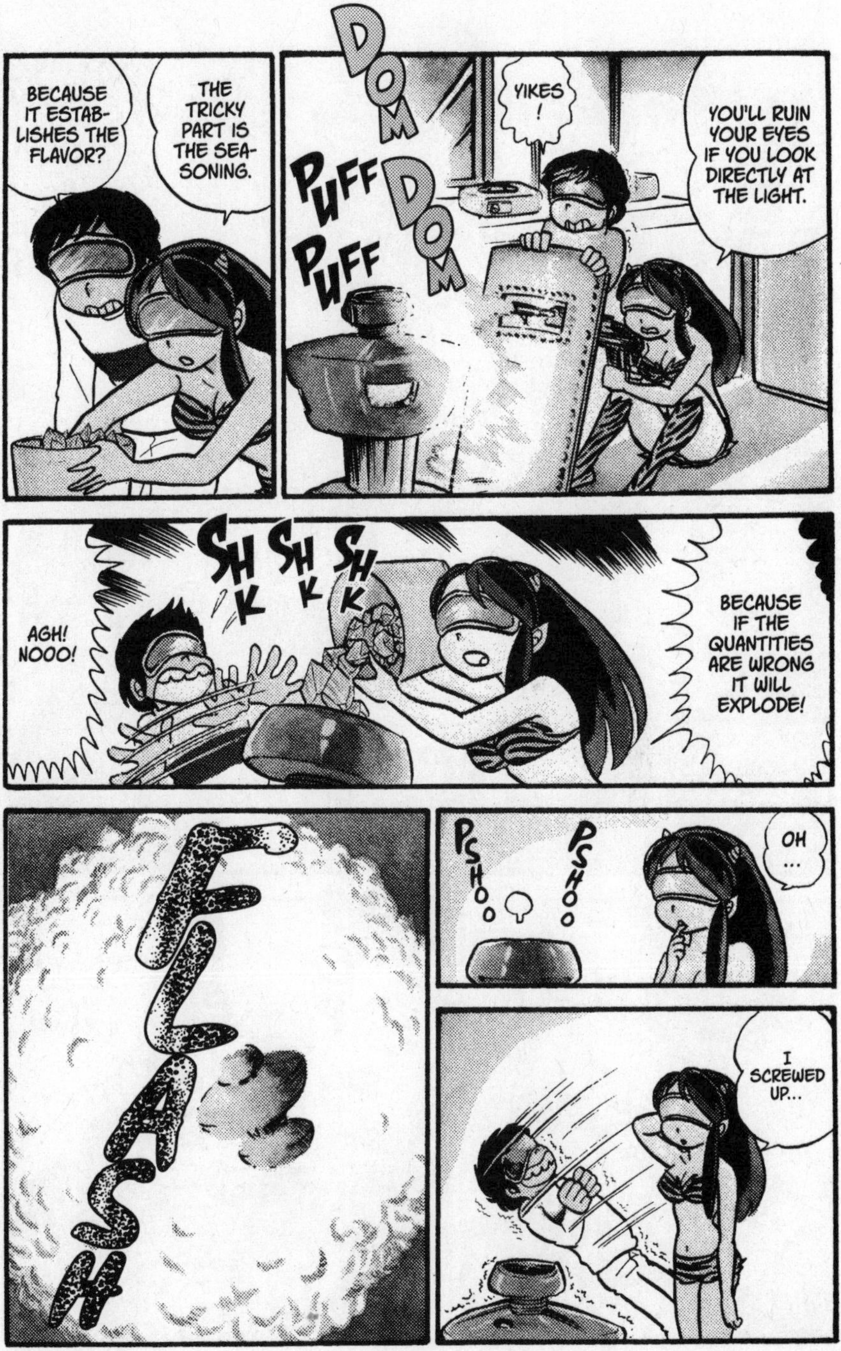
YOU'LL RUIN YOUR EYES IF YOU LOOK DIRECTLY AT THE LIGHT.
YIKES!
DOM DOM DOM
PUFF PUFF
THE TRICKY PART IS THE SEA-SONING.
BECAUSE IT ESTAB-LISHES THE FLAVOR?
BECAUSE IF THE QUANTITIES ARE WRONG IT WILL EXPLODE!
SHK SHK SHK
AGH! NOOO!
OH ...
PSHOOO
PSHOOO
I SCREWED UP...
FLASH

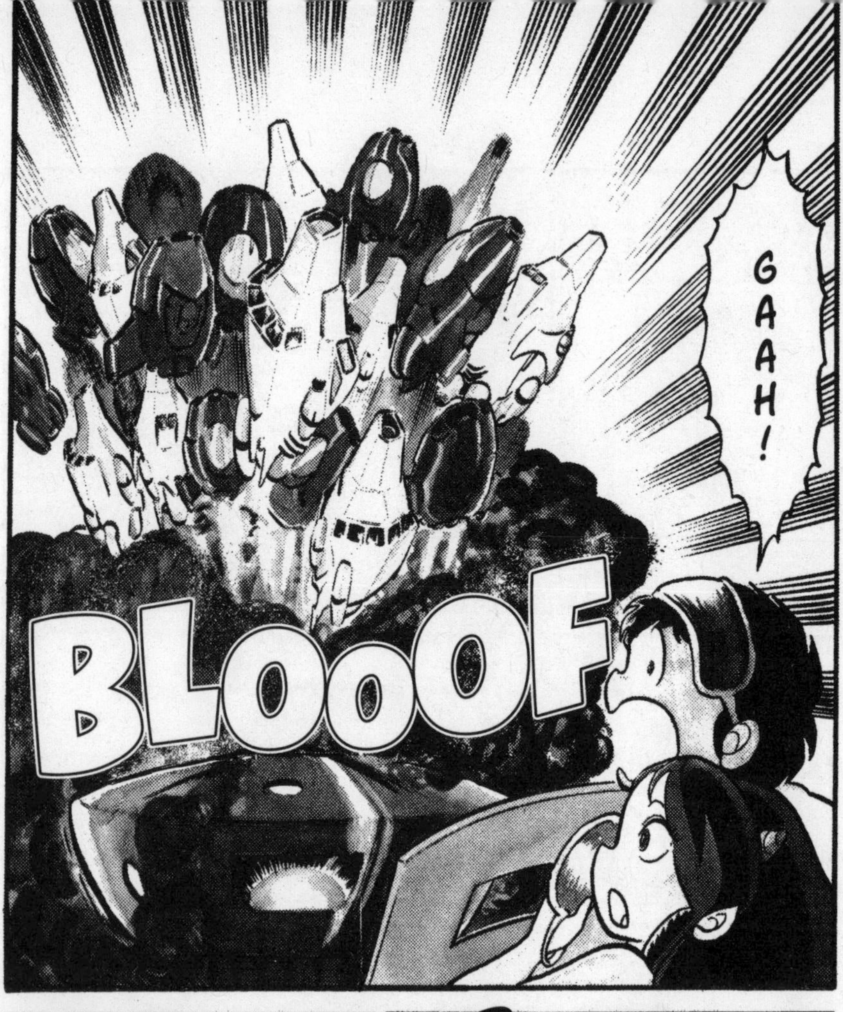
GAAH!
BLOOOF

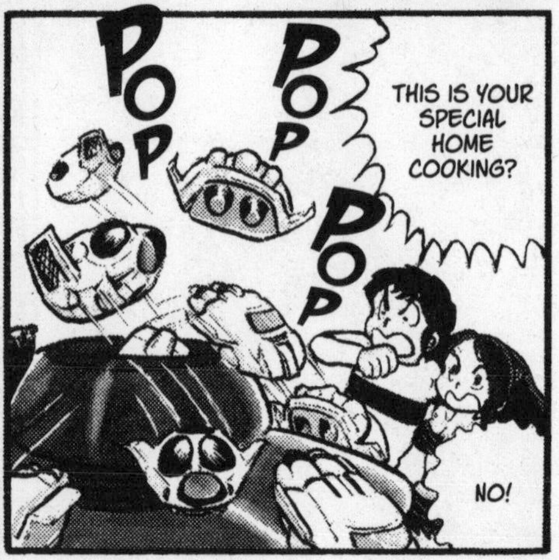
POP
POP
POP
THIS IS YOUR SPECIAL HOME COOKING?
NO!

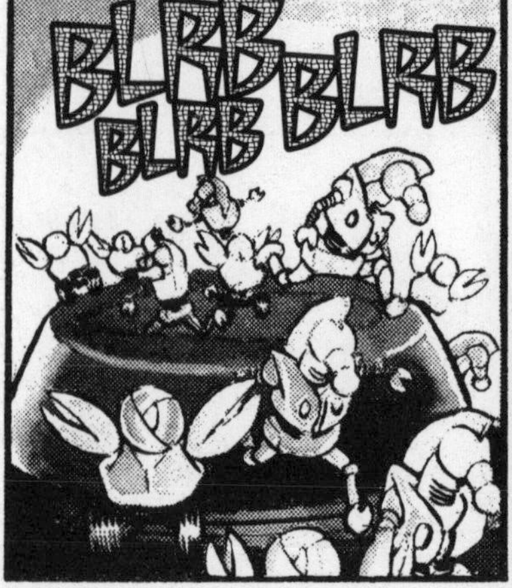
BLRB BLRB BLRB BLRB

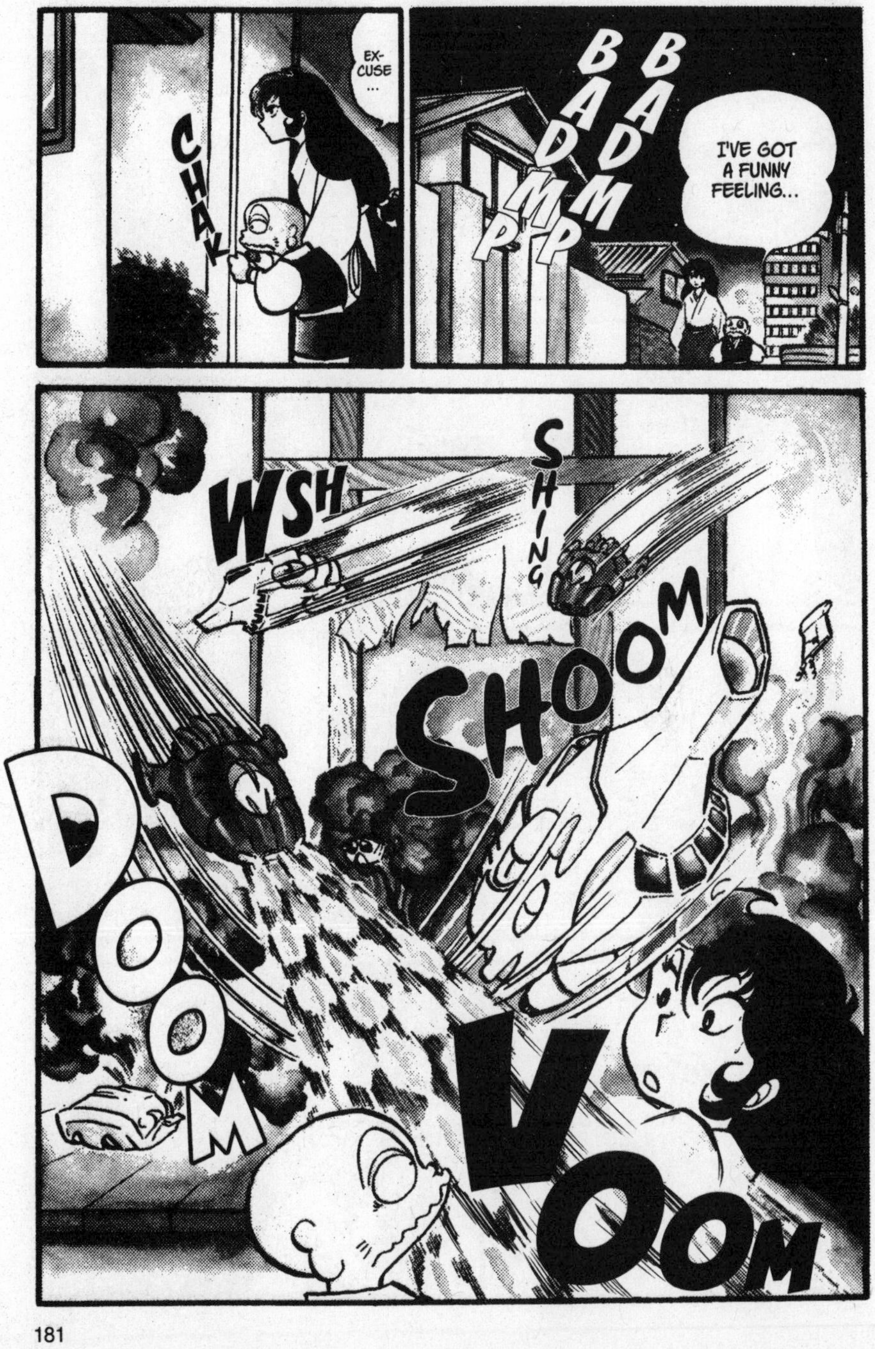
BADMP
BADMP
I'VE GOT A FUNNY FEELING...
EX-CUSE ...
CHAK
SHING
WSH
SHOOM
VOOM
DOOOM

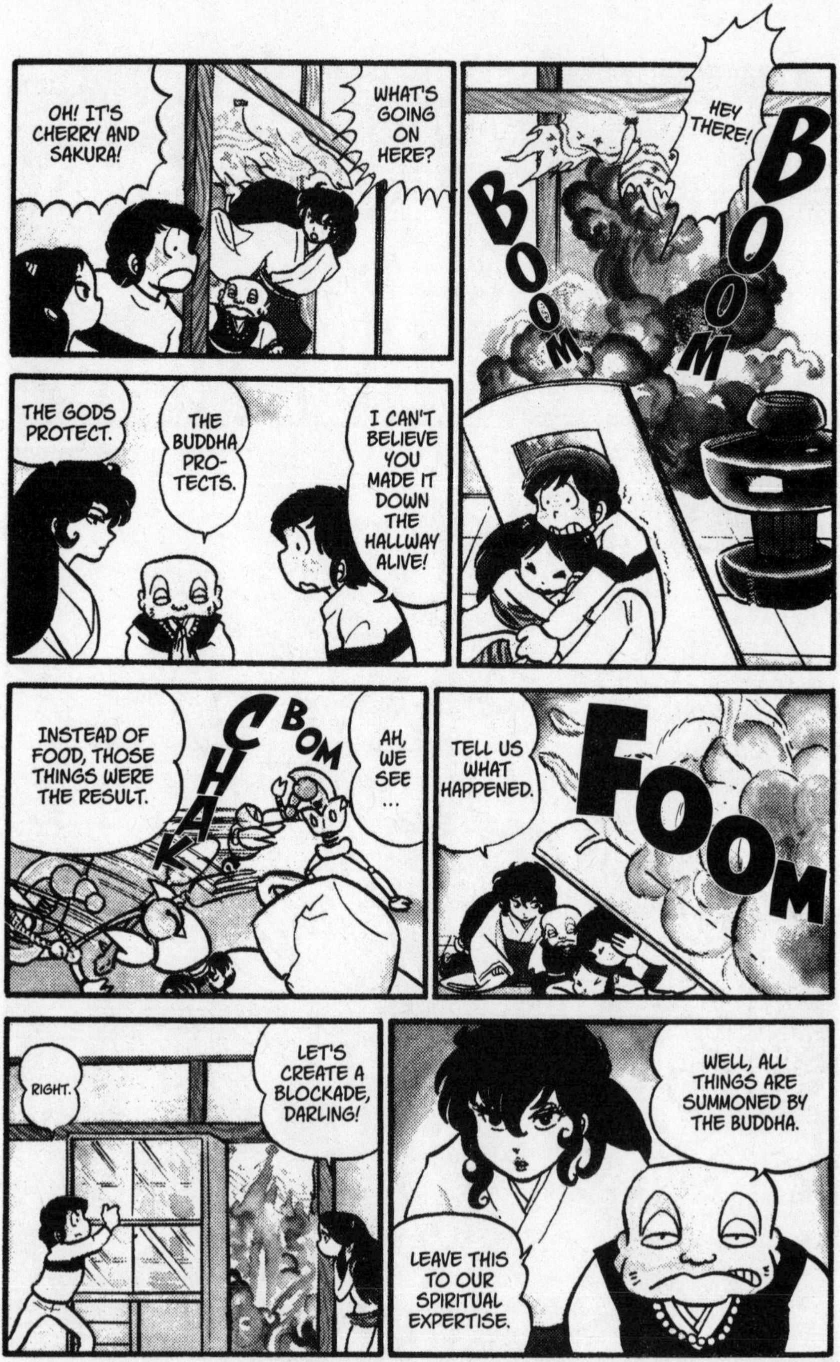
HEY THERE!
BOOM
BOOM
WHAT'S GOING ON HERE?
OH! IT'S CHERRY AND SAKURA!
I CAN'T BELIEVE YOU MADE IT DOWN THE HALLWAY ALIVE!
THE BUDDHA PROTECTS.
THE GODS PROTECT.
FOOM
TELL US WHAT HAPPENED.
AH, WE SEE ...
BOM
CHAK
INSTEAD OF FOOD, THOSE THINGS WERE THE RESULT.
WELL, ALL THINGS ARE SUMMONED BY THE BUDDHA.
LEAVE THIS TO OUR SPIRITUAL EXPERTISE.
LET'S CREATE A BLOCKADE, DARLING!
RIGHT.

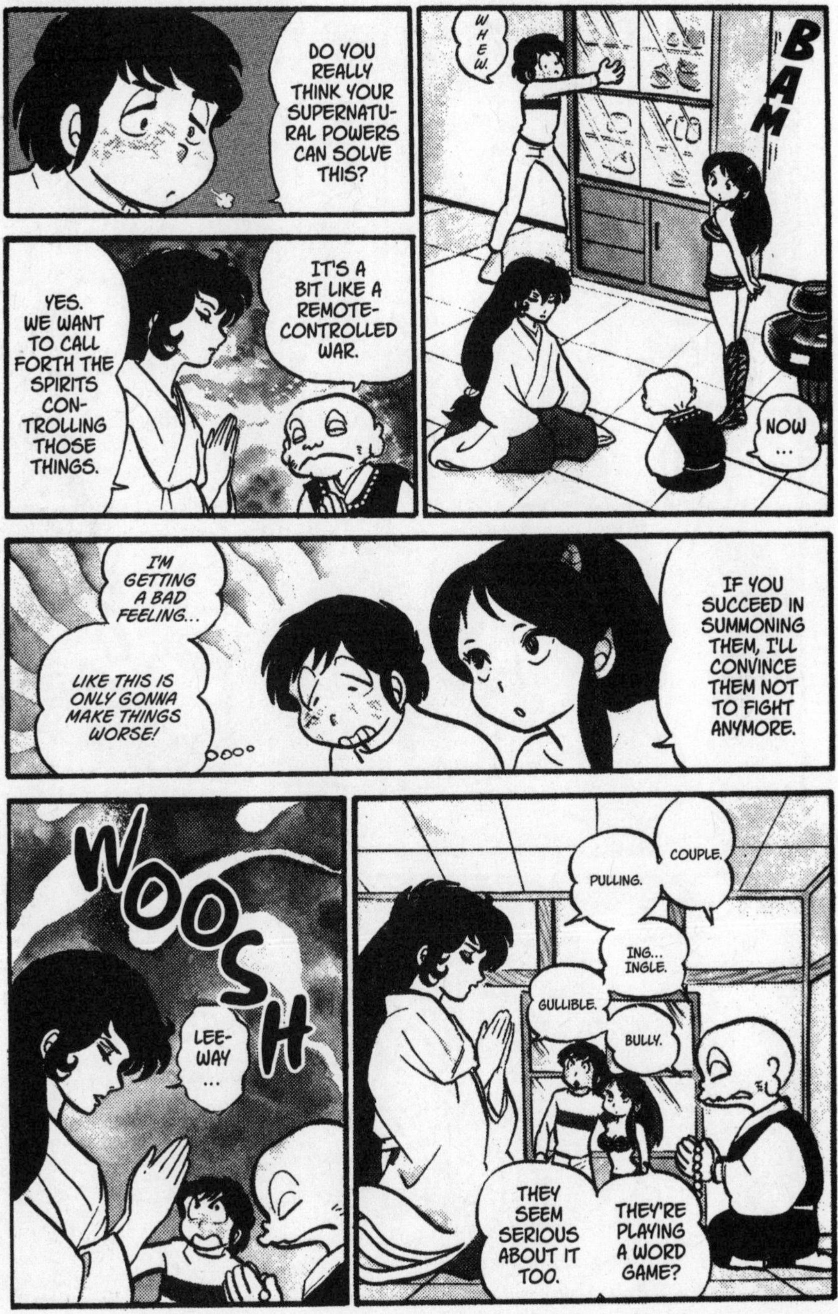
BAM
WHEW.
NOW ...
DO YOU REALLY THINK YOUR SUPERNATURAL POWERS CAN SOLVE THIS?
IT'S A BIT LIKE A REMOTE-CONTROLLED WAR.
YES. WE WANT TO CALL FORTH THE SPIRITS CONTROLLING THOSE THINGS.
IF YOU SUCCEED IN SUMMONING THEM, I'LL CONVINCE THEM NOT TO FIGHT ANYMORE.
I'M GETTING A BAD FEELING...
LIKE THIS IS ONLY GONNA MAKE THINGS WORSE!
COUPLE.
PULLING.
ING... INGLE.
GULLIBLE.
BULLY.
THEY'RE PLAYING A WORD GAME?
THEY SEEM SERIOUS ABOUT IT TOO.
WOOSH
LEE-WAY ...

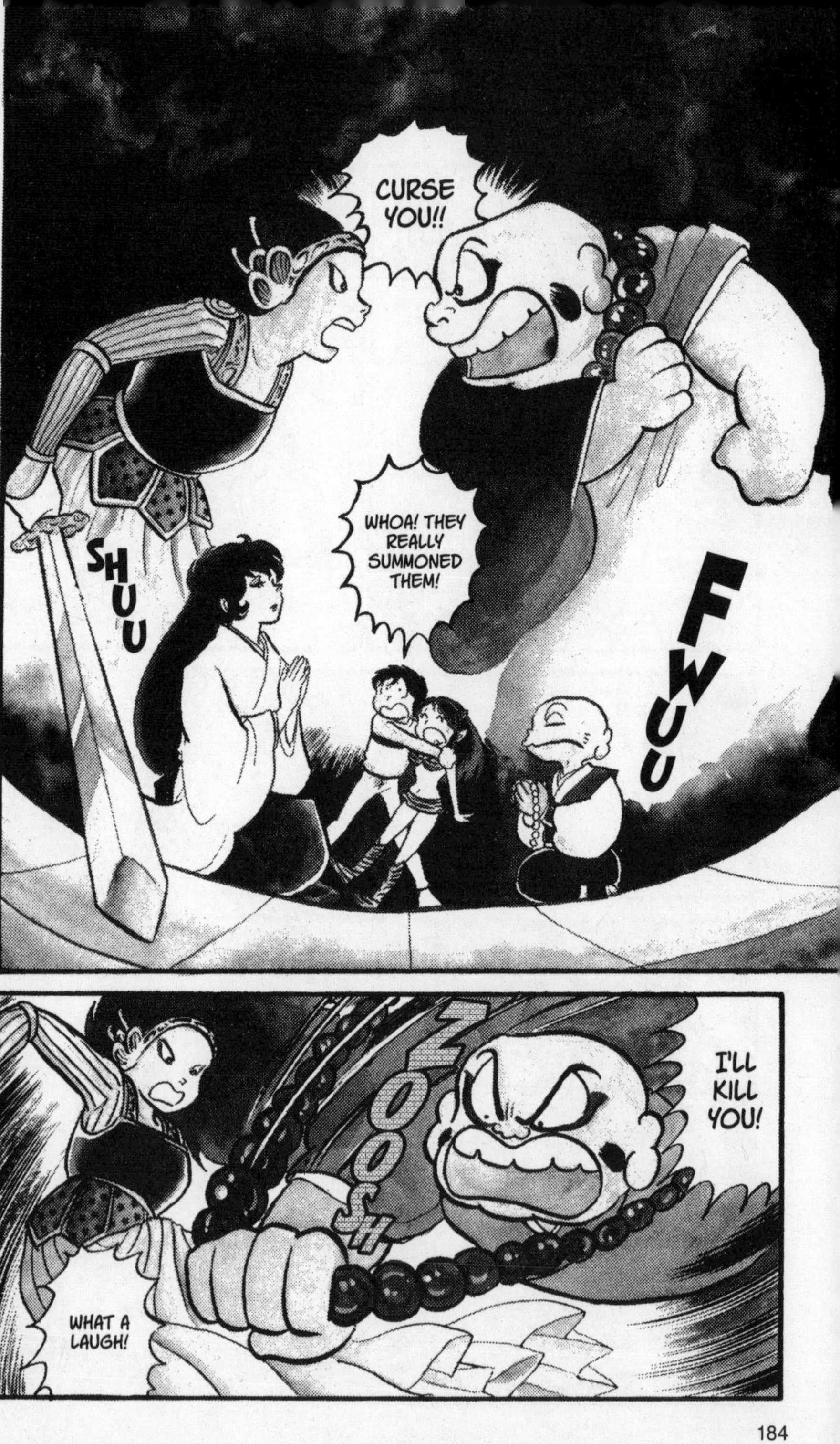
CURSE YOU!!
WHOA! THEY REALLY SUMMONED THEM!
FWUUU
SHUU
I'LL KILL YOU!
ZOOOSH
WHAT A LAUGH!

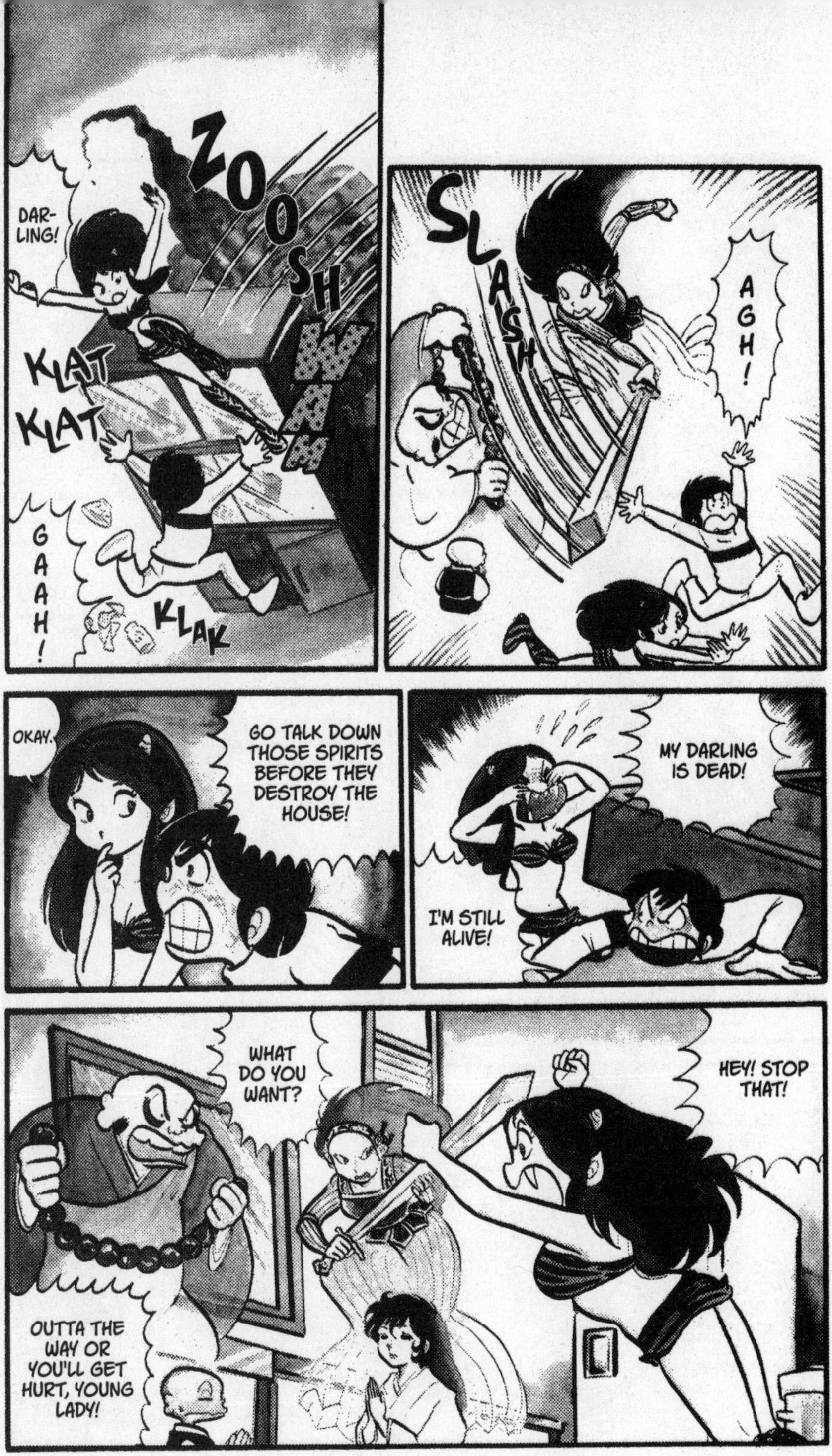
SLASH
AGH!
ZOOSH
DAR-LING!
WHAM
KLAT KLAT
GAAAH!
KLAK
MY DARLING IS DEAD!
I'M STILL ALIVE!
GO TALK DOWN THOSE SPIRITS BEFORE THEY DESTROY THE HOUSE!
OKAY.
HEY! STOP THAT!
WHAT DO YOU WANT?
OUTTA THE WAY OR YOU'LL GET HURT, YOUNG LADY!

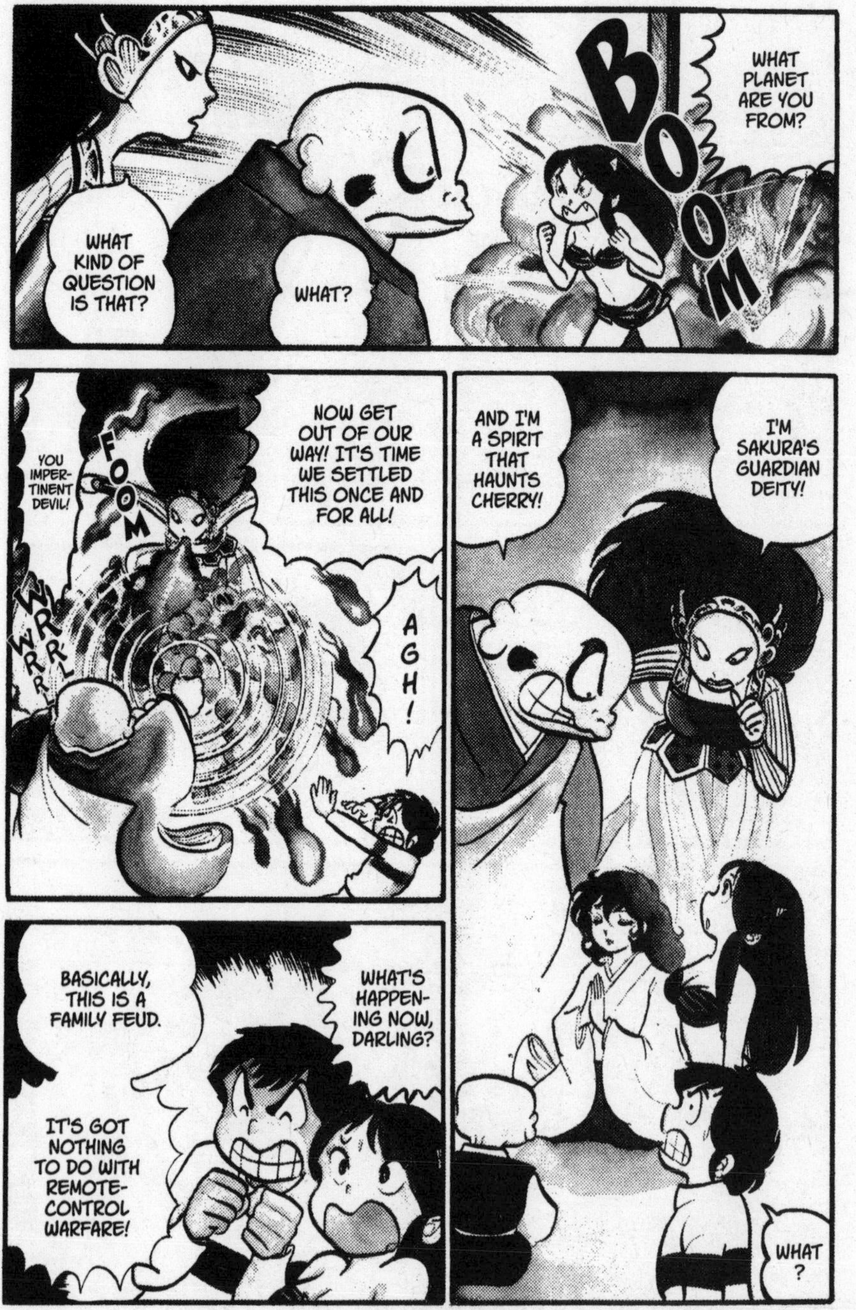

WHAT PLANET ARE YOU FROM?
BOOM
WHAT?
WHAT KIND OF QUESTION IS THAT?
I'M SAKURA'S GUARDIAN DEITY!
AND I'M A SPIRIT THAT HAUNTS CHERRY!
WHAT?
NOW GET OUT OF OUR WAY! IT'S TIME WE SETTLED THIS ONCE AND FOR ALL!
AGH!
FOOM
YOU IMPER-TINENT DEVIL!
WRRRL
WHAT'S HAPPEN-ING NOW, DARLING?
BASICALLY, THIS IS A FAMILY FEUD.
IT'S GOT NOTHING TO DO WITH REMOTE-CONTROL WARFARE!

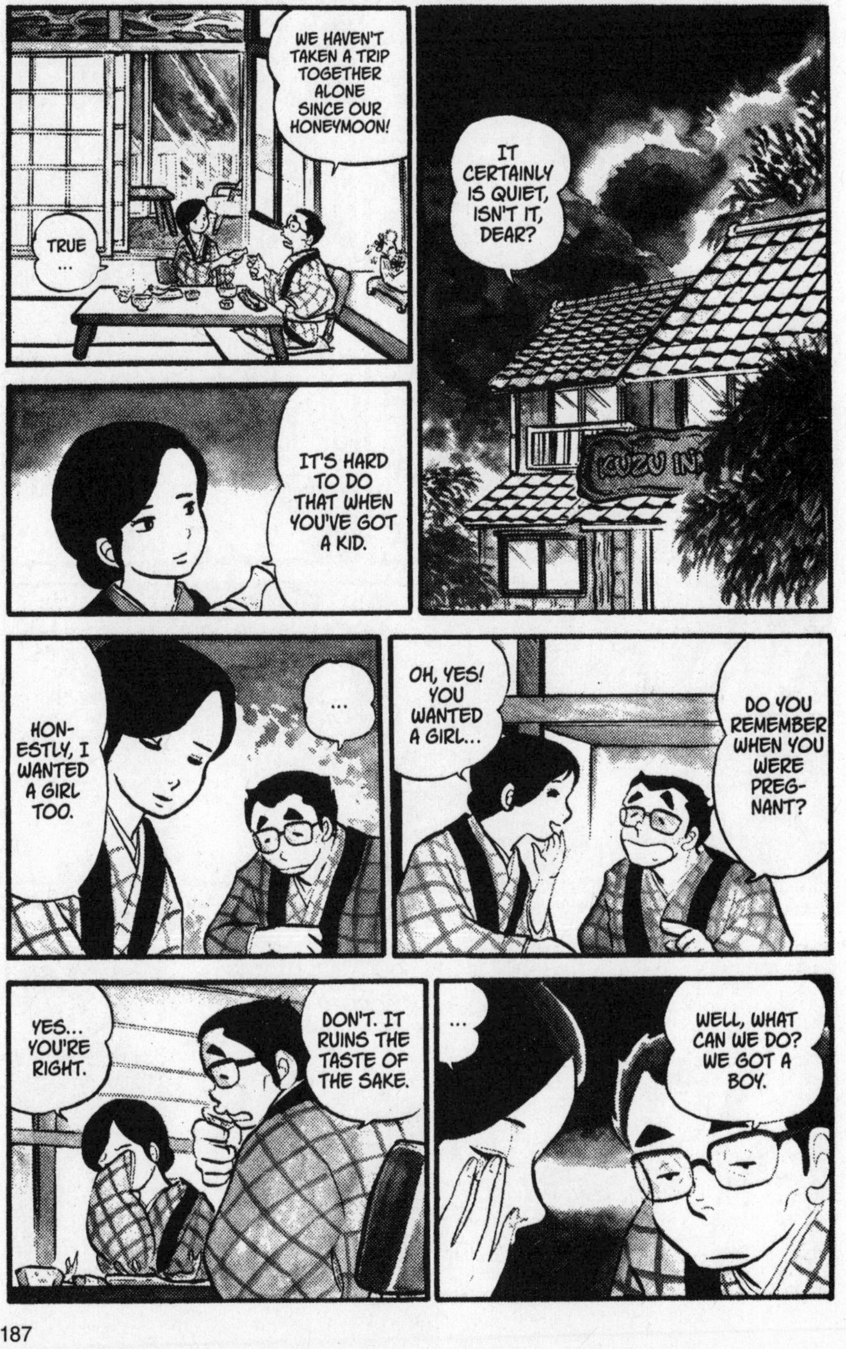
IT CERTAINLY IS QUIET, ISN'T IT, DEAR?
WE HAVEN'T TAKEN A TRIP TOGETHER ALONE SINCE OUR HONEYMOON!
TRUE ...
IT'S HARD TO DO THAT WHEN YOU'VE GOT A KID.
DO YOU REMEMBER WHEN YOU WERE PREGNANT?
OH, YES! YOU WANTED A GIRL...
...
HONESTLY, I WANTED A GIRL TOO.
WELL, WHAT CAN WE DO? WE GOT A BOY.
...
DON'T. IT RUINS THE TASTE OF THE SAKE.
YES... YOU'RE RIGHT.

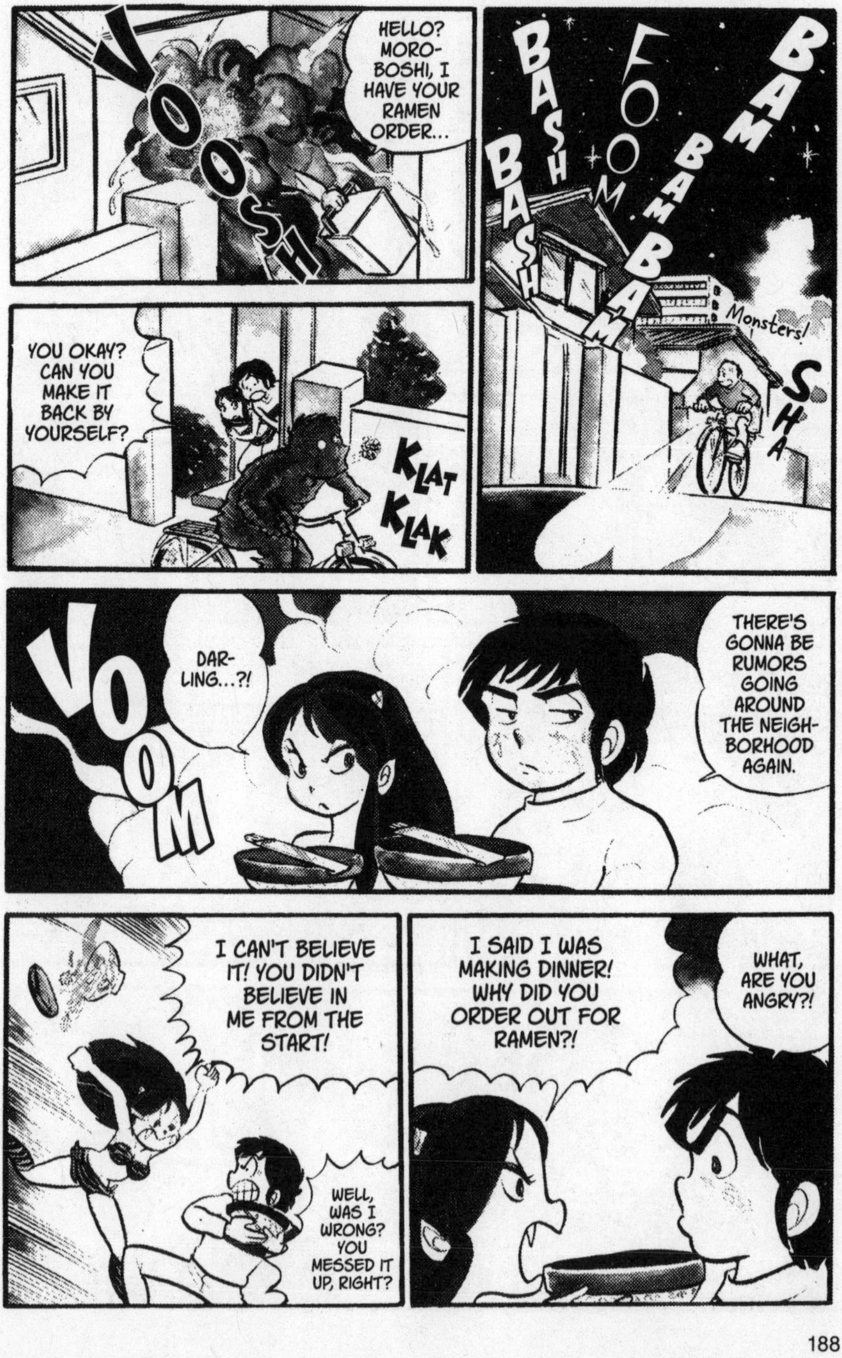
BAM
BAM BAM
FOOM
BASH
BASH
Monsters!
SHA
HELLO? MORO-BOSHI, I HAVE YOUR RAMEN ORDER...
VOOSH
YOU OKAY? CAN YOU MAKE IT BACK BY YOURSELF?
KLAT KLAK
THERE'S GONNA BE RUMORS GOING AROUND THE NEIGH-BORHOOD AGAIN.
DAR-LING...?!
VOOM
WHAT, ARE YOU ANGRY?!
I SAID I WAS MAKING DINNER! WHY DID YOU ORDER OUT FOR RAMEN?!
I CAN'T BELIEVE IT! YOU DIDN'T BELIEVE IN ME FROM THE START!
WELL, WAS I WRONG? YOU MESSED IT UP, RIGHT?

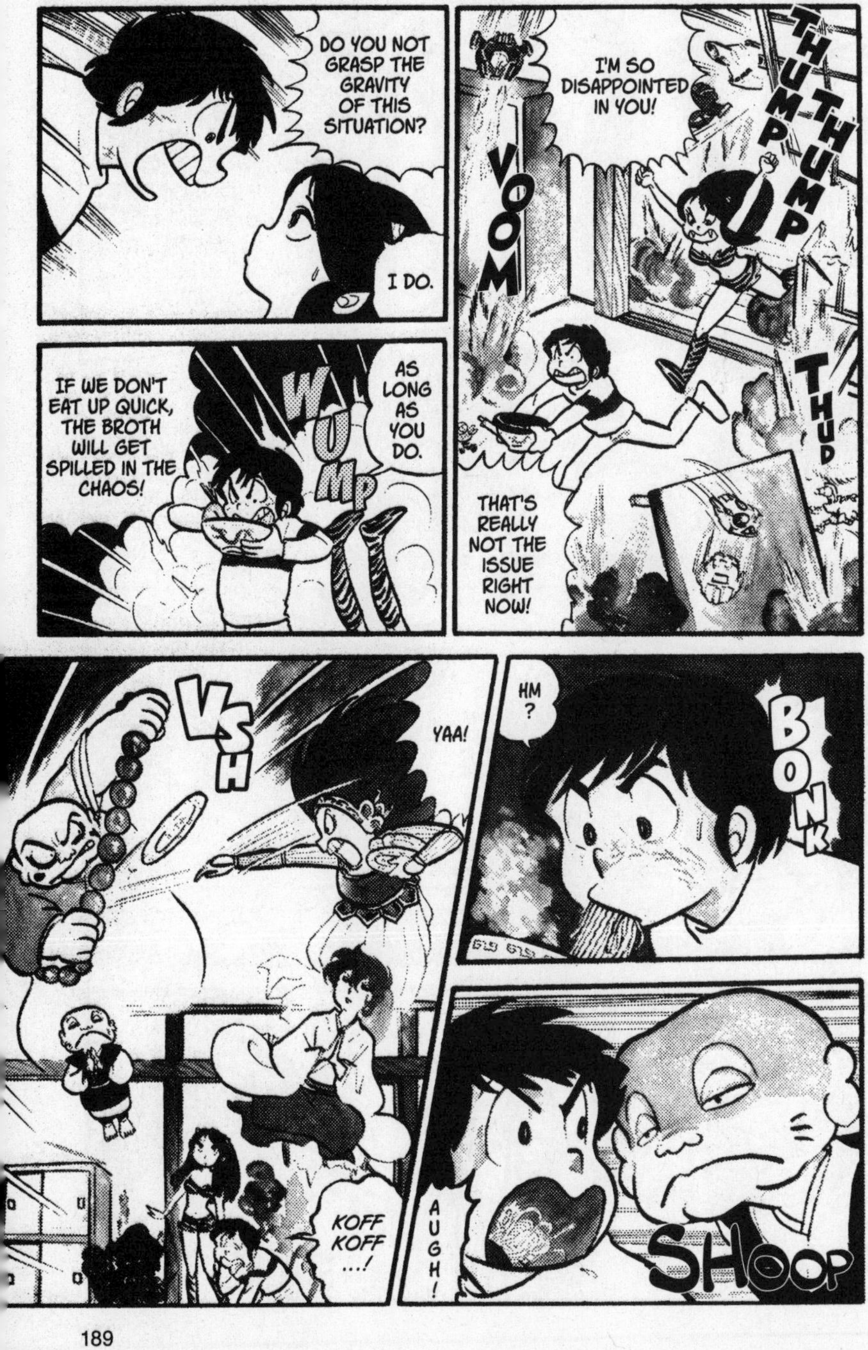
THUMP THUMP
THUMP THUMP
I'M SO DISAPPOINTED IN YOU!
VOOM
THUD
THAT'S REALLY NOT THE ISSUE RIGHT NOW!
DO YOU NOT GRASP THE GRAVITY OF THIS SITUATION?
I DO.
AS LONG AS YOU DO.
IF WE DON'T EAT UP QUICK, THE BROTH WILL GET SPILLED IN THE CHAOS!
WUMP
HM?
BONK
SHOOP
AUGH!
VSH
YAA!
KOFF KOFF ...!

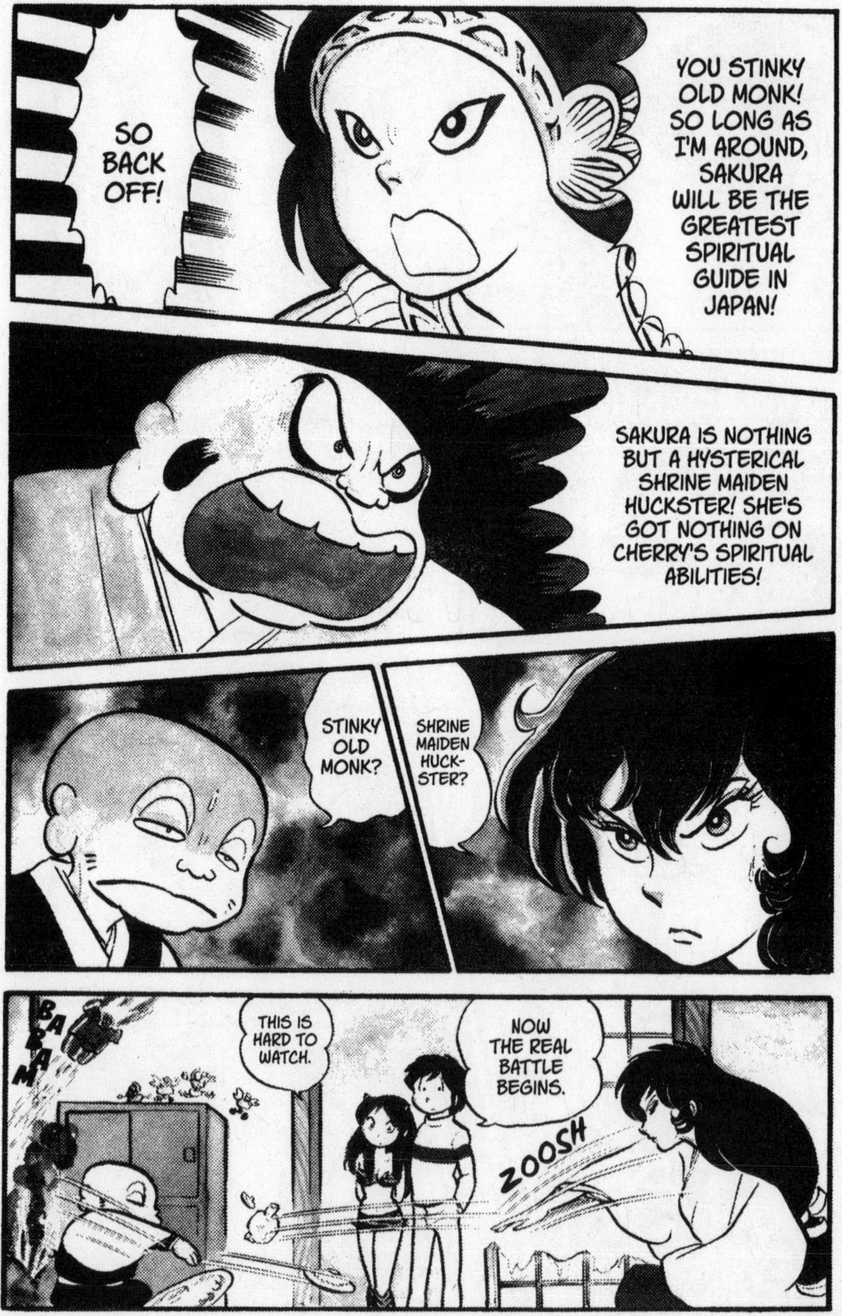
YOU STINKY OLD MONK! SO LONG AS I'M AROUND, SAKURA WILL BE THE GREATEST SPIRITUAL GUIDE IN JAPAN!
SO BACK OFF!
SAKURA IS NOTHING BUT A HYSTERICAL SHRINE MAIDEN HUCKSTER! SHE'S GOT NOTHING ON CHERRY'S SPIRITUAL ABILITIES!
SHRINE MAIDEN HUCK-STER?
STINKY OLD MONK?
NOW THE REAL BATTLE BEGINS.
THIS IS HARD TO WATCH.
BABAM
ZOOSH

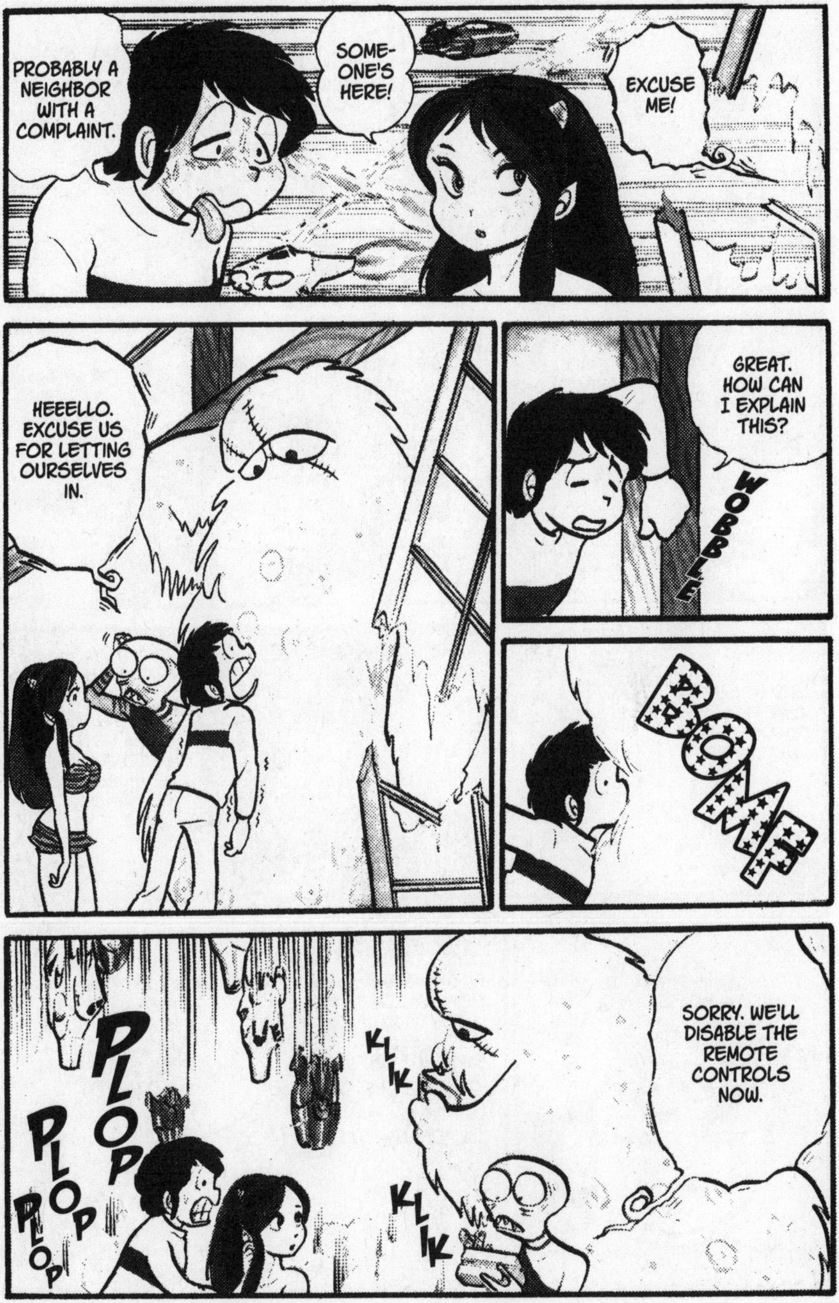
EXCUSE ME!
SOME-ONE'S HERE!
PROBABLY A NEIGHBOR WITH A COMPLAINT.
GREAT. HOW CAN I EXPLAIN THIS?
WOBBLE
BOMF
HEEELLO. EXCUSE US FOR LETTING OURSELVES IN.
SORRY. WE'LL DISABLE THE REMOTE CONTROLS NOW.
KLIK
KLIK
PLOP
PLOP
PLOP
PLOP

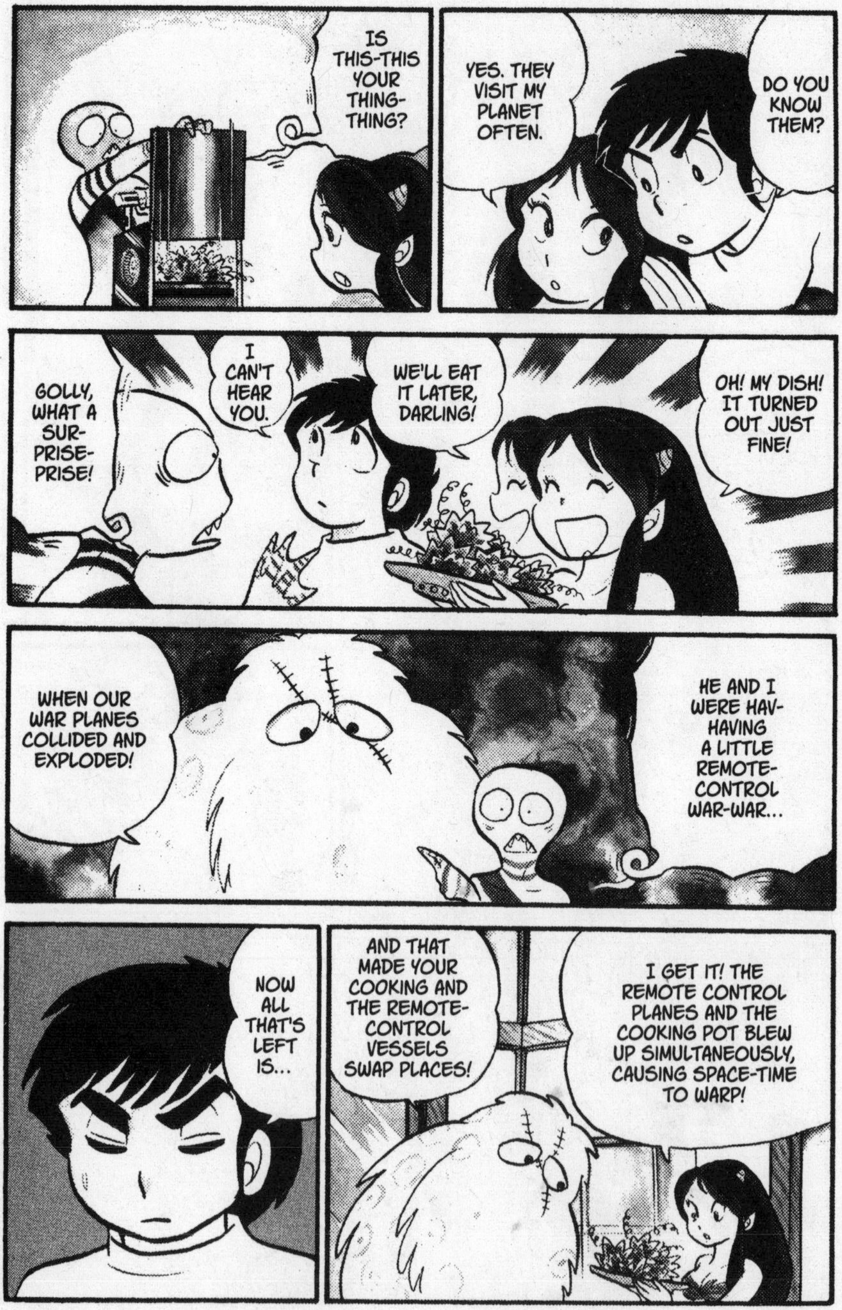
DO YOU KNOW THEM?
YES. THEY VISIT MY PLANET OFTEN.
IS THIS-THIS YOUR THING-THING?
OH! MY DISH! IT TURNED OUT JUST FINE!
WE'LL EAT IT LATER, DARLING!
I CAN'T HEAR YOU.
GOLLY, WHAT A SUR-PRISE-PRISE!
HE AND I WERE HAV-HAVING A LITTLE REMOTE-CONTROL WAR-WAR...
WHEN OUR WAR PLANES COLLIDED AND EXPLODED!
I GET IT! THE REMOTE CONTROL PLANES AND THE COOKING POT BLEW UP SIMULTANEOUSLY, CAUSING SPACE-TIME TO WARP!
AND THAT MADE YOUR COOKING AND THE REMOTE-CONTROL VESSELS SWAP PLACES!
NOW ALL THAT'S LEFT IS...

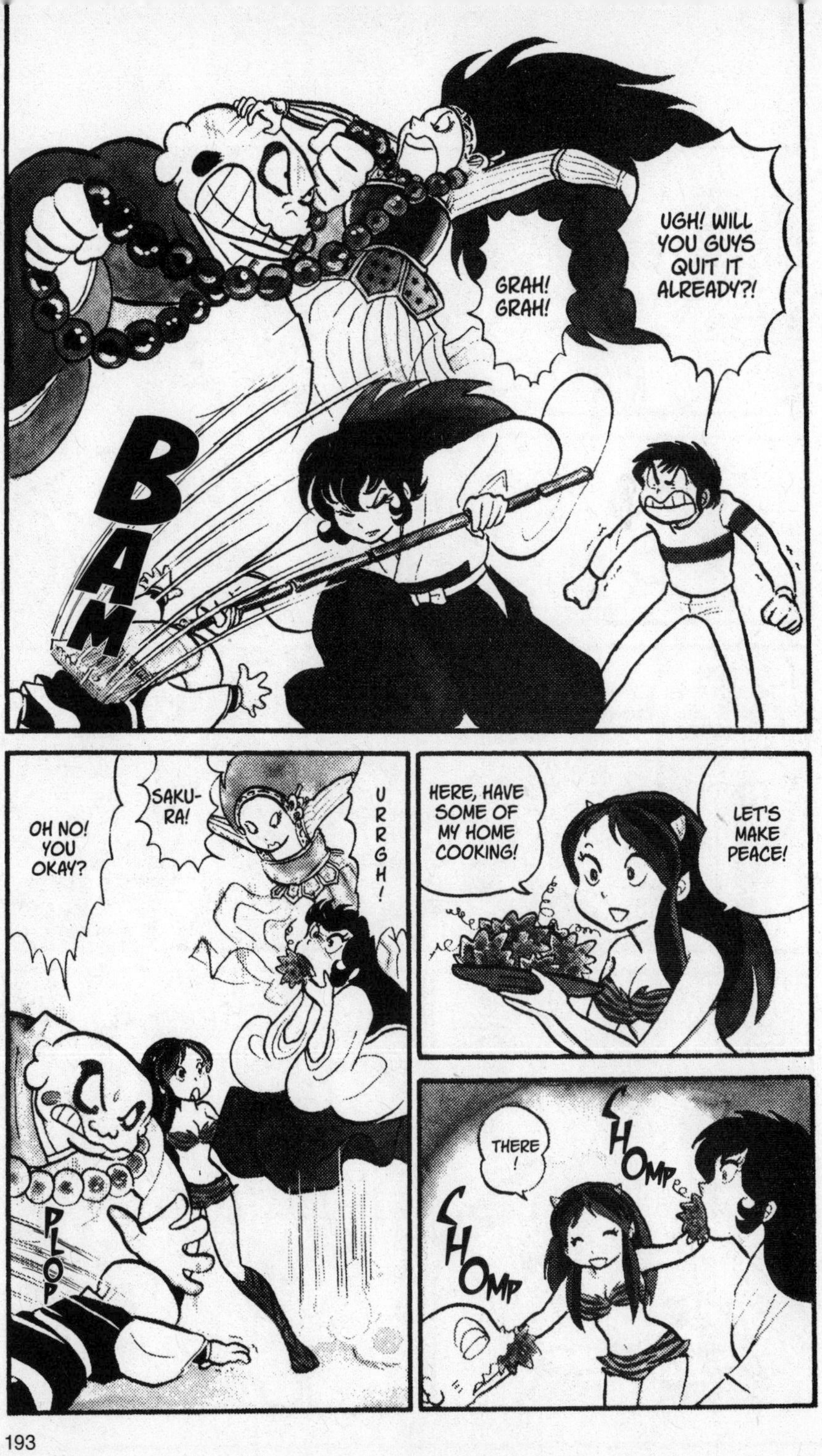
UGH! WILL YOU GUYS QUIT IT ALREADY?!
GRAH! GRAH!
BAM
LET'S MAKE PEACE!
HERE, HAVE SOME OF MY HOME COOKING!
CHOMP
THERE!
CHOMP
URRGH!
SAKU-RA!
OH NO! YOU OKAY?
PLOP

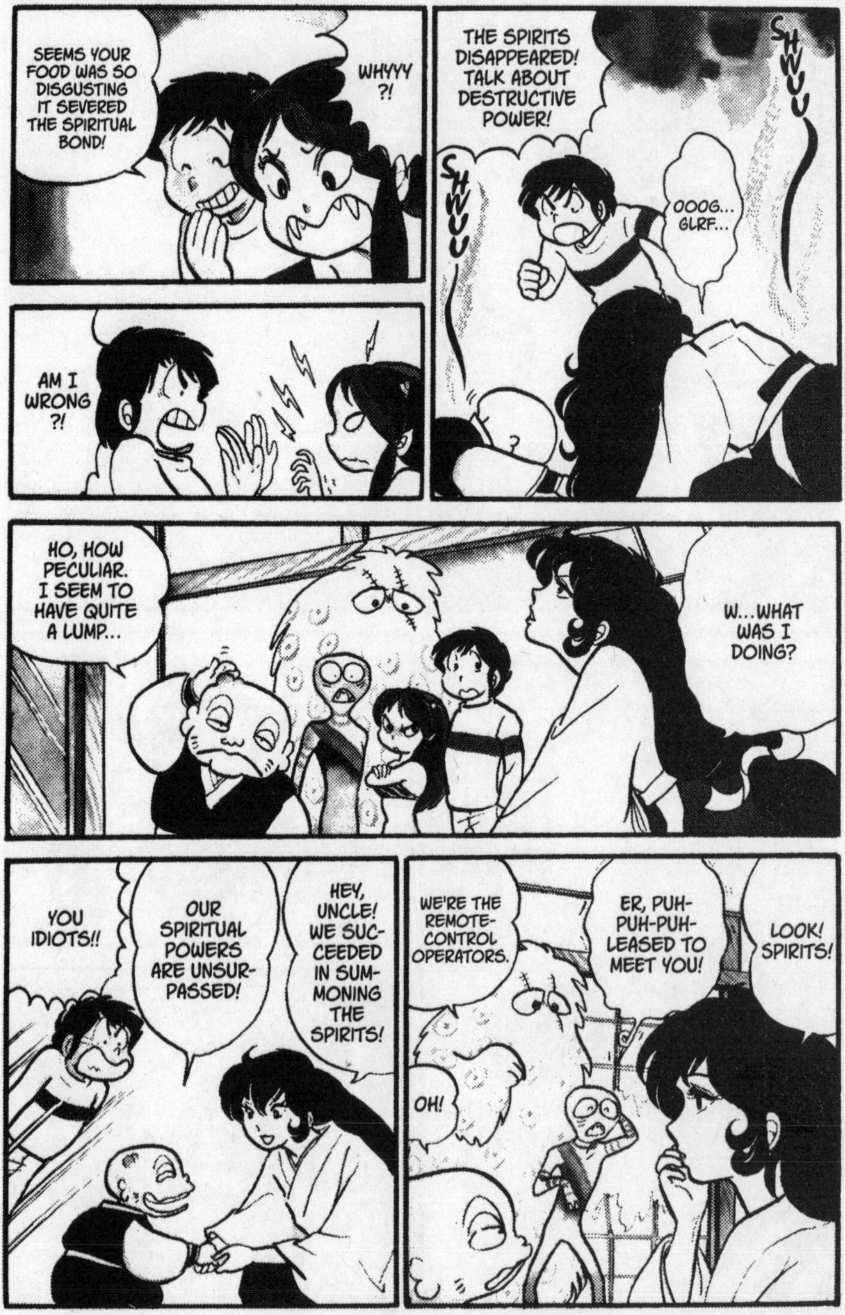
THE SPIRITS DISAPPEARED! TALK ABOUT DESTRUCTIVE POWER!
SHWUUU
OOOG... GLRF...
SHWUU
WHYYY ?!
SEEMS YOUR FOOD WAS SO DISGUSTING IT SEVERED THE SPIRITUAL BOND!
AM I WRONG ?!
W...WHAT WAS I DOING?
HO, HOW PECULIAR. I SEEM TO HAVE QUITE A LUMP...
LOOK! SPIRITS!
ER, PUH-PUH-PUH-LEASED TO MEET YOU!
WE'RE THE REMOTE-CONTROL OPERATORS.
OH!
HEY, UNCLE! WE SUCCEEDED IN SUMMONING THE SPIRITS!
OUR SPIRITUAL POWERS ARE UNSURPASSED!
YOU IDIOTS!!

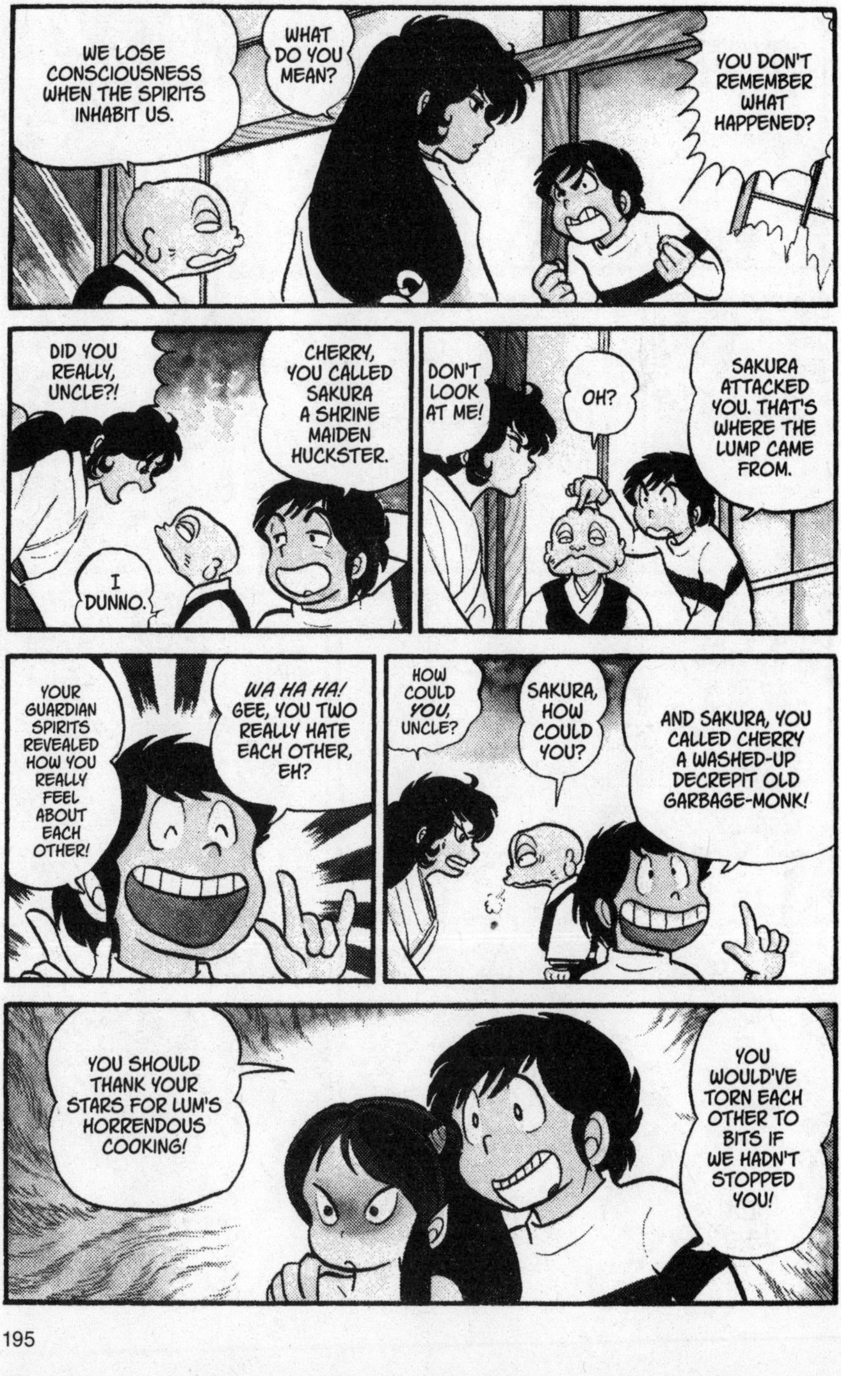
YOU DON'T REMEMBER WHAT HAPPENED?
WHAT DO YOU MEAN?
WE LOSE CONSCIOUSNESS WHEN THE SPIRITS INHABIT US.
SAKURA ATTACKED YOU. THAT'S WHERE THE LUMP CAME FROM.
OH?
DON'T LOOK AT ME!
CHERRY, YOU CALLED SAKURA A SHRINE MAIDEN HUCKSTER.
DID YOU REALLY, UNCLE?!
I DUNNO.
AND SAKURA, YOU CALLED CHERRY A WASHED-UP DECREPIT OLD GARBAGE-MONK!
SAKURA, HOW COULD YOU?
HOW COULD *YOU*, UNCLE?
WA HA HA! GEE, YOU TWO REALLY HATE EACH OTHER, EH?
YOUR GUARDIAN SPIRITS REVEALED HOW YOU REALLY FEEL ABOUT EACH OTHER!
YOU WOULD'VE TORN EACH OTHER TO BITS IF WE HADN'T STOPPED YOU!
YOU SHOULD THANK YOUR STARS FOR LUM'S HORRENDOUS COOKING!

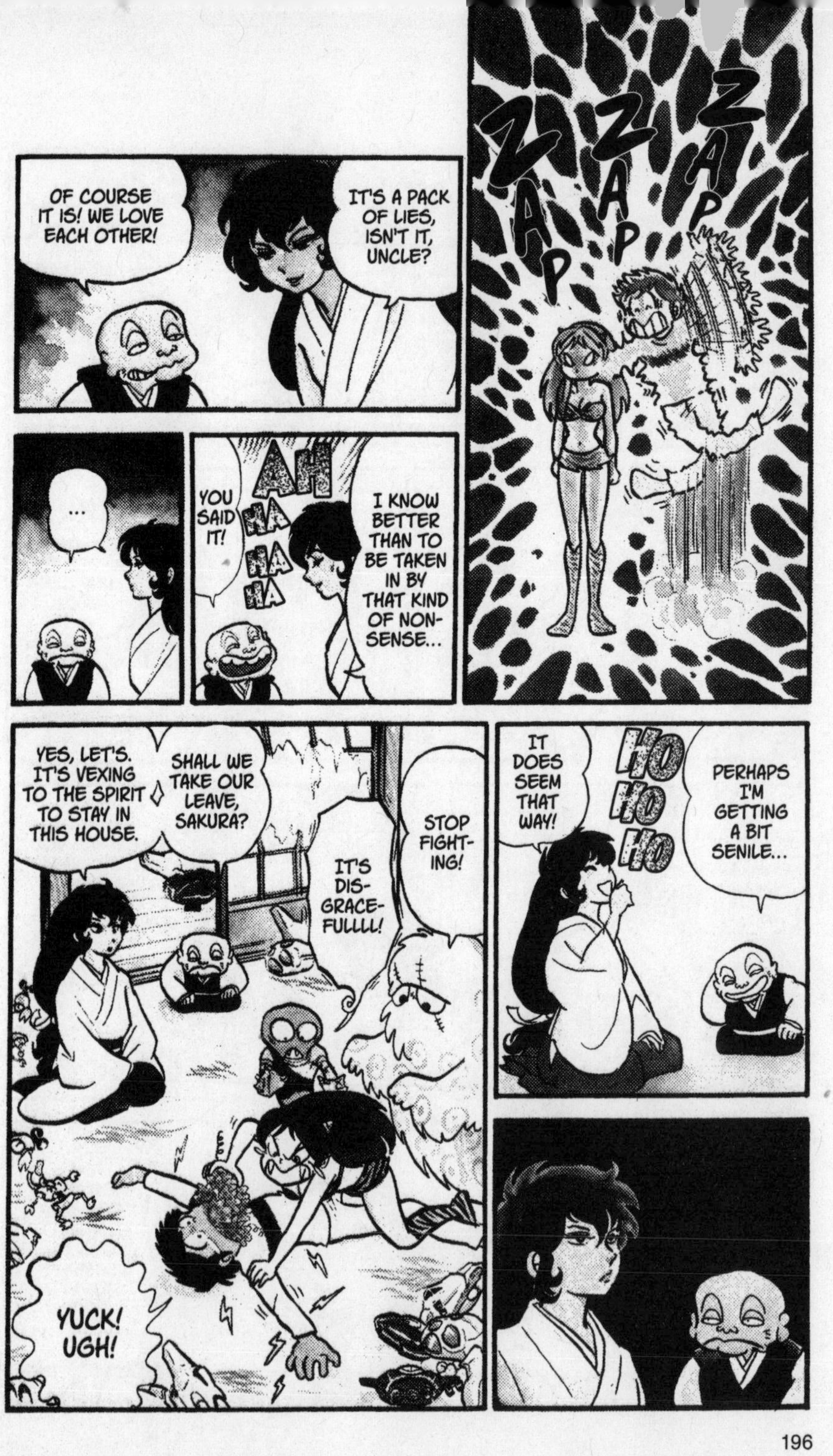
ZAP ZAP ZAP
IT'S A PACK OF LIES, ISN'T IT, UNCLE?
OF COURSE IT IS! WE LOVE EACH OTHER!
I KNOW BETTER THAN TO BE TAKEN IN BY THAT KIND OF NON-SENSE...
AH HA HA HA
YOU SAID IT!
...
PERHAPS I'M GETTING A BIT SENILE...
HO HO HO
IT DOES SEEM THAT WAY!
STOP FIGHT-ING!
IT'S DIS-GRACE-FULLLL!
SHALL WE TAKE OUR LEAVE, SAKURA?
YES, LET'S. IT'S VEXING TO THE SPIRIT TO STAY IN THIS HOUSE.
YUCK! UGH!

URUSEI YATSURA ★ DATA FILE 01

What Kind of Town is Tomobiki Town?

Happy Life in an Unlucky Town!

The town where Ataru lives, Lum settles, Cherry loiters—the most tumultuous town in Japan (and in the universe?)! Let's explore Tomobiki Town just a bit!

You might get the impression that *Urusei Yatsurai* is a school-based sci-fi comic that's set at Tomobiki High, the school that Ataru and Lum attend. But actually, Lum is absent from some of the earliest chapters, and originally the story was established as a "neighborhood manga" revolving mainly around the Moroboshi household and its surroundings. For that reason, our first Data File focuses on Ataru's hometown: Tomobiki Town!

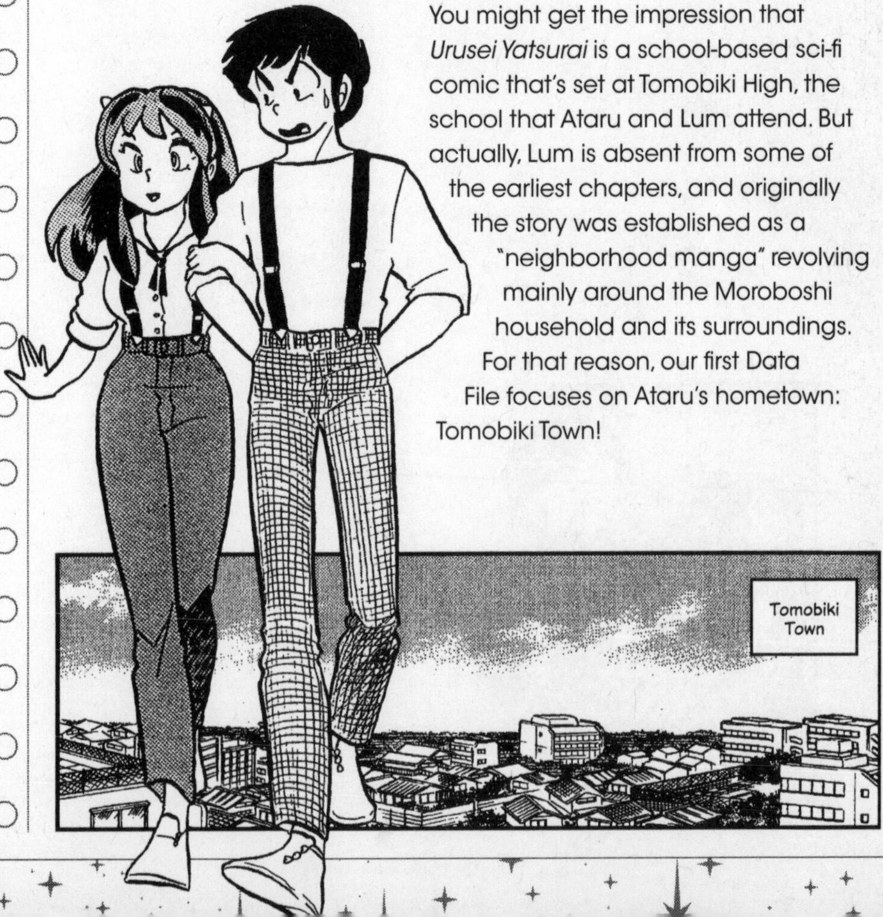
Tomobiki Town

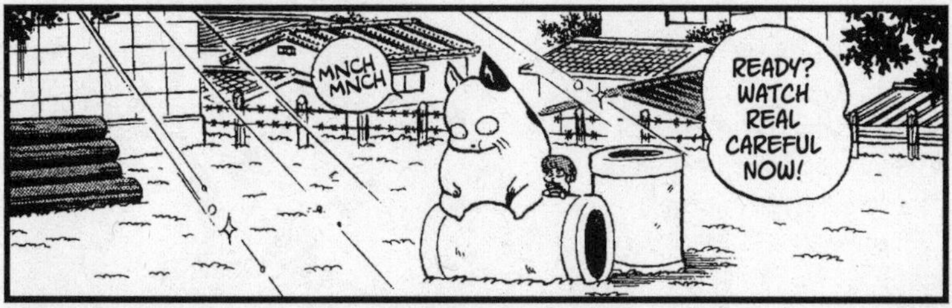
READY? WATCH REAL CAREFUL NOW!
MNCH MNCH

▲ Old-fashioned sandlot (volume 13, chapter 19 "Fantasy Bubble Gum")

STUDY 1

The Charms of Tomobiki ①

Its Inhabitants Interact a Lot!

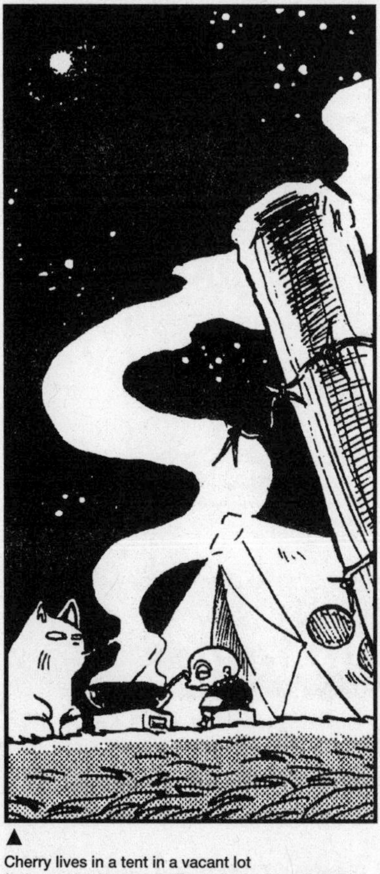

▲
Cherry lives in a tent in a vacant lot (volume 11, chapter 10 "Foxes in the Moonlight")

Tomobiki Town is located in the Nerima Ward of Tokyo. This is clear from the address on mail received at Ataru's house (volume 4, chapter 5 "Ten is Here").

As many of you probably know, Tokyo has 23 wards, and Nerima Ward is the one closest to Saitama Prefecture. It was established as a commuter town for folks working in the downtown area and was once famous as the farmland that produced Nerima daikon radishes. To this day, it remains a very humble place.

Within Nerima, Tomobiki Town is an especially relaxed place. Of course, it's a made-up town. The area surrounding Tomobiki High has a shopping street with many old shops, a number of vacant lots, and a decidedly traditional old-town feel.

It's so laid-back that kids can play baseball in the empty lots (volume 1, chapter 2 "Gentle Imp"), and nobody complains even when Cherry pitches his tent there (volume 1, chapter 6 "To Kill with Love").

The neighbors, including the Moroboshi household, are all unique characters with a strong penchant for gossip. They rubberneck during Ataru and Lum's turbulent game of tag and have no compunction about banging on the door late at night (volume 1, chapter 1 "Young Love on the Run").

They gossip shamelessly at the Moroboshi front doorstep, saying "They've finally kicked him out!" and "Well, I'm not surprised! He was on the phone for two hours! I saw him!" (volume 1, chapter 5 "Between a Rock and a Hard Place").

In a modern metropolis where people often don't know their neighbors, it's an unusually folksy place.

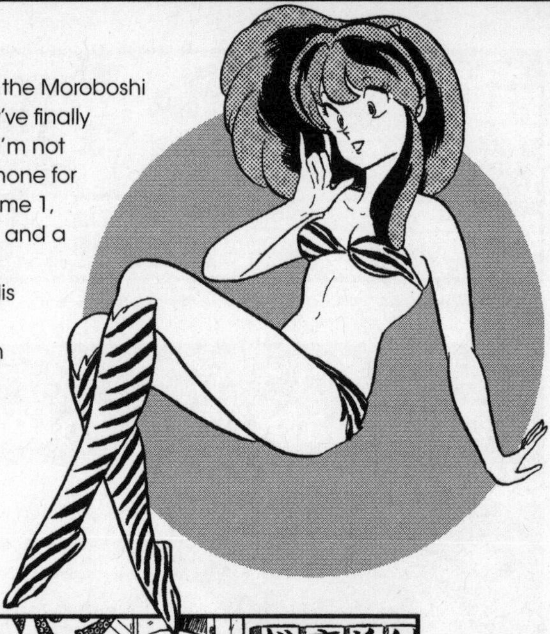

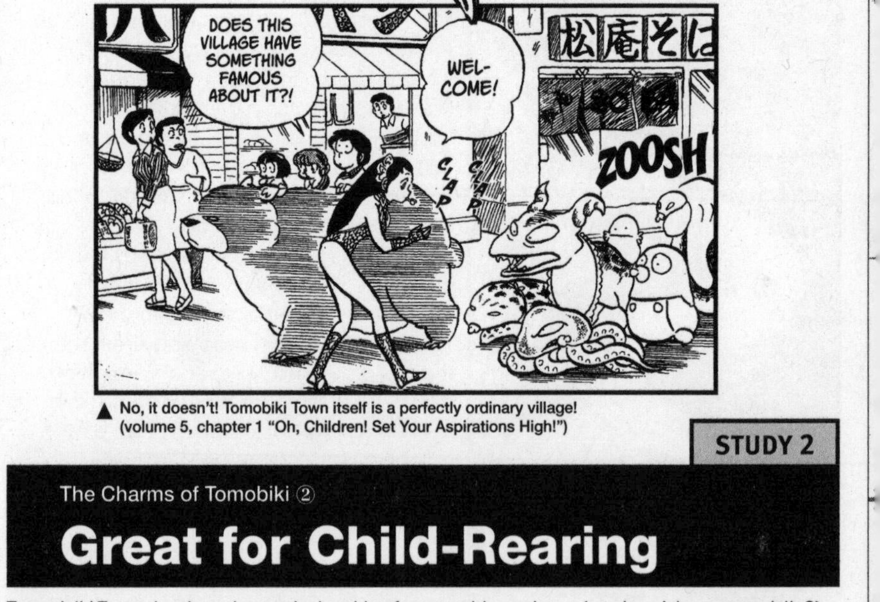

松庵そば
WEL-COME!
DOES THIS VILLAGE HAVE SOMETHING FAMOUS ABOUT IT?!
ZOOSH
CLAP
CLAP

▲ **No, it doesn't! Tomobiki Town itself is a perfectly ordinary village! (volume 5, chapter 1 "Oh, Children! Set Your Aspirations High!")**

STUDY 2

The Charms of Tomobiki ②

Great for Child-Rearing

Tomobiki Town is also characterized by frequent invasions (or should we say visits?) by aliens, starting with Lum. What's more, Tomobiki Town is a dangerous place that is frequently struck by disasters. Thanks to Lum's jealous rages, it has experienced destructive electrical storms and two military aircraft disappearances (volume 1, chapter 5 "Between a Rock and a Hard Place")!

However, the feeling of danger soon passes. Alien invasions and disasters aren't such a big deal once you get used to them.

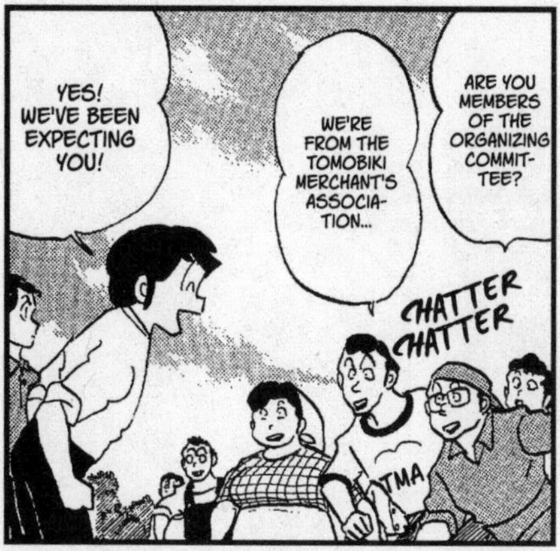
ARE YOU MEMBERS OF THE ORGANIZING COMMITTEE?
WE'RE FROM THE TOMOBIKI MERCHANT'S ASSOCIATION...
YES! WE'VE BEEN EXPECTING YOU!
CHATTER CHATTER
TMA

▲ In Tomobiki Town, the High School has a very close relationship with the Tomobiki Merchant's Association, perhaps because the school hosts so many events. (volume 9, chapter 18 "Miss Tomobiki Contest: Preliminary Round")

At first, the inhabitants of Tomobiki Town are easily irked, exclaiming "It's that Moroboshi kid again!" (volume 1, chapter 3 "The Sad Sound of Rain"), but they quickly get used to the disturbances, and even seem to enjoy them, shouting "Hey! There's something weird happening at the Moroboshi place again!" (volume 2, chapter 3 "Without Even Saying Goodbye").

If Tomobiki Town's tolerant culture and ability to accept whatever happens is one of its charms, another is the strong unity within the community. There is a particularly strong relationship between the merchants of the Tomobiki Town Shopping District and the students of Tomobiki High. On one occasion, the teachers at Tomobiki High banned students from buying snacks after school, but the merchants of the shopping district united to support the students to overturn the ban (volume 6, chapter 4 "The Great Afterschool Snack Battle").

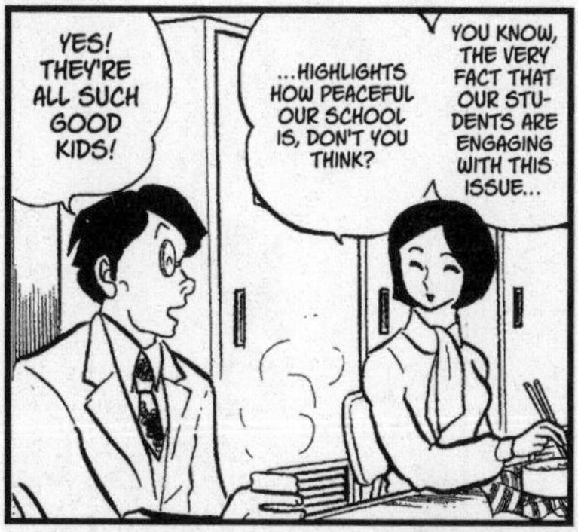
YOU KNOW, THE VERY FACT THAT OUR STUDENTS ARE ENGAGING WITH THIS ISSUE...
...HIGHLIGHTS HOW PEACEFUL OUR SCHOOL IS, DON'T YOU THINK?
YES! THEY'RE ALL SUCH GOOD KIDS!

▲ The laid-back teachers of Tomobiki High, reacting to news that the students were creating their own movie about school violence (volume 4, chapter 20 "Love and School Violence").

One reason local ties are strong is that adults keep an eye on its young people to keep them out of trouble, and the community is very healthy and safe. The student body of Tomobiki High contains not a single juvenile delinquent, there is no bullying, and the dropout rate is zero. The student body is so healthy that Sakura, who serves as the school nurse as well as the town priestess, states boldly, "I can say without hesitation that there isn't a single student with issues we should be concerned about!" (volume 11, chapter 18 "Troubled Youth")

Thus, while Tomobiki Town has an extraordinarily high incidence of natural and man-made disasters, it remains an excellent place to raise children.

STUDY 3

The Charms of Tomobiki ③

Diverse Weather Conditions!

In volume 1, chapter 1 "Young Love on the Run," Ataru is chosen for the game of tag with Lum based on a random computerized selection. But was it really pure chance?

Actually, Nerima, the district of Tokyo where Tomobiki Town is located, is famous for its unpredictable weather. It frequently has the hottest summer temperature of anywhere in Tokyo, and the weather changes quickly, with frequent rain and thunderstorms.

Tomobiki Town's frequent thunderstorms actually create quite favorable conditions for ogres who feed on electricity. Lum's ex-fiance Rei even arrives amid a thunderstorm (volume 1, chapter 6 "To Kill with Love"). In other words, it's a perfect environment for ogres.

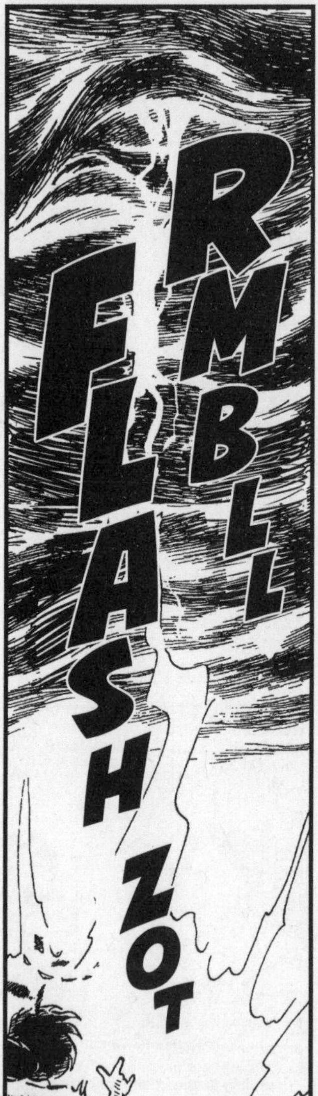
RMBLL
FLASH
ZOT

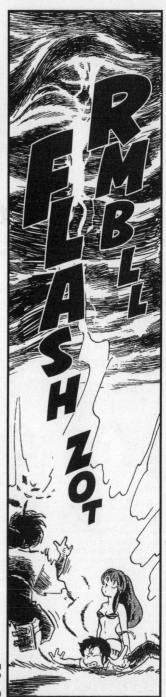

▶ A sudden bolt of lightning strikes Ataru and Lum (volume 14, chapter 15 "Siblings★ Battle of Love, Part 2")

Tomobiki Town's sky always seems always to be portending upheaval… (volume 14, chapter 8 "Ten Year Truth") ▼

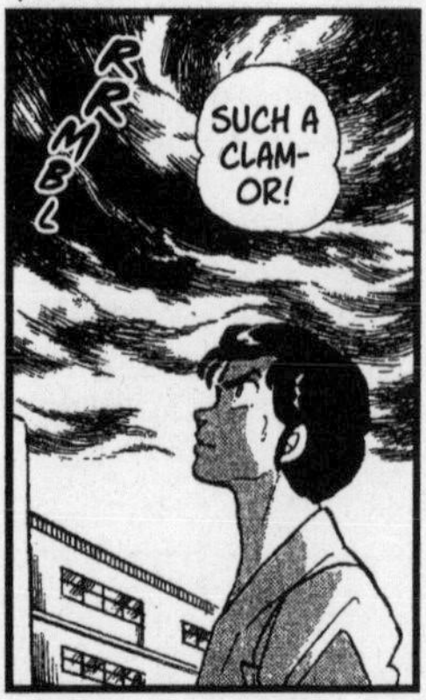
RRMBL
SUCH A CLAM-OR!

SHAAA

BOOM

KLAT
KLAT
KLAT
KLAT

HMM?!

▲ A curse by the Rainmaker Spirit brings a sudden change in weather (volume 5, chapter 12 "O, Rain! Rain and Rain More! Part 1")

It also hardly seems purely coincidental that Ataru, who has extremely poor luck (good luck for the ogres!) was selected among the residents of Tomobiki Town. In fact, it seems the ogres' computer managed to pinpoint the best possible place and contestant. The ogres have extremely advanced technology when it comes to science and engineering.

Even though it was commanded by the ogres' computer, there is no question that Lum and Ataru's meeting was ordained by the red thread of fate. It is also clear that many spirits are drawn to the Nerima district because of its bountiful rain, such as the Umbrella Ghost and the Raincloud supernatural couple (volume 3, chapter 2 "Everybody in the Rain") as well as the family of beautiful young girls cursed by the Rainmaker Spirit (volume 5, chapter 12 "O, Rain! Rain and Rain More! Part 1"). Tomobiki Town is not to be trifled with!

What do you think? This was just a simple introduction, but did it suffice to evoke a feeling that Tomobiki Town is quite a wonderful place? Why not move there and experience it for yourself—with the knowledge, of course, that occasional collateral injuries could result. If you get used to it, you're bound to love it! At least, we think so…

(Data File 01 / The End)

Author: Keiko Sugimori
Concept: Masatake Sugimori

COUNT COLUMN!

Urusei Yatsura: 366 Stories in All!

Anyway We counted them up!

The total number of Lum's electrical attacks...

A Love Barometer! But What Is Its Voltage?!

Scenes of Lum's electrical attacks are the hallmark of *Urusei Yatsura*! It turns out the total number of electrical attacks is 322. You might expect that most of them were directed at Ataru, but this is not actually the case. Some were directed at Ran or Benten (volume 11, chapter 7 "Blue-White Flames of Anger, Part 2"). Sakura has also been victimized (volume 13, chapter 2 "May We Meet in Our Dreams—The Showdown").

Is it a spiritual power? Or just a matter of dodging the electricity?

Meanwhile, there is someone who has never been attacked. Surprisingly enough, that person is Cherry. Has the karma of his spiritual practices protected him from Lum's wrath? Or does Lum simply not want to touch him, even electrically?

By the way, Lum's electrical attacks are roughly equivalent to a bolt of lightning. On average, a single attack has an electrical current of 30,000 amps and a voltage of 100 million volts. According to our calculations, Lum's total electrical capacity is enough to light roughly 107 nighttime baseball games at the Tokyo Dome.

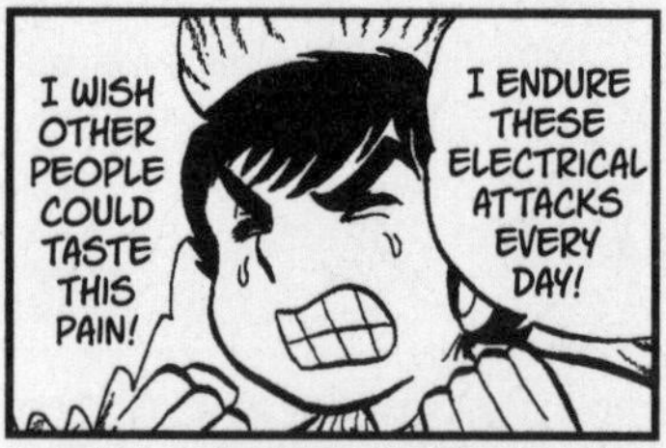
I ENDURE THESE ELECTRICAL ATTACKS EVERY DAY!
I WISH OTHER PEOPLE COULD TASTE THIS PAIN!

▲ Ataru's tearful lament. (volume 2, chapter 10 "Sake and Tears and Men and Women")

The fact that Ataru has withstood Lum's powerful attacks on his body and soul with hardly a scratch seems the ultimate proof that he's a suitable partner for her!

Lum's electrical attacks are really motivated not by jealousy or anger, but by love!

Total number of Lum's electrical attacks.......322
Of these, the number directed at Ataru.........190
Of those directed at Ataru, the number in which someone or something else was accidentally or collaterally hit by the attack: 65 out of 190. These have included a utility pole (volume 1, chapter 5 "Between a Rock and a Hard Place"), a watermelon holy relic (volume 5, chapter 17 "Beach Mystery"), a grip-strength dynamometer (volume 9, chapter 18 "Miss Tomobiki Contest: Preliminary Round") and so on.

My Lum

The eternal beauty Lum!

Special Message
From Creator Rumiko Takahashi

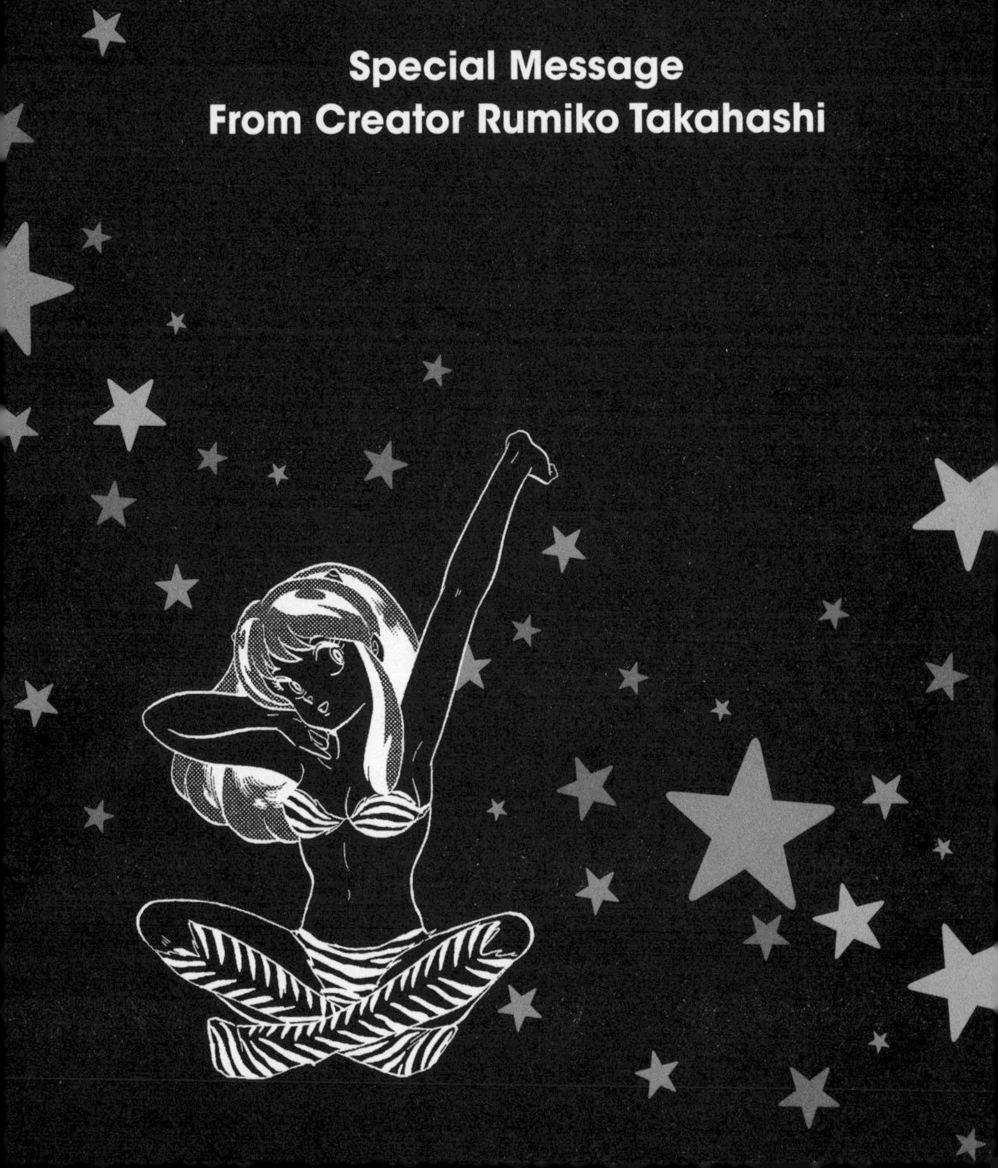

Lum is My Polar Opposite

It's been a while since I've drawn Lum, and I was very nervous. Her face was especially hard for me.

Lum is a character I created before my debut as a manga artist, for a short story I was devising at that time. I put a lot of effort into the design of her hairstyle and the shape of her body back then! (*Ha ha.*)

At the same time, Lum is the *Urusei* character who is the most beyond my comprehension. It's much easier for me to relate to insecure characters who don't express how they really feel. A character like Lum, who is absolutely direct and uninhibited, is my polar opposite. Lum showed me that I can draw characters in my own manga who don't reflect me at all.

As you read this new edition, I hope you'll be watching over Lum with love.

-Rumiko Takahashi

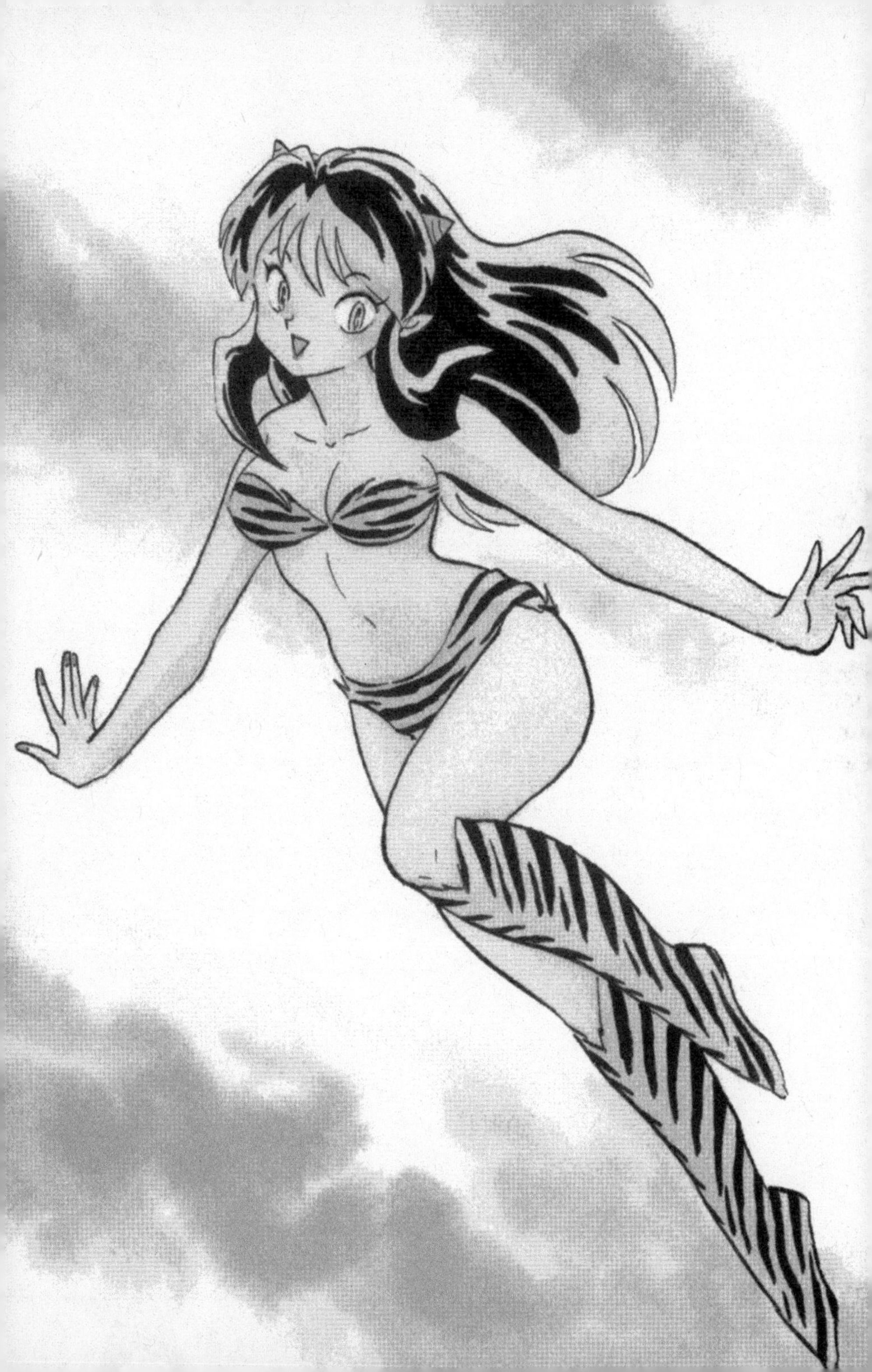

Part 1 Notes ★

The setting of *Urusei Yatsura* is in Japan, with references to cultural holidays, beliefs and practices. Check out the notes below to enrich your reading experience.

Page 3 – *Urusei Yatsura*, the title of this series, means "obnoxious people." The *sei* in "Urusei" uses the kanji character for "star."

Page 12, panel 1 – On *Setsubun*, the first day of spring, people throw beans in their houses and shout, "Ogres, begone! Happiness enter!" Ataru is simulating that action here.

Page 13, panel 6 – The game of tag is called "ogre" in Japanese. The person who is "It" is the ogre. The wordplay on "tag" and "ogre" in this scene highlights one of the many puns in this series.

Page 15, panel 7 – Ataru's father is referring to *butsumetsu* ("Buddha's death"), an extremely unlucky day according to the Japanese calendar.

Page 31, panel 6 – *Obon*, the Japanese Buddhist festival that honors the spirits of ancestors, occurs mid-July or mid-August depending on the region in Japan. It is believed that the spirits of one's ancestors visit home during this time.

Page 46, panel 5 – Shinobu asks the imp to put his *deba* away. *Deba* means "knife" in Japanese, but it can also mean protruding teeth that stick out!

Page 74, panel 2 – The 中華 sign indicates that this is a Chinese restaurant.

Page 81, panel 1 – Sakura is a *miko*, a Shinto term that means shrine maiden or priestess.

Page 84, panel 4 – *Sakura* means "**cherry** blossom."

Page 87, panel 2 – *Reiki* means "mysterious atmosphere," and this is what Sakura's mother calls the swirling energy above them.

Page 106, panel 8 – Cherry is doing a Buddhist chant for Ataru.

Page 114, panel 3 – The kanji character *kyo* in Cherry's soup literally spells "doom."

Page 132 panel 1 – Cherry is keeping score by writing the kanji 正, which is made up of five strokes. Each stroke counts as one point, or in this case, one sweet potato eaten.

Page 159, panel 6 – The celebratory dish Ataru is referring to is *sekihan*, which is made of sticky rice and red beans.

Page 159, panel 8 – *Sukiyaki* is a stew of thinly sliced beef and vegetables that is cooked on a table-top stove.

Page 163, panel 1 – The 男一匹 sign on the middle ogre god's belly is *otoko ippiki*, which means "shining example of a man."

Page 170, panel 6 – Matsusaka beef is considered to be the finest beef in Japan.

Page 176, panel 2 – The ogres are performing a *Setsubun* ritual like the one Ataru does on page 12, panel 1.

Page 183, panel 5 – The word game Cherry and Sakura are playing is *shiritori* where each player must say a word that begins with the final syllable of the last word said.

Urusei Yatsura

Part 2

Part 2 Contents

CHAPTER 10: OYUKI

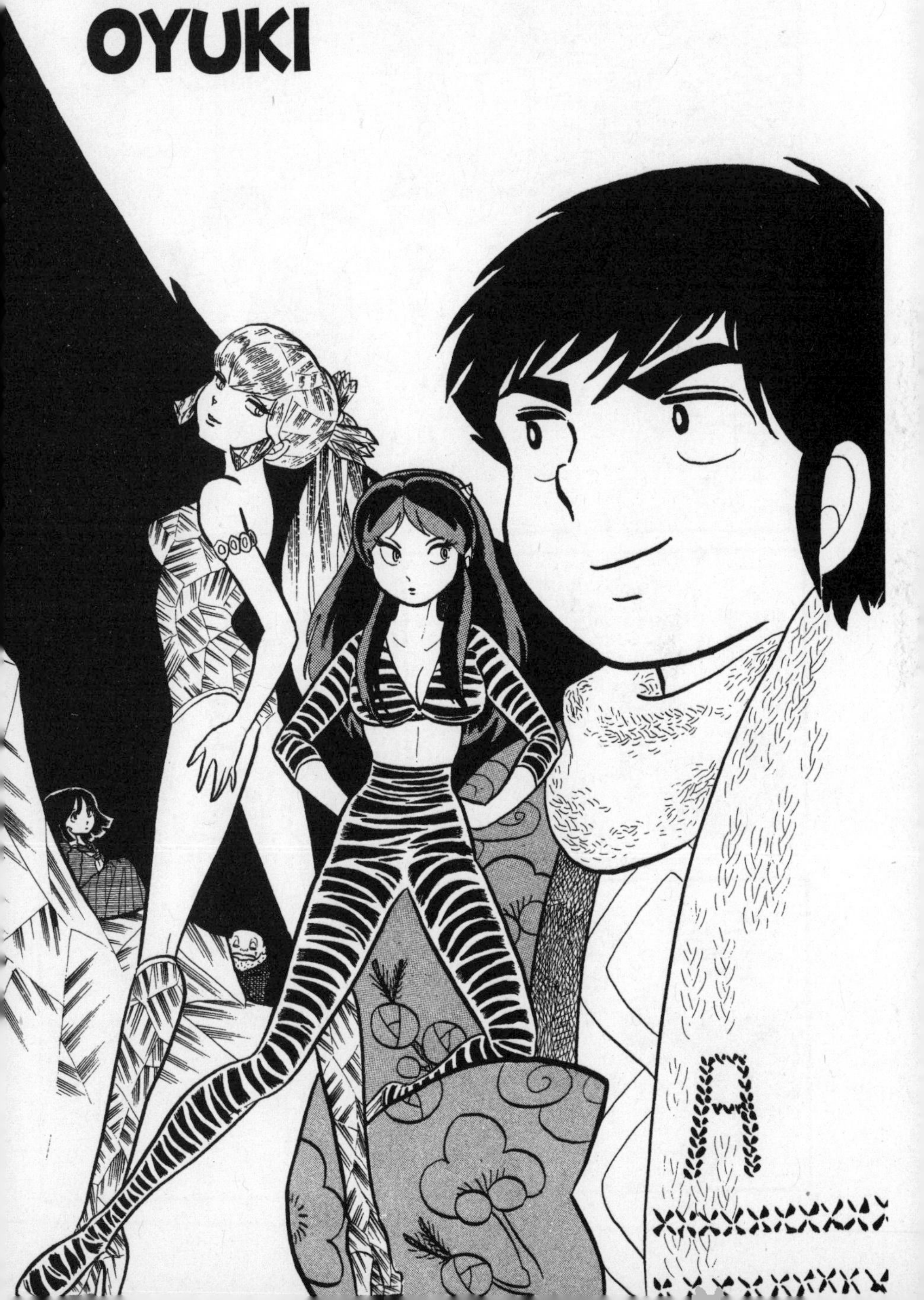

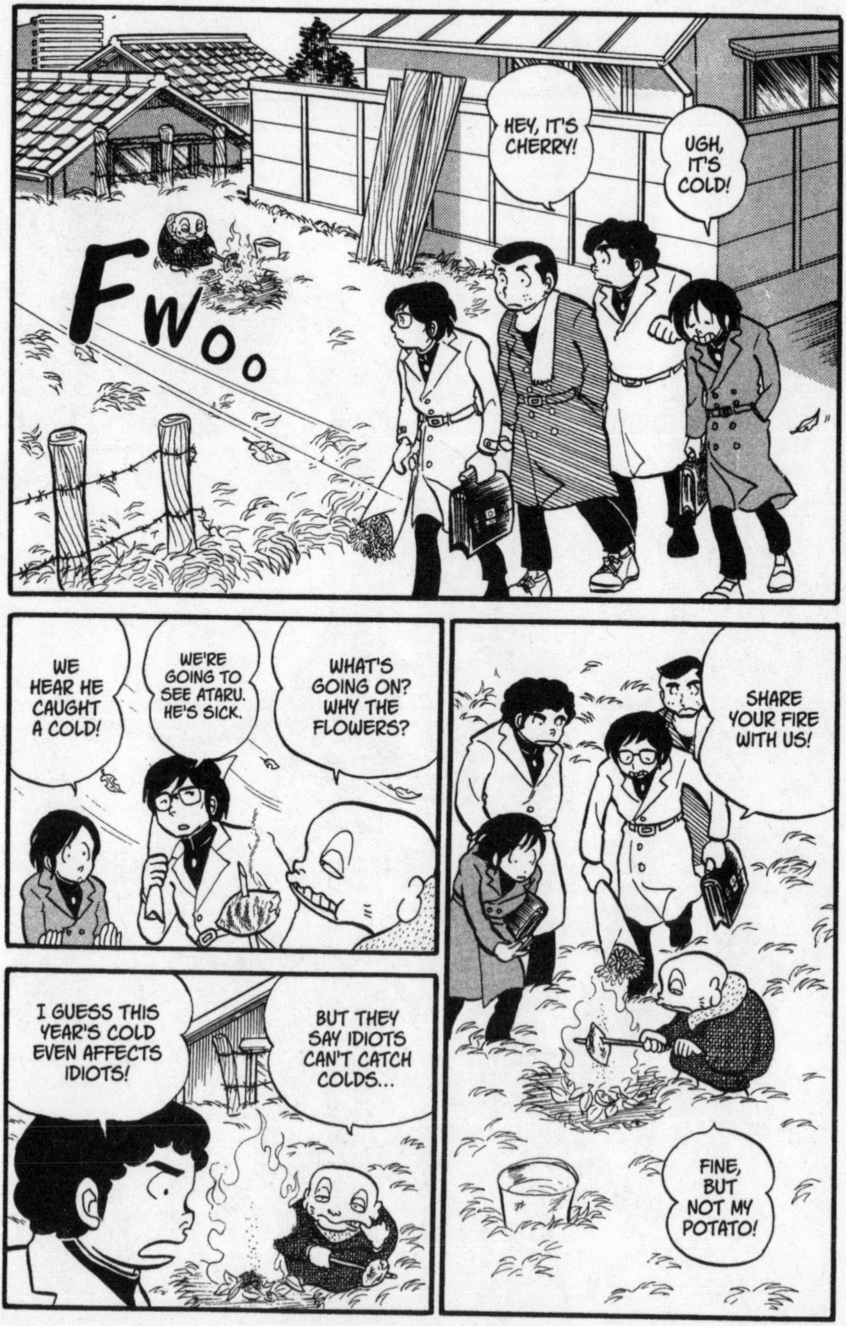
UGH, IT'S COLD!
HEY, IT'S CHERRY!
FWOO
SHARE YOUR FIRE WITH US!
FINE, BUT NOT MY POTATO!
WHAT'S GOING ON? WHY THE FLOWERS?
WE'RE GOING TO SEE ATARU. HE'S SICK.
WE HEAR HE CAUGHT A COLD!
BUT THEY SAY IDIOTS CAN'T CATCH COLDS...
I GUESS THIS YEAR'S COLD EVEN AFFECTS IDIOTS!

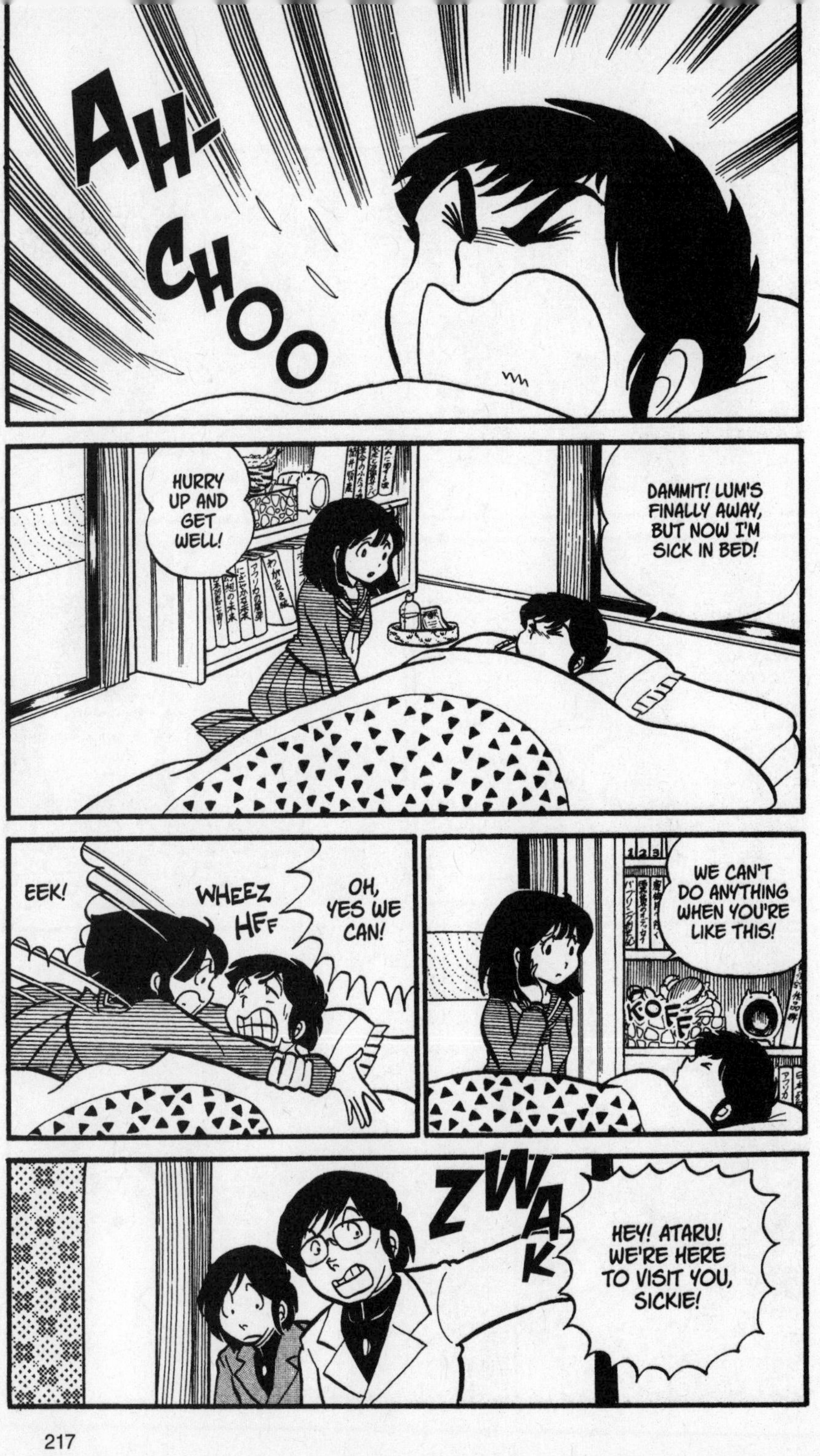
AH-CHOO
DAMMIT! LUM'S FINALLY AWAY, BUT NOW I'M SICK IN BED!
HURRY UP AND GET WELL!
WE CAN'T DO ANYTHING WHEN YOU'RE LIKE THIS!
KOFF
OH, YES WE CAN!
WHEEZ HFF
EEK!
HEY! ATARU! WE'RE HERE TO VISIT YOU, SICKIE!
ZWAK

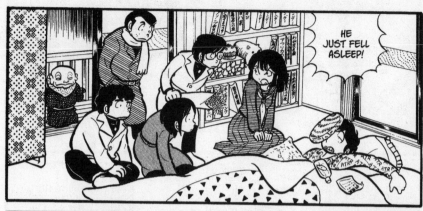

HE JUST FELL ASLEEP!
SHI-NOBU'S HERE!
AND LUM'S NOT...
SHINOBU MUST'VE CHASED HER AWAY! POOR LUM...
FEMININE RIVALRY IS SUCH AN UGLY THING...
UGH! YOU'RE SO RUDE! SHE WAS ALREADY GONE, OKAY?
HEY! WAKE UP!
BOMP
WHERE'S LUM?!
SLAP
STOP THAT! ATARU'S SICK!

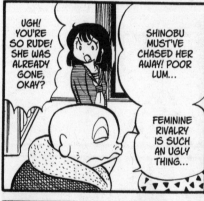

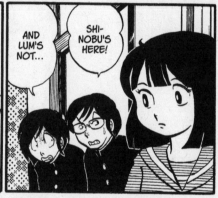

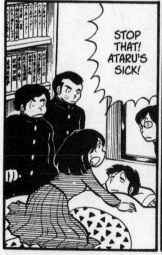

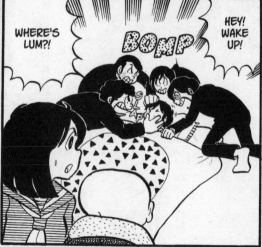

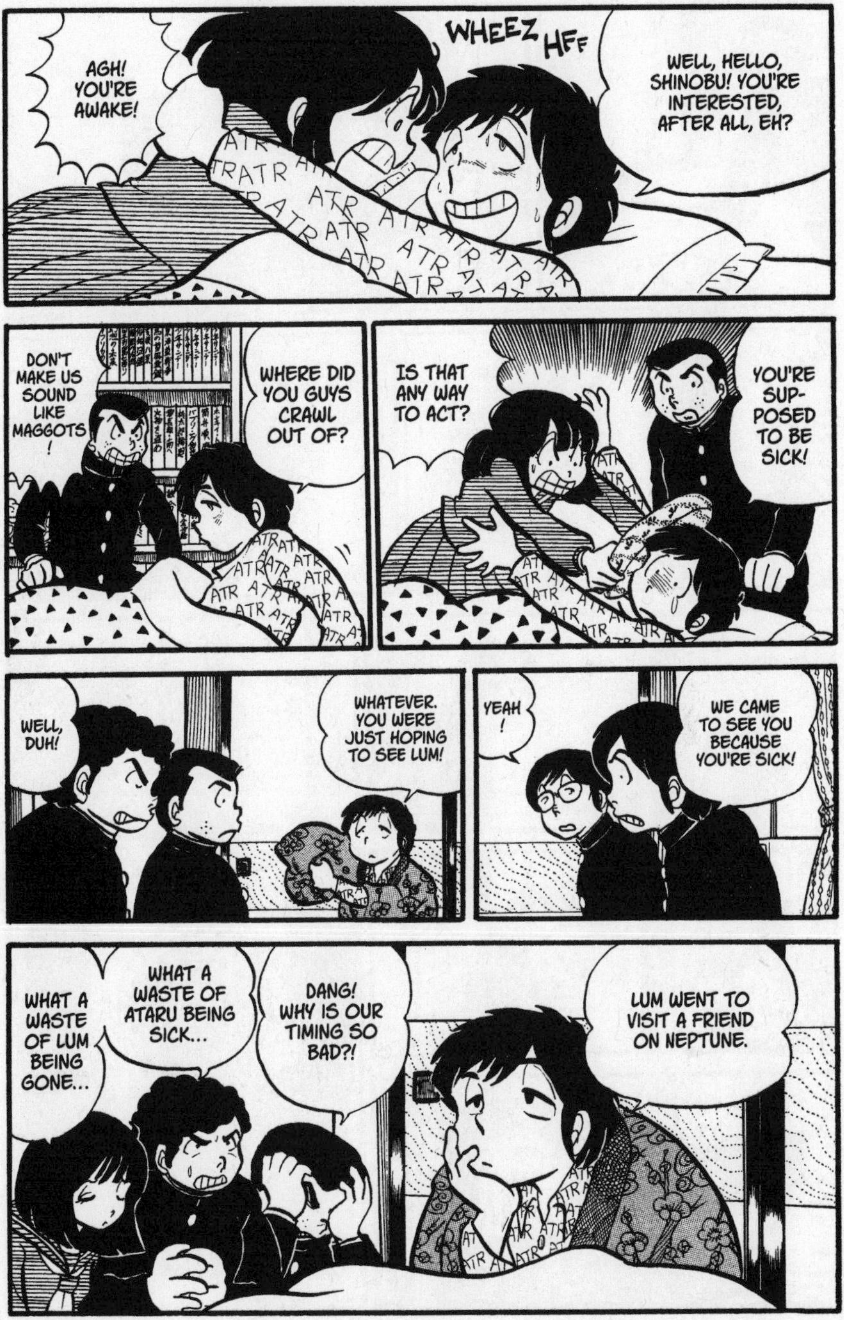
WELL, HELLO, SHINOBU! YOU'RE INTERESTED, AFTER ALL, EH?
WHEEZ HFF
AGH! YOU'RE AWAKE!
YOU'RE SUP-POSED TO BE SICK!
IS THAT ANY WAY TO ACT?
WHERE DID YOU GUYS CRAWL OUT OF?
DON'T MAKE US SOUND LIKE MAGGOTS!
WE CAME TO SEE YOU BECAUSE YOU'RE SICK!
YEAH!
WHATEVER. YOU WERE JUST HOPING TO SEE LUM!
WELL, DUH!
LUM WENT TO VISIT A FRIEND ON NEPTUNE.
DANG! WHY IS OUR TIMING SO BAD?!
WHAT A WASTE OF ATARU BEING SICK...
WHAT A WASTE OF LUM BEING GONE...

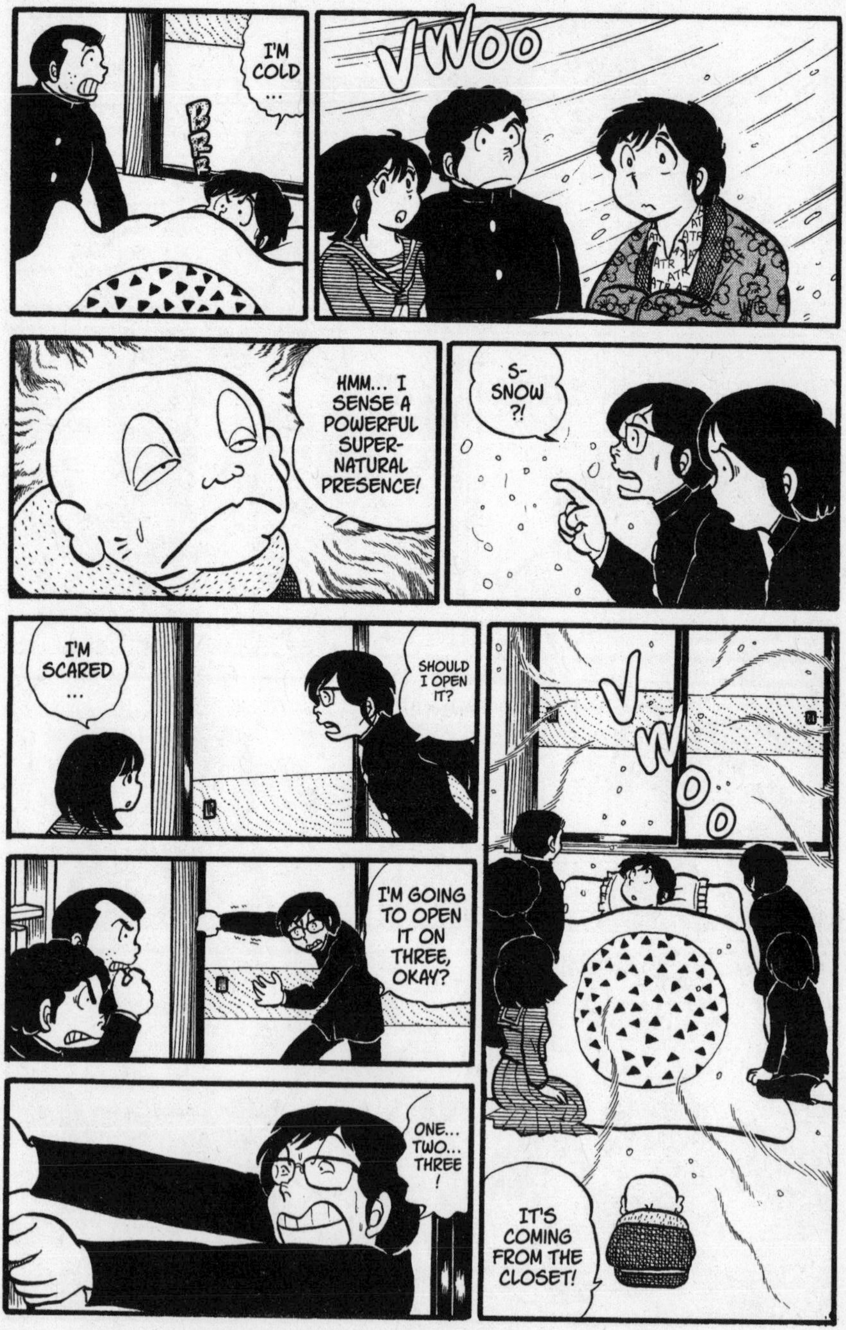
VWOO
I'M COLD ...
BRR
S-SNOW ?!
HMM... I SENSE A POWERFUL SUPER-NATURAL PRESENCE!
VWOO
IT'S COMING FROM THE CLOSET!
SHOULD I OPEN IT?
I'M SCARED ...
I'M GOING TO OPEN IT ON THREE, OKAY?
ONE... TWO... THREE !

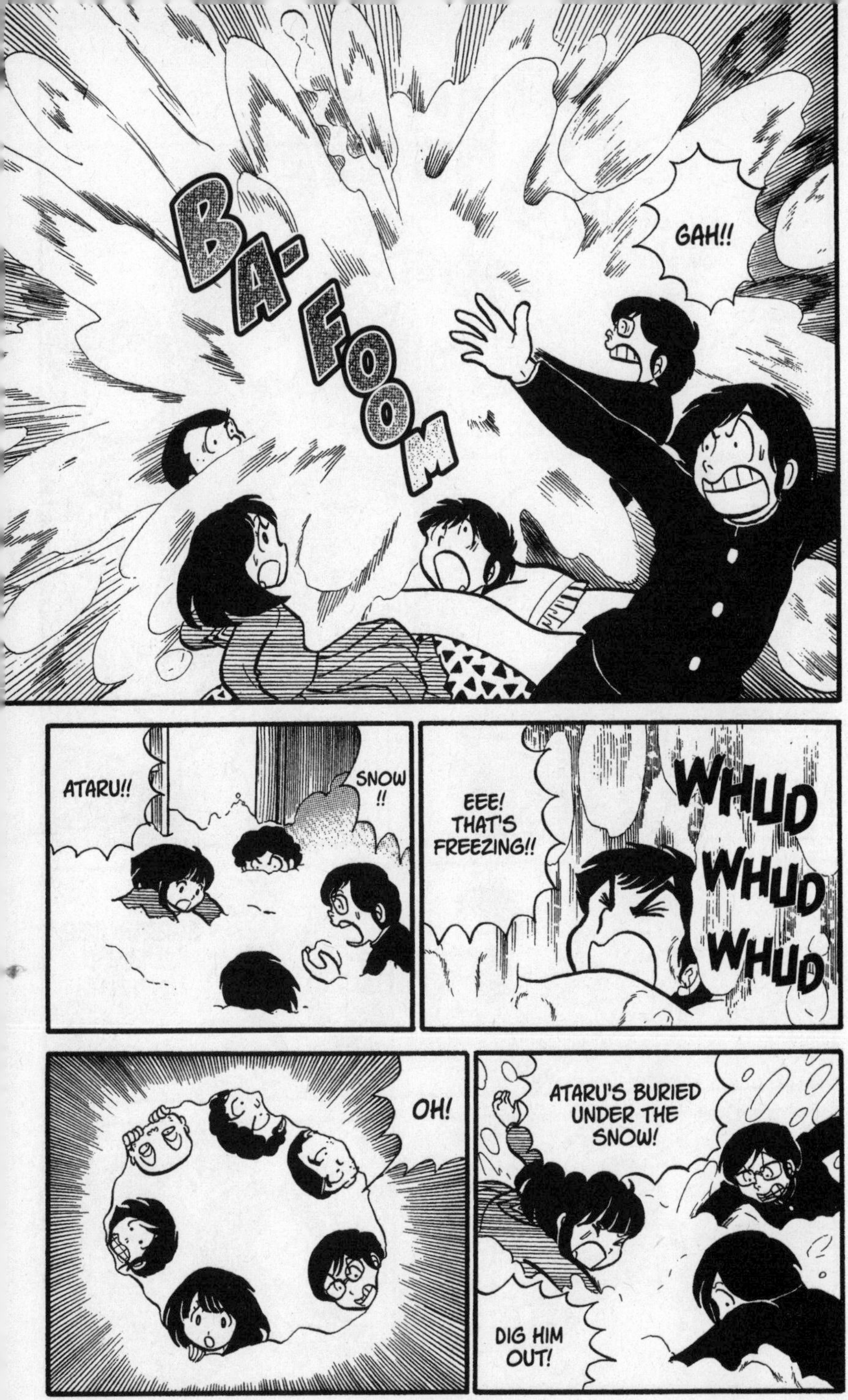
GAH!!
BA-FOOM
WHUD WHUD WHUD
EEE! THAT'S FREEZING!!
SNOW!!
ATARU!!
ATARU'S BURIED UNDER THE SNOW!
DIG HIM OUT!
OH!

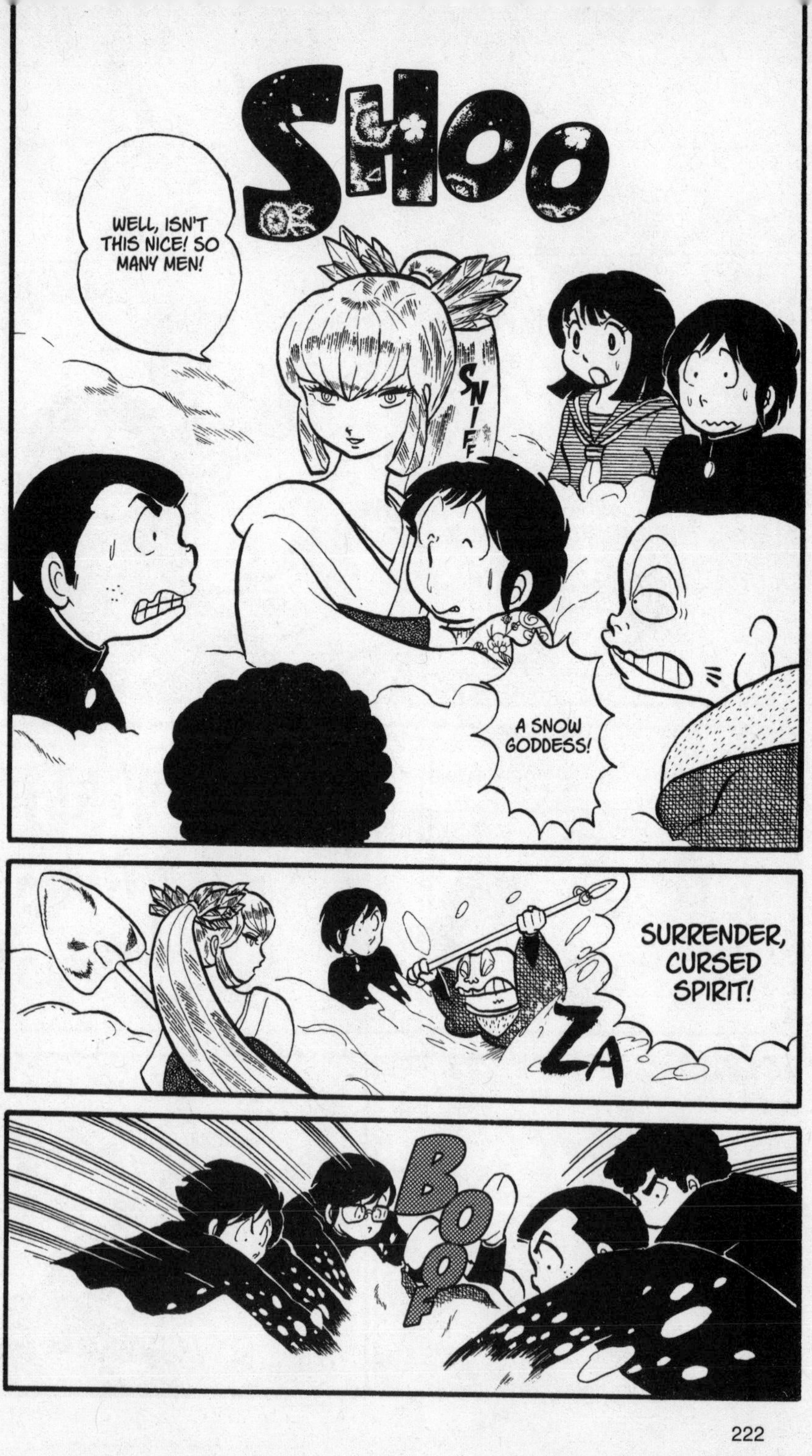
SHOO
WELL, ISN'T THIS NICE! SO MANY MEN!
SNIFF
A SNOW GODDESS!
SURRENDER, CURSED SPIRIT!
ZA
BOOF

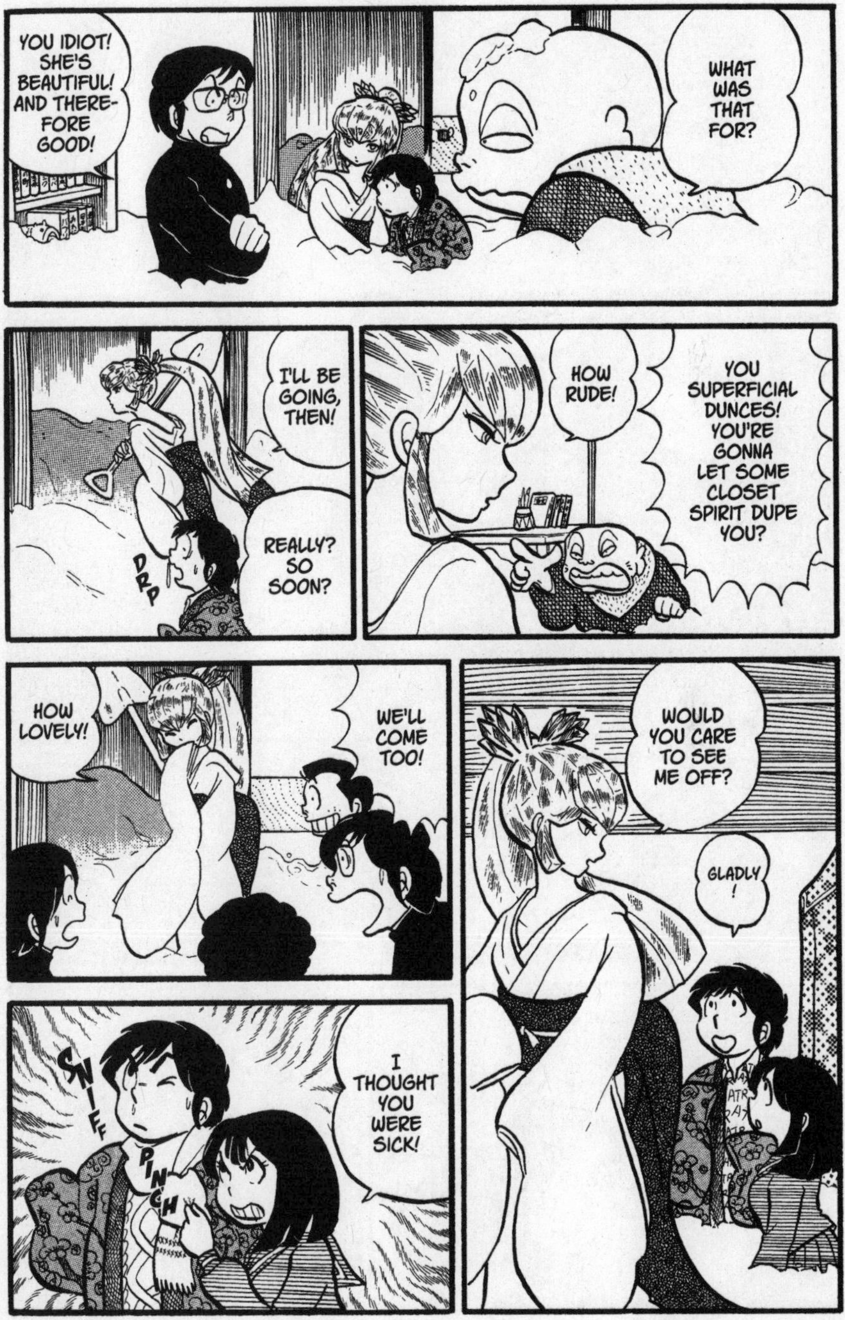
WHAT WAS THAT FOR?
YOU IDIOT! SHE'S BEAUTIFUL! AND THERE-FORE GOOD!
YOU SUPERFICIAL DUNCES! YOU'RE GONNA LET SOME CLOSET SPIRIT DUPE YOU?
HOW RUDE!
I'LL BE GOING, THEN!
REALLY? SO SOON?
DRP
WOULD YOU CARE TO SEE ME OFF?
GLADLY!
WE'LL COME TOO!
HOW LOVELY!
I THOUGHT YOU WERE SICK!
SNIFF
PINCH

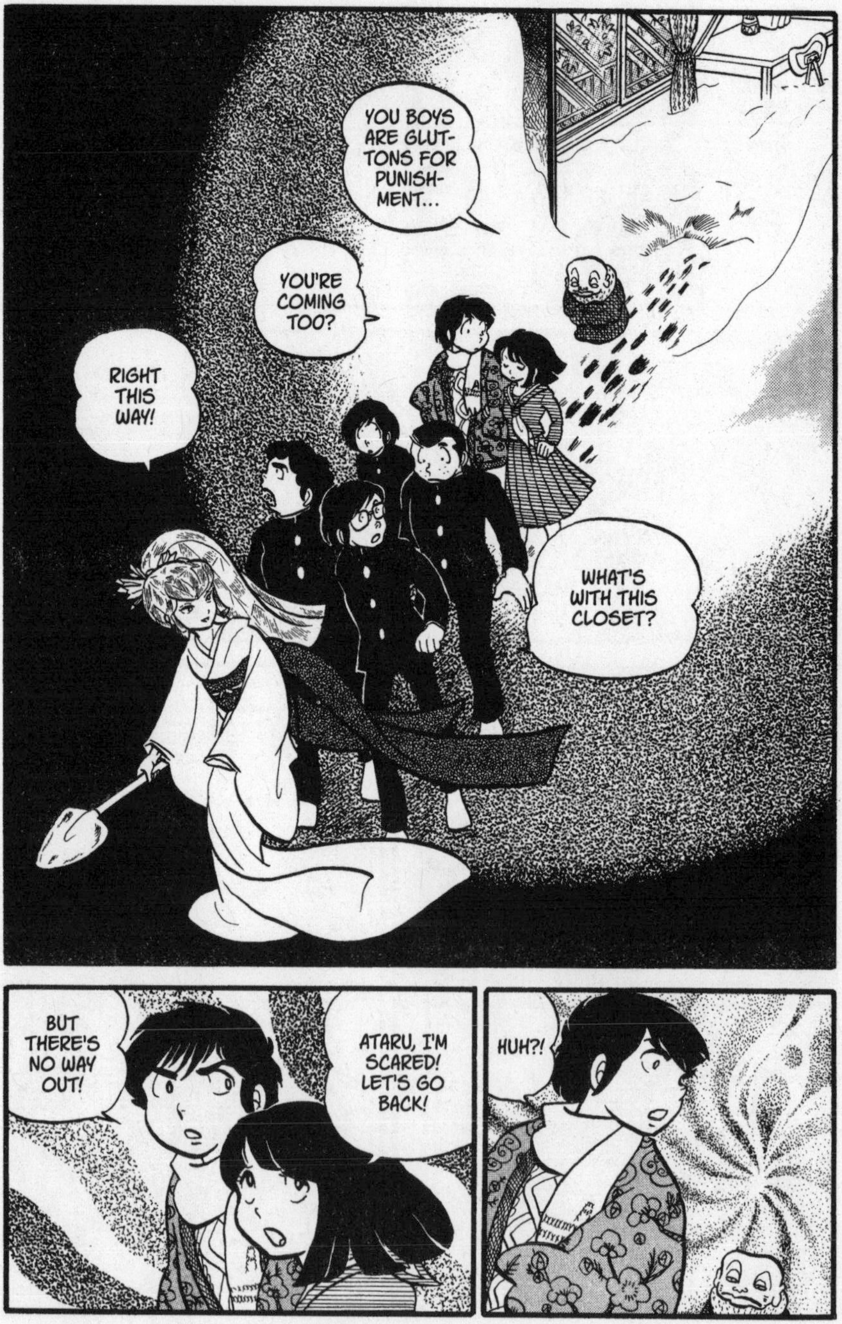
YOU BOYS ARE GLUTTONS FOR PUNISHMENT...
YOU'RE COMING TOO?
RIGHT THIS WAY!
WHAT'S WITH THIS CLOSET?
HUH?!
ATARU, I'M SCARED! LET'S GO BACK!
BUT THERE'S NO WAY OUT!

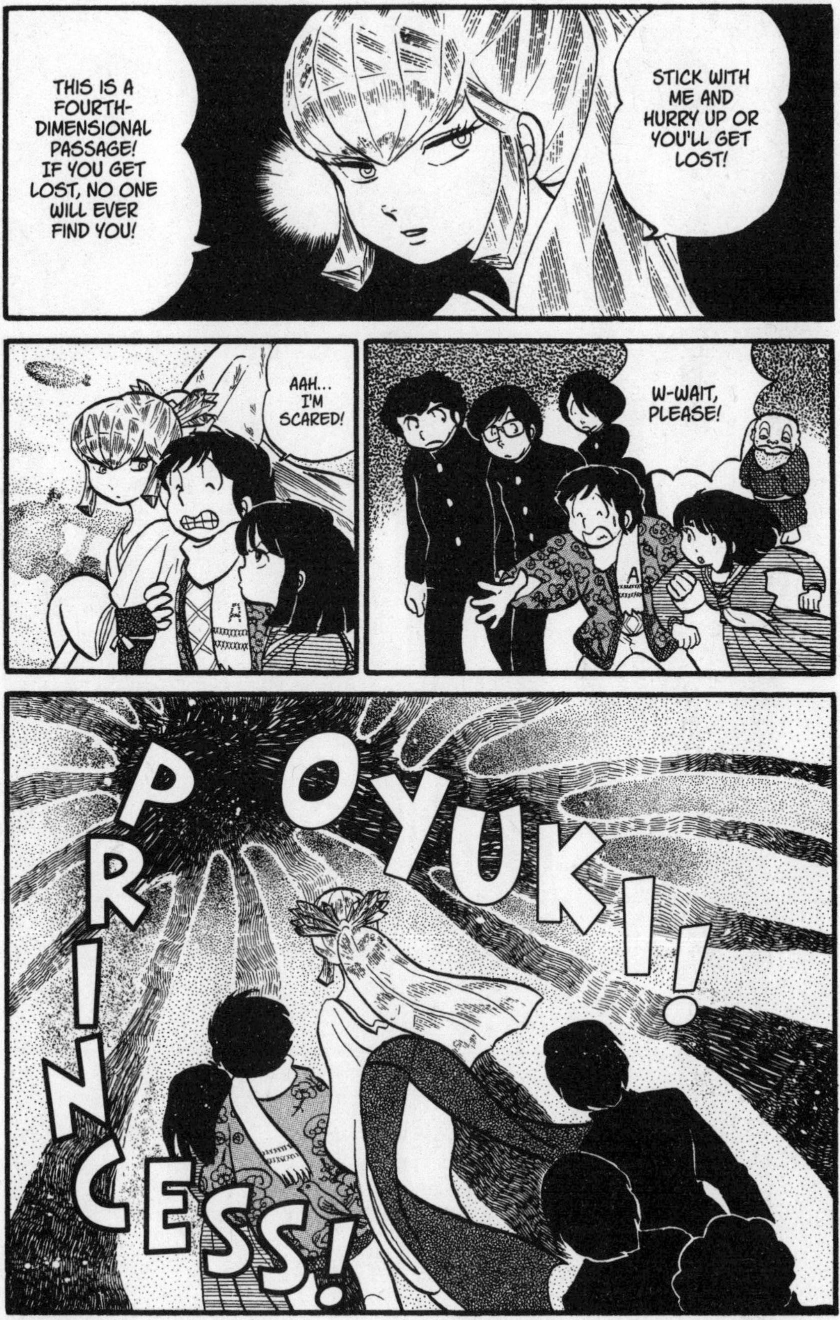

STICK WITH ME AND HURRY UP OR YOU'LL GET LOST!
THIS IS A FOURTH-DIMENSIONAL PASSAGE! IF YOU GET LOST, NO ONE WILL EVER FIND YOU!
W-WAIT, PLEASE!
AAH... I'M SCARED!
PRINCESS!
OYUKI!!

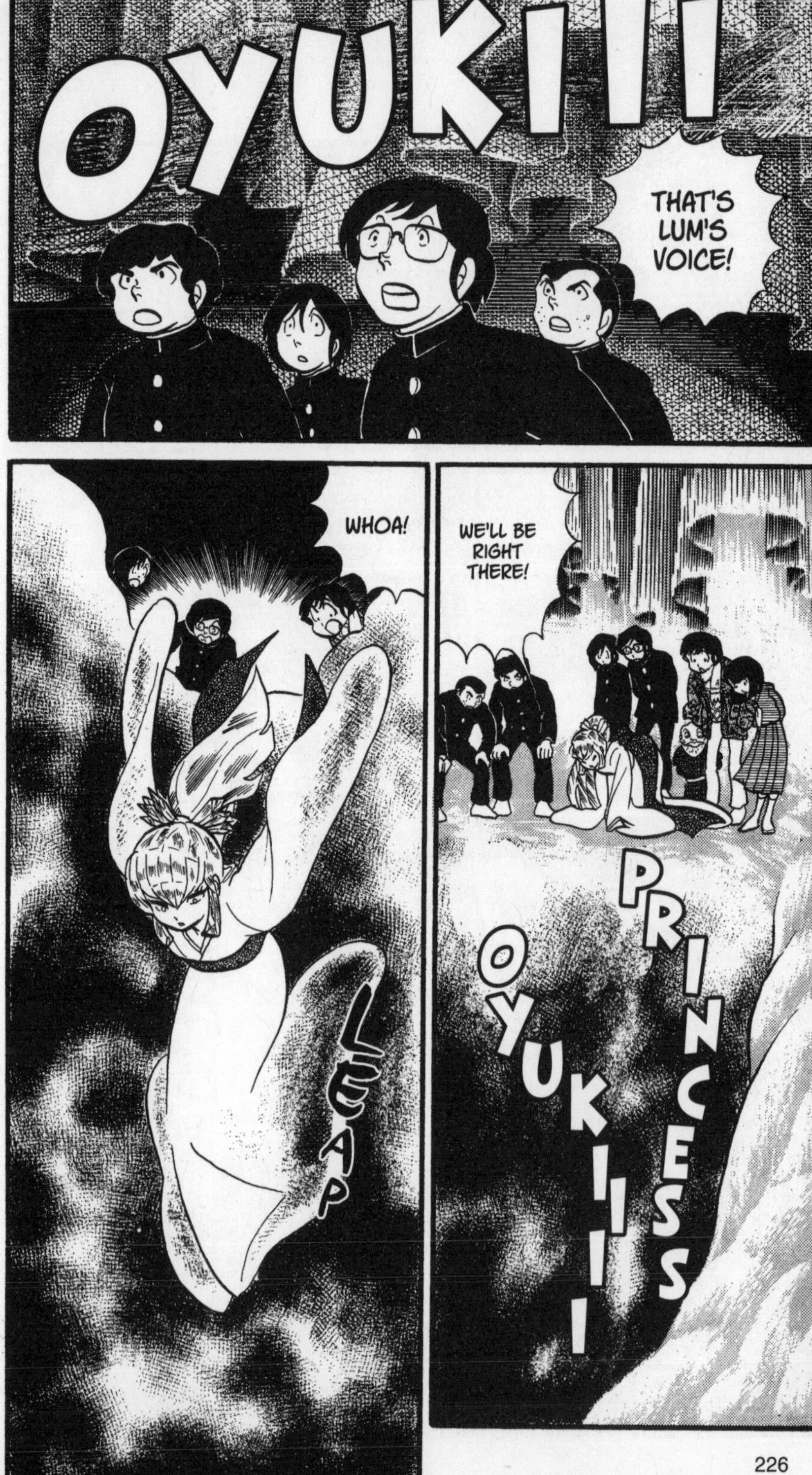
OYUKIIII
THAT'S LUM'S VOICE!
WE'LL BE RIGHT THERE!
PRINCESS
OYUKIIIII
WHOA!
LEAP

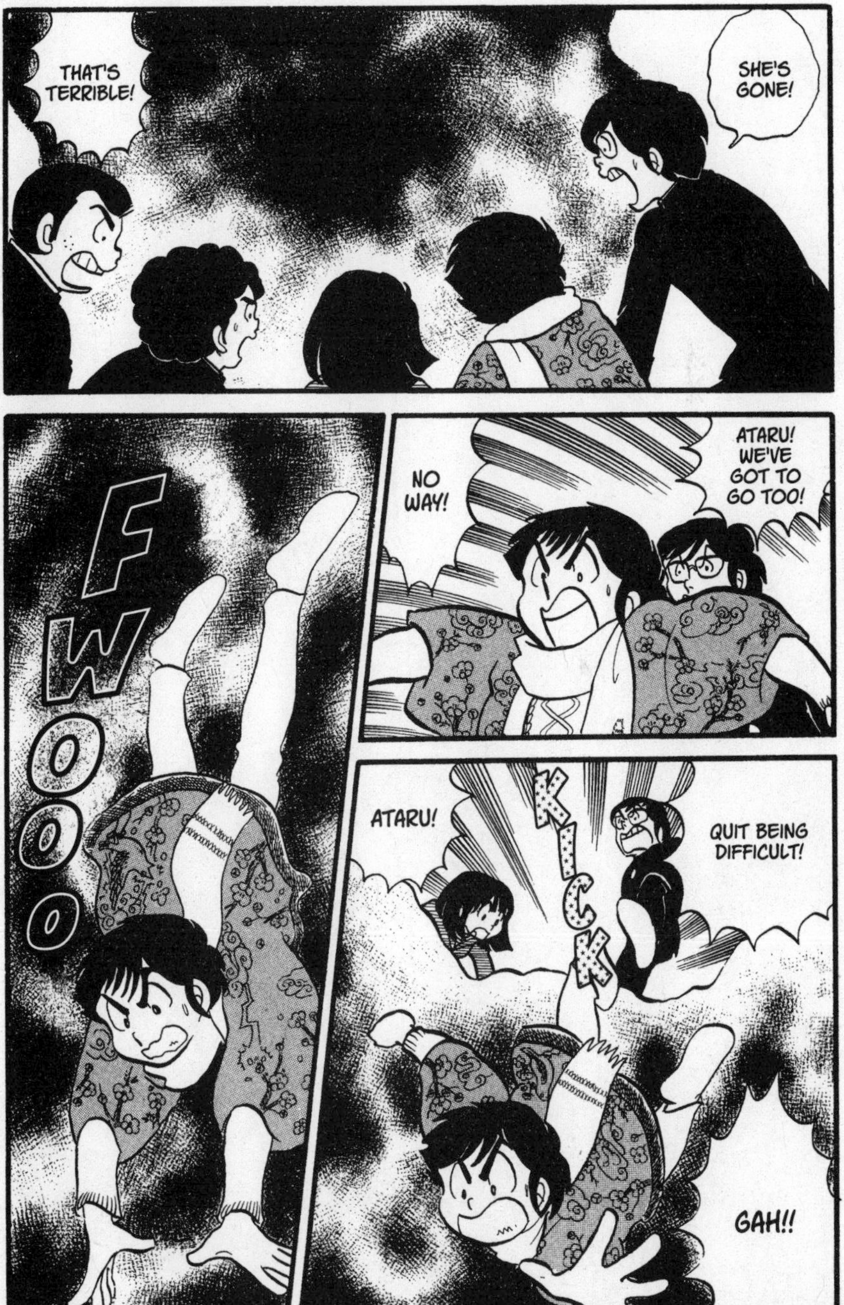
SHE'S GONE!
THAT'S TERRIBLE!
ATARU! WE'VE GOT TO GO TOO!
NO WAY!
QUIT BEING DIFFICULT!
KICK
ATARU!
GAH!!
FWOOO

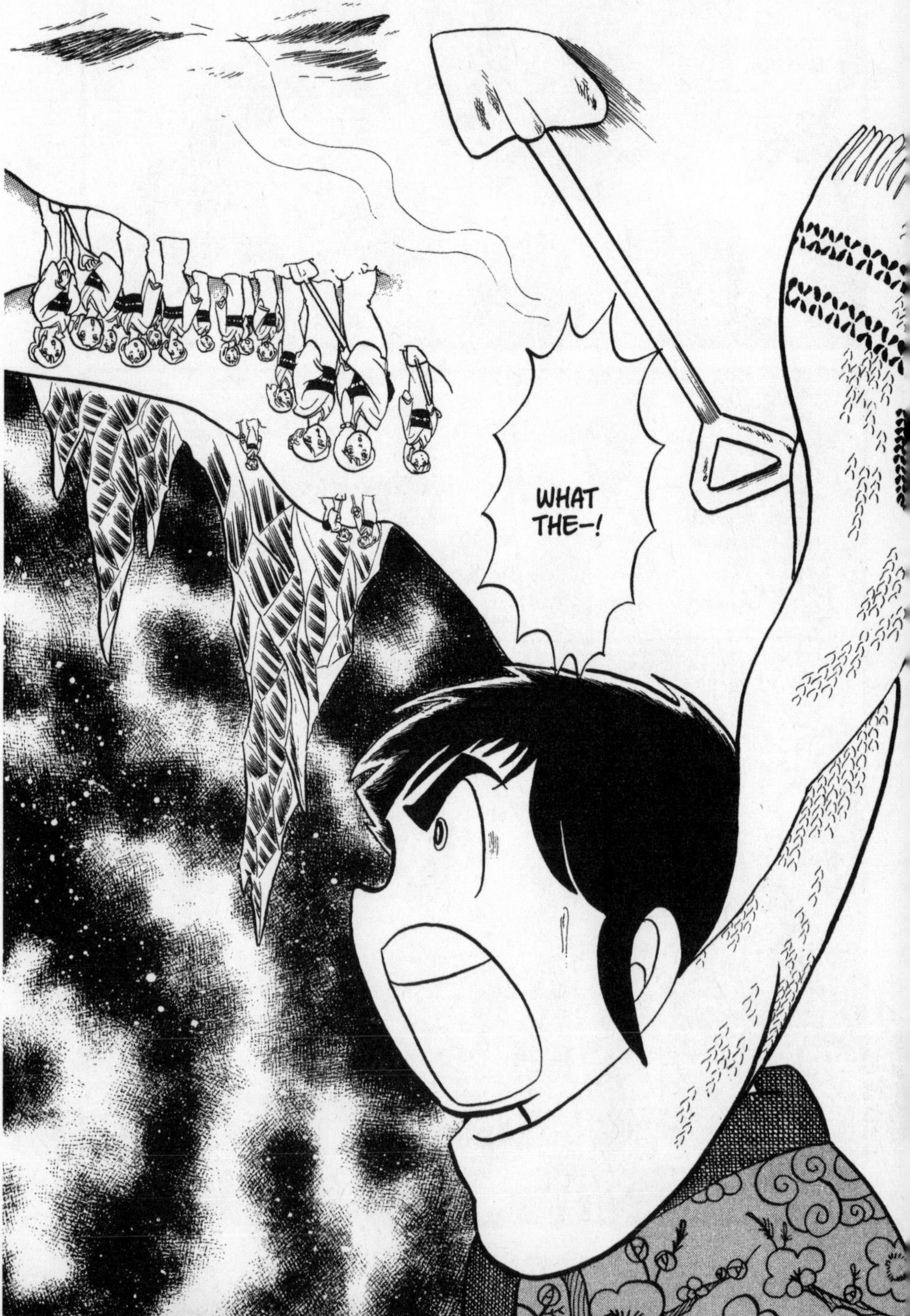
WHAT THE-!

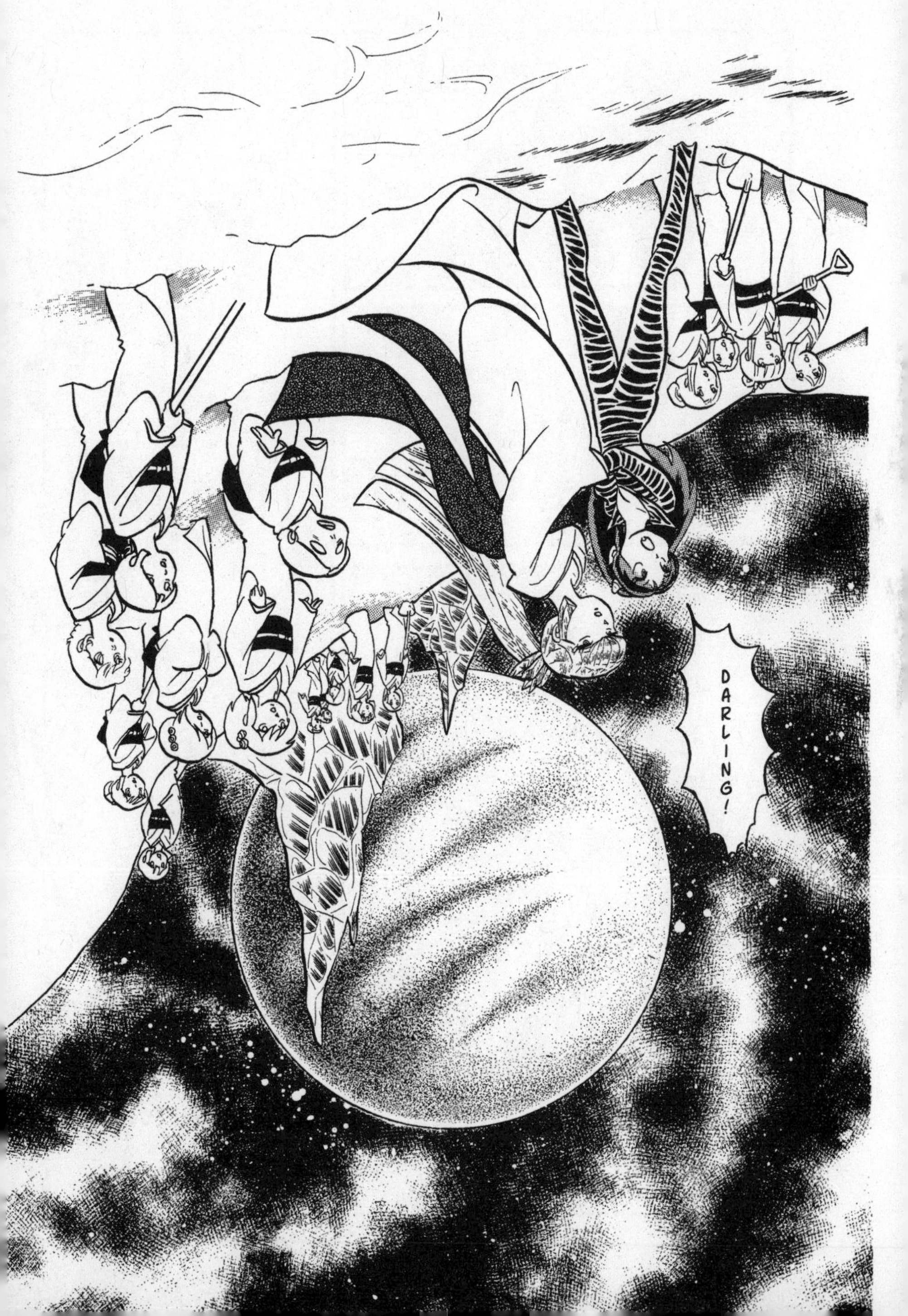
DARLING!

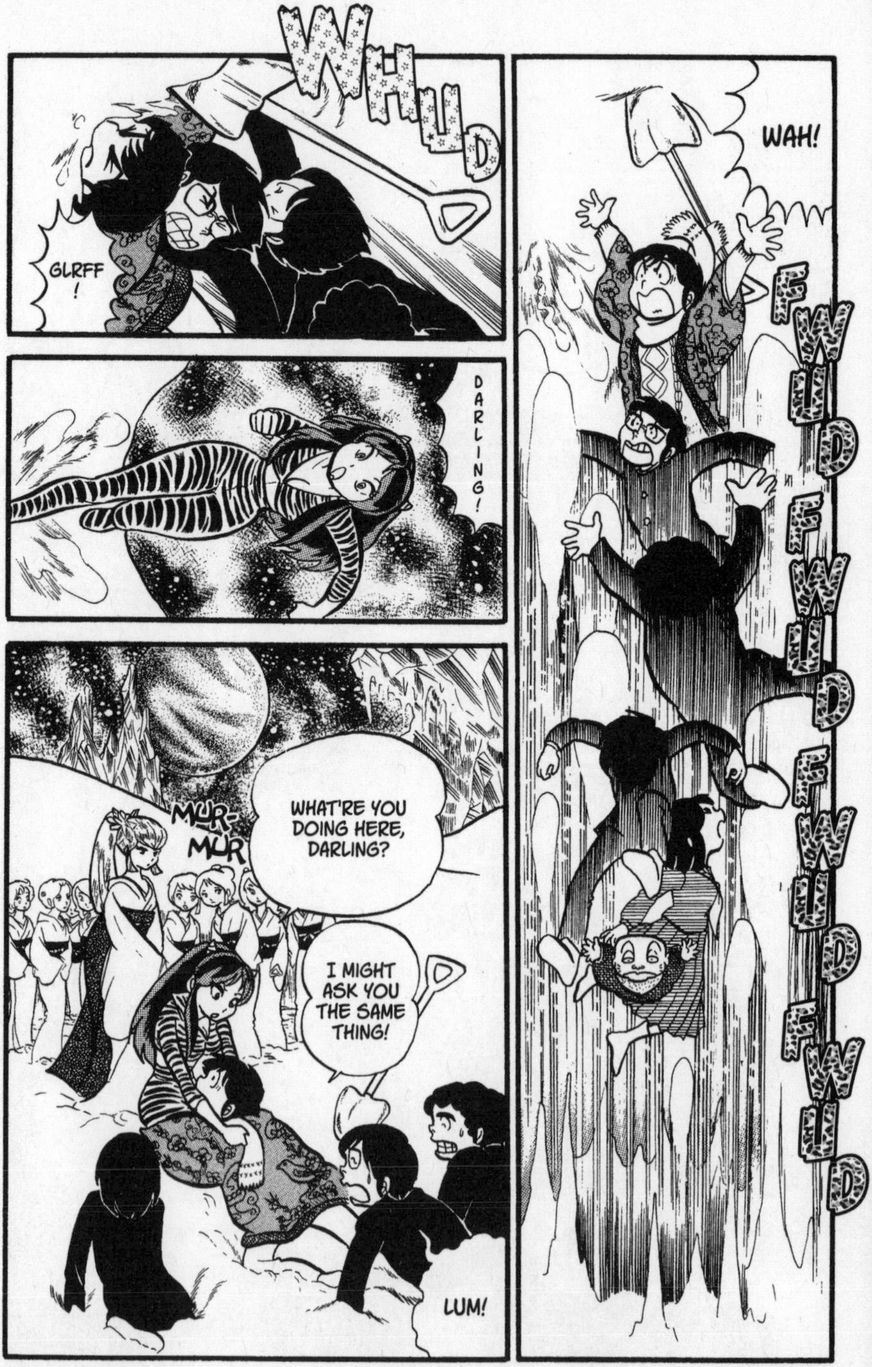
WAH!
FWUD FWUD FWUD FWUD
WHUD
GLRFF!
DARLING!
MUR-MUR
WHAT'RE YOU DOING HERE, DARLING?
I MIGHT ASK YOU THE SAME THING!
LUM!

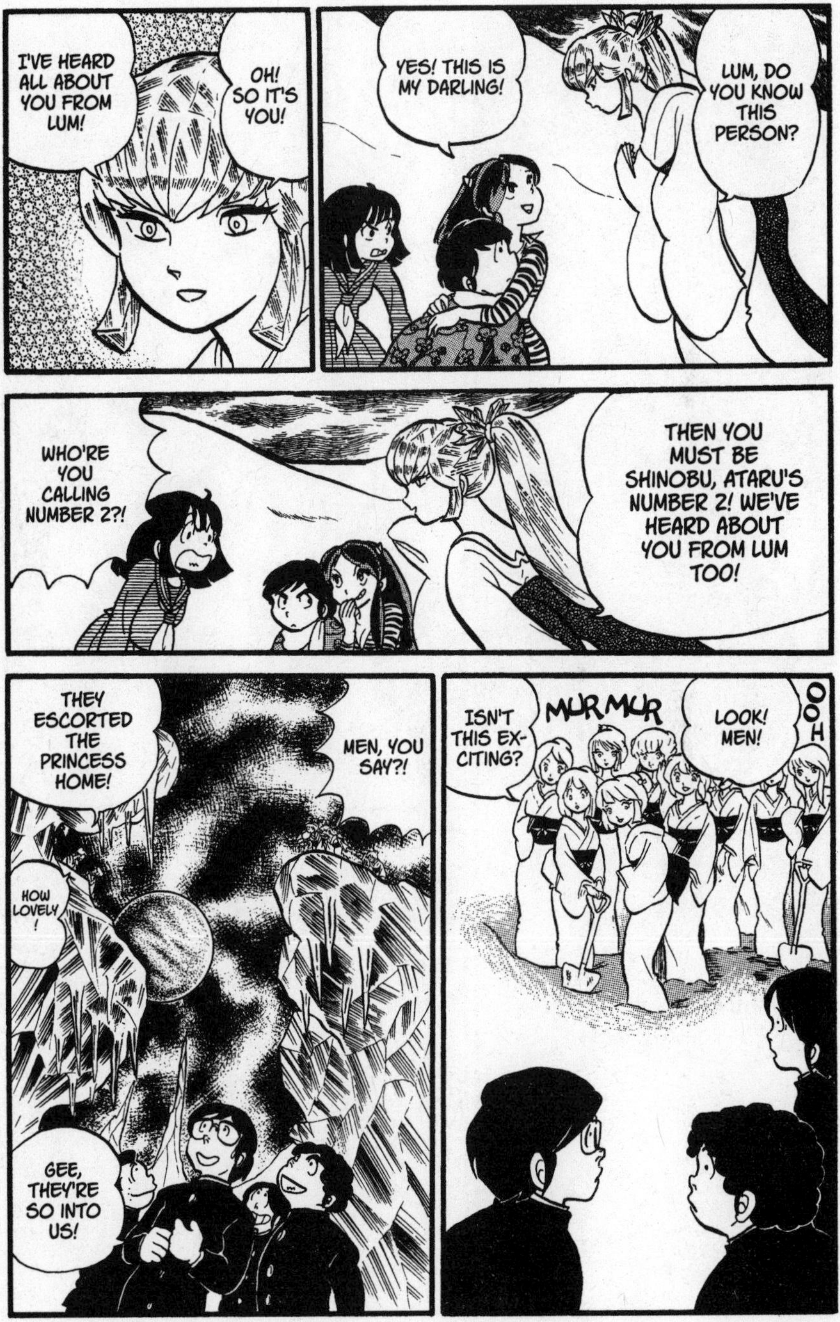
LUM, DO YOU KNOW THIS PERSON?
YES! THIS IS MY DARLING!
OH! SO IT'S YOU!
I'VE HEARD ALL ABOUT YOU FROM LUM!
THEN YOU MUST BE SHINOBU, ATARU'S NUMBER 2! WE'VE HEARD ABOUT YOU FROM LUM TOO!
WHO'RE YOU CALLING NUMBER 2?!
OOH
LOOK! MEN!
MURMUR
ISN'T THIS EX-CITING?
MEN, YOU SAY?!
THEY ESCORTED THE PRINCESS HOME!
HOW LOVELY!
GEE, THEY'RE SO INTO US!

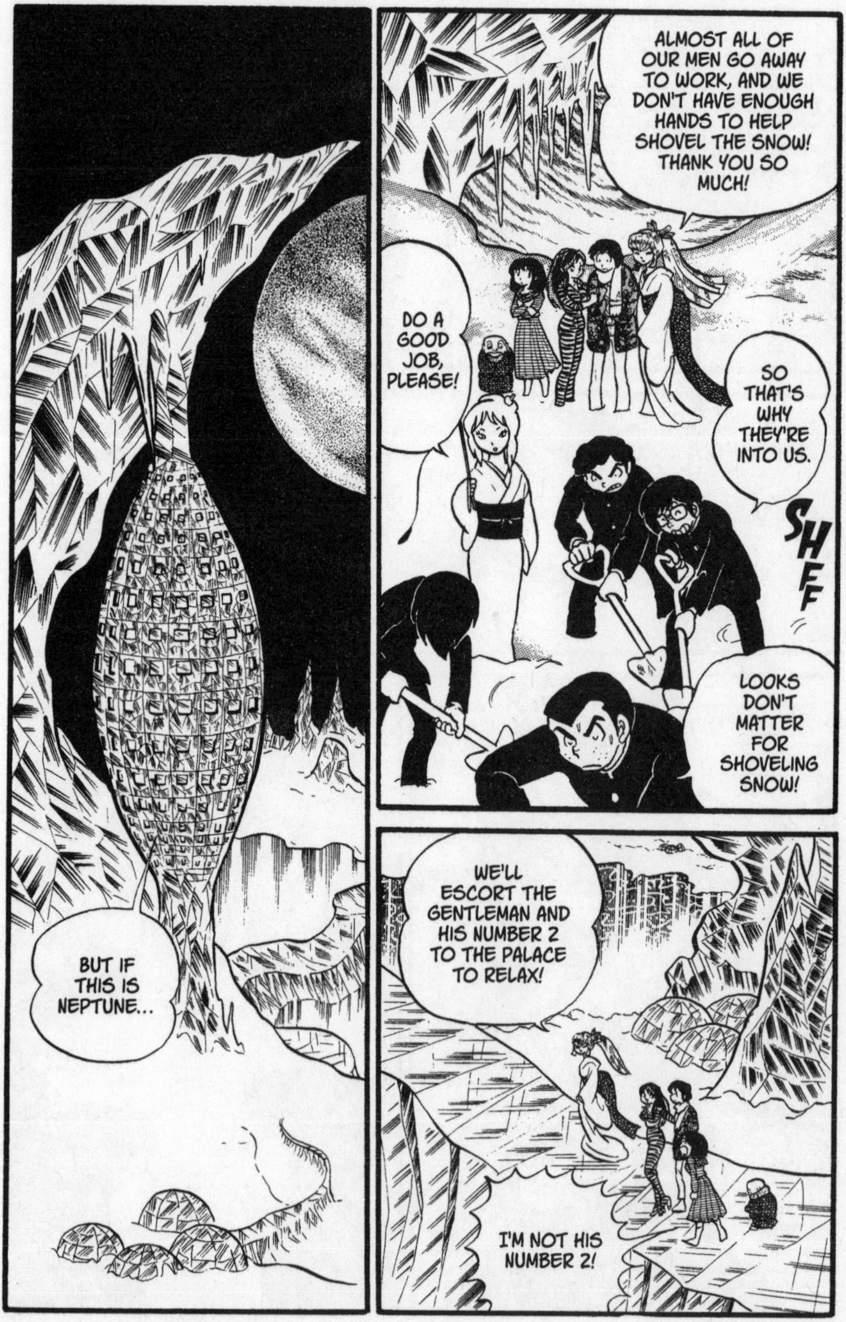
ALMOST ALL OF OUR MEN GO AWAY TO WORK, AND WE DON'T HAVE ENOUGH HANDS TO HELP SHOVEL THE SNOW! THANK YOU SO MUCH!
DO A GOOD JOB, PLEASE!
SO THAT'S WHY THEY'RE INTO US.
SHFF
LOOKS DON'T MATTER FOR SHOVELING SNOW!
WE'LL ESCORT THE GENTLEMAN AND HIS NUMBER 2 TO THE PALACE TO RELAX!
I'M NOT HIS NUMBER 2!
BUT IF THIS IS NEPTUNE...

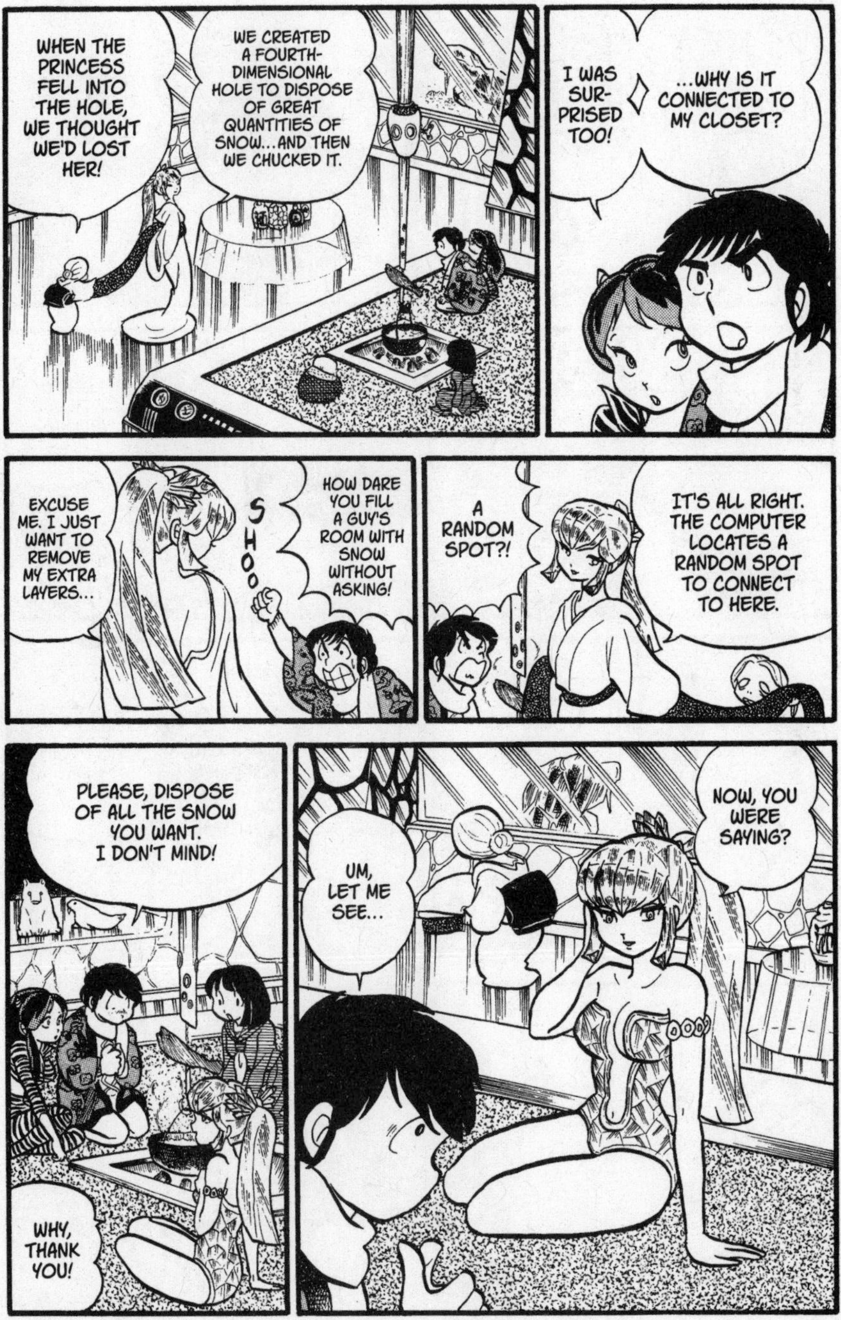
...WHY IS IT CONNECTED TO MY CLOSET?
I WAS SUR-PRISED TOO!
WE CREATED A FOURTH-DIMENSIONAL HOLE TO DISPOSE OF GREAT QUANTITIES OF SNOW...AND THEN WE CHUCKED IT.
WHEN THE PRINCESS FELL INTO THE HOLE, WE THOUGHT WE'D LOST HER!
IT'S ALL RIGHT. THE COMPUTER LOCATES A RANDOM SPOT TO CONNECT TO HERE.
A RANDOM SPOT?!
HOW DARE YOU FILL A GUY'S ROOM WITH SNOW WITHOUT ASKING!
SHOOO
EXCUSE ME. I JUST WANT TO REMOVE MY EXTRA LAYERS...
NOW, YOU WERE SAYING?
UM, LET ME SEE...
PLEASE, DISPOSE OF ALL THE SNOW YOU WANT. I DON'T MIND!
WHY, THANK YOU!

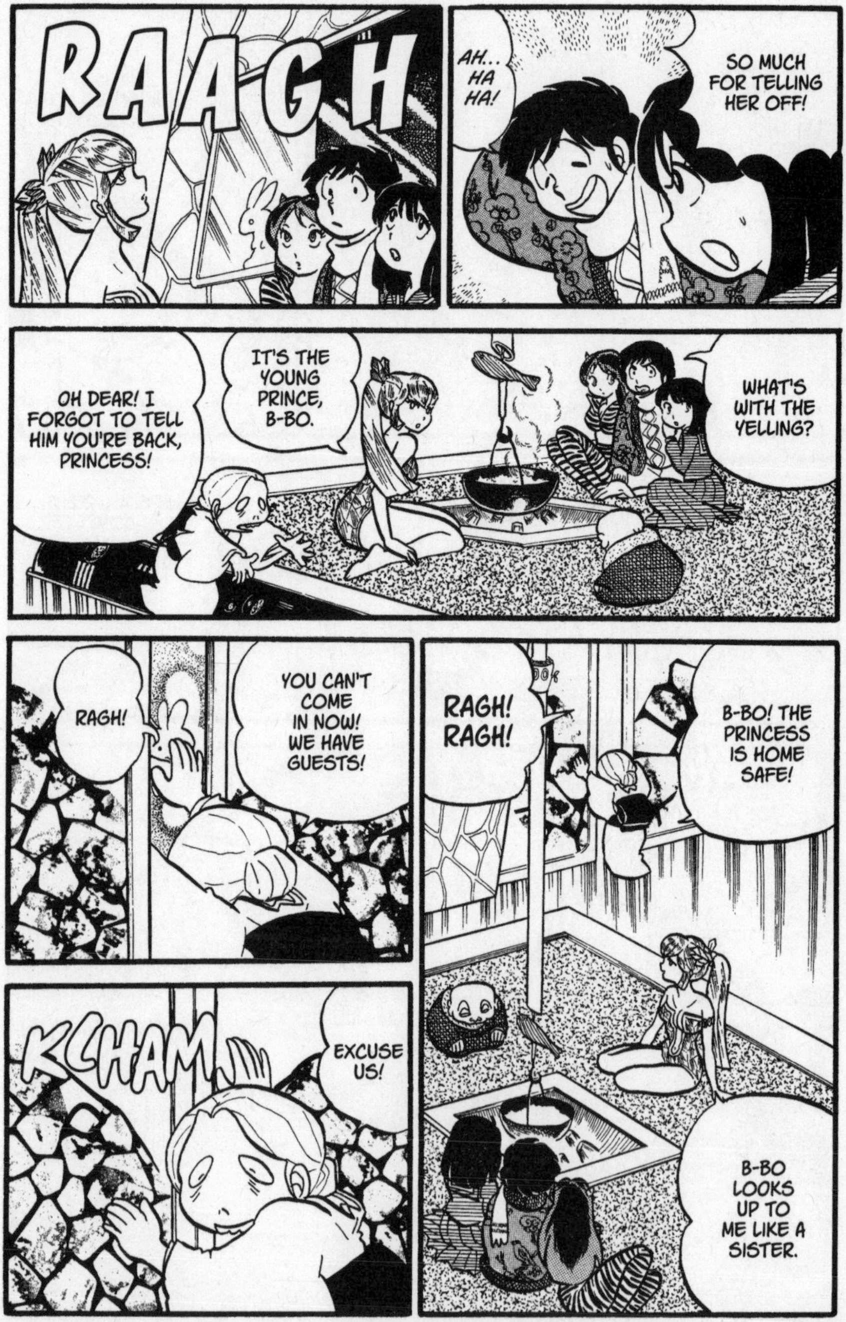
SO MUCH FOR TELLING HER OFF!
AH... HA HA!
RAAGH
WHAT'S WITH THE YELLING?
IT'S THE YOUNG PRINCE, B-BO.
OH DEAR! I FORGOT TO TELL HIM YOU'RE BACK, PRINCESS!
B-BO! THE PRINCESS IS HOME SAFE!
RAGH! RAGH!
B-BO LOOKS UP TO ME LIKE A SISTER.
YOU CAN'T COME IN NOW! WE HAVE GUESTS!
RAGH!
EXCUSE US!
KCHAM

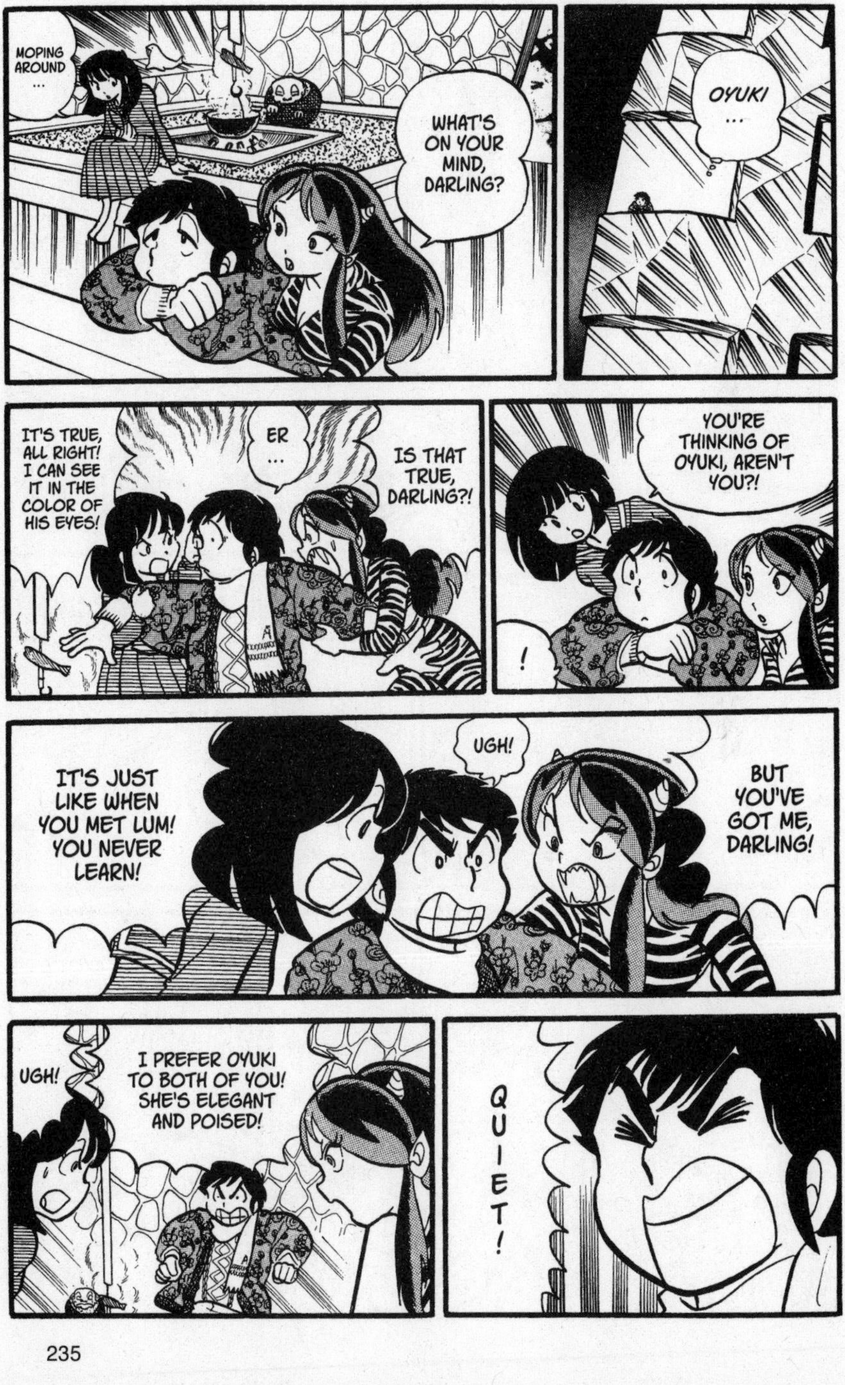

OYUKI ...
WHAT'S ON YOUR MIND, DARLING?
MOPING AROUND ...
YOU'RE THINKING OF OYUKI, AREN'T YOU?!
!
IS THAT TRUE, DARLING?!
ER ...
IT'S TRUE, ALL RIGHT! I CAN SEE IT IN THE COLOR OF HIS EYES!
BUT YOU'VE GOT ME, DARLING!
UGH!
IT'S JUST LIKE WHEN YOU MET LUM! YOU NEVER LEARN!
QUIET!
I PREFER OYUKI TO BOTH OF YOU! SHE'S ELEGANT AND POISED!
UGH!

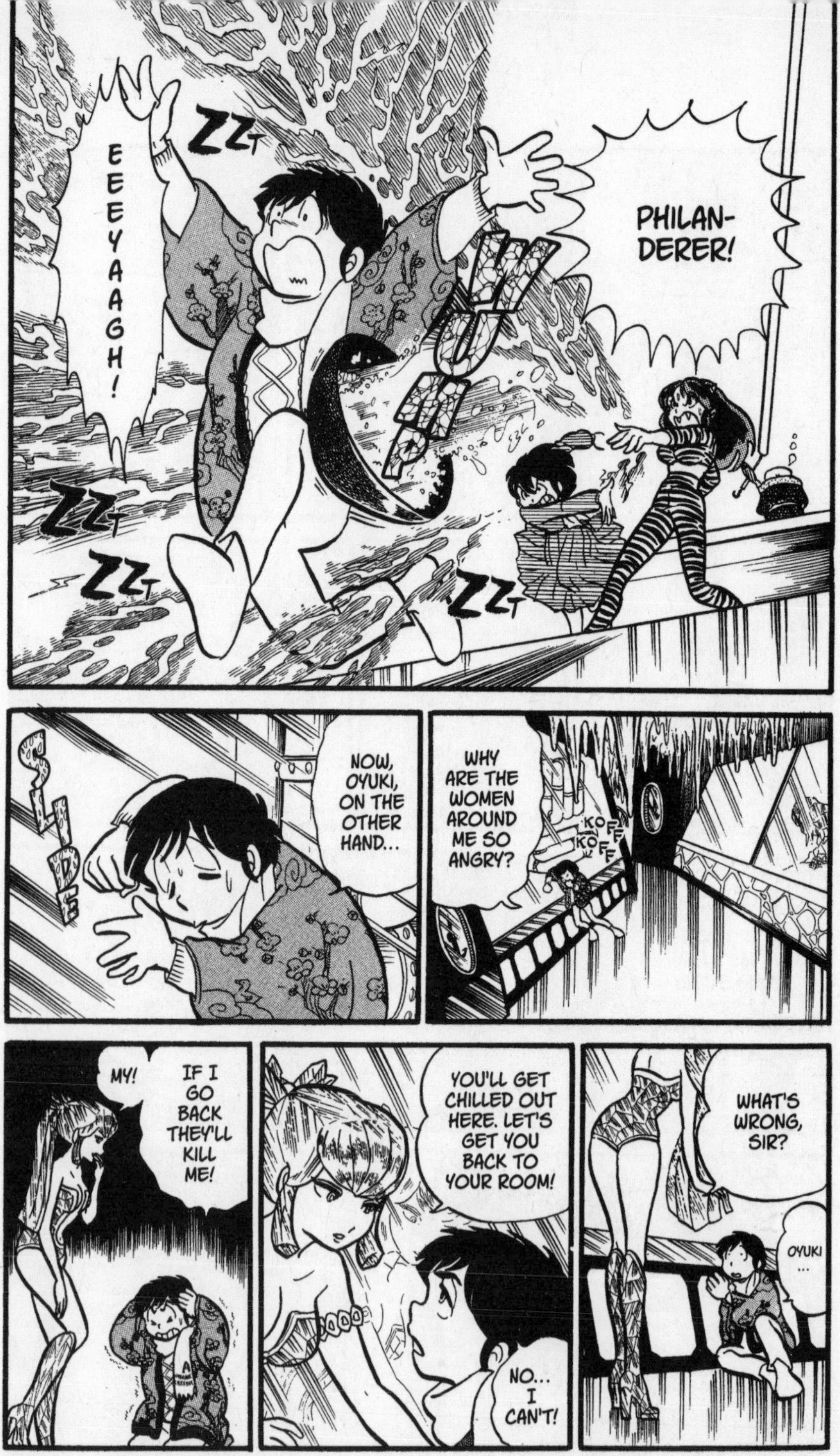

PHILAN-DERER!
ZZT
EEEYAAAGH!
ZZT
ZZT
ZZT
WHY ARE THE WOMEN AROUND ME SO ANGRY?
KOFF KOFF
NOW, OYUKI, ON THE OTHER HAND...
WHAT'S WRONG, SIR?
OYUKI...
YOU'LL GET CHILLED OUT HERE. LET'S GET YOU BACK TO YOUR ROOM!
NO... I CAN'T!
IF I GO BACK THEY'LL KILL ME!
MY!

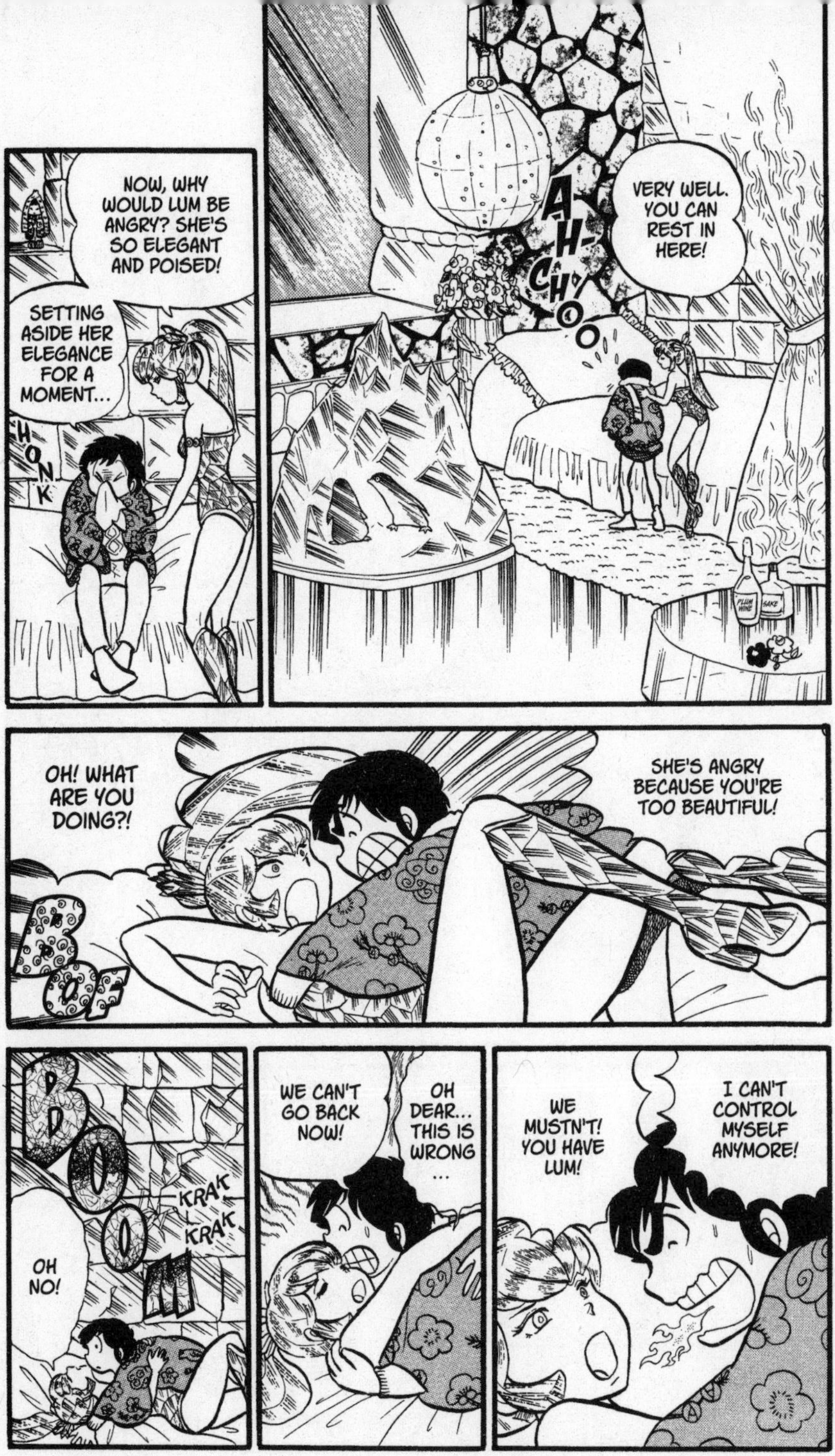
VERY WELL. YOU CAN REST IN HERE!
AH-CHOO
PLUM WINE
SAKE
NOW, WHY WOULD LUM BE ANGRY? SHE'S SO ELEGANT AND POISED!
SETTING ASIDE HER ELEGANCE FOR A MOMENT...
HONK
SHE'S ANGRY BECAUSE YOU'RE TOO BEAUTIFUL!
OH! WHAT ARE YOU DOING?!
BOOF
I CAN'T CONTROL MYSELF ANYMORE!
WE MUSTN'T! YOU HAVE LUM!
OH DEAR... THIS IS WRONG ...
WE CAN'T GO BACK NOW!
BOOOM
KRAK
KRAK
OH NO!

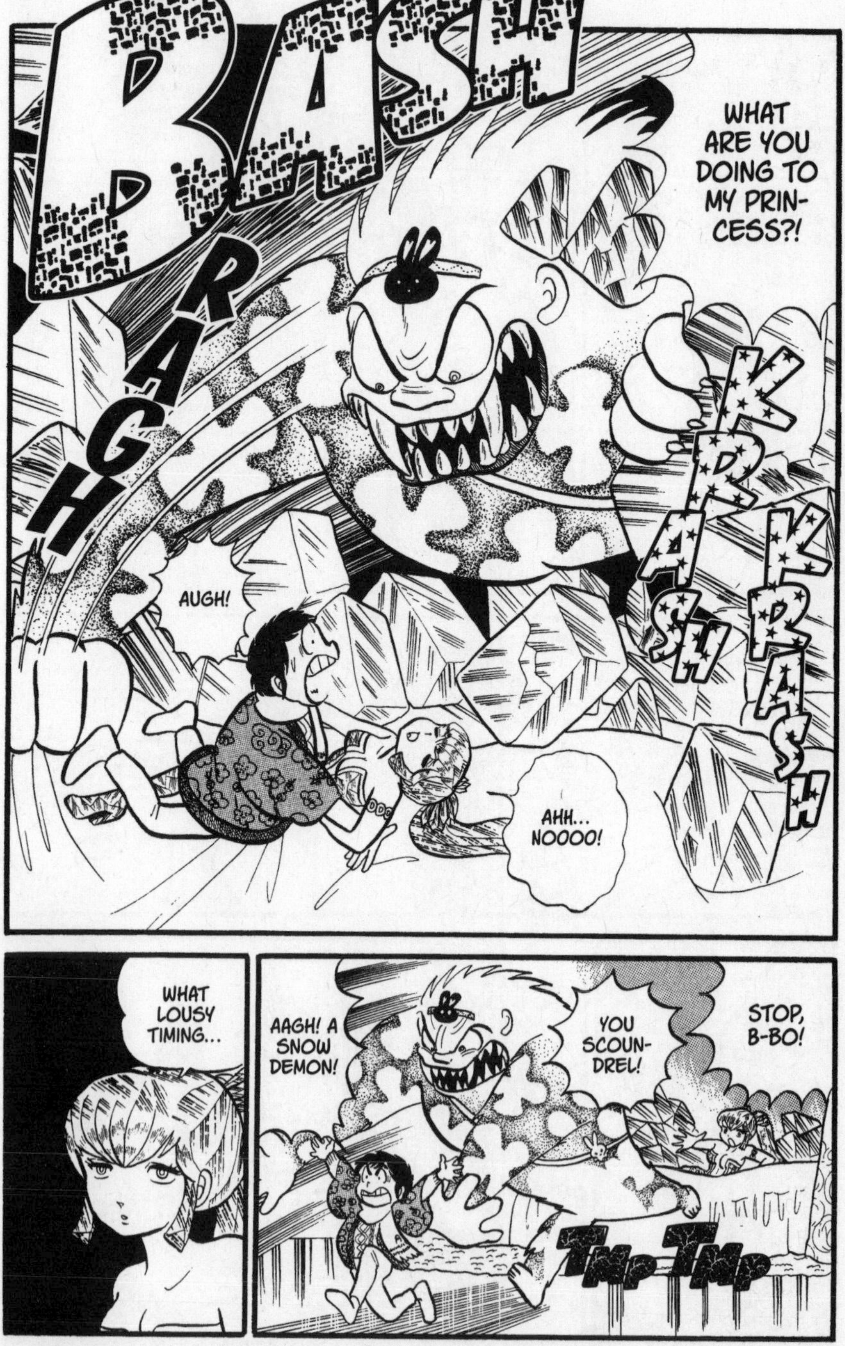
WHAT ARE YOU DOING TO MY PRIN-CESS?!
BASH
KRASH
KRASH
RAGH
AUGH!
AHH... NOOOO!
STOP, B-BO!
YOU SCOUN-DREL!
AAGH! A SNOW DEMON!
TMP TMP
WHAT LOUSY TIMING...

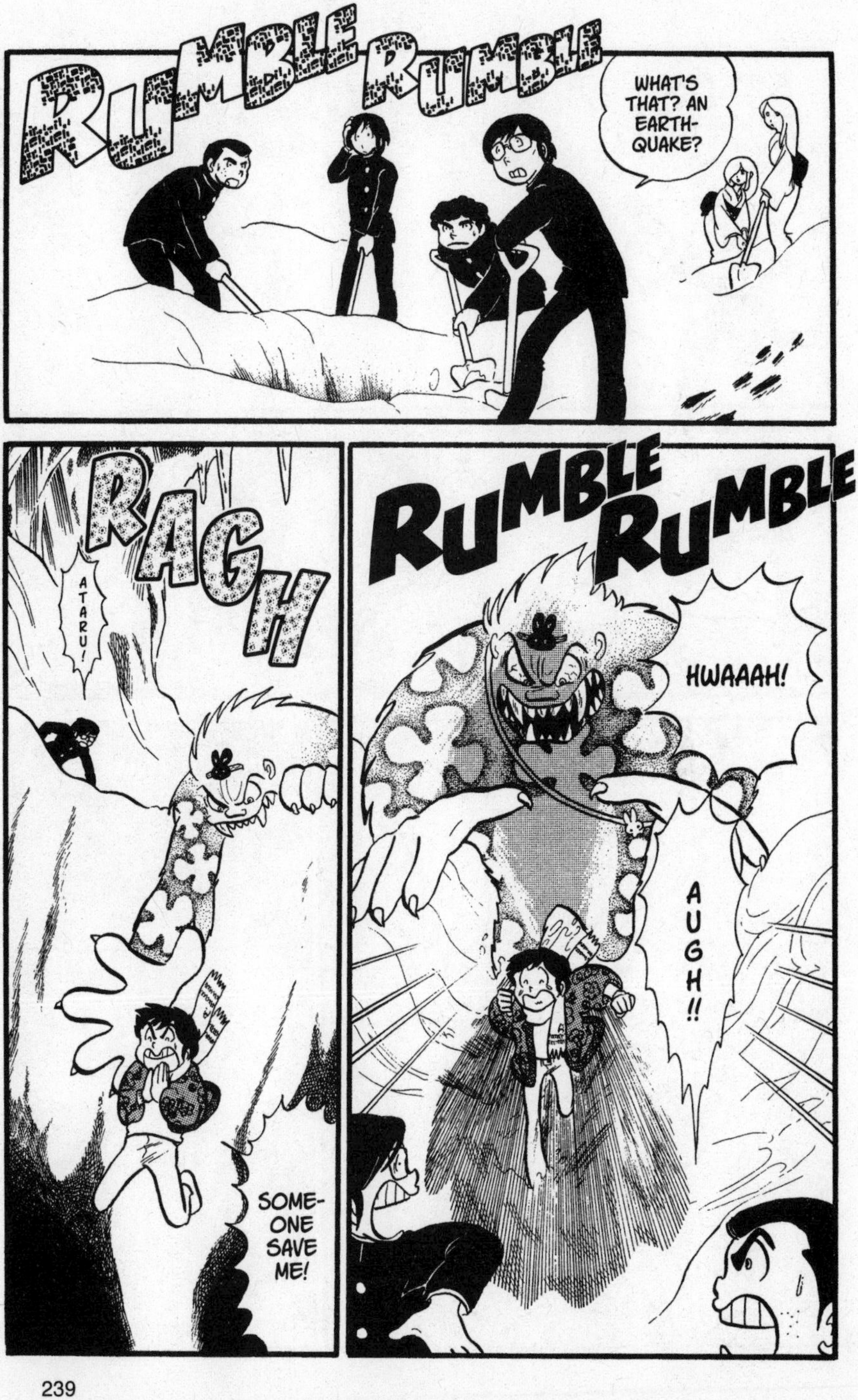
WHAT'S THAT? AN EARTH-QUAKE?
RUMBLE RUMBLE
RUMBLE RUMBLE
HWAAAH!
AUGH!!
RAGH
ATARU!
SOME-ONE SAVE ME!

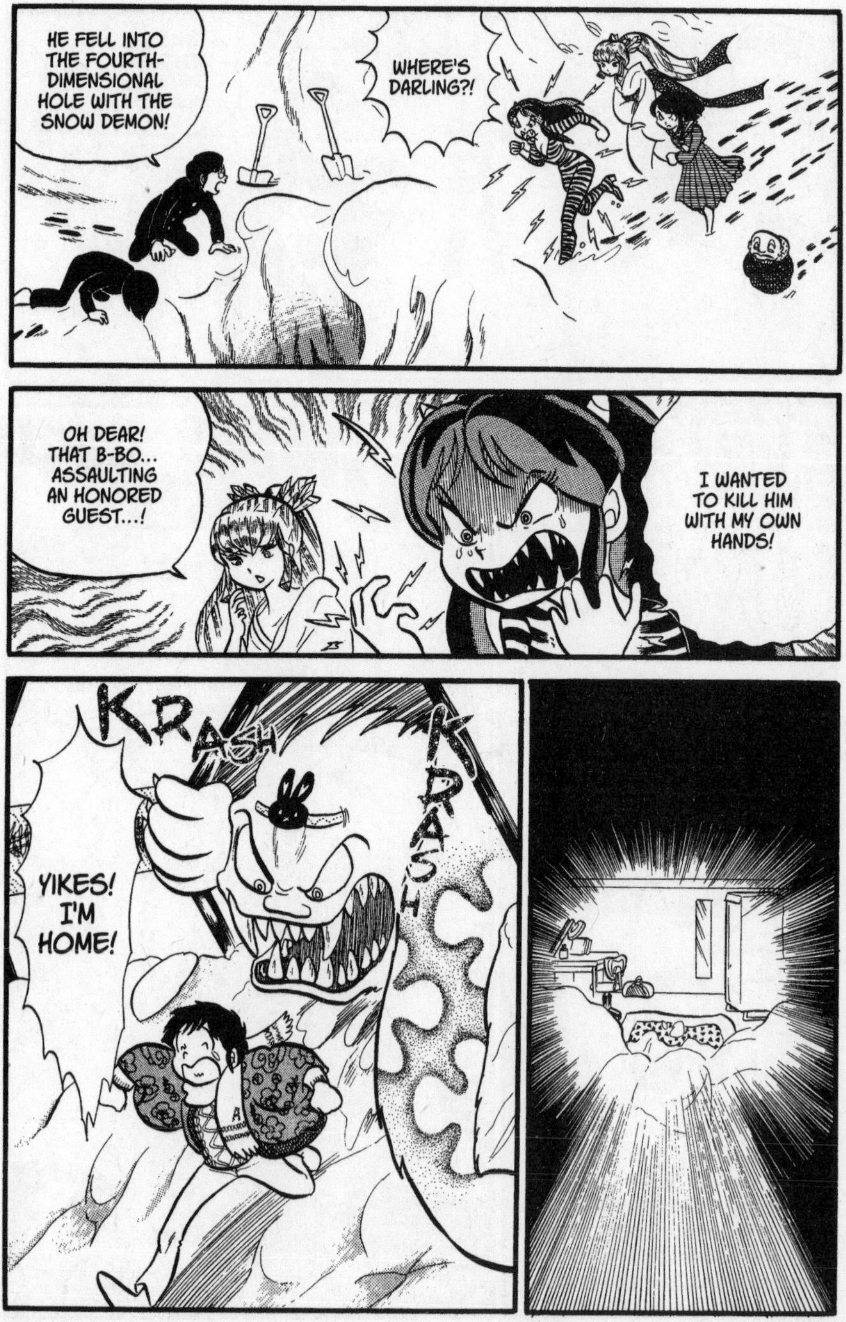
WHERE'S DARLING?!
HE FELL INTO THE FOURTH-DIMENSIONAL HOLE WITH THE SNOW DEMON!
I WANTED TO KILL HIM WITH MY OWN HANDS!
OH DEAR! THAT B-BO... ASSAULTING AN HONORED GUEST...!
KRASH
KRASH
YIKES! I'M HOME!

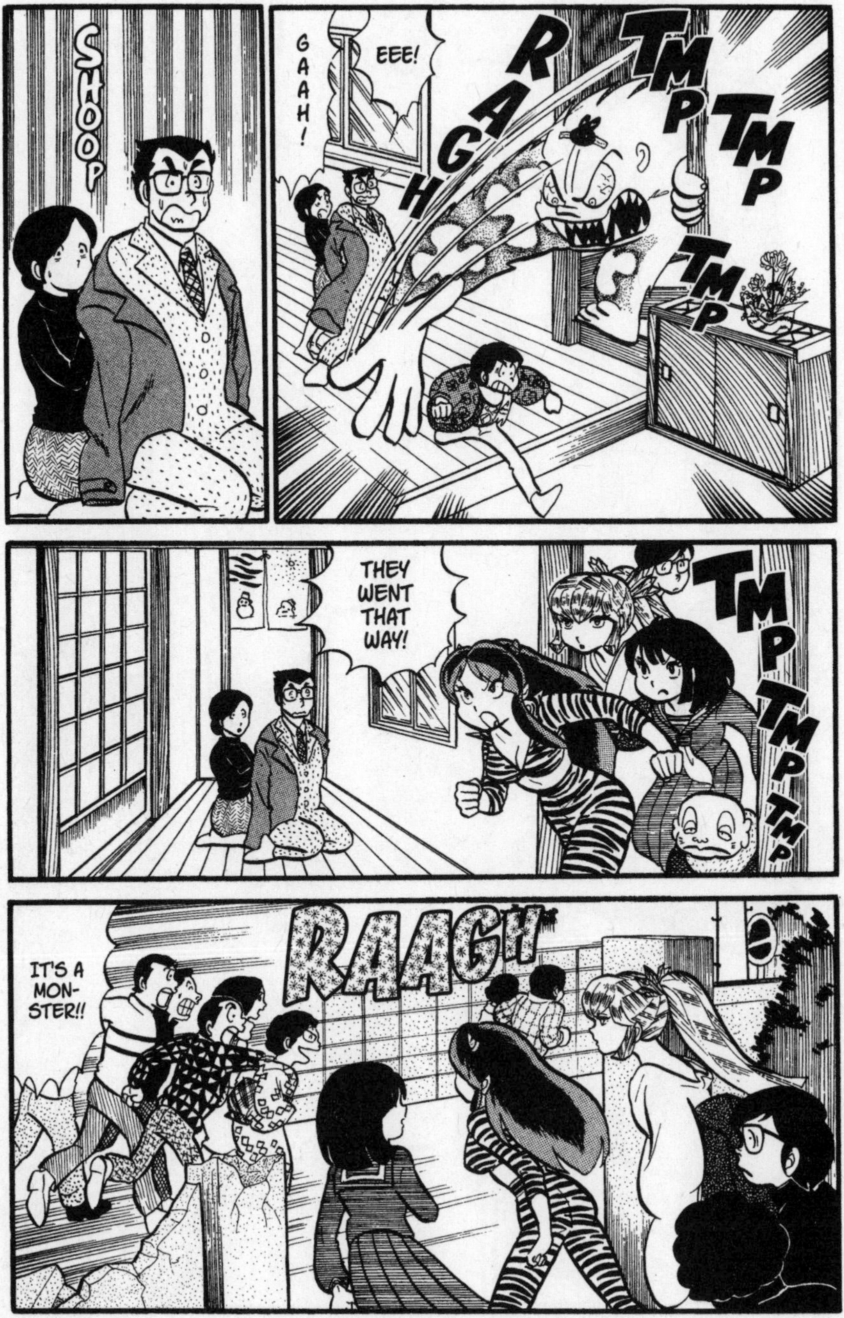
TMP
TMP
TMP
RAGH
EEE!
GAAH!
SHOOP
TMP
TMP
TMP
TMP
THEY WENT THAT WAY!
RAAGH
IT'S A MONSTER!!

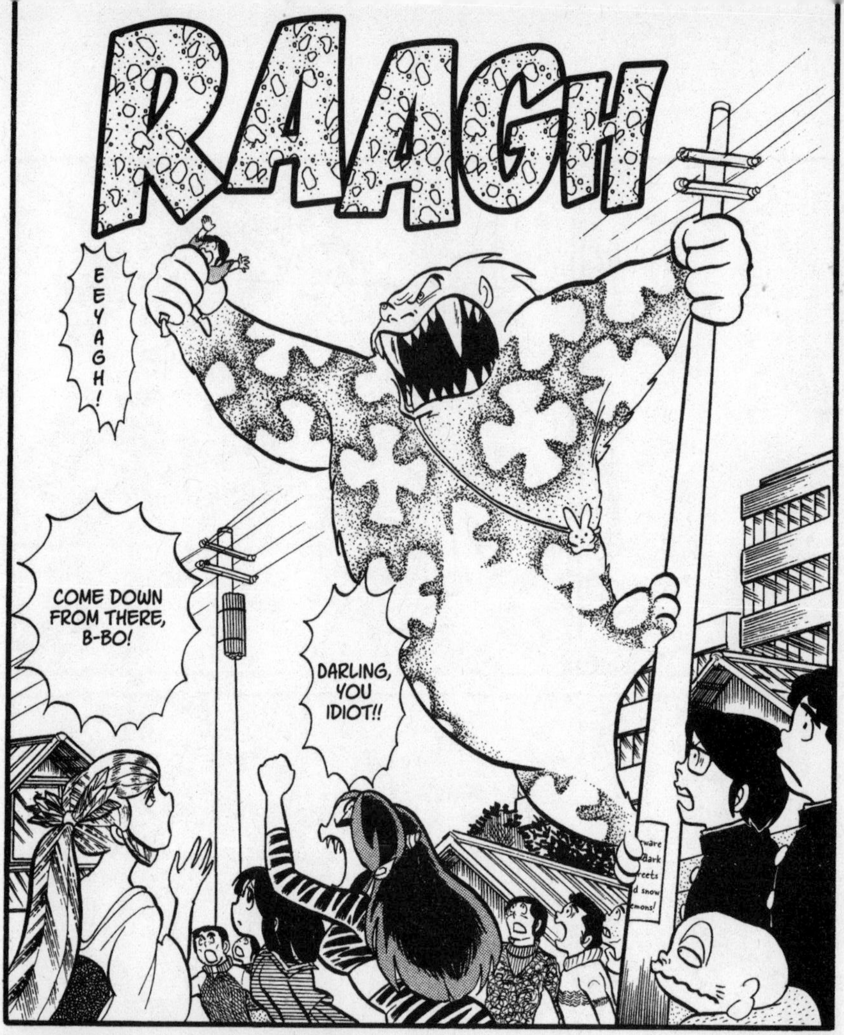
RAAGH
EEYAGH!
DARLING, YOU IDIOT!!
COME DOWN FROM THERE, B-BO!

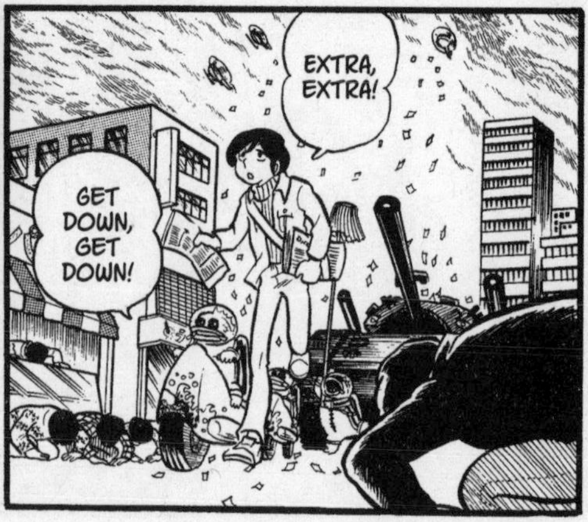
EXTRA, EXTRA!
GET DOWN, GET DOWN!

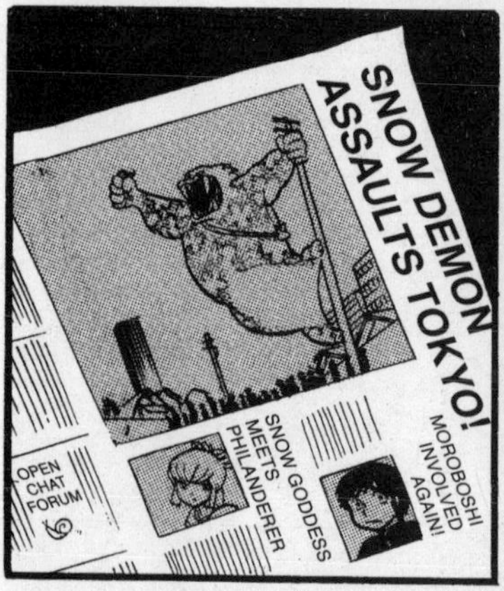
SNOW DEMON ASSAULTS TOKYO!
MOROBOSHI INVOLVED AGAIN!
SNOW GODDESS MEETS PHILANDERER
OPEN CHAT FORUM

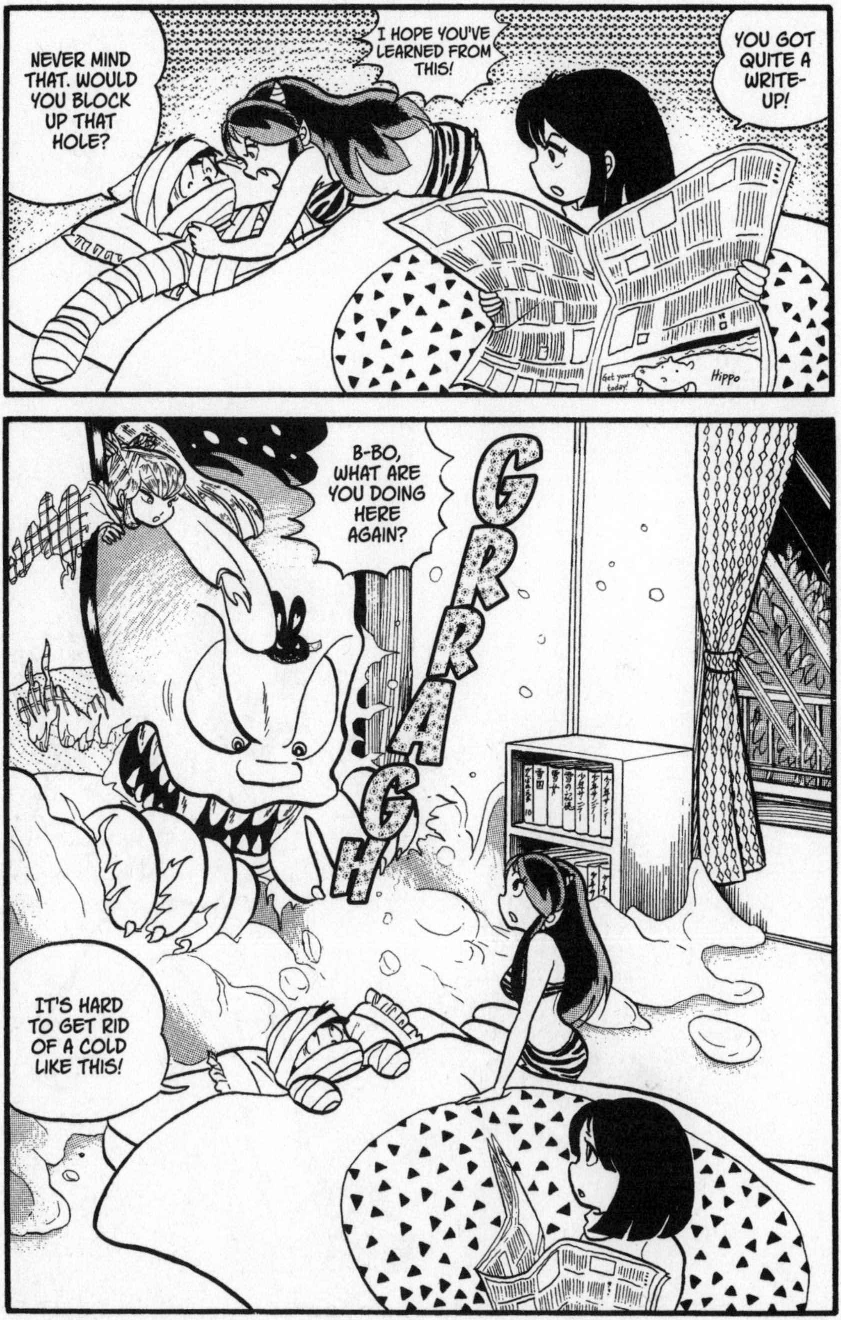
YOU GOT QUITE A WRITE-UP!
I HOPE YOU'VE LEARNED FROM THIS!
NEVER MIND THAT. WOULD YOU BLOCK UP THAT HOLE?
Hippo
Get yours today!
B-BO, WHAT ARE YOU DOING HERE AGAIN?
GRRRAGH
IT'S HARD TO GET RID OF A COLD LIKE THIS!

CHAPTER 11: EROS

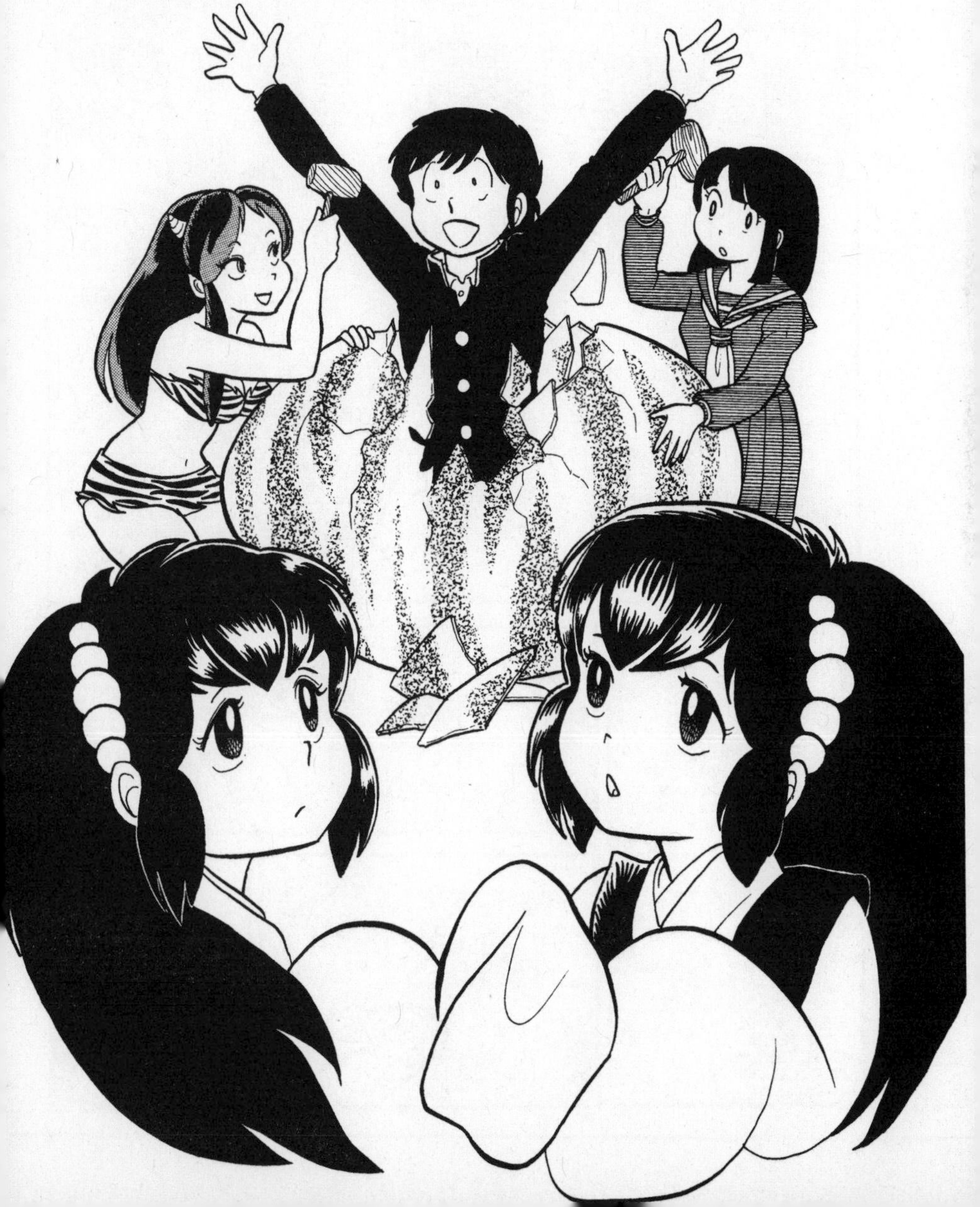

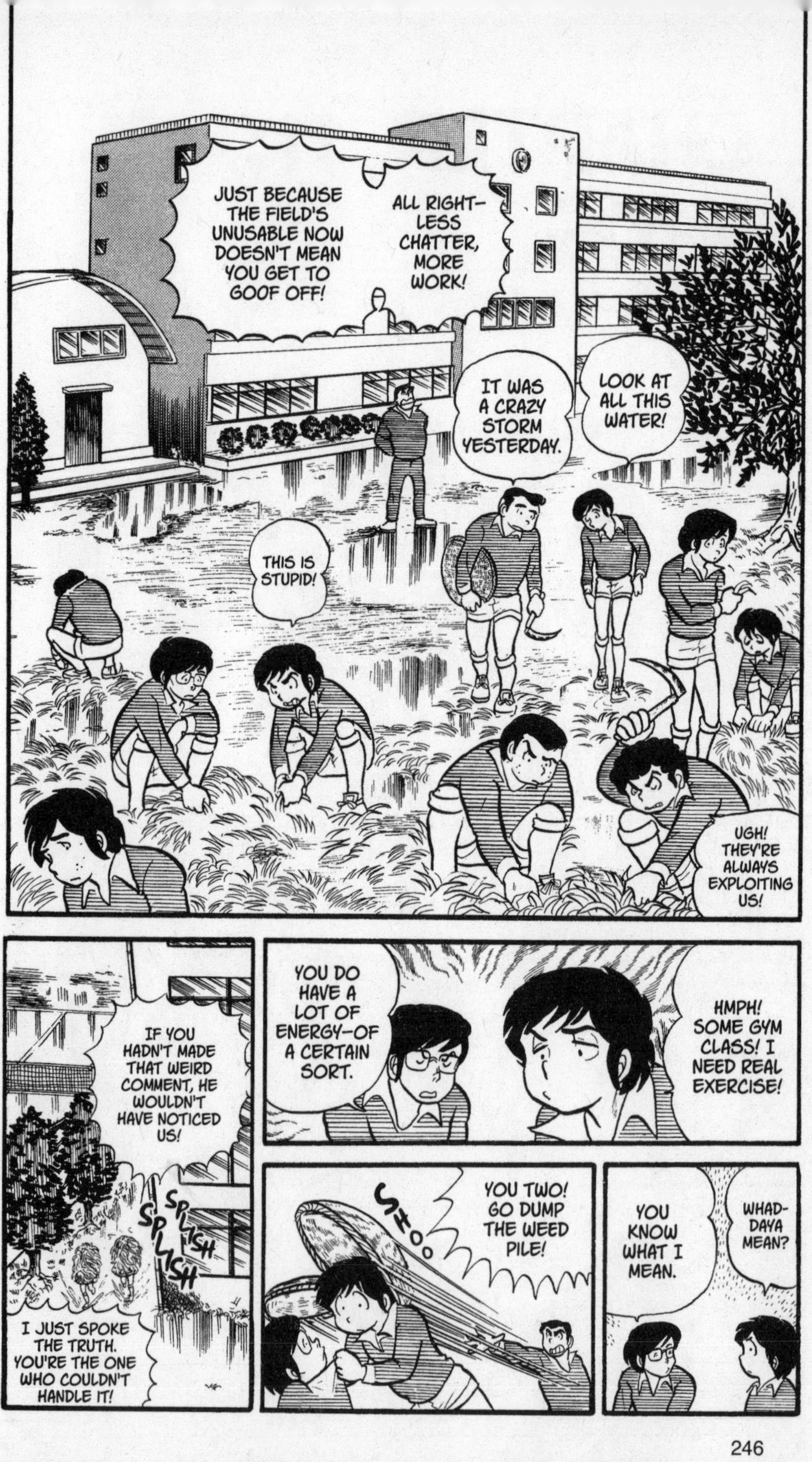
JUST BECAUSE THE FIELD'S UNUSABLE NOW DOESN'T MEAN YOU GET TO GOOF OFF!
ALL RIGHT- LESS CHATTER, MORE WORK!
LOOK AT ALL THIS WATER!
IT WAS A CRAZY STORM YESTERDAY.
THIS IS STUPID!
UGH! THEY'RE ALWAYS EXPLOITING US!
HMPH! SOME GYM CLASS! I NEED REAL EXERCISE!
YOU DO HAVE A LOT OF ENERGY—OF A CERTAIN SORT.
WHAD-DAYA MEAN?
YOU KNOW WHAT I MEAN.
YOU TWO! GO DUMP THE WEED PILE!
SHOO
IF YOU HADN'T MADE THAT WEIRD COMMENT, HE WOULDN'T HAVE NOTICED US!
SPLISH
SPLISH
I JUST SPOKE THE TRUTH. YOU'RE THE ONE WHO COULDN'T HANDLE IT!

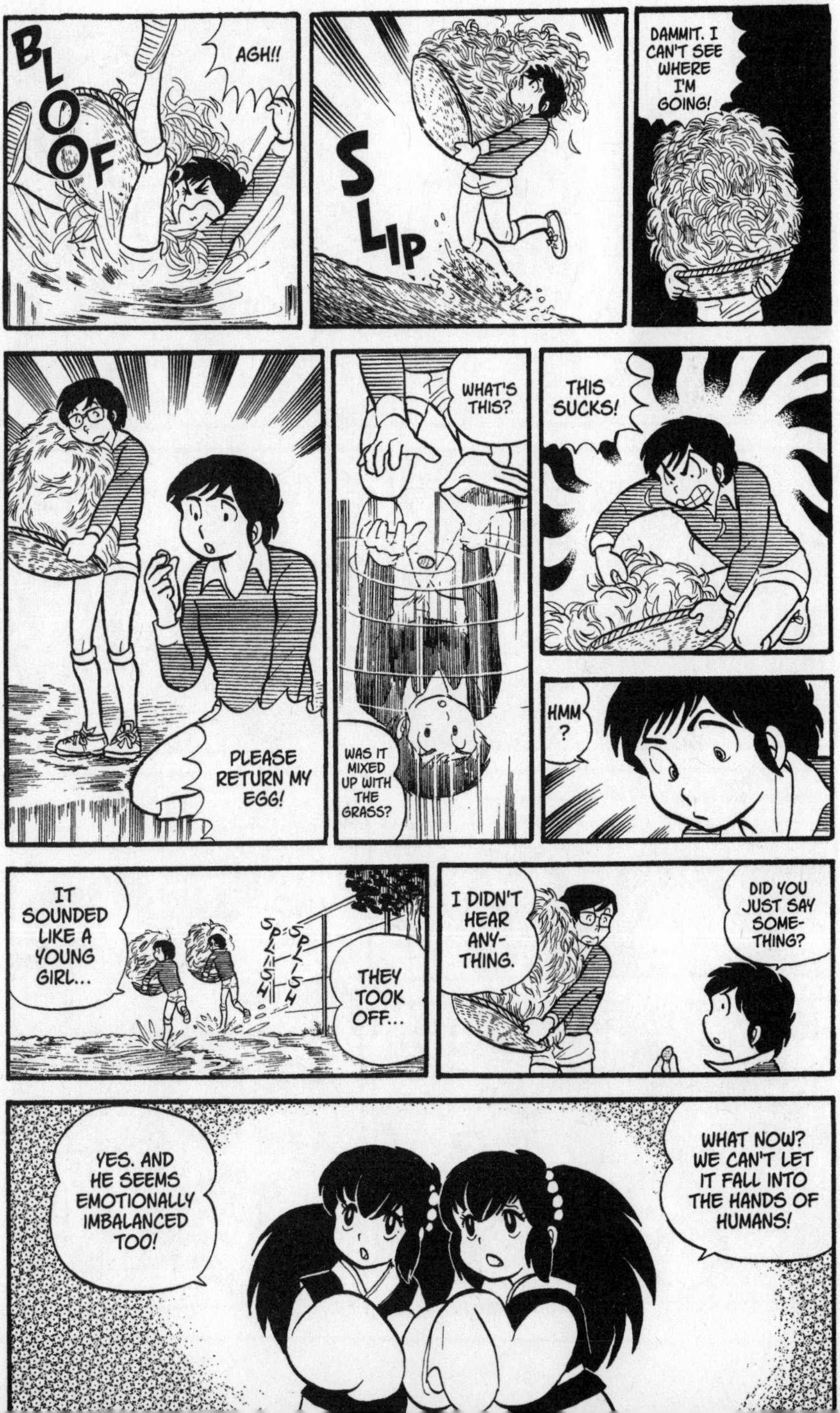
DAMMIT. I CAN'T SEE WHERE I'M GOING!
SLIP
AGH!!
BLOOF
THIS SUCKS!
HMM ?
WHAT'S THIS?
WAS IT MIXED UP WITH THE GRASS?
PLEASE RETURN MY EGG!
DID YOU JUST SAY SOME-THING?
I DIDN'T HEAR ANY-THING.
SPLISH SPLISH
THEY TOOK OFF...
IT SOUNDED LIKE A YOUNG GIRL...
WHAT NOW? WE CAN'T LET IT FALL INTO THE HANDS OF HUMANS!
YES. AND HE SEEMS EMOTIONALLY IMBALANCED TOO!

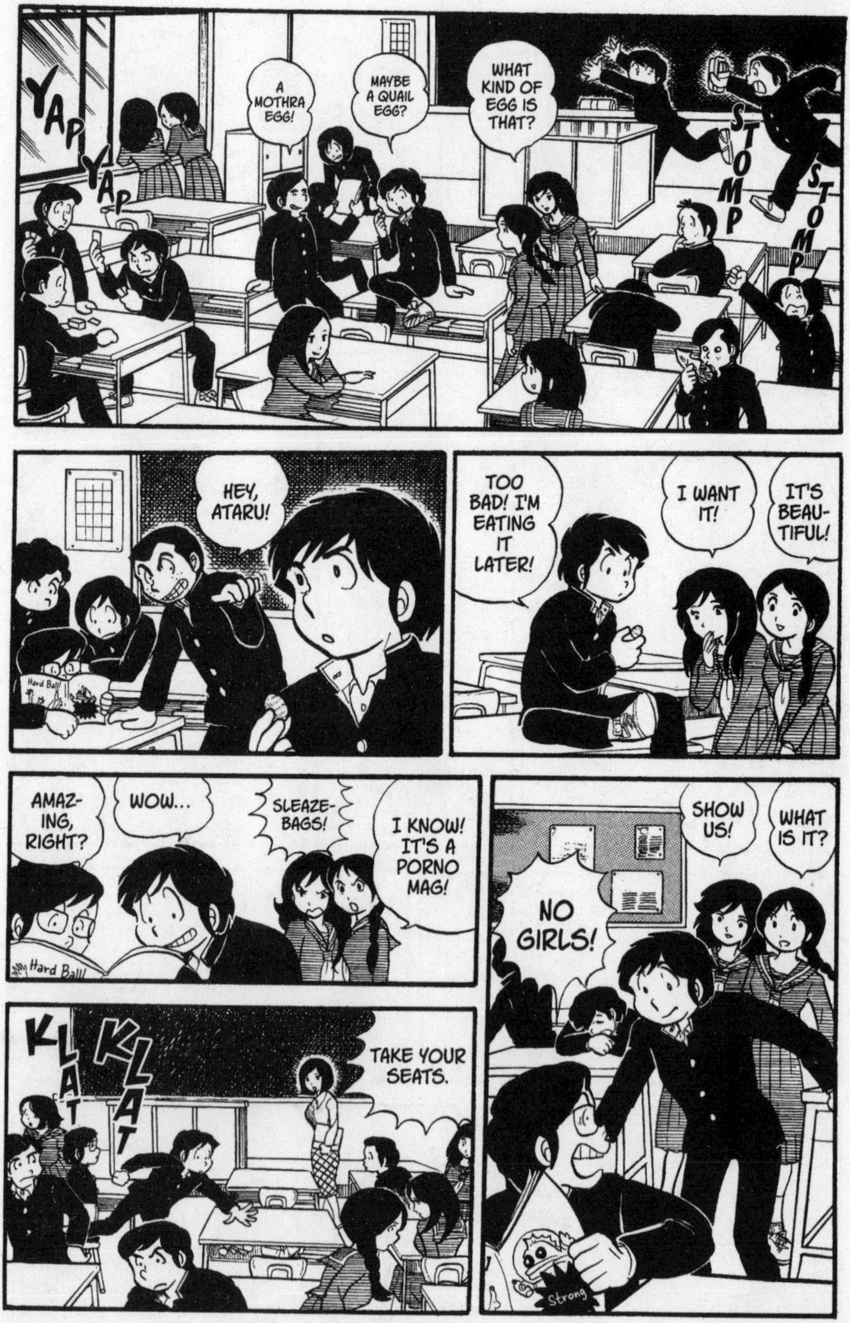
STOMP
STOMP
WHAT KIND OF EGG IS THAT?
MAYBE A QUAIL EGG?
A MOTHRA EGG!
YAP YAP
YAP
IT'S BEAU-TIFUL!
I WANT IT!
TOO BAD! I'M EATING IT LATER!
HEY, ATARU!
Hard Ball!
WHAT IS IT?
SHOW US!
NO GIRLS!
Strong
I KNOW! IT'S A PORNO MAG!
SLEAZE-BAGS!
WOW...
AMAZ-ING, RIGHT?
Hard Ball!
TAKE YOUR SEATS.
KLAT
KLAT

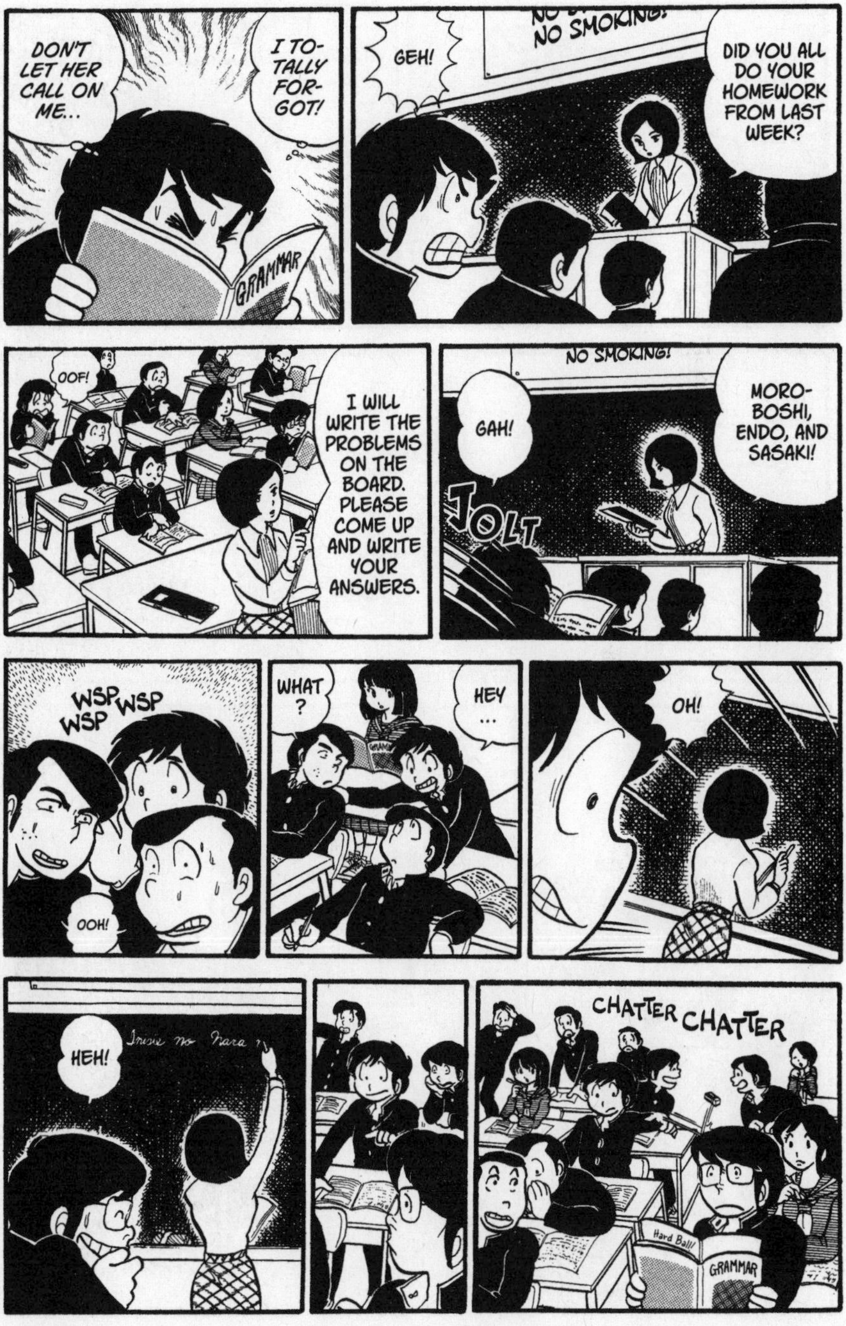
NO SMOKING!
DID YOU ALL DO YOUR HOMEWORK FROM LAST WEEK?
GEH!
I TO-TALLY FOR-GOT!
DON'T LET HER CALL ON ME...
GRAMMAR
NO SMOKING!
MORO-BOSHI, ENDO, AND SASAKI!
GAH!
JOLT
I WILL WRITE THE PROBLEMS ON THE BOARD. PLEASE COME UP AND WRITE YOUR ANSWERS.
OOF!
OH!
HEY ...
WHAT ?
WSP WSP WSP
OOH!
CHATTER CHATTER
Hard Ball!
GRAMMAR
HEH!

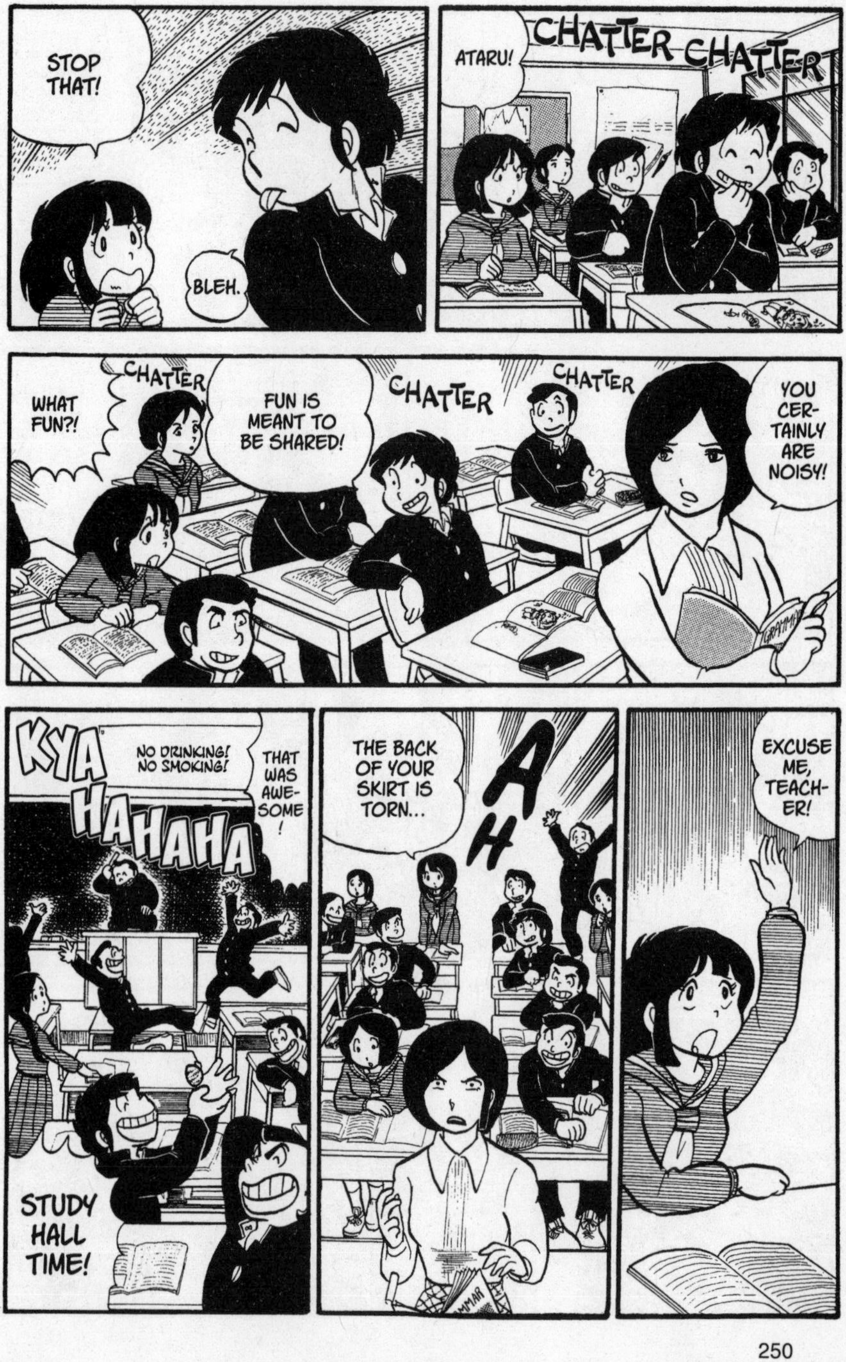
ATARU!
CHATTER CHATTER
STOP THAT!
BLEH.
YOU CERTAINLY ARE NOISY!
CHATTER
CHATTER
FUN IS MEANT TO BE SHARED!
CHATTER
WHAT FUN?!
EXCUSE ME, TEACHER!
AH
THE BACK OF YOUR SKIRT IS TORN...
THAT WAS AWESOME!
NO DRINKING! NO SMOKING!
KYA HAHAHA
STUDY HALL TIME!

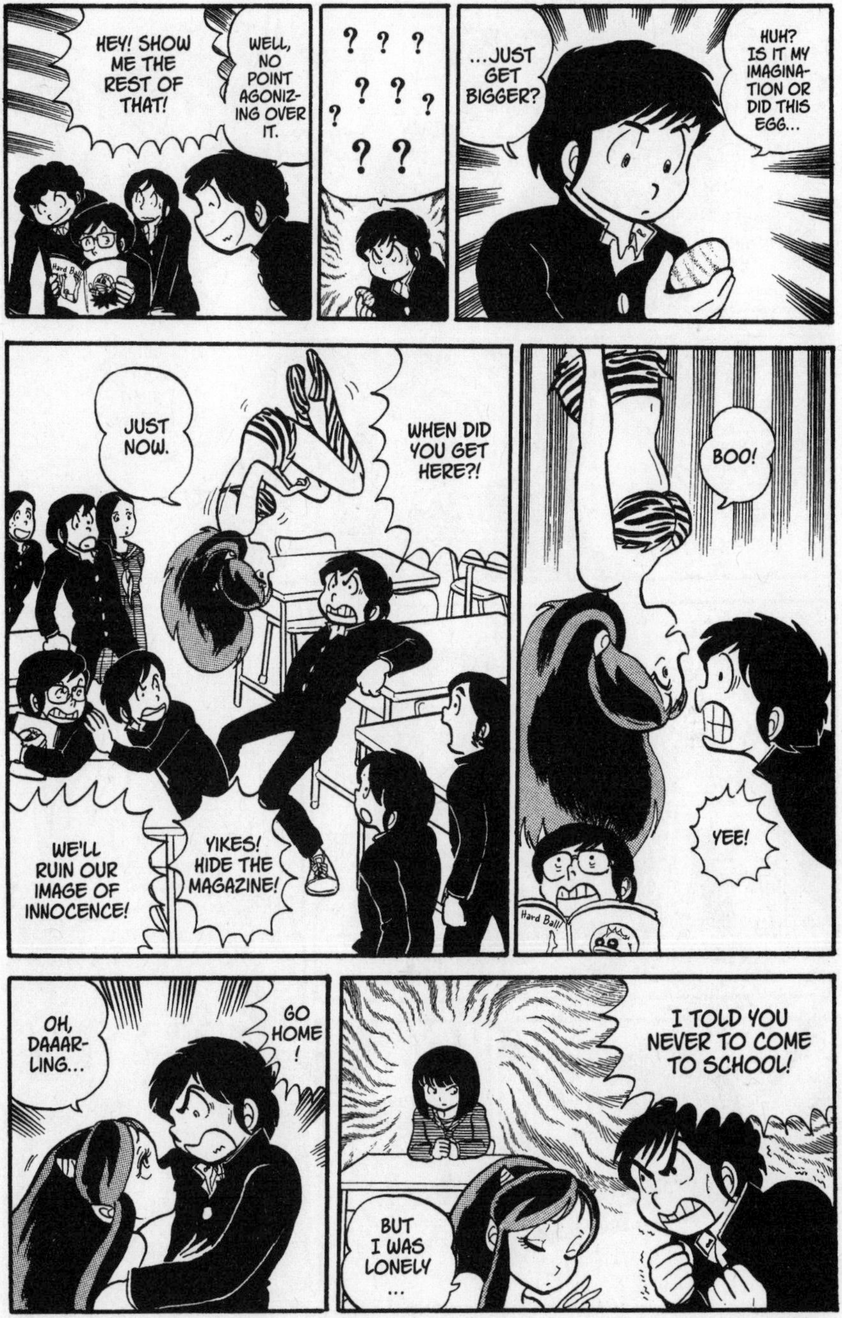
HUH? IS IT MY IMAGINATION OR DID THIS EGG…
…JUST GET BIGGER?
? ? ? ? ? ? ? ? ?
WELL, NO POINT AGONIZING OVER IT.
HEY! SHOW ME THE REST OF THAT!
Hard Ball
BOO!
YEE!
Hard Ball
WHEN DID YOU GET HERE?!
JUST NOW.
YIKES! HIDE THE MAGAZINE!
WE'LL RUIN OUR IMAGE OF INNOCENCE!
I TOLD YOU NEVER TO COME TO SCHOOL!
BUT I WAS LONELY …
GO HOME!
OH, DAAAR-LING…

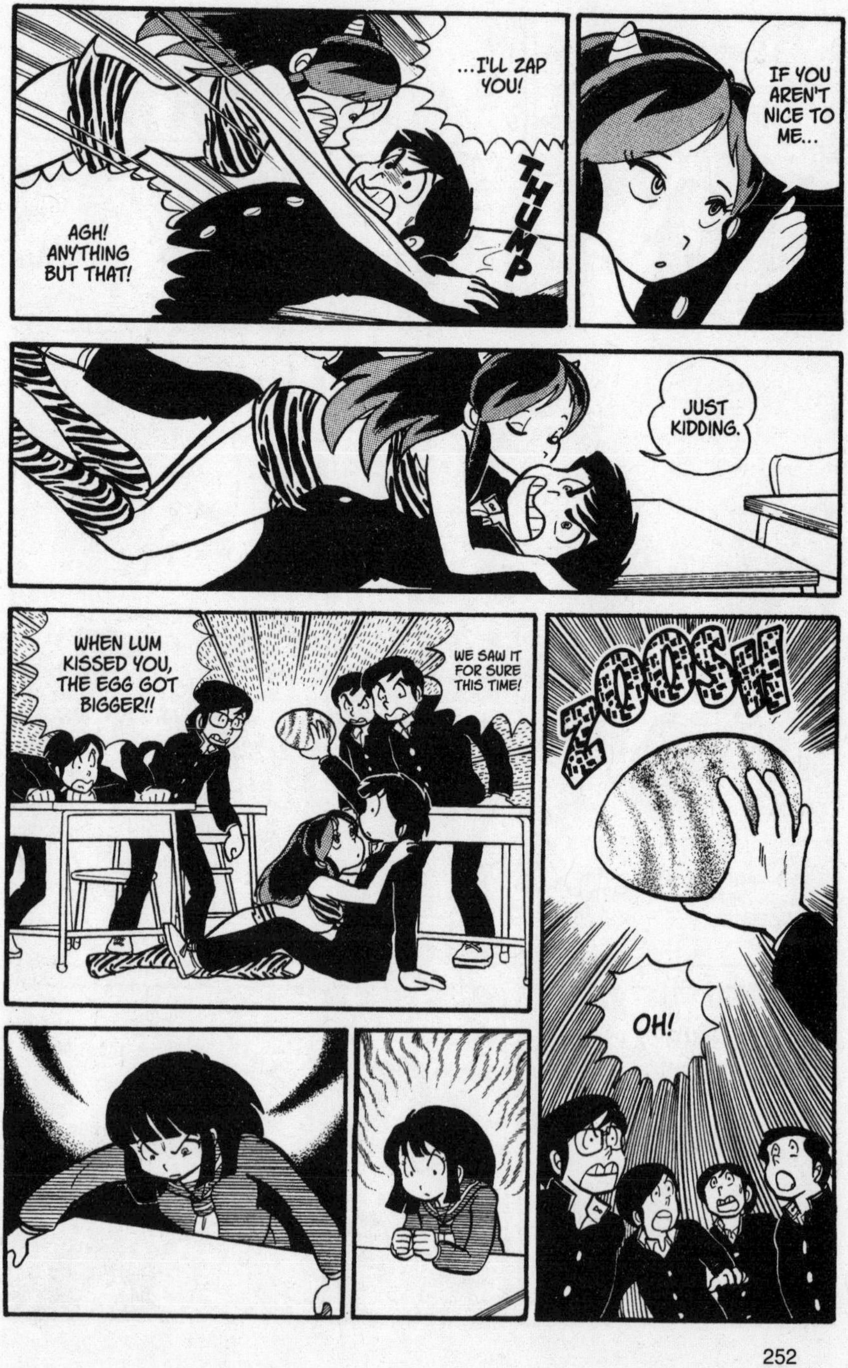
IF YOU AREN'T NICE TO ME...
...I'LL ZAP YOU!
THUMP
AGH! ANYTHING BUT THAT!
JUST KIDDING.
ZOOSH
OH!
WE SAW IT FOR SURE THIS TIME!
WHEN LUM KISSED YOU, THE EGG GOT BIGGER!!

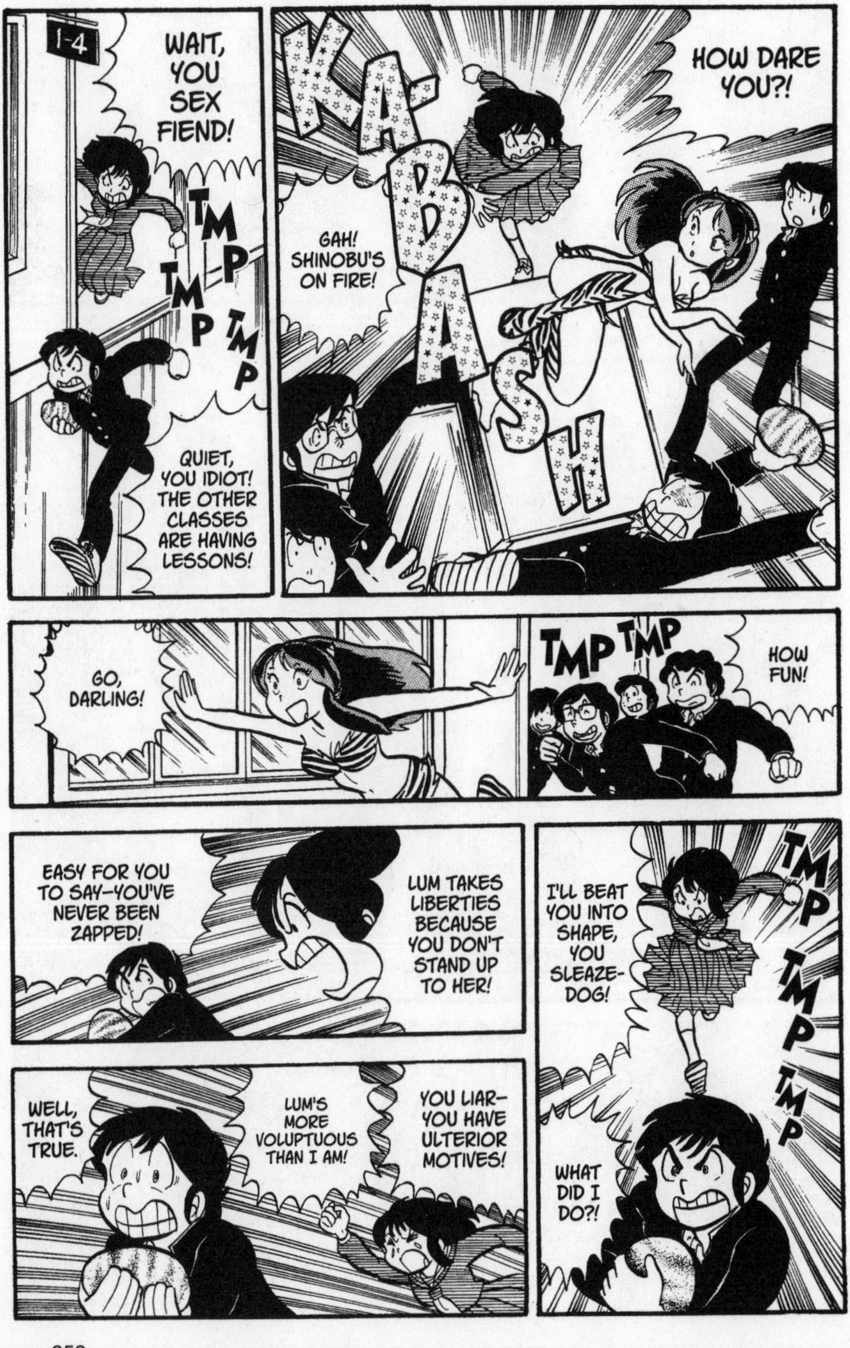
HOW DARE YOU?!
KA-BADASH
GAH! SHINOBU'S ON FIRE!
1-4
WAIT, YOU SEX FIEND!
TMP TMP
TMP TMP
QUIET, YOU IDIOT! THE OTHER CLASSES ARE HAVING LESSONS!
TMP TMP
HOW FUN!
GO, DARLING!
TMP TMP TMP TMP
I'LL BEAT YOU INTO SHAPE, YOU SLEAZE-DOG!
WHAT DID I DO?!
LUM TAKES LIBERTIES BECAUSE YOU DON'T STAND UP TO HER!
EASY FOR YOU TO SAY—YOU'VE NEVER BEEN ZAPPED!
YOU LIAR—YOU HAVE ULTERIOR MOTIVES!
LUM'S MORE VOLUPTUOUS THAN I AM!
WELL, THAT'S TRUE.

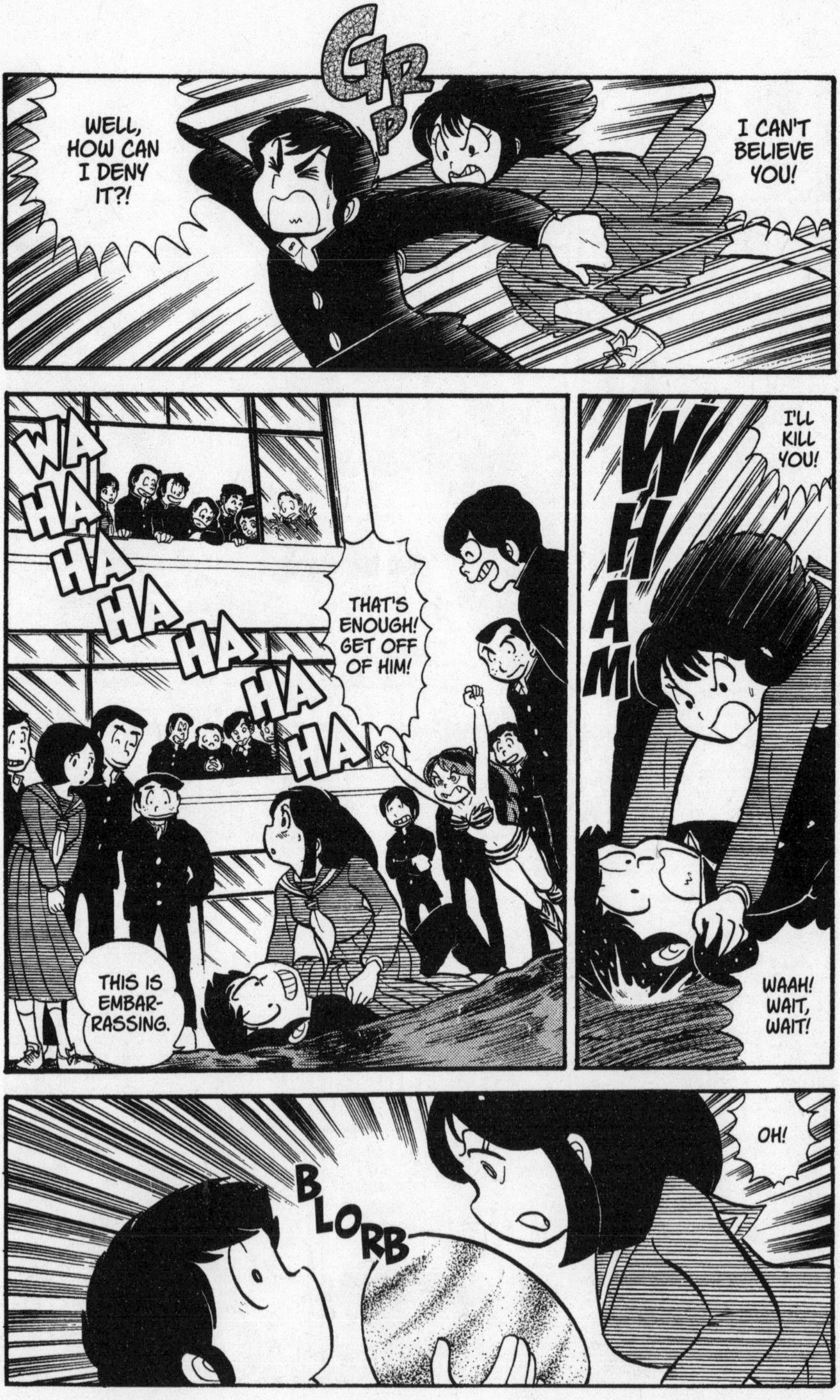
I CAN'T BELIEVE YOU!
GRP
WELL, HOW CAN I DENY IT?!
I'LL KILL YOU!
WHAM
WAAH! WAIT, WAIT!
WA HA HA HA HA HA HA
THAT'S ENOUGH! GET OFF OF HIM!
THIS IS EMBARRASSING.
OH!
BLORB

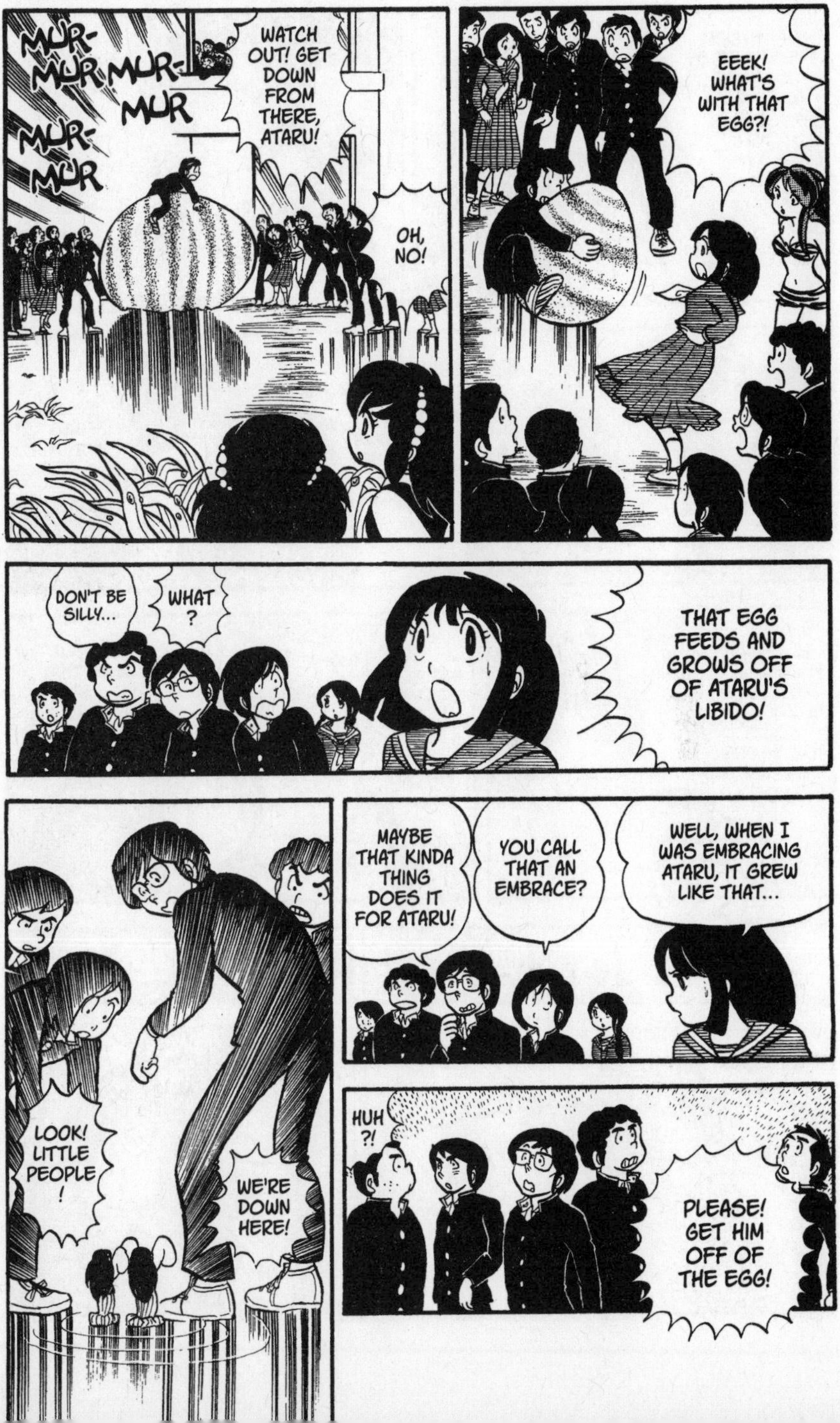
EEEK! WHAT'S WITH THAT EGG?!
WATCH OUT! GET DOWN FROM THERE, ATARU!
MUR-MUR MUR-MUR MUR-MUR
OH, NO!
THAT EGG FEEDS AND GROWS OFF OF ATARU'S LIBIDO!
WHAT?
DON'T BE SILLY...
WELL, WHEN I WAS EMBRACING ATARU, IT GREW LIKE THAT...
YOU CALL THAT AN EMBRACE?
MAYBE THAT KINDA THING DOES IT FOR ATARU!
PLEASE! GET HIM OFF OF THE EGG!
HUH?!
WE'RE DOWN HERE!
LOOK! LITTLE PEOPLE!

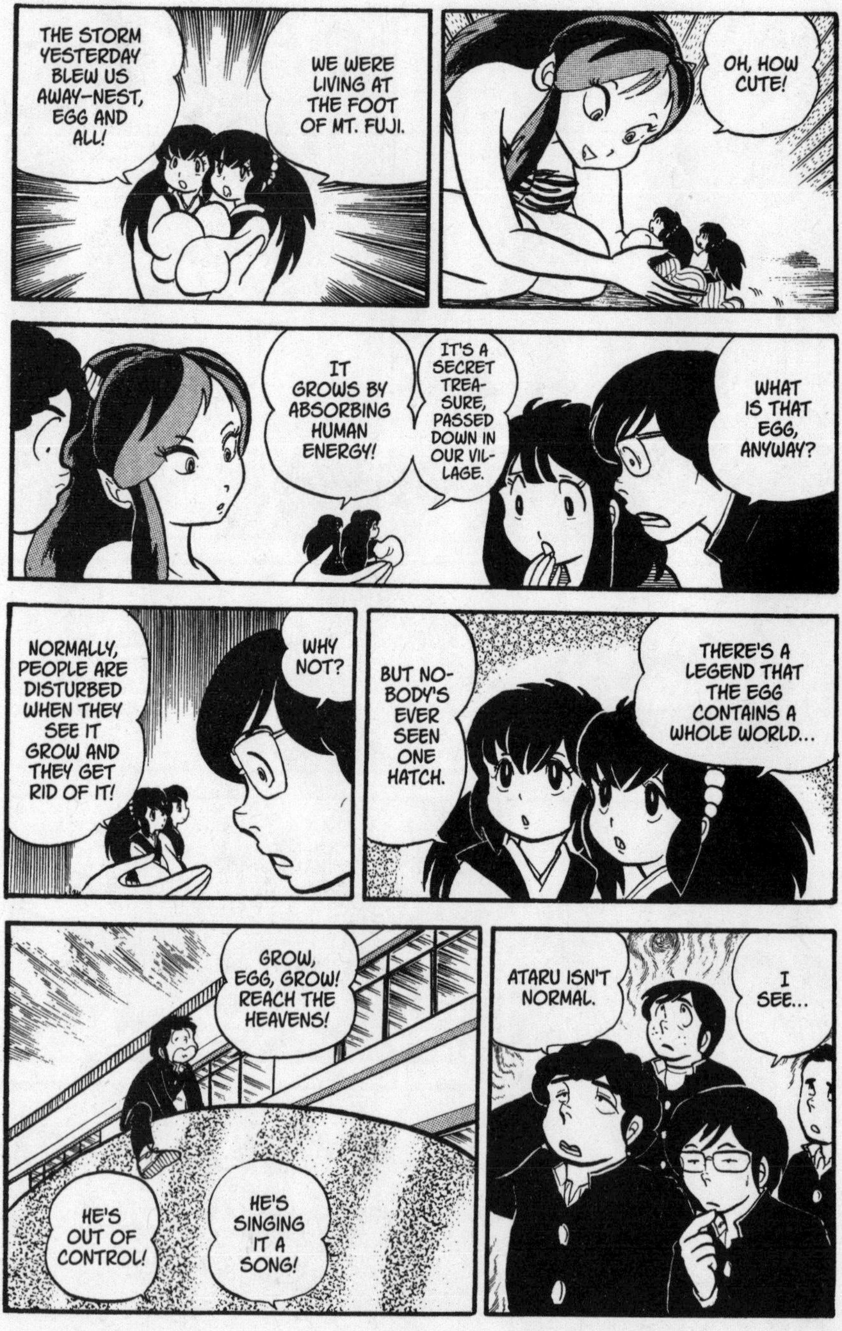
OH, HOW CUTE!
WE WERE LIVING AT THE FOOT OF MT. FUJI.
THE STORM YESTERDAY BLEW US AWAY—NEST, EGG AND ALL!
WHAT IS THAT EGG, ANYWAY?
IT'S A SECRET TREASURE, PASSED DOWN IN OUR VILLAGE.
IT GROWS BY ABSORBING HUMAN ENERGY!
THERE'S A LEGEND THAT THE EGG CONTAINS A WHOLE WORLD...
BUT NOBODY'S EVER SEEN ONE HATCH.
WHY NOT?
NORMALLY, PEOPLE ARE DISTURBED WHEN THEY SEE IT GROW AND THEY GET RID OF IT!
I SEE...
ATARU ISN'T NORMAL.
GROW, EGG, GROW! REACH THE HEAVENS!
HE'S SINGING IT A SONG!
HE'S OUT OF CONTROL!

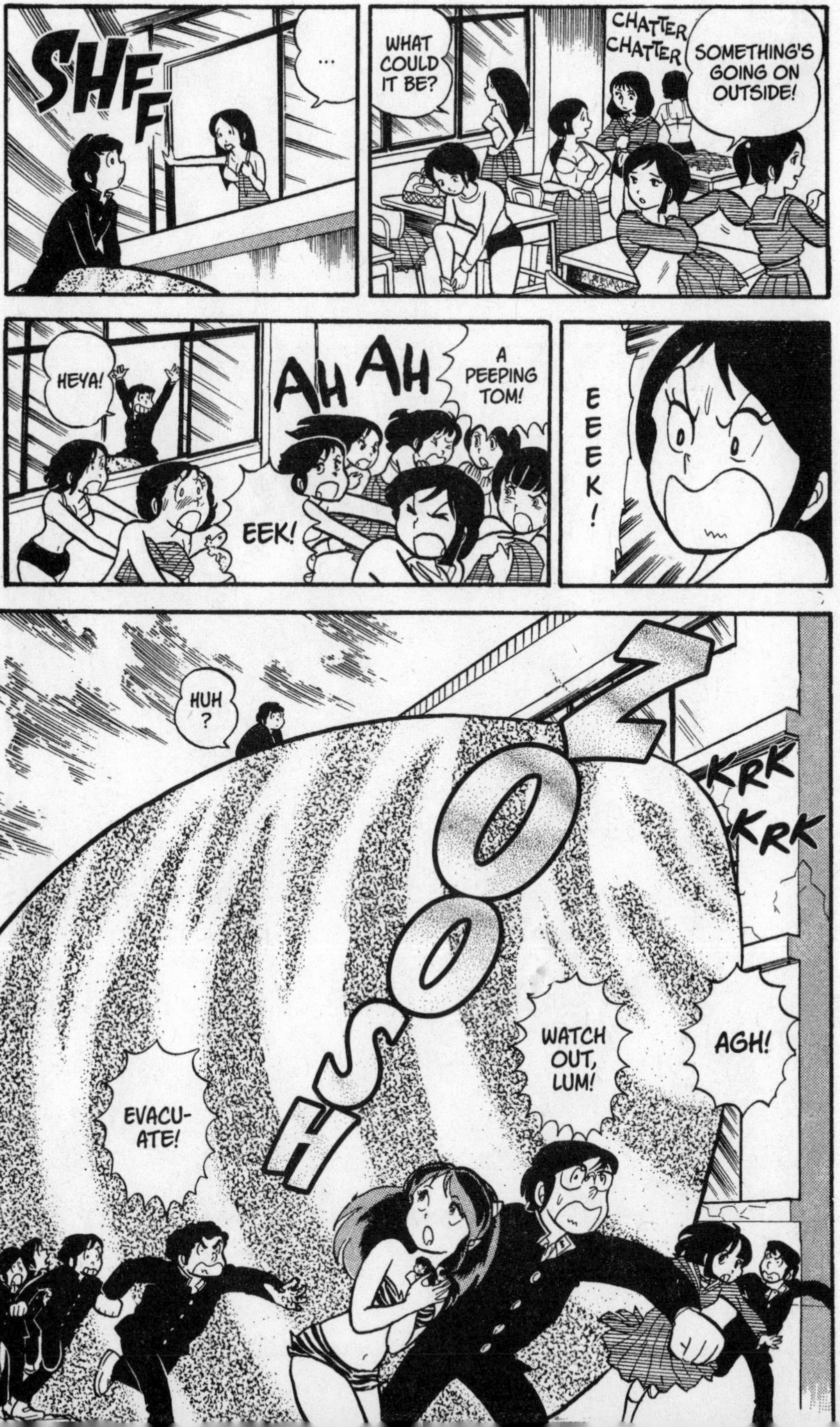
CHATTER CHATTER
SOMETHING'S GOING ON OUTSIDE!
WHAT COULD IT BE?
...
SHFF
EEEEK!
A PEEPING TOM!
AH AH
EEK!
HEYA!
ZOOSH
KRK KRK
AGH!
WATCH OUT, LUM!
HUH?
EVACU-ATE!

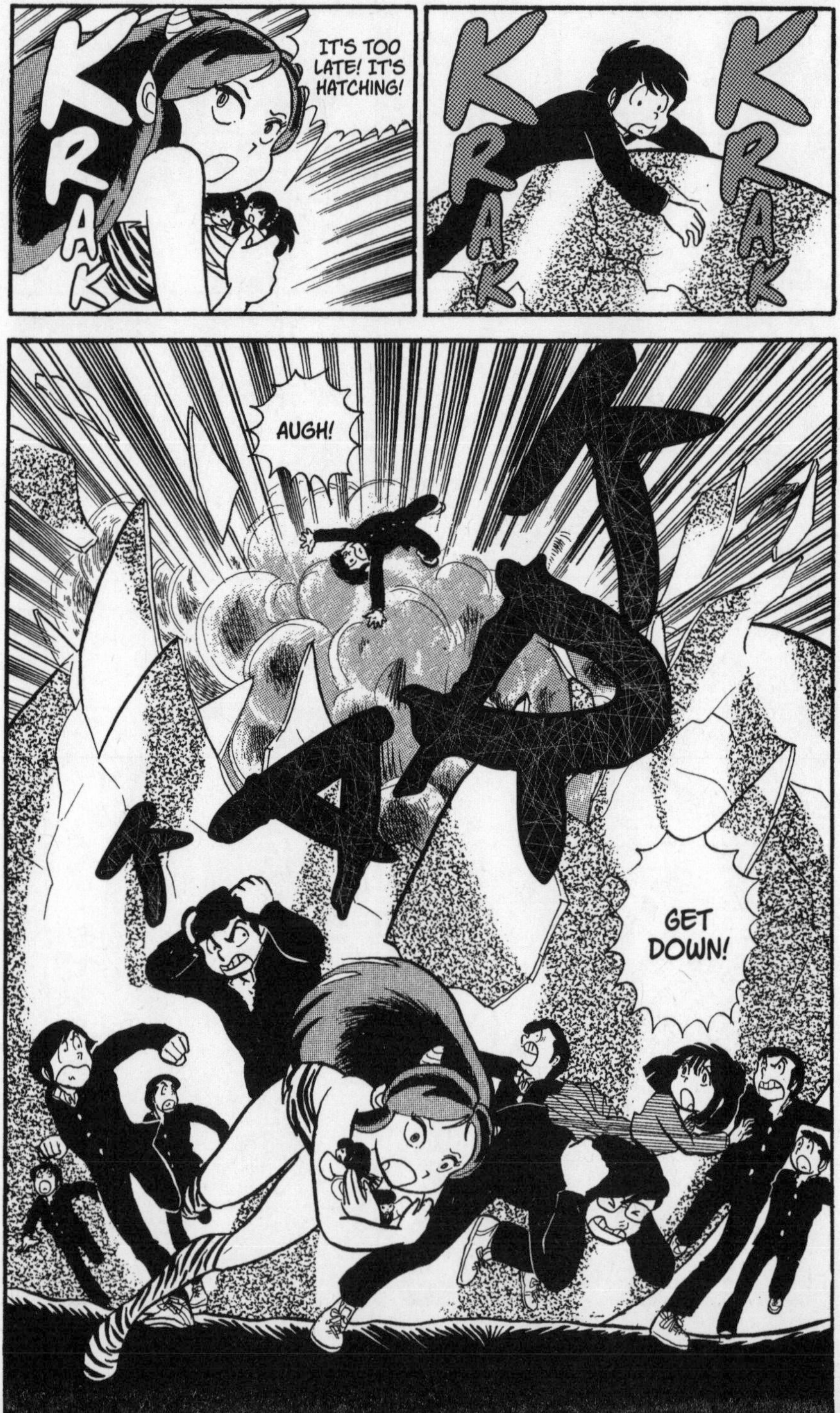
KRAK
KRAK
IT'S TOO LATE! IT'S HATCHING!
KRAK
AUGH!
GET DOWN!

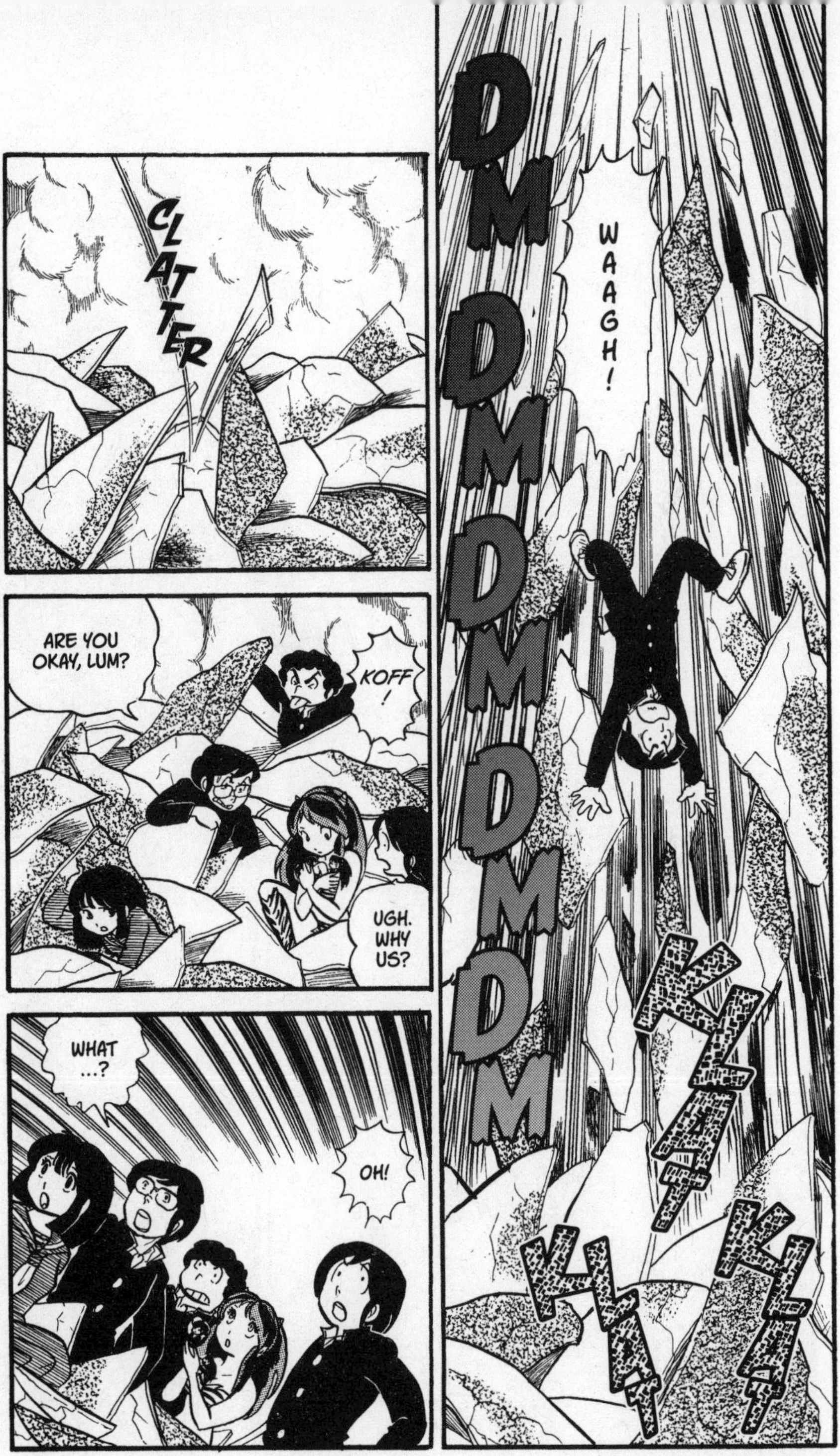
DMDMDMDMDMDM
WAAGH!
KLAK
KLAK
KLAK
CLATTER
KOFF!
ARE YOU OKAY, LUM?
UGH. WHY US?
WHAT ...?
OH!

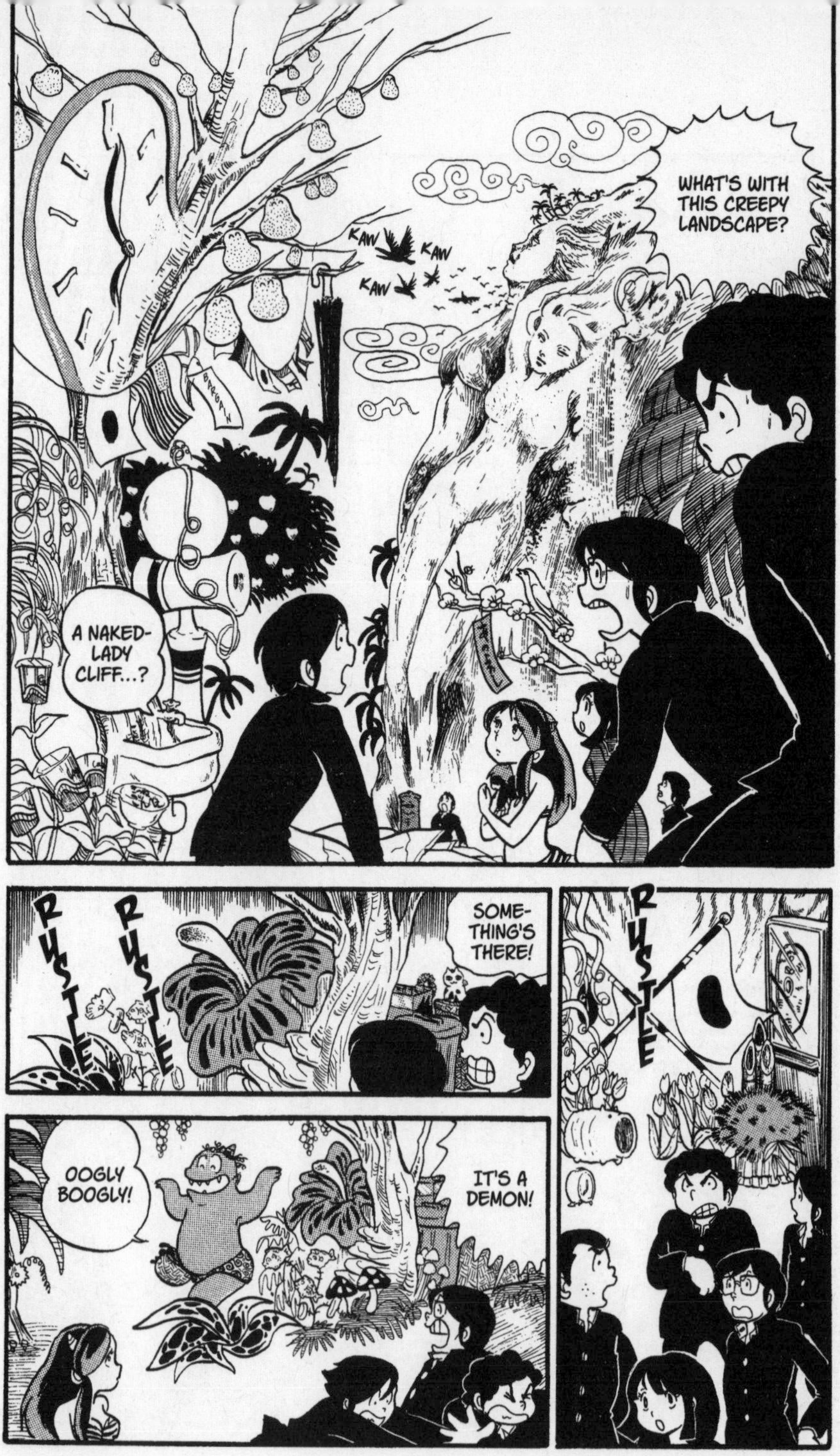

WHAT'S WITH THIS CREEPY LANDSCAPE?
KAW KAW
KAW
A NAKED-LADY CLIFF...?
RUSTLE
SOME-THING'S THERE!
RUSTLE RUSTLE
IT'S A DEMON!
OOGLY BOOGLY!

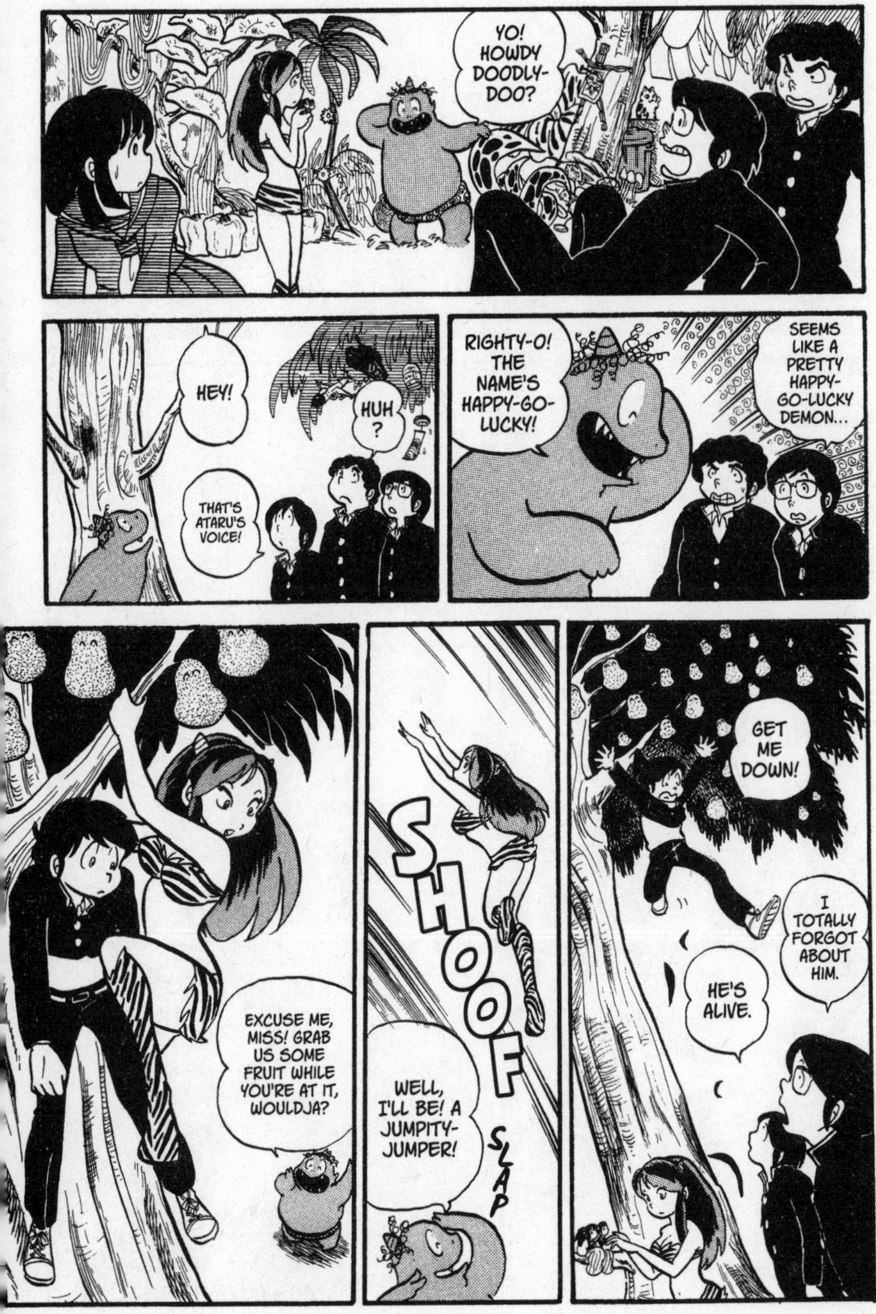
YO! HOWDY DOODLY-DOO?
SEEMS LIKE A PRETTY HAPPY-GO-LUCKY DEMON...
RIGHTY-O! THE NAME'S HAPPY-GO-LUCKY!
HEY!
HUH?
THAT'S ATARU'S VOICE!
GET ME DOWN!
I TOTALLY FORGOT ABOUT HIM.
HE'S ALIVE.
SHOOF
WELL, I'LL BE! A JUMPITY-JUMPER!
SLAP
EXCUSE ME, MISS! GRAB US SOME FRUIT WHILE YOU'RE AT IT, WOULDJA?

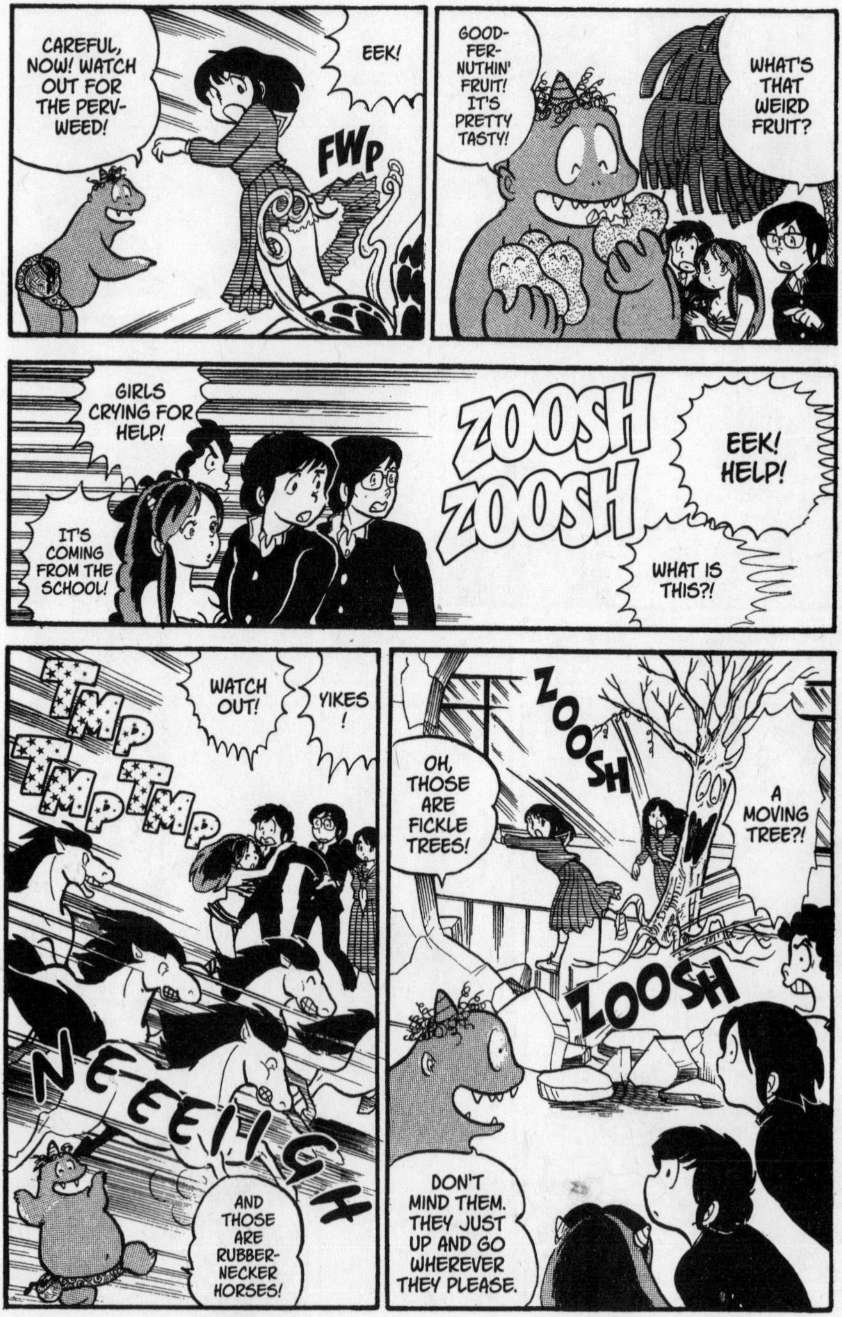
WHAT'S THAT WEIRD FRUIT?
GOOD-FER-NUTHIN' FRUIT! IT'S PRETTY TASTY!
EEK!
CAREFUL, NOW! WATCH OUT FOR THE PERV-WEED!
FWP
EEK! HELP!
WHAT IS THIS?!
ZOOSH ZOOSH
GIRLS CRYING FOR HELP!
IT'S COMING FROM THE SCHOOL!
A MOVING TREE?!
ZOOSH
OH, THOSE ARE FICKLE TREES!
ZOOSH
DON'T MIND THEM. THEY JUST UP AND GO WHEREVER THEY PLEASE.
YIKES!
WATCH OUT!
TMP TMP TMP
NEEEIIGH
AND THOSE ARE RUBBER-NECKER HORSES!

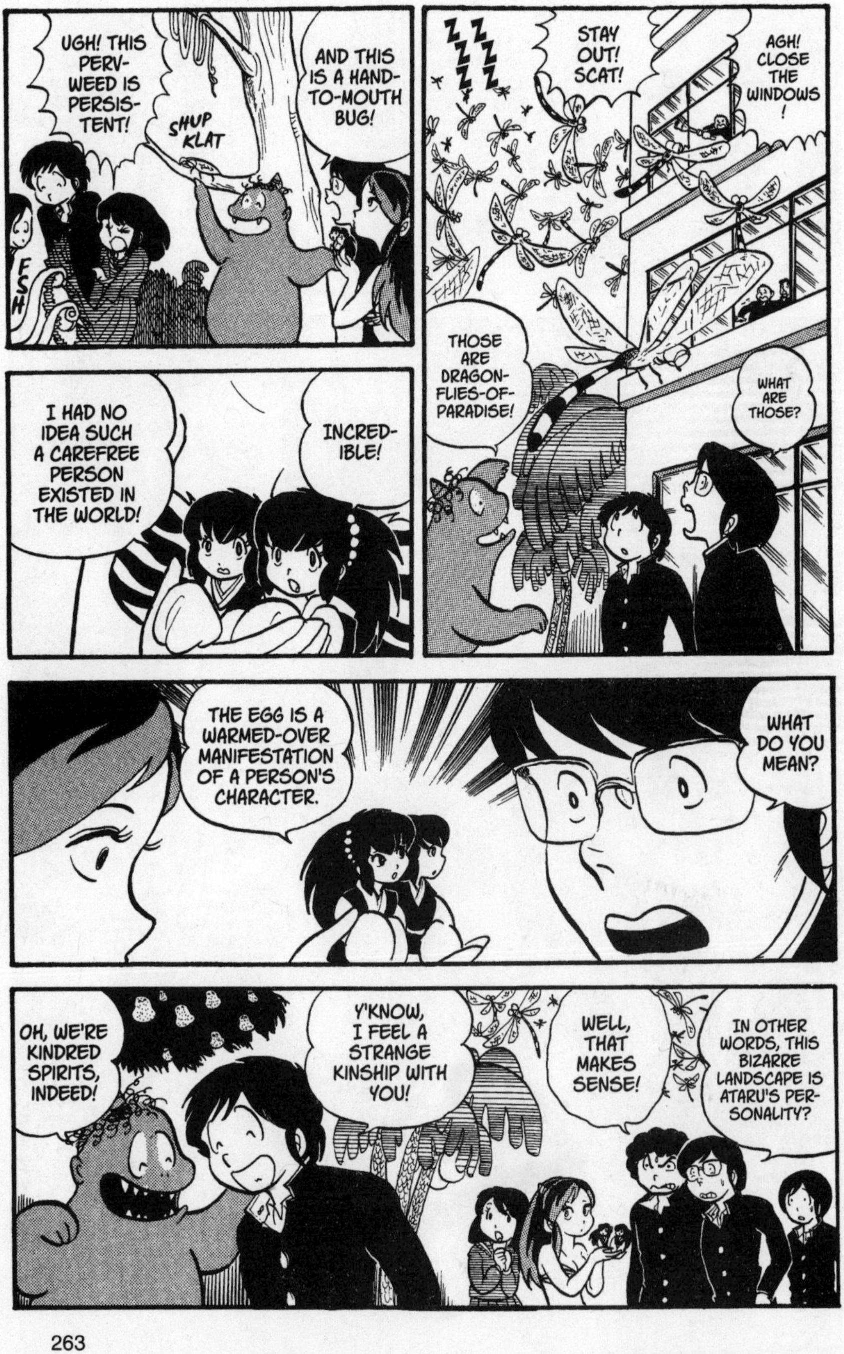
AGH! CLOSE THE WINDOWS!
STAY OUT! SCAT!
WHAT ARE THOSE?
THOSE ARE DRAGON-FLIES-OF-PARADISE!
AND THIS IS A HAND-TO-MOUTH BUG!
UGH! THIS PERV-WEED IS PERSIS-TENT!
SHUP KLAT
FSH
INCRED-IBLE!
I HAD NO IDEA SUCH A CAREFREE PERSON EXISTED IN THE WORLD!
WHAT DO YOU MEAN?
THE EGG IS A WARMED-OVER MANIFESTATION OF A PERSON'S CHARACTER.
IN OTHER WORDS, THIS BIZARRE LANDSCAPE IS ATARU'S PER-SONALITY?
WELL, THAT MAKES SENSE!
Y'KNOW, I FEEL A STRANGE KINSHIP WITH YOU!
OH, WE'RE KINDRED SPIRITS, INDEED!

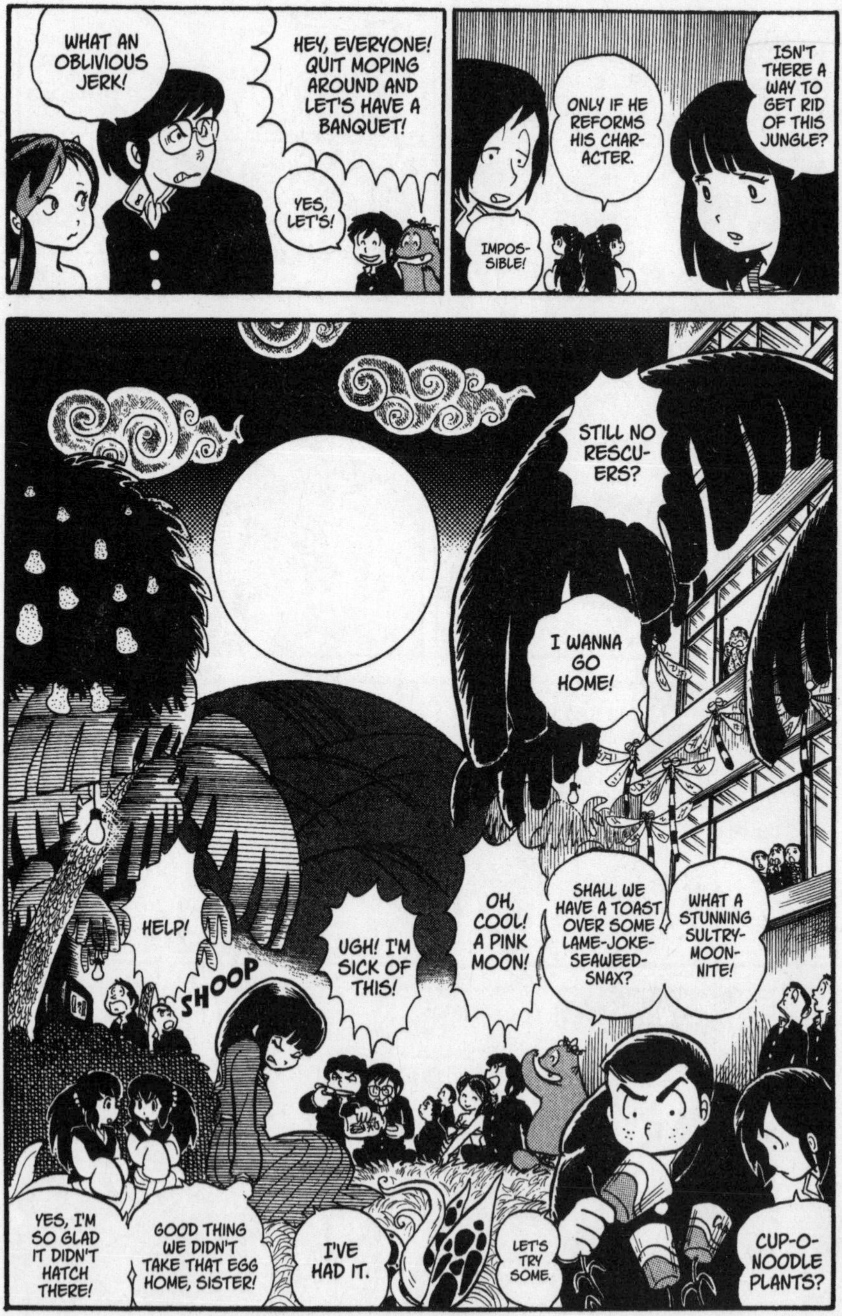
ISN'T THERE A WAY TO GET RID OF THIS JUNGLE?
ONLY IF HE REFORMS HIS CHAR-ACTER.
IMPOS-SIBLE!
HEY, EVERYONE! QUIT MOPING AROUND AND LET'S HAVE A BANQUET!
WHAT AN OBLIVIOUS JERK!
YES, LET'S!
STILL NO RESCU-ERS?
I WANNA GO HOME!
WHAT A STUNNING SULTRY-MOON-NITE!
SHALL WE HAVE A TOAST OVER SOME LAME-JOKE-SEAWEED-SNAX?
OH, COOL! A PINK MOON!
UGH! I'M SICK OF THIS!
HELP!
SHOOP
CUP-O-NOODLE PLANTS?
LET'S TRY SOME.
I'VE HAD IT.
GOOD THING WE DIDN'T TAKE THAT EGG HOME, SISTER!
YES, I'M SO GLAD IT DIDN'T HATCH THERE!

CHAPTER 12: INTENTION

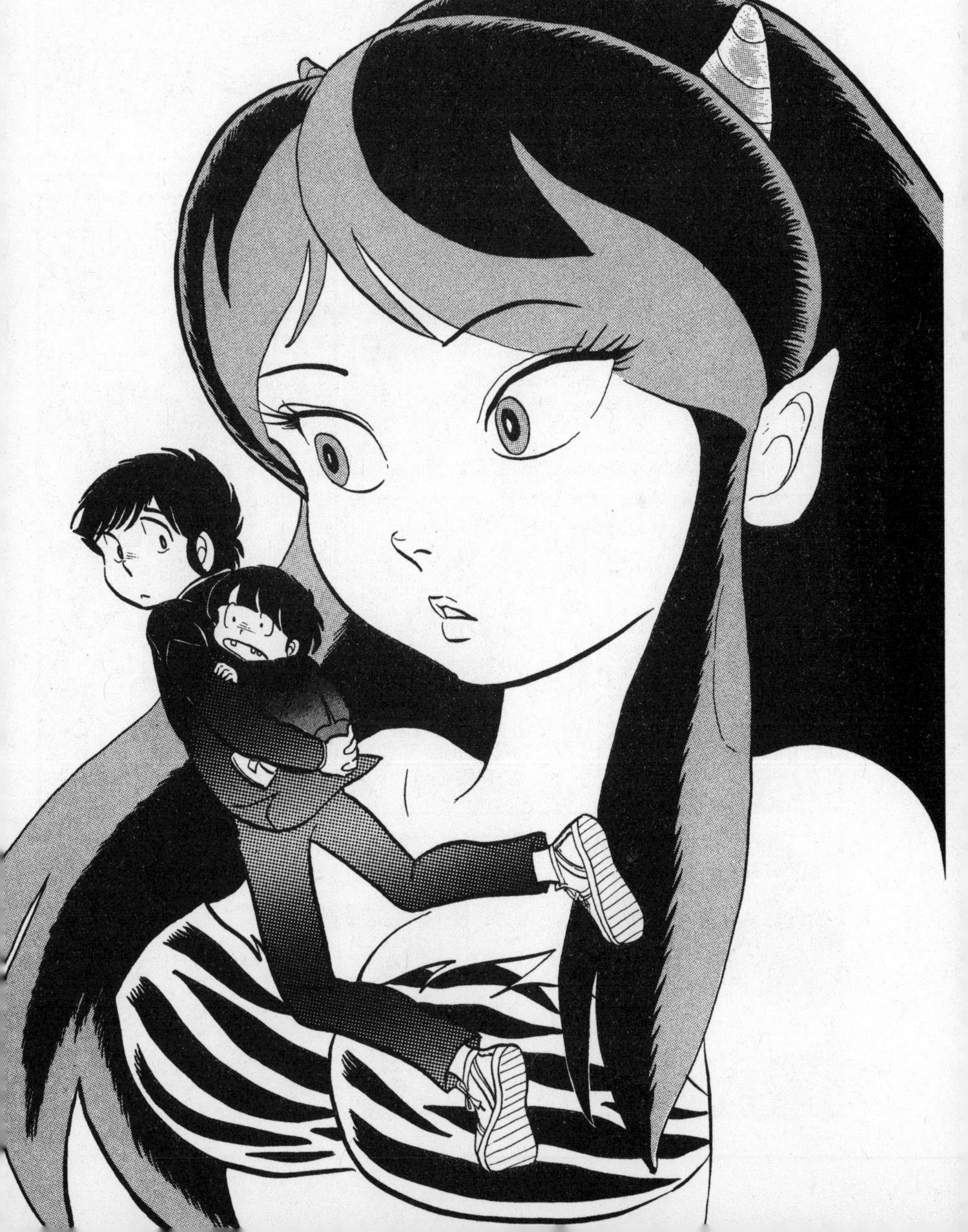

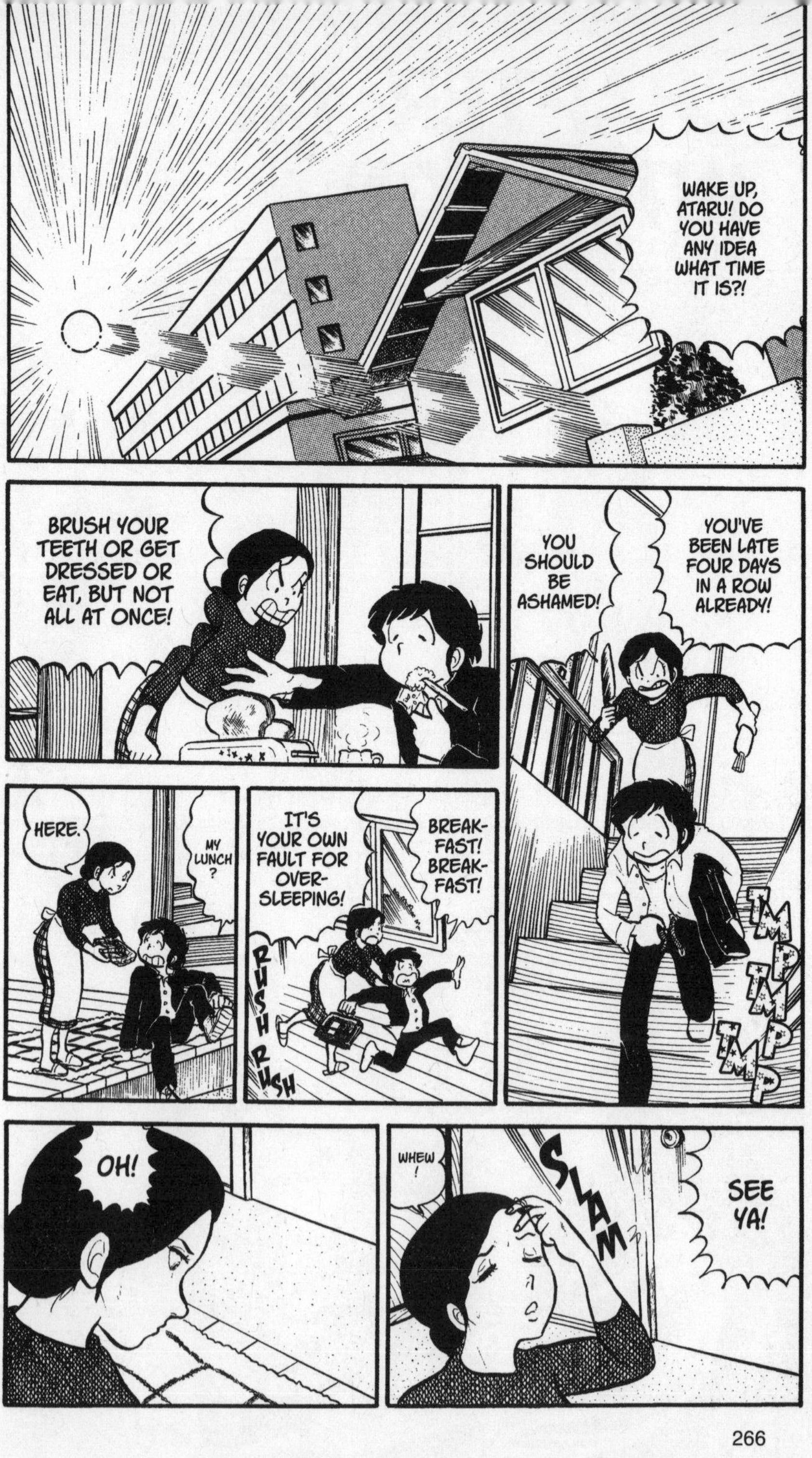
WAKE UP, ATARU! DO YOU HAVE ANY IDEA WHAT TIME IT IS?!
YOU'VE BEEN LATE FOUR DAYS IN A ROW ALREADY!
YOU SHOULD BE ASHAMED!
TMP TMP TMP
BRUSH YOUR TEETH OR GET DRESSED OR EAT, BUT NOT ALL AT ONCE!
BREAK-FAST! BREAK-FAST!
IT'S YOUR OWN FAULT FOR OVER-SLEEPING!
RUSH RUSH
MY LUNCH?
HERE.
SEE YA!
SLAM
WHEW!
OH!

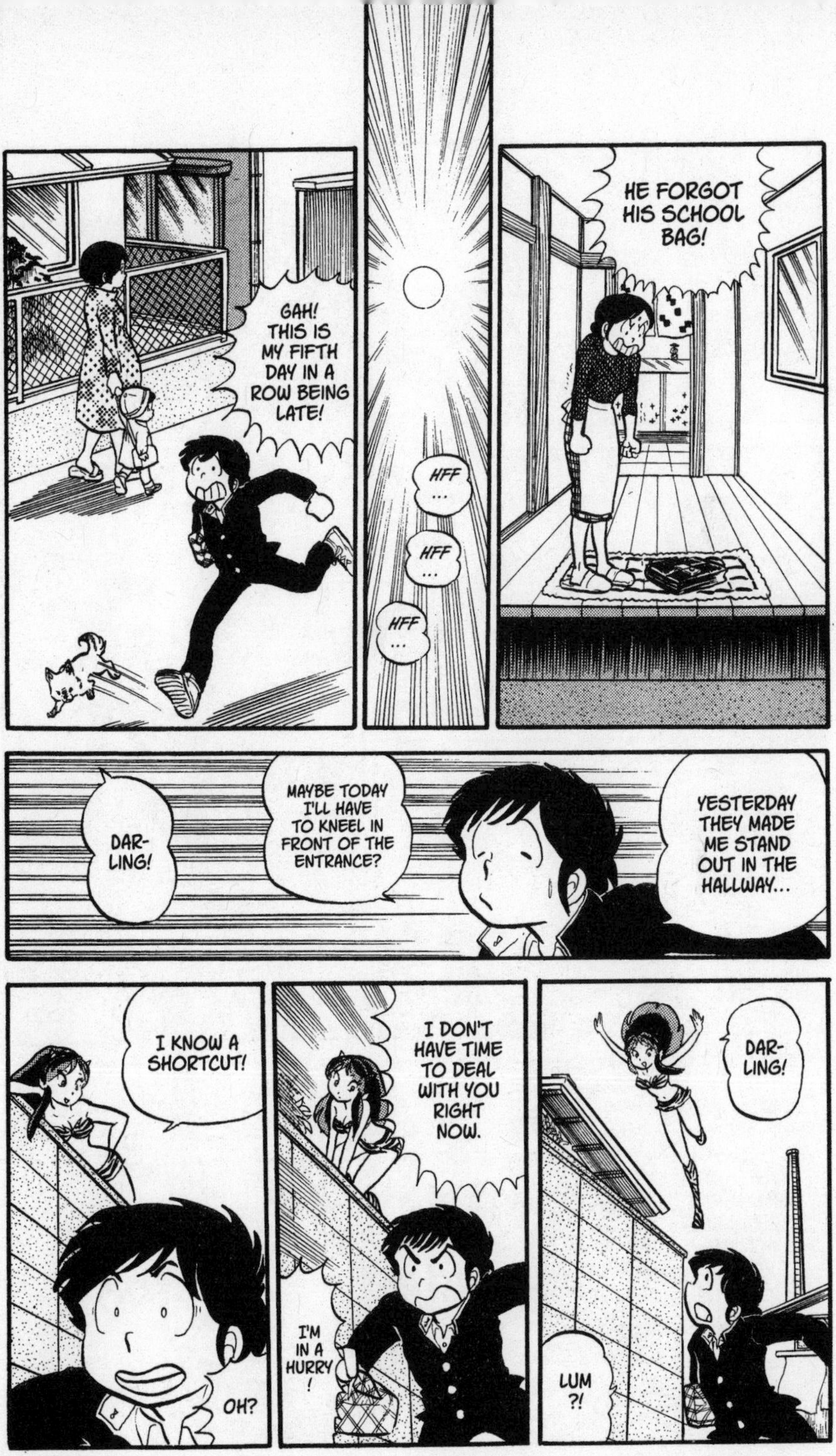
HE FORGOT HIS SCHOOL BAG!
HFF...
HFF...
HFF...
GAH! THIS IS MY FIFTH DAY IN A ROW BEING LATE!
YESTERDAY THEY MADE ME STAND OUT IN THE HALLWAY...
MAYBE TODAY I'LL HAVE TO KNEEL IN FRONT OF THE ENTRANCE?
DAR-LING!
DAR-LING!
LUM?!
I DON'T HAVE TIME TO DEAL WITH YOU RIGHT NOW.
I'M IN A HURRY!
I KNOW A SHORTCUT!
OH?

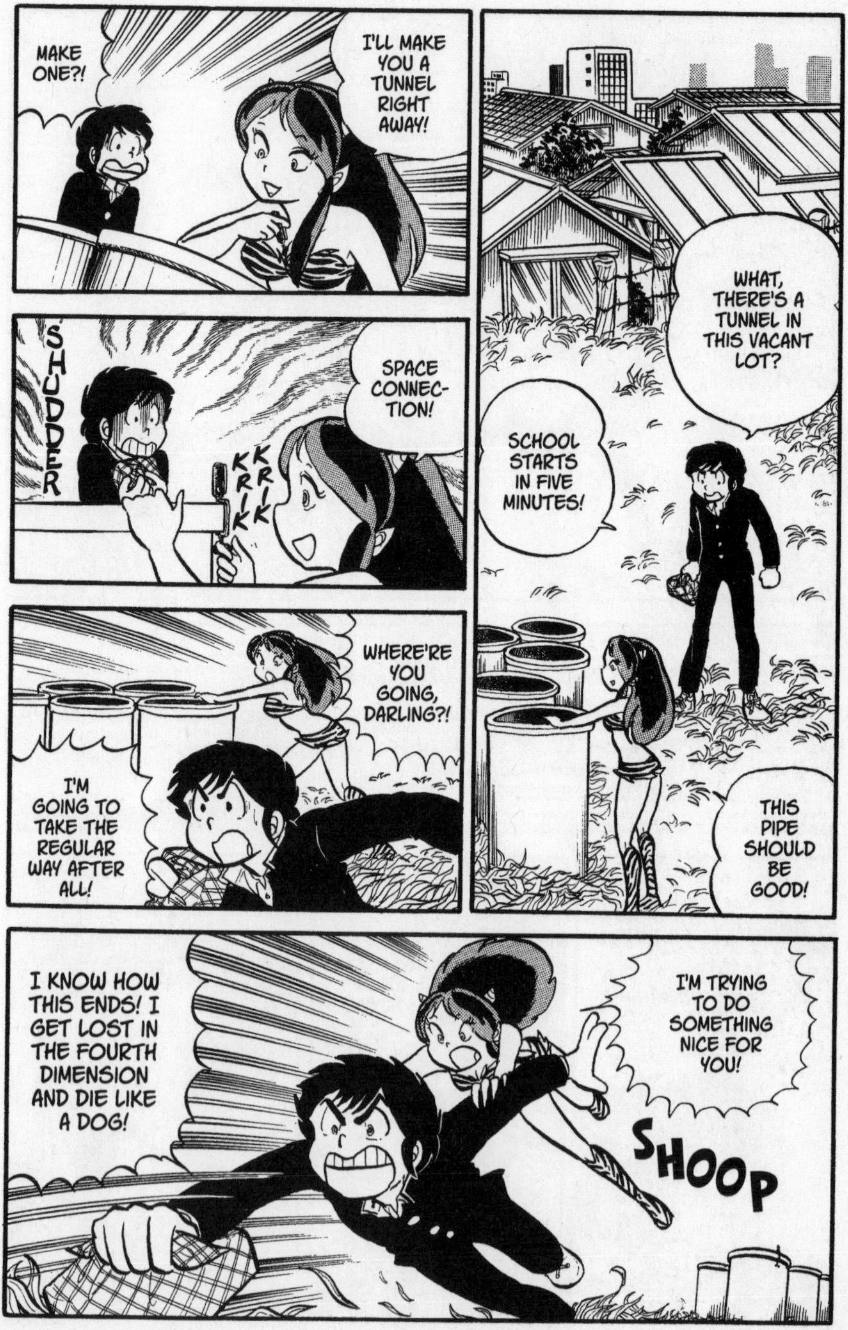
WHAT, THERE'S A TUNNEL IN THIS VACANT LOT?
SCHOOL STARTS IN FIVE MINUTES!
THIS PIPE SHOULD BE GOOD!
I'LL MAKE YOU A TUNNEL RIGHT AWAY!
MAKE ONE?!
SPACE CONNECTION!
KRIK KRIK
SHUDDER
WHERE'RE YOU GOING, DARLING?!
I'M GOING TO TAKE THE REGULAR WAY AFTER ALL!
I'M TRYING TO DO SOMETHING NICE FOR YOU!
SHOOP
I KNOW HOW THIS ENDS! I GET LOST IN THE FOURTH DIMENSION AND DIE LIKE A DOG!

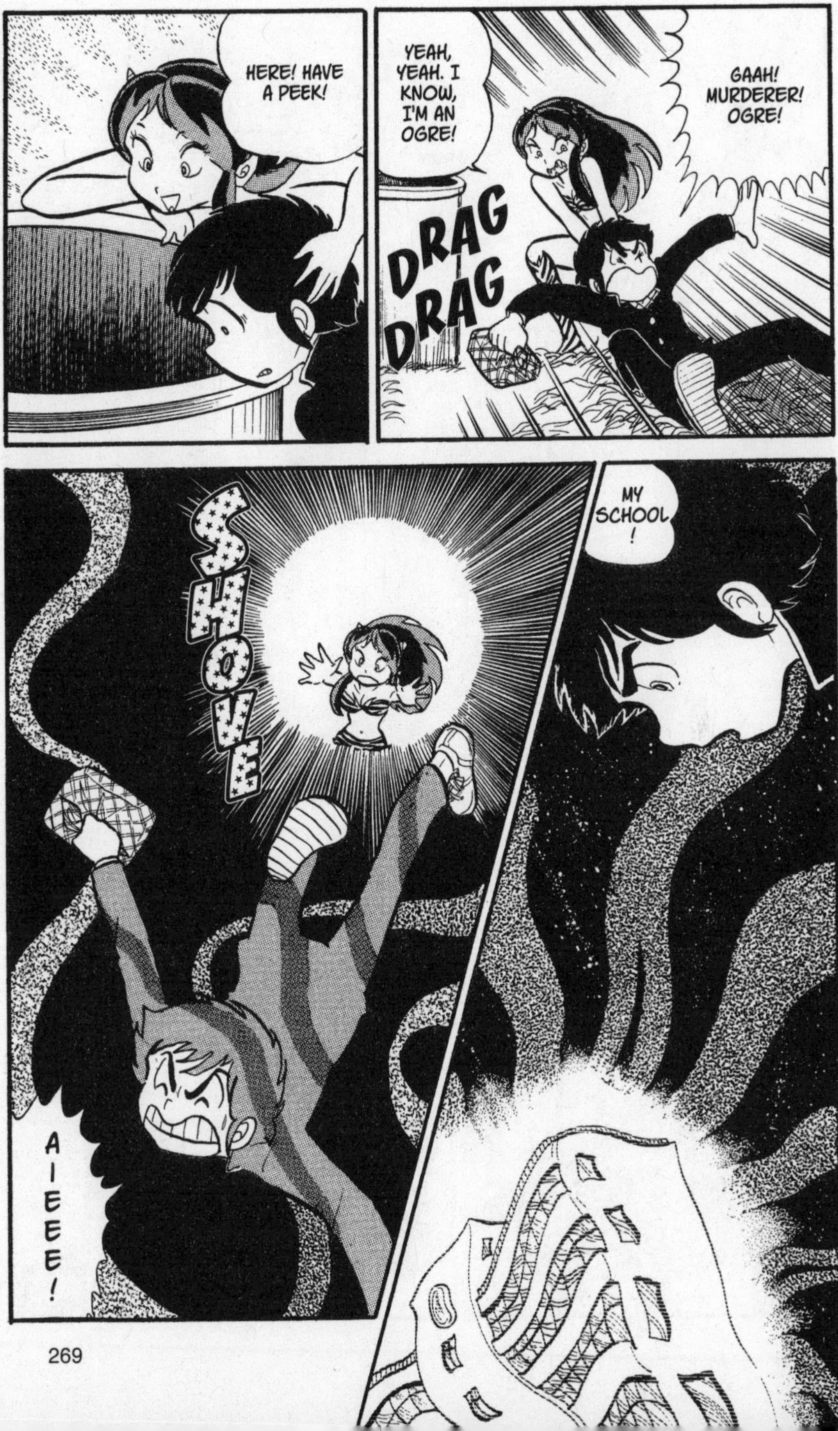
GAAH! MURDERER! OGRE!
YEAH, YEAH. I KNOW, I'M AN OGRE!
DRAG DRAG
HERE! HAVE A PEEK!
MY SCHOOL!
SHOVE
AIEEE!

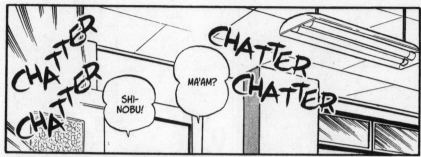

CHATTER CHATTER
MA'AM?
SHI-NOBU!
CHATTER CHATTER CHATTER
WHAT ARE YOU DOING HERE?
WELL! ATARU RAN OUT THE DOOR THIS MORNING AND FORGOT HIS BAG!
ATARU ISN'T HERE YET.
OH?!
BUT SECOND PERIOD'S STARTING!
YOU DON'T SUPPOSE HE WAS IN AN ACCIDENT, DO YOU?
OH... OH DEAR...
IT'S NOT LIKE HIM TO CUT SCHOOL BY HIMSELF.
WHEN HE GETS INTO TROUBLE HE USUALLY ROPES THOSE FOOLS IN, RIGHT?
TRUE. HE DOESN'T HAVE THE NERVE TO CUT SCHOOL ALONE!

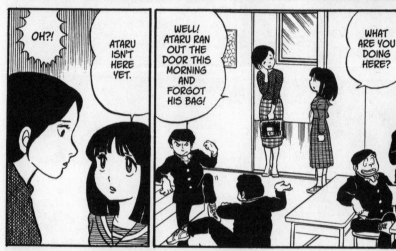

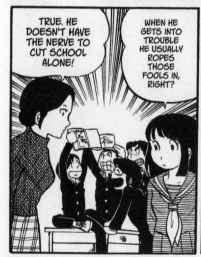

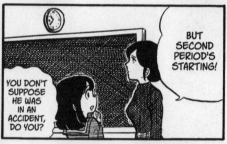

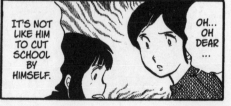

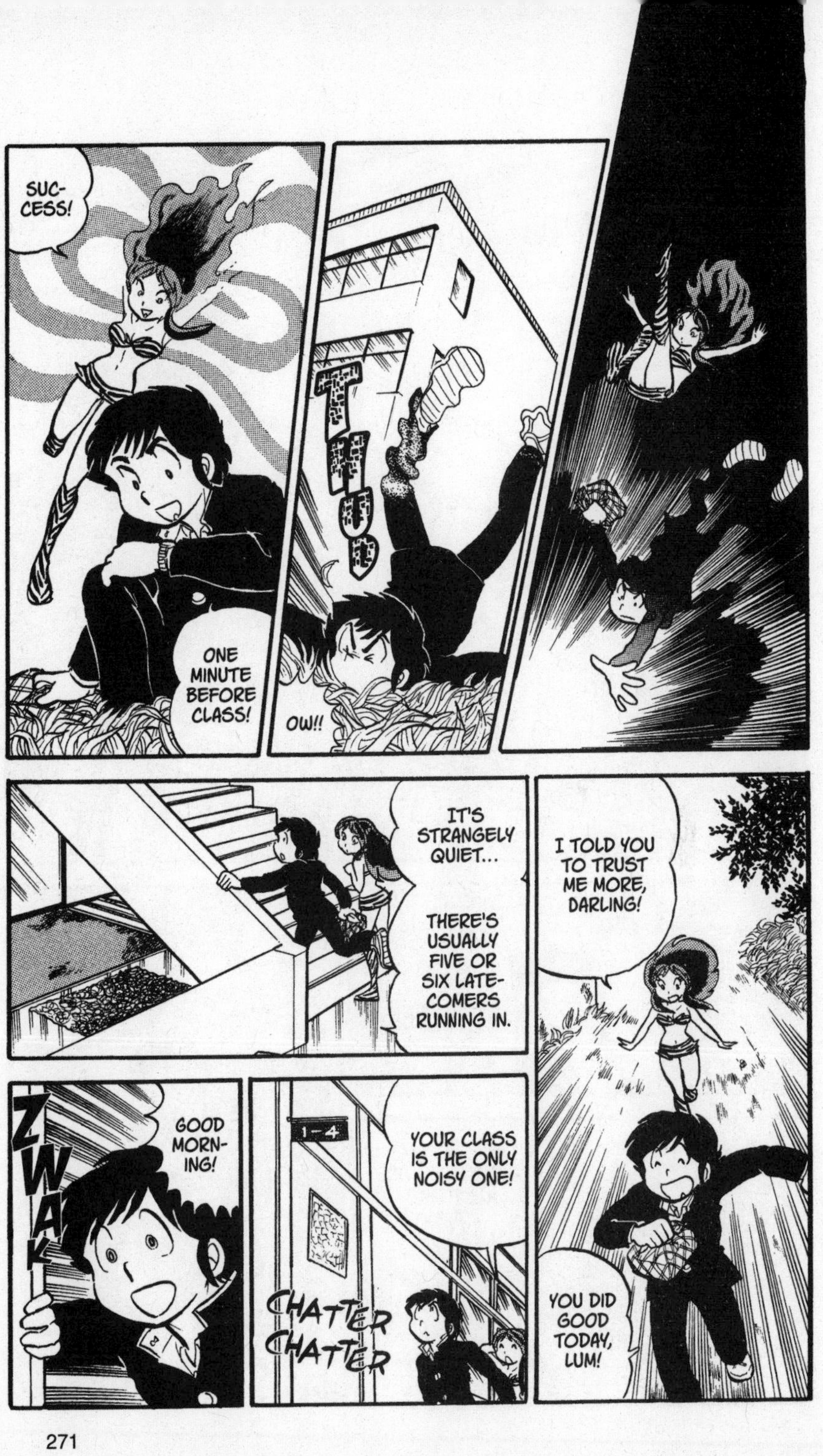
OW!!
SUC-CESS!
ONE MINUTE BEFORE CLASS!
I TOLD YOU TO TRUST ME MORE, DARLING!
YOU DID GOOD TODAY, LUM!
IT'S STRANGELY QUIET...
THERE'S USUALLY FIVE OR SIX LATE-COMERS RUNNING IN.
YOUR CLASS IS THE ONLY NOISY ONE!
1-4
CHATTER CHATTER
ZWAK
GOOD MORN-ING!

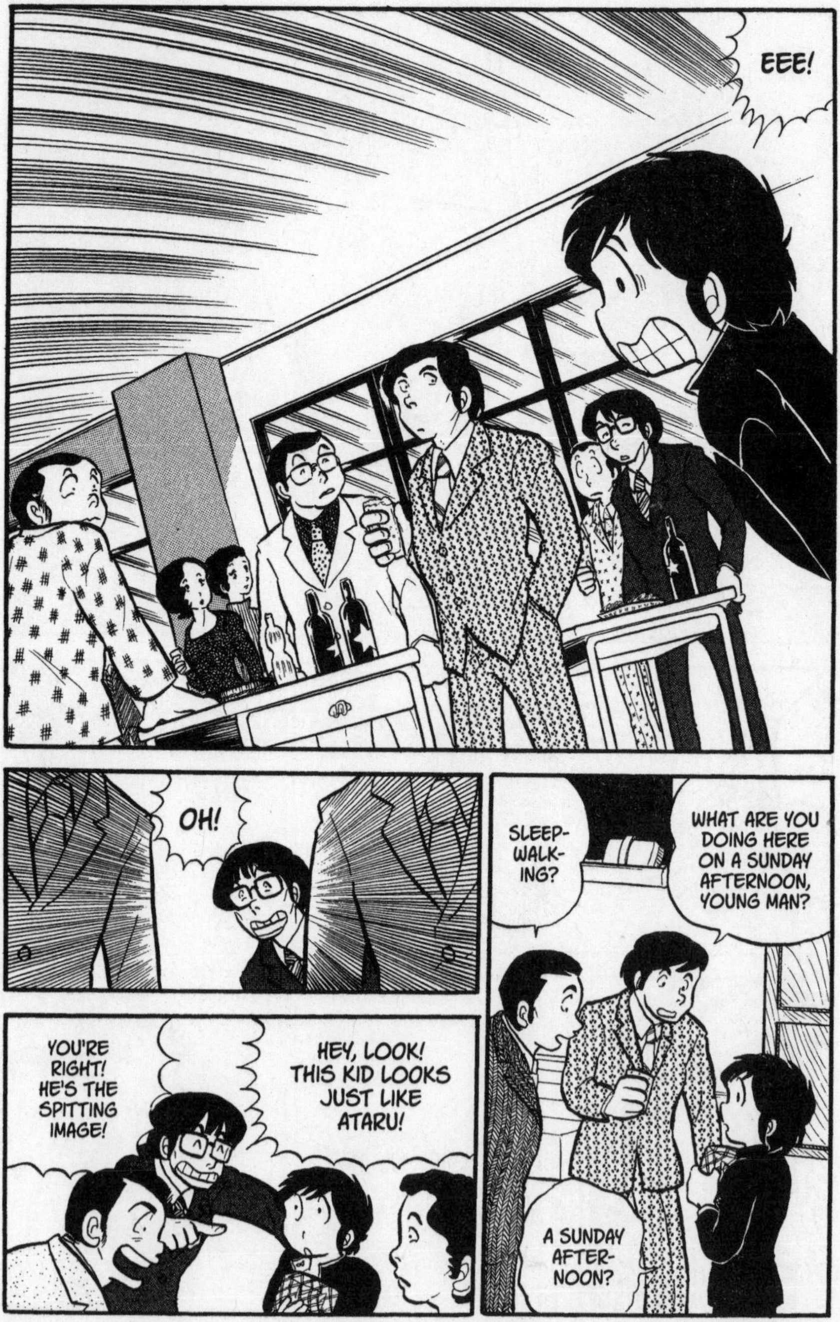
EEE!
WHAT ARE YOU DOING HERE ON A SUNDAY AFTERNOON, YOUNG MAN?
SLEEP-WALKING?
A SUNDAY AFTER-NOON?
OH!
HEY, LOOK! THIS KID LOOKS JUST LIKE ATARU!
YOU'RE RIGHT! HE'S THE SPITTING IMAGE!

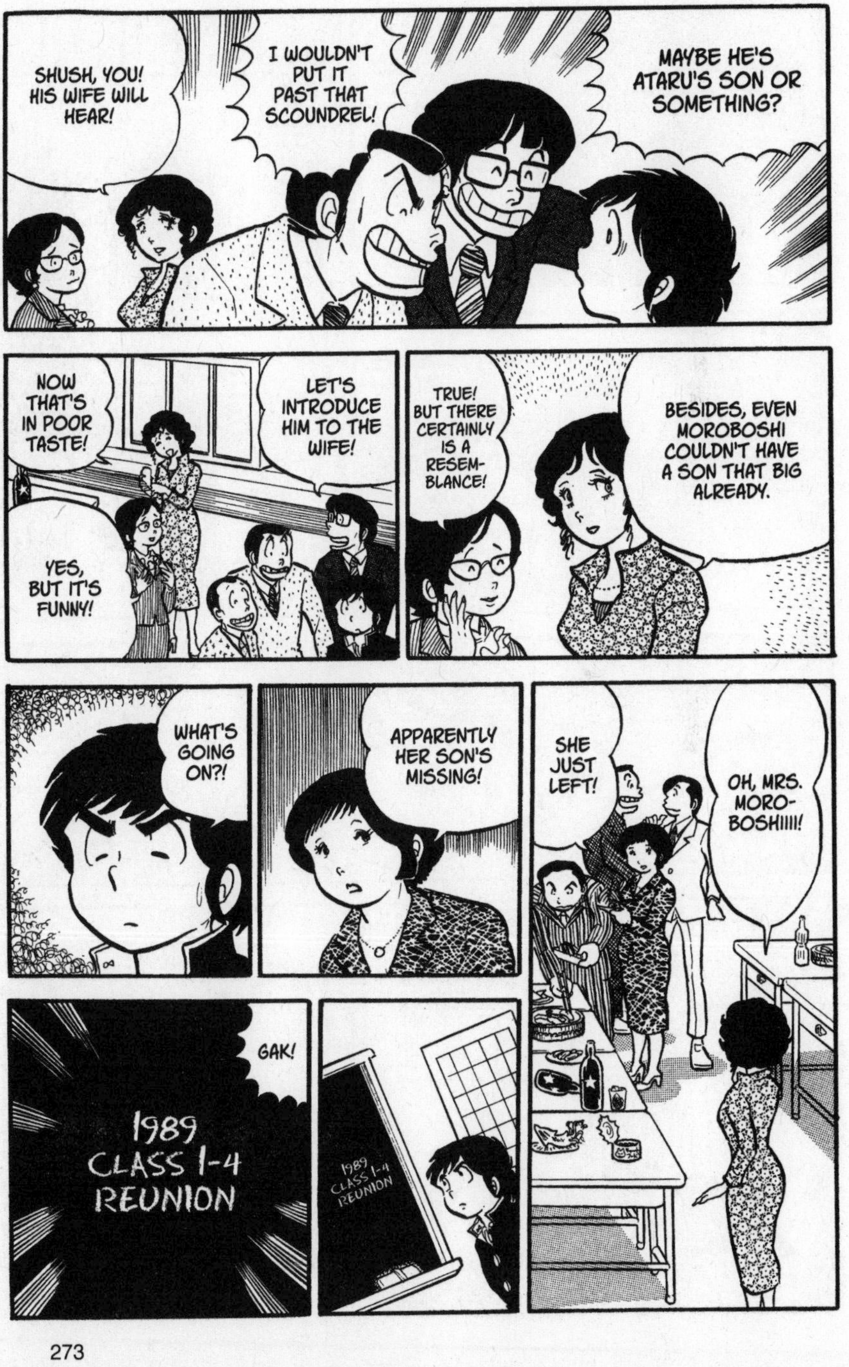
MAYBE HE'S ATARU'S SON OR SOMETHING?
I WOULDN'T PUT IT PAST THAT SCOUNDREL!
SHUSH, YOU! HIS WIFE WILL HEAR!
BESIDES, EVEN MOROBOSHI COULDN'T HAVE A SON THAT BIG ALREADY.
TRUE! BUT THERE CERTAINLY IS A RESEMBLANCE!
LET'S INTRODUCE HIM TO THE WIFE!
NOW THAT'S IN POOR TASTE!
YES, BUT IT'S FUNNY!
OH, MRS. MOROBOSHIIII!
SHE JUST LEFT!
APPARENTLY HER SON'S MISSING!
WHAT'S GOING ON?!
1989 CLASS 1-4 REUNION
GAK!
1989 CLASS 1-4 REUNION

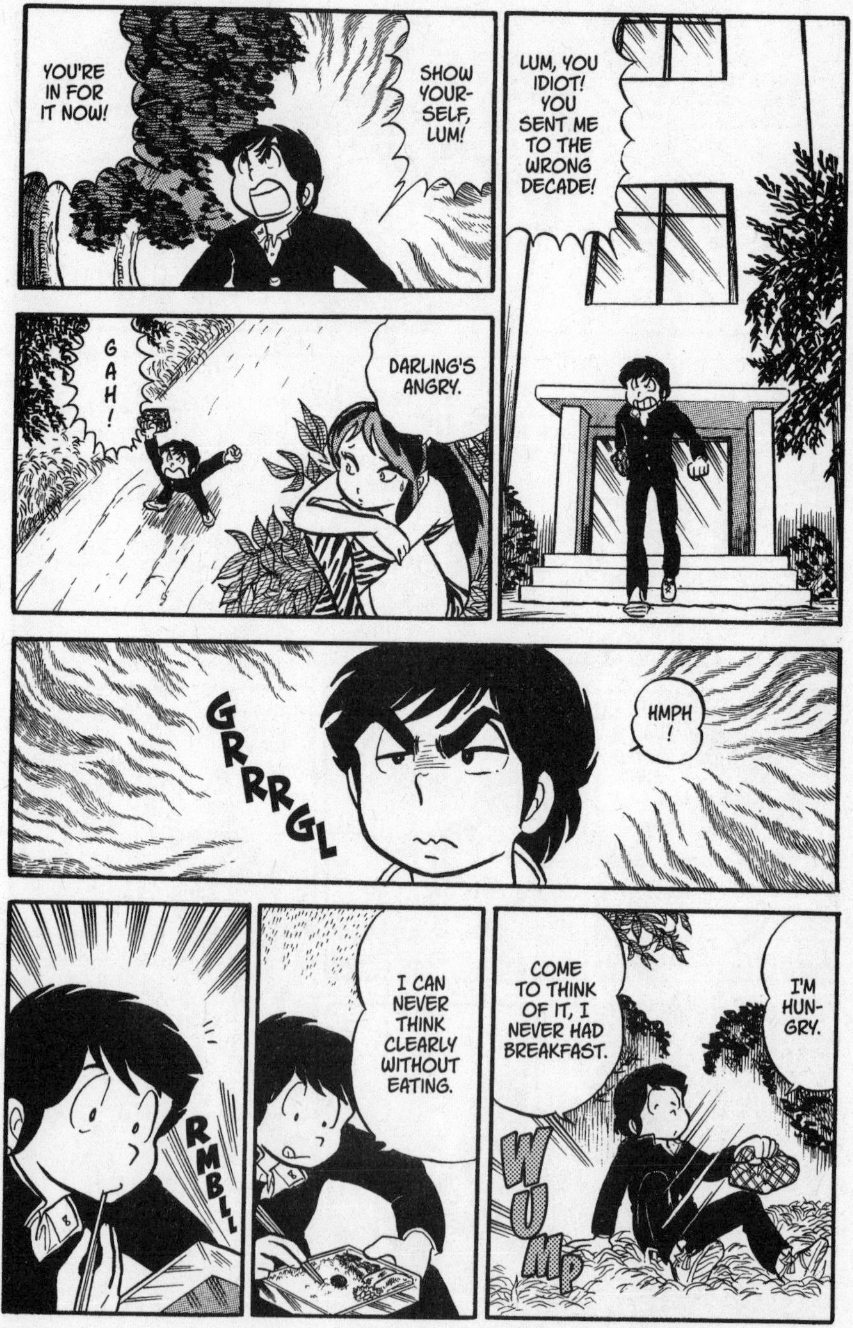
LUM, YOU IDIOT! YOU SENT ME TO THE WRONG DECADE!
SHOW YOUR-SELF, LUM!
YOU'RE IN FOR IT NOW!
DARLING'S ANGRY.
GAH!
HMPH!
GRRRGL
I'M HUN-GRY.
COME TO THINK OF IT, I NEVER HAD BREAKFAST.
WUMP
I CAN NEVER THINK CLEARLY WITHOUT EATING.
RMBLL

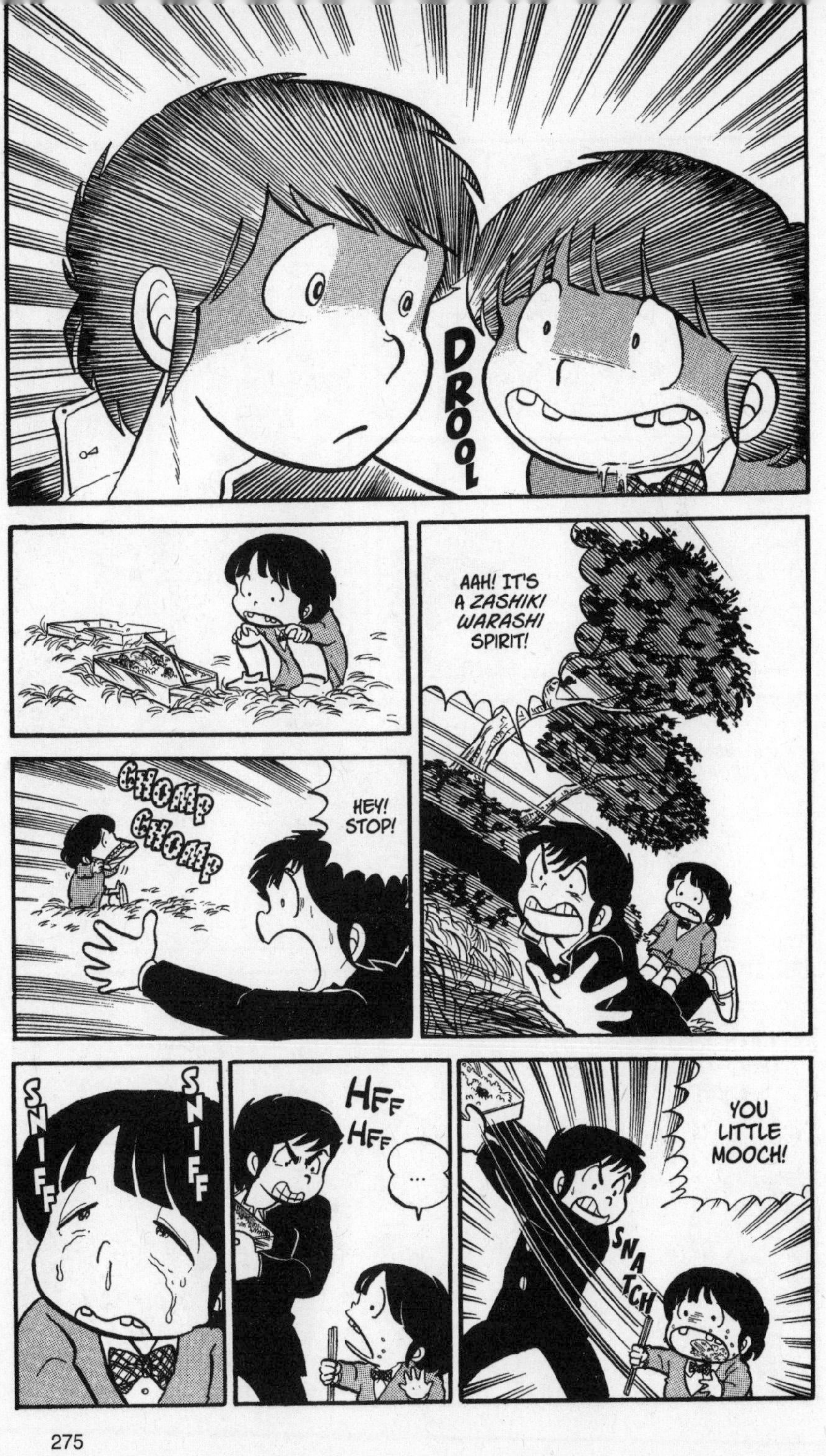
DROOL
AAH! IT'S A ZASHIKI WARASHI SPIRIT!
HEY! STOP!
CHOMP CHOMP
YOU LITTLE MOOCH!
SNATCH
HFF HFF
...
SNIFF
SNIFF

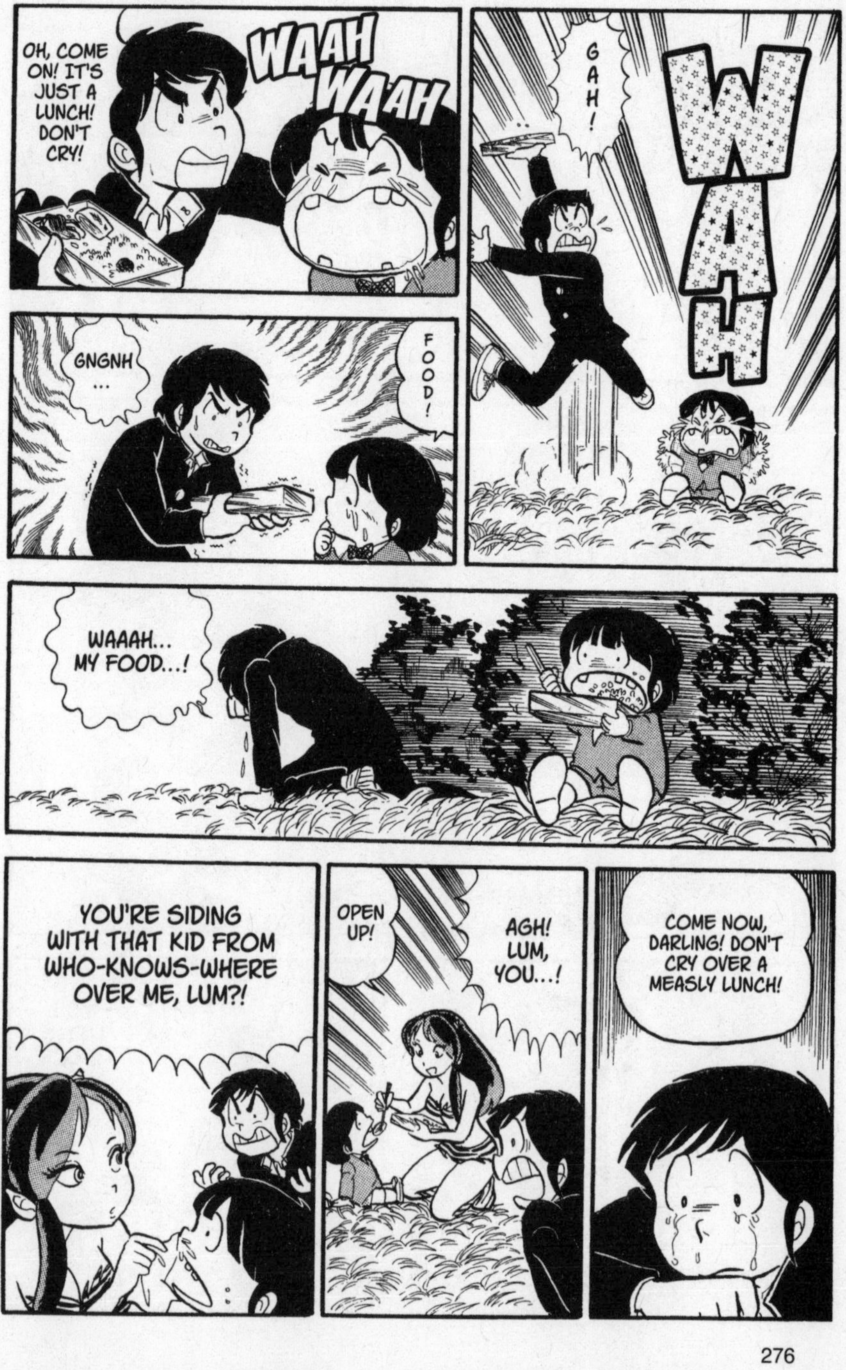
G A H !
WAH
WAAH WAAH
OH, COME ON! IT'S JUST A LUNCH! DON'T CRY!
FOOD!
GNGNH ...
WAAAH... MY FOOD...!
COME NOW, DARLING! DON'T CRY OVER A MEASLY LUNCH!
OPEN UP!
AGH! LUM, YOU...!
YOU'RE SIDING WITH THAT KID FROM WHO-KNOWS-WHERE OVER ME, LUM?!

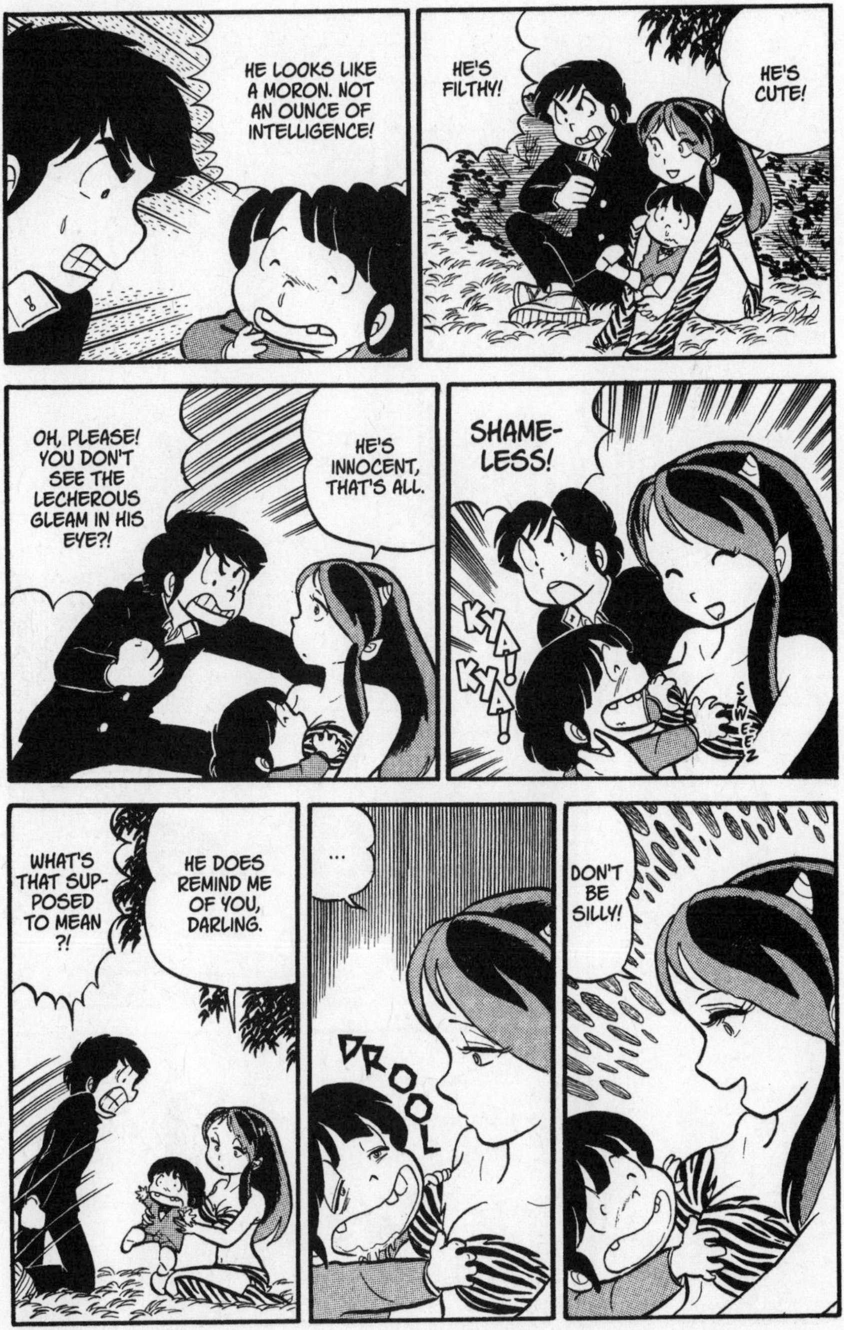
HE'S CUTE!
HE'S FILTHY!
HE LOOKS LIKE A MORON. NOT AN OUNCE OF INTELLIGENCE!
SHAME-LESS!
KYA! KYA!
SKWEEZ
HE'S INNOCENT, THAT'S ALL.
OH, PLEASE! YOU DON'T SEE THE LECHEROUS GLEAM IN HIS EYE?!
DON'T BE SILLY!
...
DROOL
HE DOES REMIND ME OF YOU, DARLING.
WHAT'S THAT SUP-POSED TO MEAN ?!

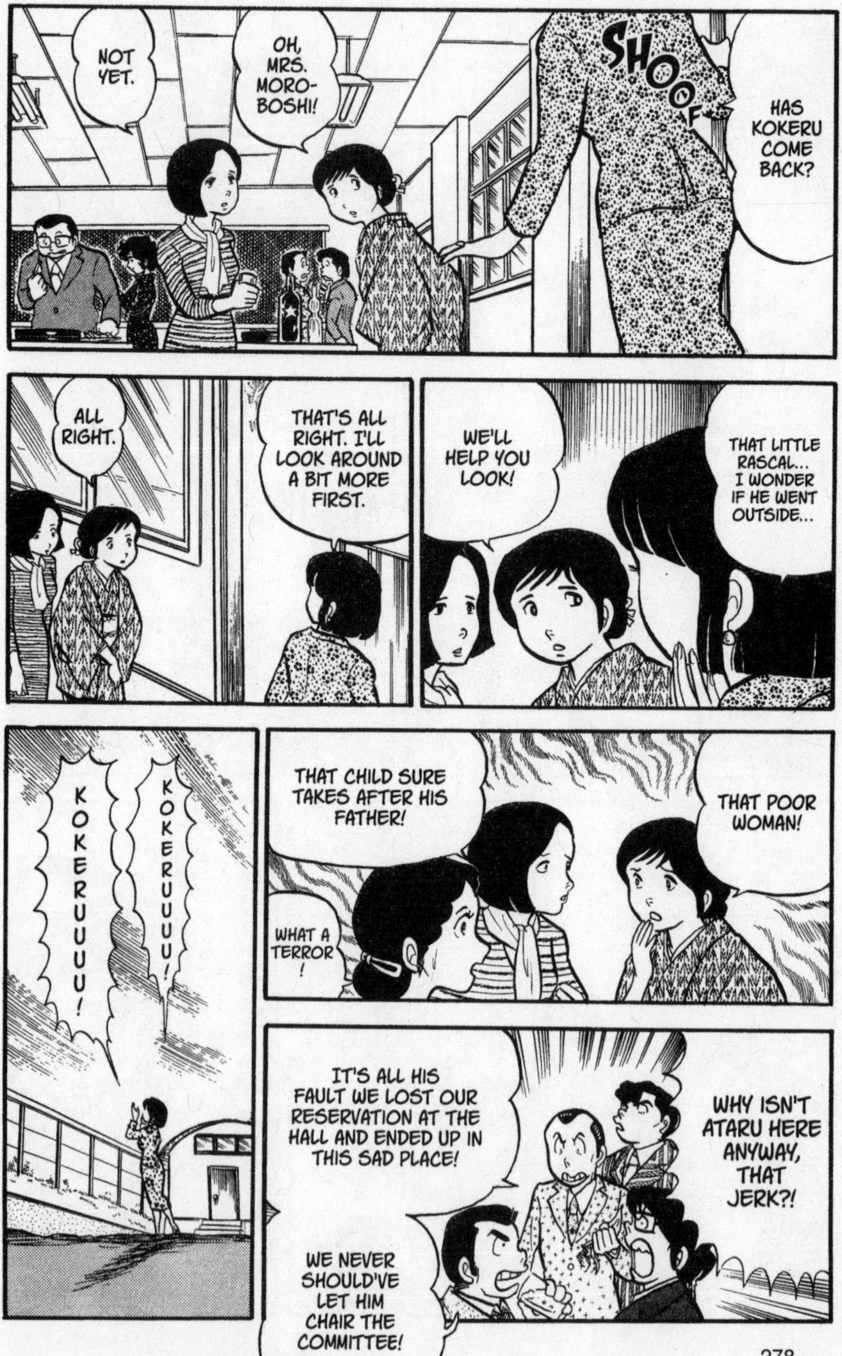
HAS KOKERU COME BACK?
SHOOF
OH, MRS. MOROBOSHI!
NOT YET.
THAT LITTLE RASCAL... I WONDER IF HE WENT OUTSIDE...
WE'LL HELP YOU LOOK!
THAT'S ALL RIGHT. I'LL LOOK AROUND A BIT MORE FIRST.
ALL RIGHT.
THAT POOR WOMAN!
THAT CHILD SURE TAKES AFTER HIS FATHER!
WHAT A TERROR!
WHY ISN'T ATARU HERE ANYWAY, THAT JERK?!
IT'S ALL HIS FAULT WE LOST OUR RESERVATION AT THE HALL AND ENDED UP IN THIS SAD PLACE!
WE NEVER SHOULD'VE LET HIM CHAIR THE COMMITTEE!
KOKERUUUU!
KOKERUUUU!

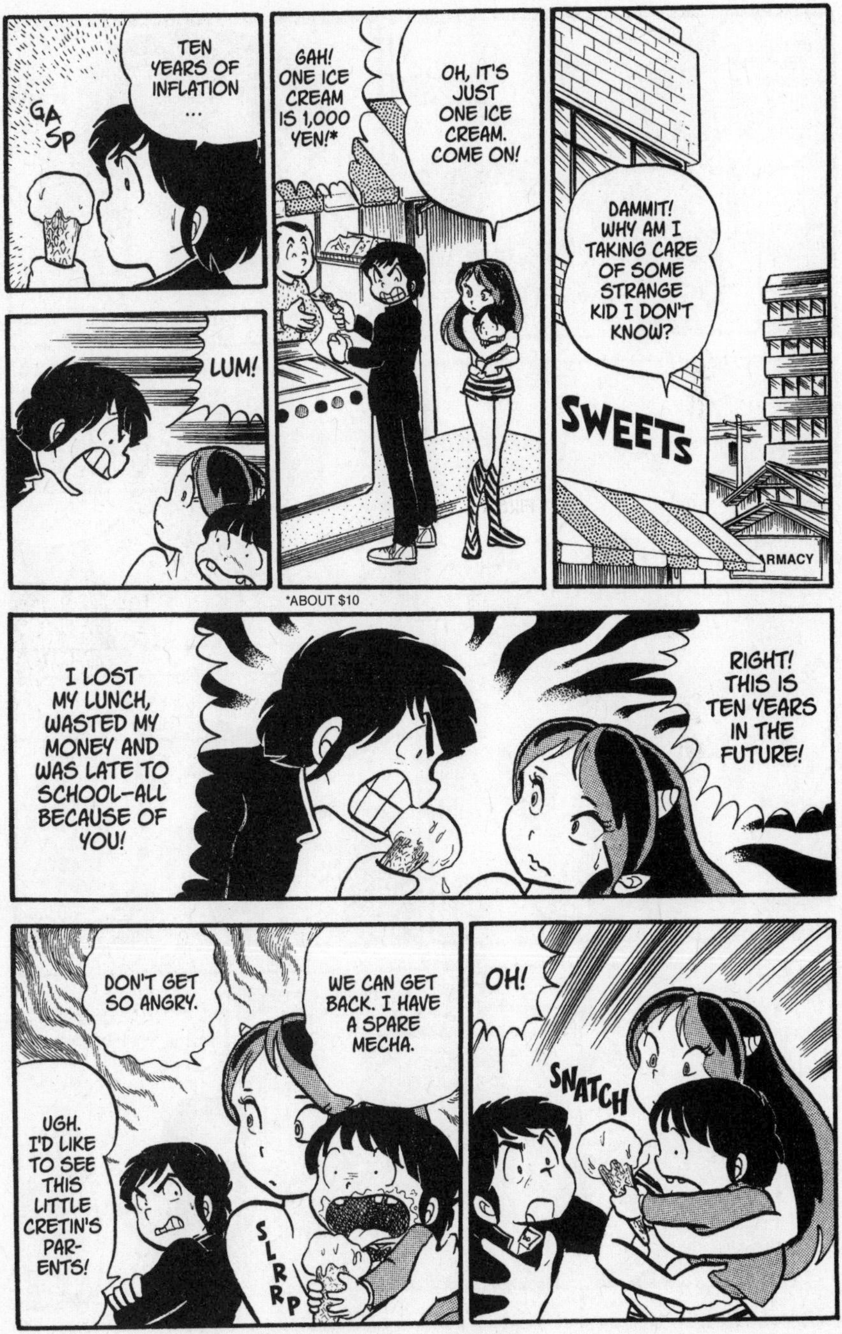
SWEETS
DAMMIT! WHY AM I TAKING CARE OF SOME STRANGE KID I DON'T KNOW?
ARMACY
OH, IT'S JUST ONE ICE CREAM. COME ON!
GAH! ONE ICE CREAM IS 1,000 YEN!*
TEN YEARS OF INFLATION ...
GASP
LUM!
*ABOUT $10
RIGHT! THIS IS TEN YEARS IN THE FUTURE!
I LOST MY LUNCH, WASTED MY MONEY AND WAS LATE TO SCHOOL—ALL BECAUSE OF YOU!
OH!
SNATCH
WE CAN GET BACK. I HAVE A SPARE MECHA.
DON'T GET SO ANGRY.
UGH. I'D LIKE TO SEE THIS LITTLE CRETIN'S PAR-ENTS!
SLRRP

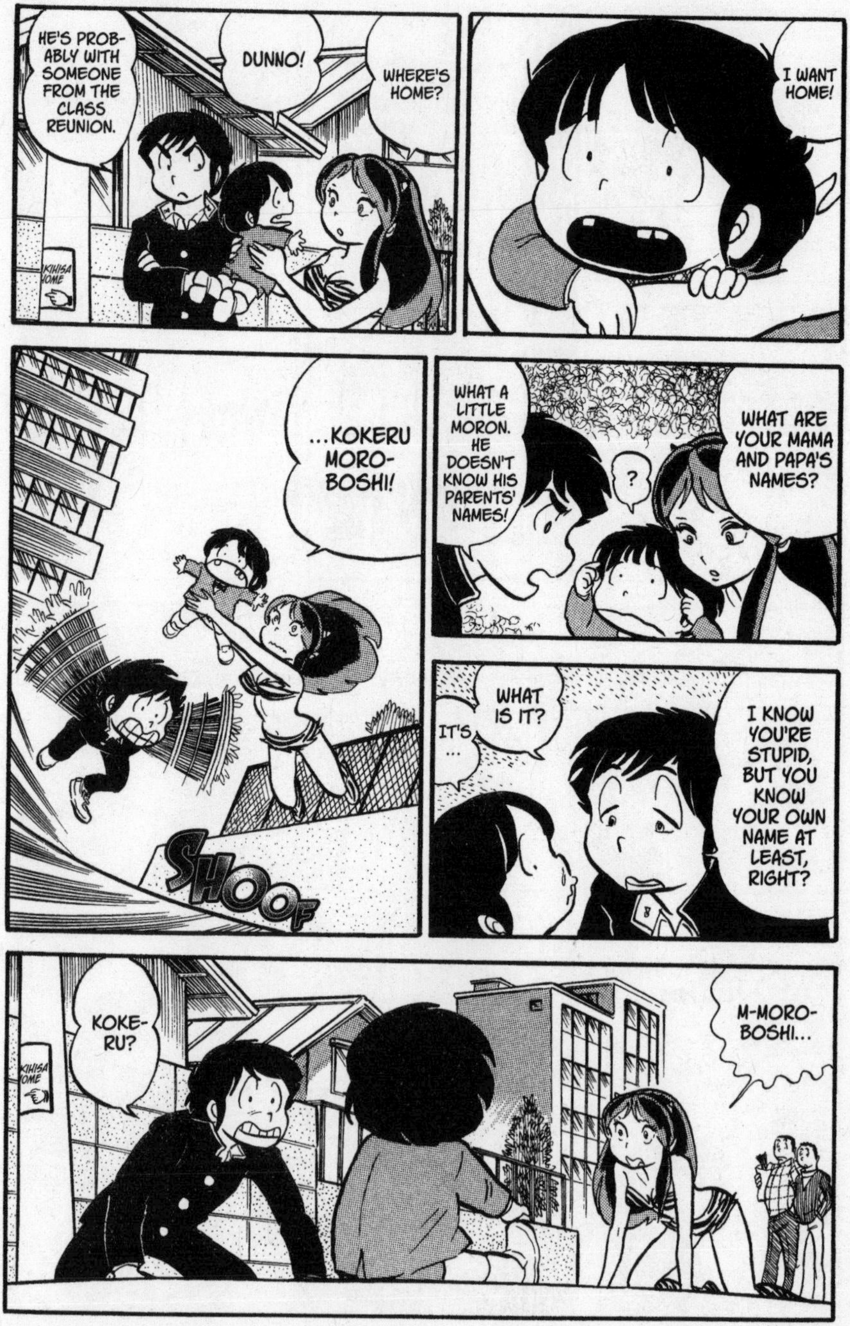

I WANT HOME!
WHERE'S HOME?
DUNNO!
HE'S PROB-ABLY WITH SOMEONE FROM THE CLASS REUNION.
WHAT ARE YOUR MAMA AND PAPA'S NAMES?
?
WHAT A LITTLE MORON. HE DOESN'T KNOW HIS PARENTS' NAMES!
I KNOW YOU'RE STUPID, BUT YOU KNOW YOUR OWN NAME AT LEAST, RIGHT?
WHAT IS IT?
IT'S ...
...KOKERU MORO-BOSHI!
SHOOF
M-MORO-BOSHI...
KOKE-RU?

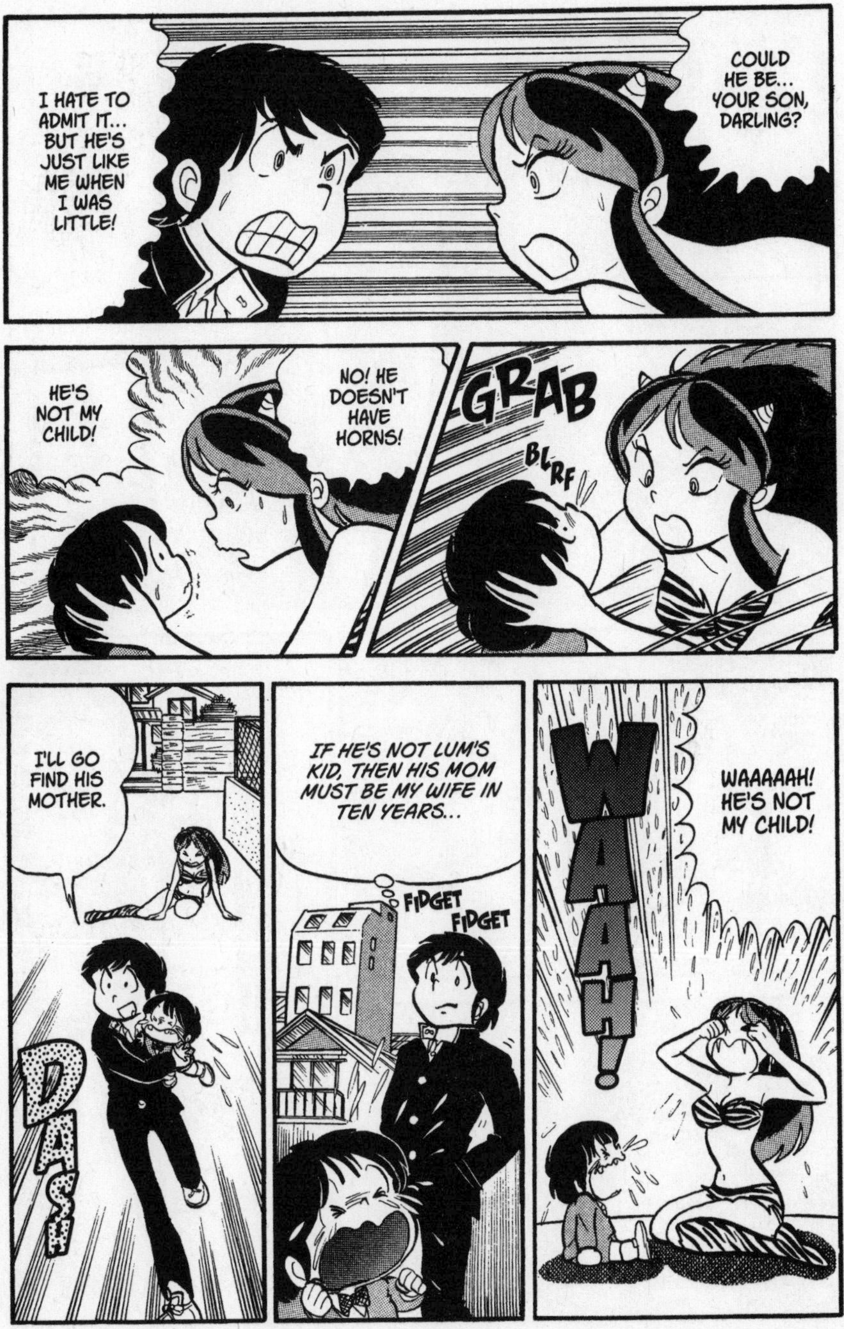
COULD HE BE... YOUR SON, DARLING?
I HATE TO ADMIT IT... BUT HE'S JUST LIKE ME WHEN I WAS LITTLE!
GRAB
BLRF
NO! HE DOESN'T HAVE HORNS!
HE'S NOT MY CHILD!
WAAAH!
WAAAAAH! HE'S NOT MY CHILD!
IF HE'S NOT LUM'S KID, THEN HIS MOM MUST BE MY WIFE IN TEN YEARS...
FIDGET FIDGET
I'LL GO FIND HIS MOTHER.
DASH!

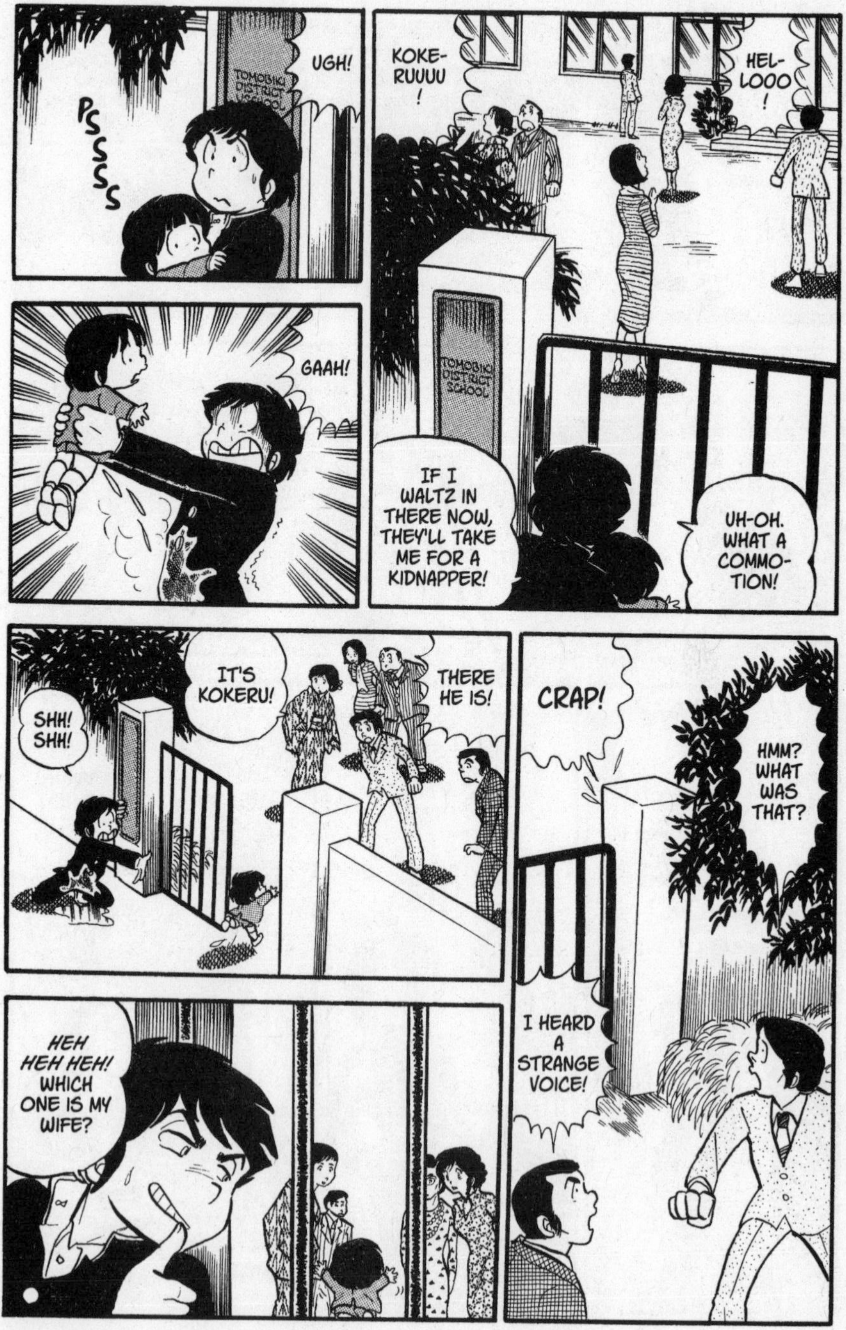
HEL-LOOO!
KOKE-RUUUU!
TOMOBIKI DISTRICT SCHOOL
UH-OH. WHAT A COMMOTION!
IF I WALTZ IN THERE NOW, THEY'LL TAKE ME FOR A KIDNAPPER!
UGH!
TOMOBIKI DISTRICT SCHOOL
PSSSS
GAAH!
HMM? WHAT WAS THAT?
CRAP!
I HEARD A STRANGE VOICE!
THERE HE IS!
IT'S KOKERU!
SHH! SHH!
HEH HEH HEH! WHICH ONE IS MY WIFE?

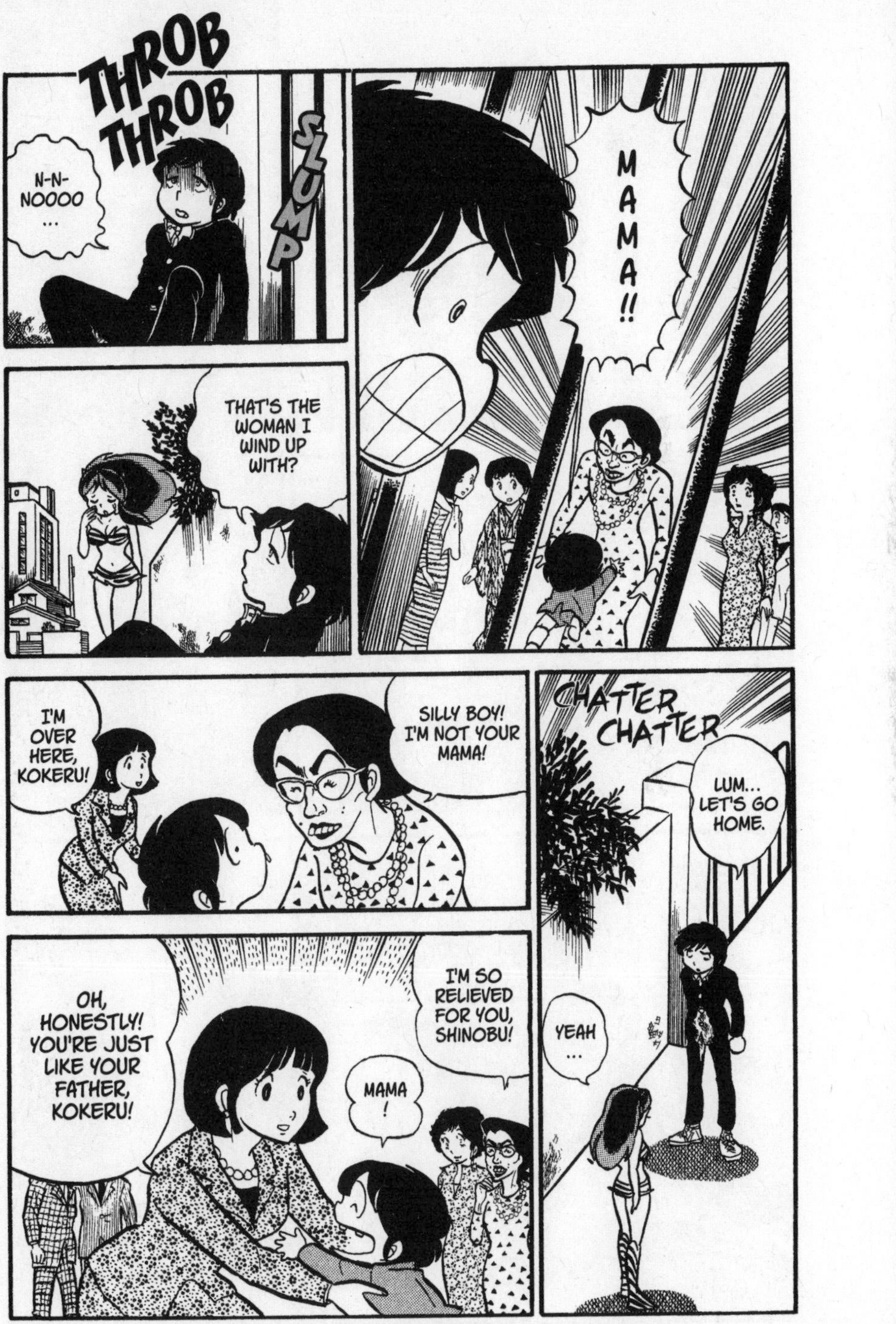
MAMA!!
THROB THROB
SLUMP
N-N-NOOOO ...
THAT'S THE WOMAN I WIND UP WITH?
CHATTER CHATTER
LUM... LET'S GO HOME.
YEAH ...
SILLY BOY! I'M NOT YOUR MAMA!
I'M OVER HERE, KOKERU!
I'M SO RELIEVED FOR YOU, SHINOBU!
MAMA !
OH, HONESTLY! YOU'RE JUST LIKE YOUR FATHER, KOKERU!

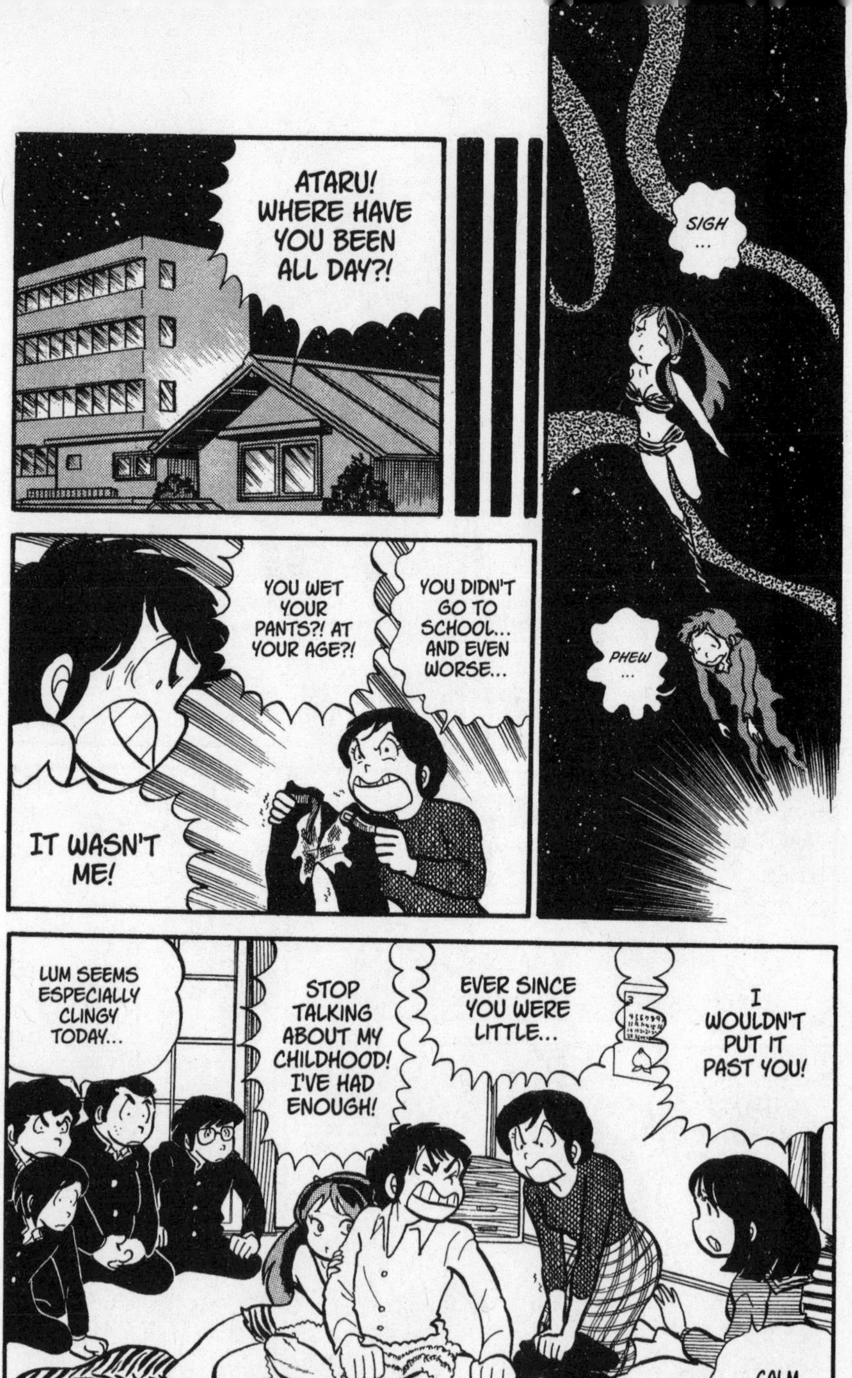
SIGH ...
PHEW ...
ATARU! WHERE HAVE YOU BEEN ALL DAY?!
YOU DIDN'T GO TO SCHOOL... AND EVEN WORSE...
YOU WET YOUR PANTS?! AT YOUR AGE?!
IT WASN'T ME!
I WOULDN'T PUT IT PAST YOU!
EVER SINCE YOU WERE LITTLE...
STOP TALKING ABOUT MY CHILDHOOD! I'VE HAD ENOUGH!
LUM SEEMS ESPECIALLY CLINGY TODAY...
CALM DOWN, MA'AM...

CHAPTER 13: PUPPET

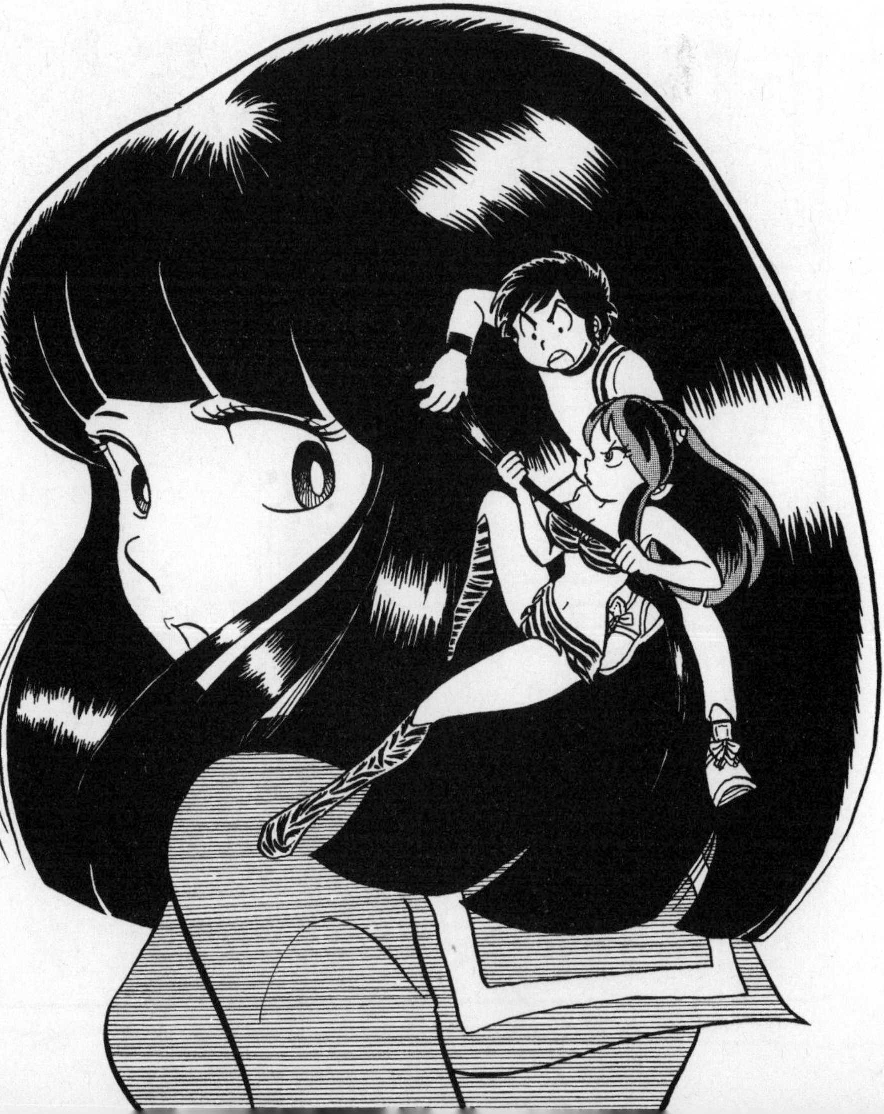

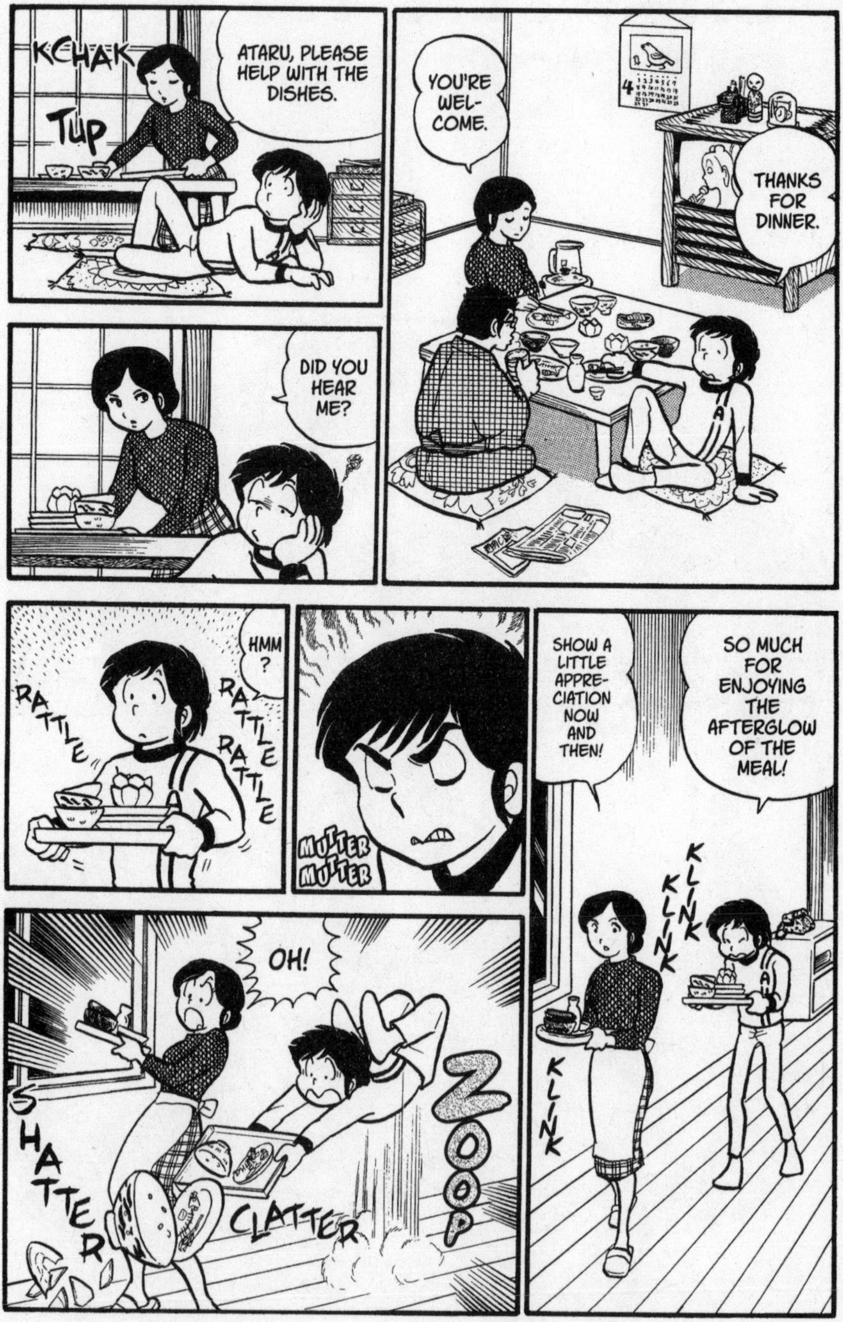
THANKS FOR DINNER.
YOU'RE WEL-COME.
ATARU, PLEASE HELP WITH THE DISHES.
KCHAK
TUP
DID YOU HEAR ME?
SO MUCH FOR ENJOYING THE AFTERGLOW OF THE MEAL!
SHOW A LITTLE APPRE-CIATION NOW AND THEN!
KLINK
KLINK
KLINK
MUTTER MUTTER
HMM?
RATTLE
RATTLE
RATTLE
OH!
ZOOP
SHATTER
CLATTER

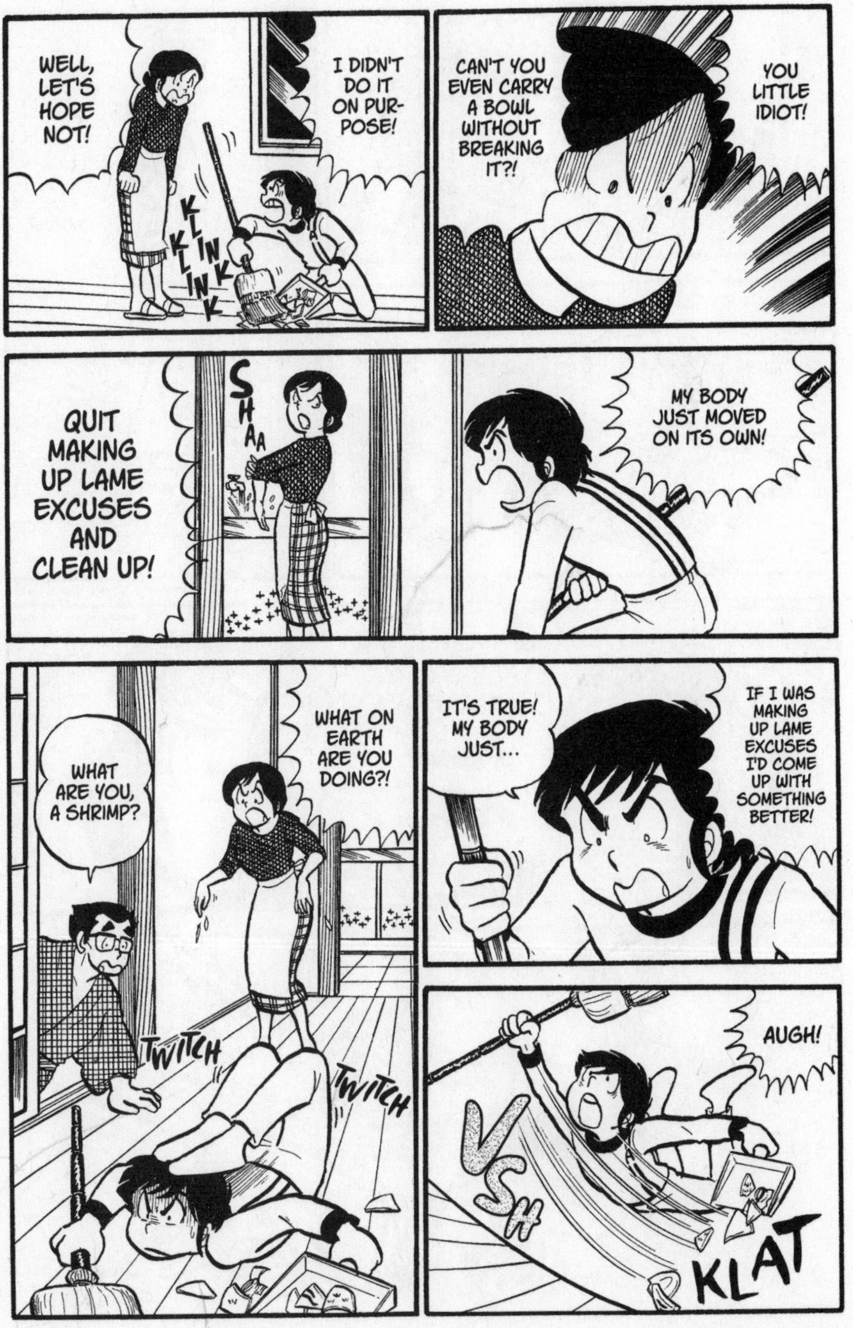
YOU LITTLE IDIOT!
CAN'T YOU EVEN CARRY A BOWL WITHOUT BREAKING IT?!
I DIDN'T DO IT ON PURPOSE!
WELL, LET'S HOPE NOT!
KLINK
KLINK
MY BODY JUST MOVED ON ITS OWN!
SHAA
QUIT MAKING UP LAME EXCUSES AND CLEAN UP!
IT'S TRUE! MY BODY JUST...
IF I WAS MAKING UP LAME EXCUSES I'D COME UP WITH SOMETHING BETTER!
AUGH!
VSH
KLAT
WHAT ON EARTH ARE YOU DOING?!
WHAT ARE YOU, A SHRIMP?
TWITCH
TWITCH

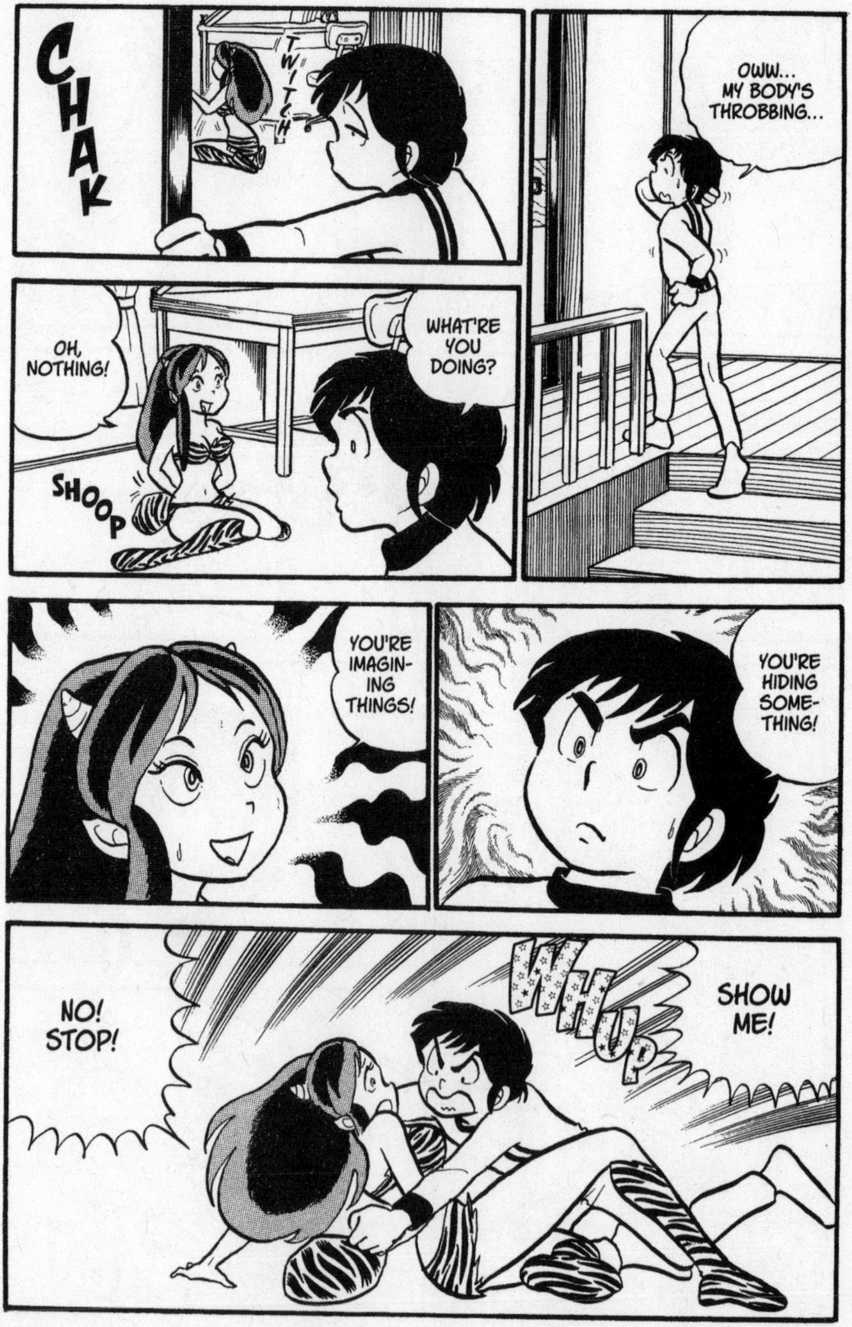

OWW... MY BODY'S THROBBING...
CHAK
TWITCH
WHAT'RE YOU DOING?
OH, NOTHING!
SHOOP
YOU'RE HIDING SOMETHING!
YOU'RE IMAGINING THINGS!
SHOW ME!
WHUP
NO! STOP!

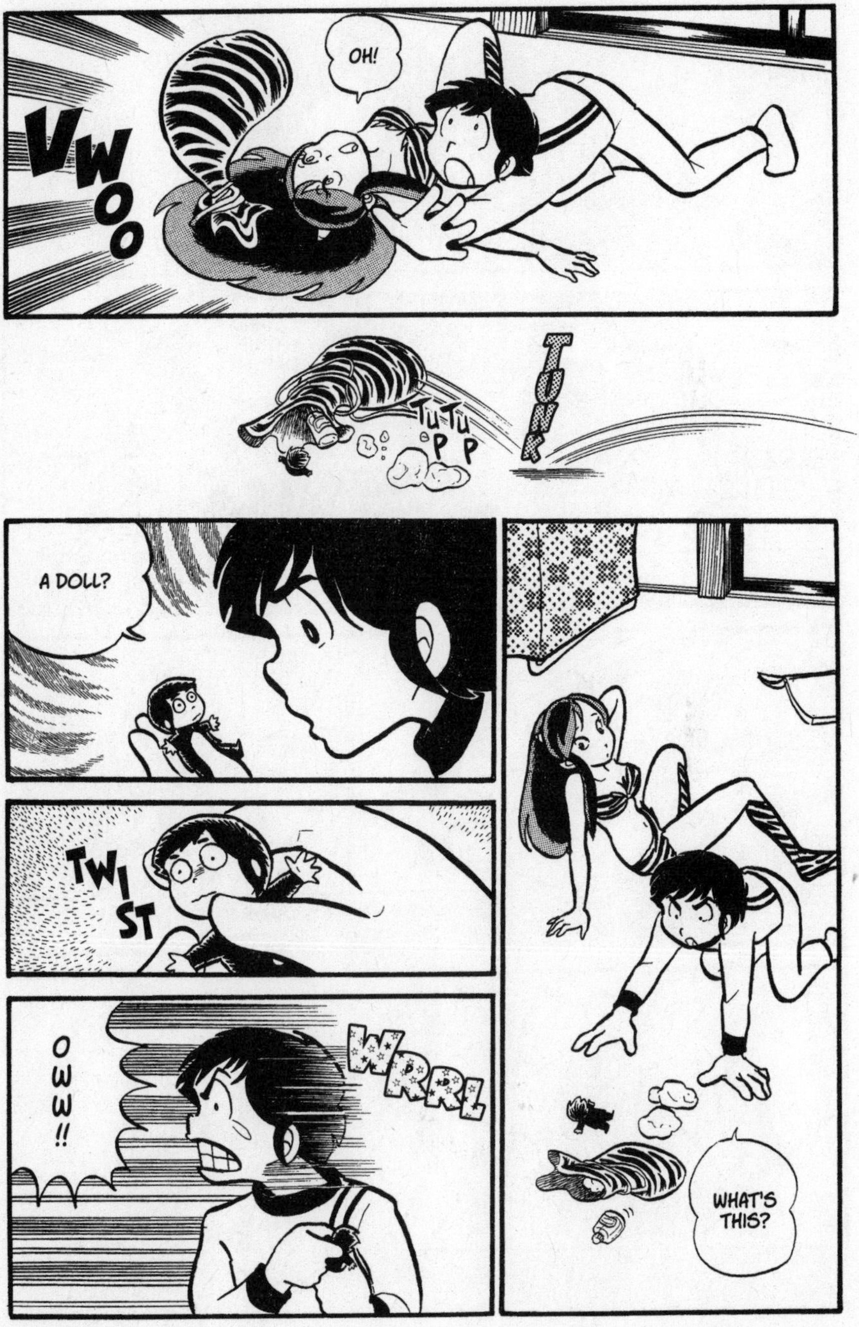
OH!
VWOOO
TONK
TUP
TUP
WHAT'S THIS?
A DOLL?
TWIST
WRRL
OWW!!

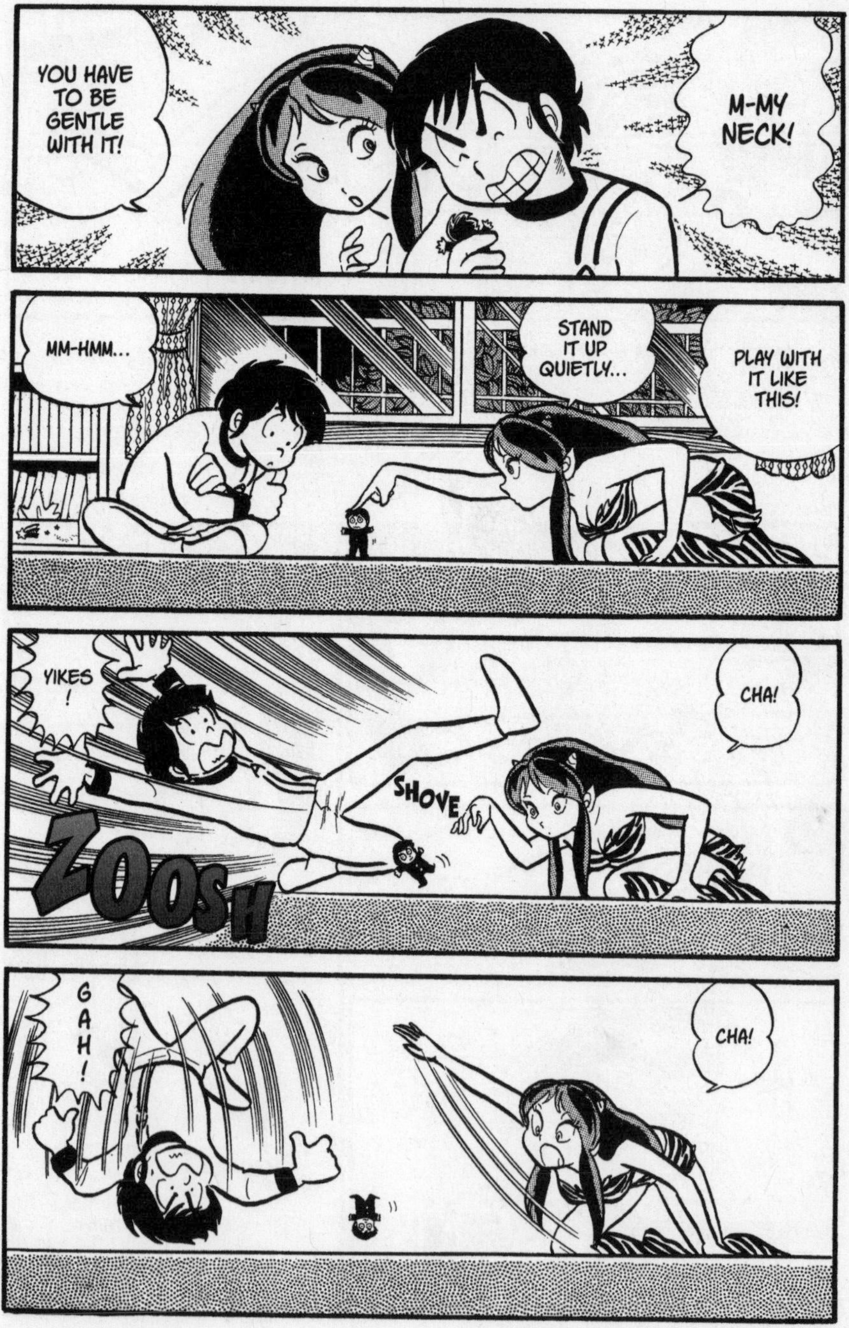
M-MY NECK!
YOU HAVE TO BE GENTLE WITH IT!
PLAY WITH IT LIKE THIS!
STAND IT UP QUIETLY...
MM-HMM...
CHA!
SHOVE
YIKES!
ZOOSH
CHA!
GAH!

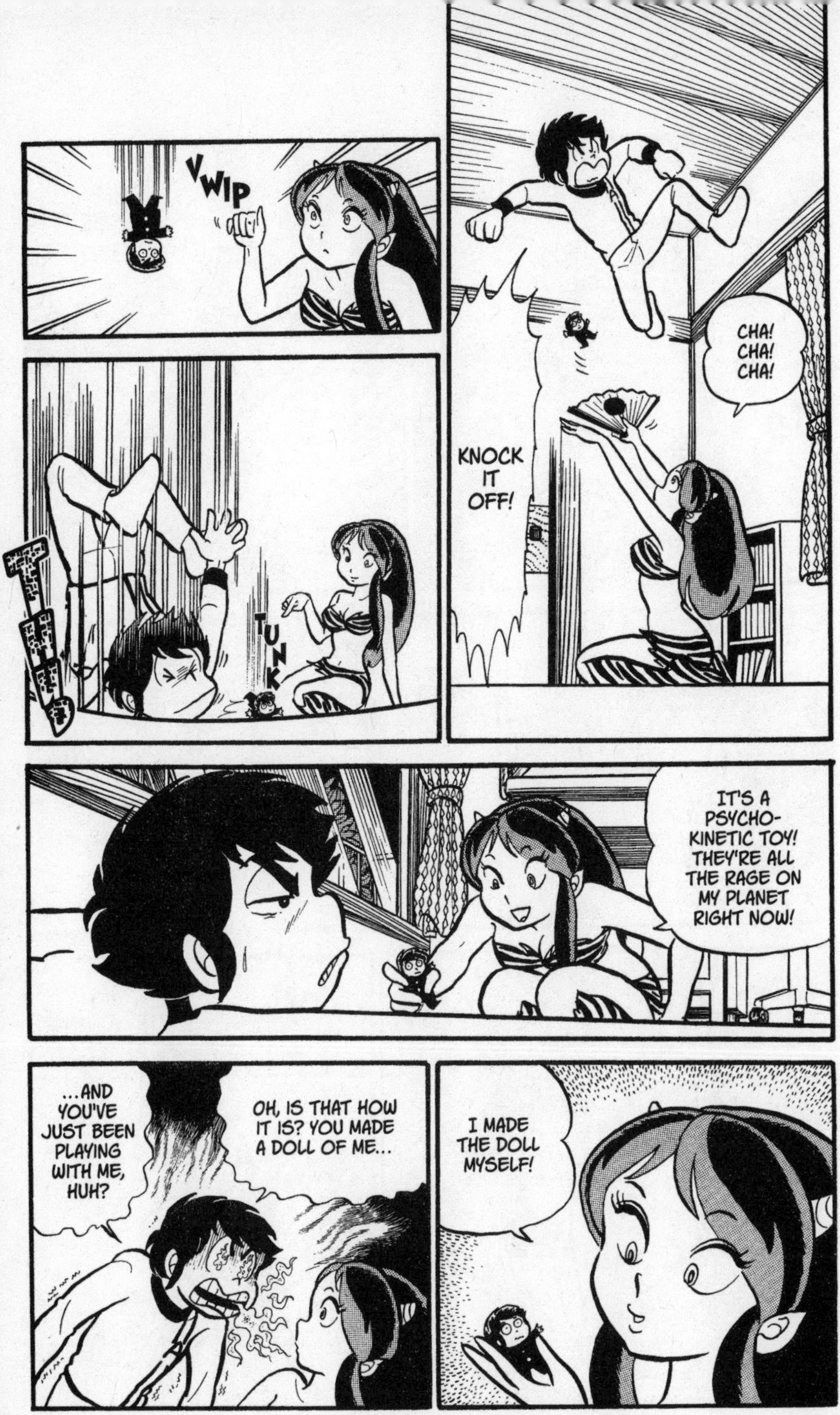
CHA! CHA! CHA!
KNOCK IT OFF!
VWIP
TUNK
IT'S A PSYCHO-KINETIC TOY! THEY'RE ALL THE RAGE ON MY PLANET RIGHT NOW!
I MADE THE DOLL MYSELF!
OH, IS THAT HOW IT IS? YOU MADE A DOLL OF ME...
...AND YOU'VE JUST BEEN PLAYING WITH ME, HUH?

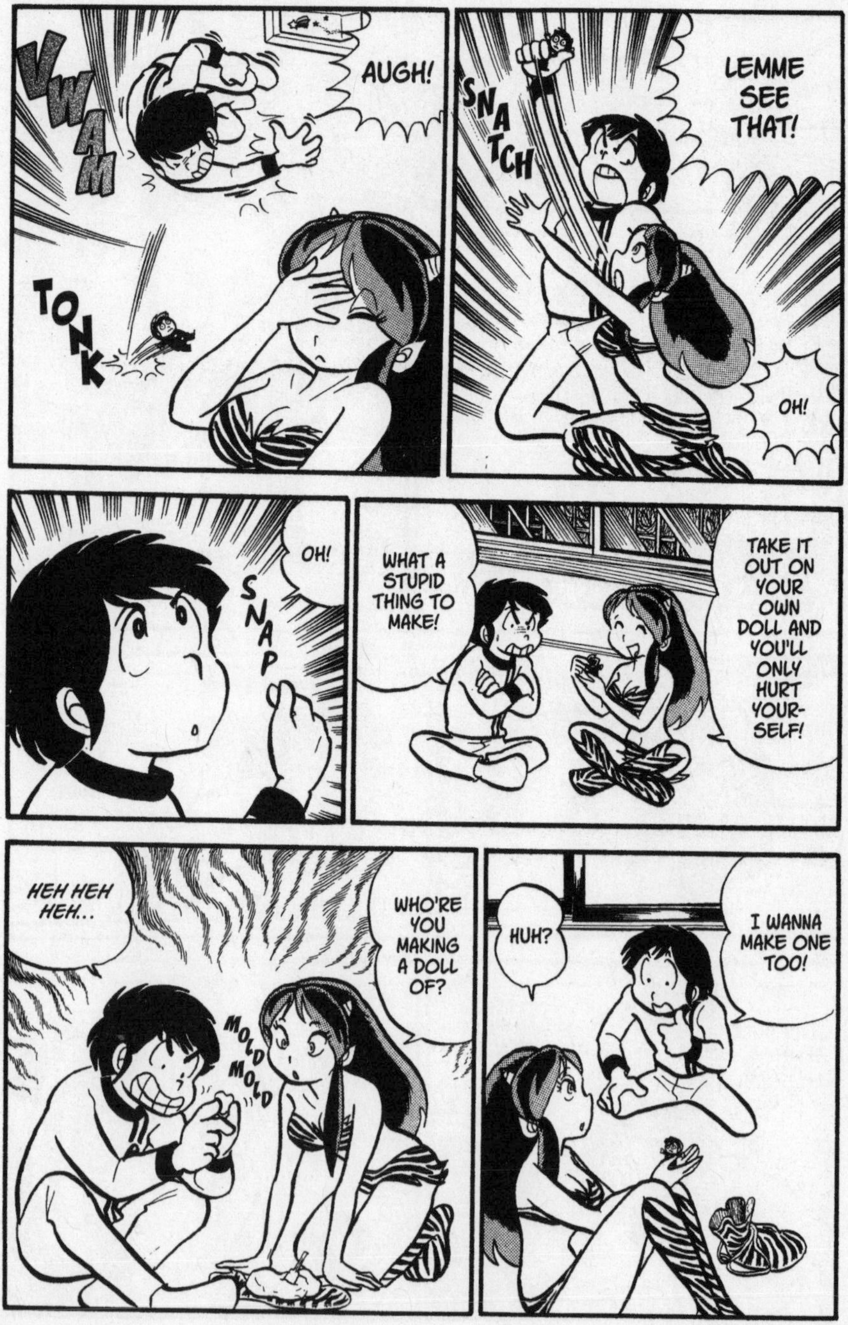
LEMME SEE THAT!
SNATCH
OH!
AUGH!
VWAM
TONK
TAKE IT OUT ON YOUR OWN DOLL AND YOU'LL ONLY HURT YOUR-SELF!
WHAT A STUPID THING TO MAKE!
OH!
SNAP
I WANNA MAKE ONE TOO!
HUH?
WHO'RE YOU MAKING A DOLL OF?
HEH HEH HEH...
MOLD MOLD

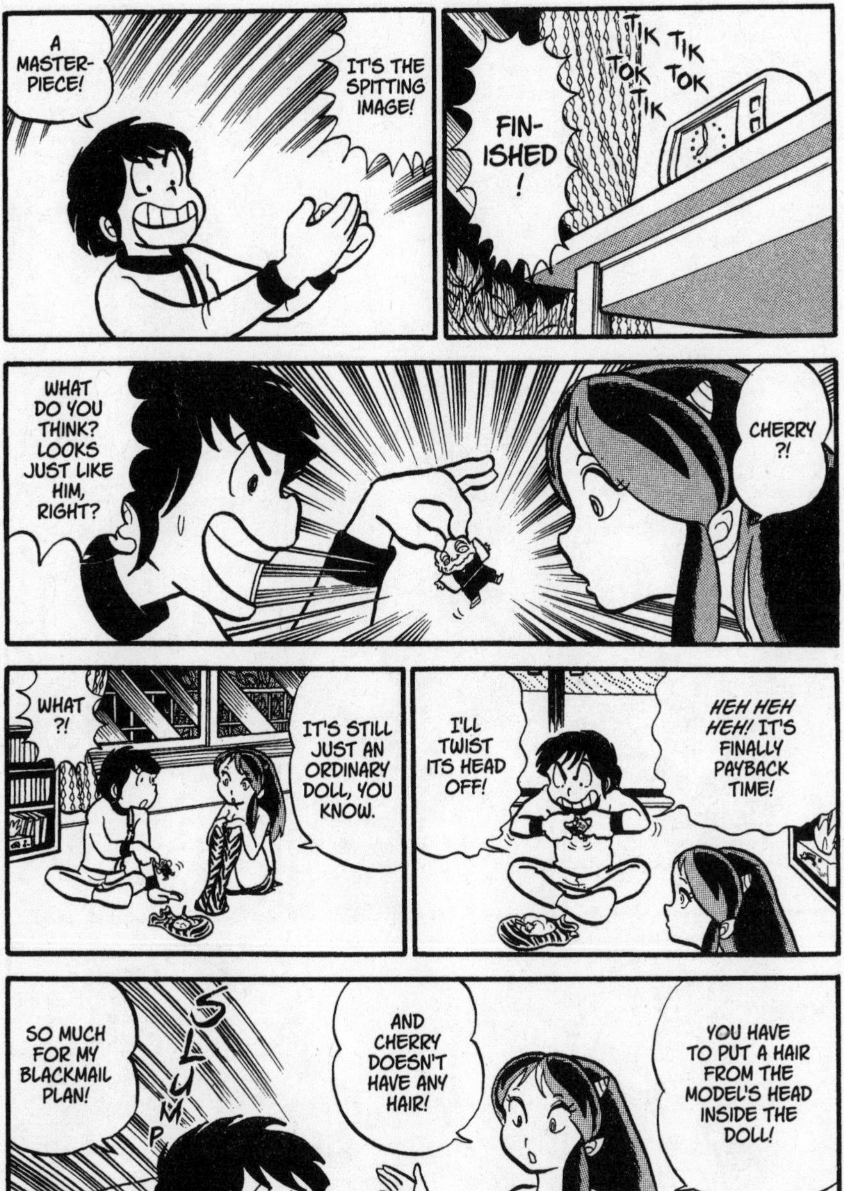
TIK TIK TOK TOK TIK
FIN-ISHED!
IT'S THE SPITTING IMAGE!
A MASTER-PIECE!
CHERRY?!
WHAT DO YOU THINK? LOOKS JUST LIKE HIM, RIGHT?
HEH HEH HEH! IT'S FINALLY PAYBACK TIME!
I'LL TWIST ITS HEAD OFF!
IT'S STILL JUST AN ORDINARY DOLL, YOU KNOW.
WHAT?!
YOU HAVE TO PUT A HAIR FROM THE MODEL'S HEAD INSIDE THE DOLL!
AND CHERRY DOESN'T HAVE ANY HAIR!
SLUMP
SO MUCH FOR MY BLACKMAIL PLAN!

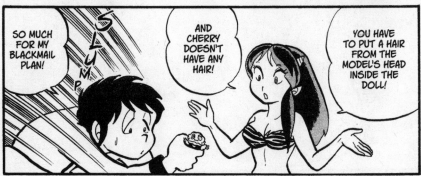

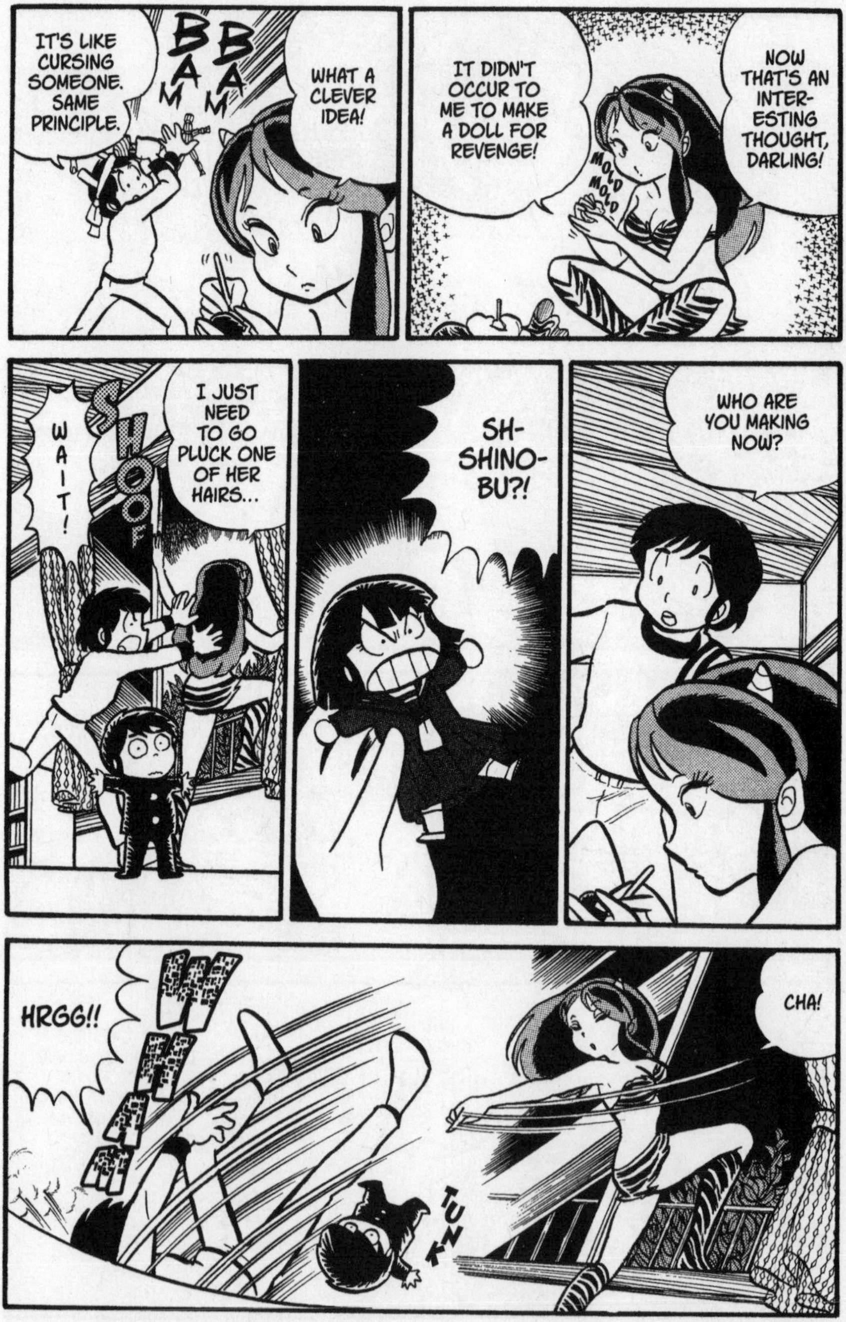
NOW THAT'S AN INTERESTING THOUGHT, DARLING!
IT DIDN'T OCCUR TO ME TO MAKE A DOLL FOR REVENGE!
MOLD MOLD
WHAT A CLEVER IDEA!
BAM BAM
IT'S LIKE CURSING SOMEONE. SAME PRINCIPLE.
WHO ARE YOU MAKING NOW?
SH-SHINOBU?!
I JUST NEED TO GO PLUCK ONE OF HER HAIRS...
SHOOF
WAIT!
CHA!
TUNK
HRGG!!

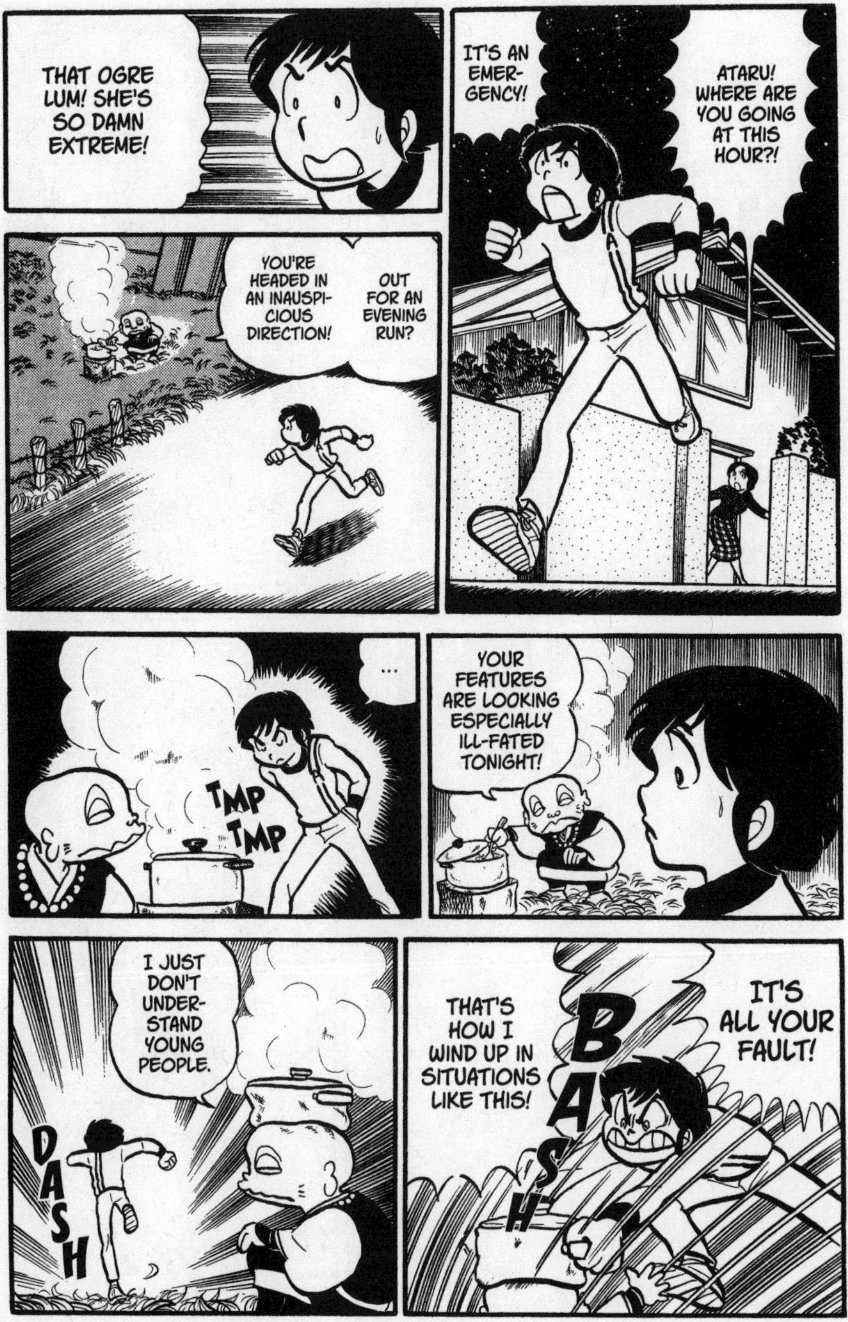
ATARU! WHERE ARE YOU GOING AT THIS HOUR?!
IT'S AN EMERGENCY!
THAT OGRE LUM! SHE'S SO DAMN EXTREME!
OUT FOR AN EVENING RUN?
YOU'RE HEADED IN AN INAUSPICIOUS DIRECTION!
YOUR FEATURES ARE LOOKING ESPECIALLY ILL-FATED TONIGHT!
...
TMP TMP
IT'S ALL YOUR FAULT!
THAT'S HOW I WIND UP IN SITUATIONS LIKE THIS!
BASH
I JUST DON'T UNDERSTAND YOUNG PEOPLE.
DASH

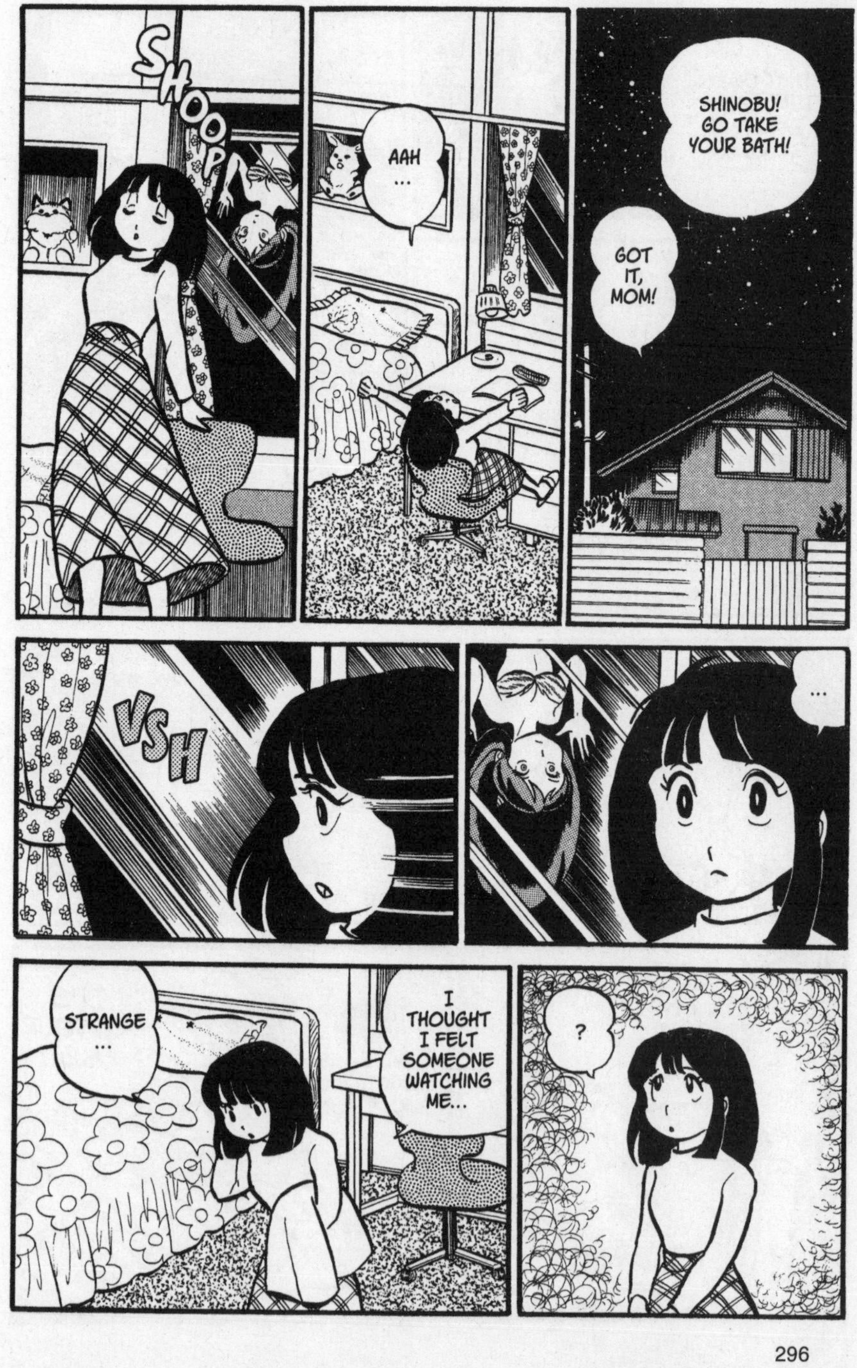
SHINOBU! GO TAKE YOUR BATH!
GOT IT, MOM!
AAH ...
SHOOP
...
VSH
?
STRANGE ...
I THOUGHT I FELT SOMEONE WATCHING ME...

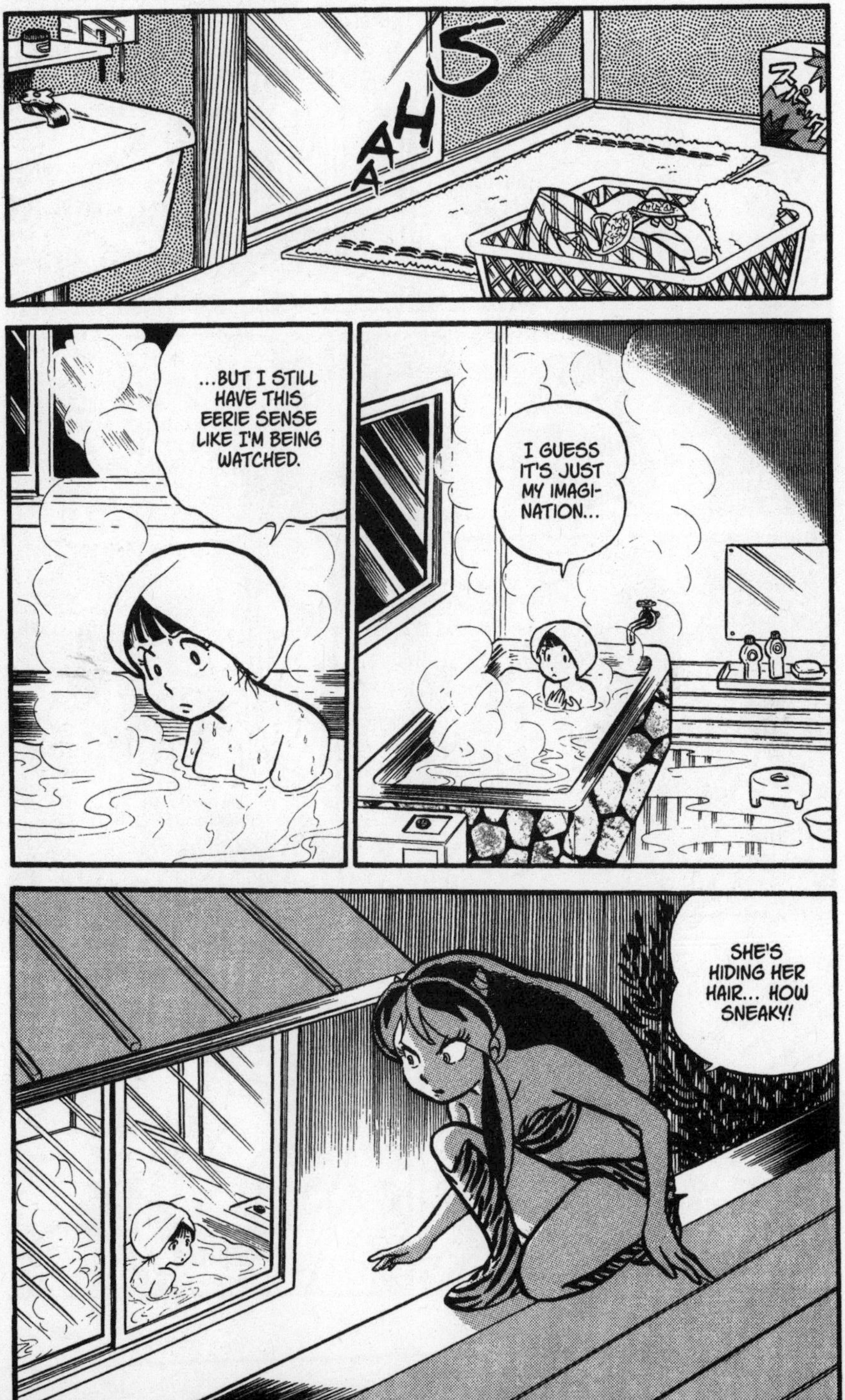
AAHS
I GUESS IT'S JUST MY IMAGINATION...
...BUT I STILL HAVE THIS EERIE SENSE LIKE I'M BEING WATCHED.
SHE'S HIDING HER HAIR... HOW SNEAKY!

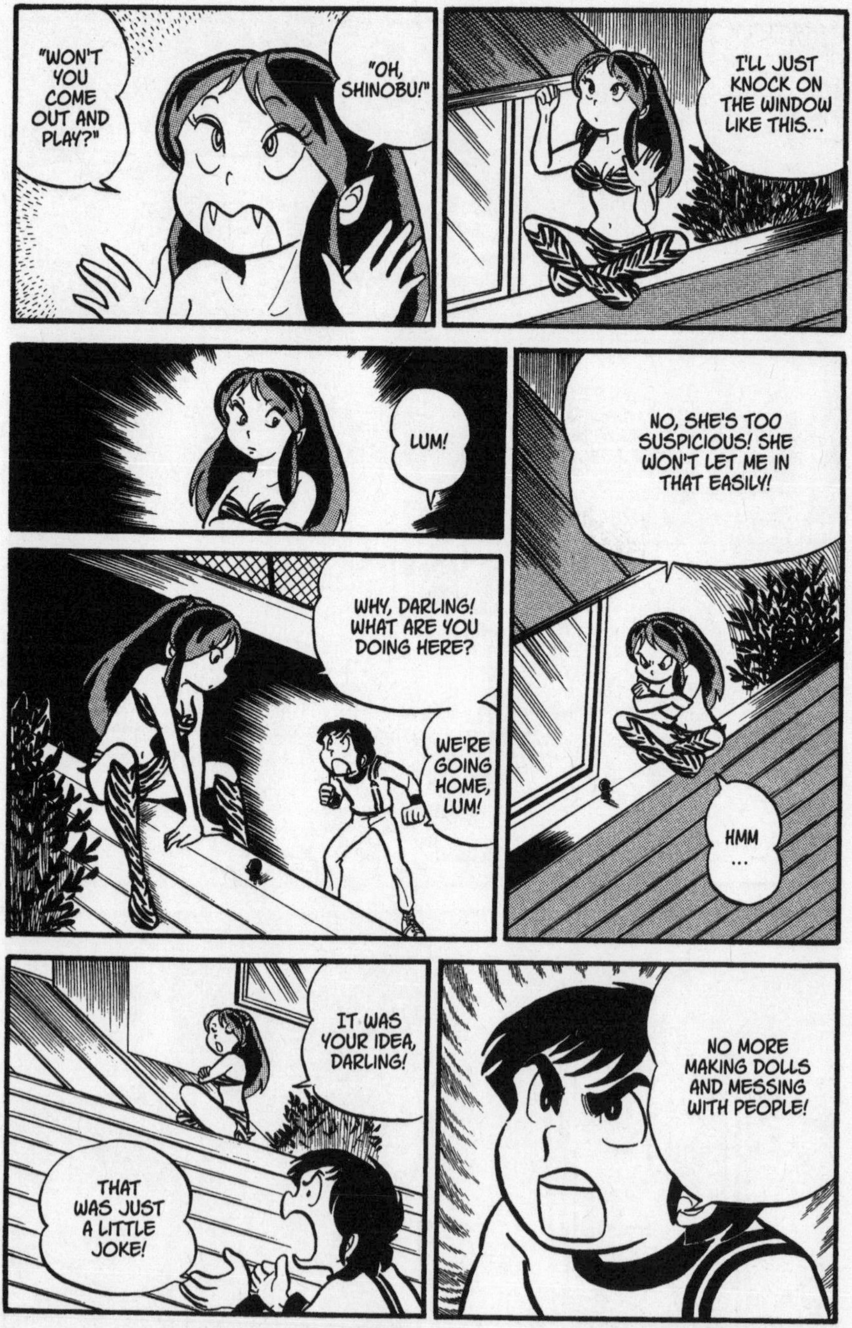
I'LL JUST KNOCK ON THE WINDOW LIKE THIS...
"OH, SHINOBU!"
"WON'T YOU COME OUT AND PLAY?"
NO, SHE'S TOO SUSPICIOUS! SHE WON'T LET ME IN THAT EASILY!
HMM ...
LUM!
WHY, DARLING! WHAT ARE YOU DOING HERE?
WE'RE GOING HOME, LUM!
NO MORE MAKING DOLLS AND MESSING WITH PEOPLE!
IT WAS YOUR IDEA, DARLING!
THAT WAS JUST A LITTLE JOKE!

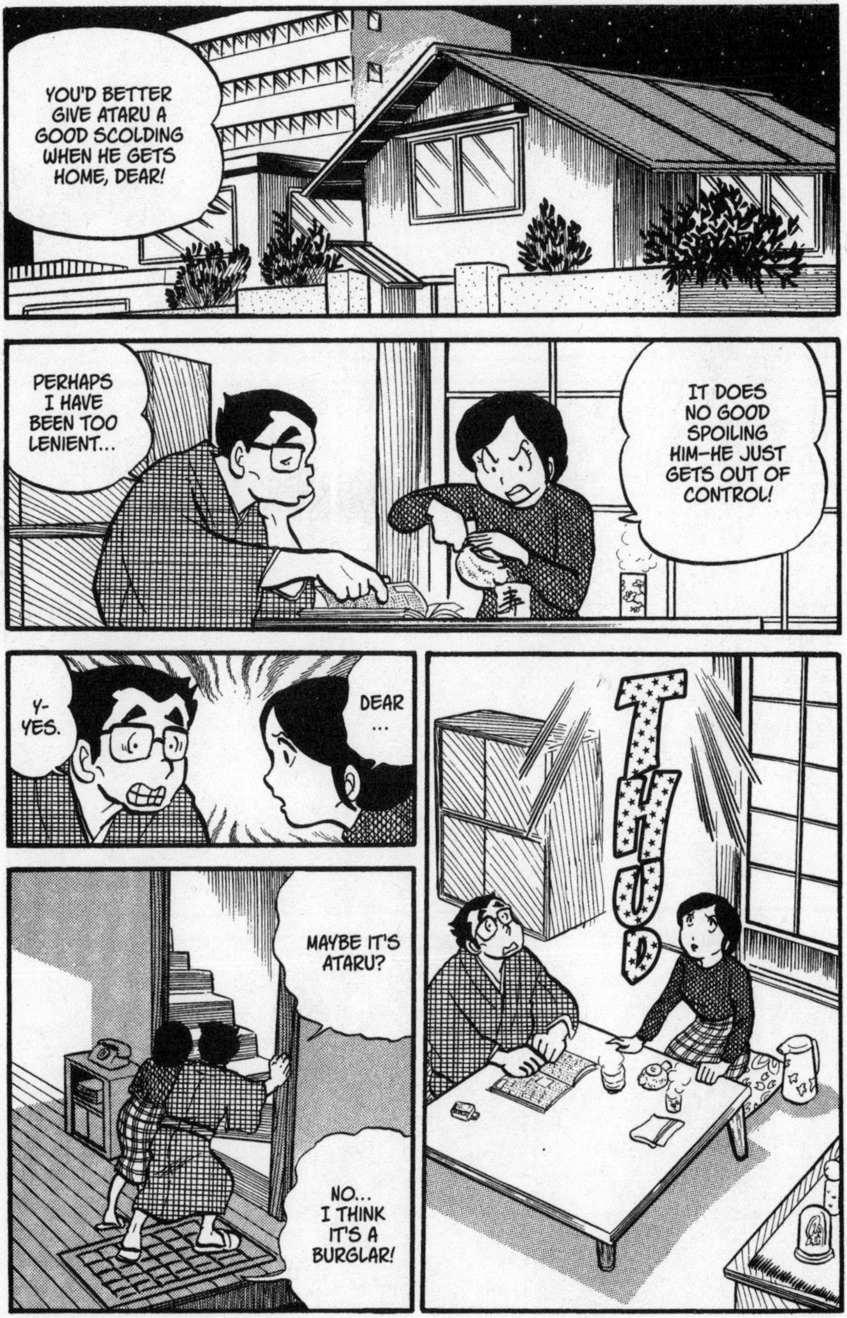
YOU'D BETTER GIVE ATARU A GOOD SCOLDING WHEN HE GETS HOME, DEAR!
IT DOES NO GOOD SPOILING HIM—HE JUST GETS OUT OF CONTROL!
PERHAPS I HAVE BEEN TOO LENIENT...
THUD
DEAR ...
Y- YES.
MAYBE IT'S ATARU?
NO... I THINK IT'S A BURGLAR!

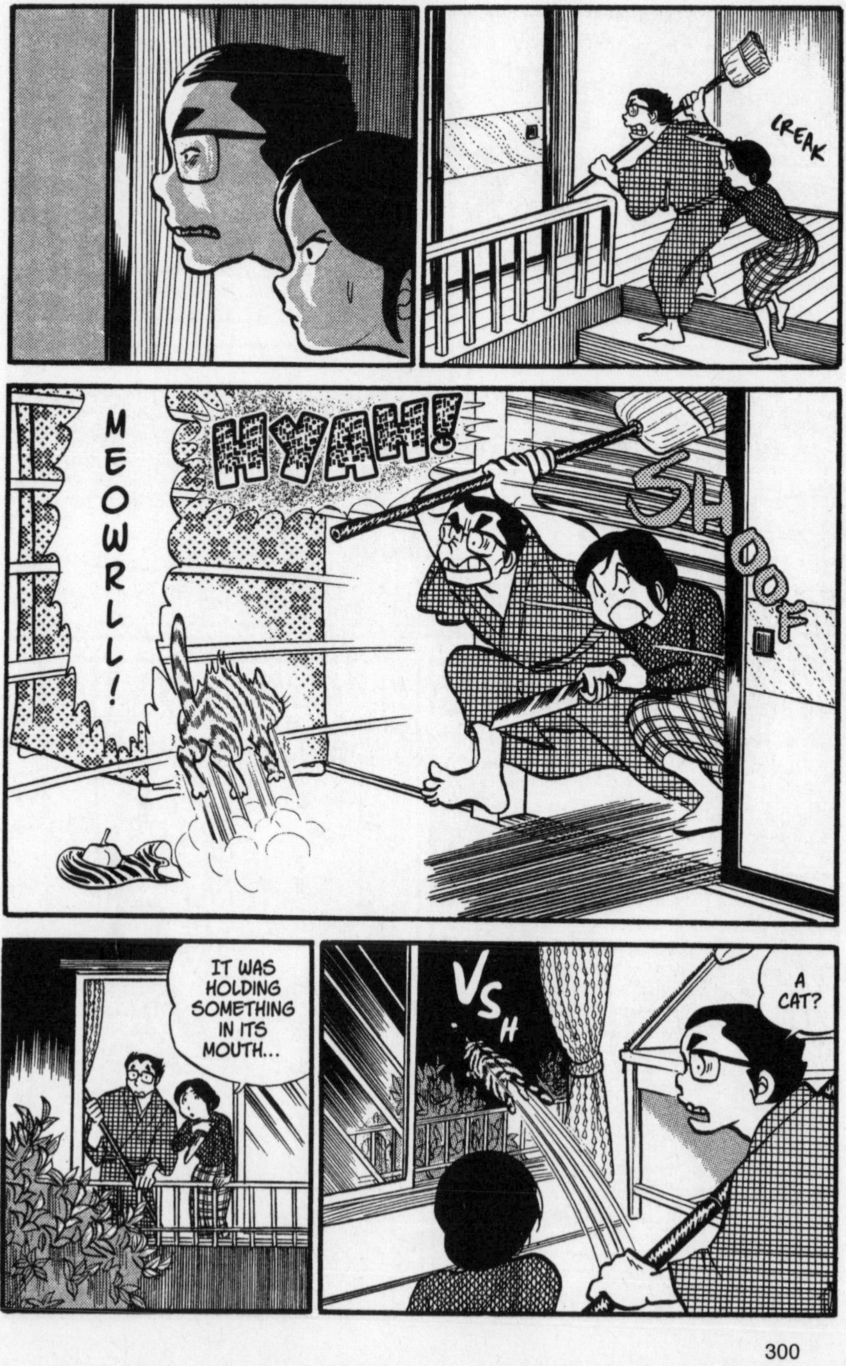
CREAK
SHOOOF
HYAH!
MEOWRLLL!
A CAT?
VSH
IT WAS HOLDING SOMETHING IN ITS MOUTH...

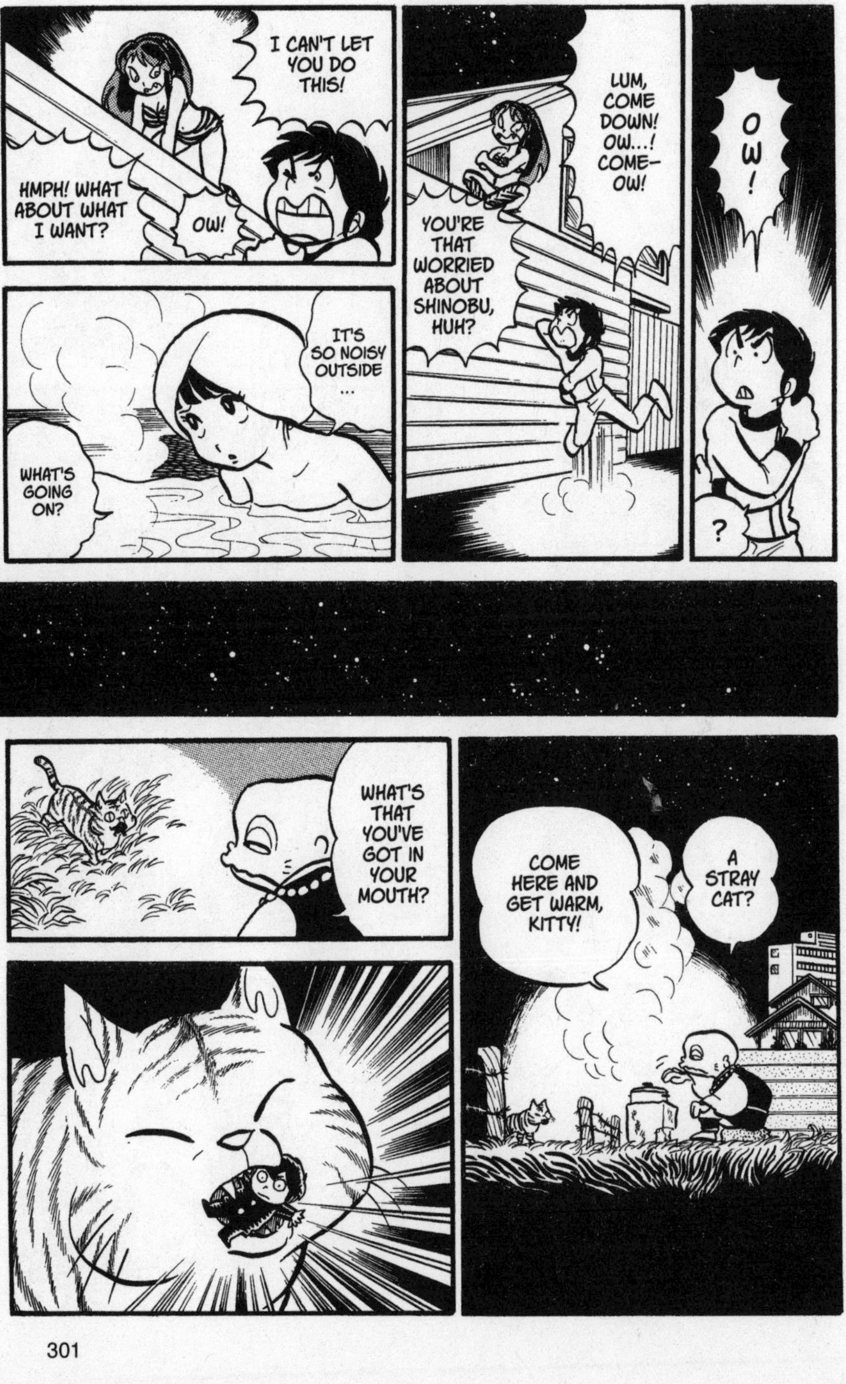
OW!
?
LUM, COME DOWN! OW...! COME-OW!
YOU'RE THAT WORRIED ABOUT SHINOBU, HUH?
I CAN'T LET YOU DO THIS!
OW!
HMPH! WHAT ABOUT WHAT I WANT?
IT'S SO NOISY OUTSIDE ...
WHAT'S GOING ON?
A STRAY CAT?
COME HERE AND GET WARM, KITTY!
WHAT'S THAT YOU'VE GOT IN YOUR MOUTH?

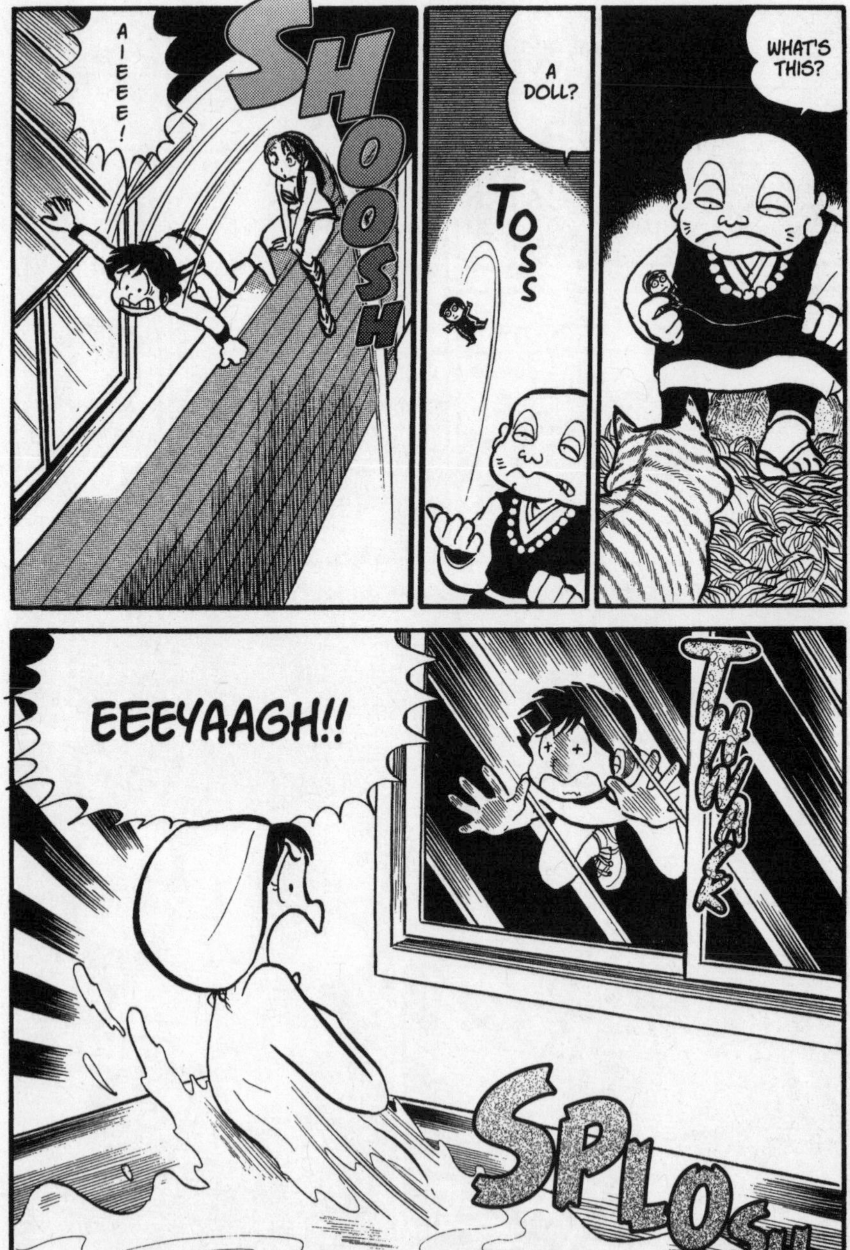
WHAT'S THIS?
A DOLL?
TOSS
AIEEE!
SHOOSH
EEEYAAGH!!
THWACK
SPLOSH

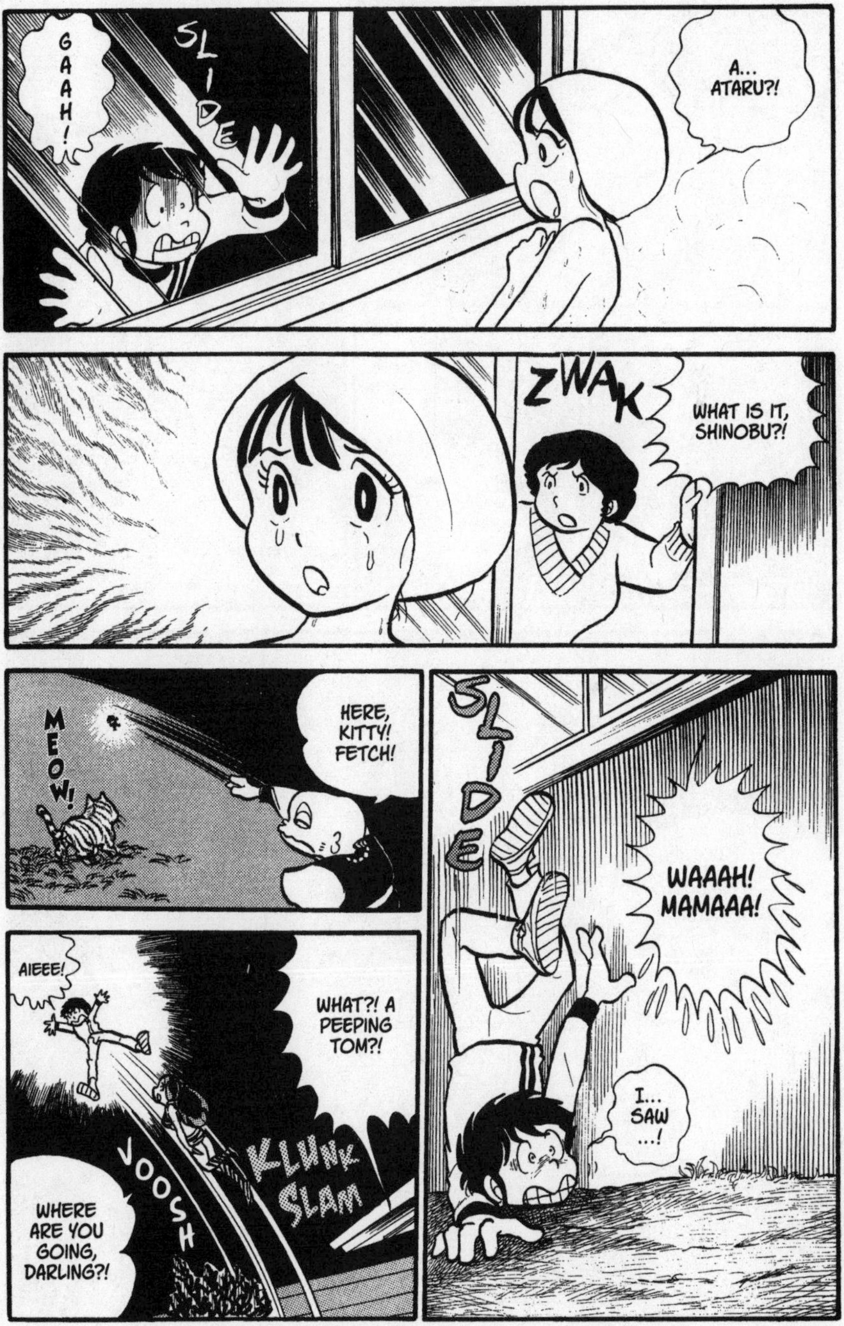
A... ATARU?!
SLIDE
GAAH!
ZWAK
WHAT IS IT, SHINOBU?!
SLIDE
WAAAH! MAMAAA!
I... SAW ...!
HERE, KITTY! FETCH!
MEOW!
WHAT?! A PEEPING TOM?!
AIEEE!
KLUNK SLAM
VOOSH
WHERE ARE YOU GOING, DARLING?!

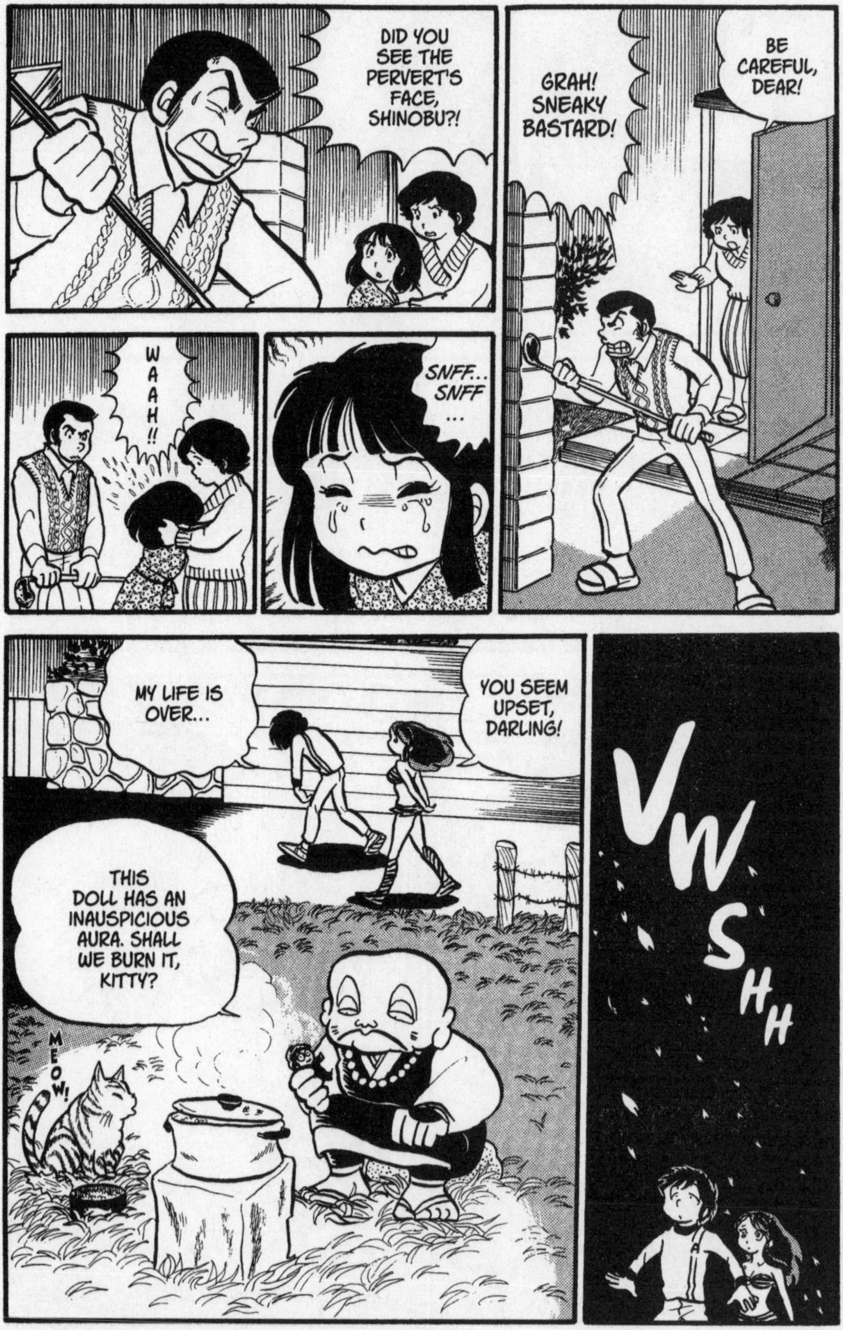
BE CAREFUL, DEAR!
GRAH! SNEAKY BASTARD!
DID YOU SEE THE PERVERT'S FACE, SHINOBU?!
SNFF... SNFF ...
WAAAH!!
VWSHH
YOU SEEM UPSET, DARLING!
MY LIFE IS OVER...
THIS DOLL HAS AN INAUSPICIOUS AURA. SHALL WE BURN IT, KITTY?
MEOW!

CHAPTER 14: STILL WATERS RUN DEEP

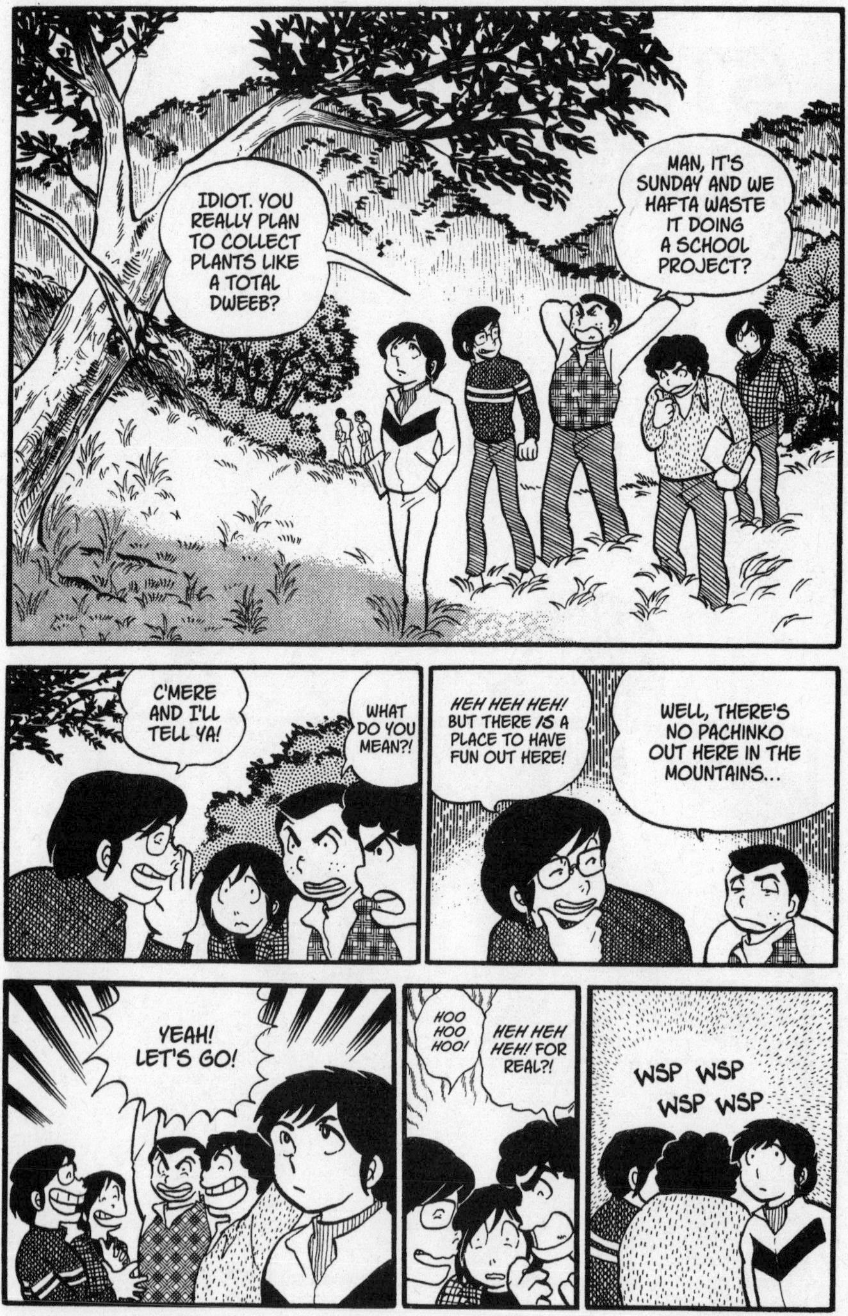
MAN, IT'S SUNDAY AND WE HAFTA WASTE IT DOING A SCHOOL PROJECT?
IDIOT. YOU REALLY PLAN TO COLLECT PLANTS LIKE A TOTAL DWEEB?
WELL, THERE'S NO PACHINKO OUT HERE IN THE MOUNTAINS...
HEH HEH HEH! BUT THERE IS A PLACE TO HAVE FUN OUT HERE!
WHAT DO YOU MEAN?!
C'MERE AND I'LL TELL YA!
WSP WSP WSP WSP
HEH HEH HEH! FOR REAL?!
HOO HOO HOO!
YEAH! LET'S GO!

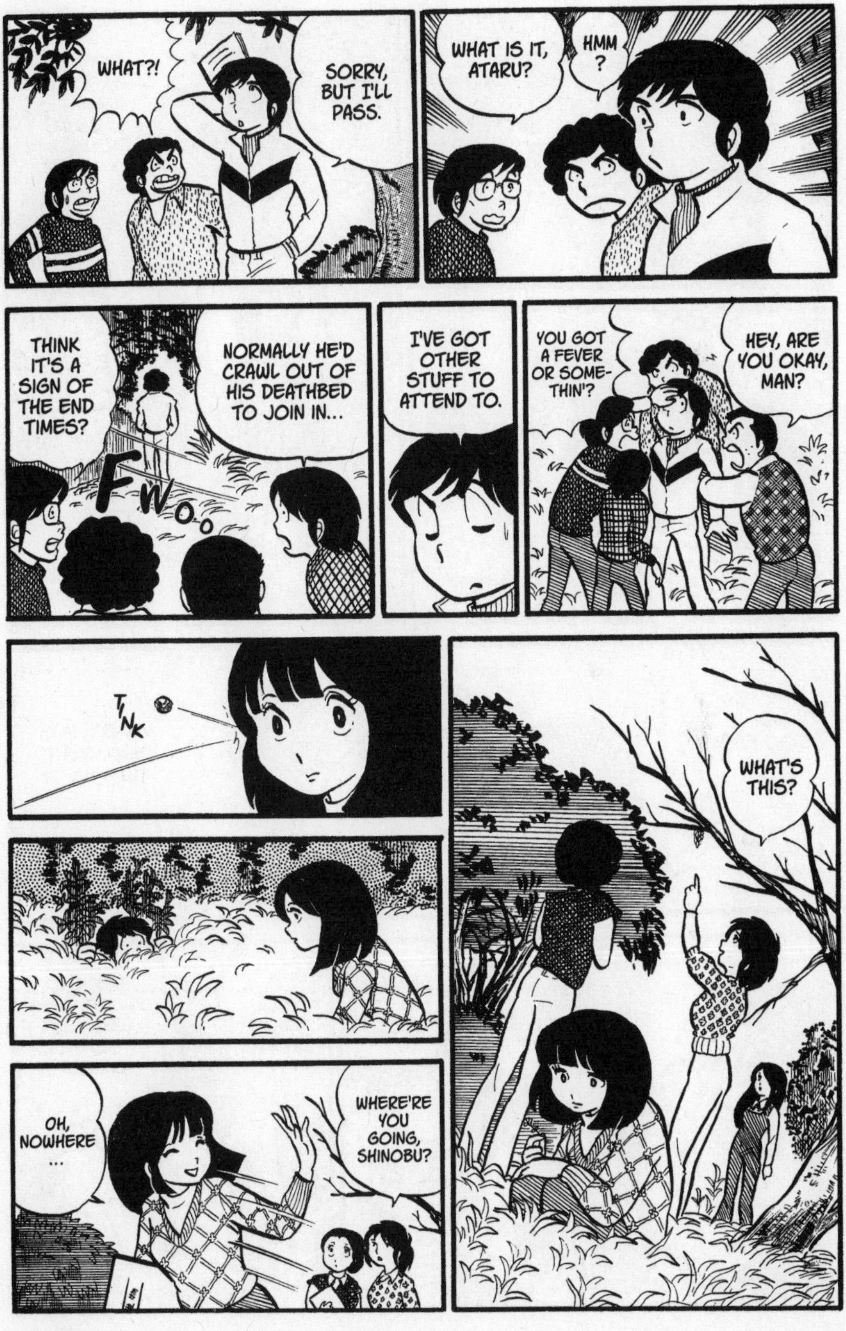
HMM ?
WHAT IS IT, ATARU?
SORRY, BUT I'LL PASS.
WHAT?!
HEY, ARE YOU OKAY, MAN?
YOU GOT A FEVER OR SOME-THIN'?
I'VE GOT OTHER STUFF TO ATTEND TO.
NORMALLY HE'D CRAWL OUT OF HIS DEATHBED TO JOIN IN...
THINK IT'S A SIGN OF THE END TIMES?
FWOO
WHAT'S THIS?
TINK
WHERE'RE YOU GOING, SHINOBU?
OH, NOWHERE ...

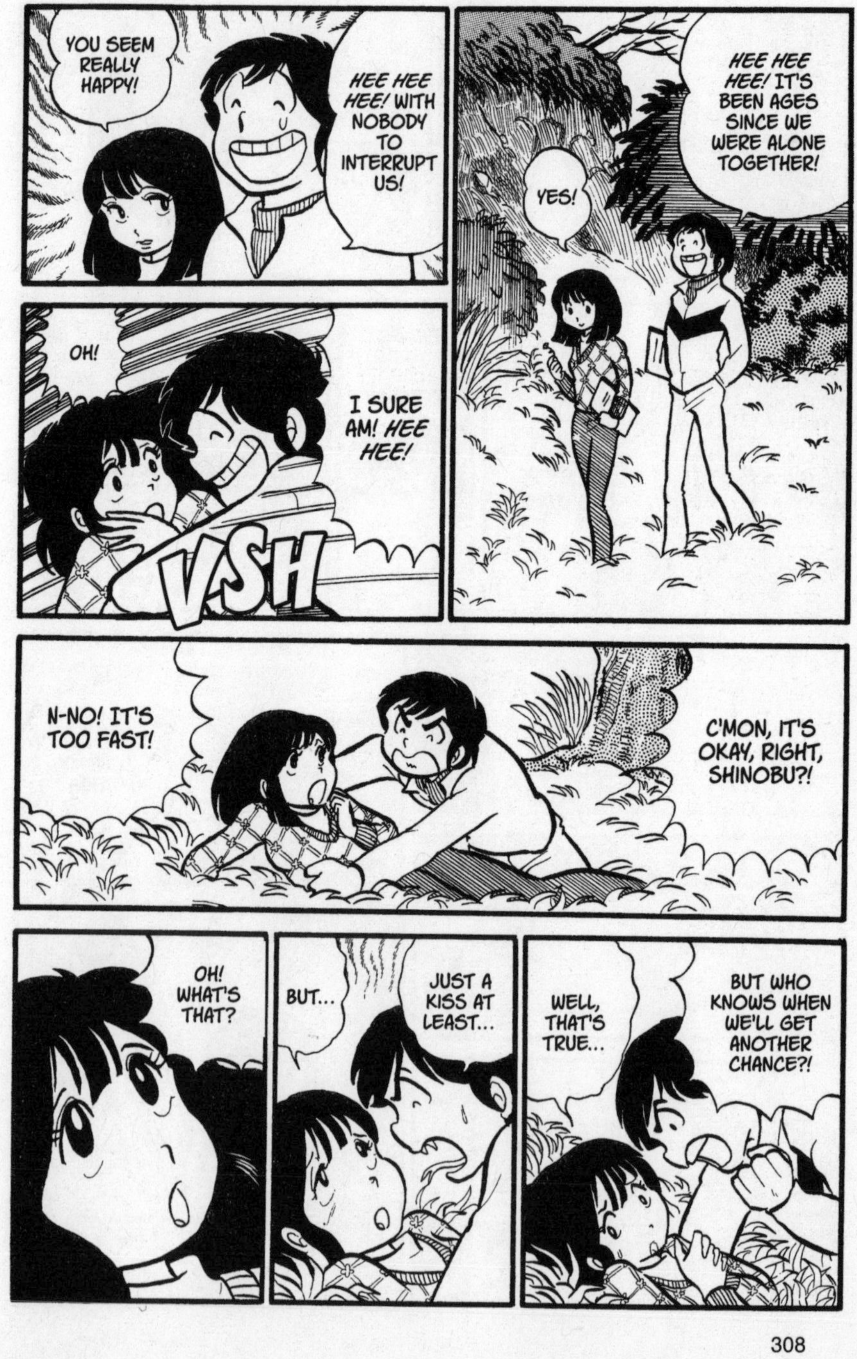
HEE HEE HEE! IT'S BEEN AGES SINCE WE WERE ALONE TOGETHER!
YES!
HEE HEE HEE! WITH NOBODY TO INTERRUPT US!
YOU SEEM REALLY HAPPY!
I SURE AM! HEE HEE!
OH!
VSH
C'MON, IT'S OKAY, RIGHT, SHINOBU?!
N-NO! IT'S TOO FAST!
BUT WHO KNOWS WHEN WE'LL GET ANOTHER CHANCE?!
WELL, THAT'S TRUE...
JUST A KISS AT LEAST...
BUT...
OH! WHAT'S THAT?

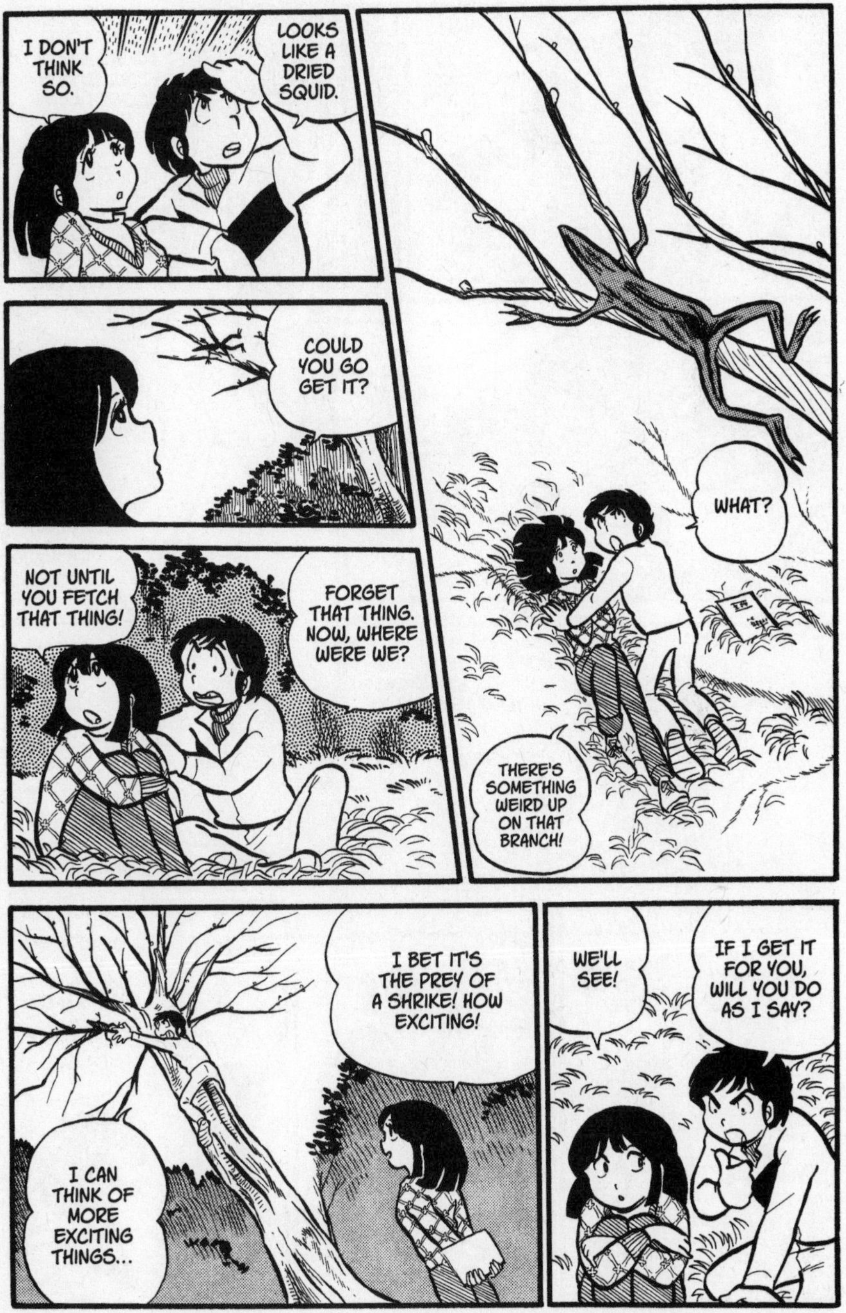
WHAT?
THERE'S SOMETHING WEIRD UP ON THAT BRANCH!
LOOKS LIKE A DRIED SQUID.
I DON'T THINK SO.
COULD YOU GO GET IT?
FORGET THAT THING. NOW, WHERE WERE WE?
NOT UNTIL YOU FETCH THAT THING!
IF I GET IT FOR YOU, WILL YOU DO AS I SAY?
WE'LL SEE!
I BET IT'S THE PREY OF A SHRIKE! HOW EXCITING!
I CAN THINK OF MORE EXCITING THINGS...

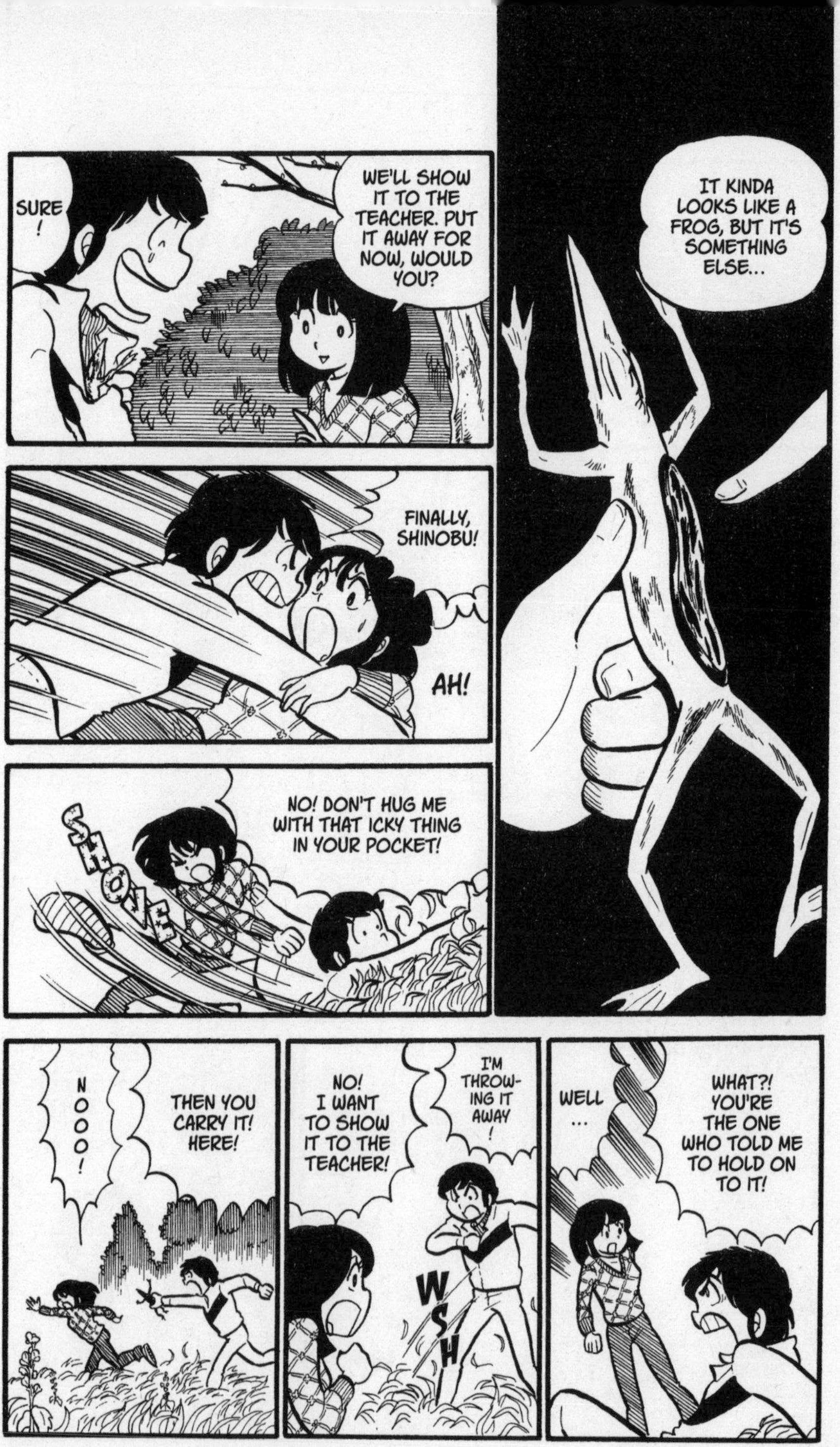
IT KINDA LOOKS LIKE A FROG, BUT IT'S SOMETHING ELSE...
WE'LL SHOW IT TO THE TEACHER. PUT IT AWAY FOR NOW, WOULD YOU?
SURE!
FINALLY, SHINOBU!
AH!
NO! DON'T HUG ME WITH THAT ICKY THING IN YOUR POCKET!
SHOVE
WHAT?! YOU'RE THE ONE WHO TOLD ME TO HOLD ON TO IT!
WELL...
I'M THROWING IT AWAY!
NO! I WANT TO SHOW IT TO THE TEACHER!
WSH
THEN YOU CARRY IT! HERE!
NOOOO!

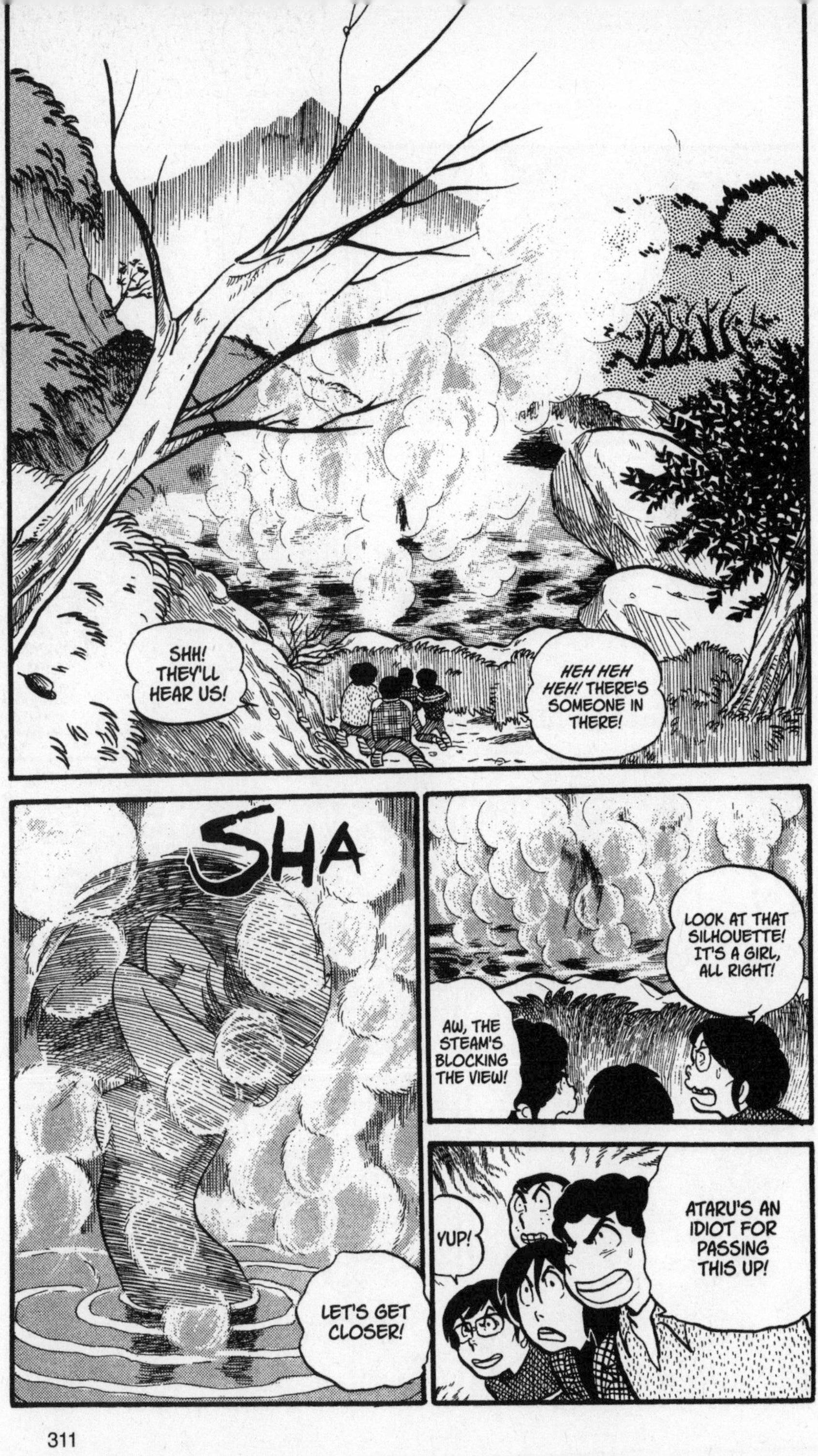
HEH HEH HEH! THERE'S SOMEONE IN THERE!
SHH! THEY'LL HEAR US!
LOOK AT THAT SILHOUETTE! IT'S A GIRL, ALL RIGHT!
AW, THE STEAM'S BLOCKING THE VIEW!
ATARU'S AN IDIOT FOR PASSING THIS UP!
YUP!
SHA
LET'S GET CLOSER!

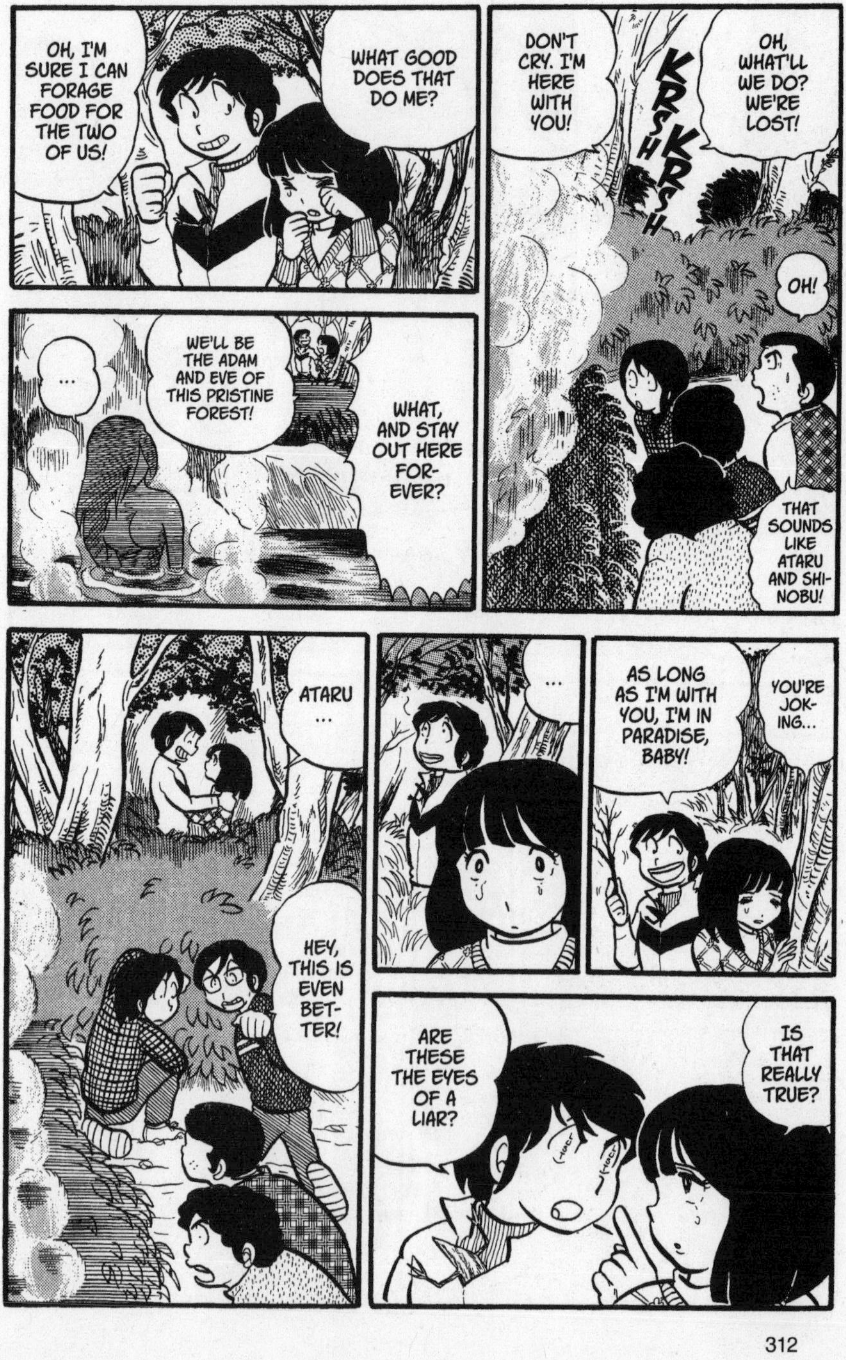
OH, WHAT'LL WE DO? WE'RE LOST!
DON'T CRY. I'M HERE WITH YOU!
KRSH KRSH
OH!
THAT SOUNDS LIKE ATARU AND SHI-NOBU!
WHAT GOOD DOES THAT DO ME?
OH, I'M SURE I CAN FORAGE FOOD FOR THE TWO OF US!
WHAT, AND STAY OUT HERE FOR-EVER?
WE'LL BE THE ADAM AND EVE OF THIS PRISTINE FOREST!
...
YOU'RE JOK-ING...
AS LONG AS I'M WITH YOU, I'M IN PARADISE, BABY!
...
IS THAT REALLY TRUE?
ARE THESE THE EYES OF A LIAR?
ATARU ...
HEY, THIS IS EVEN BET-TER!

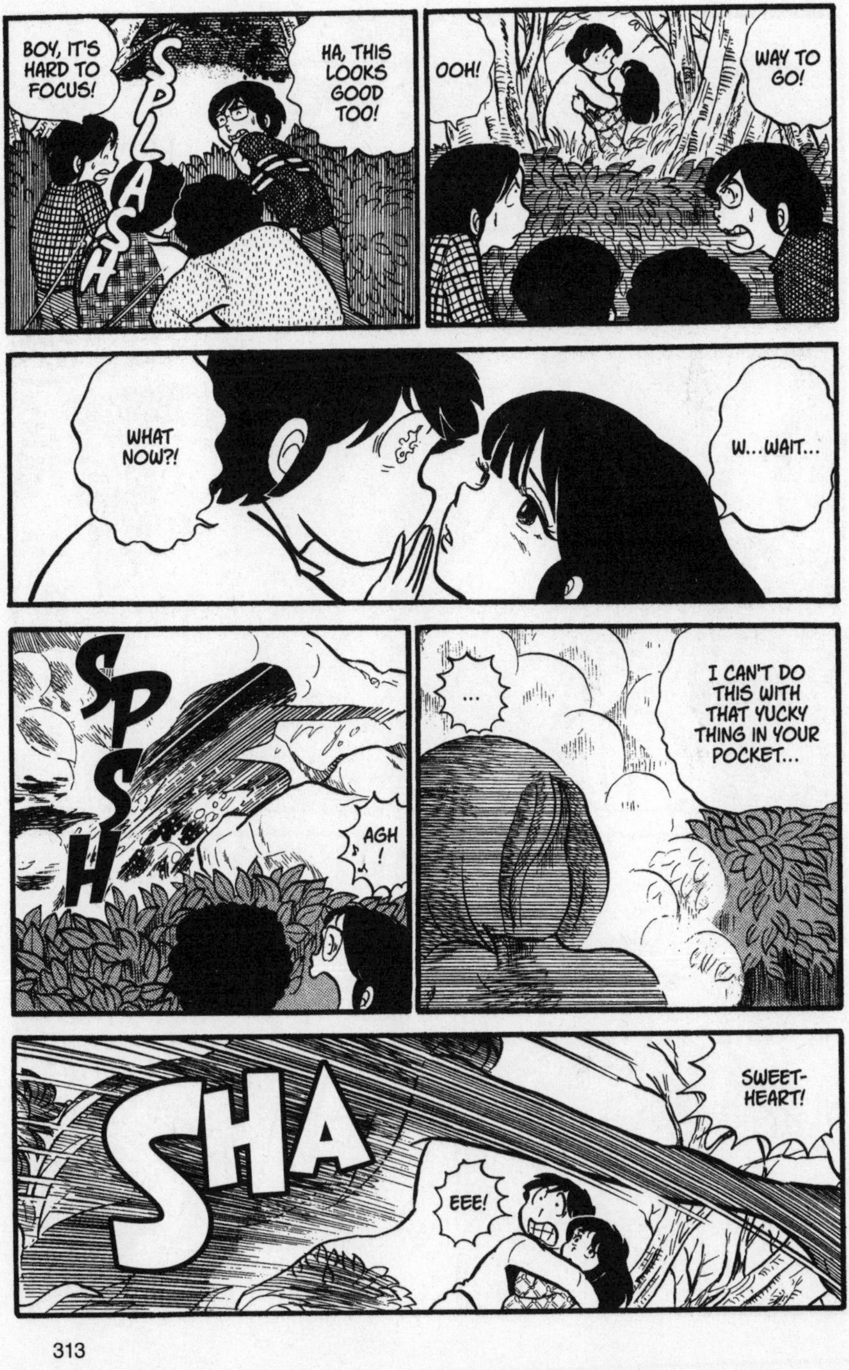
WAY TO GO!
OOH!
HA, THIS LOOKS GOOD TOO!
BOY, IT'S HARD TO FOCUS!
SPLASH
W...WAIT...
WHAT NOW?!
I CAN'T DO THIS WITH THAT YUCKY THING IN YOUR POCKET...
...
AGH!
SPSH
SWEET-HEART!
EEE!
SHA

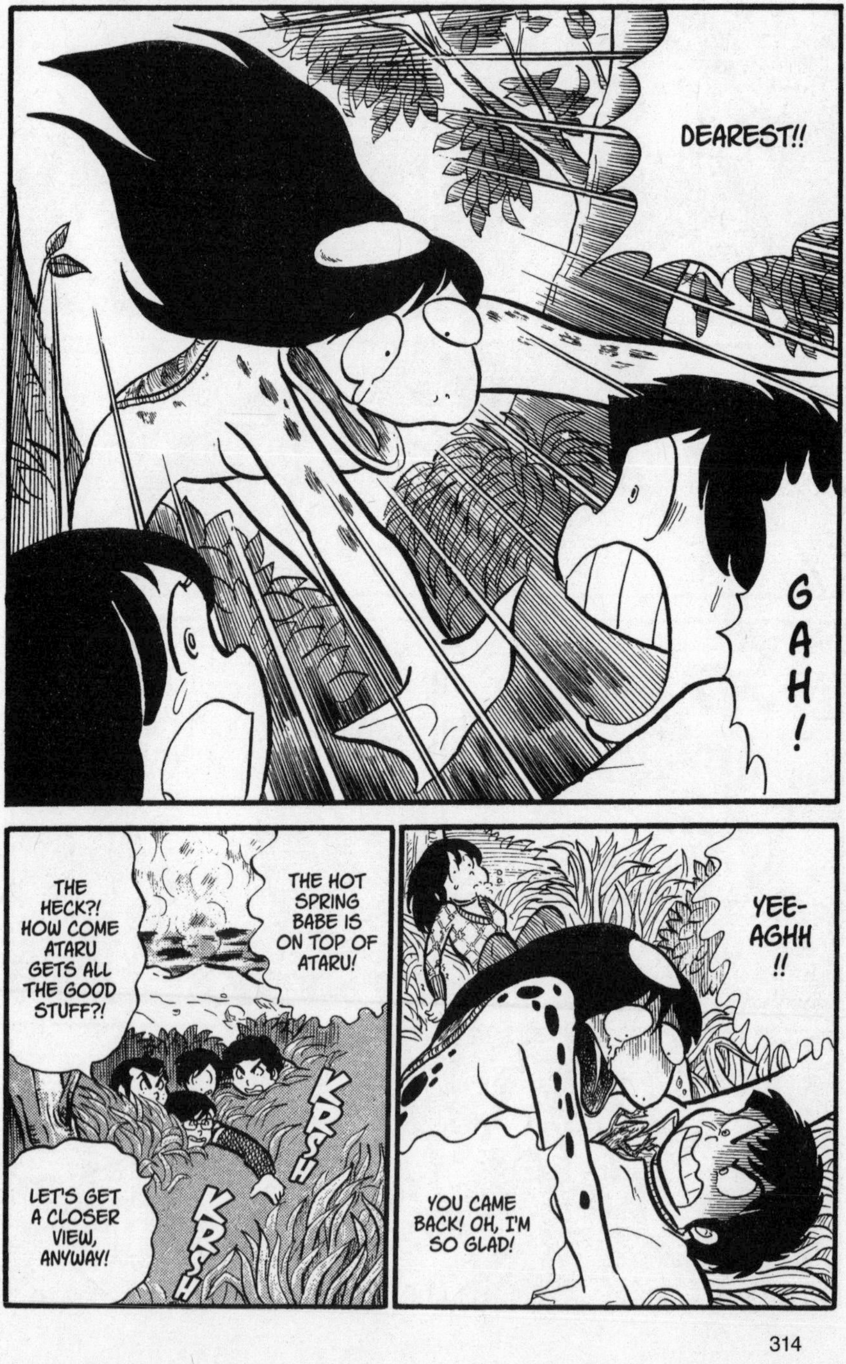
DEAREST!!
GAH!
YEE-AGHH!!
YOU CAME BACK! OH, I'M SO GLAD!
THE HOT SPRING BABE IS ON TOP OF ATARU!
THE HECK?! HOW COME ATARU GETS ALL THE GOOD STUFF?!
KRSH
KRSH
LET'S GET A CLOSER VIEW, ANYWAY!

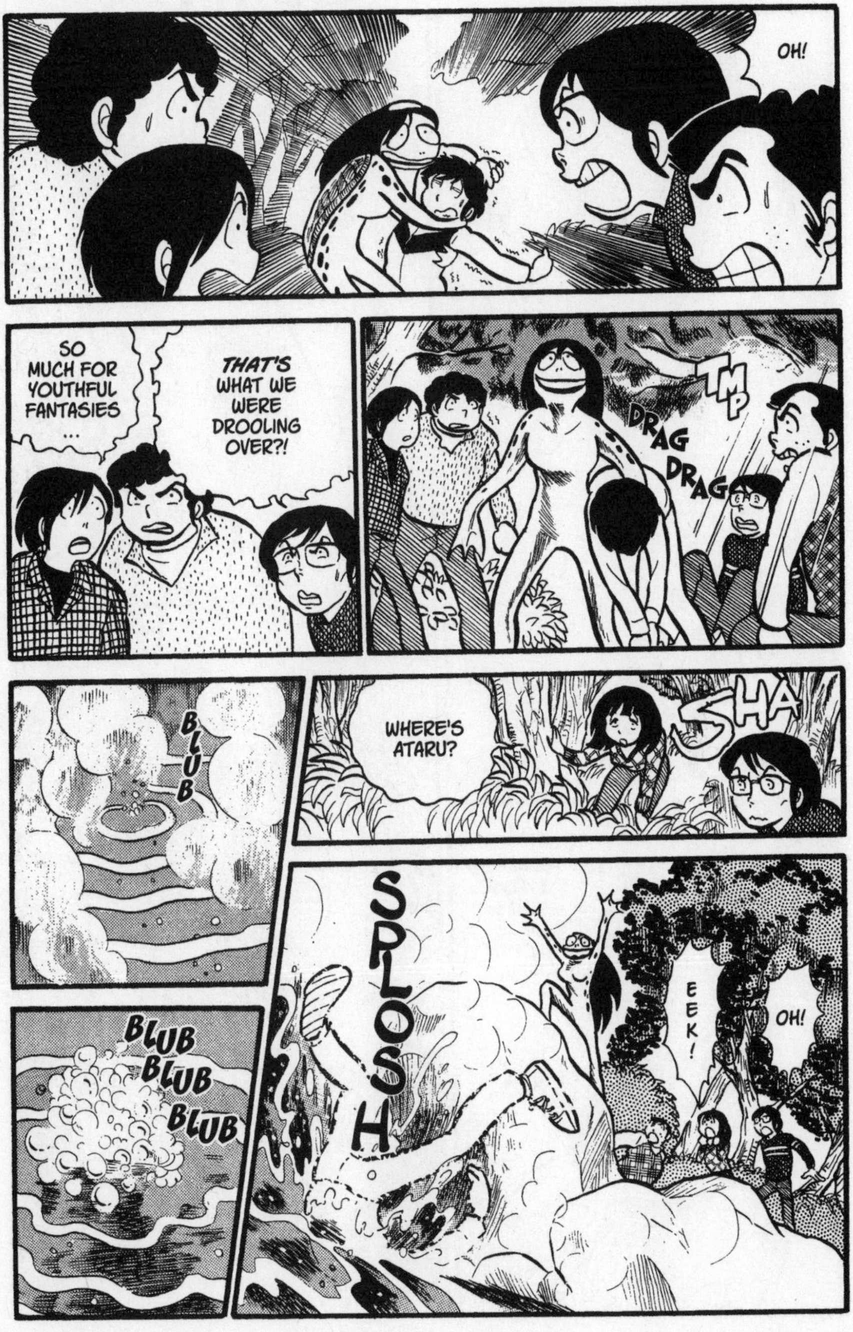
OH!
TMP
DRAG DRAG
THAT'S WHAT WE WERE DROOLING OVER?!
SO MUCH FOR YOUTHFUL FANTASIES ...
SHA
WHERE'S ATARU?
BLUB
BLUB BLUB BLUB
SPLOSH
OH!
EEK!

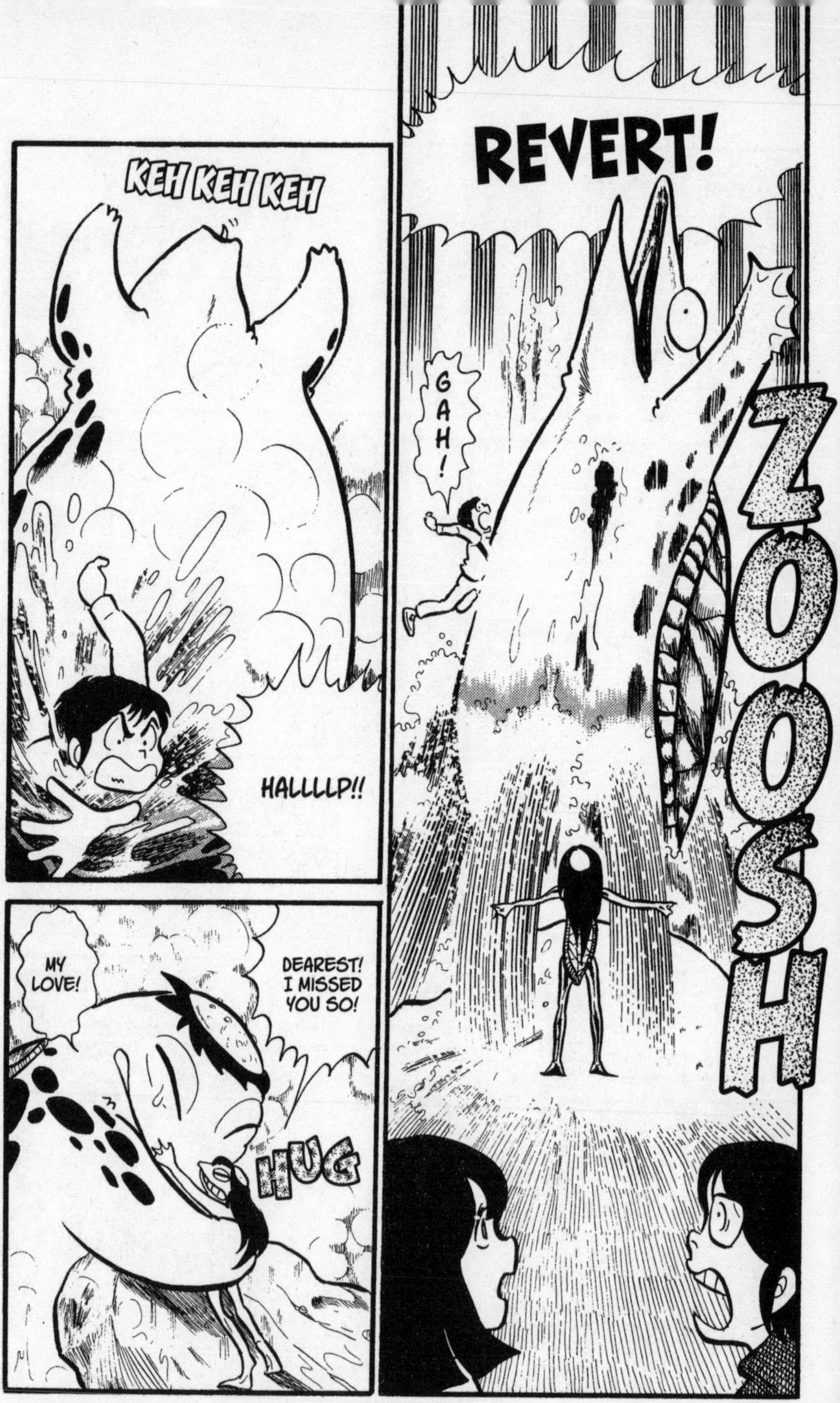
REVERT!
GAH!
ZOOSH
KEH KEH KEH
HALLLLP!!
DEAREST! I MISSED YOU SO!
MY LOVE!
HUG

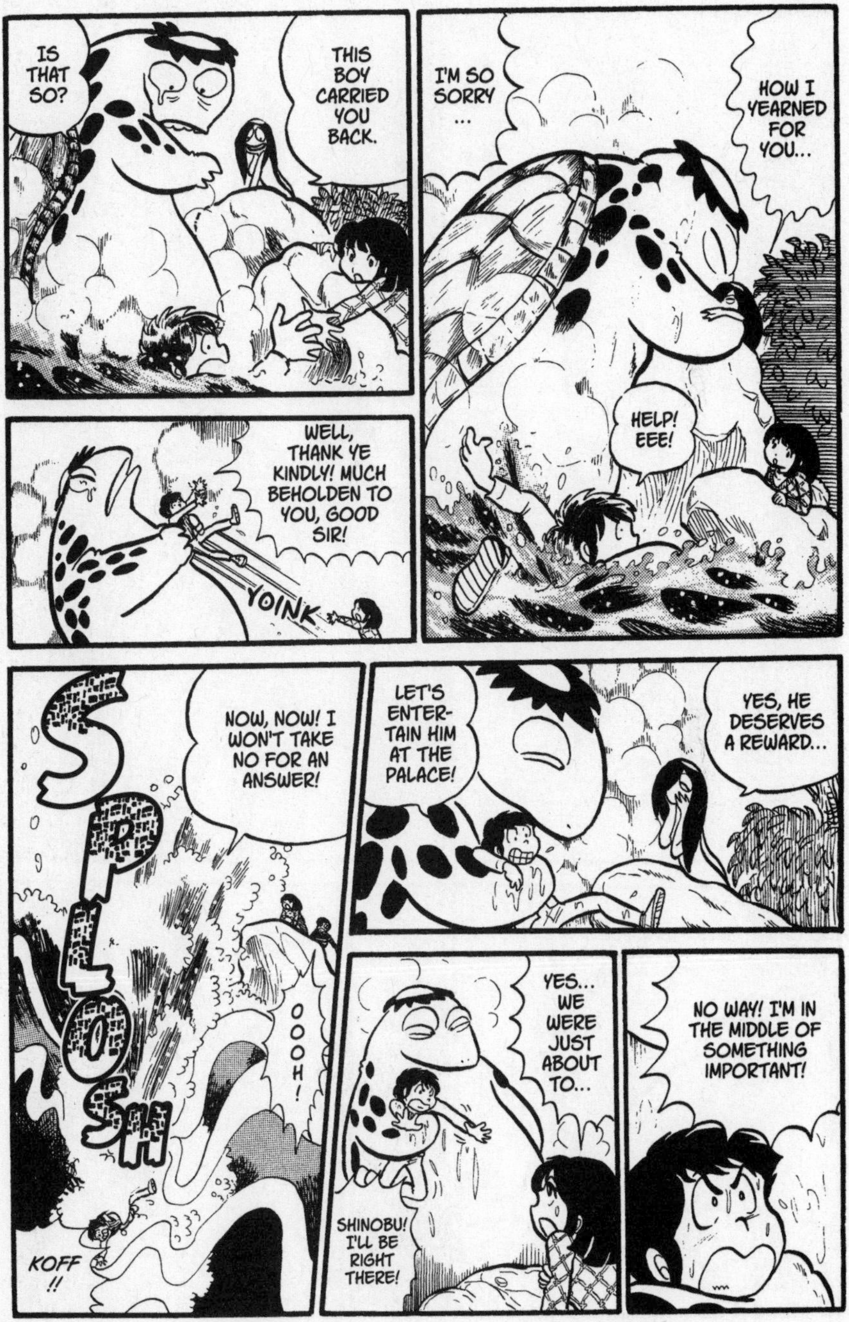
HOW I YEARNED FOR YOU...
I'M SO SORRY ...
HELP! EEE!
THIS BOY CARRIED YOU BACK.
IS THAT SO?
WELL, THANK YE KINDLY! MUCH BEHOLDEN TO YOU, GOOD SIR!
YOINK
YES, HE DESERVES A REWARD...
LET'S ENTER-TAIN HIM AT THE PALACE!
NO WAY! I'M IN THE MIDDLE OF SOMETHING IMPORTANT!
YES... WE WERE JUST ABOUT TO...
SHINOBU! I'LL BE RIGHT THERE!
NOW, NOW! I WON'T TAKE NO FOR AN ANSWER!
SPLOOSH
OOOOH!
KOFF !!

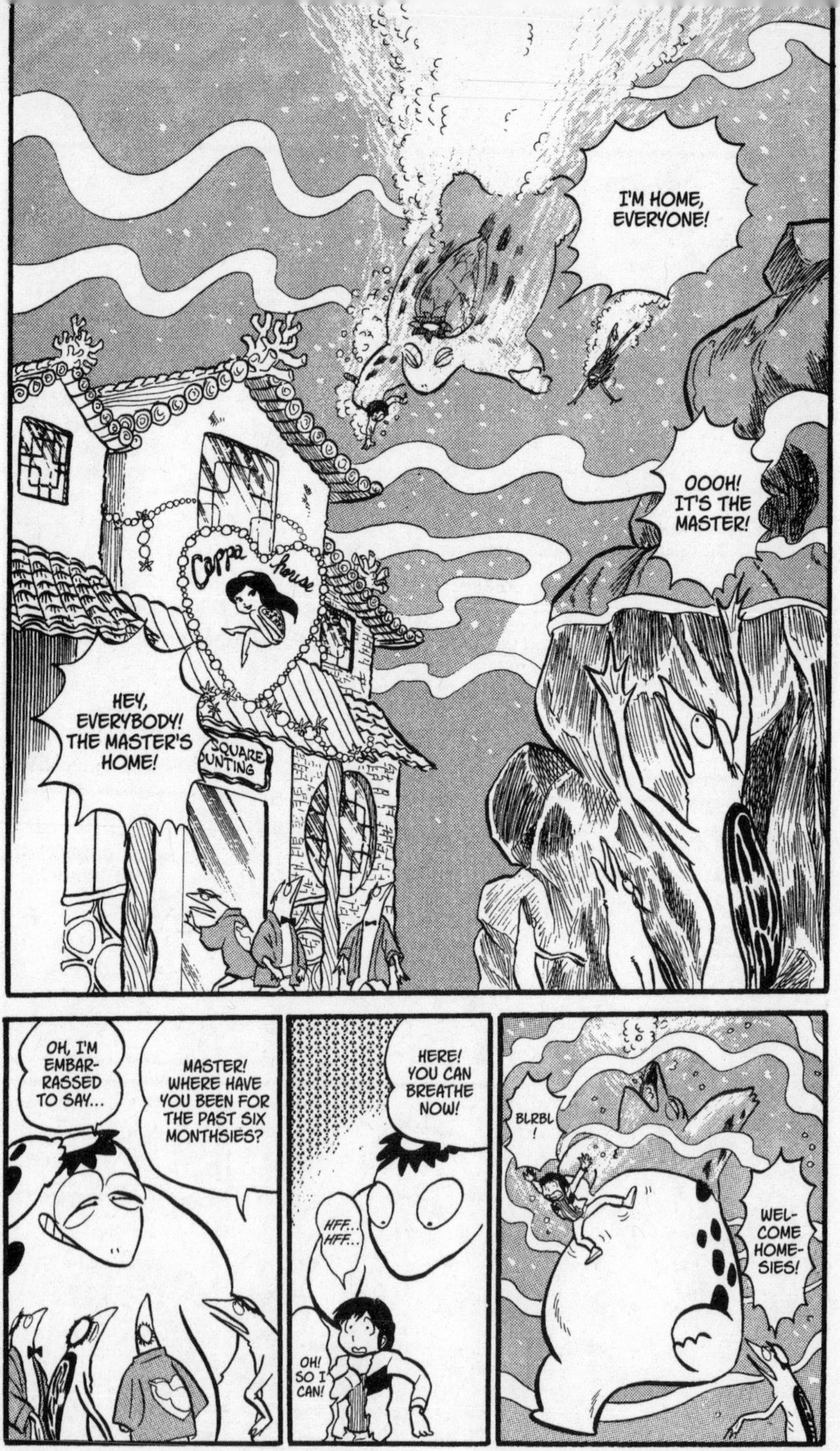
I'M HOME, EVERYONE!
OOOH! IT'S THE MASTER!
Cappa house
HEY, EVERYBODY! THE MASTER'S HOME!
BLRBL!
WEL-COME HOME-SIES!
HERE! YOU CAN BREATHE NOW!
HFF... HFF...
OH! SO I CAN!
MASTER! WHERE HAVE YOU BEEN FOR THE PAST SIX MONTHSIES?
OH, I'M EMBAR-RASSED TO SAY...

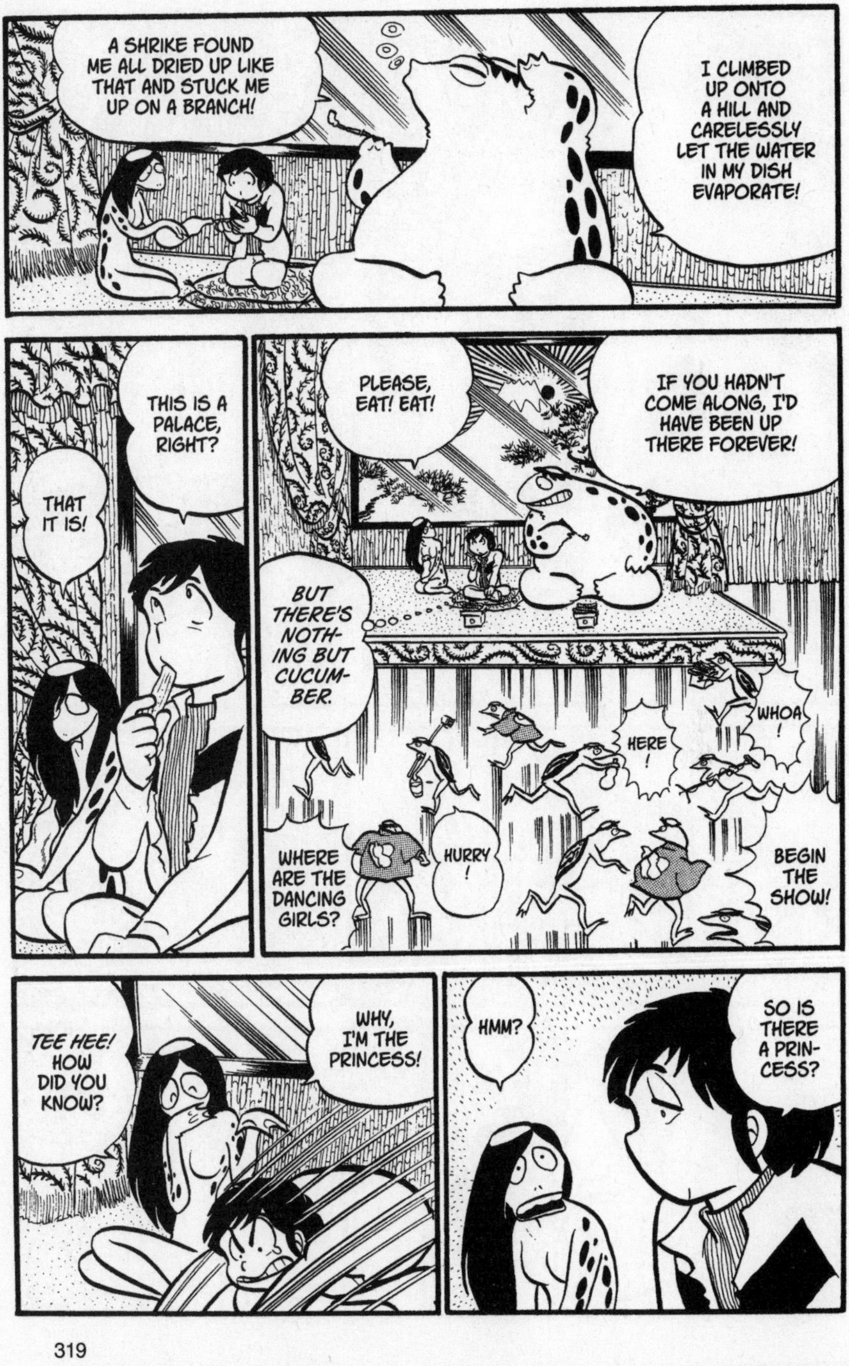
I CLIMBED UP ONTO A HILL AND CARELESSLY LET THE WATER IN MY DISH EVAPORATE!
A SHRIKE FOUND ME ALL DRIED UP LIKE THAT AND STUCK ME UP ON A BRANCH!
IF YOU HADN'T COME ALONG, I'D HAVE BEEN UP THERE FOREVER!
PLEASE, EAT! EAT!
BUT THERE'S NOTHING BUT CUCUMBER.
WHOA!
HERE!
BEGIN THE SHOW!
HURRY!
WHERE ARE THE DANCING GIRLS?
THIS IS A PALACE, RIGHT?
THAT IT IS!
SO IS THERE A PRINCESS?
HMM?
WHY, I'M THE PRINCESS!
TEE HEE! HOW DID YOU KNOW?

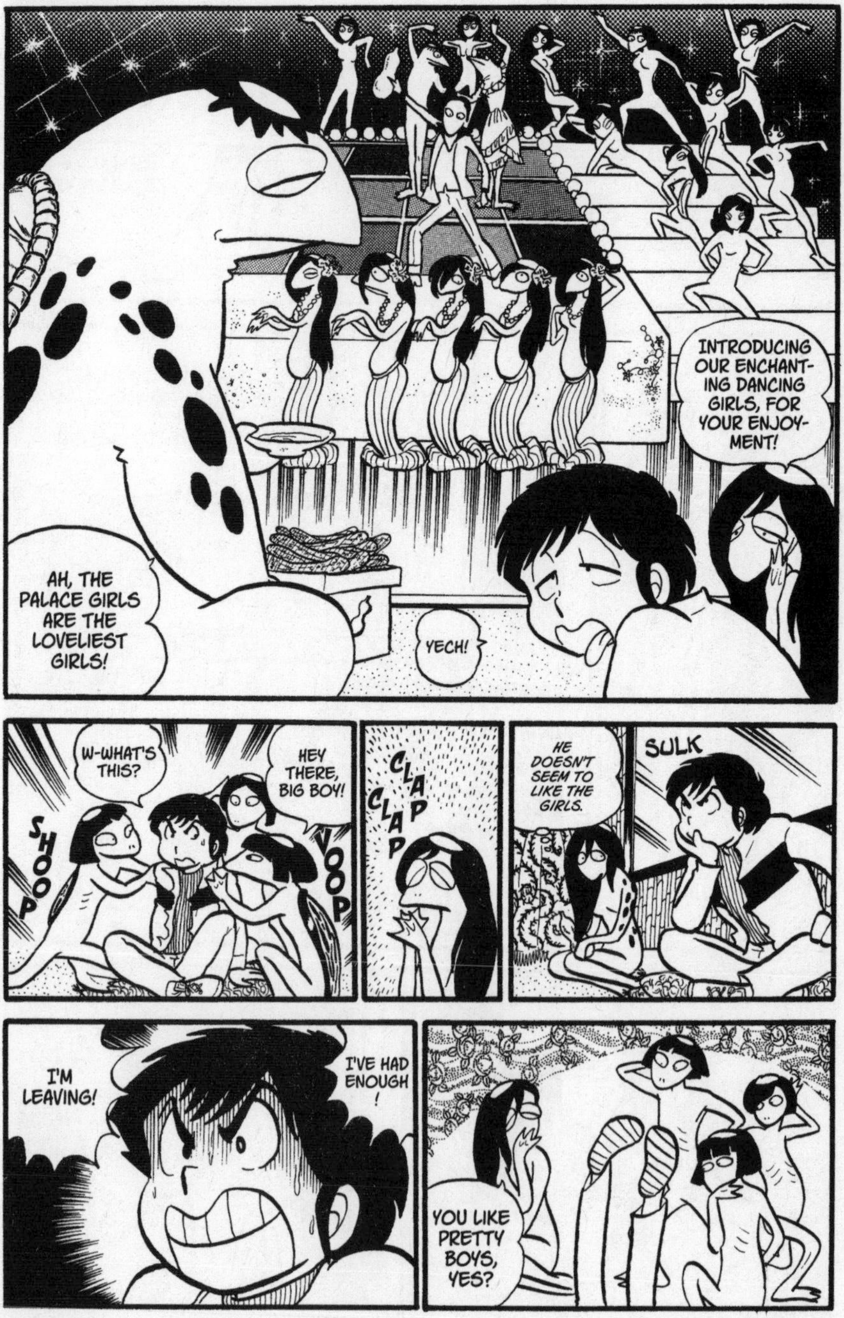
INTRODUCING OUR ENCHANTING DANCING GIRLS, FOR YOUR ENJOYMENT!
AH, THE PALACE GIRLS ARE THE LOVELIEST GIRLS!
YECH!
SULK
HE DOESN'T SEEM TO LIKE THE GIRLS.
CLAP CLAP
HEY THERE, BIG BOY!
VOOP
W-WHAT'S THIS?
SHOOP
YOU LIKE PRETTY BOYS, YES?
I'VE HAD ENOUGH!
I'M LEAVING!

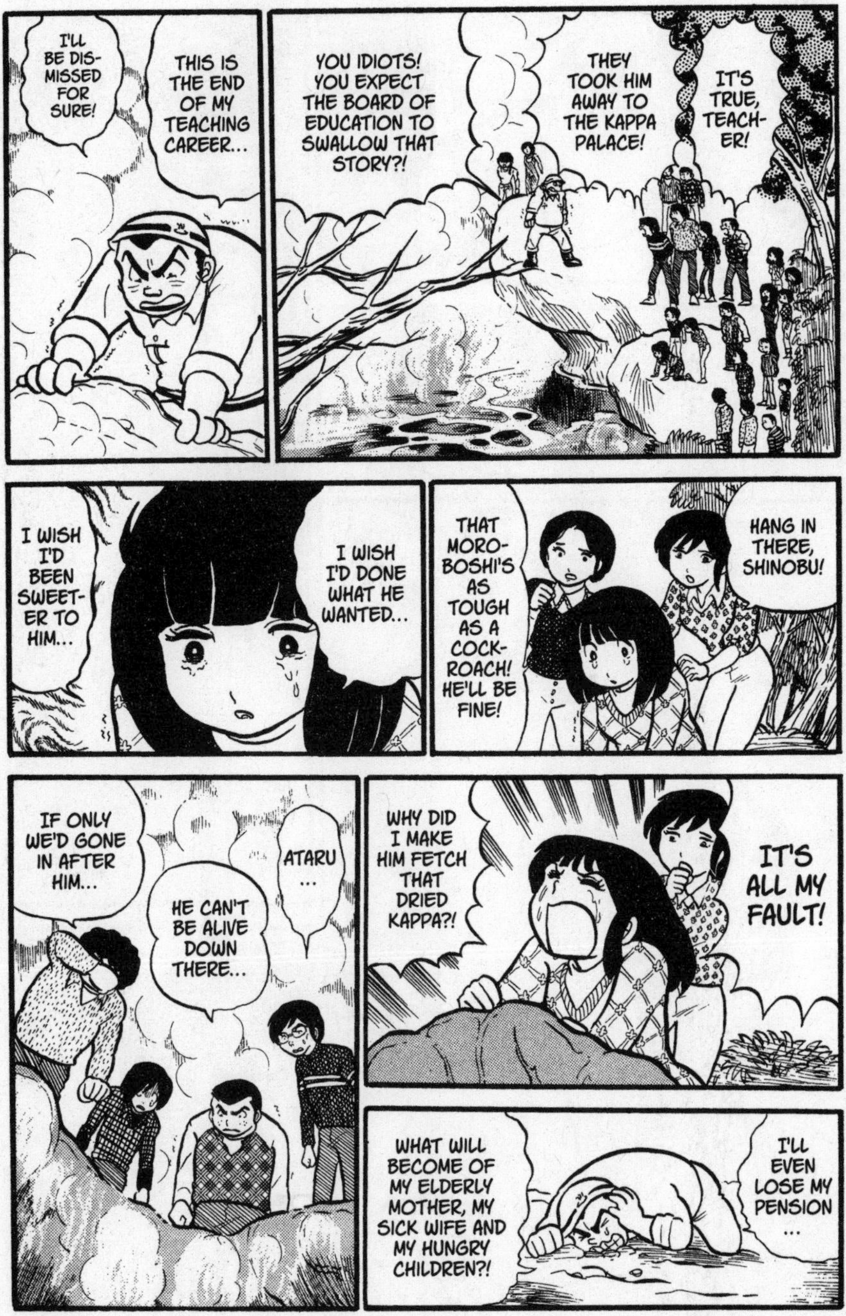
IT'S TRUE, TEACHER!
THEY TOOK HIM AWAY TO THE KAPPA PALACE!
YOU IDIOTS! YOU EXPECT THE BOARD OF EDUCATION TO SWALLOW THAT STORY?!
THIS IS THE END OF MY TEACHING CAREER...
I'LL BE DIS-MISSED FOR SURE!
HANG IN THERE, SHINOBU!
THAT MORO-BOSHI'S AS TOUGH AS A COCK-ROACH! HE'LL BE FINE!
I WISH I'D DONE WHAT HE WANTED...
I WISH I'D BEEN SWEET-ER TO HIM...
IT'S ALL MY FAULT!
WHY DID I MAKE HIM FETCH THAT DRIED KAPPA?!
I'LL EVEN LOSE MY PENSION ...
WHAT WILL BECOME OF MY ELDERLY MOTHER, MY SICK WIFE AND MY HUNGRY CHILDREN?!
ATARU ...
HE CAN'T BE ALIVE DOWN THERE...
IF ONLY WE'D GONE IN AFTER HIM...

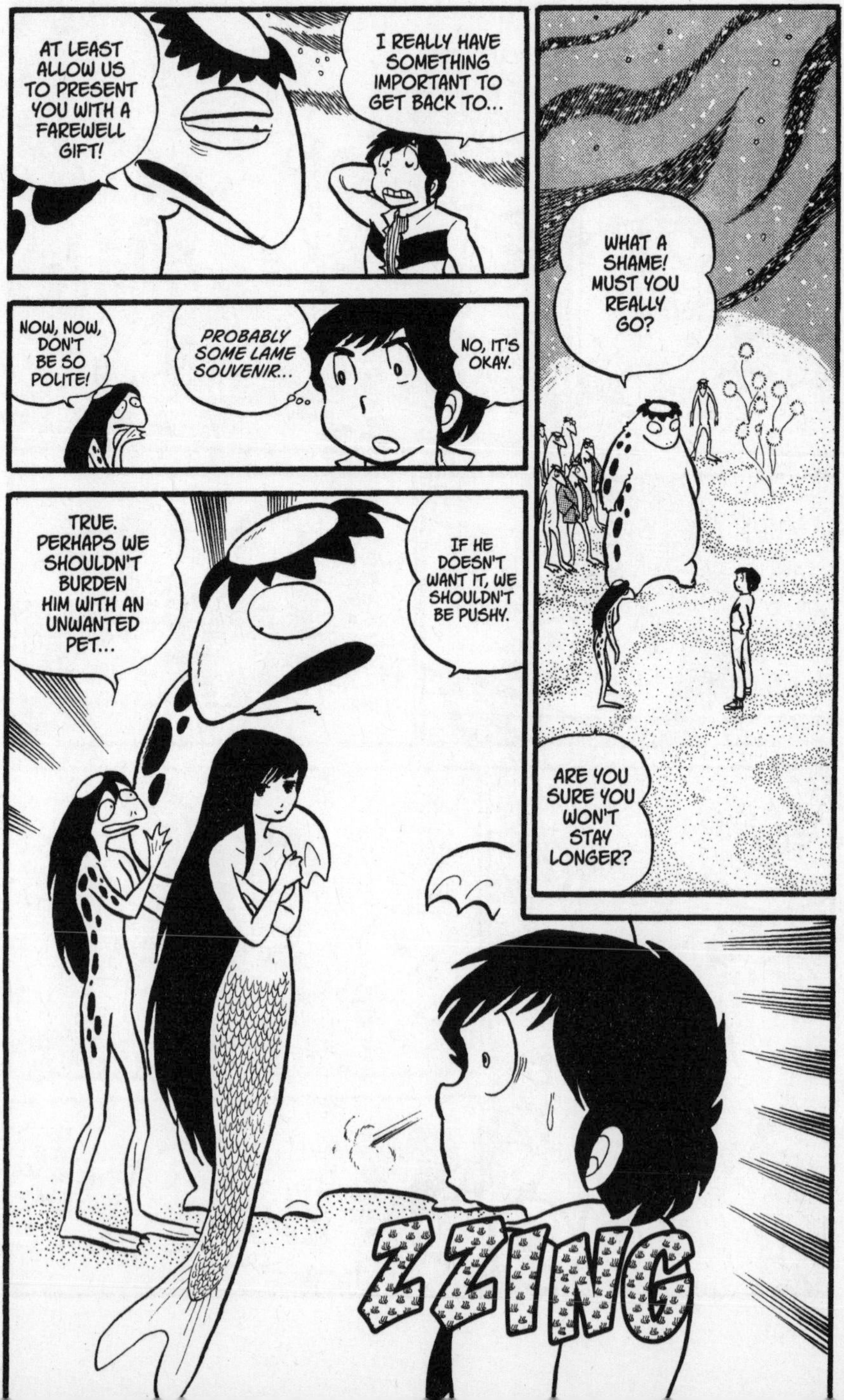
WHAT A SHAME! MUST YOU REALLY GO?
ARE YOU SURE YOU WON'T STAY LONGER?
I REALLY HAVE SOMETHING IMPORTANT TO GET BACK TO...
AT LEAST ALLOW US TO PRESENT YOU WITH A FAREWELL GIFT!
NO, IT'S OKAY.
PROBABLY SOME LAME SOUVENIR...
NOW, NOW, DON'T BE SO POLITE!
IF HE DOESN'T WANT IT, WE SHOULDN'T BE PUSHY.
TRUE. PERHAPS WE SHOULDN'T BURDEN HIM WITH AN UNWANTED PET...
ZZING

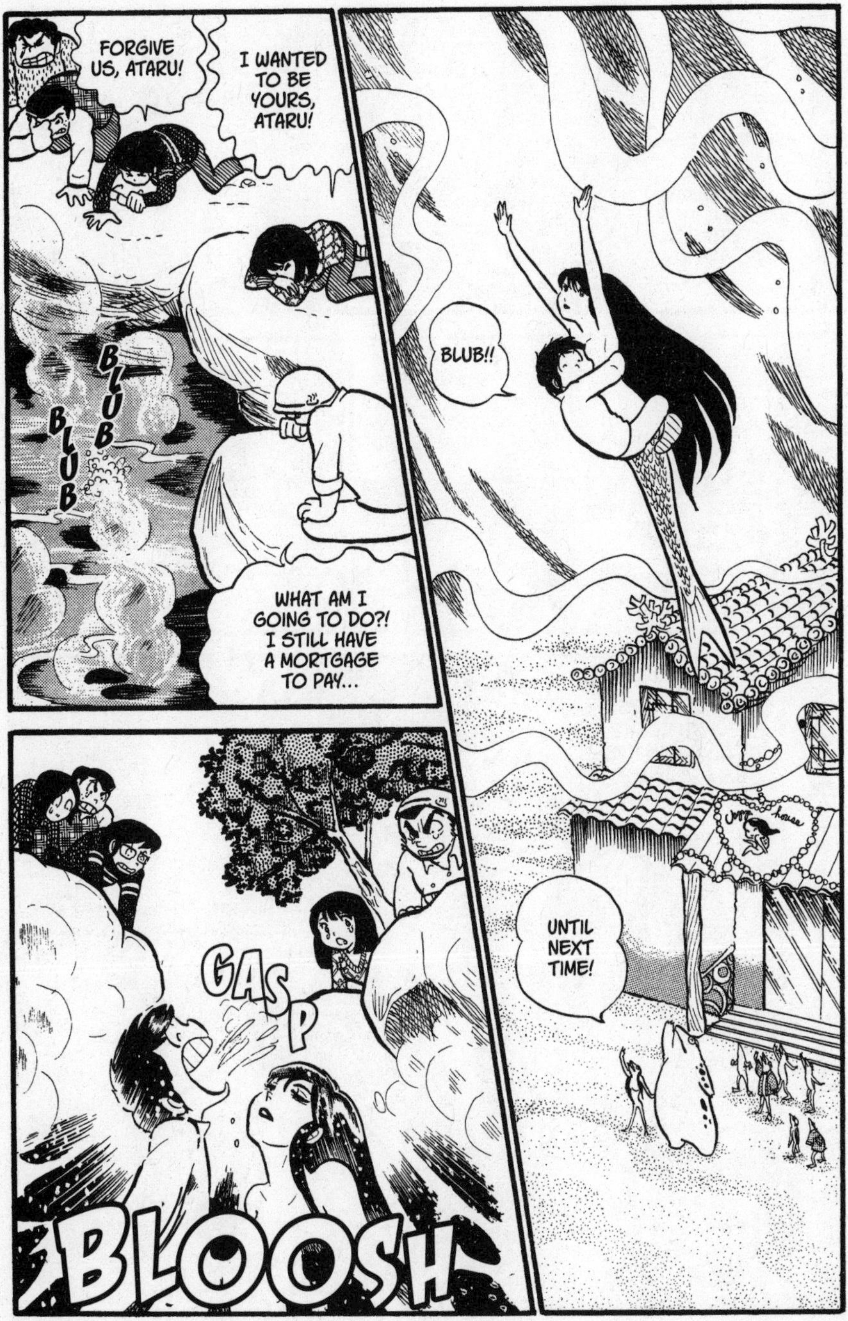
BLUB!!
UNTIL NEXT TIME!
FORGIVE US, ATARU!
I WANTED TO BE YOURS, ATARU!
BLUB BLUB
WHAT AM I GOING TO DO?! I STILL HAVE A MORTGAGE TO PAY...
GASP
BLOOSH

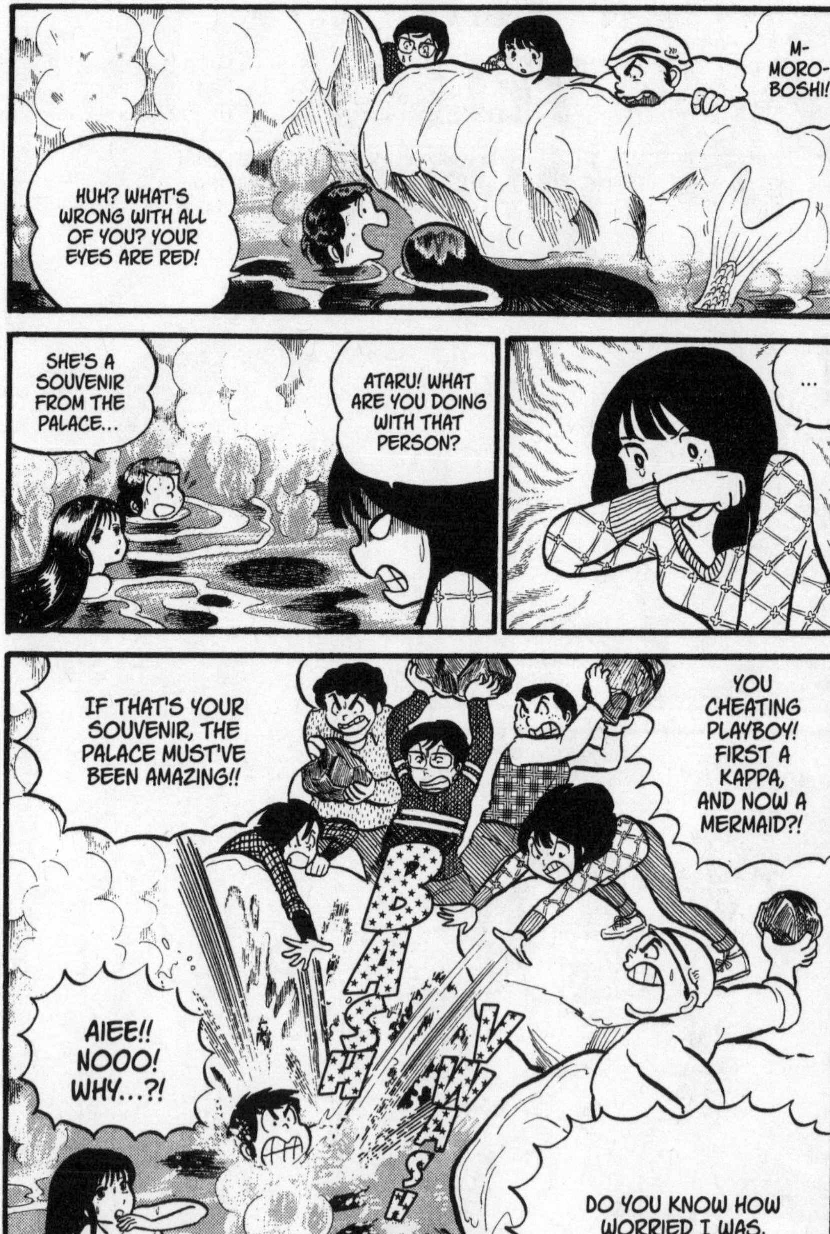
M-MORO-BOSHI!
HUH? WHAT'S WRONG WITH ALL OF YOU? YOUR EYES ARE RED!
...
ATARU! WHAT ARE YOU DOING WITH THAT PERSON?
SHE'S A SOUVENIR FROM THE PALACE...
YOU CHEATING PLAYBOY! FIRST A KAPPA, AND NOW A MERMAID?!
IF THAT'S YOUR SOUVENIR, THE PALACE MUST'VE BEEN AMAZING!!
BASH
AIEE!! NOOO! WHY...?!
DO YOU KNOW HOW WORRIED I WAS, YOU LITTLE...?!

CHAPTER 15: THE YELLOW RIBBON OF HAPPINESS

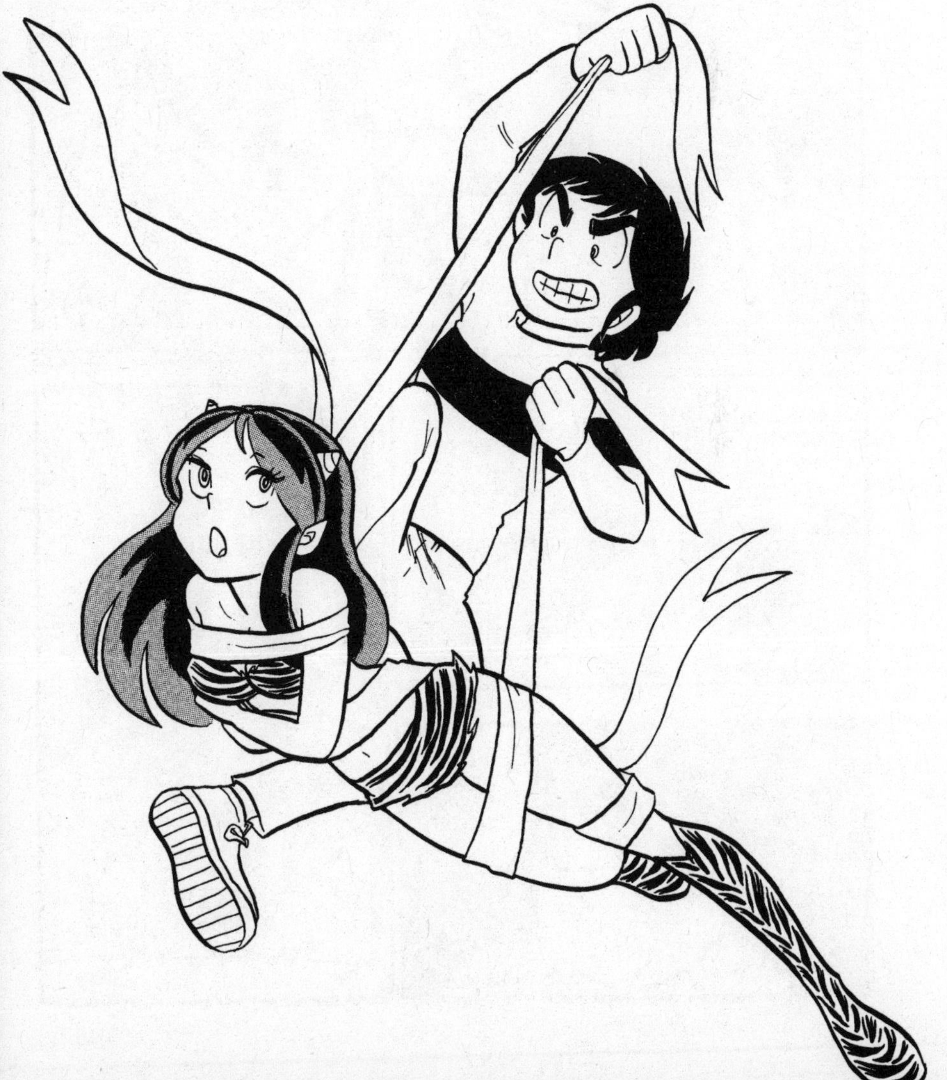

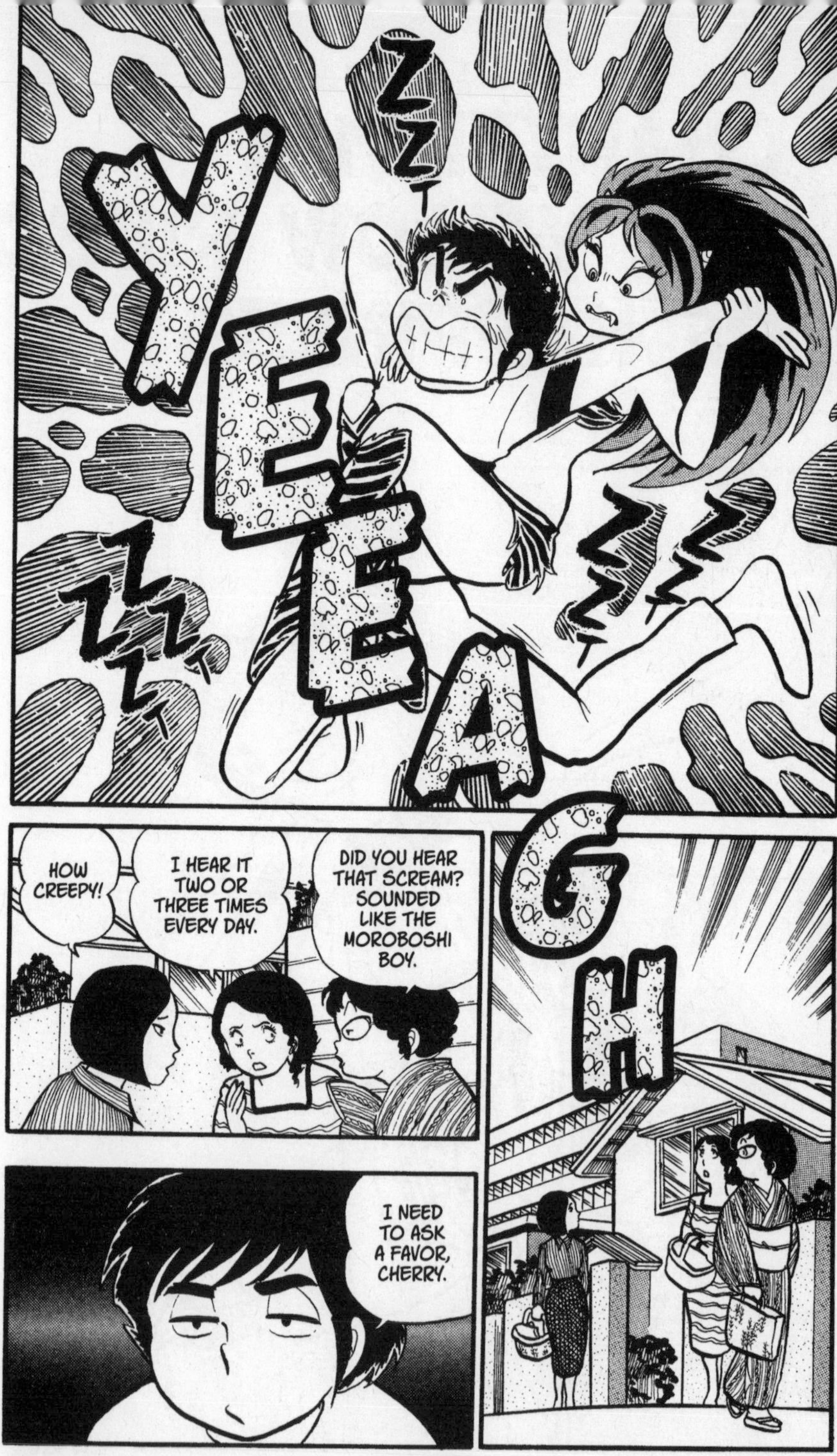
ZZZ
YEEAAGH
ZZZZ
DID YOU HEAR THAT SCREAM? SOUNDED LIKE THE MOROBOSHI BOY.
I HEAR IT TWO OR THREE TIMES EVERY DAY.
HOW CREEPY!
I NEED TO ASK A FAVOR, CHERRY.

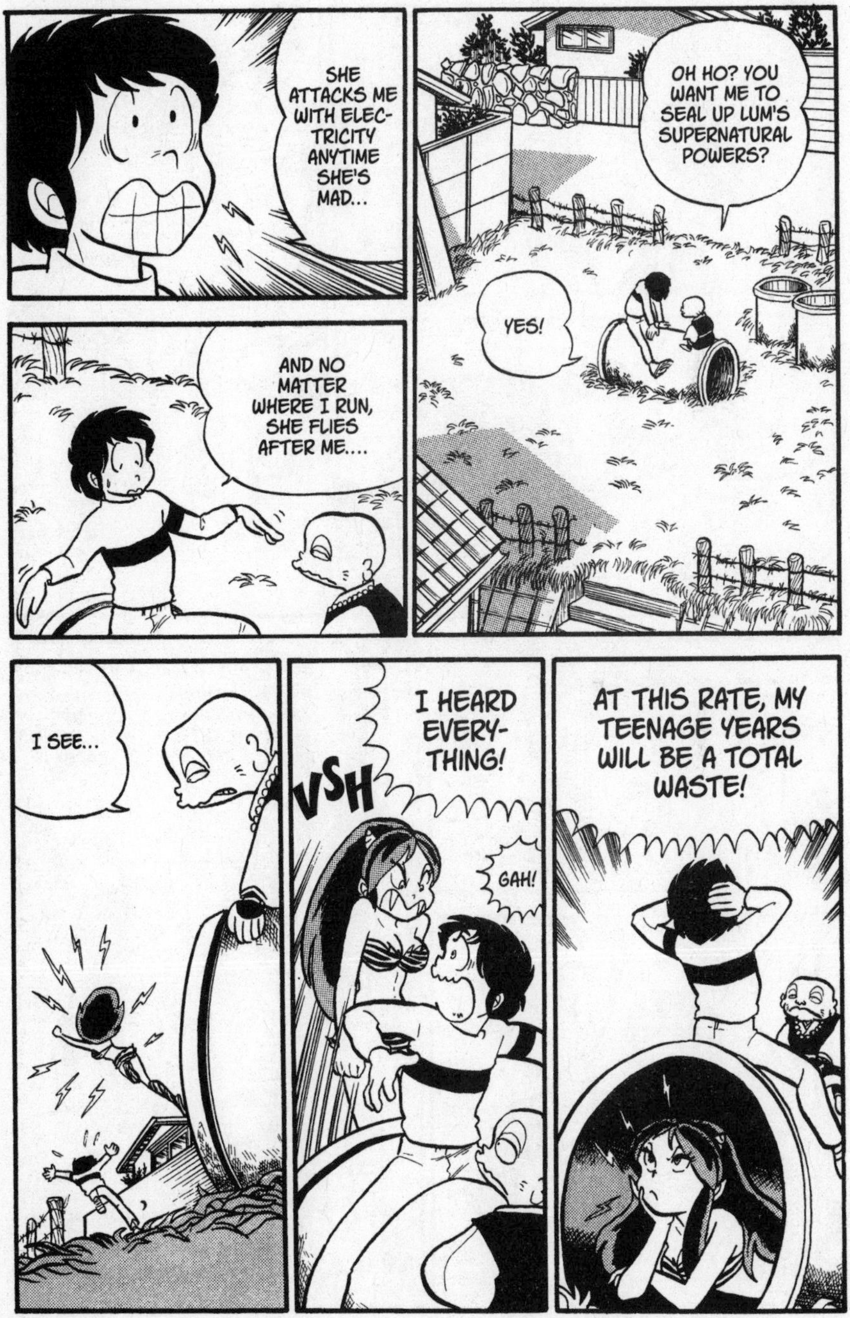
OH HO? YOU WANT ME TO SEAL UP LUM'S SUPERNATURAL POWERS?
YES!
SHE ATTACKS ME WITH ELEC-TRICITY ANYTIME SHE'S MAD...
AND NO MATTER WHERE I RUN, SHE FLIES AFTER ME....
AT THIS RATE, MY TEENAGE YEARS WILL BE A TOTAL WASTE!
I HEARD EVERY-THING!
VSH
GAH!
I SEE...

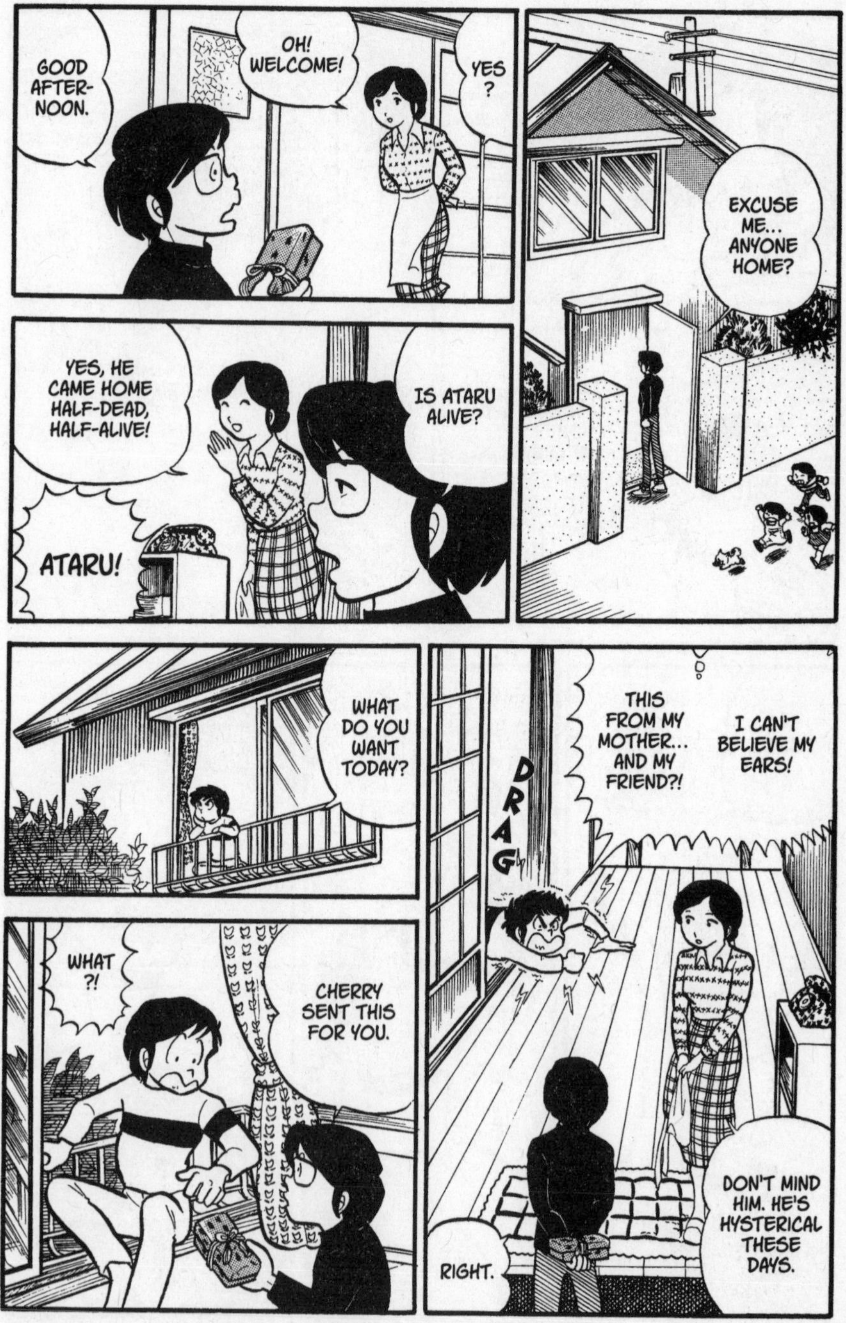
EXCUSE ME... ANYONE HOME?
YES ?
OH! WELCOME!
GOOD AFTER-NOON.
IS ATARU ALIVE?
YES, HE CAME HOME HALF-DEAD, HALF-ALIVE!
ATARU!
I CAN'T BELIEVE MY EARS!
THIS FROM MY MOTHER... AND MY FRIEND?!
DRAG
DON'T MIND HIM. HE'S HYSTERICAL THESE DAYS.
RIGHT.
WHAT DO YOU WANT TODAY?
CHERRY SENT THIS FOR YOU.
WHAT ?!

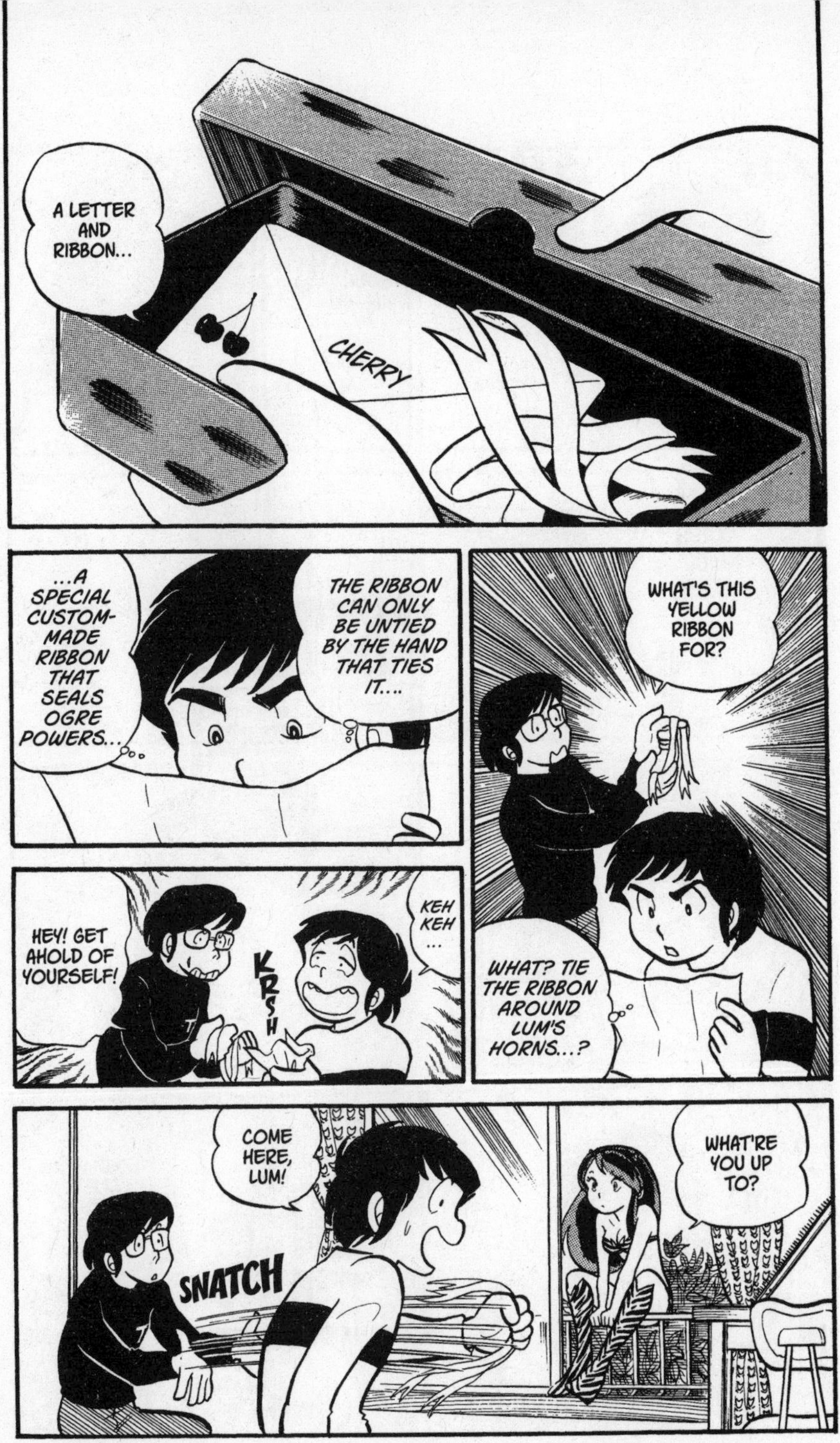
A LETTER AND RIBBON...
CHERRY
WHAT'S THIS YELLOW RIBBON FOR?
WHAT? TIE THE RIBBON AROUND LUM'S HORNS...?
THE RIBBON CAN ONLY BE UNTIED BY THE HAND THAT TIES IT....
...A SPECIAL CUSTOM-MADE RIBBON THAT SEALS OGRE POWERS...
KEH KEH ...
KRSH
HEY! GET AHOLD OF YOURSELF!
WHAT'RE YOU UP TO?
COME HERE, LUM!
SNATCH

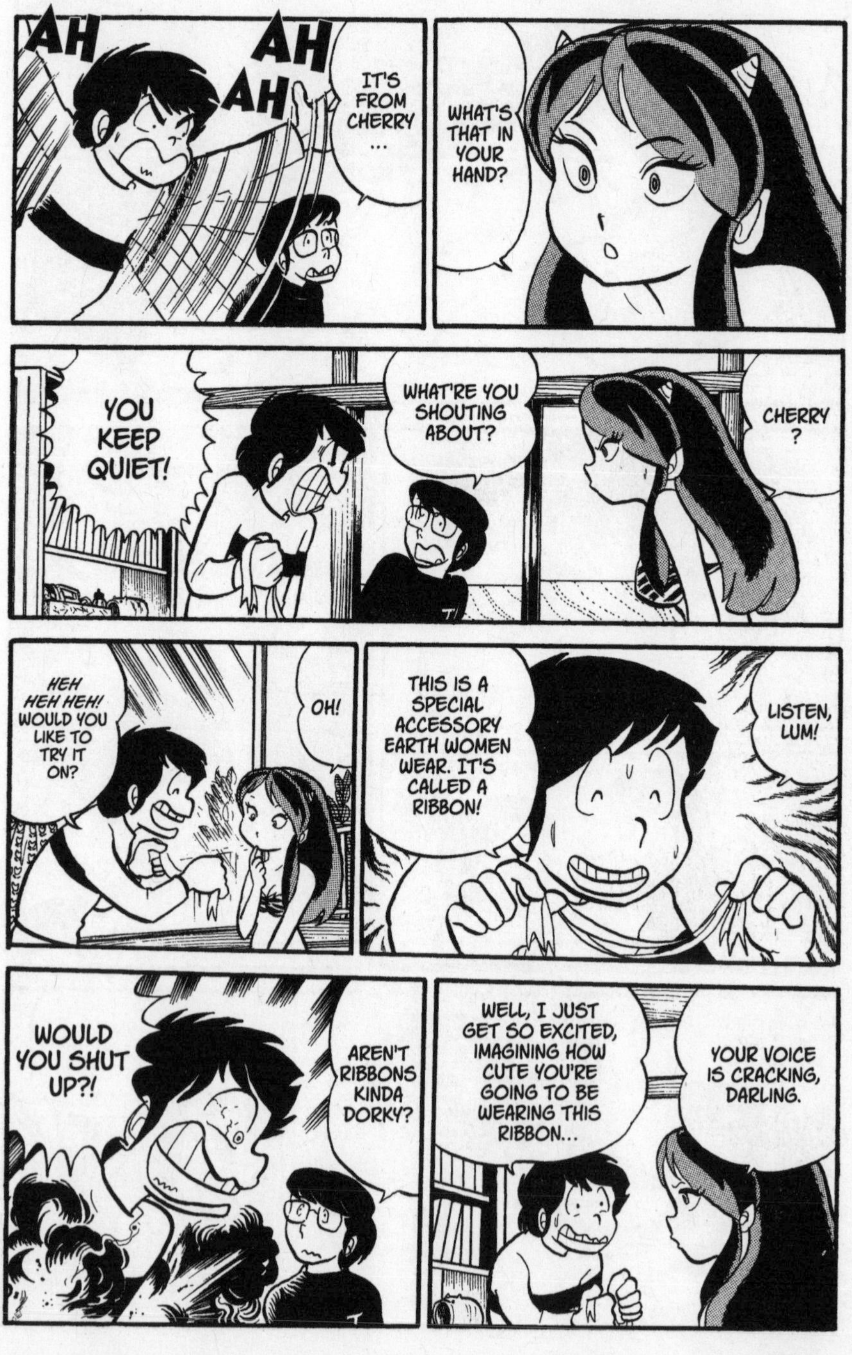
WHAT'S THAT IN YOUR HAND?
IT'S FROM CHERRY ...
AH
AH
AH
CHERRY ?
WHAT'RE YOU SHOUTING ABOUT?
YOU KEEP QUIET!
LISTEN, LUM!
THIS IS A SPECIAL ACCESSORY EARTH WOMEN WEAR. IT'S CALLED A RIBBON!
OH!
HEH HEH HEH! WOULD YOU LIKE TO TRY IT ON?
YOUR VOICE IS CRACKING, DARLING.
WELL, I JUST GET SO EXCITED, IMAGINING HOW CUTE YOU'RE GOING TO BE WEARING THIS RIBBON...
AREN'T RIBBONS KINDA DORKY?
WOULD YOU SHUT UP?!

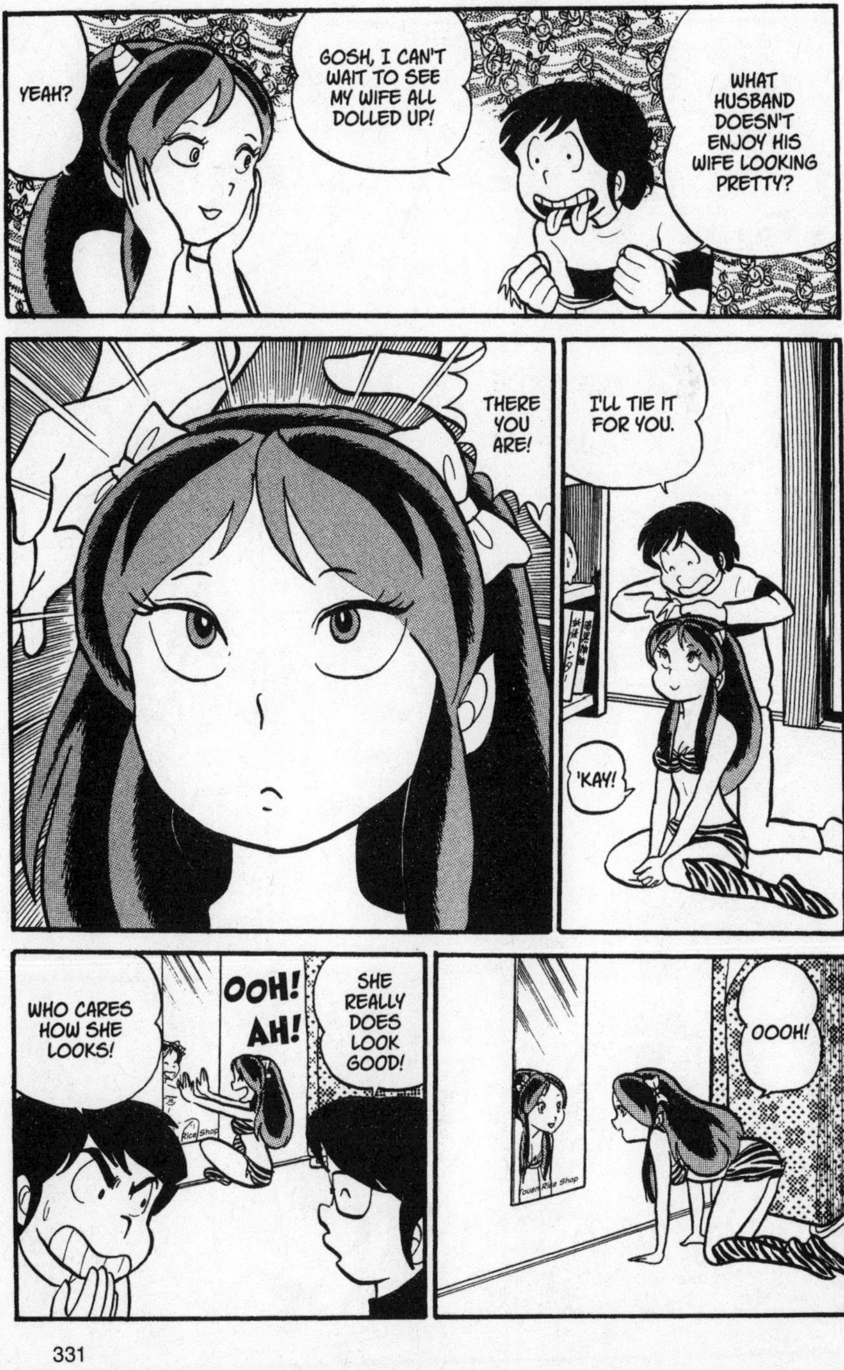
WHAT HUSBAND DOESN'T ENJOY HIS WIFE LOOKING PRETTY?
GOSH, I CAN'T WAIT TO SEE MY WIFE ALL DOLLED UP!
YEAH?
I'LL TIE IT FOR YOU.
'KAY!
THERE YOU ARE!
OOOH!
Touen Rice Shop
SHE REALLY DOES LOOK GOOD!
OOH! AH!
Rice Shop
WHO CARES HOW SHE LOOKS!

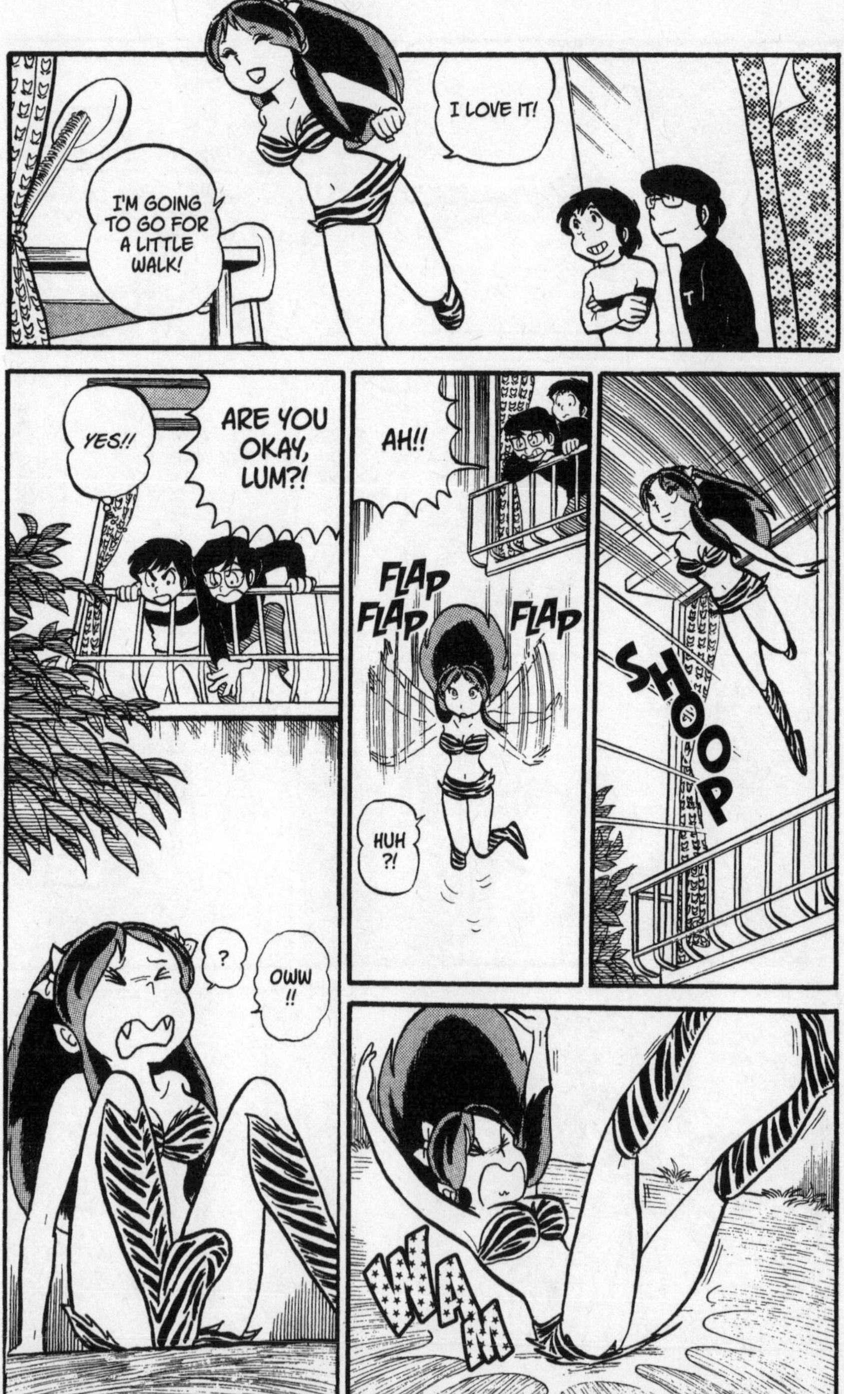
I LOVE IT!
I'M GOING TO GO FOR A LITTLE WALK!
SHOOP
AH!!
FLAP FLAP
FLAP
HUH ?!
WHAM
ARE YOU OKAY, LUM?!
YES!!
OWW !!
?

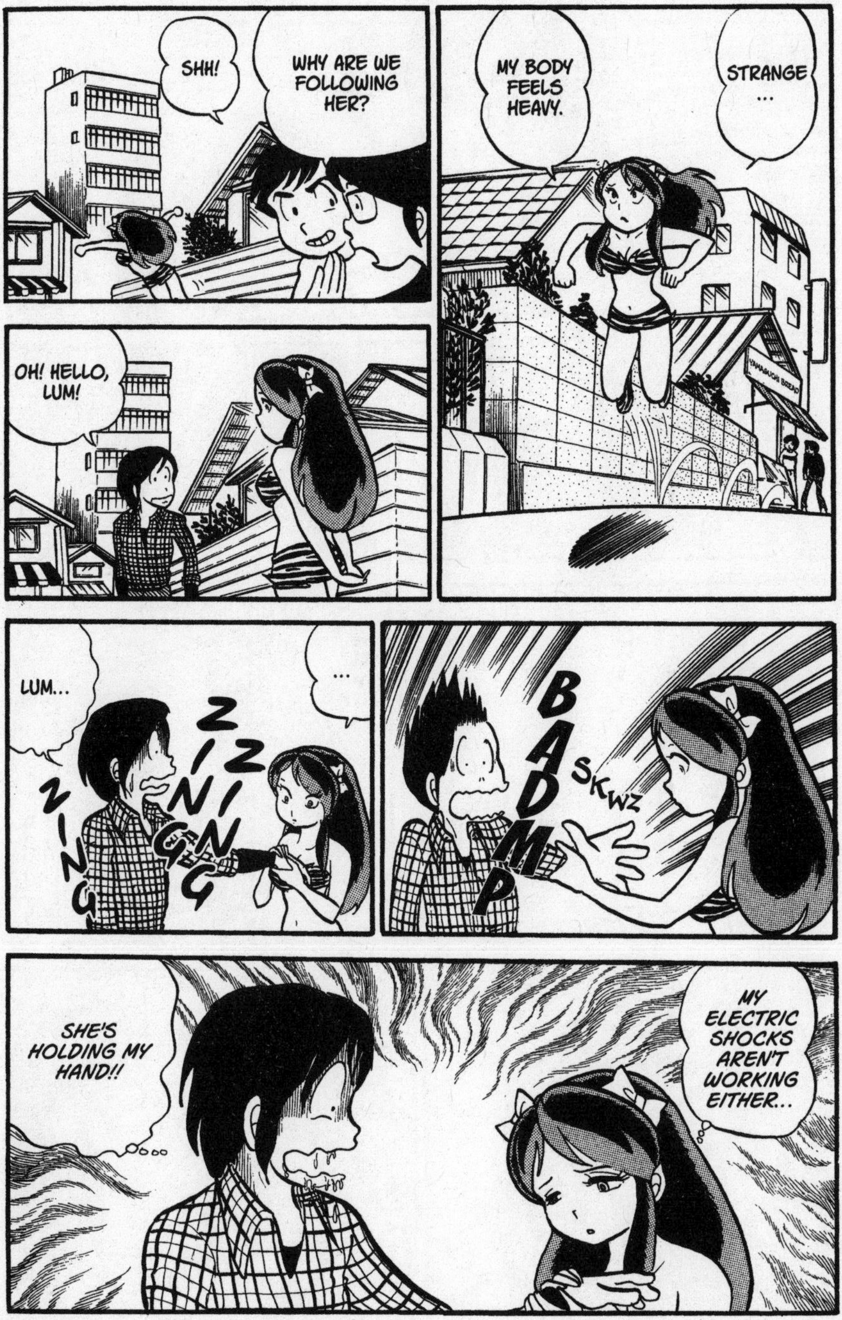
STRANGE ...
MY BODY FEELS HEAVY.
WHY ARE WE FOLLOWING HER?
SHH!
OH! HELLO, LUM!
BADMP
SKWZ
...
ZING
ZING
LUM...
ZING
MY ELECTRIC SHOCKS AREN'T WORKING EITHER...
SHE'S HOLDING MY HAND!!

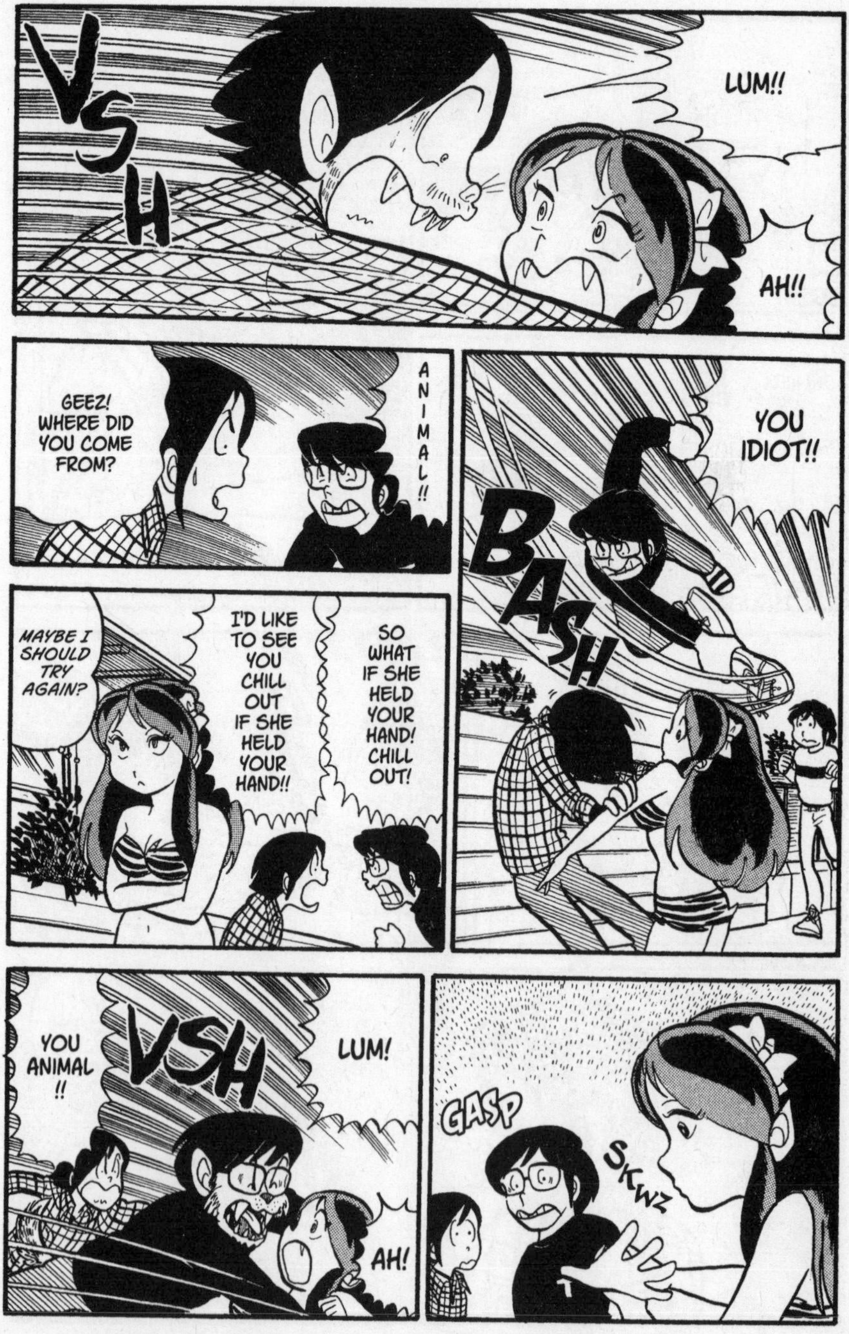
LUM!!
VSH
AH!!
YOU IDIOT!!
BASH
ANIMAL!!
GEEZ! WHERE DID YOU COME FROM?
SO WHAT IF SHE HELD YOUR HAND! CHILL OUT!
I'D LIKE TO SEE YOU CHILL OUT IF SHE HELD YOUR HAND!!
MAYBE I SHOULD TRY AGAIN?
SKWZ
GASP
LUM!
VSH
YOU ANIMAL !!
AH!

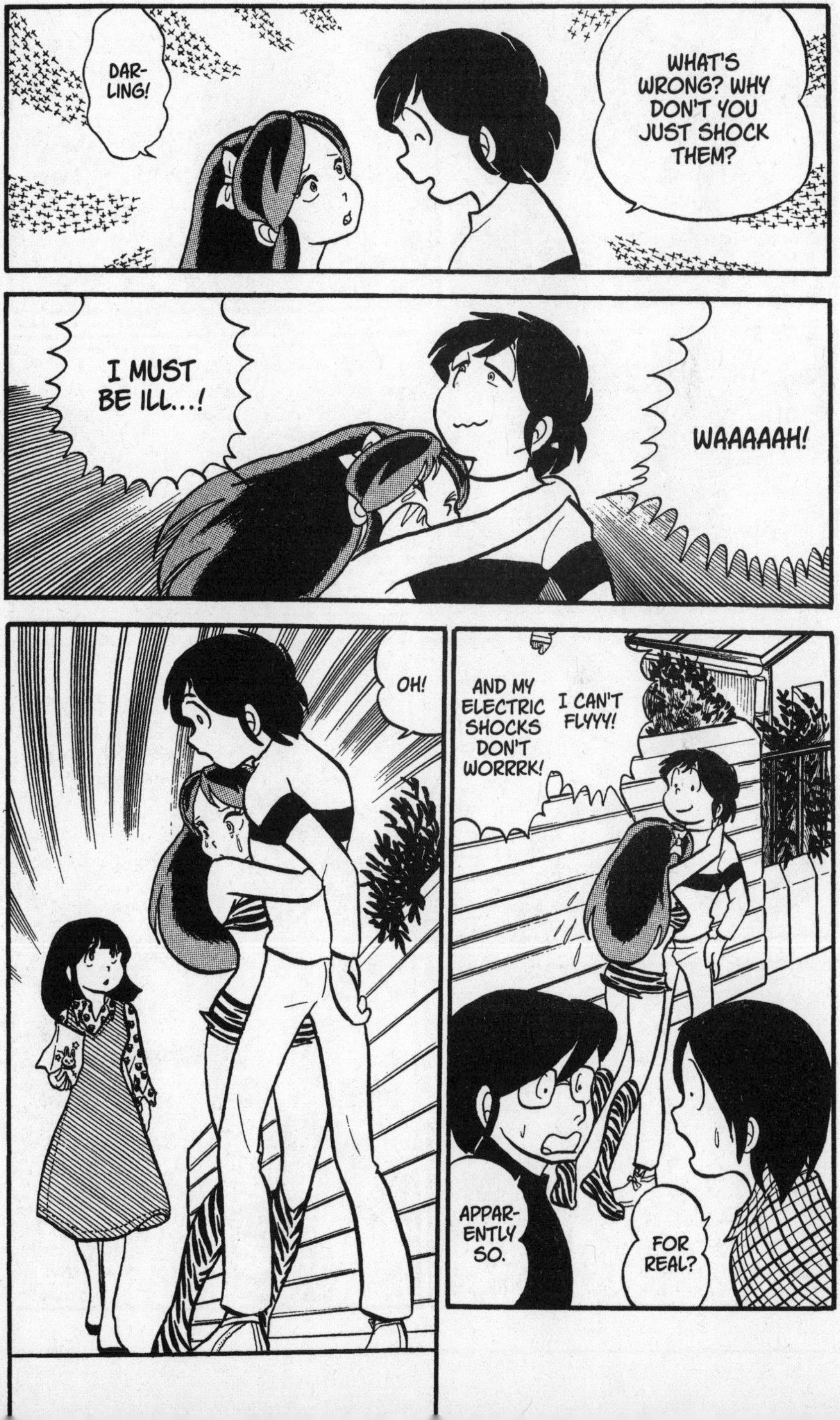
WHAT'S WRONG? WHY DON'T YOU JUST SHOCK THEM?
DAR-LING!
WAAAAAH!
I MUST BE ILL...!
I CAN'T FLYYY!
AND MY ELECTRIC SHOCKS DON'T WORRRK!
FOR REAL?
APPAR-ENTLY SO.
OH!

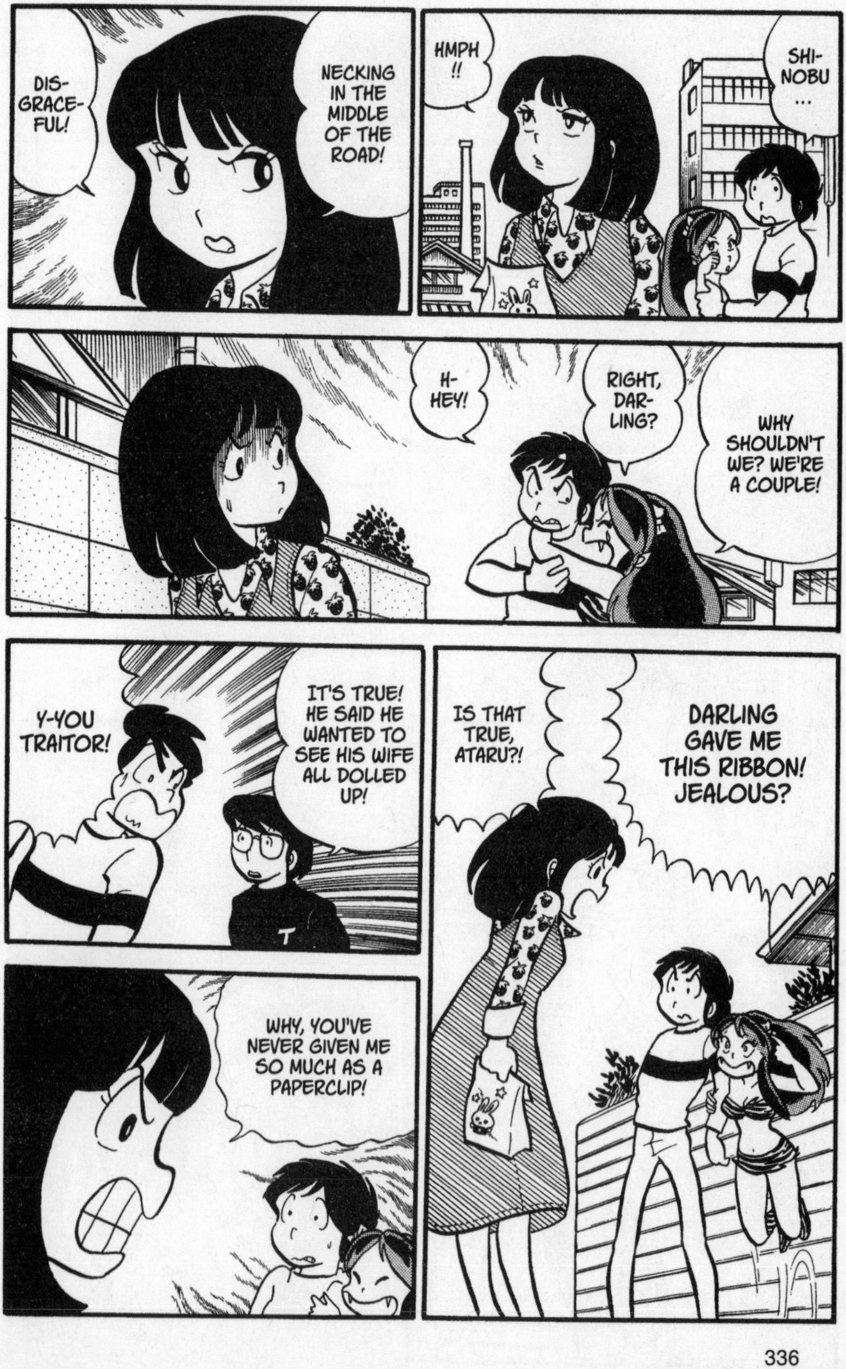
SHI-NOBU ...
HMPH !!
NECKING IN THE MIDDLE OF THE ROAD!
DIS-GRACE-FUL!
WHY SHOULDN'T WE? WE'RE A COUPLE!
RIGHT, DAR-LING?
H-HEY!
DARLING GAVE ME THIS RIBBON! JEALOUS?
IS THAT TRUE, ATARU?!
IT'S TRUE! HE SAID HE WANTED TO SEE HIS WIFE ALL DOLLED UP!
Y-YOU TRAITOR!
WHY, YOU'VE NEVER GIVEN ME SO MUCH AS A PAPERCLIP!

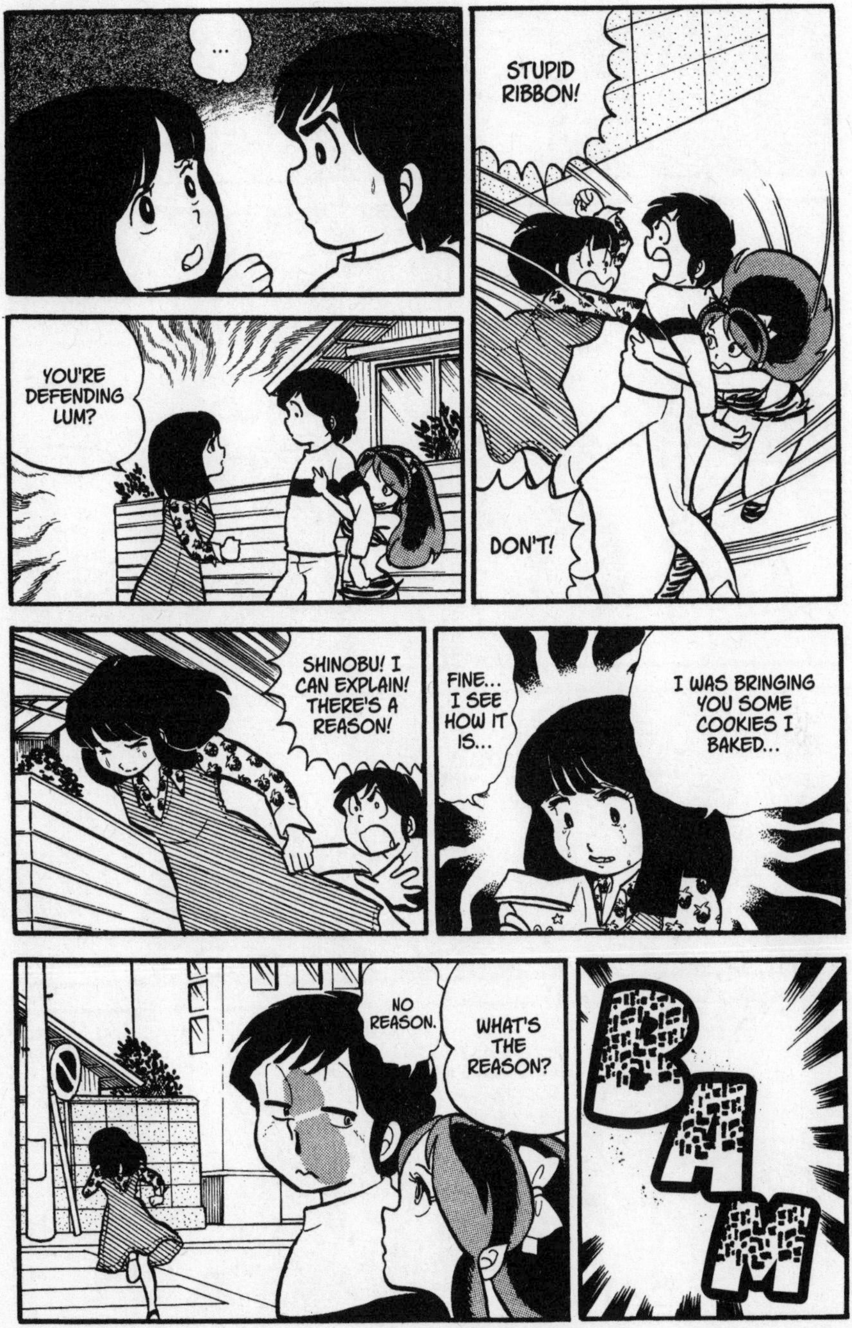
STUPID RIBBON!
DON'T!
...
YOU'RE DEFENDING LUM?
I WAS BRINGING YOU SOME COOKIES I BAKED...
FINE... I SEE HOW IT IS...
SHINOBU! I CAN EXPLAIN! THERE'S A REASON!
BAM
WHAT'S THE REASON?
NO REASON.

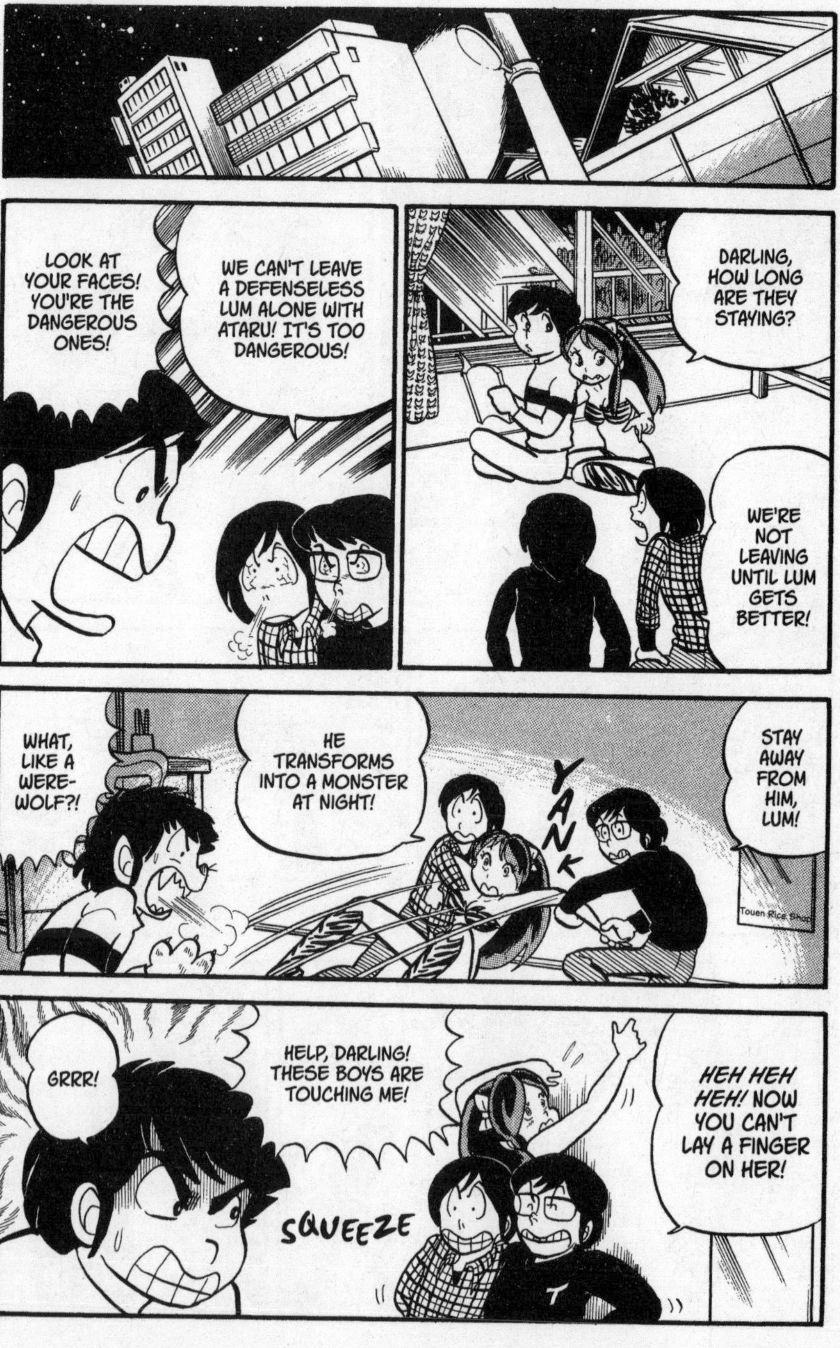
DARLING, HOW LONG ARE THEY STAYING?
WE'RE NOT LEAVING UNTIL LUM GETS BETTER!
WE CAN'T LEAVE A DEFENSELESS LUM ALONE WITH ATARU! IT'S TOO DANGEROUS!
LOOK AT YOUR FACES! YOU'RE THE DANGEROUS ONES!
STAY AWAY FROM HIM, LUM!
Touen Rice Shop
YANK
HE TRANSFORMS INTO A MONSTER AT NIGHT!
WHAT, LIKE A WERE-WOLF?!
HEH HEH HEH! NOW YOU CAN'T LAY A FINGER ON HER!
HELP, DARLING! THESE BOYS ARE TOUCHING ME!
SQUEEZE
GRRR!

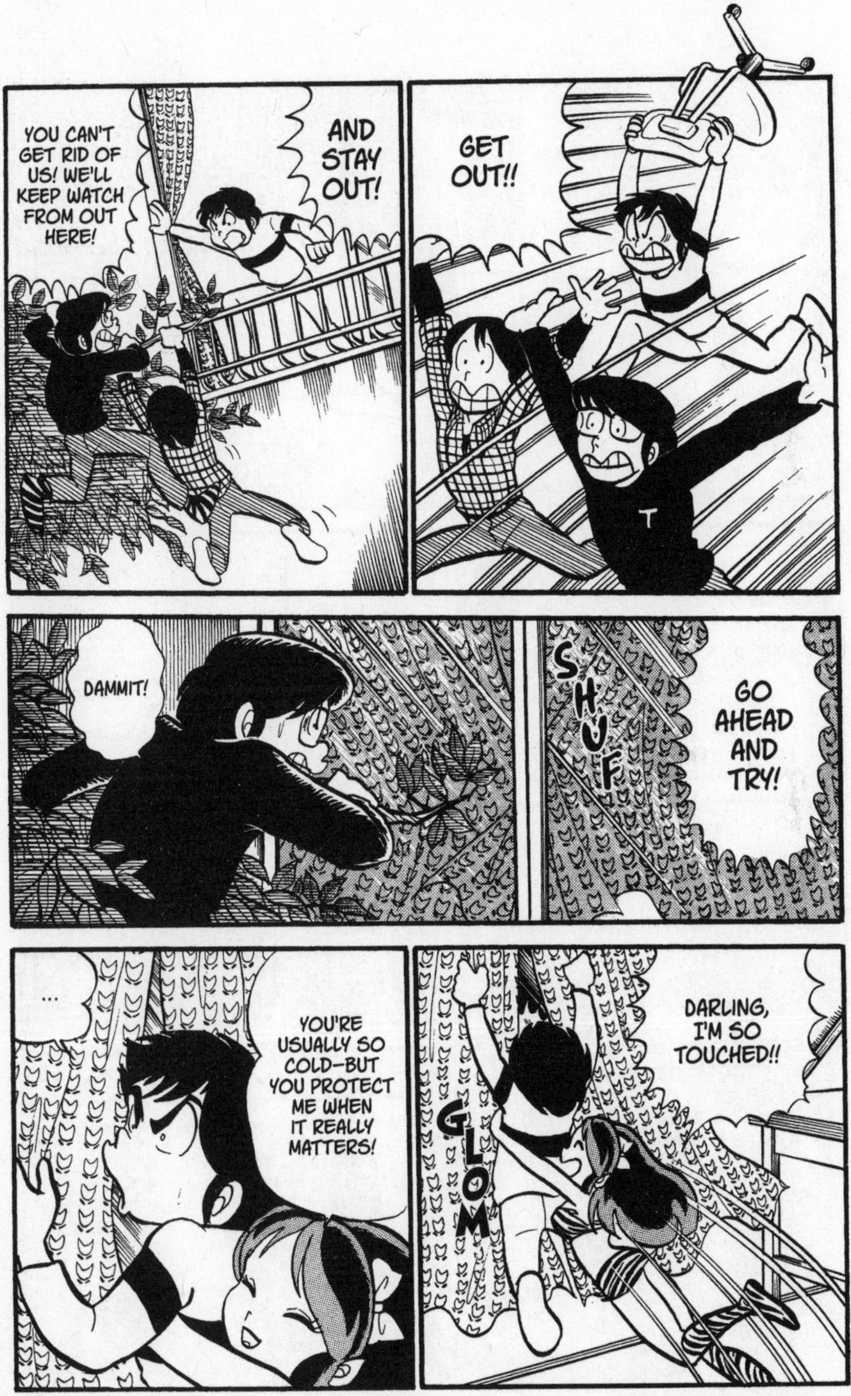
GET OUT!!
AND STAY OUT!
YOU CAN'T GET RID OF US! WE'LL KEEP WATCH FROM OUT HERE!
GO AHEAD AND TRY!
SHUF
DAMMIT!
DARLING, I'M SO TOUCHED!!
GLOM
YOU'RE USUALLY SO COLD—BUT YOU PROTECT ME WHEN IT REALLY MATTERS!
...

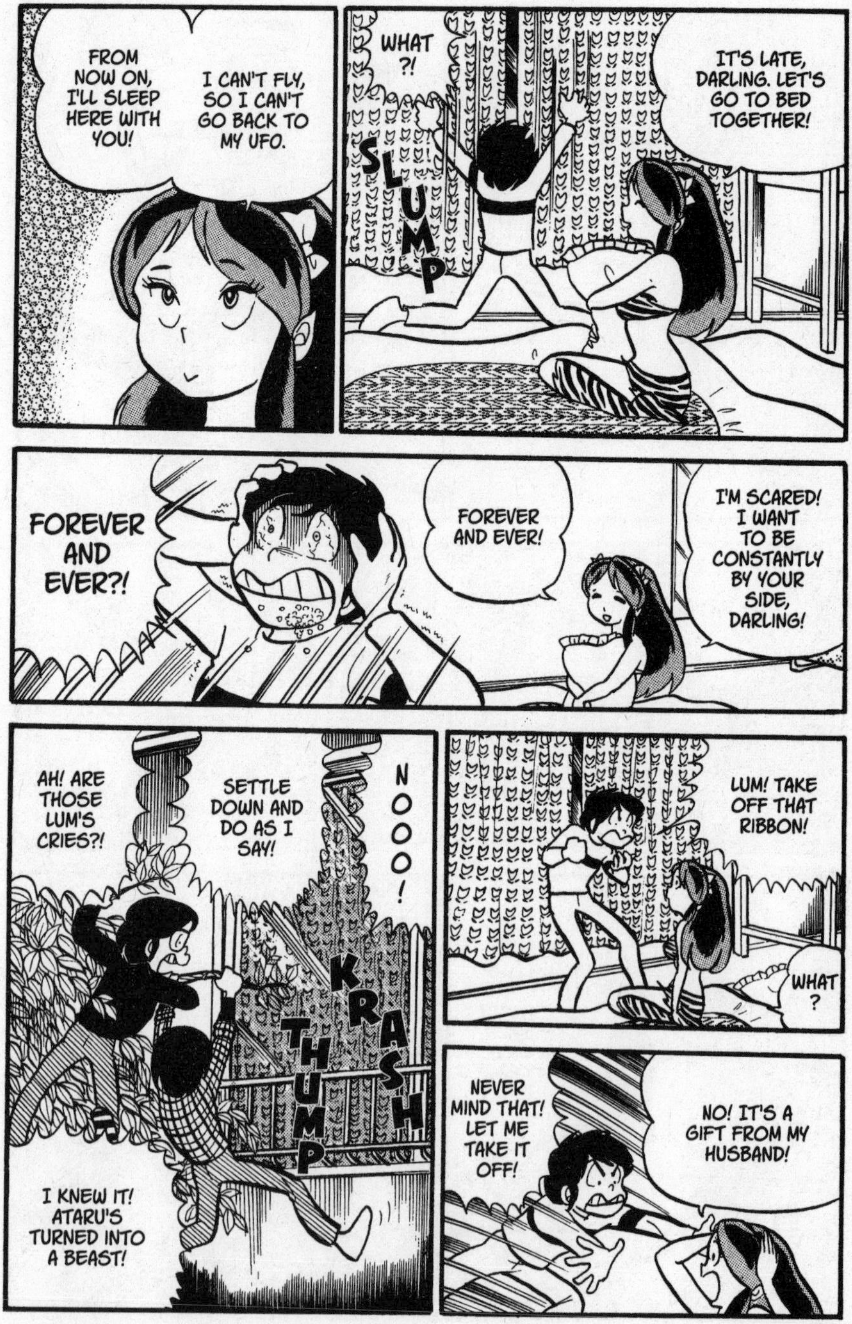
IT'S LATE, DARLING. LET'S GO TO BED TOGETHER!
WHAT ?!
SLUMP
I CAN'T FLY, SO I CAN'T GO BACK TO MY UFO.
FROM NOW ON, I'LL SLEEP HERE WITH YOU!
I'M SCARED! I WANT TO BE CONSTANTLY BY YOUR SIDE, DARLING!
FOREVER AND EVER!
FOREVER AND EVER?!
LUM! TAKE OFF THAT RIBBON!
WHAT ?
NO! IT'S A GIFT FROM MY HUSBAND!
NEVER MIND THAT! LET ME TAKE IT OFF!
NOOOO!
SETTLE DOWN AND DO AS I SAY!
AH! ARE THOSE LUM'S CRIES?!
KRASH
THUMP
I KNEW IT! ATARU'S TURNED INTO A BEAST!

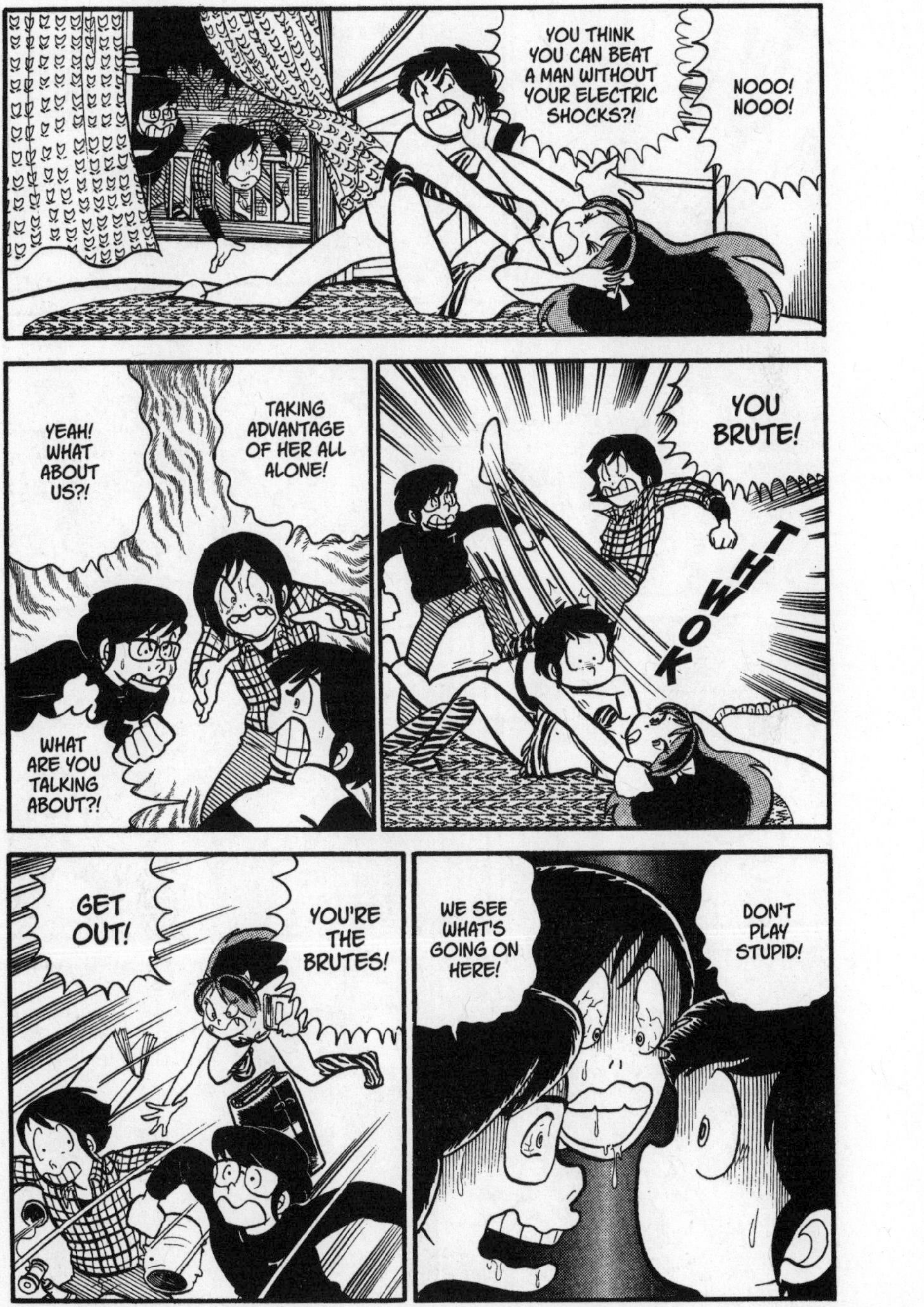
NOOO! NOOO!
YOU THINK YOU CAN BEAT A MAN WITHOUT YOUR ELECTRIC SHOCKS?!
YOU BRUTE!
THWOK
TAKING ADVANTAGE OF HER ALL ALONE!
YEAH! WHAT ABOUT US?!
WHAT ARE YOU TALKING ABOUT?!
DON'T PLAY STUPID!
WE SEE WHAT'S GOING ON HERE!
YOU'RE THE BRUTES!
GET OUT!

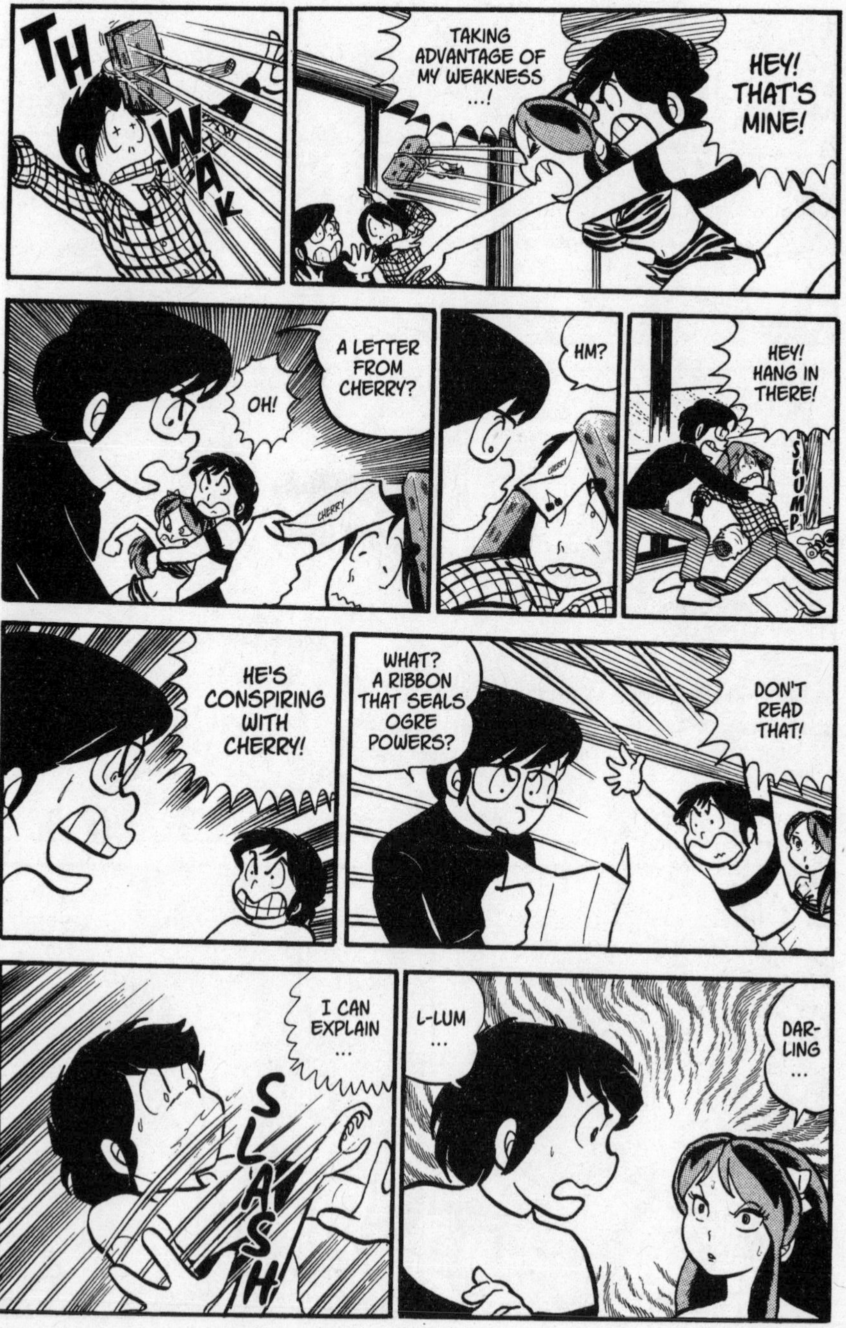
HEY! THAT'S MINE!
TAKING ADVANTAGE OF MY WEAKNESS ...!
THWAK
HEY! HANG IN THERE!
SLUMP
HM?
CHERRY
A LETTER FROM CHERRY?
OH!
CHERRY
DON'T READ THAT!
WHAT? A RIBBON THAT SEALS OGRE POWERS?
HE'S CONSPIRING WITH CHERRY!
DAR-LING ...
L-LUM ...
I CAN EXPLAIN ...
SLASH

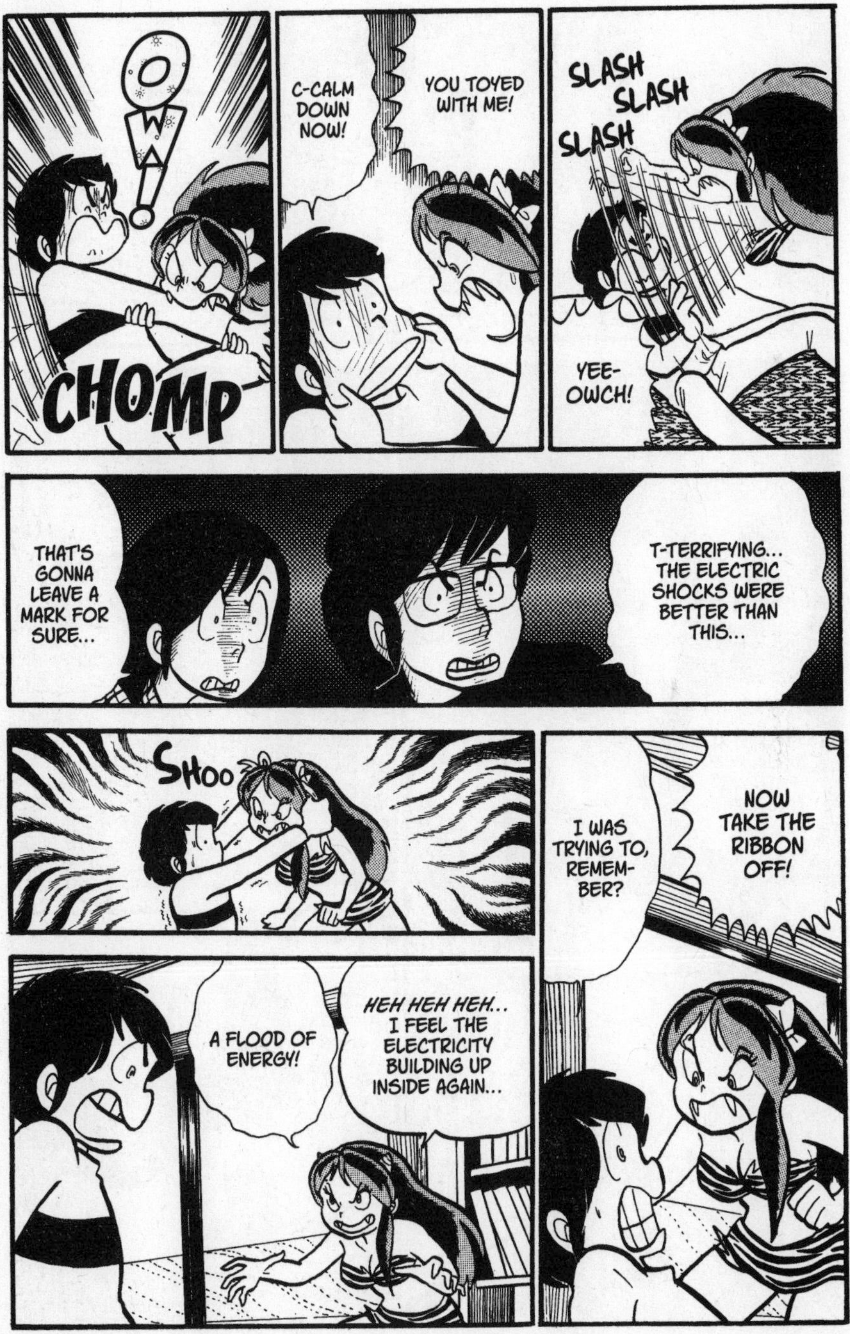
SLASH
SLASH
SLASH
YEE-OWCH!
YOU TOYED WITH ME!
C-CALM DOWN NOW!
OWA!
CHOMP
T-TERRIFYING... THE ELECTRIC SHOCKS WERE BETTER THAN THIS...
THAT'S GONNA LEAVE A MARK FOR SURE...
NOW TAKE THE RIBBON OFF!
I WAS TRYING TO, REMEMBER?
SHOO
HEH HEH HEH... I FEEL THE ELECTRICITY BUILDING UP INSIDE AGAIN...
A FLOOD OF ENERGY!

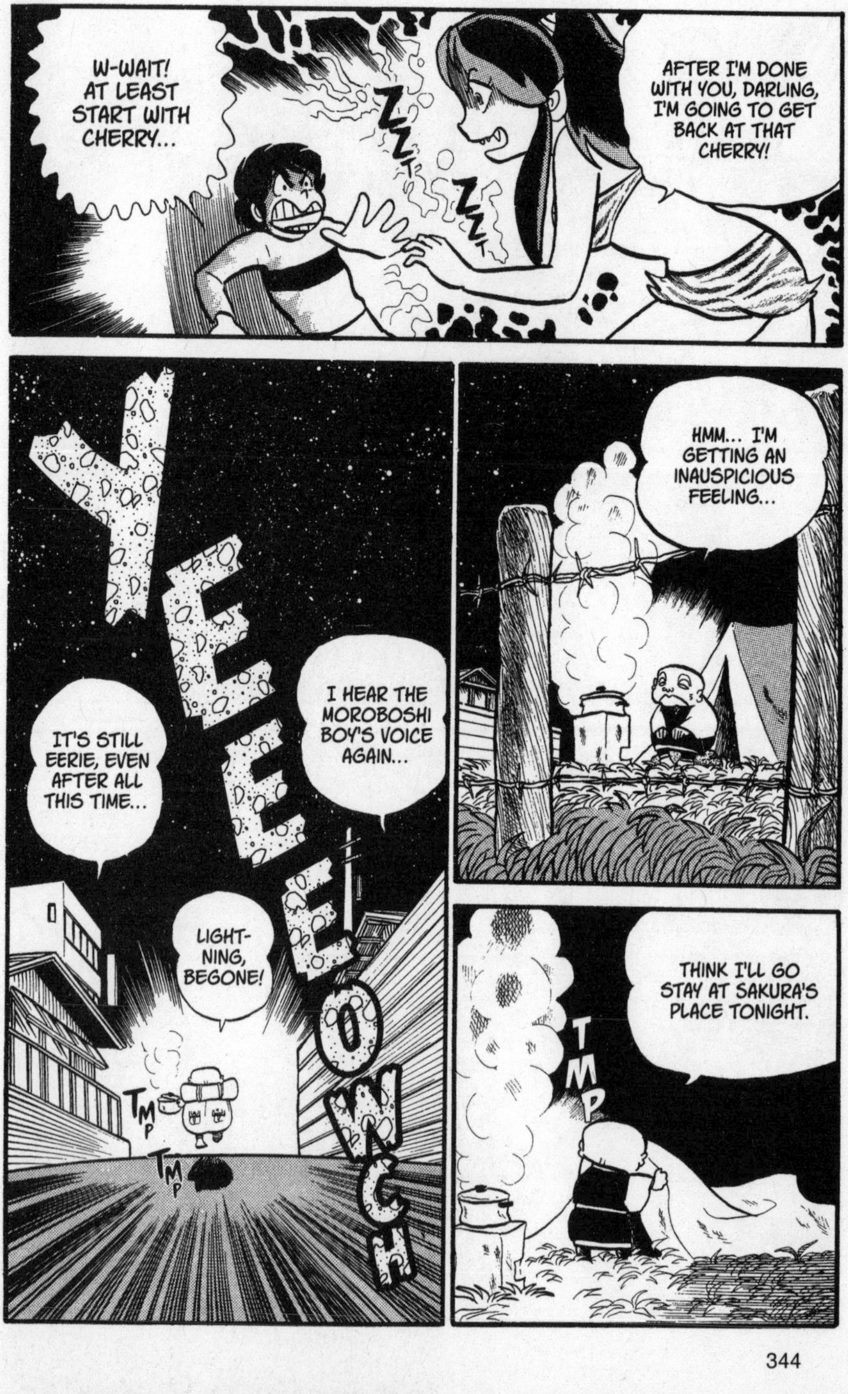
AFTER I'M DONE WITH YOU, DARLING, I'M GOING TO GET BACK AT THAT CHERRY!
ZZZT
ZZZT
W-WAIT! AT LEAST START WITH CHERRY...
HMM... I'M GETTING AN INAUSPICIOUS FEELING...
TMP
THINK I'LL GO STAY AT SAKURA'S PLACE TONIGHT.
YEEEEOWCH
I HEAR THE MOROBOSHI BOY'S VOICE AGAIN...
IT'S STILL EERIE, EVEN AFTER ALL THIS TIME...
LIGHT-NING, BEGONE!
TMP
TMP

CHAPTER 16: BECOME A WOMAN AND START OVER!

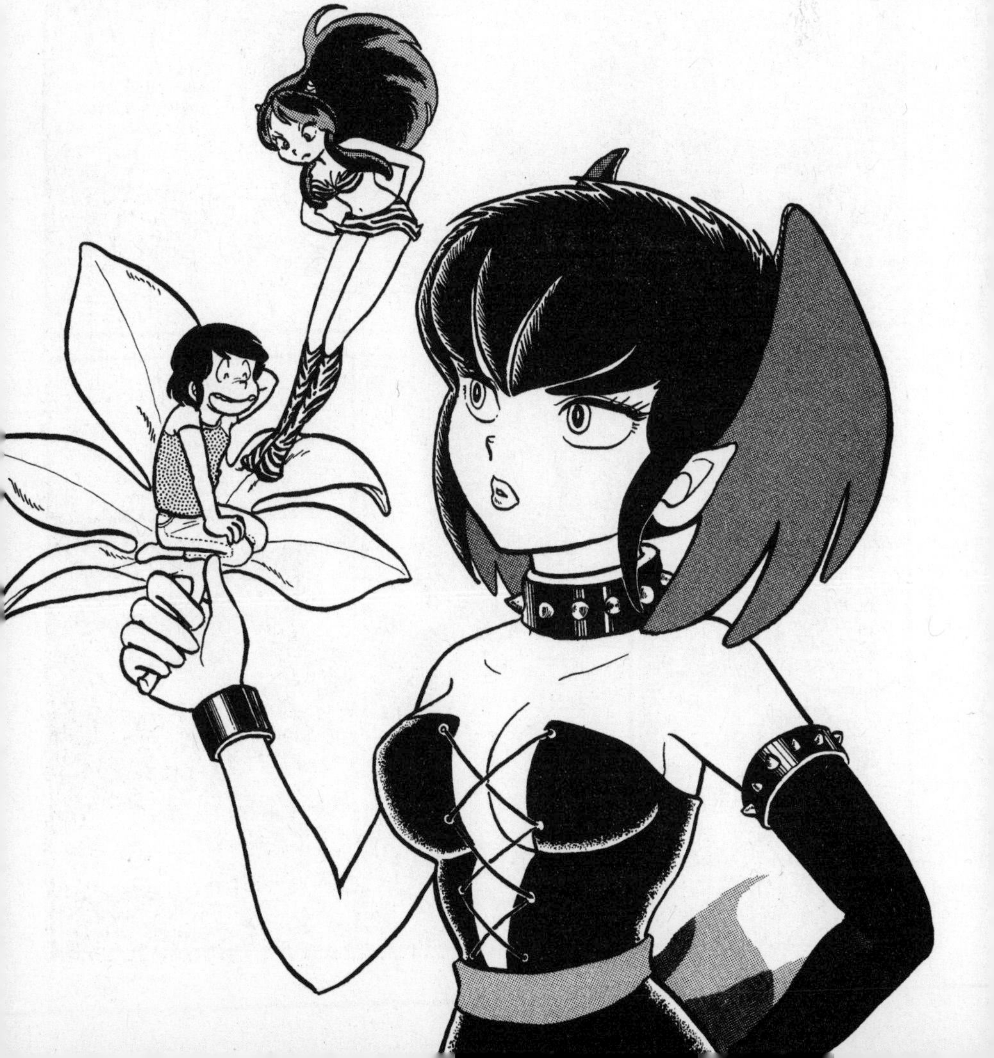

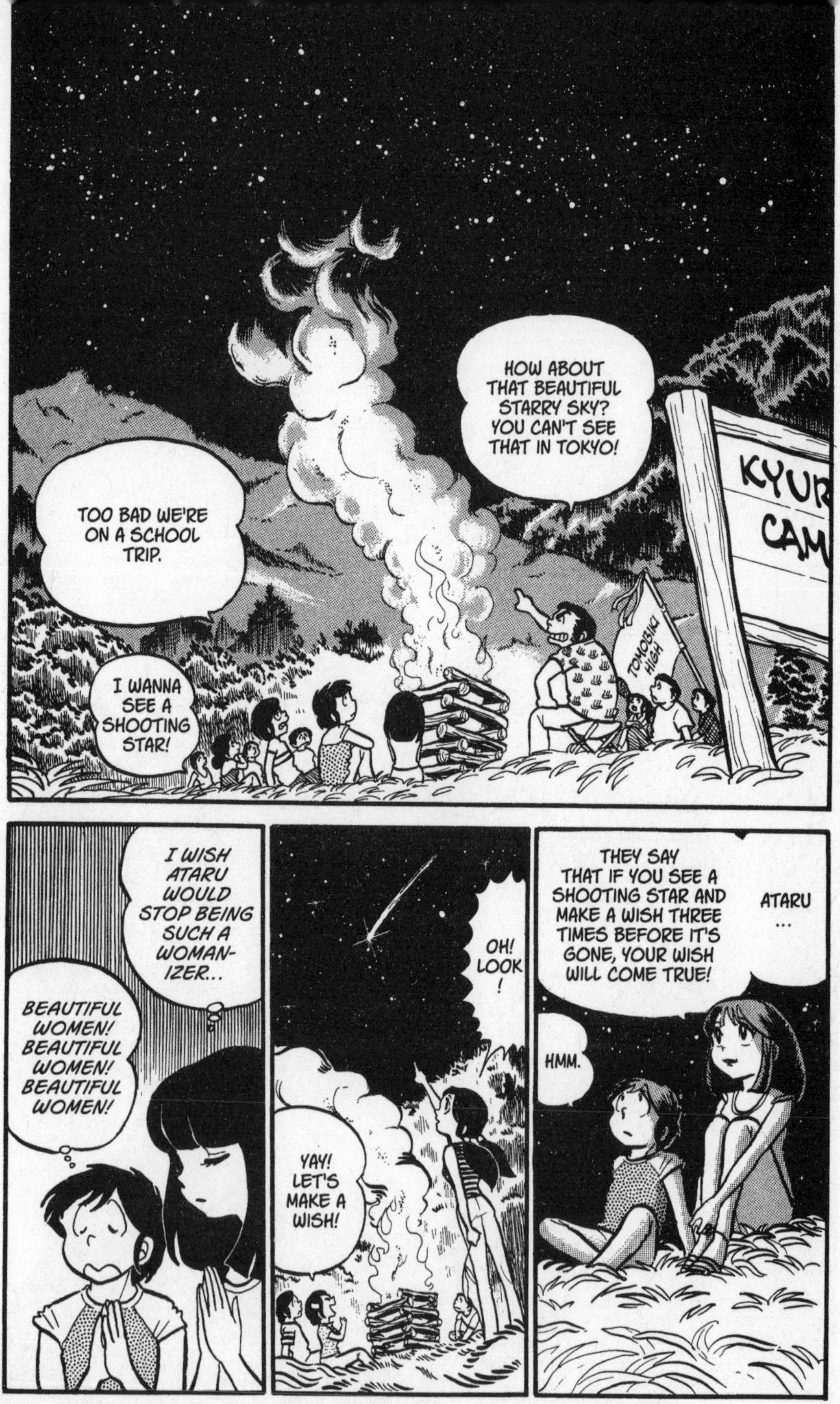
HOW ABOUT THAT BEAUTIFUL STARRY SKY? YOU CAN'T SEE THAT IN TOKYO!
TOMOBIKI HIGH
TOO BAD WE'RE ON A SCHOOL TRIP.
I WANNA SEE A SHOOTING STAR!
ATARU ...
THEY SAY THAT IF YOU SEE A SHOOTING STAR AND MAKE A WISH THREE TIMES BEFORE IT'S GONE, YOUR WISH WILL COME TRUE!
HMM.
OH! LOOK!
YAY! LET'S MAKE A WISH!
I WISH ATARU WOULD STOP BEING SUCH A WOMANIZER...
BEAUTIFUL WOMEN! BEAUTIFUL WOMEN! BEAUTIFUL WOMEN!

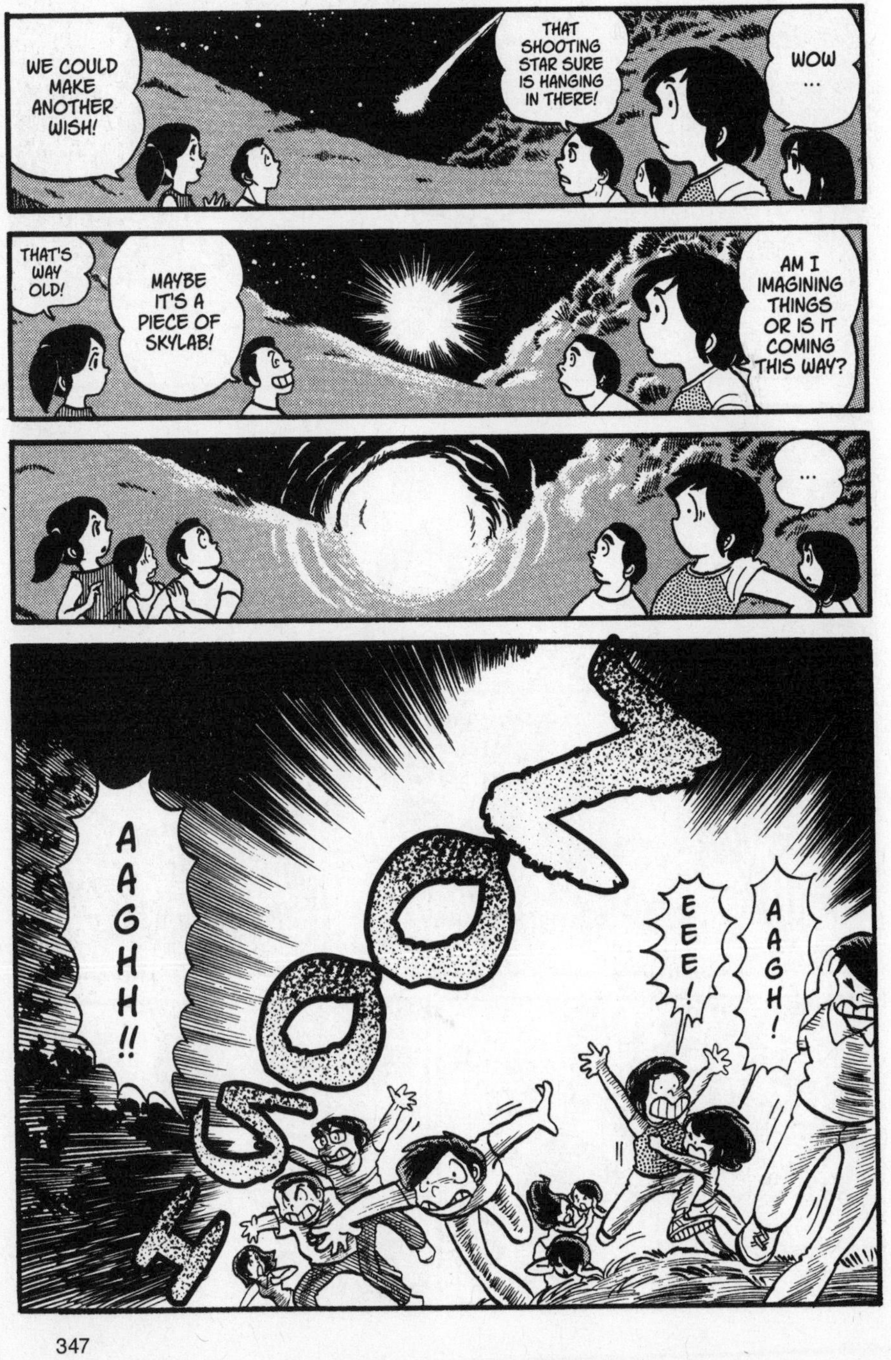
WOW ...
THAT SHOOTING STAR SURE IS HANGING IN THERE!
WE COULD MAKE ANOTHER WISH!
AM I IMAGINING THINGS OR IS IT COMING THIS WAY?
MAYBE IT'S A PIECE OF SKYLAB!
THAT'S WAY OLD!
...
AAGH!
EEE!
AAGHH!!

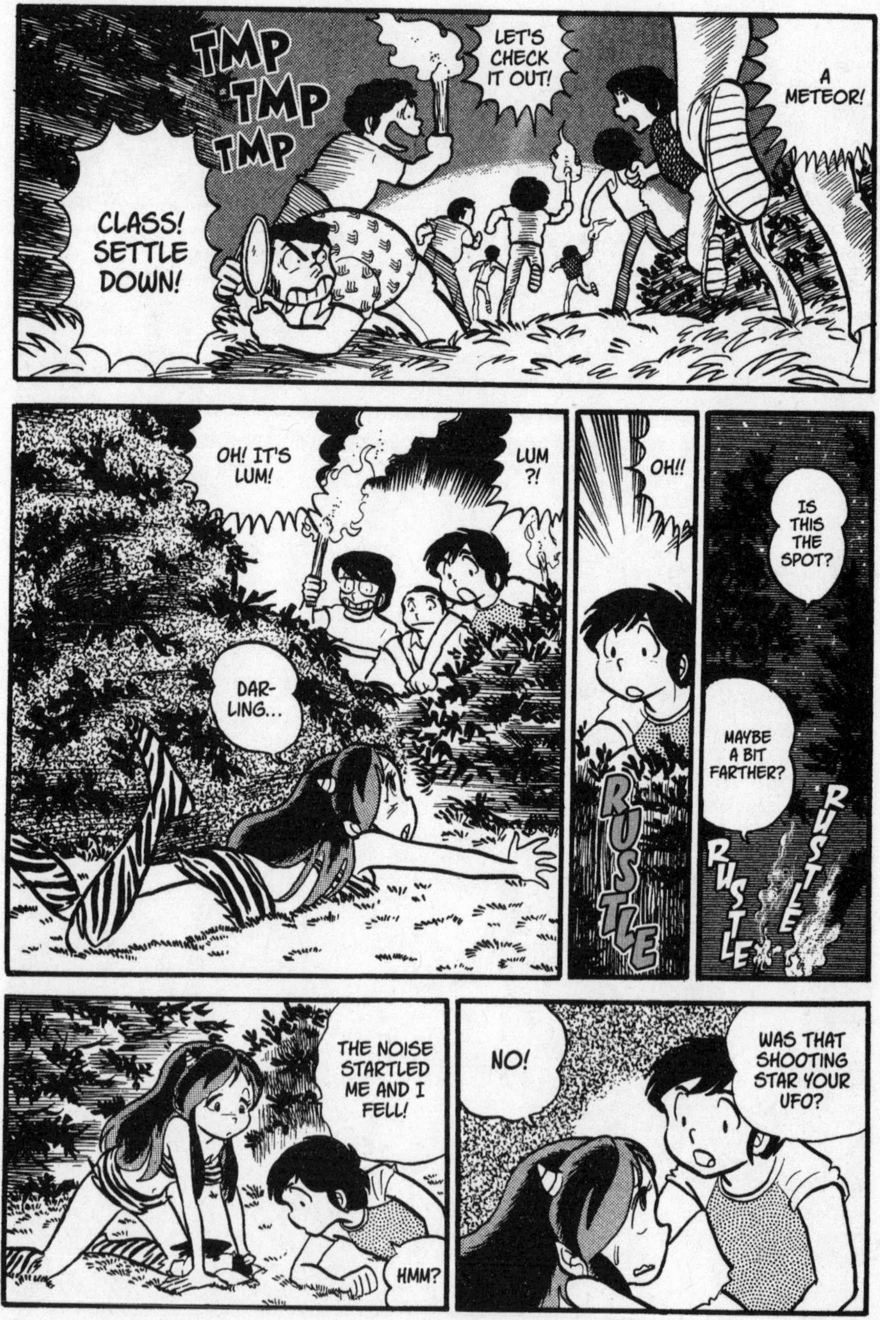
A METEOR!
LET'S CHECK IT OUT!
TMP TMP TMP
CLASS! SETTLE DOWN!
IS THIS THE SPOT?
MAYBE A BIT FARTHER?
RUSTLE RUSTLE
OH!!
RUSTLE
LUM ?!
OH! IT'S LUM!
DAR-LING...
WAS THAT SHOOTING STAR YOUR UFO?
NO!
THE NOISE STARTLED ME AND I FELL!
HMM?

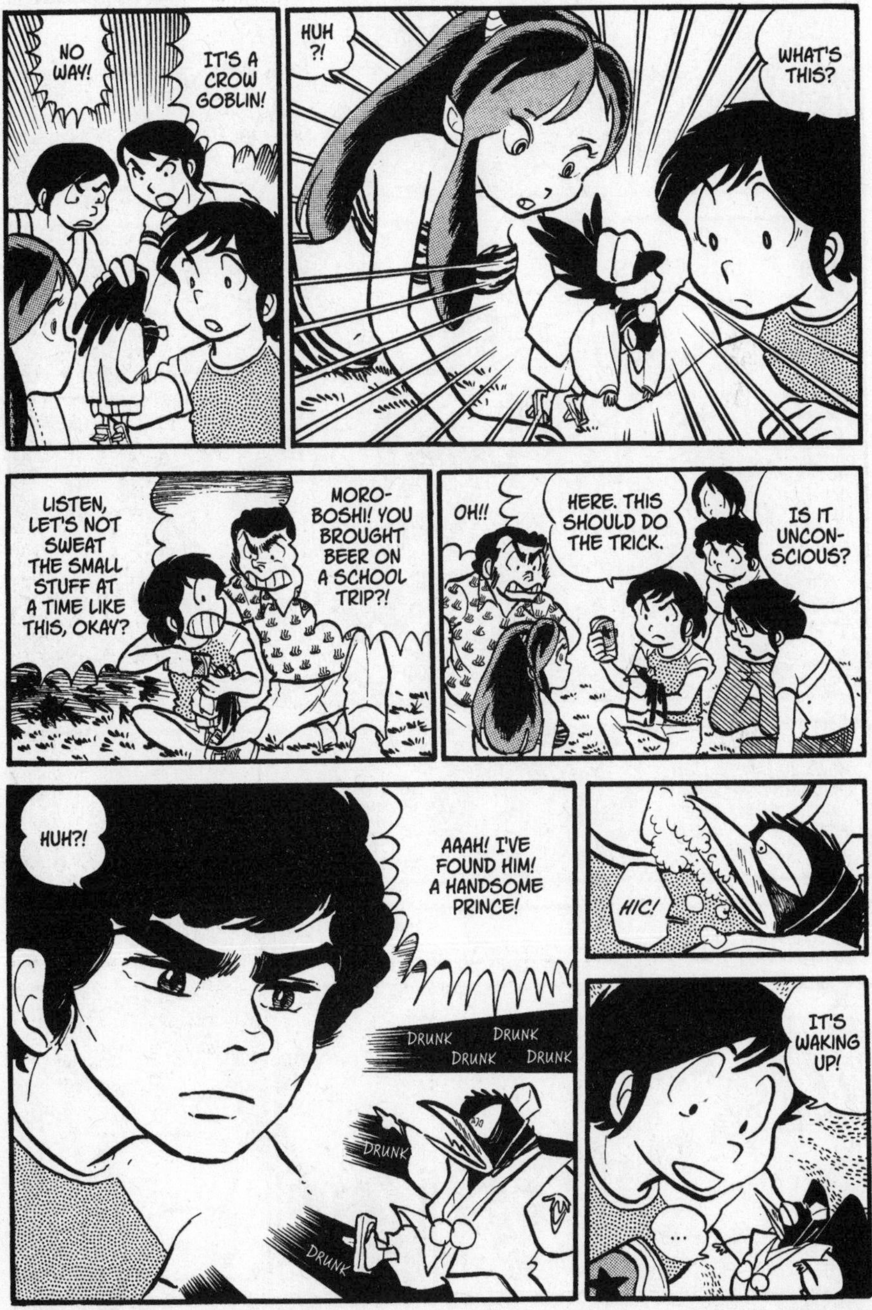
WHAT'S THIS?
HUH ?!
IT'S A CROW GOBLIN!
NO WAY!
IS IT UNCONSCIOUS?
HERE. THIS SHOULD DO THE TRICK.
OH!!
MORO-BOSHI! YOU BROUGHT BEER ON A SCHOOL TRIP?!
LISTEN, LET'S NOT SWEAT THE SMALL STUFF AT A TIME LIKE THIS, OKAY?
HIC!
IT'S WAKING UP!
...
AAAH! I'VE FOUND HIM! A HANDSOME PRINCE!
HUH?!
DRUNK DRUNK DRUNK DRUNK
DRUNK
DRUNK

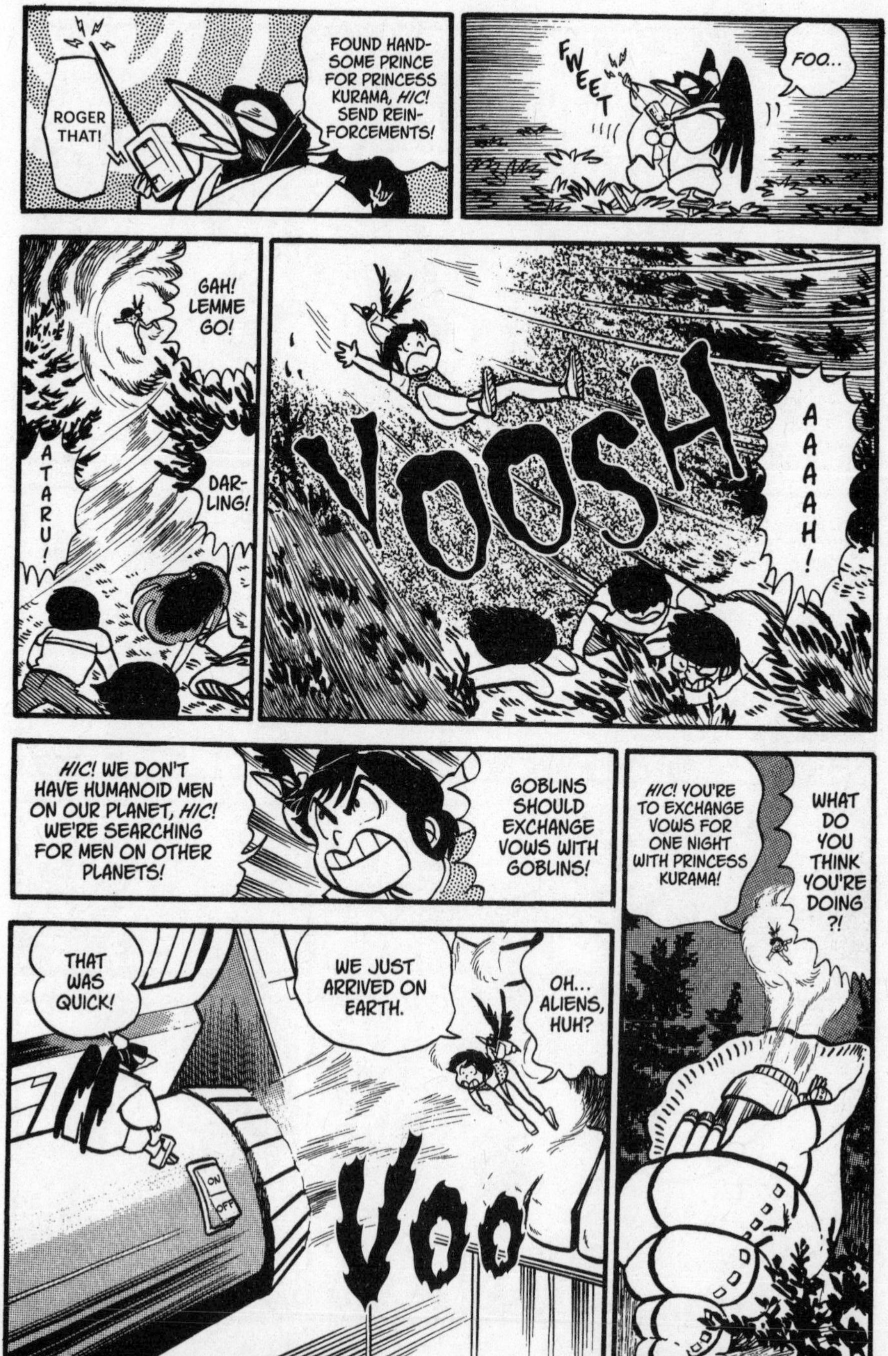
FOO...
FWEET
FOUND HAND-SOME PRINCE FOR PRINCESS KURAMA, *HIC!* SEND REIN-FORCEMENTS!
ROGER THAT!
AAAAAH!
VOOSH
GAH! LEMME GO!
DAR-LING!
ATARU!
WHAT DO YOU THINK YOU'RE DOING ?!
HIC! YOU'RE TO EXCHANGE VOWS FOR ONE NIGHT WITH PRINCESS KURAMA!
GOBLINS SHOULD EXCHANGE VOWS WITH GOBLINS!
HIC! WE DON'T HAVE HUMANOID MEN ON OUR PLANET, *HIC!* WE'RE SEARCHING FOR MEN ON OTHER PLANETS!
OH... ALIENS, HUH?
WE JUST ARRIVED ON EARTH.
THAT WAS QUICK!
VOO
ON
OFF

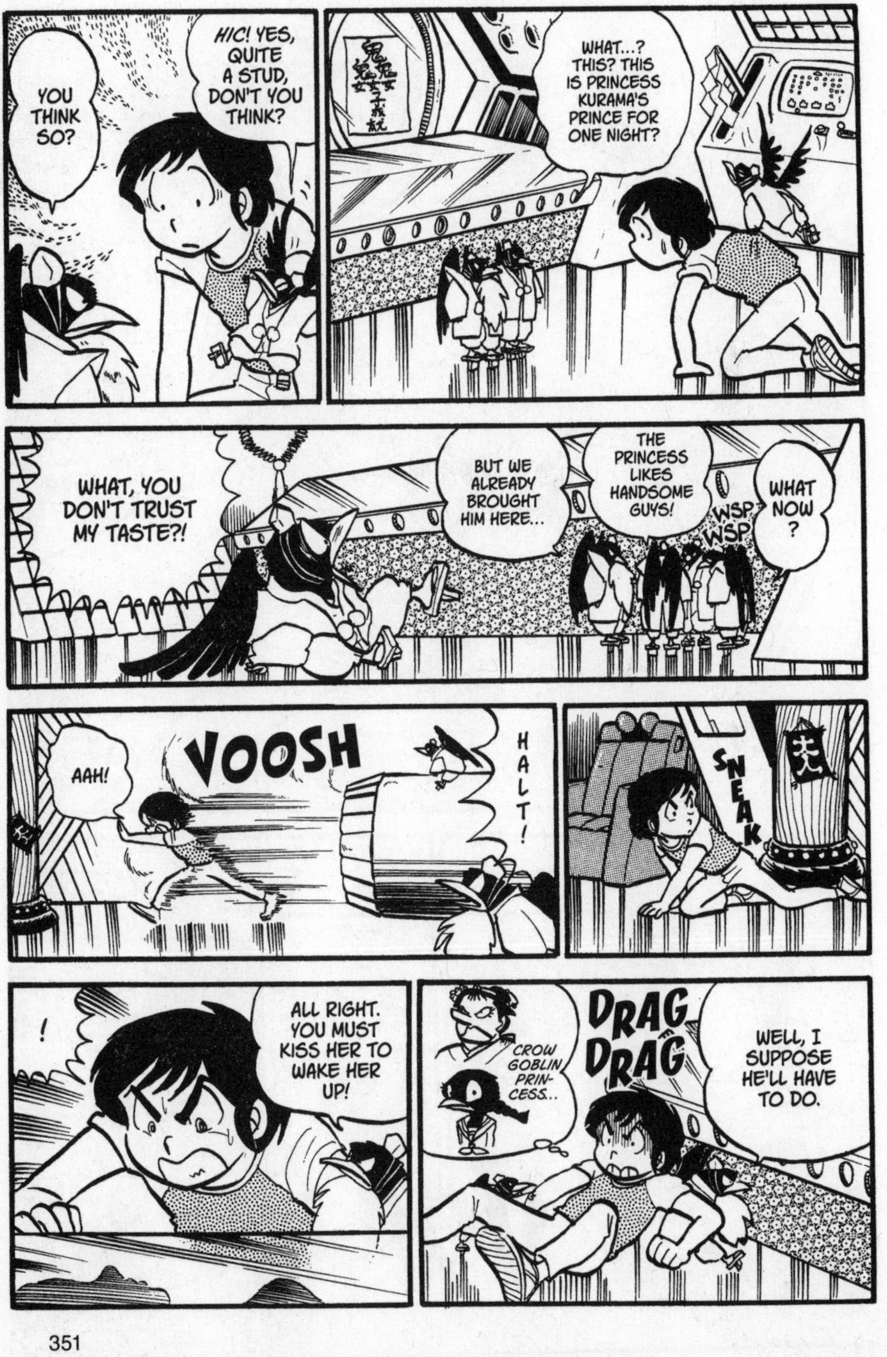
WHAT...? THIS? THIS IS PRINCESS KURAMA'S PRINCE FOR ONE NIGHT?
HIC! YES, QUITE A STUD, DON'T YOU THINK?
YOU THINK SO?
WHAT NOW ?
WSP WSP
THE PRINCESS LIKES HANDSOME GUYS!
BUT WE ALREADY BROUGHT HIM HERE...
WHAT, YOU DON'T TRUST MY TASTE?!
SNEAK
HALT!
VOOSH
AAH!
WELL, I SUPPOSE HE'LL HAVE TO DO.
DRAG DRAG
CROW GOBLIN PRINCESS...
ALL RIGHT. YOU MUST KISS HER TO WAKE HER UP!
!

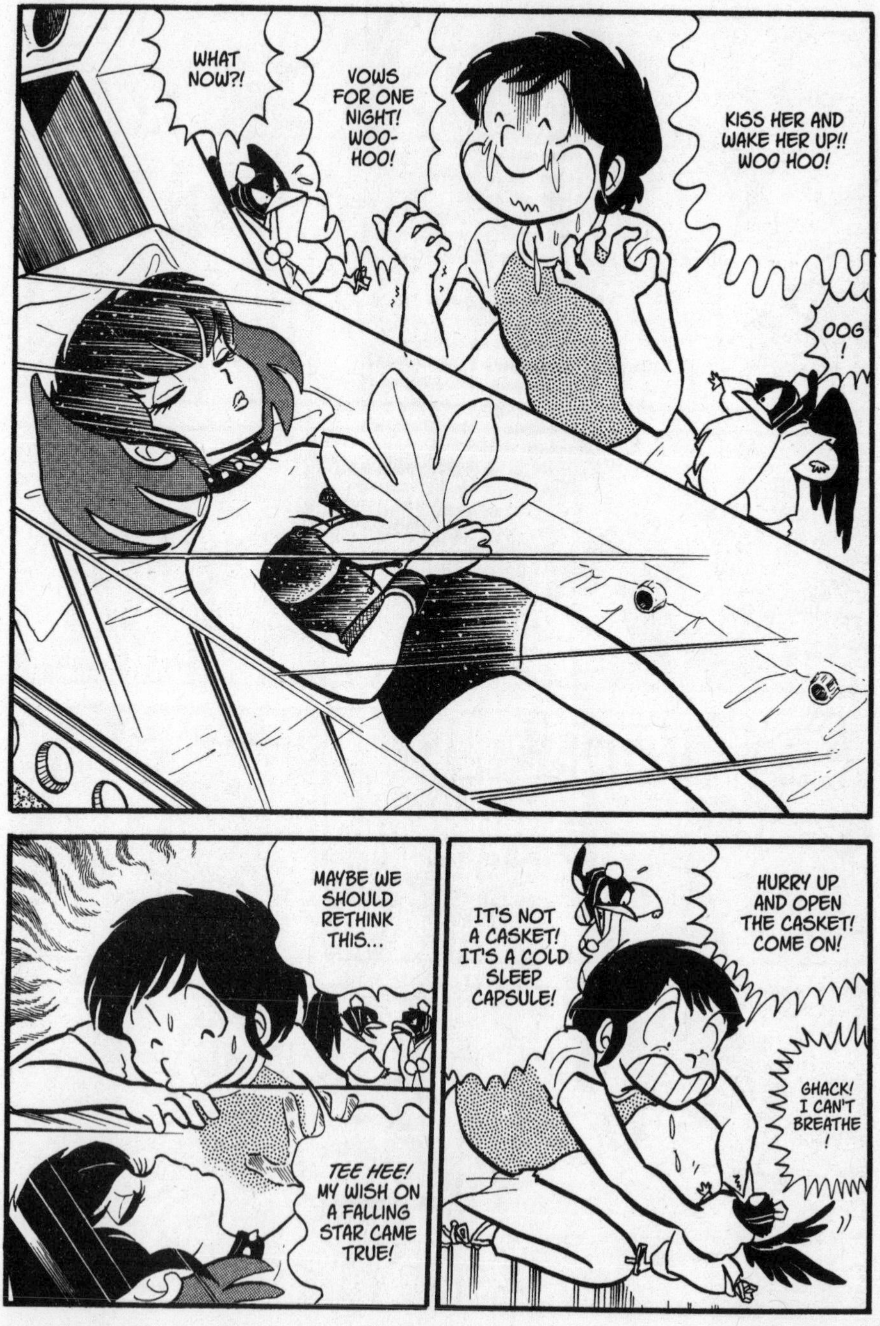
KISS HER AND WAKE HER UP!! WOO HOO!
VOWS FOR ONE NIGHT! WOO-HOO!
WHAT NOW?!
OOG!
HURRY UP AND OPEN THE CASKET! COME ON!
IT'S NOT A CASKET! IT'S A COLD SLEEP CAPSULE!
GHACK! I CAN'T BREATHE!
MAYBE WE SHOULD RETHINK THIS...
TEE HEE! MY WISH ON A FALLING STAR CAME TRUE!

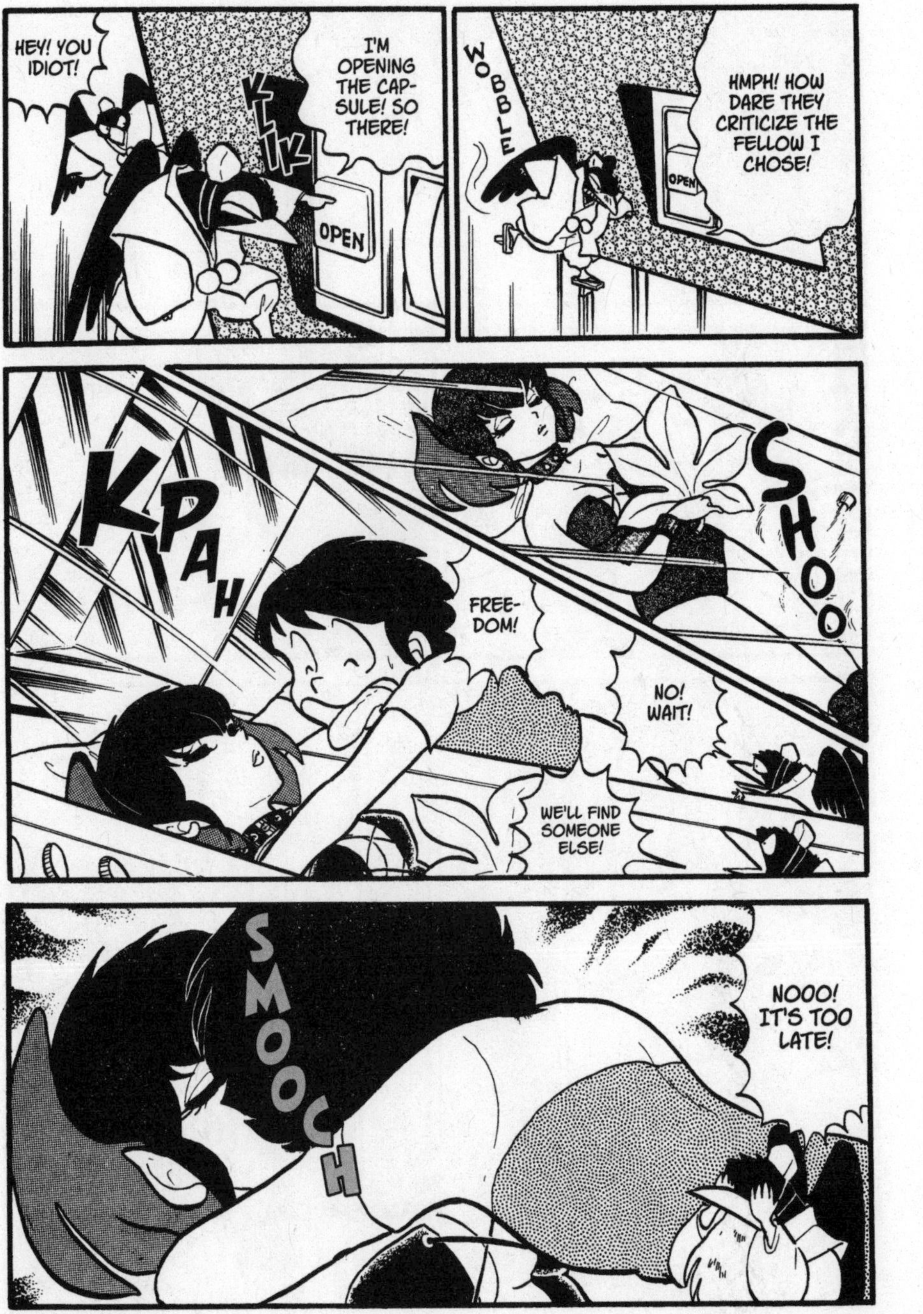
HMPH! HOW DARE THEY CRITICIZE THE FELLOW I CHOSE!
WOBBLE
OPEN
I'M OPENING THE CAP-SULE! SO THERE!
HEY! YOU IDIOT!
KLIK
OPEN
SHOO
FREE-DOM!
NO! WAIT!
KPAH
WE'LL FIND SOMEONE ELSE!
NOOO! IT'S TOO LATE!
SMOOCH

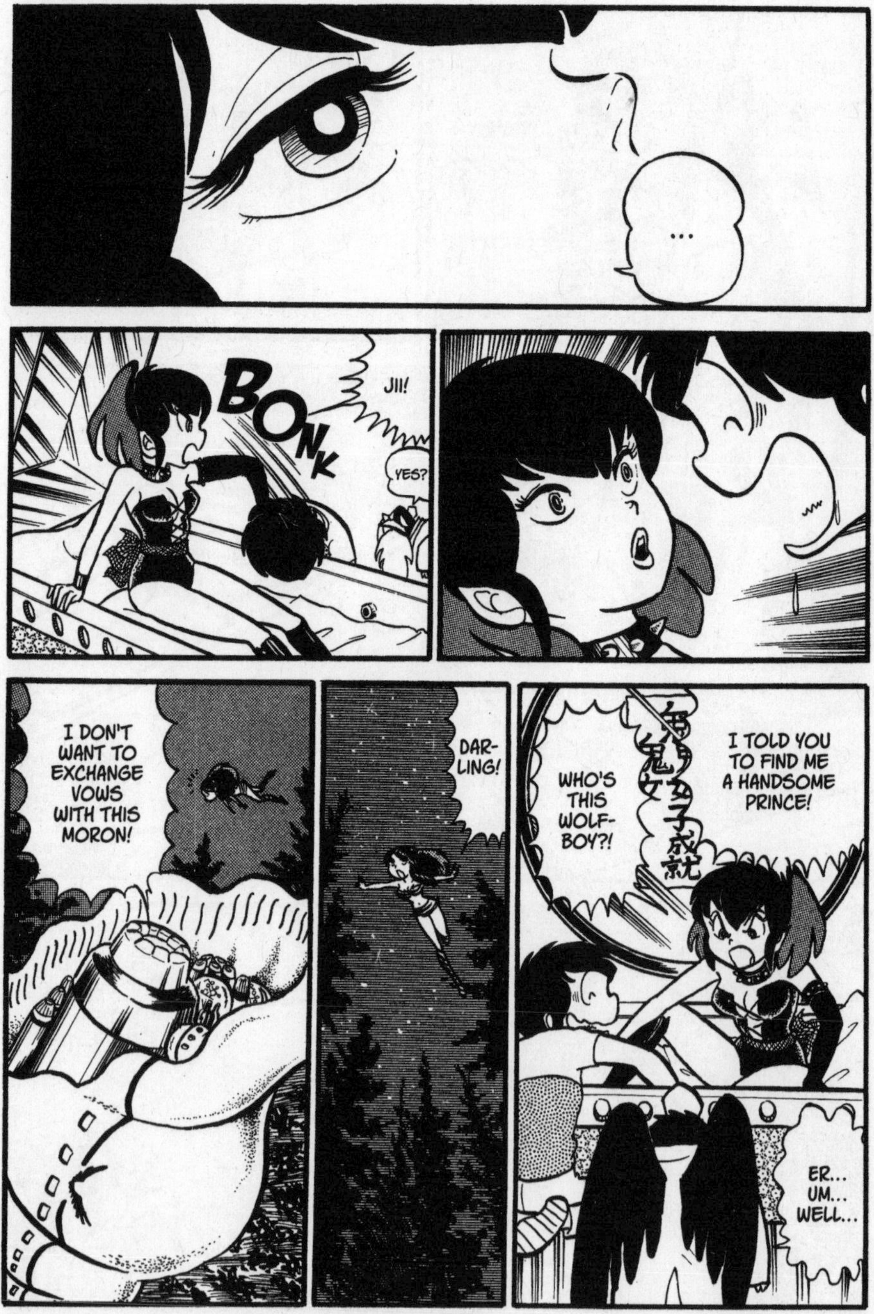
...
JII!
BONK
YES?
I TOLD YOU TO FIND ME A HANDSOME PRINCE!
WHO'S THIS WOLF-BOY?!
ER... UM... WELL...
DAR-LING!
I DON'T WANT TO EXCHANGE VOWS WITH THIS MORON!

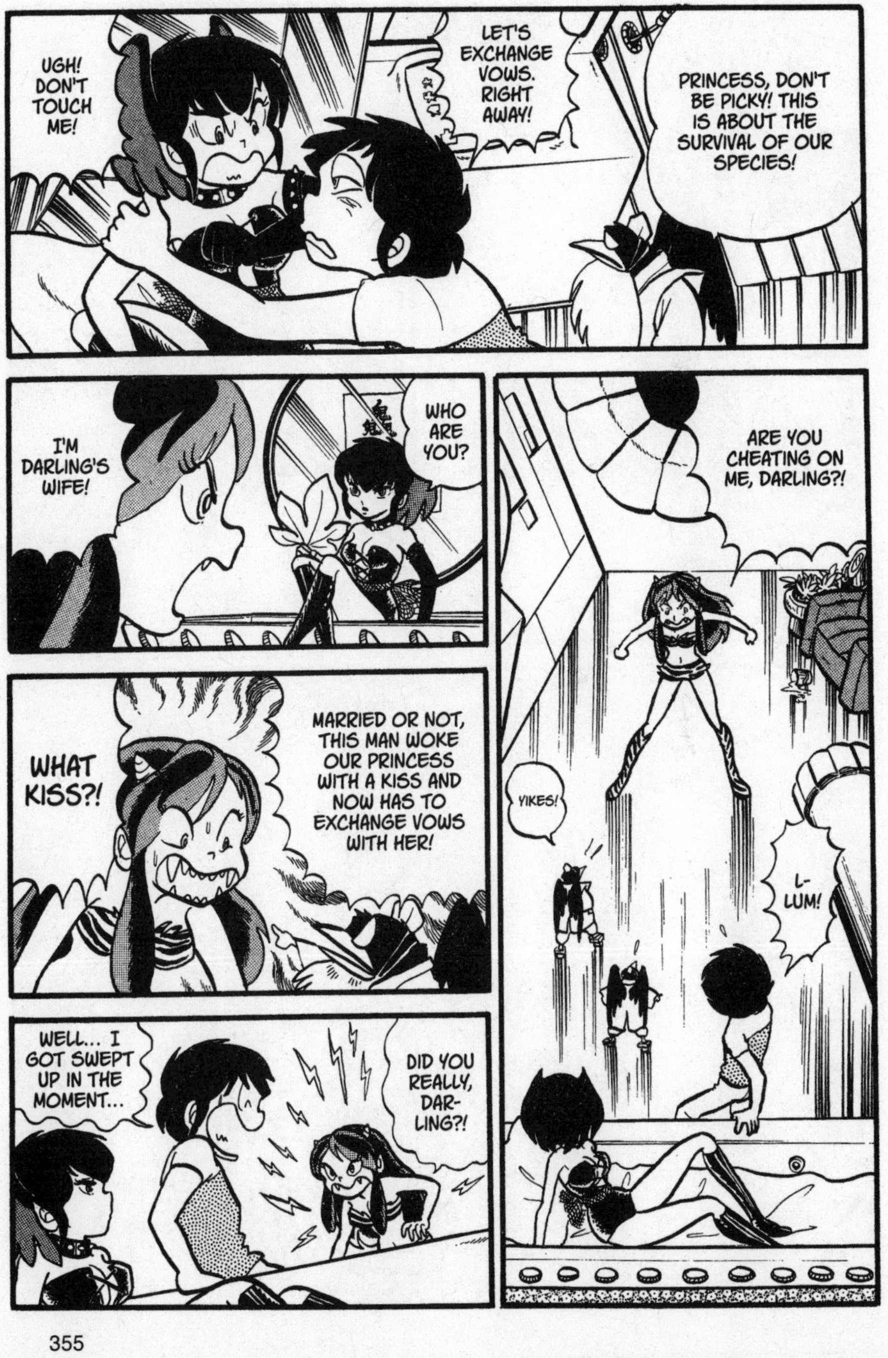
PRINCESS, DON'T BE PICKY! THIS IS ABOUT THE SURVIVAL OF OUR SPECIES!
LET'S EXCHANGE VOWS. RIGHT AWAY!
UGH! DON'T TOUCH ME!
ARE YOU CHEATING ON ME, DARLING?!
L-LUM!
YIKES!
WHO ARE YOU?
I'M DARLING'S WIFE!
MARRIED OR NOT, THIS MAN WOKE OUR PRINCESS WITH A KISS AND NOW HAS TO EXCHANGE VOWS WITH HER!
WHAT KISS?!
DID YOU REALLY, DAR-LING?!
WELL... I GOT SWEPT UP IN THE MOMENT...

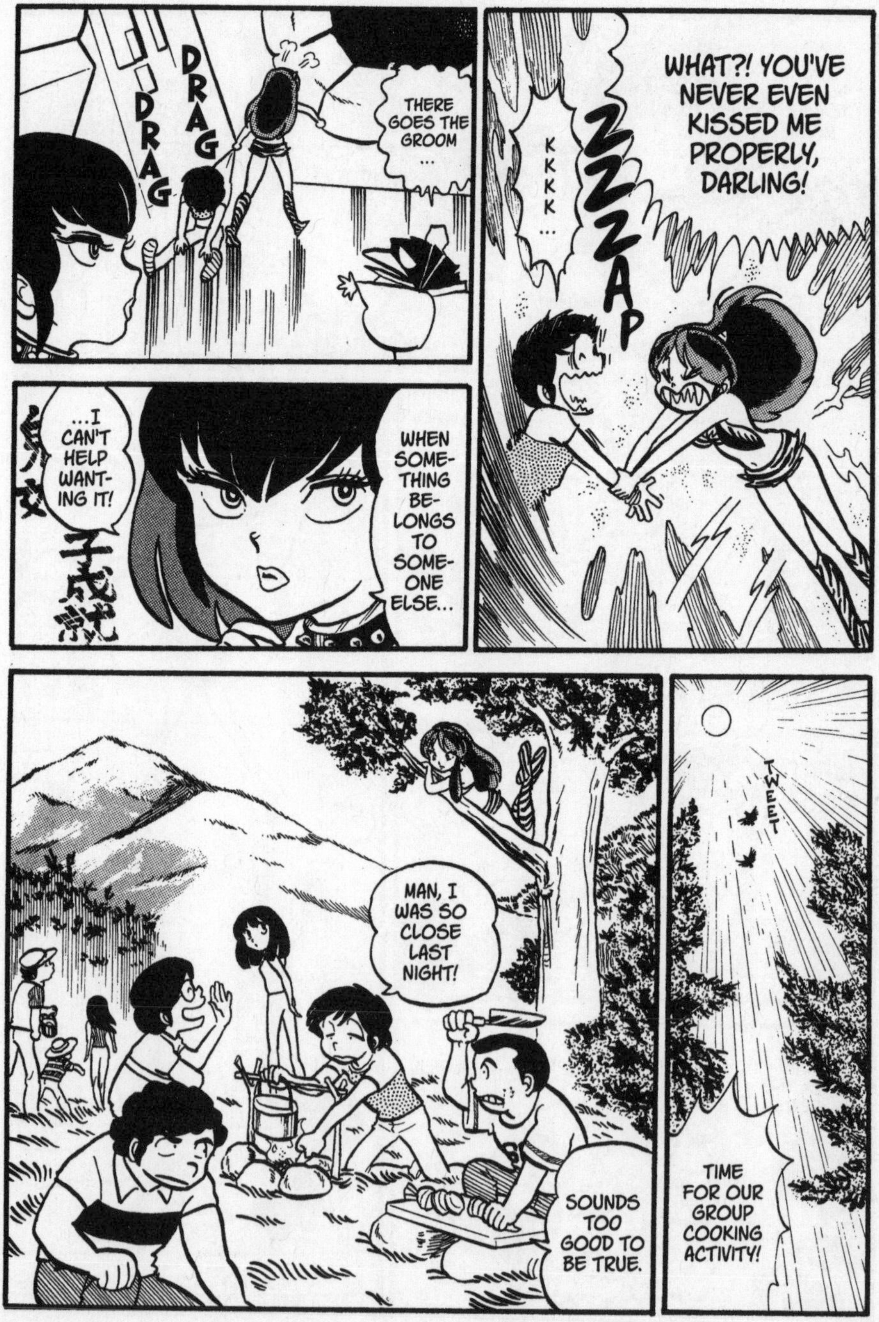
WHAT?! YOU'VE NEVER EVEN KISSED ME PROPERLY, DARLING!
ZZZAP
KKKK...
THERE GOES THE GROOM ...
DRAG
DRAG
WHEN SOMETHING BELONGS TO SOMEONE ELSE...
...I CAN'T HELP WANTING IT!
TWEET
TIME FOR OUR GROUP COOKING ACTIVITY!
MAN, I WAS SO CLOSE LAST NIGHT!
SOUNDS TOO GOOD TO BE TRUE.

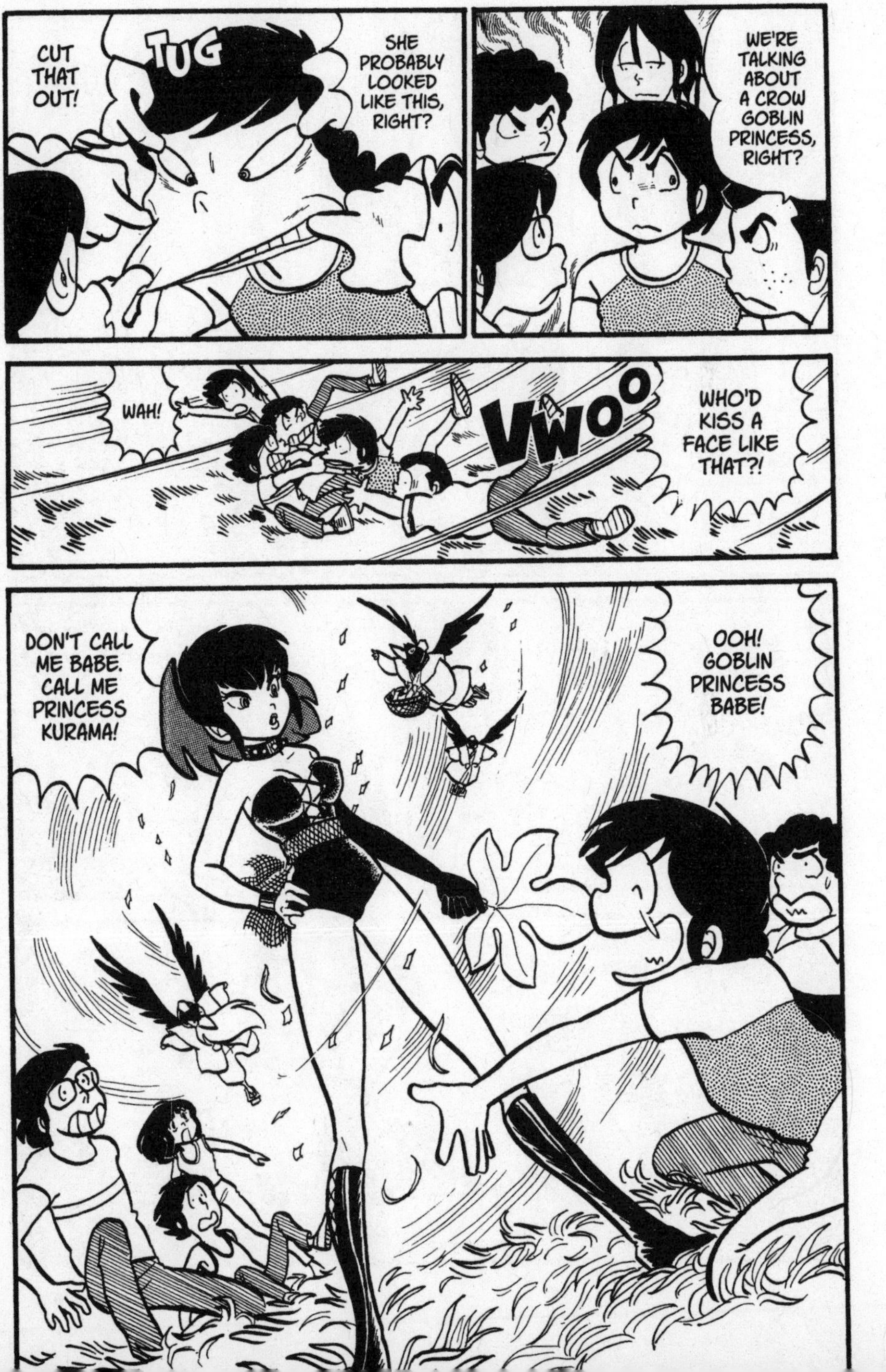
WE'RE TALKING ABOUT A CROW GOBLIN PRINCESS, RIGHT?
SHE PROBABLY LOOKED LIKE THIS, RIGHT?
TUG
CUT THAT OUT!
WHO'D KISS A FACE LIKE THAT?!
VWOO
WAH!
OOH! GOBLIN PRINCESS BABE!
DON'T CALL ME BABE. CALL ME PRINCESS KURAMA!

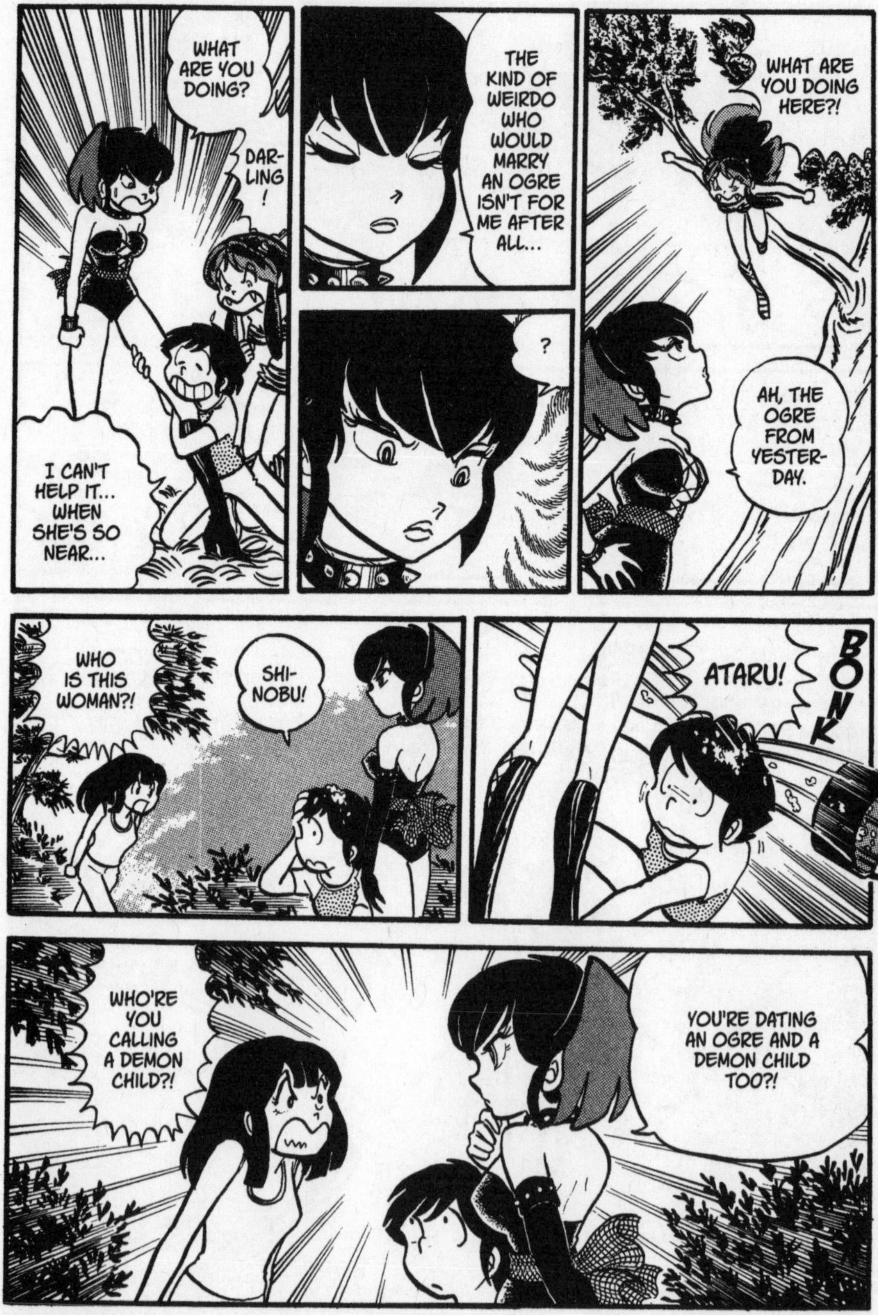
WHAT ARE YOU DOING HERE?!
AH, THE OGRE FROM YESTER-DAY.
THE KIND OF WEIRDO WHO WOULD MARRY AN OGRE ISN'T FOR ME AFTER ALL...
?
WHAT ARE YOU DOING?
DAR-LING!
I CAN'T HELP IT... WHEN SHE'S SO NEAR...
ATARU!
BONK
SHI-NOBU!
WHO IS THIS WOMAN?!
YOU'RE DATING AN OGRE AND A DEMON CHILD TOO?!
WHO'RE YOU CALLING A DEMON CHILD?!

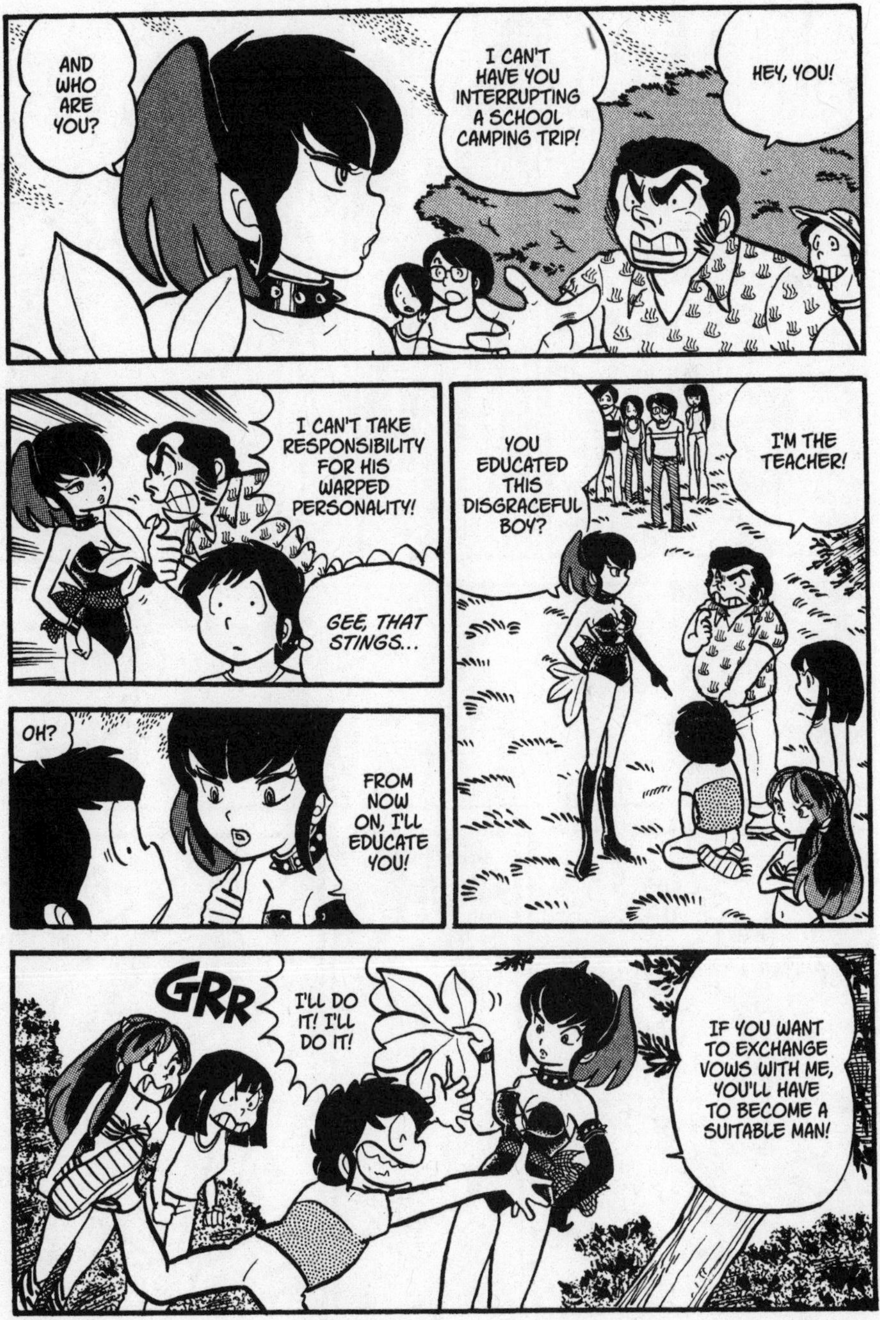
HEY, YOU!
I CAN'T HAVE YOU INTERRUPTING A SCHOOL CAMPING TRIP!
AND WHO ARE YOU?
I'M THE TEACHER!
YOU EDUCATED THIS DISGRACEFUL BOY?
I CAN'T TAKE RESPONSIBILITY FOR HIS WARPED PERSONALITY!
GEE, THAT STINGS...
FROM NOW ON, I'LL EDUCATE YOU!
OH?
IF YOU WANT TO EXCHANGE VOWS WITH ME, YOU'LL HAVE TO BECOME A SUITABLE MAN!
I'LL DO IT! I'LL DO IT!
GRR

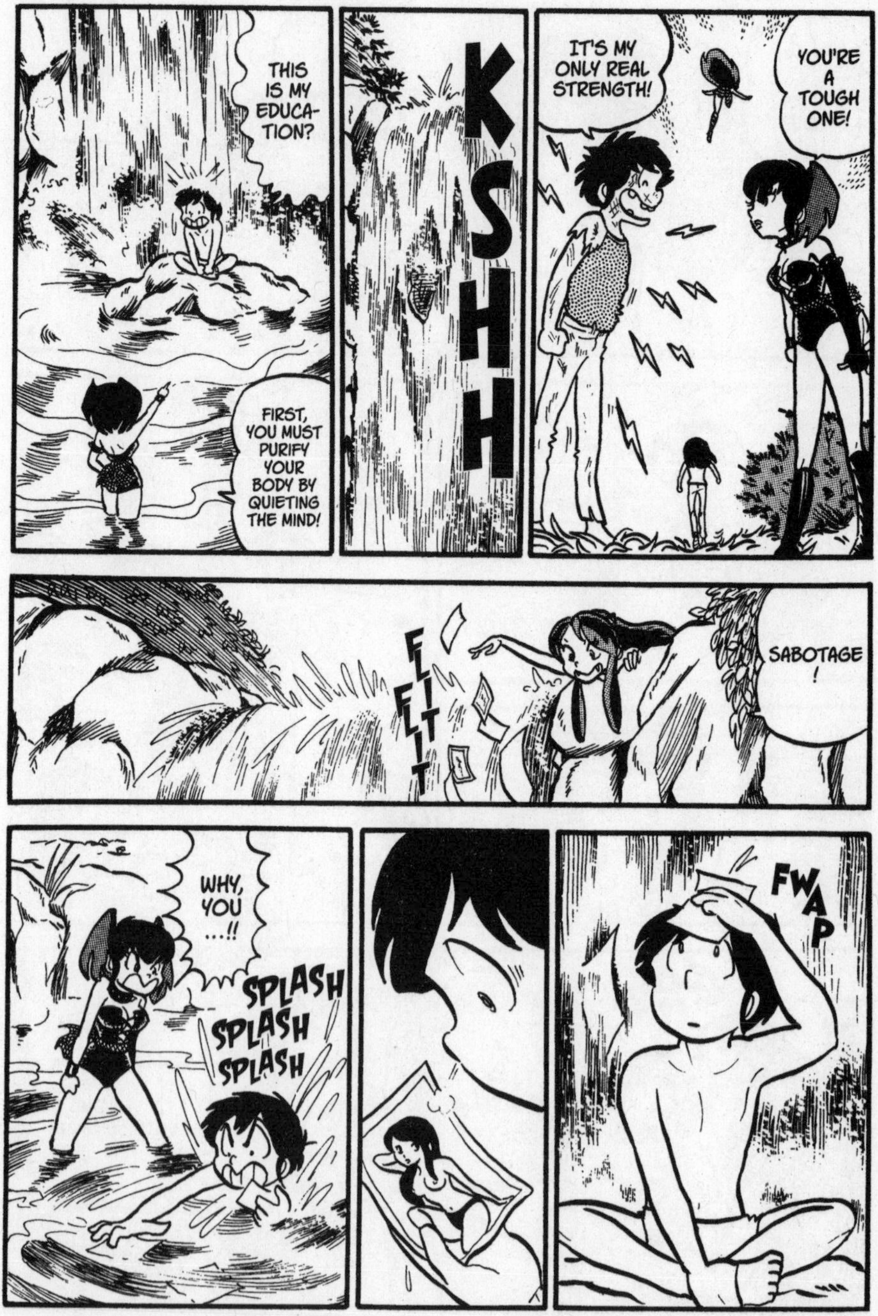
YOU'RE A TOUGH ONE!
IT'S MY ONLY REAL STRENGTH!
KSHH
THIS IS MY EDUCA-TION?
FIRST, YOU MUST PURIFY YOUR BODY BY QUIETING THE MIND!
SABOTAGE!
FLIT FLIT
FWAP
WHY, YOU ...!!
SPLASH SPLASH SPLASH

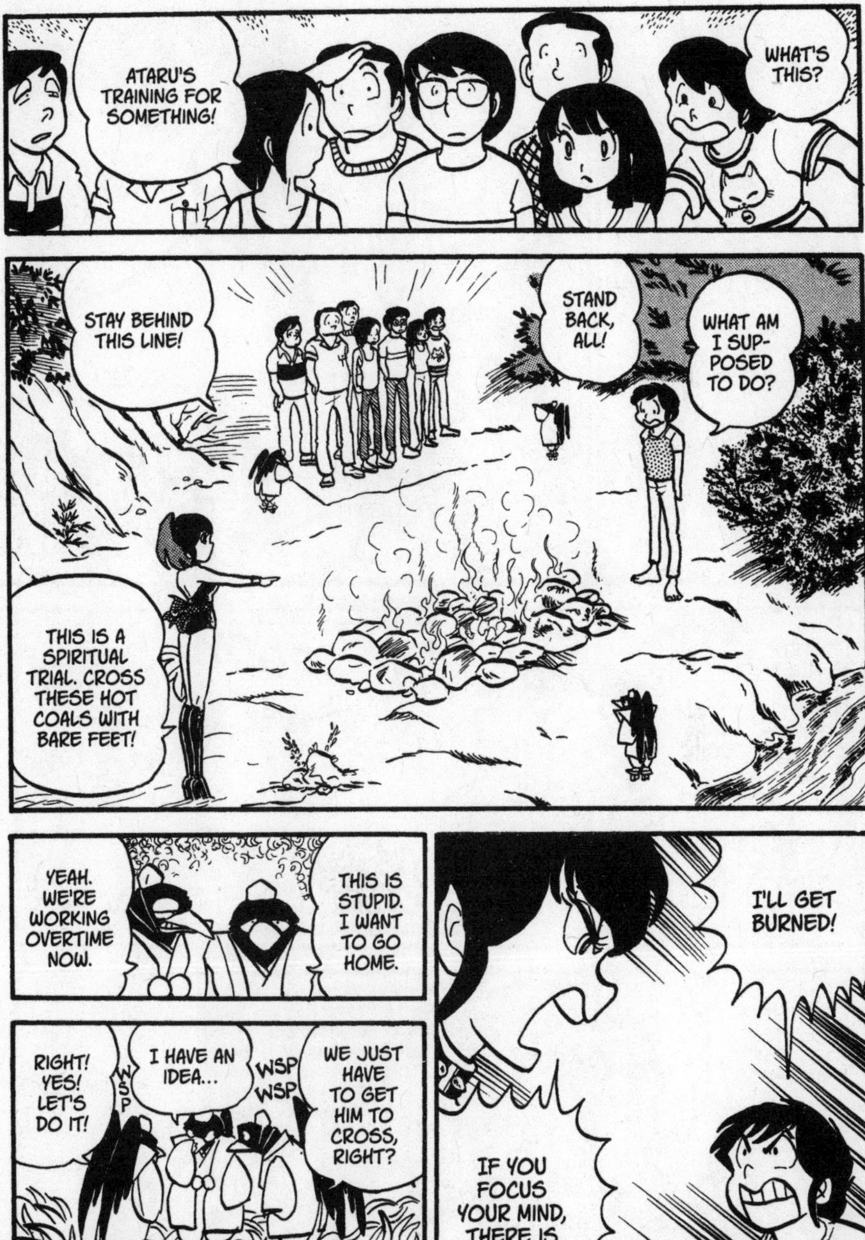
WHAT'S THIS?
ATARU'S TRAINING FOR SOMETHING!
STAND BACK, ALL!
WHAT AM I SUP-POSED TO DO?
STAY BEHIND THIS LINE!
THIS IS A SPIRITUAL TRIAL. CROSS THESE HOT COALS WITH BARE FEET!
I'LL GET BURNED!
IF YOU FOCUS YOUR MIND, THERE IS NO HEAT!
THIS IS STUPID. I WANT TO GO HOME.
YEAH. WE'RE WORKING OVERTIME NOW.
WE JUST HAVE TO GET HIM TO CROSS, RIGHT?
WSP WSP
I HAVE AN IDEA...
WSP
RIGHT! YES! LET'S DO IT!

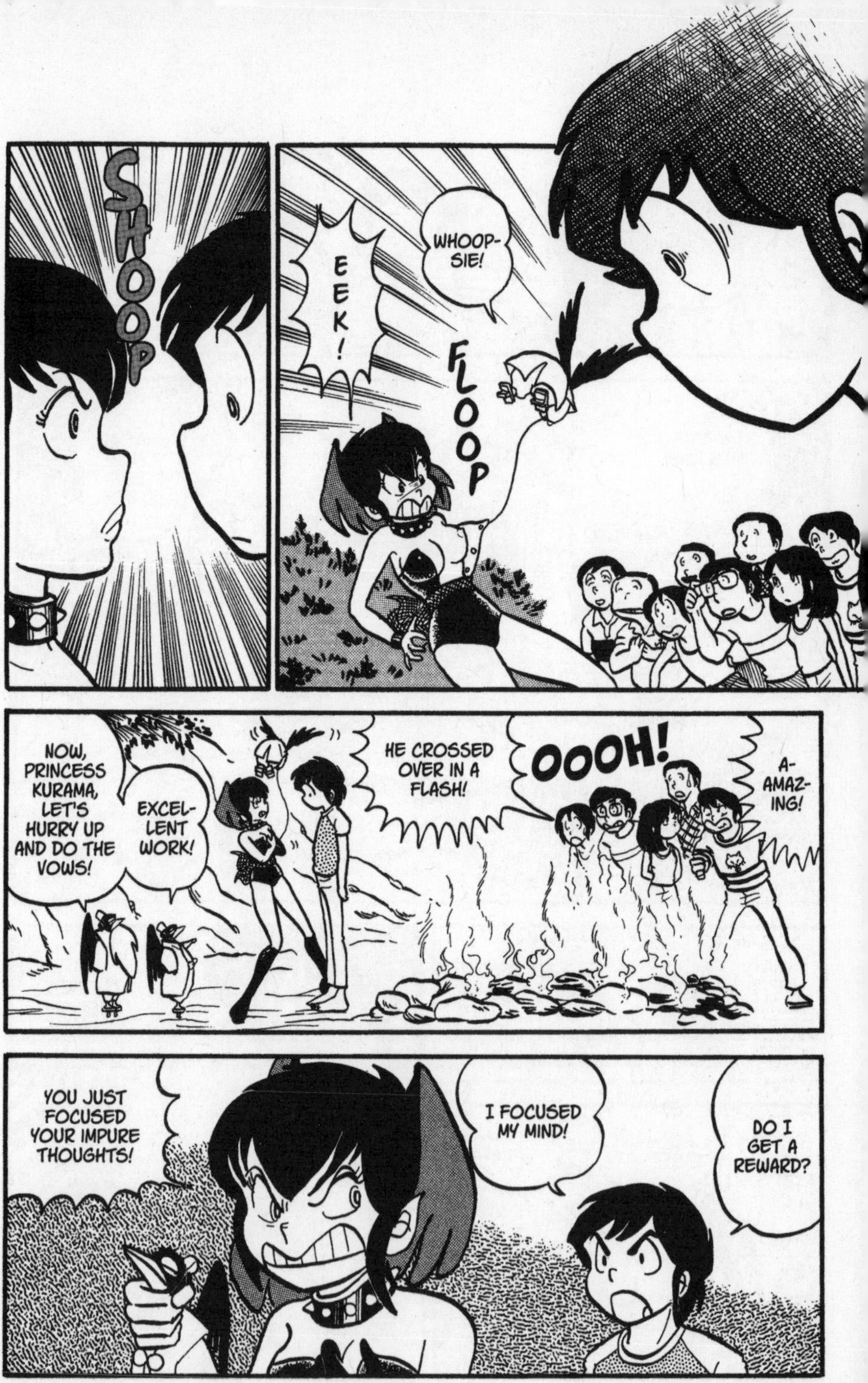
WHOOP-SIE!
EEK!
FLOOP
SHOOP
A-AMAZ-ING!
OOOH!
HE CROSSED OVER IN A FLASH!
EXCEL-LENT WORK!
NOW, PRINCESS KURAMA, LET'S HURRY UP AND DO THE VOWS!
DO I GET A REWARD?
I FOCUSED MY MIND!
YOU JUST FOCUSED YOUR IMPURE THOUGHTS!

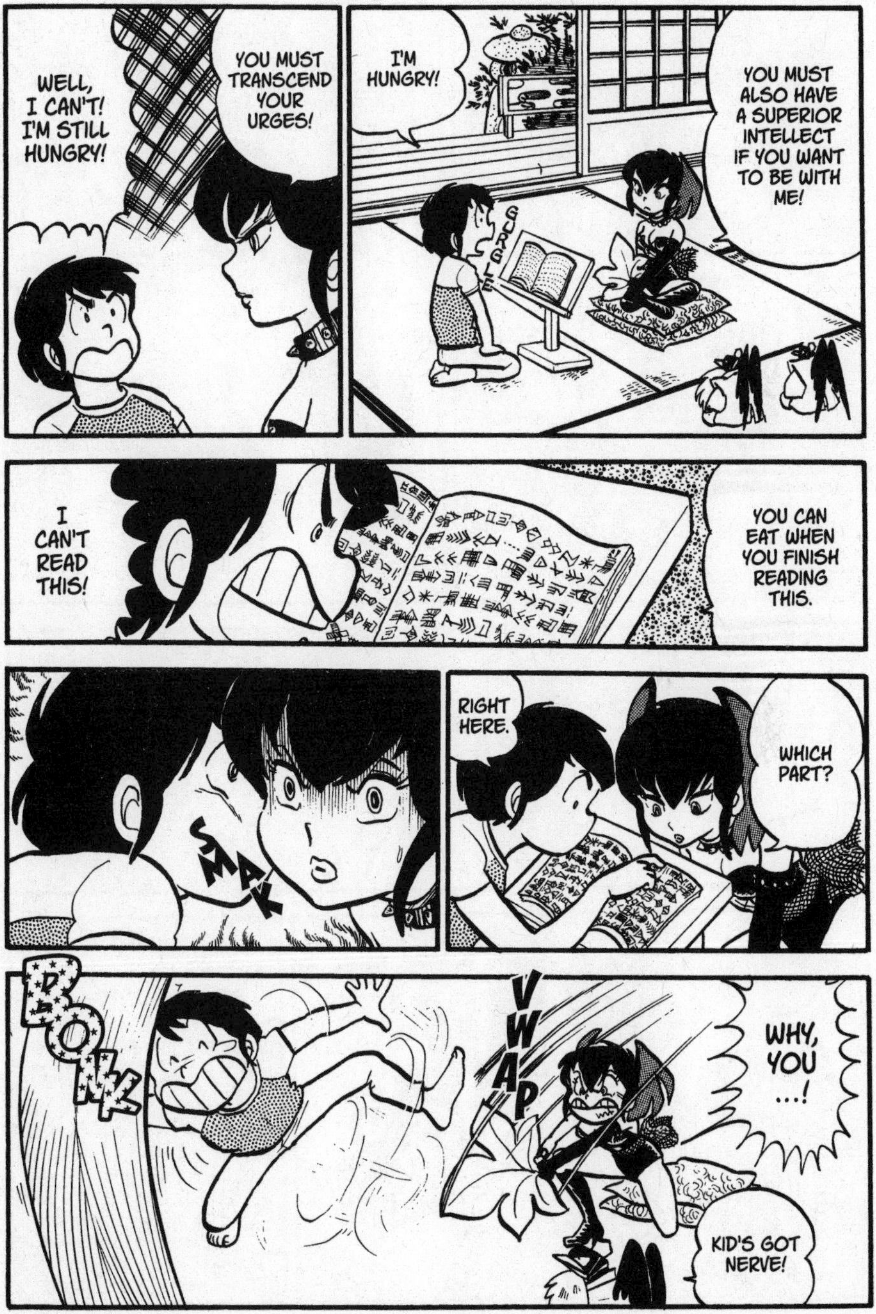
YOU MUST ALSO HAVE A SUPERIOR INTELLECT IF YOU WANT TO BE WITH ME!
I'M HUNGRY!
GURGLE
YOU MUST TRANSCEND YOUR URGES!
WELL, I CAN'T! I'M STILL HUNGRY!
YOU CAN EAT WHEN YOU FINISH READING THIS.
I CAN'T READ THIS!
WHICH PART?
RIGHT HERE.
SMAK
WHY, YOU ...!
KID'S GOT NERVE!
VWAP
BONK

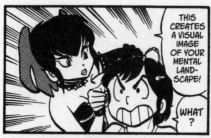

WHAT NOW?
WE'RE GOING TO FIND OUT WHY YOUR BRAIN IS SO WARPED!
THIS CREATES A VISUAL IMAGE OF YOUR MENTAL LAND-SCAPE!
WHAT ?
STOP! THIS IS A VIOLATION OF PRIVACY!
CHAK
LUM! DON'T JUST HANG THERE! HELP ME!
YOU MADE YOUR BED, DARLING!
...
HMPH!
MFF!
FWAP
WHOA!
THIS IS INTER-ESTING!

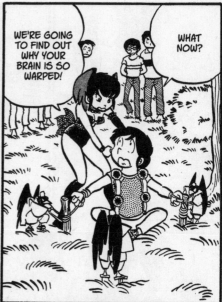

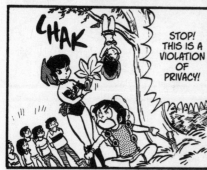

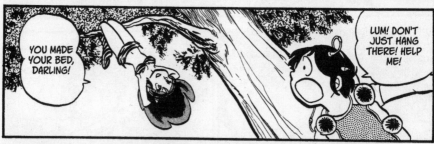

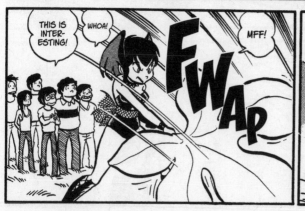

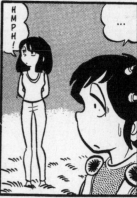

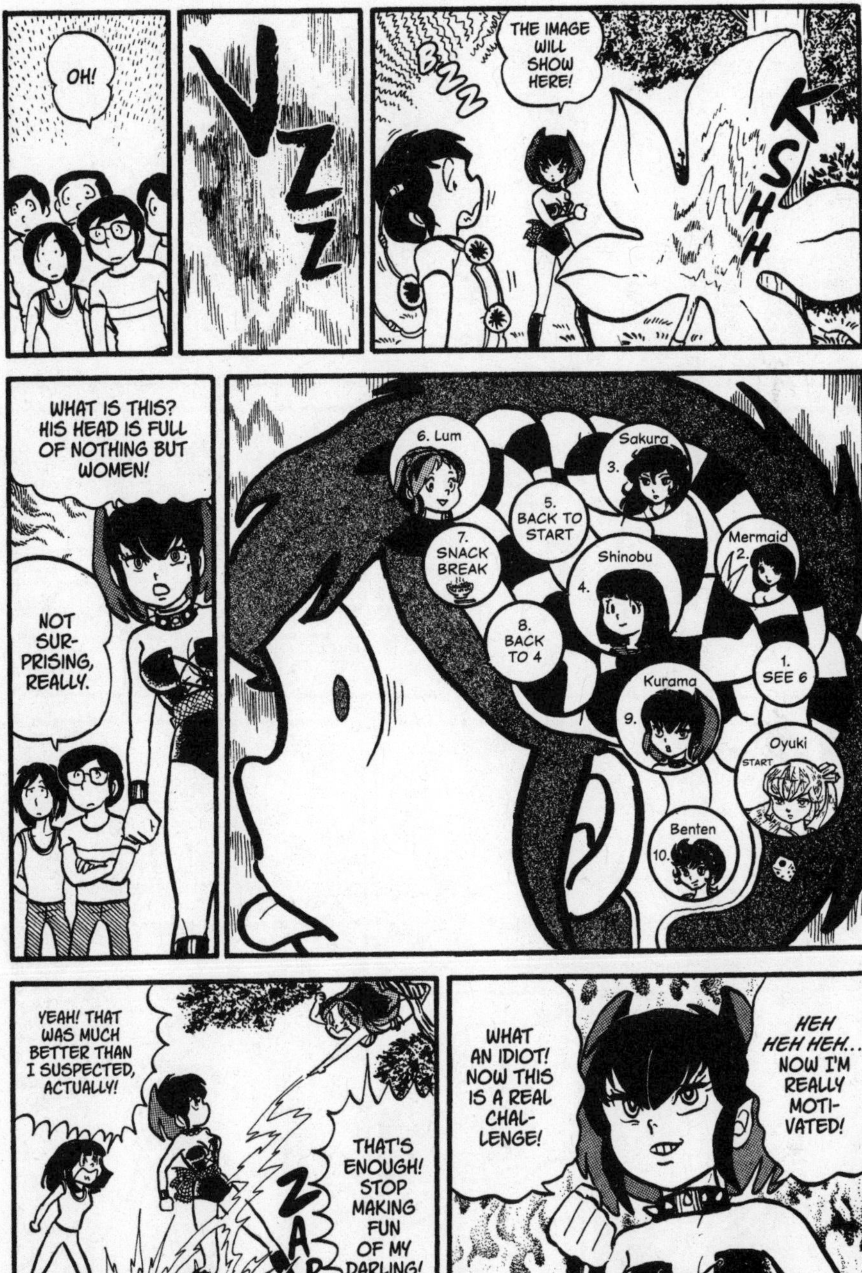
THE IMAGE WILL SHOW HERE!
BZZZ
KSHH
VZZZ
OH!
6. Lum
Sakura
3.
5. BACK TO START
Mermaid
2.
7. SNACK BREAK
Shinobu
4.
8. BACK TO 4
1. SEE 6
Kurama
9.
Oyuki
START
Benten
10.
WHAT IS THIS? HIS HEAD IS FULL OF NOTHING BUT WOMEN!
NOT SUR-PRISING, REALLY.
HEH HEH HEH... NOW I'M REALLY MOTI-VATED!
WHAT AN IDIOT! NOW THIS IS A REAL CHAL-LENGE!
YEAH! THAT WAS MUCH BETTER THAN I SUSPECTED, ACTUALLY!
THAT'S ENOUGH! STOP MAKING FUN OF MY DARLING!
ZAP

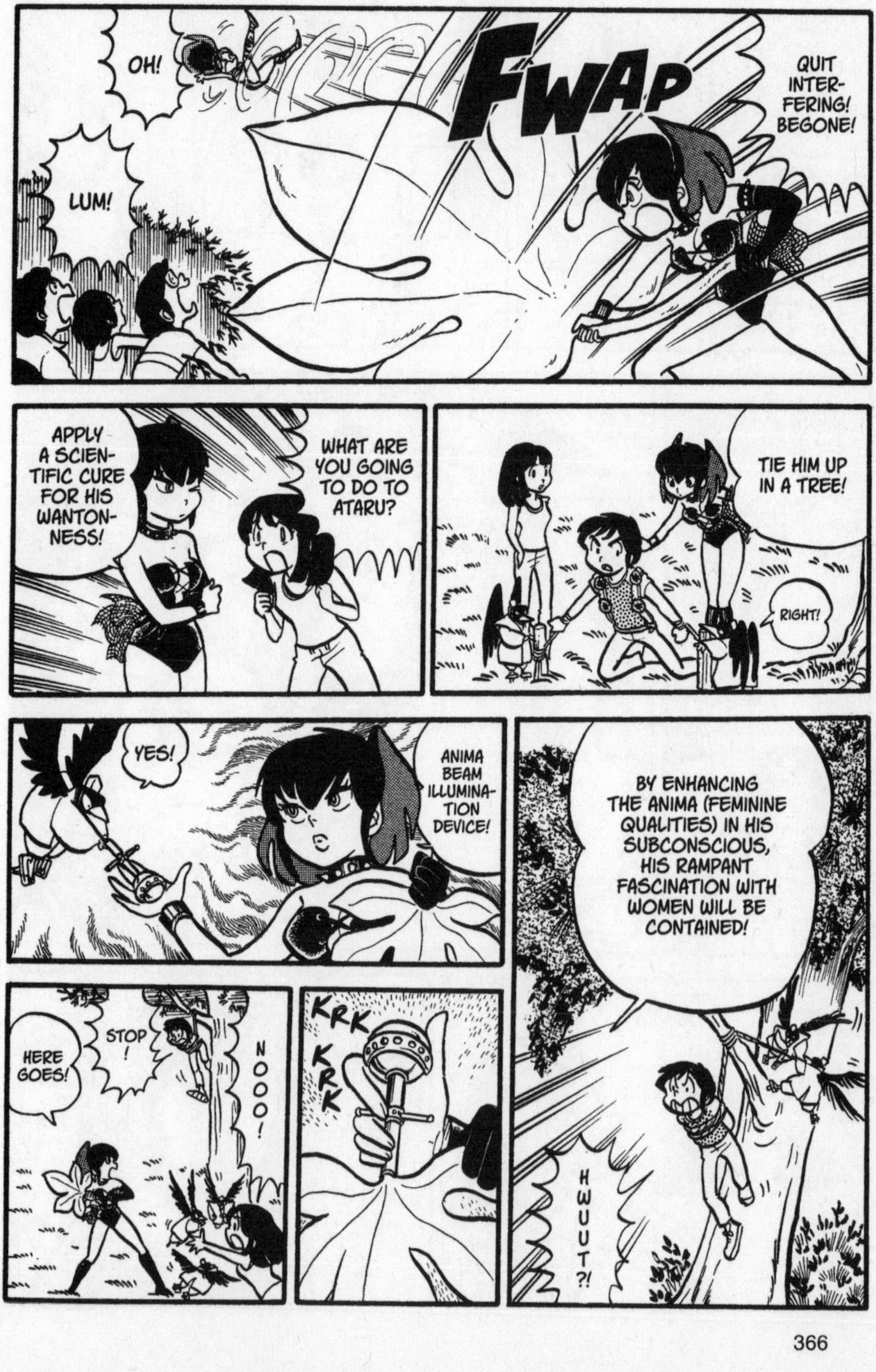
QUIT INTER-FERING! BEGONE!
FWAP
OH!
LUM!
TIE HIM UP IN A TREE!
RIGHT!
WHAT ARE YOU GOING TO DO TO ATARU?
APPLY A SCIEN-TIFIC CURE FOR HIS WANTON-NESS!
BY ENHANCING THE ANIMA (FEMININE QUALITIES) IN HIS SUBCONSCIOUS, HIS RAMPANT FASCINATION WITH WOMEN WILL BE CONTAINED!
HWUUT?!
ANIMA BEAM ILLUMINA-TION DEVICE!
YES!
KRK
KRK
KRK
NOOO!
STOP!
HERE GOES!

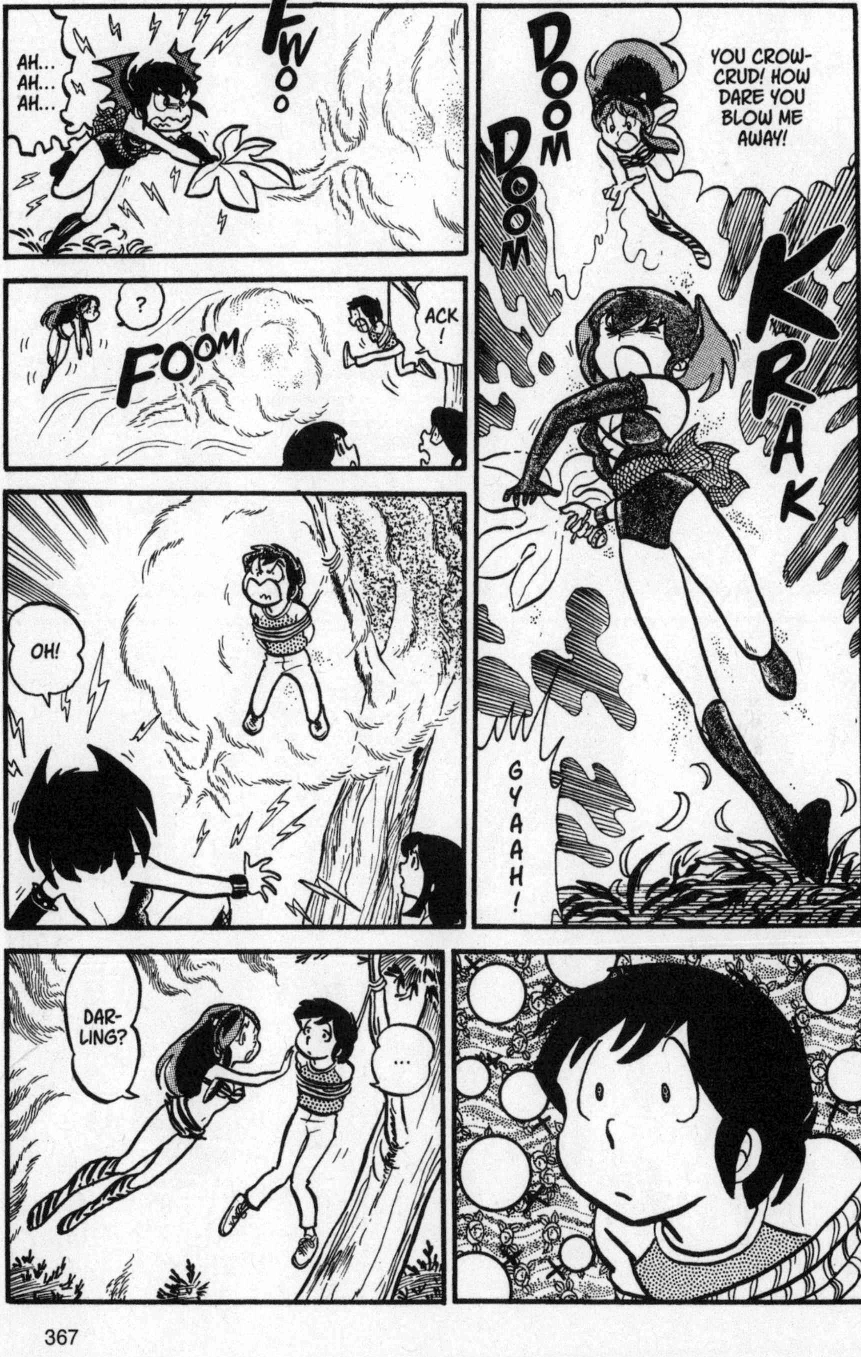
YOU CROW-CRUD! HOW DARE YOU BLOW ME AWAY!
DOOM
DOOM
KRAK
GYAAH!
AH... AH... AH...
FWOOO
ACK!
?
FOOM
OH!
DAR-LING?
...

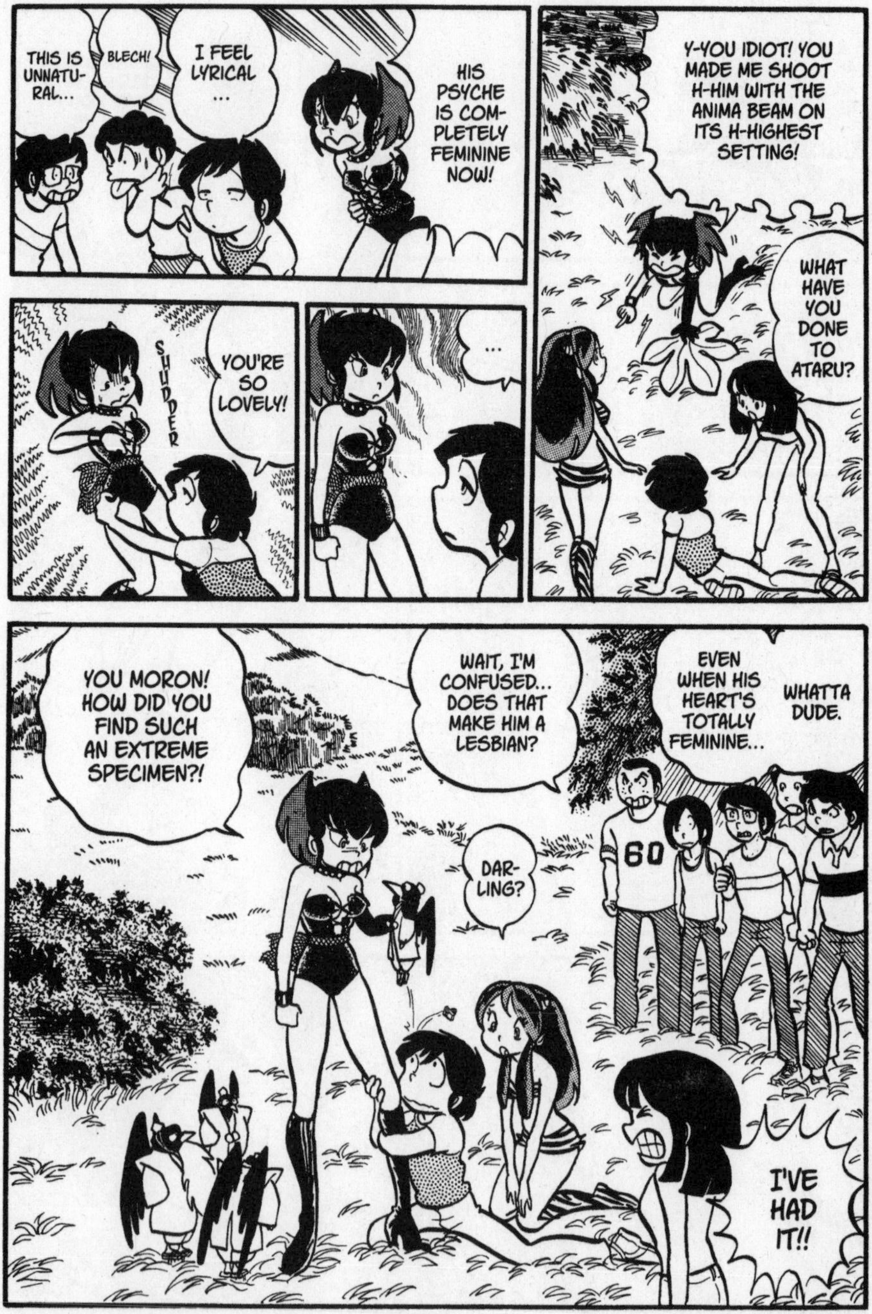
Y-YOU IDIOT! YOU MADE ME SHOOT H-HIM WITH THE ANIMA BEAM ON ITS H-HIGHEST SETTING!
WHAT HAVE YOU DONE TO ATARU?
HIS PSYCHE IS COMPLETELY FEMININE NOW!
I FEEL LYRICAL...
BLECH!
THIS IS UNNATURAL...
...
YOU'RE SO LOVELY!
SHUDDER
EVEN WHEN HIS HEART'S TOTALLY FEMININE...
WHATTA DUDE.
WAIT, I'M CONFUSED... DOES THAT MAKE HIM A LESBIAN?
YOU MORON! HOW DID YOU FIND SUCH AN EXTREME SPECIMEN?!
DARLING?
60
I'VE HAD IT!!

CHAPTER 17: OBSESSION IS A PART OF LOVE

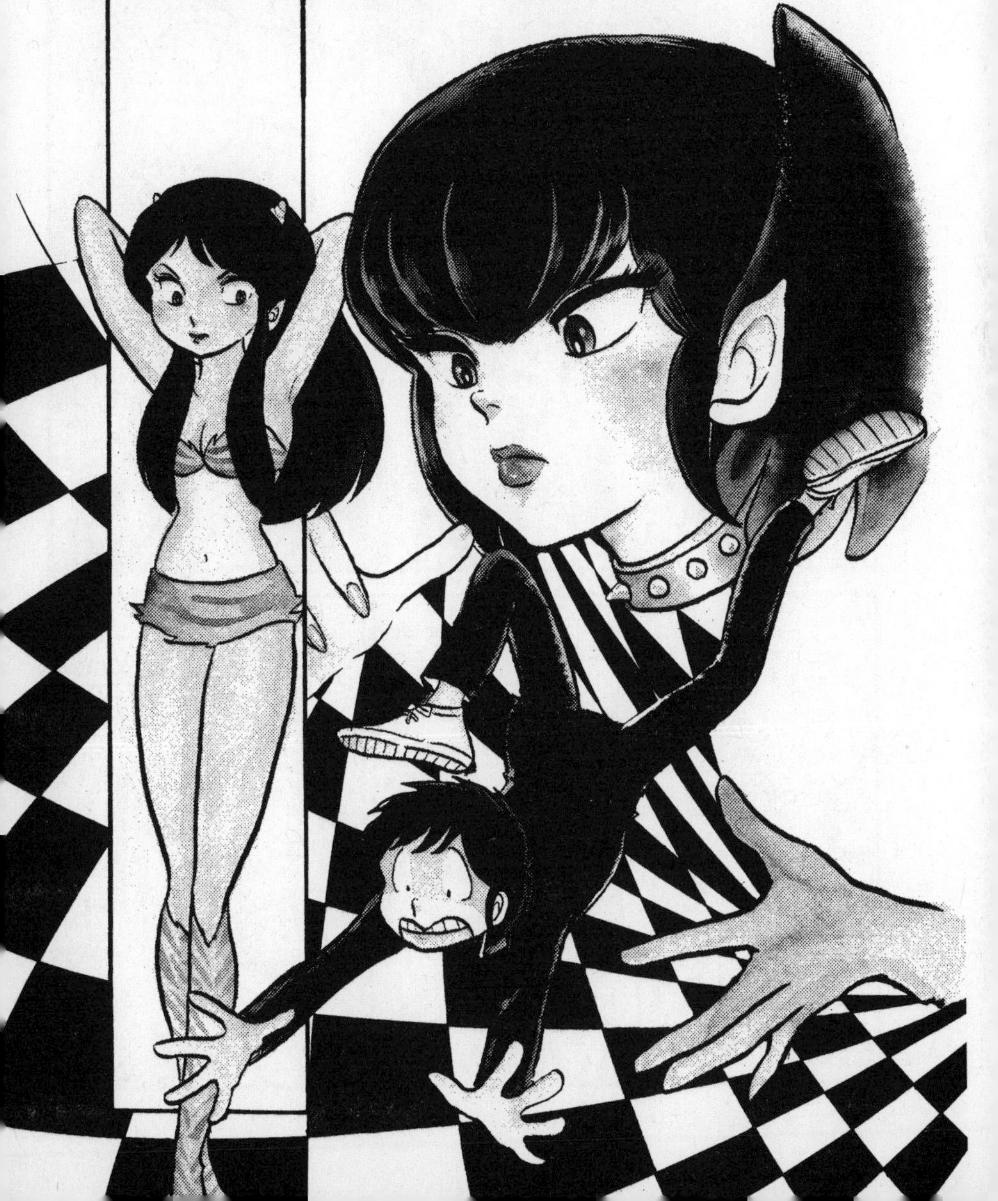

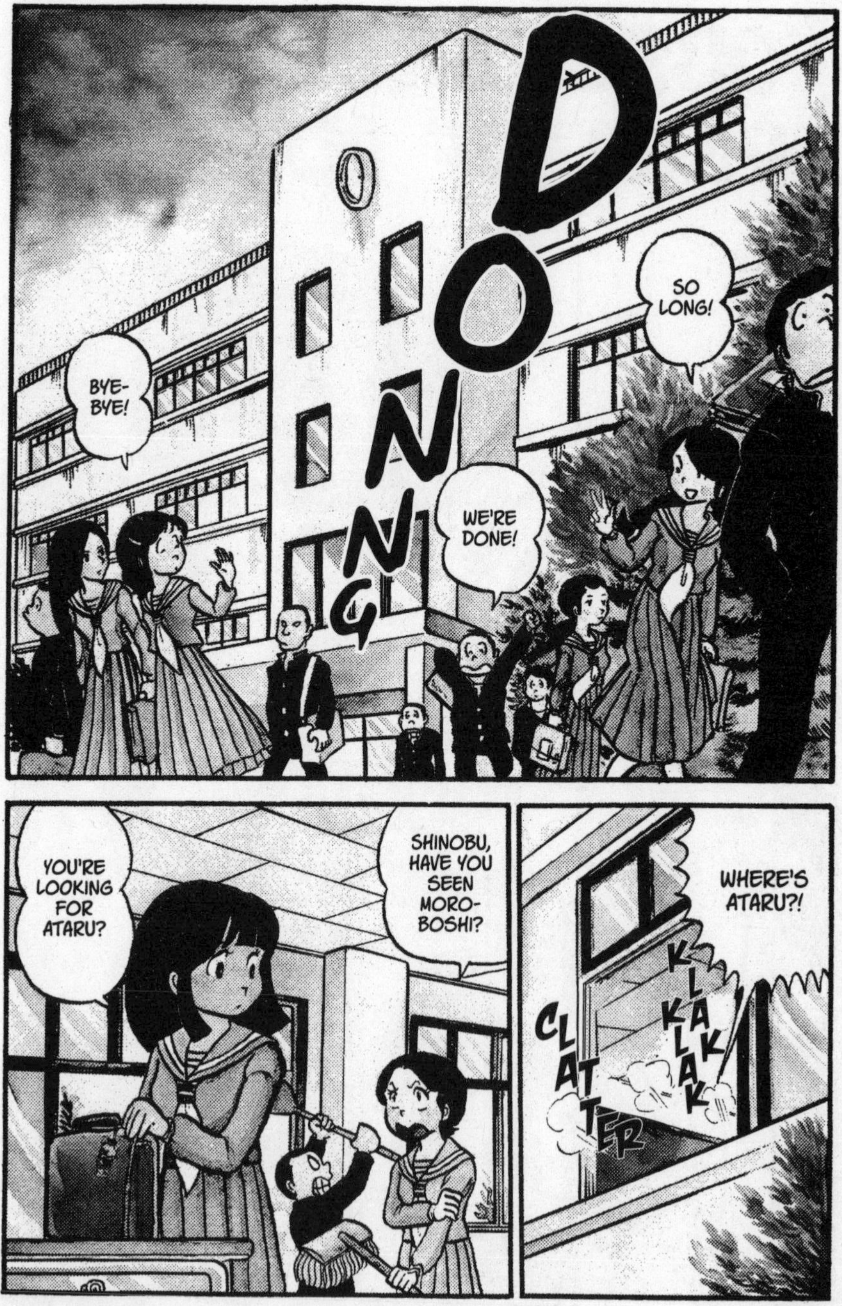
SO LONG!
DONNG
BYE-BYE!
WE'RE DONE!
WHERE'S ATARU?!
KLAK KLAK
CLATTER
SHINOBU, HAVE YOU SEEN MOROBOSHI?
YOU'RE LOOKING FOR ATARU?

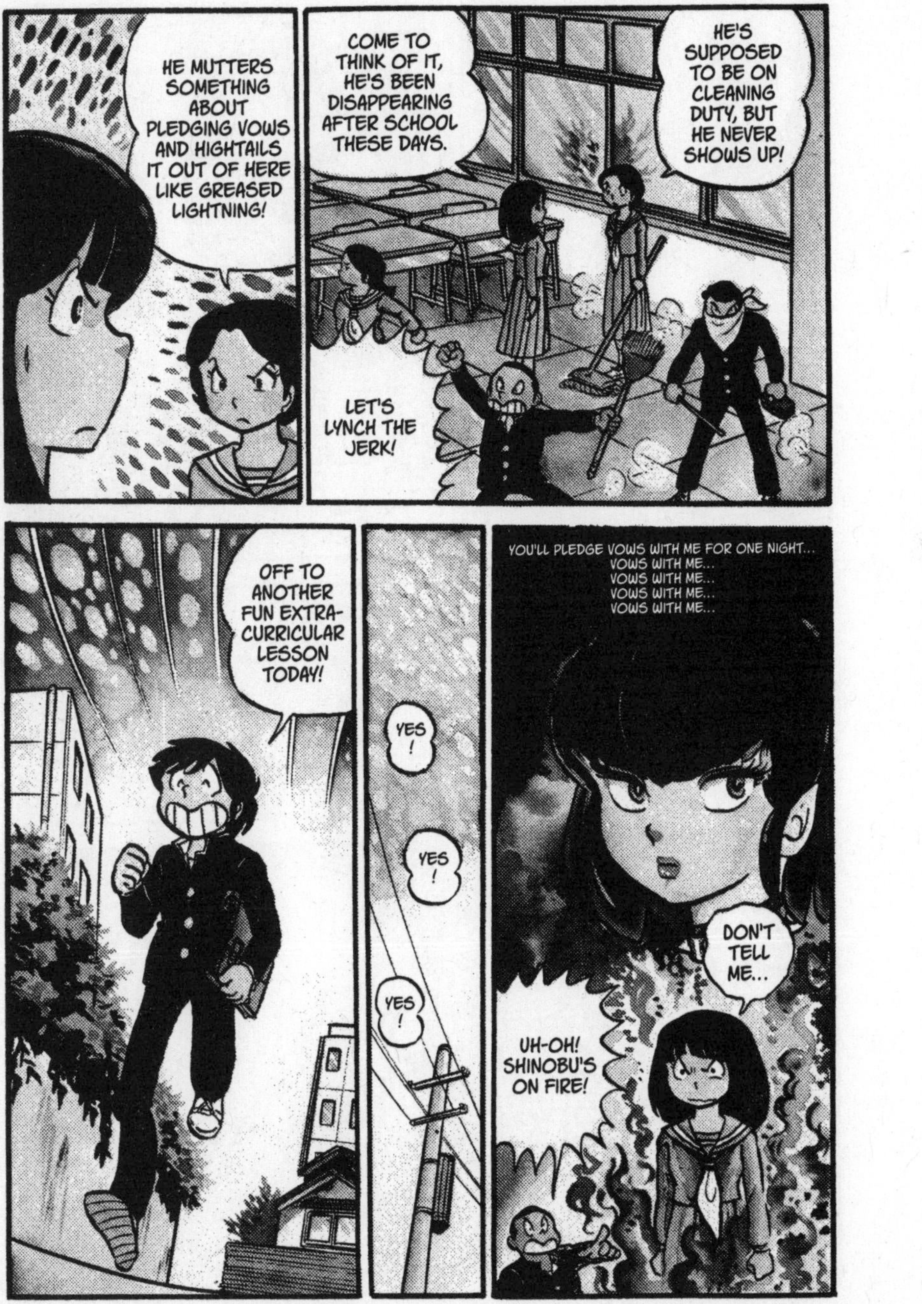
HE'S SUPPOSED TO BE ON CLEANING DUTY, BUT HE NEVER SHOWS UP!
COME TO THINK OF IT, HE'S BEEN DISAPPEARING AFTER SCHOOL THESE DAYS.
LET'S LYNCH THE JERK!
HE MUTTERS SOMETHING ABOUT PLEDGING VOWS AND HIGHTAILS IT OUT OF HERE LIKE GREASED LIGHTNING!
YOU'LL PLEDGE VOWS WITH ME FOR ONE NIGHT... VOWS WITH ME... VOWS WITH ME... VOWS WITH ME... VOWS WITH ME...
DON'T TELL ME...
UH-OH! SHINOBU'S ON FIRE!
YES!
YES!
YES!
OFF TO ANOTHER FUN EXTRA-CURRICULAR LESSON TODAY!

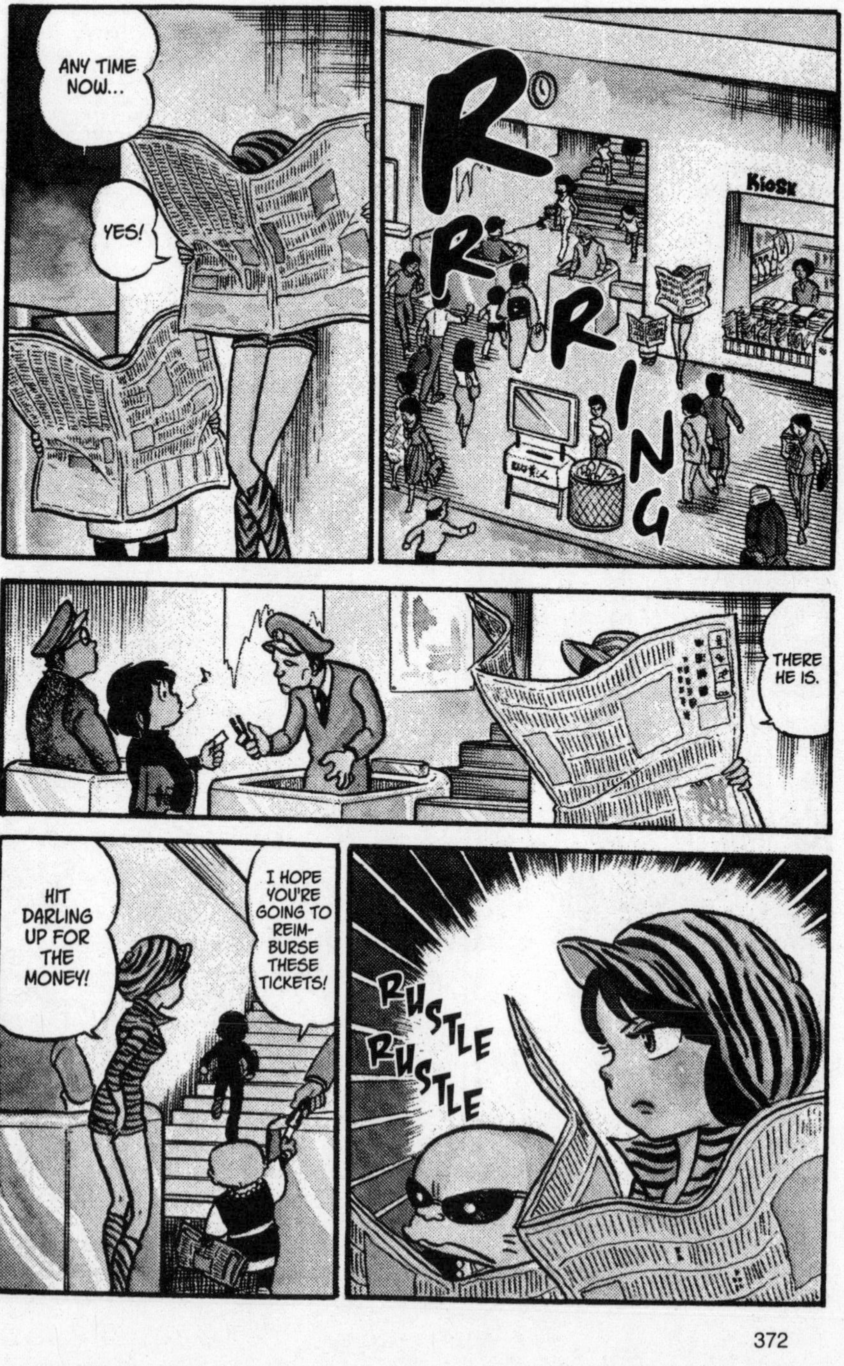
RRRRING
ANY TIME NOW...
YES!
THERE HE IS.
RUSTLE RUSTLE
I HOPE YOU'RE GOING TO REIMBURSE THESE TICKETS!
HIT DARLING UP FOR THE MONEY!

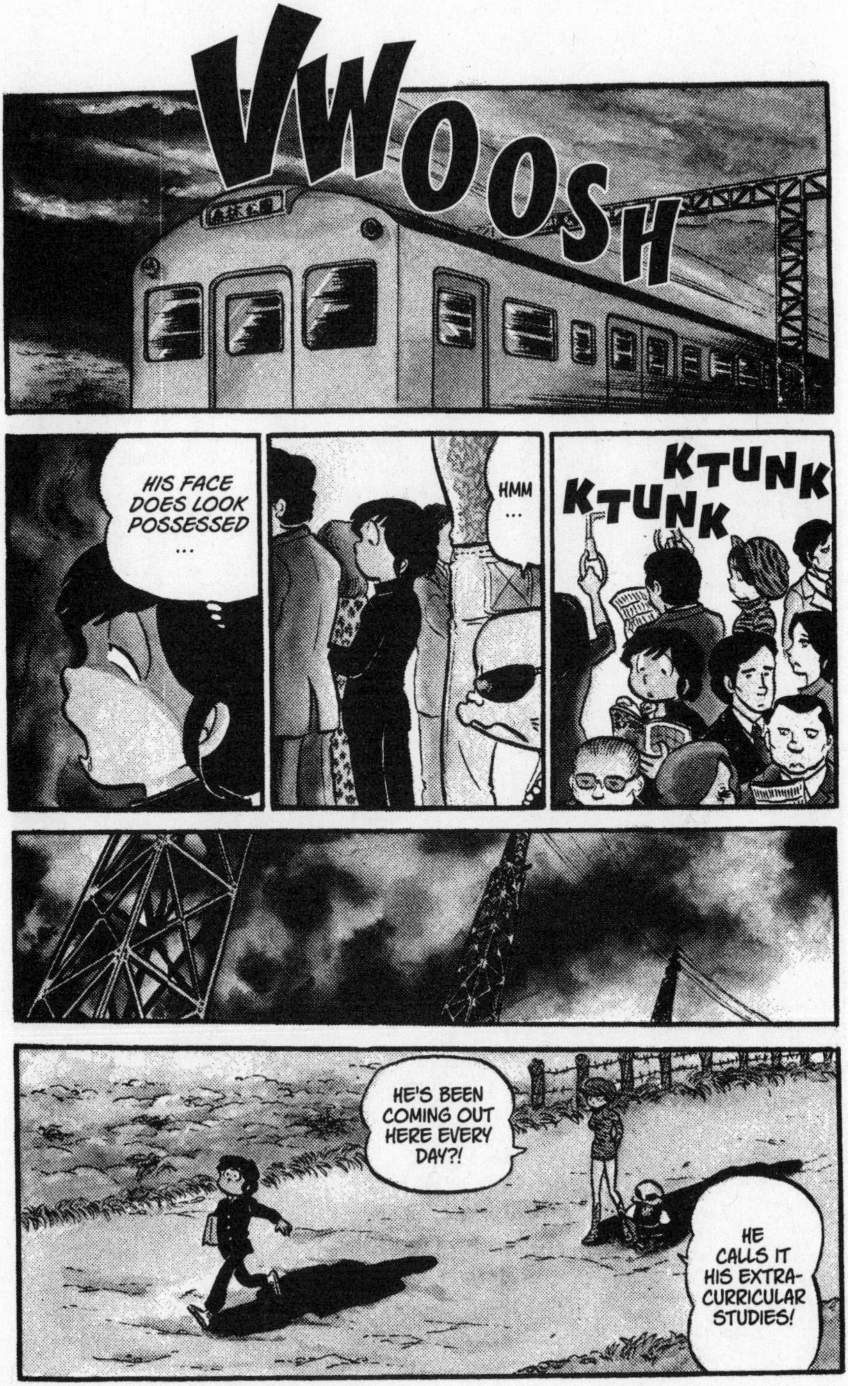
VWOOSH
KTUNK KTUNK
HMM ...
HIS FACE DOES LOOK POSSESSED ...
HE'S BEEN COMING OUT HERE EVERY DAY?!
HE CALLS IT HIS EXTRA-CURRICULAR STUDIES!

KR!!

KCHAM

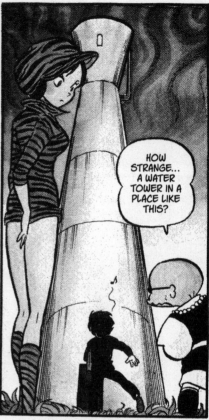

HOW STRANGE... A WATER TOWER IN A PLACE LIKE THIS?

HEY NOW! THE MORON'S HERE!

KURA-MAAAA!

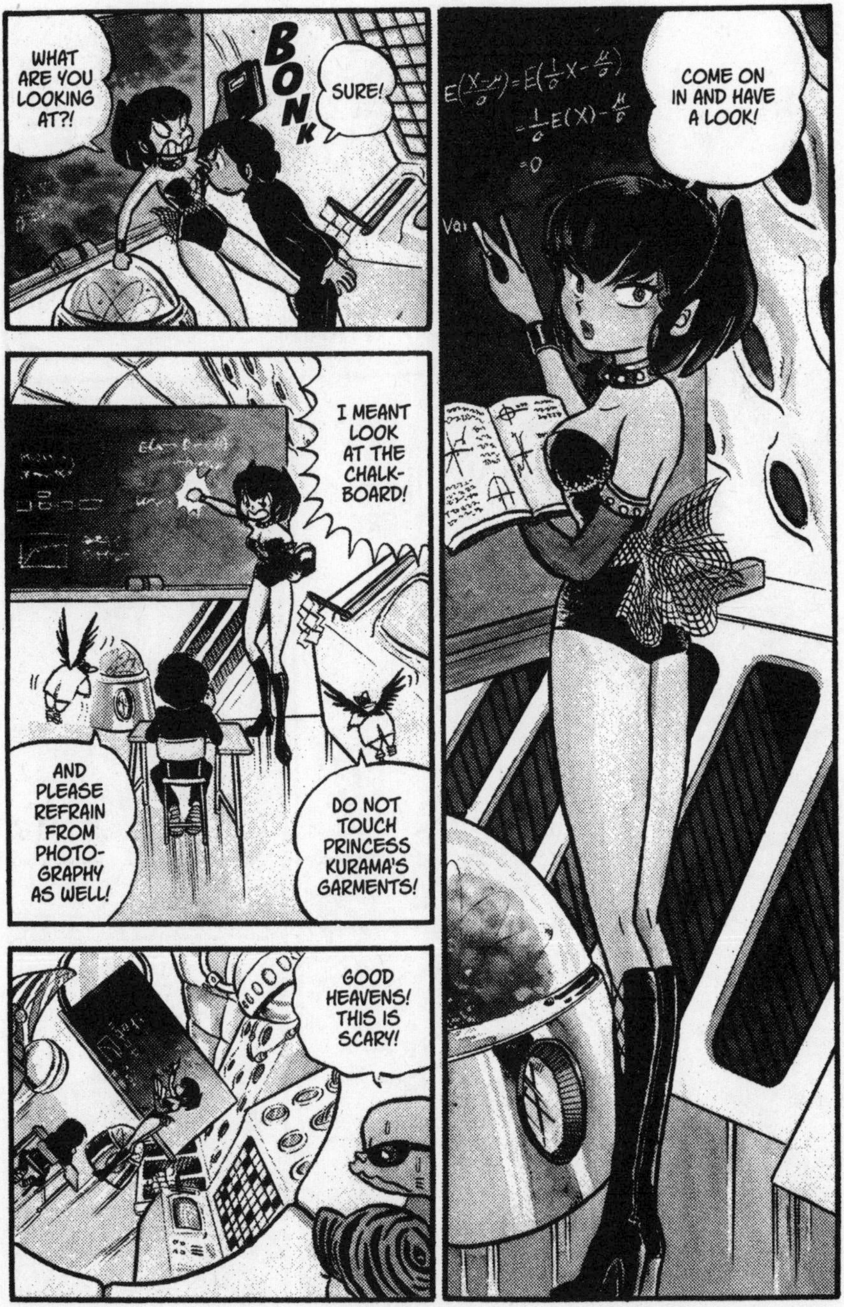
COME ON IN AND HAVE A LOOK!
SURE!
BONK
WHAT ARE YOU LOOKING AT?!
I MEANT LOOK AT THE CHALK-BOARD!
DO NOT TOUCH PRINCESS KURAMA'S GARMENTS!
AND PLEASE REFRAIN FROM PHOTOGRAPHY AS WELL!
GOOD HEAVENS! THIS IS SCARY!

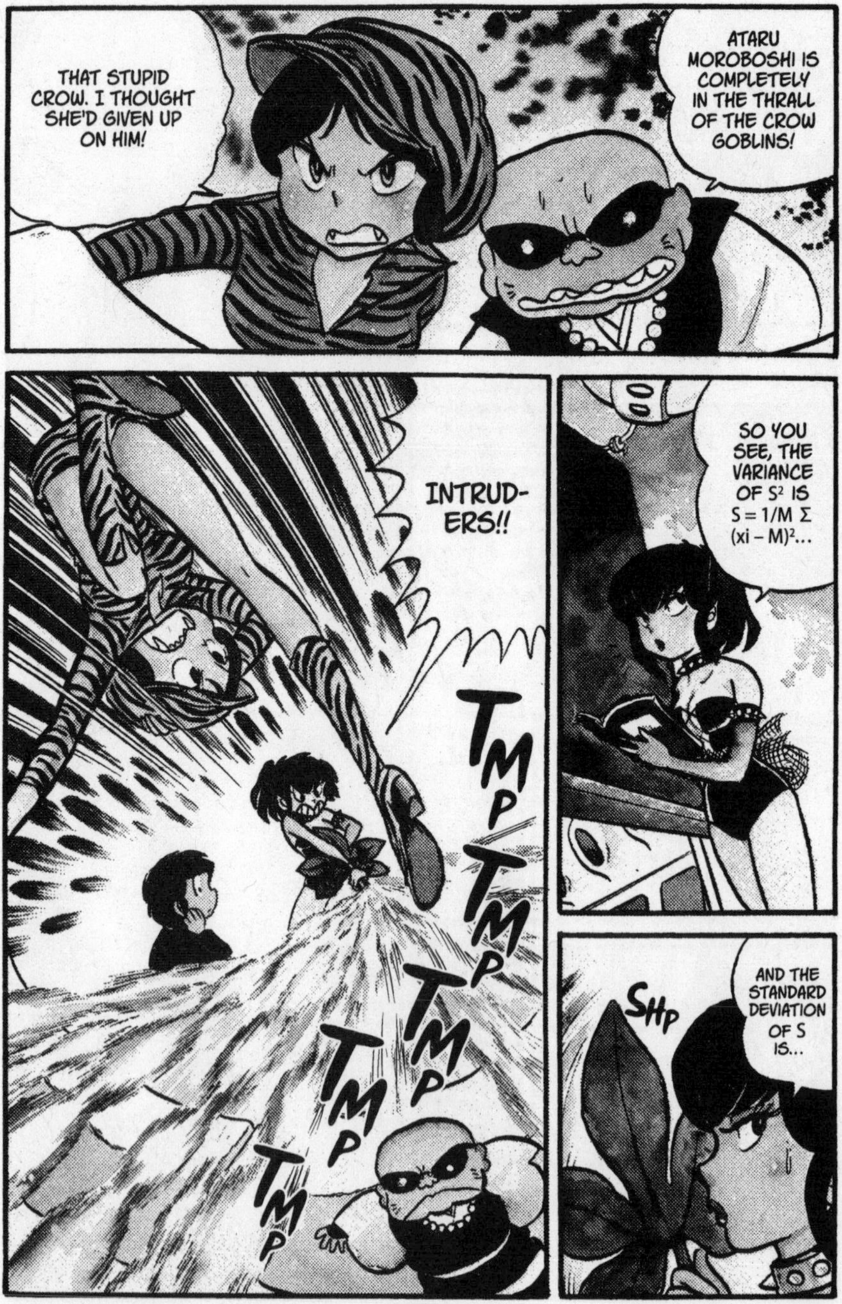
ATARU MOROBOSHI IS COMPLETELY IN THE THRALL OF THE CROW GOBLINS!
THAT STUPID CROW. I THOUGHT SHE'D GIVEN UP ON HIM!
SO YOU SEE, THE VARIANCE OF S^2 IS $S = 1/M\ \Sigma\ (xi - M)^2$…
SHP
AND THE STANDARD DEVIATION OF S IS…
INTRUD-ERS!!
TMP TMP TMP TMP TMP TMP

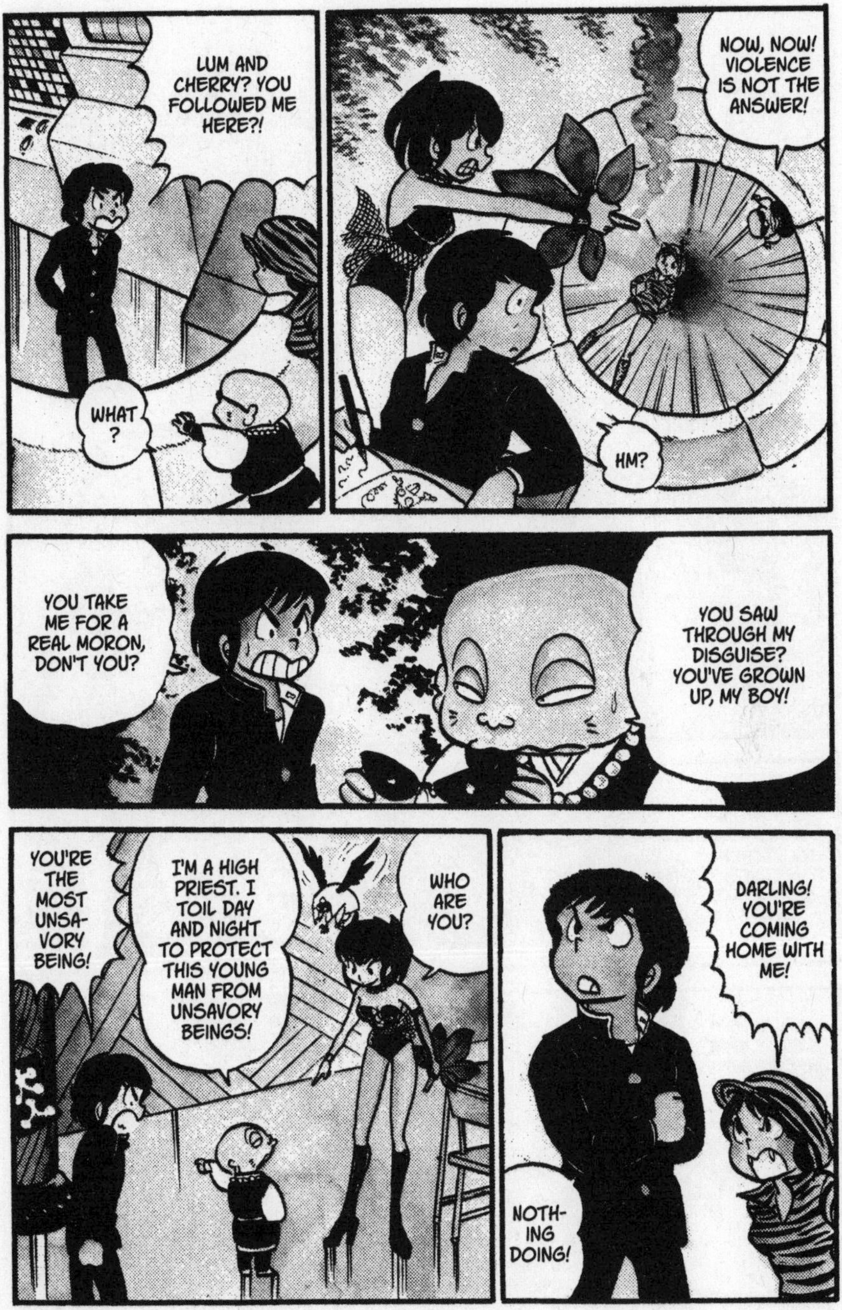
NOW, NOW! VIOLENCE IS NOT THE ANSWER!
HM?
LUM AND CHERRY? YOU FOLLOWED ME HERE?!
WHAT ?
YOU SAW THROUGH MY DISGUISE? YOU'VE GROWN UP, MY BOY!
YOU TAKE ME FOR A REAL MORON, DON'T YOU?
DARLING! YOU'RE COMING HOME WITH ME!
NOTH-ING DOING!
WHO ARE YOU?
I'M A HIGH PRIEST. I TOIL DAY AND NIGHT TO PROTECT THIS YOUNG MAN FROM UNSAVORY BEINGS!
YOU'RE THE MOST UNSA-VORY BEING!

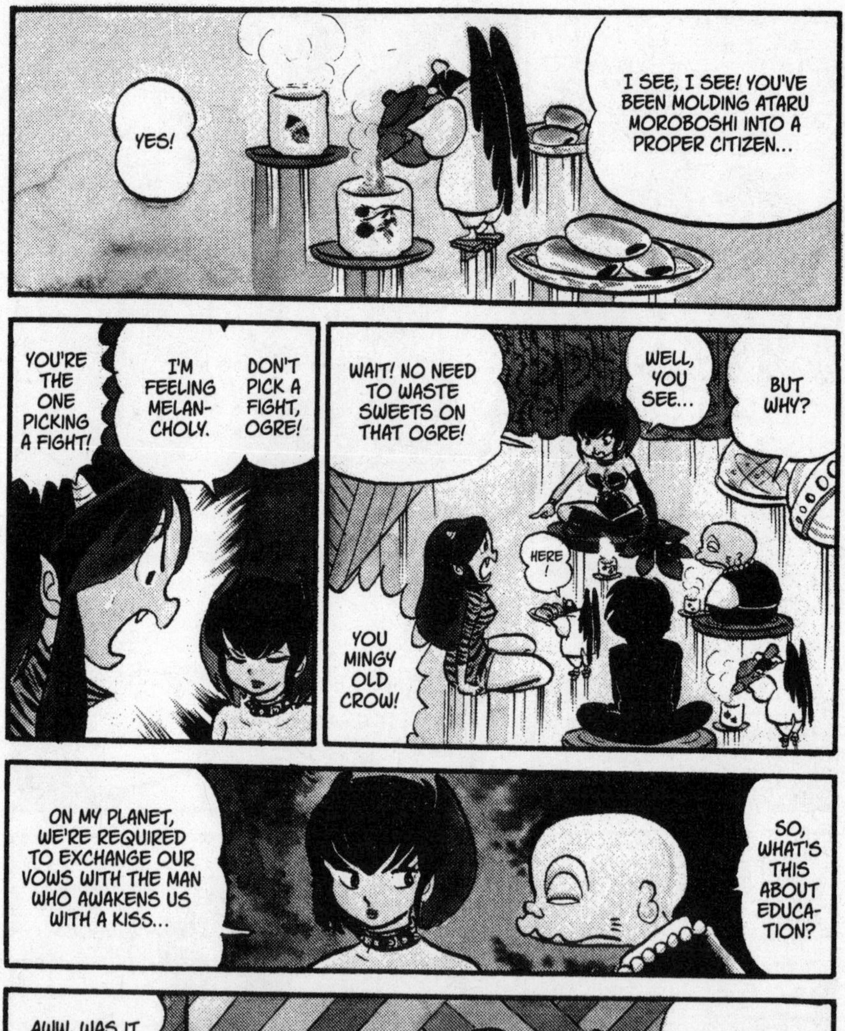
I SEE, I SEE! YOU'VE BEEN MOLDING ATARU MOROBOSHI INTO A PROPER CITIZEN...
YES!
BUT WHY?
WELL, YOU SEE...
WAIT! NO NEED TO WASTE SWEETS ON THAT OGRE!
HERE!
YOU MINGY OLD CROW!
DON'T PICK A FIGHT, OGRE!
I'M FEELING MELAN-CHOLY.
YOU'RE THE ONE PICKING A FIGHT!
SO, WHAT'S THIS ABOUT EDUCA-TION?
ON MY PLANET, WE'RE REQUIRED TO EXCHANGE OUR VOWS WITH THE MAN WHO AWAKENS US WITH A KISS...
UNFORTUNATELY FOR ME, THAT MAN WAS HIM!
AWW, WAS IT REALLY THAT UNFORTUNATE?
YES!!

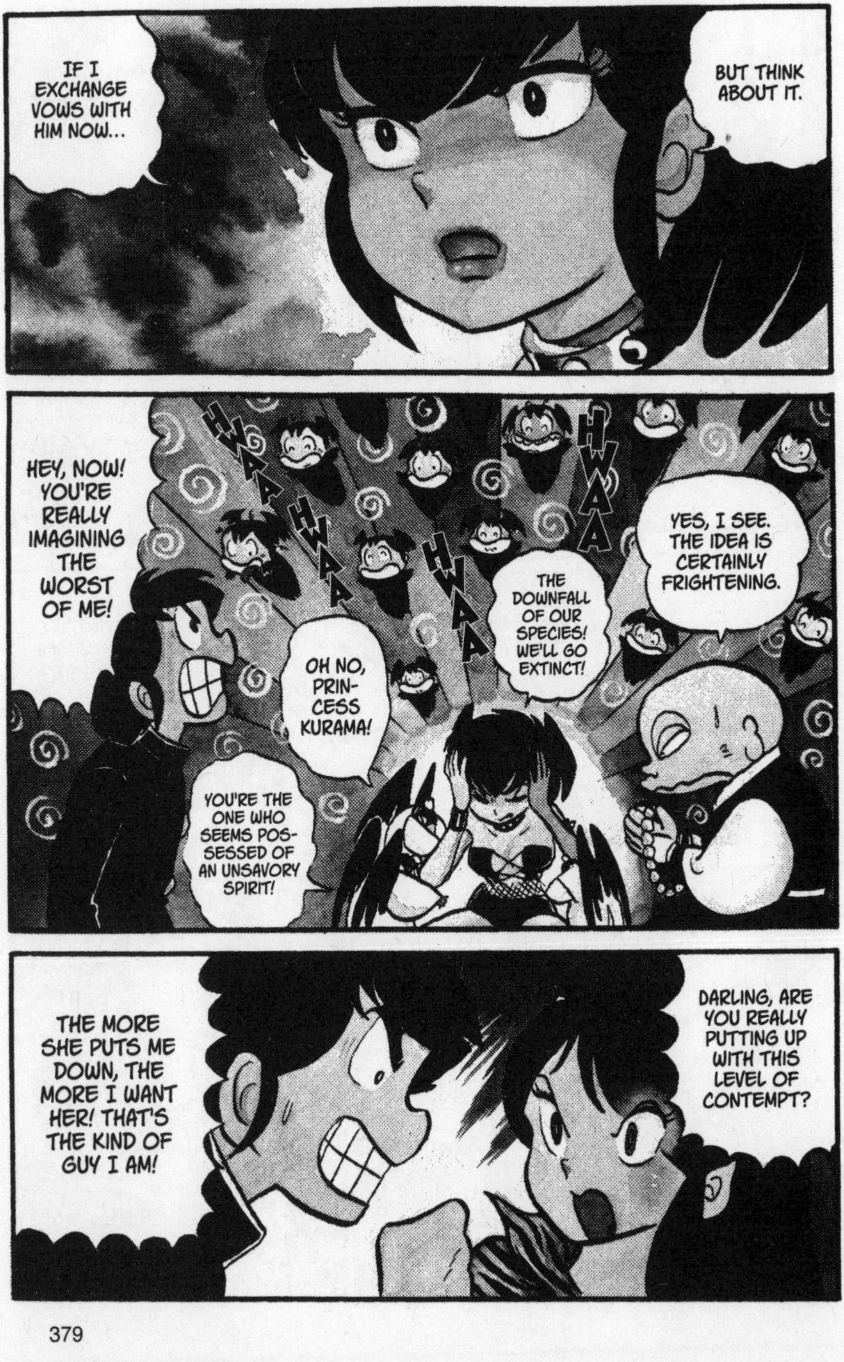
BUT THINK ABOUT IT.
IF I EXCHANGE VOWS WITH HIM NOW...
HWAA
YES, I SEE. THE IDEA IS CERTAINLY FRIGHTENING.
THE DOWNFALL OF OUR SPECIES! WE'LL GO EXTINCT!
HWAA
HWAA
HWAA
OH NO, PRINCESS KURAMA!
HEY, NOW! YOU'RE REALLY IMAGINING THE WORST OF ME!
YOU'RE THE ONE WHO SEEMS POSSESSED OF AN UNSAVORY SPIRIT!
DARLING, ARE YOU REALLY PUTTING UP WITH THIS LEVEL OF CONTEMPT?
THE MORE SHE PUTS ME DOWN, THE MORE I WANT HER! THAT'S THE KIND OF GUY I AM!

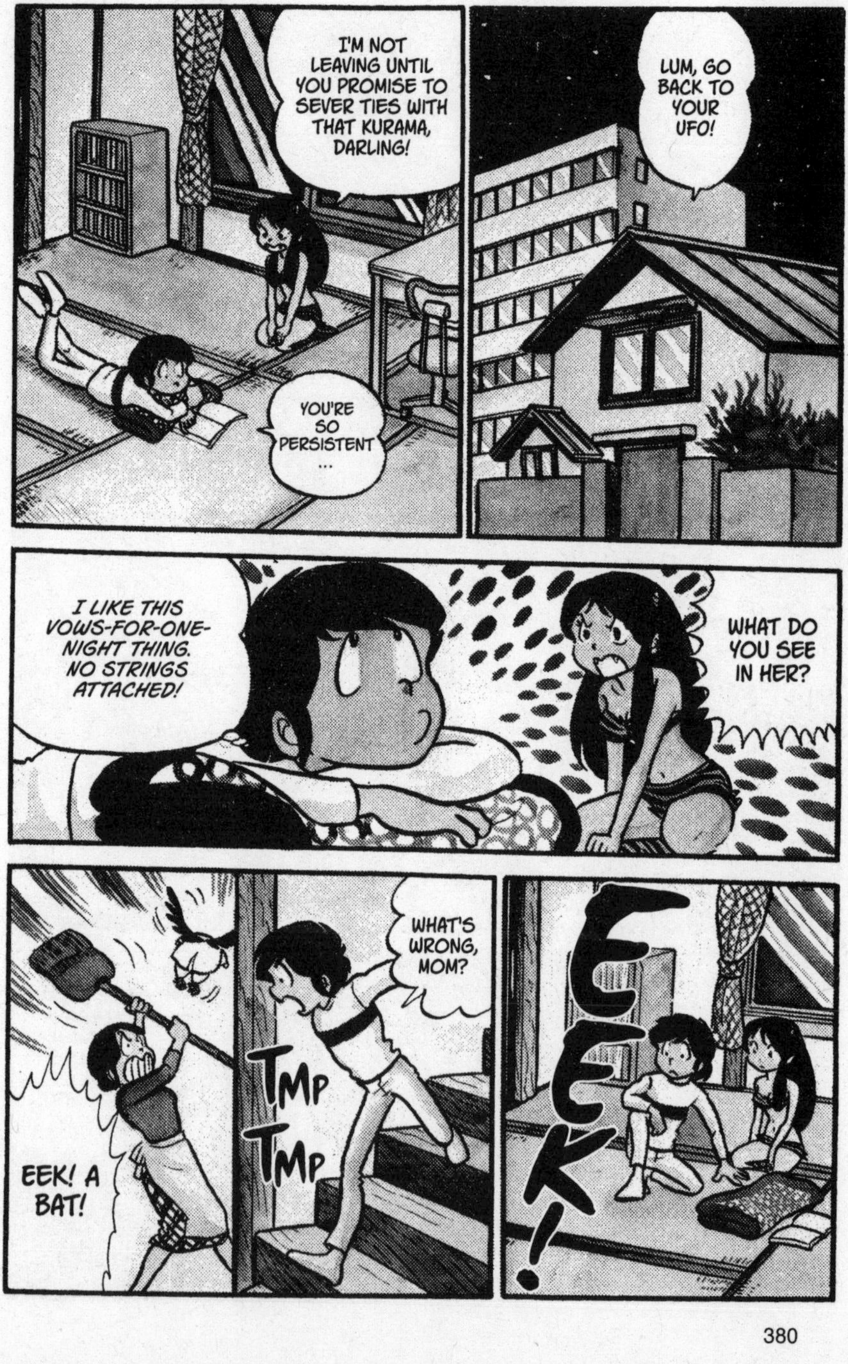
LUM, GO BACK TO YOUR UFO!
I'M NOT LEAVING UNTIL YOU PROMISE TO SEVER TIES WITH THAT KURAMA, DARLING!
YOU'RE SO PERSISTENT ...
WHAT DO YOU SEE IN HER?
I LIKE THIS VOWS-FOR-ONE-NIGHT THING. NO STRINGS ATTACHED!
EEEK!
WHAT'S WRONG, MOM?
TMP TMP
EEK! A BAT!

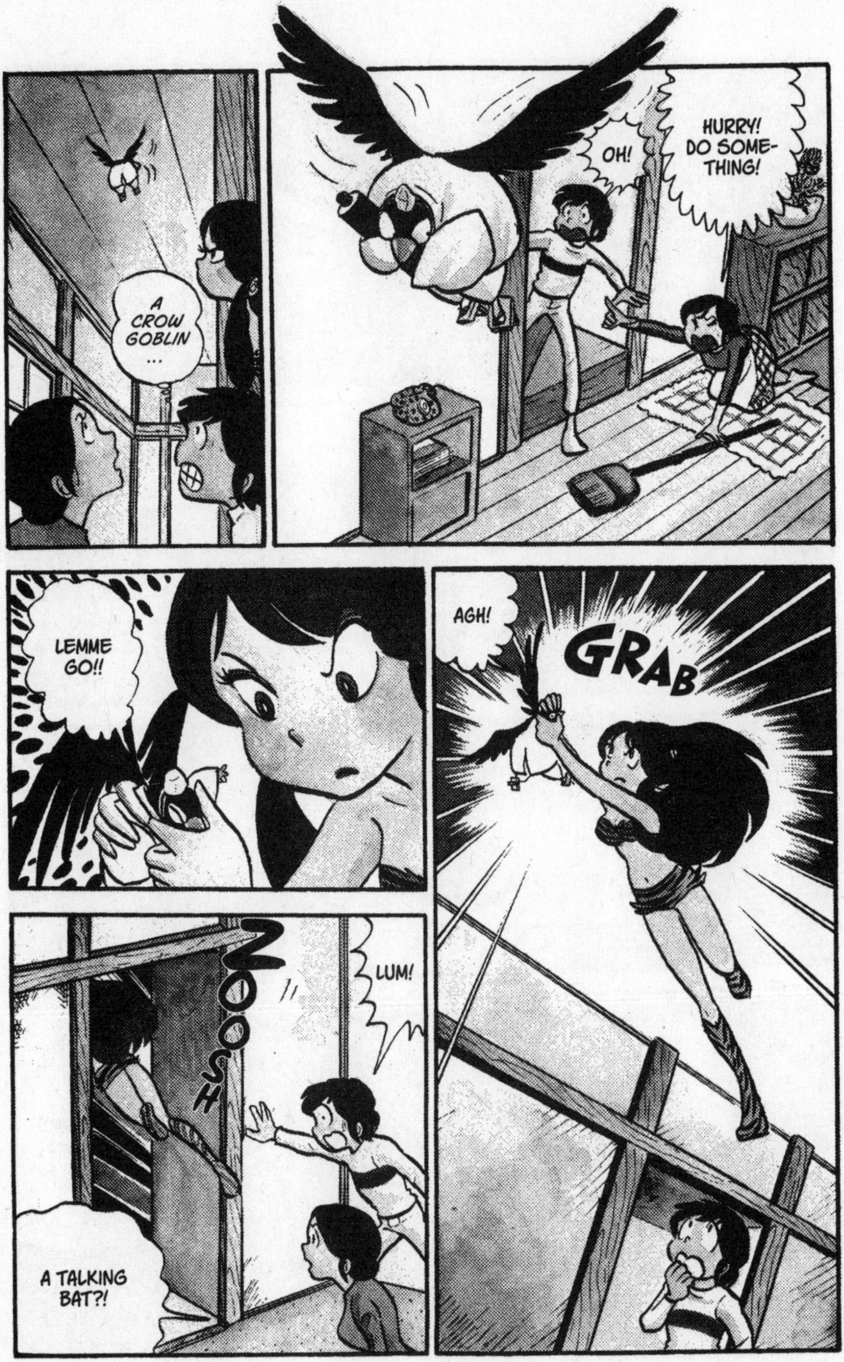
HURRY! DO SOME-THING!
OH!
A CROW GOBLIN ...
AGH!
GRAB
LEMME GO!!
LUM!
ZOOSH
A TALKING BAT?!

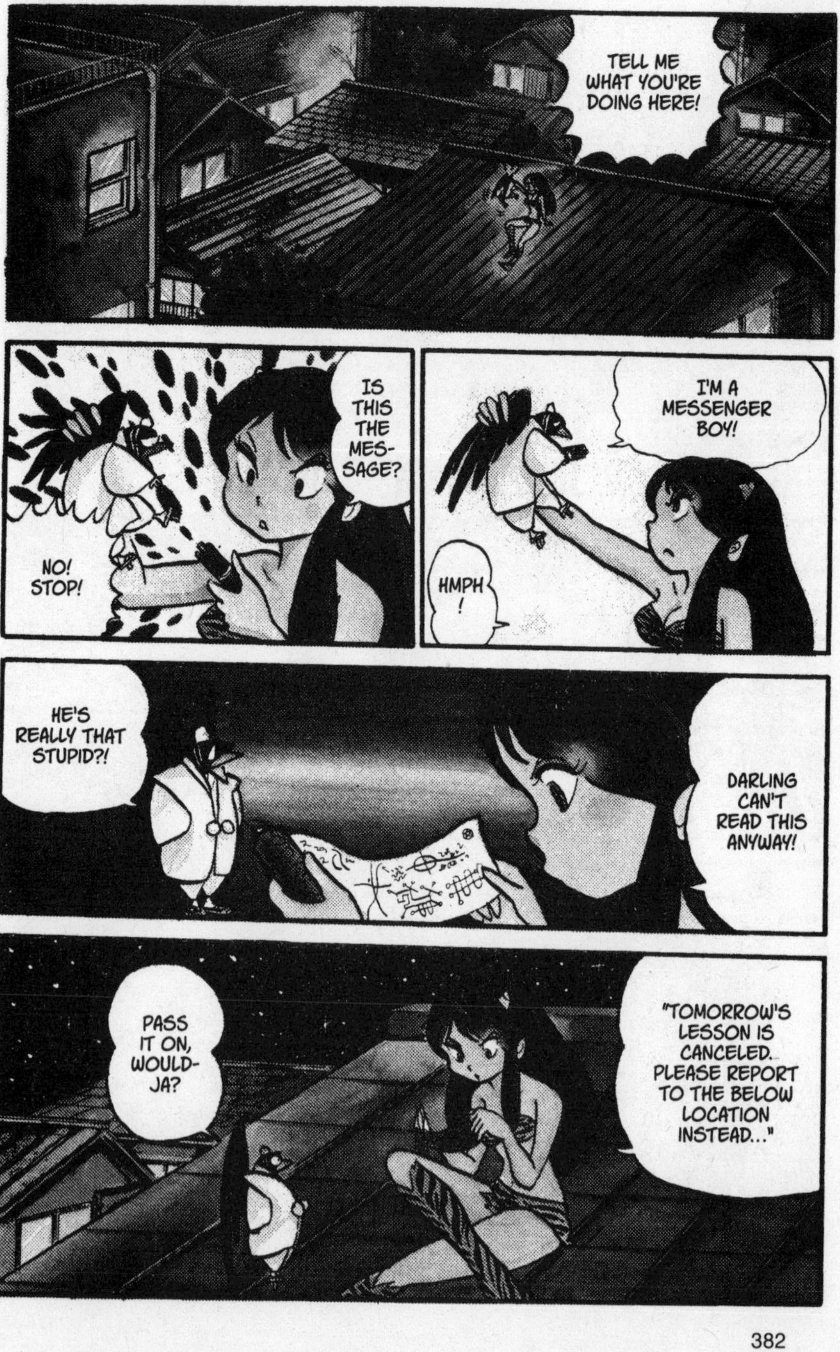
TELL ME WHAT YOU'RE DOING HERE!
I'M A MESSENGER BOY!
HMPH!
IS THIS THE MESSAGE?
NO! STOP!
DARLING CAN'T READ THIS ANYWAY!
HE'S REALLY THAT STUPID?!
"TOMORROW'S LESSON IS CANCELED. PLEASE REPORT TO THE BELOW LOCATION INSTEAD..."
PASS IT ON, WOULDJA?

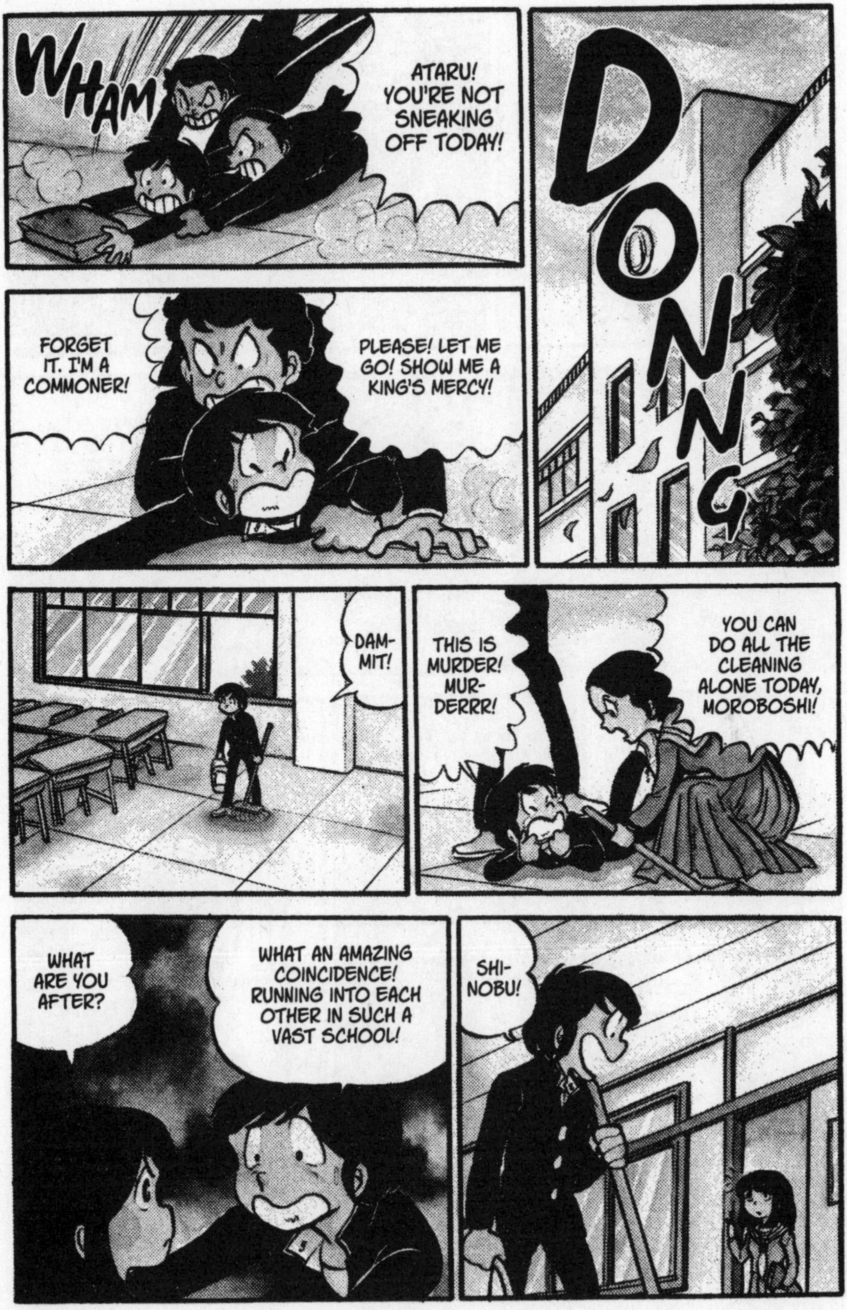
DONNG
WHAM
ATARU! YOU'RE NOT SNEAKING OFF TODAY!
PLEASE! LET ME GO! SHOW ME A KING'S MERCY!
FORGET IT. I'M A COMMONER!
YOU CAN DO ALL THE CLEANING ALONE TODAY, MOROBOSHI!
THIS IS MURDER! MUR-DERRR!
DAM-MIT!
SHI-NOBU!
WHAT AN AMAZING COINCIDENCE! RUNNING INTO EACH OTHER IN SUCH A VAST SCHOOL!
WHAT ARE YOU AFTER?

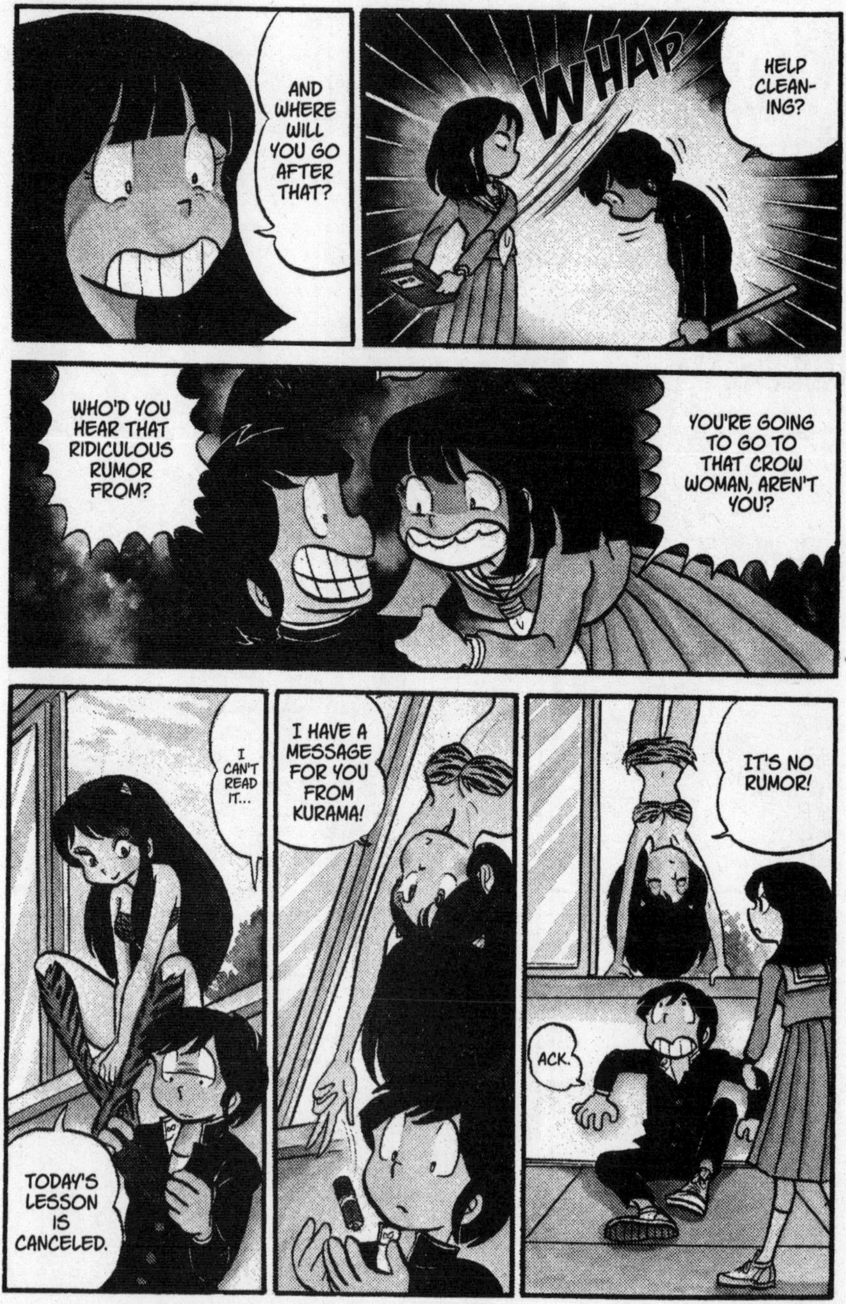
WHAP
HELP CLEAN-ING?
AND WHERE WILL YOU GO AFTER THAT?
YOU'RE GOING TO GO TO THAT CROW WOMAN, AREN'T YOU?
WHO'D YOU HEAR THAT RIDICULOUS RUMOR FROM?
IT'S NO RUMOR!
ACK.
I HAVE A MESSAGE FOR YOU FROM KURAMA!
I CAN'T READ IT...
TODAY'S LESSON IS CANCELED.

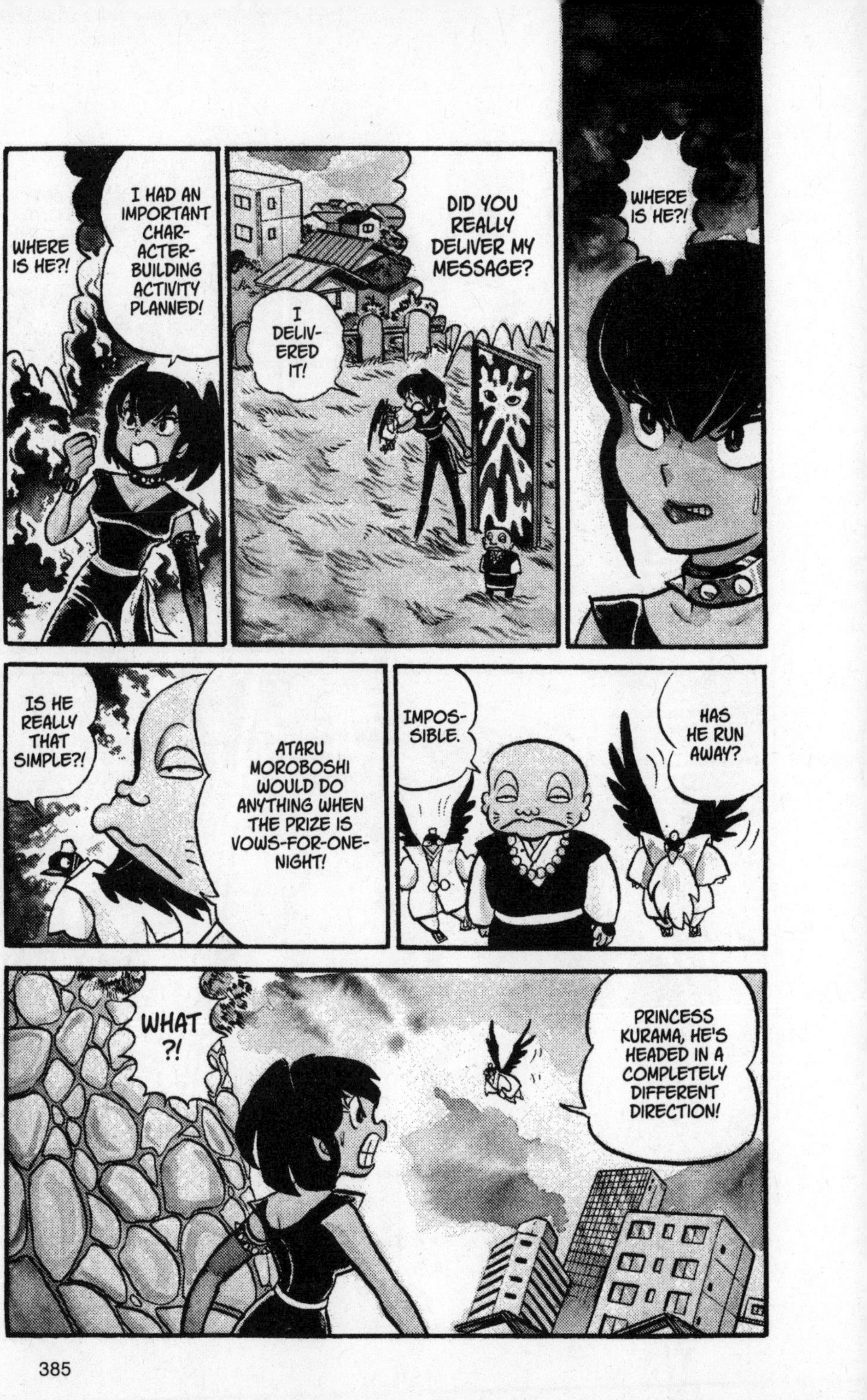
WHERE IS HE?!
DID YOU REALLY DELIVER MY MESSAGE?
I DELIVERED IT!
I HAD AN IMPORTANT CHARACTER-BUILDING ACTIVITY PLANNED!
WHERE IS HE?!
HAS HE RUN AWAY?
IMPOSSIBLE.
ATARU MOROBOSHI WOULD DO ANYTHING WHEN THE PRIZE IS VOWS-FOR-ONE-NIGHT!
IS HE REALLY THAT SIMPLE?!
PRINCESS KURAMA, HE'S HEADED IN A COMPLETELY DIFFERENT DIRECTION!
WHAT?!

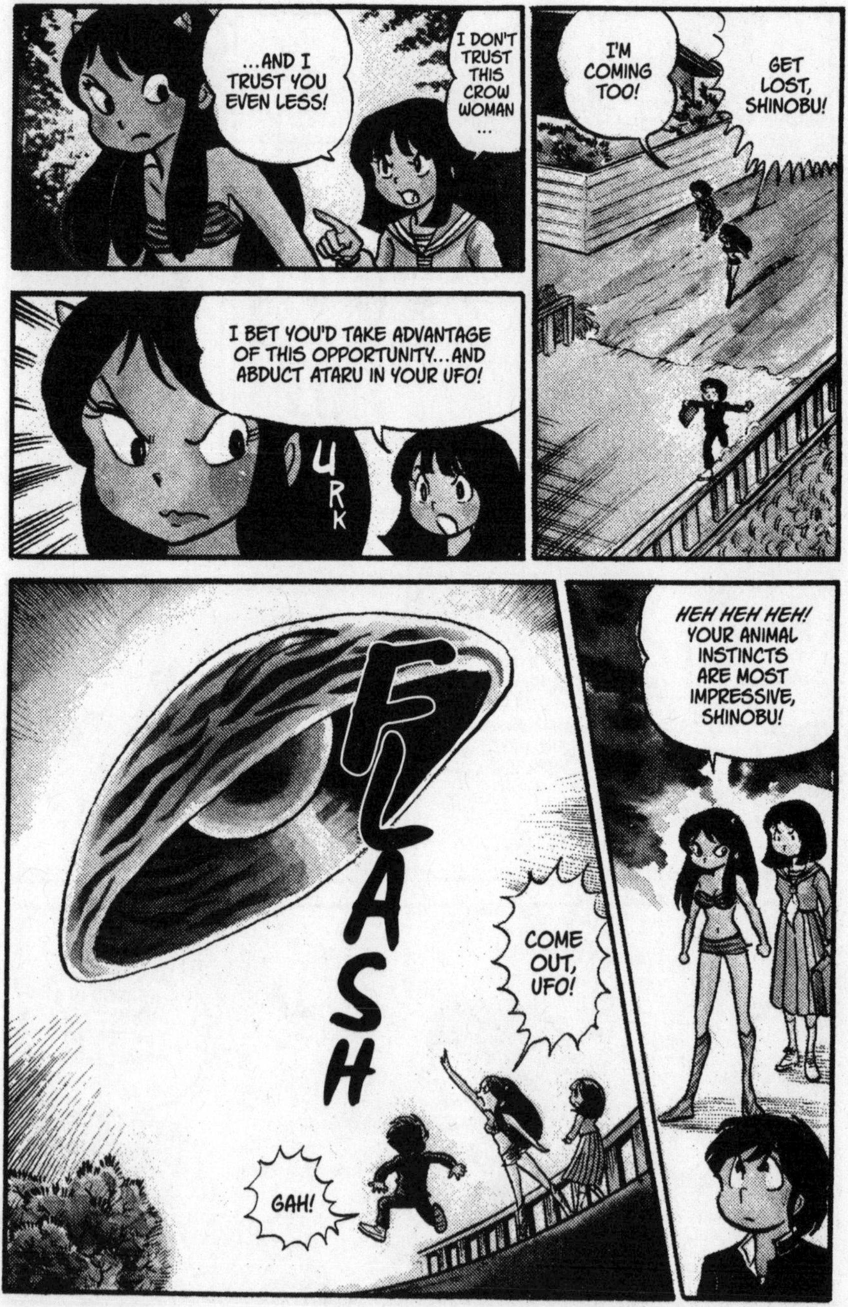
GET LOST, SHINOBU!
I'M COMING TOO!
I DON'T TRUST THIS CROW WOMAN ...
...AND I TRUST YOU EVEN LESS!
I BET YOU'D TAKE ADVANTAGE OF THIS OPPORTUNITY...AND ABDUCT ATARU IN YOUR UFO!
URK
HEH HEH HEH! YOUR ANIMAL INSTINCTS ARE MOST IMPRESSIVE, SHINOBU!
FLASH
COME OUT, UFO!
GAH!

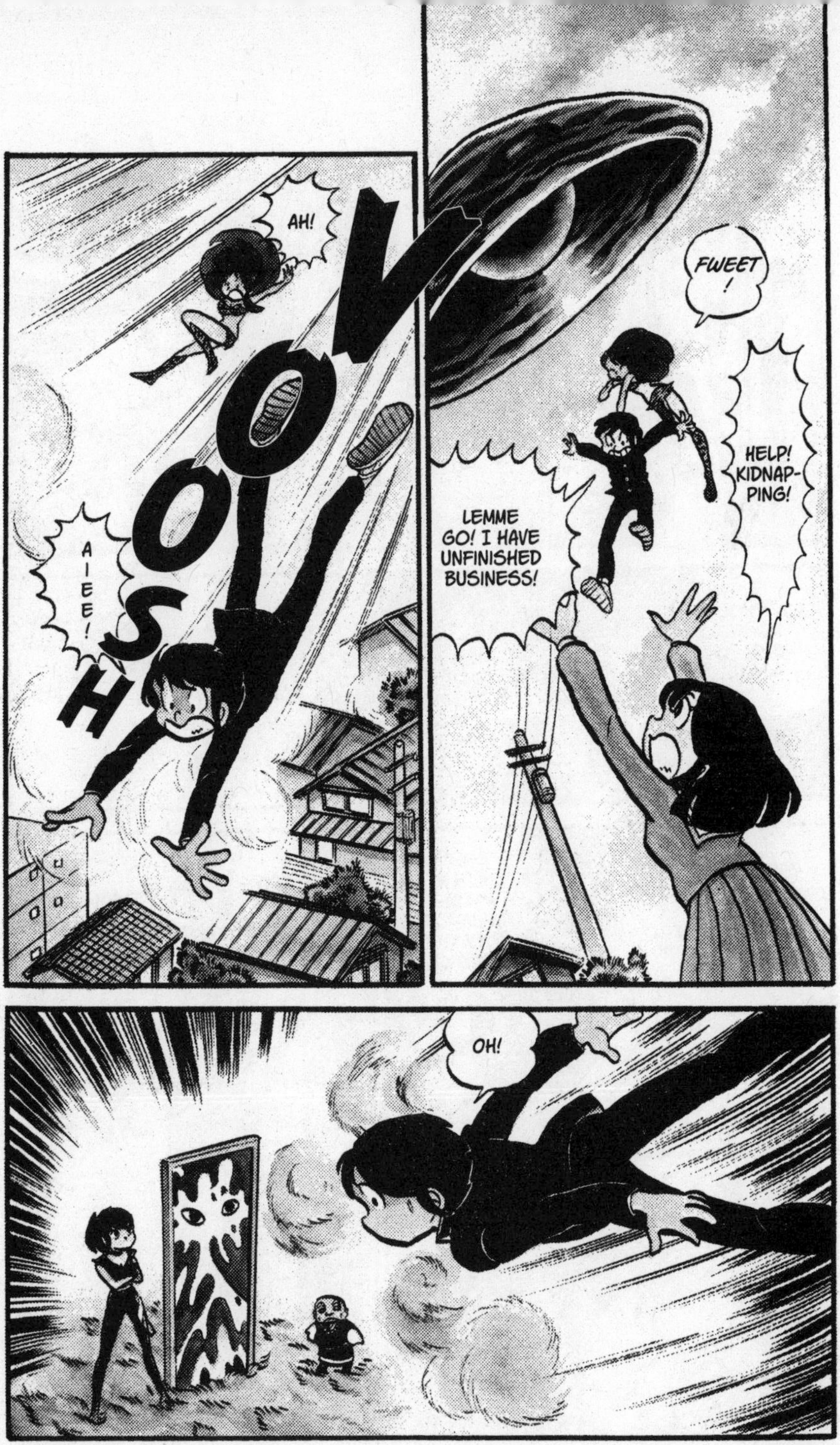
FWEET!
HELP! KIDNAPPING!
LEMME GO! I HAVE UNFINISHED BUSINESS!
AH!
WOOSH
AIEE!
OH!

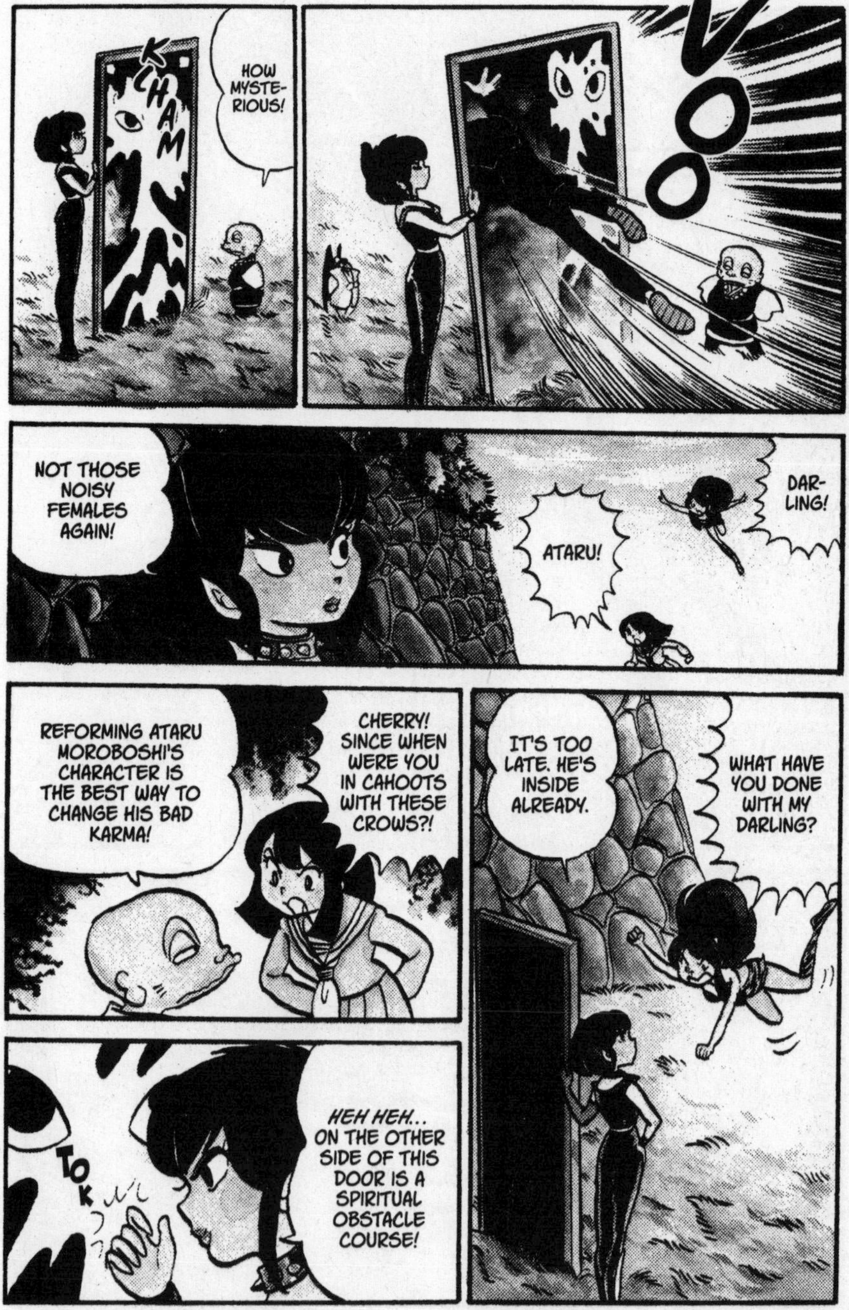
VOOO
KLHAM
HOW MYSTE-RIOUS!
DAR-LING!
ATARU!
NOT THOSE NOISY FEMALES AGAIN!
WHAT HAVE YOU DONE WITH MY DARLING?
IT'S TOO LATE. HE'S INSIDE ALREADY.
CHERRY! SINCE WHEN WERE YOU IN CAHOOTS WITH THESE CROWS?!
REFORMING ATARU MOROBOSHI'S CHARACTER IS THE BEST WAY TO CHANGE HIS BAD KARMA!
TOK
HEH HEH... ON THE OTHER SIDE OF THIS DOOR IS A SPIRITUAL OBSTACLE COURSE!

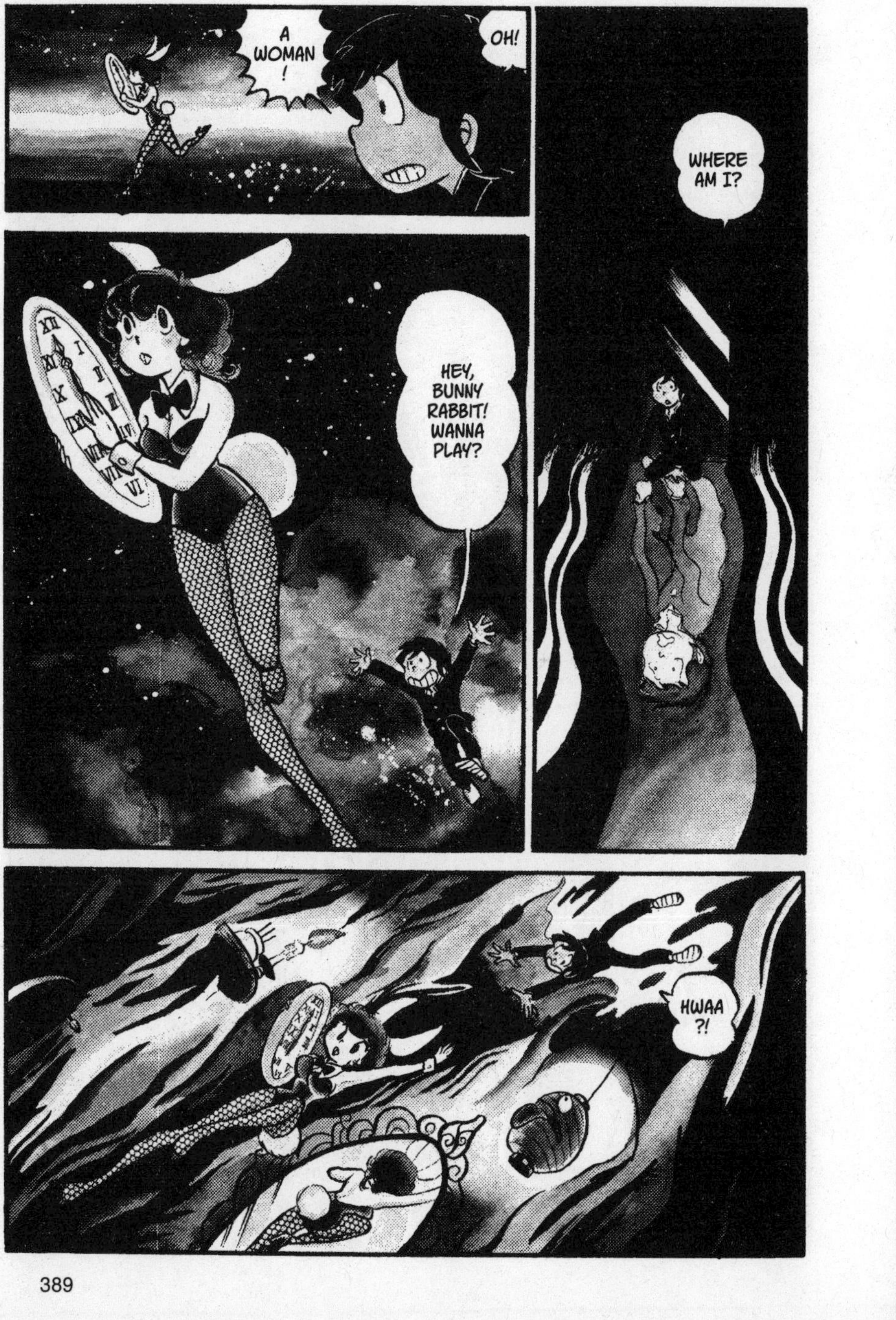
WHERE AM I?
OH!
A WOMAN!
HEY, BUNNY RABBIT! WANNA PLAY?
HWAA?!

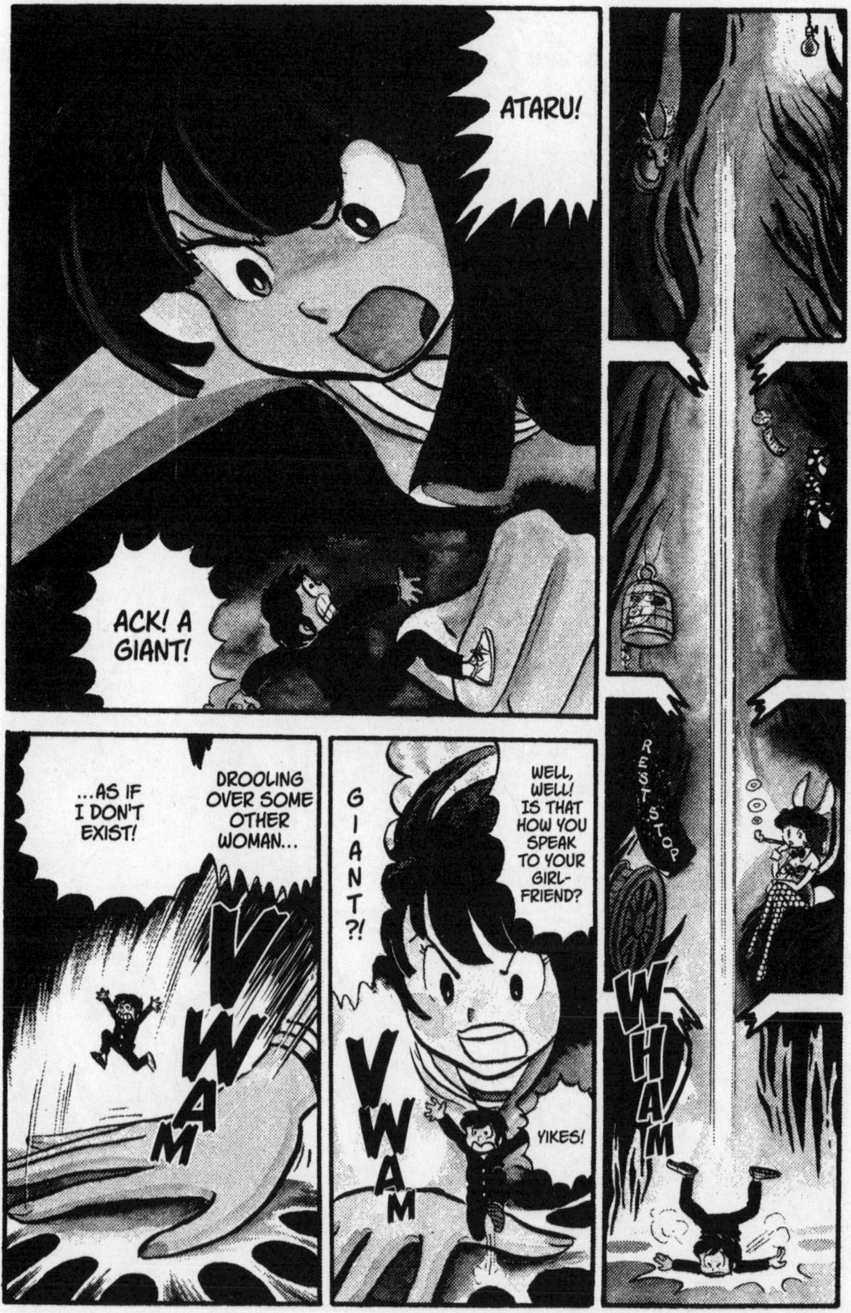
REST STOP
WHAM
ATARU!
ACK! A GIANT!
WELL, WELL! IS THAT HOW YOU SPEAK TO YOUR GIRL-FRIEND?
GIANT?!
VWAM
YIKES!
DROOLING OVER SOME OTHER WOMAN...
...AS IF I DON'T EXIST!
VWAM

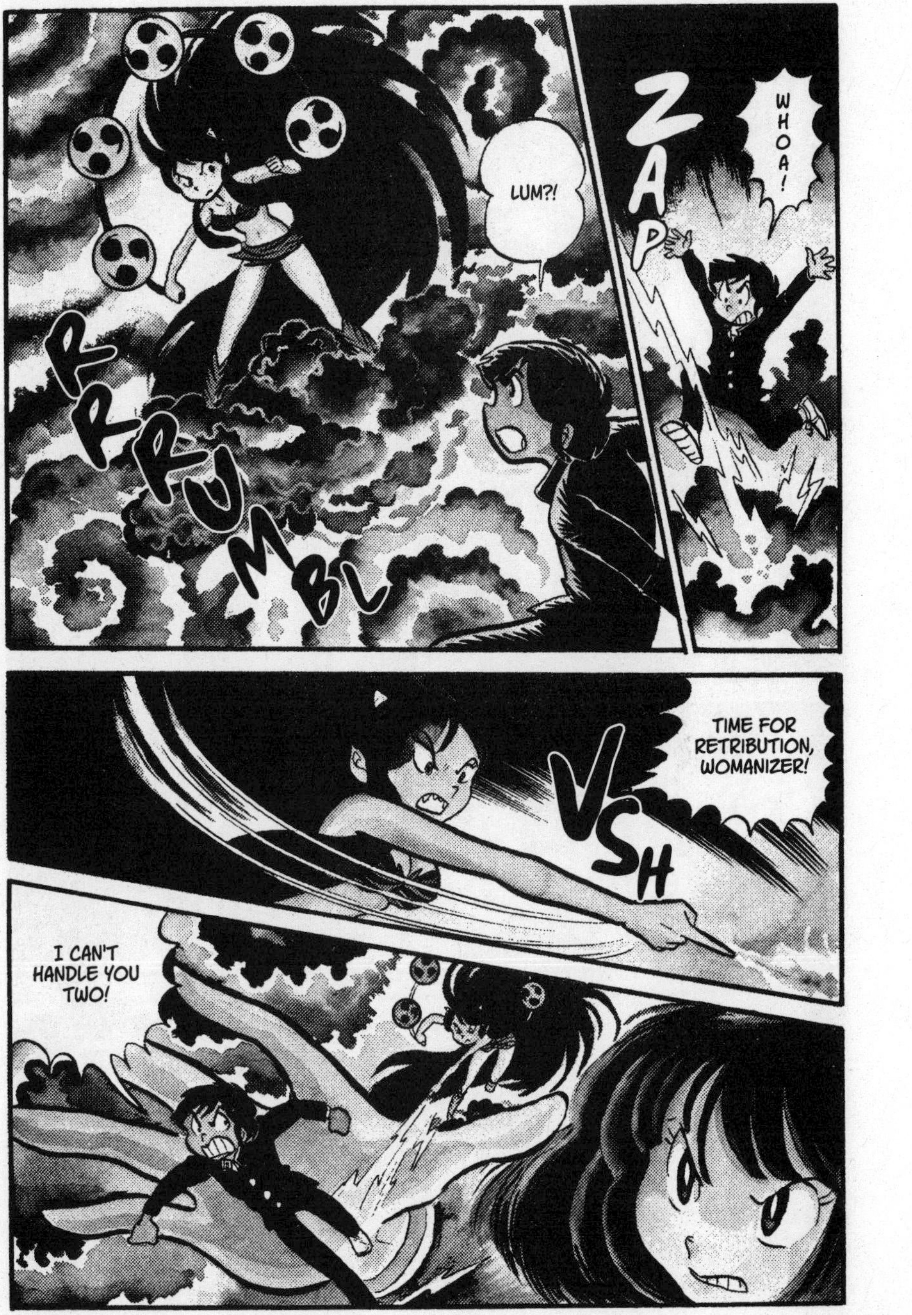
WHOA!
ZAP
LUM?!
RRRUMBL
TIME FOR RETRIBUTION, WOMANIZER!
VSH
I CAN'T HANDLE YOU TWO!

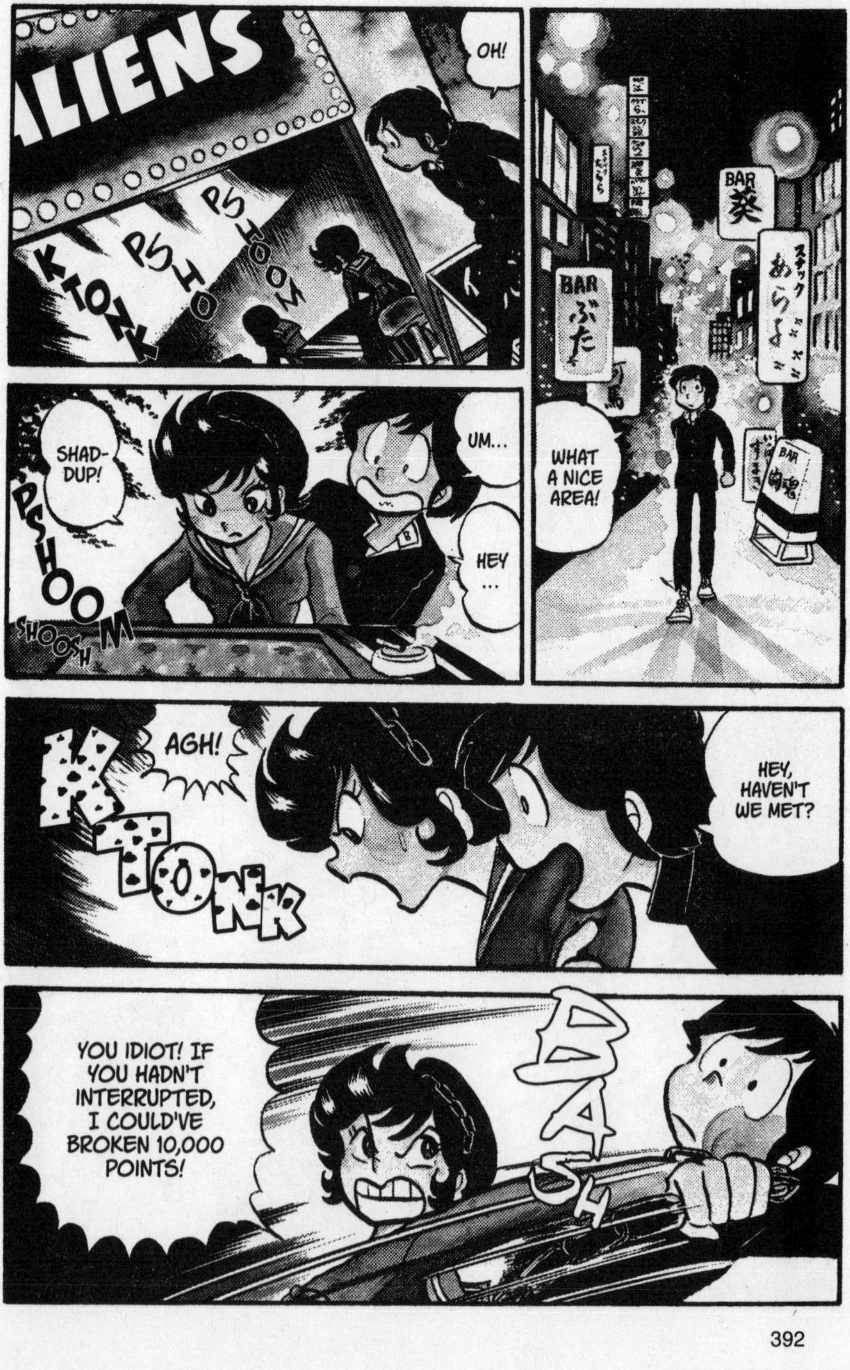
BAR 葵
スナック あらよ
BAR ぶた
WHAT A NICE AREA!
OH!
ALIENS
PSHOOM
PSHOOM
KTONK
UM...
HEY ...
SHAD-DUP!
PSHOOOM
SHOOSH
HEY, HAVEN'T WE MET?
AGH!
KTONK
BASH
YOU IDIOT! IF YOU HADN'T INTERRUPTED, I COULD'VE BROKEN 10,000 POINTS!

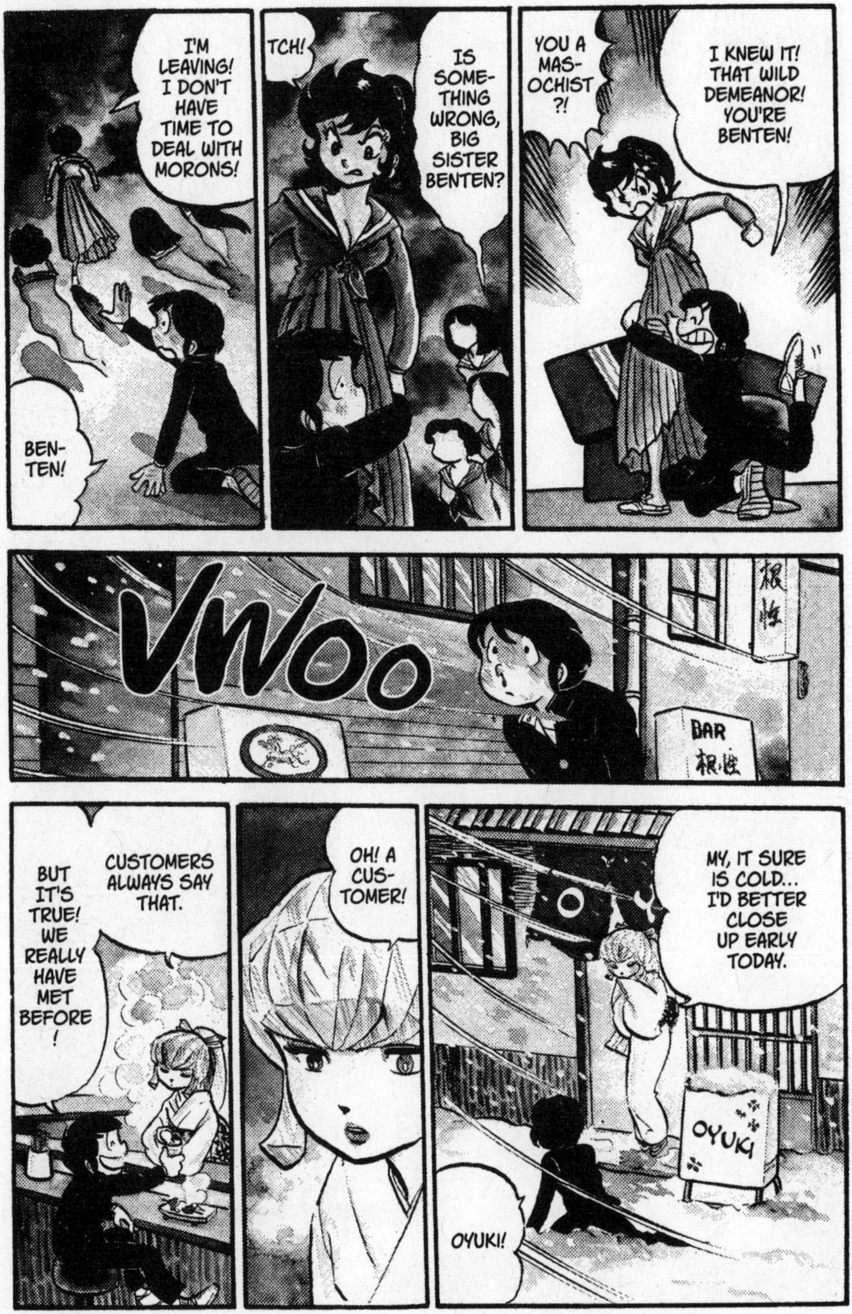

I KNEW IT! THAT WILD DEMEANOR! YOU'RE BENTEN!
YOU A MASOCHIST?!
IS SOMETHING WRONG, BIG SISTER BENTEN?
TCH!
I'M LEAVING! I DON'T HAVE TIME TO DEAL WITH MORONS!
BENTEN!
VWOO
BAR
MY, IT SURE IS COLD... I'D BETTER CLOSE UP EARLY TODAY.
OYUKI
OYUKI!
OH! A CUSTOMER!
CUSTOMERS ALWAYS SAY THAT.
BUT IT'S TRUE! WE REALLY HAVE MET BEFORE!

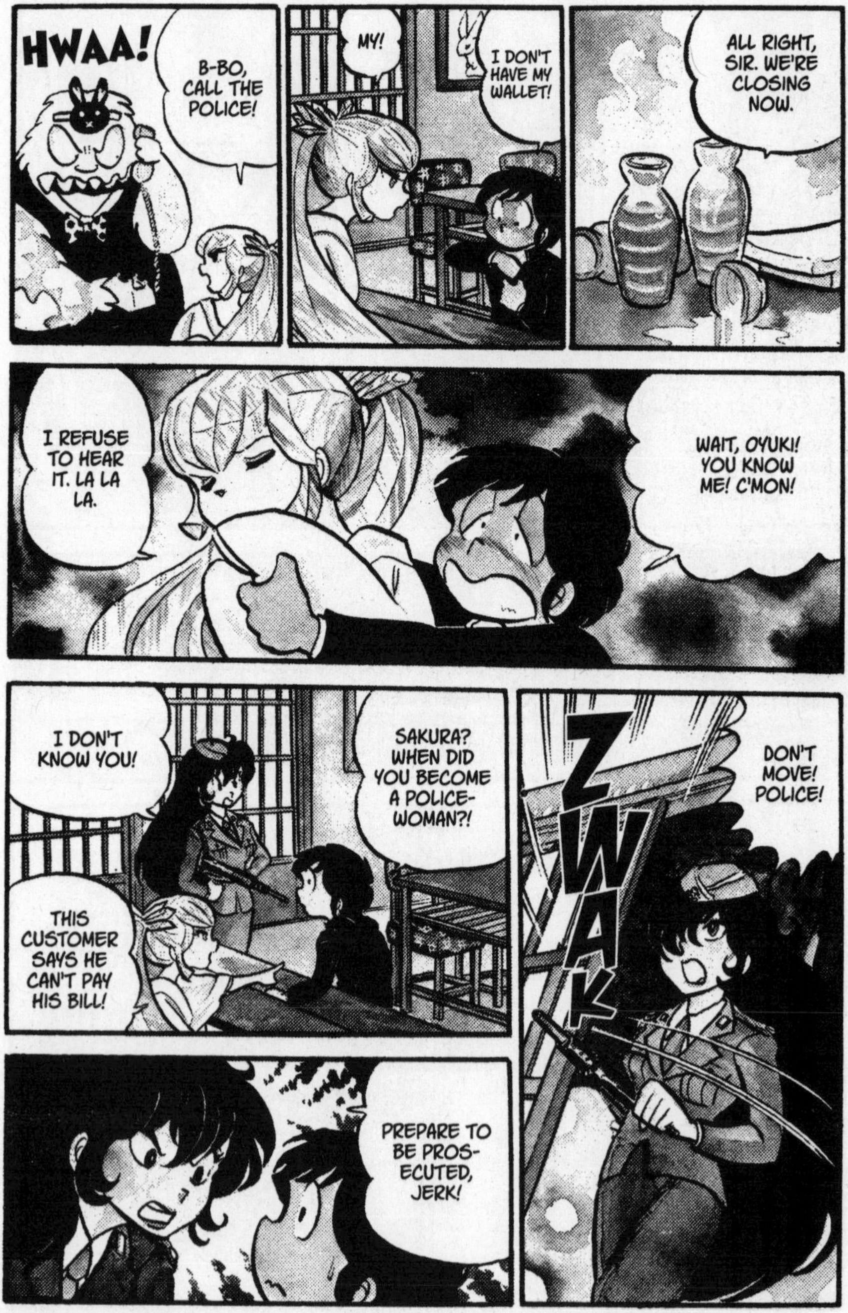
ALL RIGHT, SIR. WE'RE CLOSING NOW.
I DON'T HAVE MY WALLET!
MY!
B-BO, CALL THE POLICE!
HWAA!
WAIT, OYUKI! YOU KNOW ME! C'MON!
I REFUSE TO HEAR IT. LA LA LA.
DON'T MOVE! POLICE!
ZWAK
SAKURA? WHEN DID YOU BECOME A POLICE-WOMAN?!
I DON'T KNOW YOU!
THIS CUSTOMER SAYS HE CAN'T PAY HIS BILL!
PREPARE TO BE PROS-ECUTED, JERK!

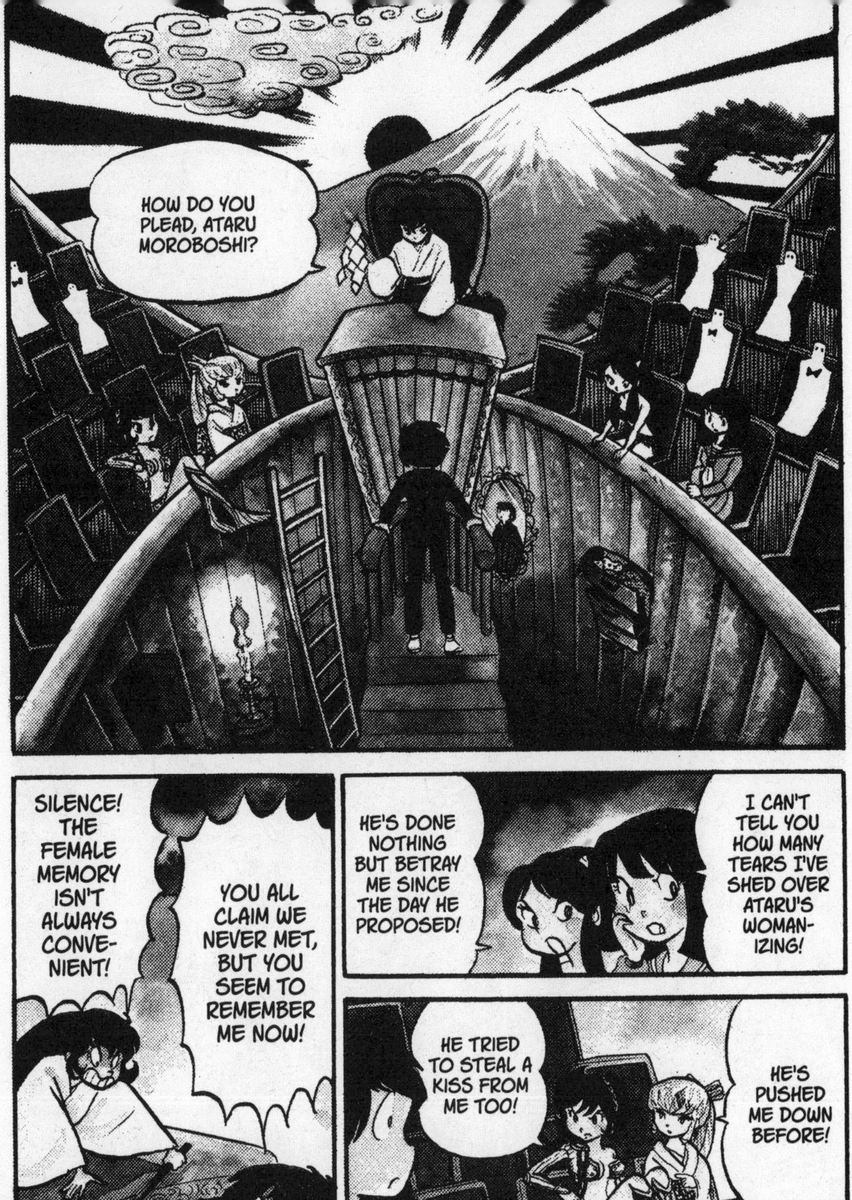
HOW DO YOU PLEAD, ATARU MOROBOSHI?
I CAN'T TELL YOU HOW MANY TEARS I'VE SHED OVER ATARU'S WOMAN-IZING!
HE'S DONE NOTHING BUT BETRAY ME SINCE THE DAY HE PROPOSED!
HE'S PUSHED ME DOWN BEFORE!
HE TRIED TO STEAL A KISS FROM ME TOO!
I'VE BEEN SUBJECTED TO MULTIPLE LEWD ADVANCES AS WELL.
WHAT'S ALL THIS?!
YOU ALL CLAIM WE NEVER MET, BUT YOU SEEM TO REMEMBER ME NOW!
SILENCE! THE FEMALE MEMORY ISN'T ALWAYS CONVE-NIENT!

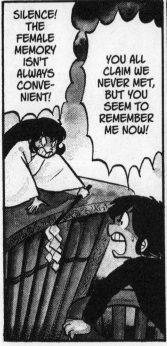

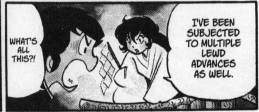

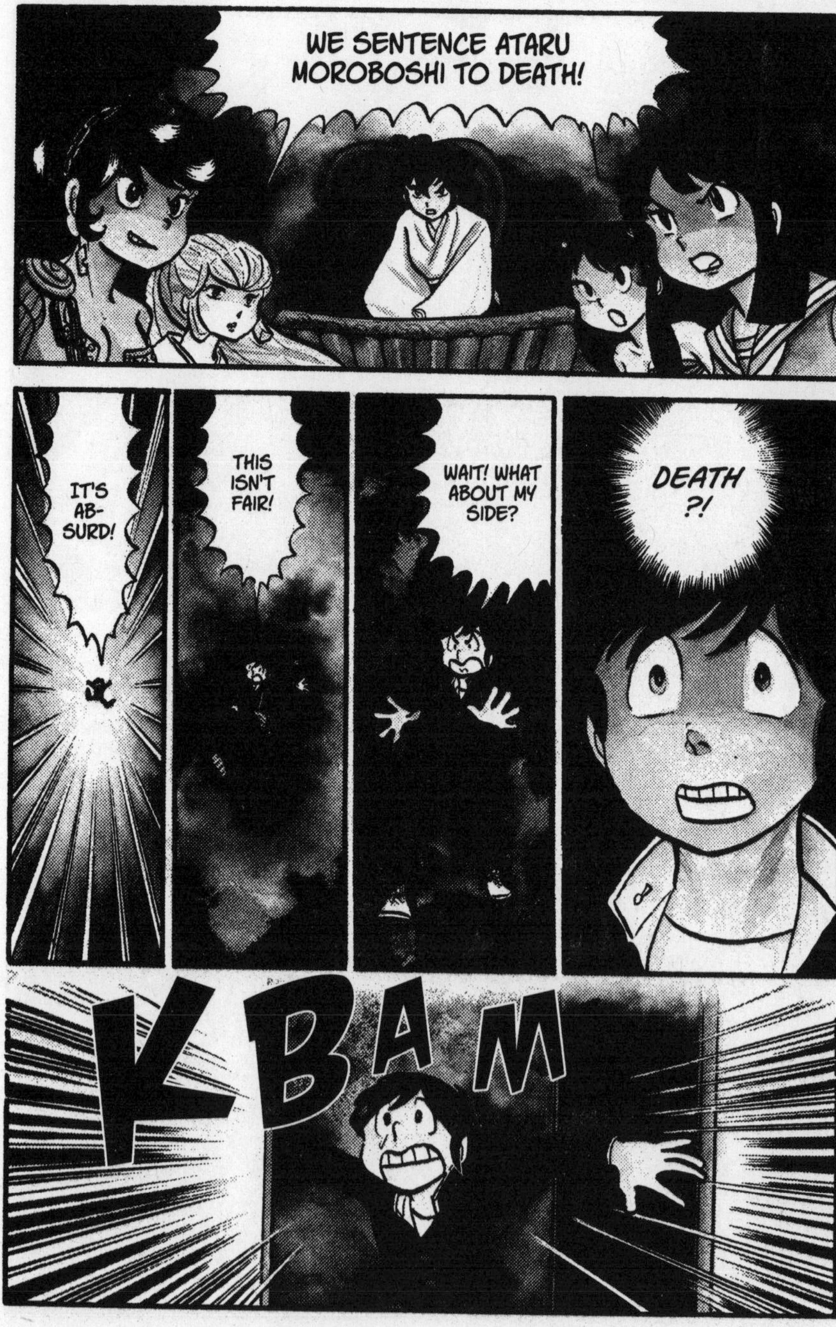
WE SENTENCE ATARU MOROBOSHI TO DEATH!
DEATH ?!
WAIT! WHAT ABOUT MY SIDE?
THIS ISN'T FAIR!
IT'S AB-SURD!
KBAM

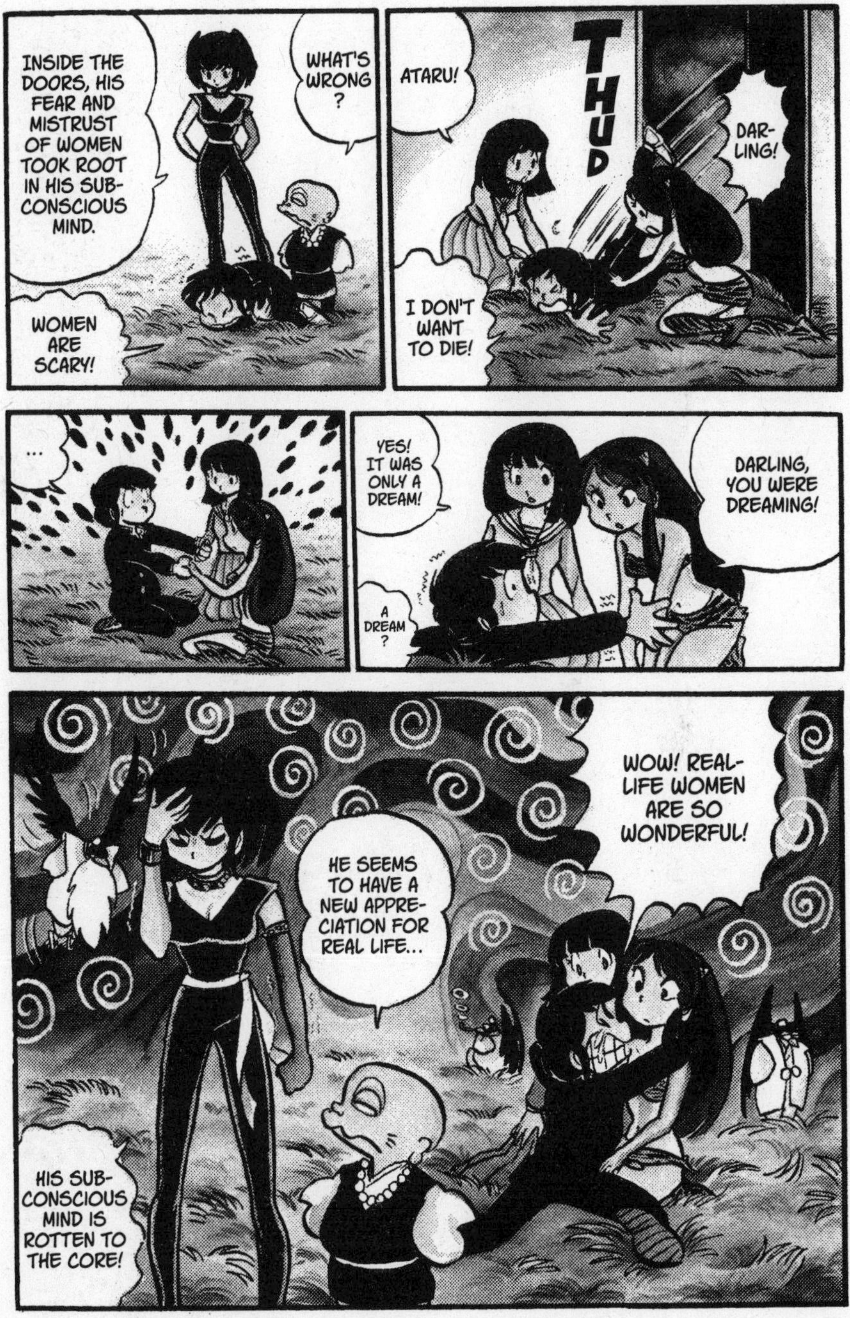
DARLING!
THUD
ATARU!
I DON'T WANT TO DIE!
WHAT'S WRONG?
INSIDE THE DOORS, HIS FEAR AND MISTRUST OF WOMEN TOOK ROOT IN HIS SUBCONSCIOUS MIND.
WOMEN ARE SCARY!
DARLING, YOU WERE DREAMING!
YES! IT WAS ONLY A DREAM!
A DREAM?
...
WOW! REAL-LIFE WOMEN ARE SO WONDERFUL!
HE SEEMS TO HAVE A NEW APPRECIATION FOR REAL LIFE...
HIS SUBCONSCIOUS MIND IS ROTTEN TO THE CORE!

URUSEI YATSURA ★ DATA FILE 02

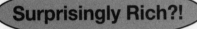

Surprisingly Rich?!

Sakura's Financial Life?!

In *Urusei Yatsura,* the character with the most beauty and talent is Sakura, who is a priestess as well as a nurse at Tomobiki High School. We all know Sakura is gorgeous and has a perfect figure, but beyond that she is also a surprisingly accomplished career woman with tremendous business acumen.

When Sakura first appears in the series, she lives in a humble one-story house (volume 1, chapter 4 "Present for You"), which later becomes a luxurious two-story home (volume 4, chapter 6 "Ten's Love"). She always wears stylish clothing, and her stomach is large enough to win an eating contest, implying a substantial food budget.

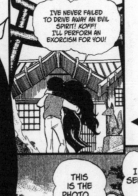

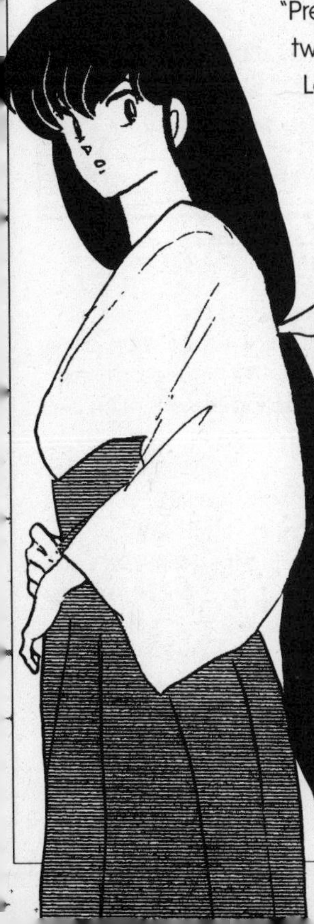

I'VE NEVER FAILED TO DRIVE AWAY AN EVIL SPIRIT! KOFF! I'LL PERFORM AN EXORCISM FOR YOU!

◀ Sakura's initial one-story home... (volume 1, chapter 4 "Present for You")

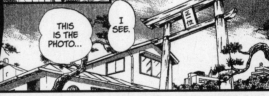

I SEE.
THIS IS THE PHOTO...

▲ It becomes—BAM!—a two-story home! Was it rebuilt? Or modified? (volume 17, chapter 8 "Goat and Cheese")

Yes, next to billionaire Shutaro Mendo, Sakura's wealth pales, but she is in fact unusually rich for a young woman. Let us shine a spotlight on her hidden business know-how!

STUDY 1

Success Secrets ①

Unusual Levels of Beauty and Skill!

As a priestess, Sakura has very high-level spiritual powers. Initially Cherry takes charge of driving away supernatural beings, but later Sakura's skills threaten his dominance.

Moreover, the jobs she is tasked with are clearly quite extraordinary, such as exorcising a watermelon (volume 5, chapter 17 "Beach Mystery"), laying to rest a cursed boxing glove (volume 11, chapter 4 "The Glove of Love and Conflict") or exorcising a sake spirit (volume 13, chapter 22 "Exorcism Three-Way"). These are all quite challenging feats where one would expect to command a particularly high exorcism fee.

Sakura is also quite enterprising. She rakes in the profits by hiring Ran as a part-time priestess for the paper fortune business during New Year's, the most profitable period at a shrine (volume 4, chapter 4 "Fortune Fear").

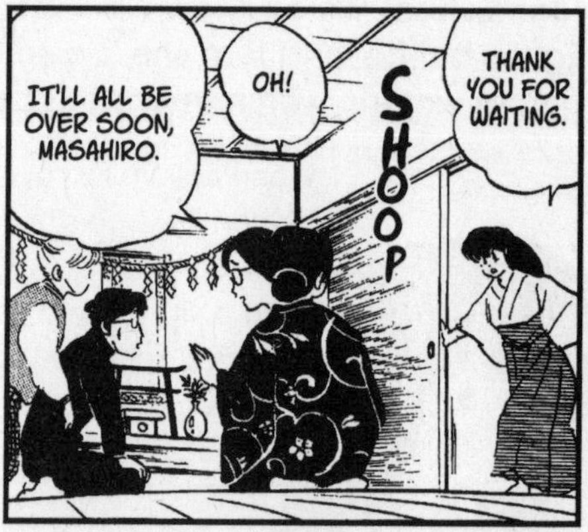
THANK YOU FOR WAITING.
SHOOP
OH!
IT'LL ALL BE OVER SOON, MASAHIRO.

▲ **Business is booming, and the customers are nonstop (volume 15, chapter 19 "Date with a Spirit")**

Obviously, with two gorgeous priestesses like Sakura and Ran on deck, the customers are drawn like moths to a flame. The fortune business is a big success, even attracting the attention of a slew of amateur photographers!

Sakura's colleagues clearly hold her in high regard. When an injured priest solicits her to recruit some youngsters to ring the New Year's bell, she refers Ataru and the gang for the job. (volume 13, chapter 8 "Ringing in the New Year"). Her broad network and support of her professional relationships must certainly contribute to her prosperity.

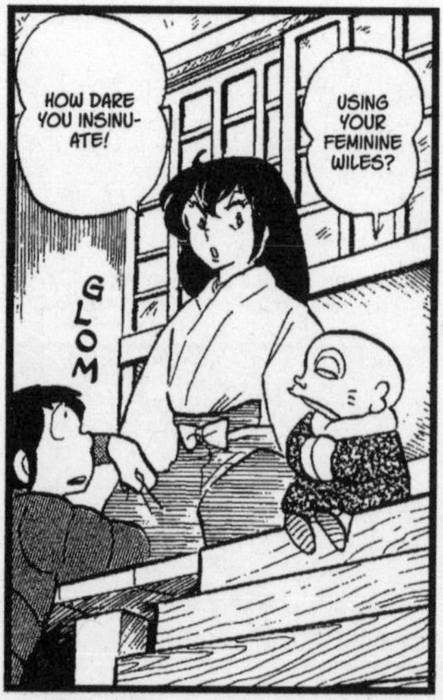
USING YOUR FEMININE WILES?
HOW DARE YOU INSINU-ATE!
GLOM

◀ **Earning extra cash hawking fortunes (volume 4, chapter 4 "Fortune Fear")**

STUDY 2

Success Secrets ②

A Civil Servant with a Solid Income

While Sakura's priestess work doubtlessly provides ample income, she also sidelines as a school nurse. Sakura's personal interests may have factored into her choice, but we suspect she was attracted by the stability of a career in the public sector. Priestess work may be lucrative, but it's also unstable.

Tomobiki High is a public school, so Sakura has the same status as a civil servant. Naturally, it has excellent benefits and a solid pension plan. Regardless of the economic climate, her wages and yearly bonus are assured, and she's eligible for maternity leave and paid leave. She also gets spring, summer, and winter breaks just like the students, so it's an ideal second career for a priestess. The stable paychecks probably made it easier for her to get her home improvement loan.

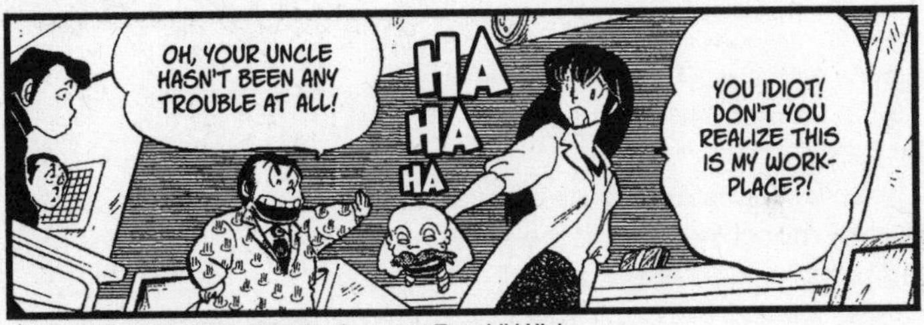
YOU IDIOT! DON'T YOU REALIZE THIS IS MY WORK-PLACE?!
HA HA HA
OH, YOUR UNCLE HASN'T BEEN ANY TROUBLE AT ALL!

▲ **Sakura also works as the school nurse at Tomobiki High (volume 6, chapter 16 "Intruder")**

While it's easy to see the advantages of the job, it's also a very hard post. Only an elite few can pass through the narrow gateway that leads down this illustrious career path.

First, a candidate must obtain specialized training through the education department of a university, trade school, or college, and then undergo the requisite practicum to get licensed. There is also an employment exam to pass. These hurdles must have been particularly daunting in light of Sakura's frail health in her youth.

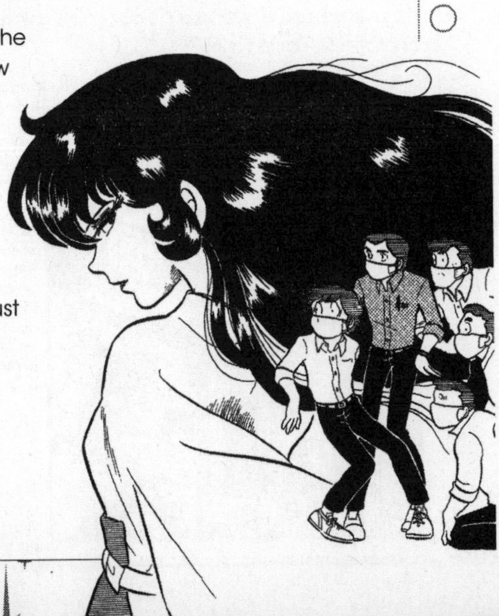

Moreover, there is only one post available per school, so openings are few and far between. Sakura must have gotten lucky, as she seems to have arrived at her post in the middle of the first semester (volume 3, chapter 1 "Sakura Sensei, Enchanted Blossom"). Leave it to a priestess to get fortune on her side!

STUDY 3

Success Secrets ③

Sakura is Far From Stingy
(As in she spends a lot!)

Sakura is engaged to be married to her fiancé, Tsubame. Not only is her everyday life expensive, but she must also save up for marriage.

Her food costs are formidable. She consumes enormous quantities: a light breakfast for Sakura consists of a large wooden container of steamed rice and a whole box of sake-pickled vegetables (volume 13, chapter 22 "Exorcism Three-Way"), a regular breakfast consists of a giant portion of stew (volume 10, chapter 8 "Sakura's Sorrowful Childhood") and a snack at school consists of at least five Chinese steamed buns (volume 13, chapter 5 "The Tragic Twilight Hour of Autumn Potatoes"). Truly, no amount of income would ever suffice.

This creates a need for supplementary methods. Sakura manages this by mooching food. In the early volumes, Sakura's mooching skills are not yet well-developed. She seems even to consider mooching shameful, and rebukes Cherry disapprovingly when he mooches: "Have you no shame!!" (volume 3, chapter 9 "Food Fight")

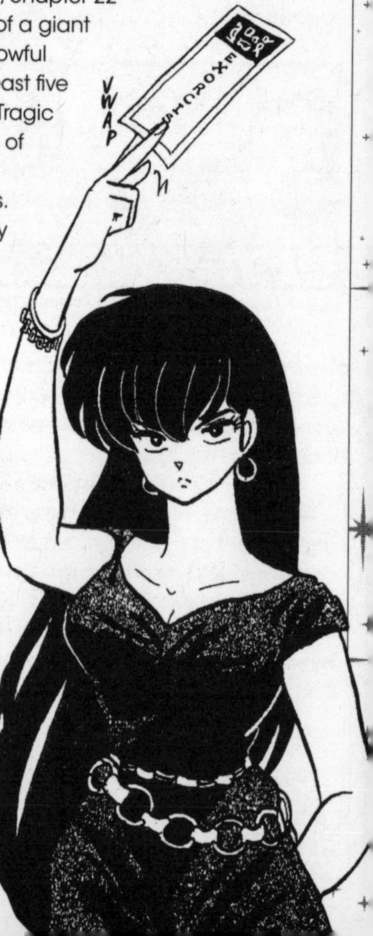
VWAP

Sakura's style is traditional but she loves to dress up... (volume 17, chapter 5 "One Night's Battle, Part 1") ▶

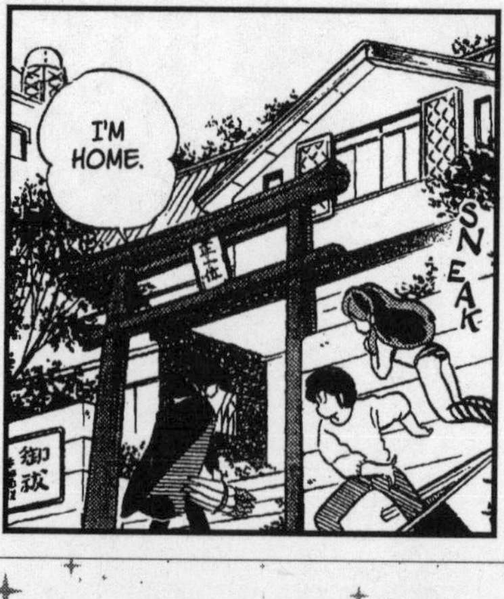
I'M HOME.
SNEAK

◀ Ataru and Lum see Tsubame and Sakura's new home when they visit the future; it looks quite nice (volume 16, chapter 8 "The Ends of Love and Sadness")

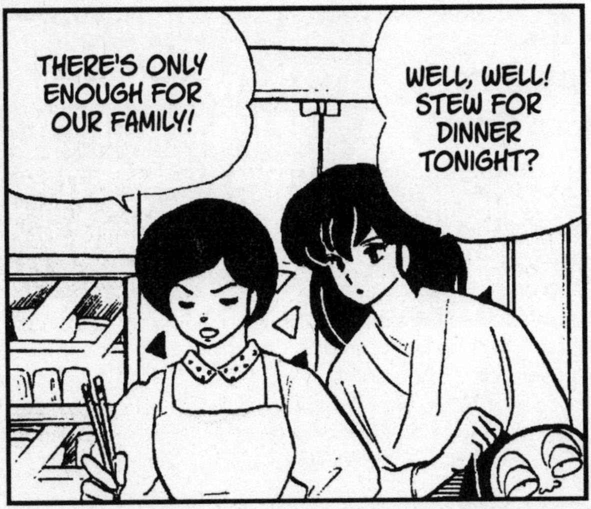
WELL, WELL! STEW FOR DINNER TONIGHT?
THERE'S ONLY ENOUGH FOR OUR FAMILY!

◀ Repeated skirmishes with Mrs. Moroboshi... (volume 15, chapter 5 "Magical Hat")

Later, however, Sakura's mooching evolves. She approaches the Moroboshi house unbidden to offer spiritual services and goes as far as to solicit a dish of *unaju* (volume 6, chapter 9 "There's a Cat on the Stairs!"). Considering the economic status of the Moroboshi family, mooching unaju is quite a brazen action. Perhaps this suggests an awareness of the need to save up money for her marriage.

While Sakura is a good moocher, she is also generous.

She invites Ataru and friends to her home and serves tea (volume 8, chapter 13 "Haunted Bottle") and on another occasion she serves them eel—albeit eel gifted from someone else (volume 10, chapter 2 "Ten Floats in Space?!"). She is not simply a miser. This delicate balance between mooching and generosity can be seen as one of Sakura's attractive qualities.

With her lucrative priestess work for big windfalls, her school nurse job for steady income and mooching skills to make ends meet, Sakura runs her shrine with a surprising tri-pronged reverse-sliding scale three-step business approach. In essence, she's a very competent woman.

(Data File 02 / The End)

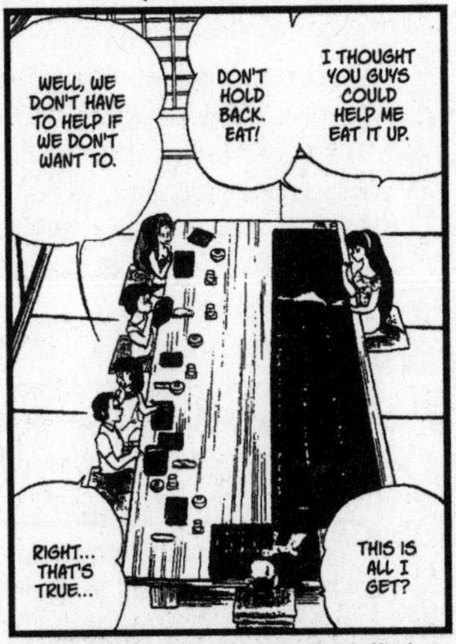
I THOUGHT YOU GUYS COULD HELP ME EAT IT UP.
DON'T HOLD BACK. EAT!
WELL, WE DON'T HAVE TO HELP IF WE DON'T WANT TO.
THIS IS ALL I GET?
RIGHT... THAT'S TRUE...

▲ Sakura shares her excess eel—regifted from someone else—with the gang, explaining it's "more than I can eat." Does she have a generous side too?! (volume 10, chapter 2 "Ten Floats in Space?!")

Author: Keiko Sugimori
Concept: Masatake Sugimori

COUNT COLUMN!

Urusei Yatsura: 366 Stories in All!

Anyway We counted them up!

The total number of times Ataru buys snacks...

Sprinting to the Tomobiki Shopping Arcade with an Empty Stomach!

At Tomobiki High School, stopping for take-out treats like ice cream or *taiyaki* is considered snacking, but so is sitting down to eat at a café or ramen shop (volume 6, chapter 4 "The Great Afterschool Snack Battle"). We counted the number of times Ataru has bought snacks in the series—and the answer was a whopping sixty-six times!

On one strange occasion, Ataru even takes on the "Hell Course" challenge—a torturously-portioned full-course meal that is free to those who can finish it (volume 3, chapter 9 "Food Fight"). He consumes 68,000 yen worth of food, including spaghetti, buttered rice, a 10 oz. steak, piping-hot steamed rice, seared raw bonito, roast chicken, and subgum yakisoba, but unfortunately capitulates before the end of the meal. Mendo winds up with the bill.

Ataru is human too—he treats his own son!

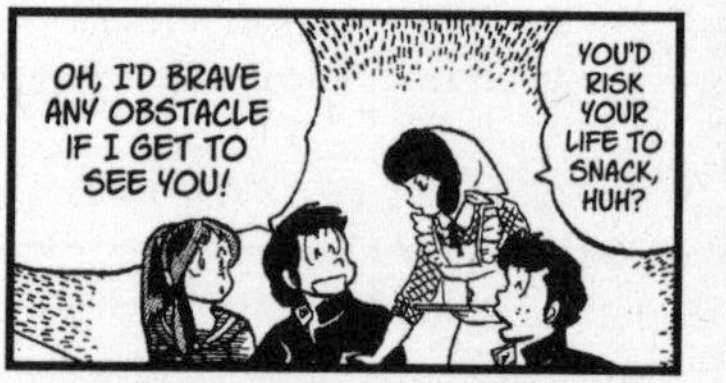
YOU'D RISK YOUR LIFE TO SNACK, HUH?
OH, I'D BRAVE ANY OBSTACLE IF I GET TO SEE YOU!
▲ Ataru sneaks off-campus during lunch hour (volume 6, chapter 4 "The Great Afterschool Snack Battle")

Ataru is stingy. Of the 66 times he buys food, only twice does he treat someone else. The first time is when he buys an ice cream for his own future child for 1,000 yen (volume 1, chapter 12 "Intention"). The second time is when he buys a whole mountain of roasted sweet potatoes for Lum when she is angry (volume 13, chapter 5 "The Tragic Twilight Hour of Autumn Potatoes").

These instances are in fact somewhat miraculous since Ataru frequently avoids spending money (even on his own food) by running off and ditching the bill.

When the teachers of Tomobiki High institute a "snack ban," the merchants of the Tomobiki shopping arcade side with the students and provide all-encompassing support (volume 6, chapter 4 "The Great Afterschool Snack Battle"). But actually, Ataru does not seem to spend much of his money in the shopping arcade...

Total number of Ataru's snacks.......66
Of these, the number of times he dines in at a café or ramen shop..........20
Of these, the number of times Ataru treats someone else, and the total cost...........A mere two occasions. Ice cream (1,000 yen), and a mountain of sweet potatoes (roughly 2,000 yen's worth if calculated at 1,000 yen per kilo), for a total of 3,000 yen (estimated).

Urusei Yatsura

Part 2 Notes

The world of *Urusei Yatsura* takes place in Japan, with references to cultural holidays, beliefs and practices. Check out the notes below to enrich your reading experience.

Page 216, panel 4 – The phrase that Cherry is referring to is "*Baka wa kaze wo hikanai,*" an idiom that means "Idiots can't catch colds." One explanation is that idiots are not in tune with their bodies and therefore don't even realize that they're sick.

Page 217, panel 1 – In Japanese culture, one superstitious belief dictates that if you sneeze, others are talking about you behind your back.

Page 219, panel 3 – Some of the magazines in Ataru's bookshelf include *Shonen Sunday,* the manga magazine that *Urusei Yatsura* originally ran in.

Page 222, panel 1 – This snow goddess is an iteration of the *Yuki-onna* ("snow woman") spirit that appears in Japanese folklore—often in stories involving marriage with a human man.

Page 225, panel 4 – The snow goddess's name is Oyuki, which means "snow" in Japanese.

Page 239, panel 3 – In the original manga, Ataru says, "*Namusan!*" which is a Buddhist incantation that literally means Buddha, Dharma and Sangha. This word is used casually as an exclamation of surprise or frustration.

Page 248, panel 1 – Mothra is a giant moth goddess that first appeared in the 1961 film *Mothra*. She is the most common recurring monster in the Godzilla series besides Godzilla himself.

Page 255, panel 6 – *Kobito* literally translates to "little people" and refers to mythical dwarfs.

Page 275, panel 2 – *Zashiki warashi* is a house spirit that's fond of mischief and believed to bring great fortune and riches to those whose house it haunts. It appears as a ghostlike child with a blushing red face who looks about five or six years old.

Page 294, panel 2 – Ataru is holding a straw effigy and hammers a nail into it. He is performing a modern-day version of *ushi no koku mairi*, which literally means "ox-hour shrine visit" and refers to a specified method of cursing someone. Traditionally, this practice occurs between the hours of 1 a.m. and 3 a.m. (a.k.a., Hours of the Ox according to the Chinese zodiac), and it is performed by a woman dressed in white wearing an iron crown set with three lit candles in it.

Page 306, panel 2 – *Pachinko* is a type of arcade game that resembles an arcade pinball machine with its steel balls. It is associated with gambling where the winner eventually trades prizes for cash in a roundabout way. Gambling for cash is illegal in Japan.

Page 319, panel 1 – *Kappa* are mythological creatures who are said to carry a dish moist with water on their heads. If the dish gets dry, they become immobilized. The kappa's favorite food is cucumber.

Page 349, panel 2 – *Karasu tengu* are crow goblins, mythological birdlike creatures with wings that inhabit the mountains.

Page 351, panel 1 – The poster on the wall has kanji characters for "demon" on the first two lines, "woman" on the third, "child" on the fourth, and "achievement" on the last two.

Page 403 – *Unaju* is a dish consisting of eel filets over rice, served in a lacquered box.

Page 404 – *Taiyaki* is a fish-shaped molded cake with sweet-bean filling.

Rumiko Takahashi

The spotlight on Rumiko Takahashi's career began in 1978 when she won an honorable mention in Shogakukan's prestigious New Comic Artist Contest for *Those Selfish Aliens*. Later that same year, her boy-meets-alien comedy series, *Urusei Yatsura*, was serialized in *Weekly Shonen Sunday*. This phenomenally successful manga series was adapted into anime format and spawned a TV series and half a dozen theatrical-release movies, all incredibly popular in their own right. Takahashi followed up the success of her debut series with one blockbuster hit after another—*Maison Ikkoku* ran from 1980 to 1987, *Ranma 1/2* from 1987 to 1996, and *Inuyasha* from 1996 to 2008. Other notable works include *Mermaid Saga*, *Rumic Theater*, and *One-Pound Gospel*.

Takahashi was inducted into the Will Eisner Comic Awards Hall of Fame in 2018. She won the prestigious Shogakukan Manga Award twice in her career, once for *Urusei Yatsura* in 1981 and the second time for *Inuyasha* in 2002. Her series have sold over 200 million copies worldwide as of March 2017. A majority of the Takahashi canon has been adapted into other media such as anime, live-action TV series, and film. Takahashi's manga, as well as the other formats her work has been adapted into, have continued to delight generations of fans around the world. Distinguished by her wonderfully endearing characters, Takahashi's work adeptly incorporates a wide variety of elements such as comedy, romance, fantasy, and martial arts. While her series are difficult to pin down into one simple genre, the signature style she has created has come to be known as the "Rumic World." Rumiko Takahashi is an artist who truly represents the very best from the world of manga. Her current series *RIN-NE* is available in North America from VIZ Media.

URUSEI YATSURA
VIZ Signature Edition
Vol. 1

STORY AND ART BY
RUMIKO TAKAHASHI

URUSEI YATSURA [SHINSOBAN] Vol.1, 2
by Rumiko TAKAHASHI
© 2006 Rumiko TAKAHASHI
All rights reserved.
Original Japanese edition published by SHOGAKUKAN.
English translation rights in the United States of America,
Canada, the United Kingdom, Ireland, Australia and New
Zealand arranged with SHOGAKUKAN.

Translation & English Adaptation/Camellia Nieh
Lettering/Erika Terriquez
Design/Yukiko Whitley
Editor/Amy Yu

The stories, characters and incidents mentioned in
this publication are entirely fictional.

Printed in the U.S.A.

Published by VIZ Media, LLC
P.O. Box 77010
San Francisco, CA 94107

10 9 8 7 6 5 4 3 2 1
First printing, February 2019

VIZ MEDIA
viz.com

VIZ SIGNATURE

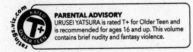

Urusei Yatsura

Hey! You're Reading in the Wrong Direction!

This is the end of this graphic novel!

To properly enjoy this VIZ graphic novel, please turn it around and begin reading from right to left. Unlike English, Japanese is read right to left, so Japanese comics are read in reverse order from the way English comics are typically read.

This book has been printed in the original Japanese format in order to preserve the orientation of the original artwork. Have fun with it!

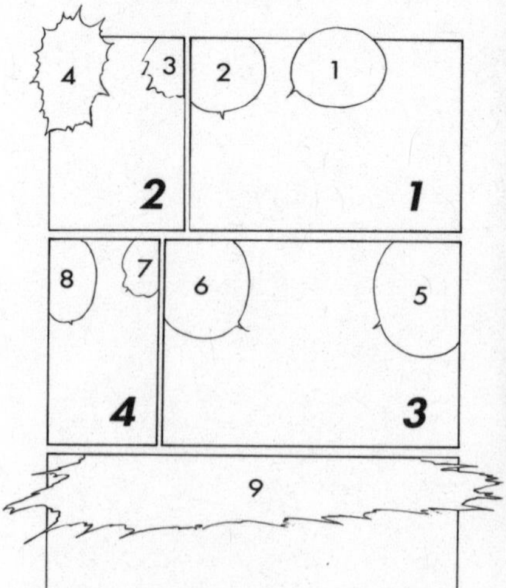

1
2
3
4
1
2
5
6
7
8
3
4
9
5
142

Follow the action this way

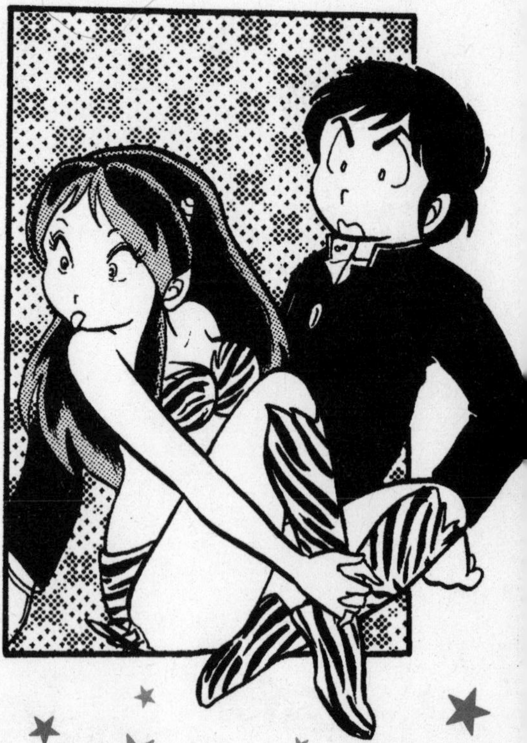